ARISTOPHANES
THE DEMOCRAT

This book provides a new interpretation of the nature of Old Comedy and its place at the heart of Athenian democratic politics. Professor Sidwell argues that Aristophanes and his rivals belonged to opposing political groups, each with their own political agenda. Through disguised caricature and parody of their rivals' work, the poets expressed and fuelled the political conflict between their factions. Professor Sidwell rereads the principal texts of Aristophanes and the fragmented remains of the work of his rivals in the light of his arguments for the political foundations of the genre.

KEITH SIDWELL is Adjunct Professor in the Department of Greek and Roman Studies, University of Calgary. He has written on Greek drama, later Greek literature – including, most recently, *Lucian: Chattering Courtesans and Other Sardonic Sketches* (2004) – and on Neo-Latin writing, and is a co-author of the Reading Greek and Reading Latin series, and author of *Reading Medieval Latin* (1995).

ARISTOPHANES THE DEMOCRAT

The Politics of Satirical Comedy during the Peloponnesian War

KEITH SIDWELL

*Adjunct Professor in the Department of Greek and Roman Studies,
University of Calgary*

CAMBRIDGE UNIVERSITY PRESS

CAMBRIDGE
UNIVERSITY PRESS

University Printing House, Cambridge CB2 8BS, United Kingdom

One Liberty Plaza, 20th Floor, New York, NY 10006, USA

477 Williamstown Road, Port Melbourne, VIC 3207, Australia

314-321, 3rd Floor, Plot 3, Splendor Forum, Jasola District Centre, New Delhi - 110025, India

79 Anson Road, #06-04/06, Singapore 079906

Cambridge University Press is part of the University of Cambridge.

It furthers the University's mission by disseminating knowledge in the pursuit of education, learning and research at the highest international levels of excellence.

www.cambridge.org
Information on this title: www.cambridge.org/9781009073202

© Keith Sidwell 2009

This publication is in copyright. Subject to statutory exception and to the provisions of relevant collective licensing agreements, no reproduction of any part may take place without the written permission of Cambridge University Press.

First published 2009
First paperback edition 2021

A catalogue record for this publication is available from the British Library

Library of Congress Cataloging in Publication data
Sidwell, Keith C.
Aristophanes the democrat : the politics of satirical comedy during the Peloponnesian War / by Keith Sidwell.
p. cm.
Includes bibliographical references and index.
ISBN 978-0-521-51998-4
1. Aristophanes – Political and social views. 2. Greek drama (Comedy) – History and criticism.
3. Satire, Greek – History and criticism. 4. Politics and literature – Greece. I. Title.
PA3879.S53   2009
882'.01 – dc22   2009017687

ISBN 978-0-521-51998-4 Hardback
ISBN 978-1-009-07320-2 Paperback

Cambridge University Press has no responsibility for the persistence or accuracy of URLs for external or third-party internet websites referred to in this publication, and does not guarantee that any content on such websites is, or will remain, accurate or appropriate.

This *book is for Jess*

Contents

Detail of illustration	*page* viii
Preface	ix
Acknowledgements	xii
List of abbreviations	xiv

PART I	SETTING THE STAGE	1
1	Getting to grips with the politics of Old Comedy	3
2	Metacomedy and politics	31
3	Metacomedy and caricature	45

PART II	THE POETS' WAR	105
4	*Acharnians*: Parabasis versus play	107
5	Metacomedy, caricature and politics from *Knights* to *Peace*	155
6	Metacomedy, caricature and politics from *Autolycus* to *Frogs*	217

Conclusions and consequences   299

PART III APPENDICES	303
Appendix 1 The view from the theatron	305
Appendix 2 Metacomedy and caricature in the surviving fourth-century plays of Aristophanes	337
Appendix 3 Timeline and proposed relationships between comedies	341
Appendix 4 The date of Eupolis' Taxiarchoi	346
Appendix 5 Clouds *868–73 and* τραυλίζω	349
Appendix 6 Michael Vickers on Strepsiades and Pericles	350
Bibliography	352
Index	363
Index Locorum	382
Index of Modern Scholars	406

Illustration

Figure 1 Mid-fourth century Apulian bell-crater, perhaps illustrating Cratinus' *Pytine*. Formerly Berlin, Staatliche Museum F3047 (lost during World War II). Taken from T. Panofka, 'Komödienscenen auf Thongefässen', *Archäologische Zeitung* 7 (1849), Tafel IV. Used by permission of the Syndics of Cambridge University Library. *page* 65

Preface

The reader may reasonably enquire, 'Why (yet) another book on Old Comedy?' I sympathise. We have for some time been pretty well equipped with texts and commentaries and scholars have recently raced to pack the bookshelves with volumes devoted to the interpretation of Aristophanes, of Eupolis and of the genre as a whole. Yet I have felt obliged to add to this stockpile because I think that still we have not reached any real understanding of several crucial matters which relate to the context and impact of satirical comedy in the fifth century, and that I have discovered a new way to resolve them. In the welter of severe ignorance which pervades the study even of Aristophanes, to say nothing of his fragmentary rivals, this may seem like a bold claim. Nonetheless, since what I have to say arises in the first instance from an authorial address (the revised parabasis of *Clouds*) and then from external evidence, I feel that it is worth proceeding, even if the journey ahead is parlous and fraught with lacunae.

I begin by challenging the general assumption (for which see among others Ste Croix, Sommerstein, Henderson and Edwards) that insofar as we can know where Aristophanes stood politically, it was on the 'right' of Athenian politics. A new interpretation of the context envisaged for the *Clouds* revision, together with a reexamination of some external evidence, points in a very different direction, towards an Aristophanes whose ideological anchor is at the radical end of the democratic spectrum. This same context, together with some meagre, but important and neglected, evidence for Eupolis will suggest equally that Aristophanes' main rival set up his political stall at the opposite extreme. It is the stark contrast between these findings and the usual inferences from the interpretation of Aristophanic plots which impels a reevaluation of the role of irony in these plays and thence of the modes of satire employed in the pieces.

The basic proposition that we can begin our study of Aristophanes and Eupolis from the premiss that they were politically opposed, but in a way previously unthought of, not only provides a new key into the political agenda of the surviving and fragmentary plays, but also helps us gain a new handle on the 'poets' war', that series of attacks and counter-attacks which can be seen in various parabatic comments and is most prominent in our evidence in relation to the *Knights*. And here too, reinterpretation of the *Clouds* parabasis both casts new light upon the attitude of Aristophanes towards politically oriented poetic rivals like Eupolis, and also reveals the possible existence of a satirical method – metacomedy – which brings into play a whole swathe of lost dramas by competitors which will have been reused, in full expectation of audience recognition, in order to subvert and satirise rival poets' earlier political satires. The role of metacomic intertexts in Aristophanic drama especially, when examined via a process for detection of them decocted from parabatic statements, reveals in fact that Aristophanes appears to have conducted a campaign against Eupolis which continued (despite Eupolis' absence from the comic competitions after around 411) right down to the end of the war.

The same text, the *Clouds* parabasis, may reveal a third tool for reinterpretation of Old Comedies. For in the course of determining what it is that Aristophanes can possibly be defending as he stresses his rivals' repetitiveness versus his own originality *in a play which is clearly a repeat*, and attacks some of them for their attacks on Hyperbolus, it becomes a reasonable inference that he regards the central satirical device available to him (and his rivals) as *on-stage caricature of real individuals*. Since the main characters in his *Clouds* apart from Socrates are not given real names, it appears that the type of subterfuge we can detect in Paphlagon/Cleon or Labes/Laches because it is blatant was in fact the norm, except that it is (for some reason) normally textually understated. Once this aperçu is applied to the on-stage representation of comic poets (as with the main character of Cratinus' *Pytine*, Ephialtes and his mentor in Eupolis' *Autolycus*, and Dicaeopolis in Aristophanes' *Acharnians*), we can begin to locate the main lines of the poetic-ideological debates of the war period, and to suggest new interpretations of Aristophanic dramas, together with reconstructions of the rival plays which they often parody and subvert. The book thus proceeds from detailed re-examination of a single – authorial – statement towards a reconsideration of the author's politics, relationships with his rivals and their plays, and modes of satirical engagement, to a detailed reconsideration of the meanings of individual plays and their avatars.

To some, the book may seem under-theorised, especially in comparison to recent work (such as that of von Moellendorf (Bakhtinian analysis of the grotesque), Kloss (Pragmatics), Robson (Humour Theory). Revermann (Performance Theory) and Platter (Bakhtinian dialogism)). The work's basic premiss, that we can recover something vital about fifth-century assumptions about the genre from Aristophanes' own words, disallows the application of theory in advance of the articulation of the consequences of this reorientation. In fact, however, the need to treat much fragmentary material, especially in the detailed second half, will necessitate the formulation of a clearly articulated methodology, which may stand as my contribution to such theorisation. Moreover, since part of the basic thrust of the work is to reveal how Aristophanes in particular (but his rivals too) made constant use of the fact that the audience for the dramatic festival was fairly consistent in order to make fun of verbal and visual material from their rivals' comedies to satirise them and their political coteries, it is clear that recent ideas about 'intertextuality' will be important to the argument. In particular, it is crucial at the outset that the reader be clear that what I mean by this term is specifically *the intended reuse by an author of an existing text (in the widest sense) known to the audience, as a tool with which the audience may construct the meaning of his own new text.*

One final point needs to be made in respect of intertextuality. In order to illuminate comic techniques – especially those involving visual intertextuality – I have occasionally had recourse (in footnotes) to modern examples (in particular from the TV cartoon series 'The Simpsons' and the now defunct satirical puppet-show 'Spitting Image'). In a modern drama we can actually know and, more importantly, *see* what is going on when such intertextuality is used – unlike in Old Comedy. For example where Homer Simpson is clubbed by baby Maggie in the basement of their home, the scene then unfolds visually and musically precisely in terms of Hitchcock's *Psycho*. The viewer who has not seen *Psycho* will still be able to follow the narrative and some of the humour, but the intertextual layer will escape her. Meanwhile, the dialogue itself makes no reference at all to the intertext. Readers should not infer that the use of such analogies is an *argument*: it is, rather, an *illustration of possibilities*. It is important to bear in mind that much of what I suggest here can readily be paralleled in modern culture.

Acknowledgements

This book has taken a long time to write. This can be put down to a number of factors: the sheer difficulty of writing against the grain of modern scholarship on the subject, the amount of time spent (as it turns out *wasted*) in running a small department constantly under threat, and the development of other areas of research at the same time. Still, now it is done, I have many debts of gratitude to repay and I do so with great pleasure.

In the course of investigating the angle from which I approach Old Comedy, I have had the pleasure of conversations and correspondence with many exceptional scholars, including (but by no means listing exhaustively): Ewen Bowie, Chris Carey, Greg Dobrov, Simon Goldhill, Alan Griffiths, Eric Handley, David Harvey, Jeff Henderson, Nick Lowe, Antonia Marchiori, Toph Marshall, Susanna Morton-Braund, Robin Osborne, Martin Revermann, Ralph Rosen, Ian Ruffell, Michael Silk, Alan Sommerstein, Ian Storey, Oliver Taplin and John Wilkins. Among these I owe particular thanks to Jeff Henderson and Ralph Rosen, who invited me to give seminars at their respective universities (Boston University and the University of Pennsylvania), and to Michael Silk, who facilitated my appointment as a Visiting Lecturer at King's College London during a sabbatical in 1993–4. Three different universities have fostered my comic muse, Lancaster (1981–5), where my teaching commitments in tragedy and comedy sparked an interest in the politics of Greek drama, Maynooth (1985–1998), where I first published on this subject, and University College Cork (1998–2008), where I have brought the book to a conclusion. In Maynooth and Cork, periods of sabbatical leave in 1993–4, 2001 and 2008 (and a Senior Research Fellowship from the *IRCHSS* in 2004–5) have made the difference between finishing and not. My thanks are also due to the University of Calgary, Alberta, Canada and to Peter Toohey, Head of the Department of Greek and Roman Studies, for inviting me as a Visiting Professor for the winter term of 2008, where I completed work on the manuscript.

Acknowledgements

Special thanks are due to my own readers: to David Braund, David Caulfield, John Dillon, Konstantin Doulamis and Oliver Ranner who each gave judicious critiques which have helped shape the final version; to Noreen Humble, whose perceptiveness has aided in mending many a lacuna of thought and expression; and to my son Marc, whose lively intelligence and vast practical experience of the theatre, as actor, drama historian and dramatist, have been of great moral support throughout the project and have left their own impact on the volume. The Press' readers produced insightful reports which I like to think have helped to make this a better book than it was when they saw it. My thanks are due to them, as they are to Michael Sharp for his strong support.

My final debts are personal, innumerable, and impossible to repay with so small a thing as even a very big book. Those who have supported me through this project and its many black moments know who they are. For their love and understanding I shall always be grateful.

Abbreviations

CAH²	*Cambridge Ancient History*, 2nd edn, Cambridge 1992–.
CGFP	*Comicorum Graecorum Fragmenta in Papyris Reperta*, ed. C. Austin, Berlin 1973.
Davies *APF*	J. K. Davies, *Athenian Propertied Families 600–300 BC*, Oxford 1971.
DFA²	A. Pickard-Cambridge, *The Dramatic Festivals of Athens*, 2nd edn, rev. J. Gould and D. M. Lewis, reissued with new suppl., Oxford 1988.
Gomme-Andrewes-Dover	W. Gomme, A. Andrewes and K. J. Dover, *A Historical Commentary on Thucydides*, 5 vols., Oxford 1959–81.
IG II²	*Inscriptiones Graecae*, vol. II², ed. J. Kirchner, Berlin 1913–40.
K-A	Kassel and Austin: see *PCG* below.
Koster, *Prolegomena*	*Scholia in Aristophanem* I. IA, *Prolegomena de Comoedia*, ed. W. J. W. Koster, Groningen 1975.
LGPN	*A Lexicon of Greek Personal Names*, ed. P. M. Fraser and E. Matthews, Oxford 1987–.
PA	*Prosopographia Attica*, ed. J. Kirchner, Berlin 1901–3.
PAA	*Persons of Ancient Athens*, ed. J. S. Traill, Toronto 1994–.
PCG	*Poetae Comici Graeci*, ed. R. Kassell and C. Austin, Berlin 1983–.
RE	A. Pauly, G. Wissowa, and W. Kroll, *Real-Encyclopädie der klassischen Altertumswissenschaft*, 1893–.

Schol. Ar.	*Scholia in Aristophanem*, ed. W. J. W. Koster and D. Holwerda, Groningen, 1960–2007.
SEG	*Supplementum Epigraphicum Graecum*, Leiden 1923–.

PART I

Setting the stage

CHAPTER I

Getting to grips with the politics of Old Comedy

[W]e must never consider in isolation a few lines in a comedy or even the speech in which they occur, but look at the play as a whole and indeed the dramatist's entire output, in so far as it is known to us.
G. E. M. de Ste Croix, *The Origins of the Peloponnesian War*, 369

Ideally... one would wish to find some kind of external control, evidence independent of our reading of the plays that would help us to calibrate our estimation of their tone or mood. Evidence about the poet, for example, might usefully restrict the range of intentions which could plausibly be ascribed to him; evidence about his audience might help us to reconstruct the expectations and preferences with which he had to reckon, and so indicate the kinds of response and effect which he might have intended to achieve; evidence about the context in which a play was composed and received, and the consequent constraints on poet and audience, might also help us to determine their respective intentions and receptive dispositions... [E]vidence of this kind is, by and large, not forthcoming...
Malcolm Heath, *Political Comedy in Aristophanes*, 8

Finding a way into the politics of Old Comedy is not easy. Starting from the plays requires the assumption that we can rely on our interpretations of them (a simple case of *petitio principii*?). If we nonetheless take this route (as for example does Ste Croix) and are tempted to take any individual utterance from a play at face value, we will be instantly reminded by others that it is bounded by its dramatic context: it is after all spoken by a *character* and not directly by the author and its political meaning will thus depend crucially upon a much wider context (including the now inaccessible original performance). Even if we were to accept the Croixian 'sandwich' hypothesis (that serious material is inserted into comedy like meat in a panino),[1] we would have to admit that we are thus made over-reliant on modern judgements of what is funny and may be missing

---
[1] Ste Croix 1972, 234, 357.

something fundamental which would have made even such an utterance amusing for its original audience. But if we attempt to approach the wider context, whether the individual play or the 'dramatist's entire output', we are again faced with apparently insuperable difficulties. If *Acharnians* is a 'peace-play', in the sense that it argues for peace with Sparta, why does the chorus in the parabasis (653–5) ask the Athenians to reject Spartan peace overtures? If Lamachus is a target in *Acharnians* (566f.) and *Peace* (304, 473–4, 1290–4), why is he praised in *Thesmophoriazousai* (841) and *Frogs* (1039)? It is not that answers of some kind cannot be found to such problems, merely that they are all speculative and not the stuff of which consensus is made.

Heath's starting point is, theoretically speaking, more satisfactory. The problem is that there is in the first place hardly any external evidence against which to test the plays' political stance or tone, and where there is, scholars again disagree fundamentally about its meaning and validity. If *Knights* satirises the *demos*, one might ask how this squares with the *Old Oligarch's* contention ([Xen.]*Ath Pol.* 2.18) that satire of the *demos* was forbidden. On the other hand, since we do not know precisely when the *Athenian Constitution* was composed, nor by whom, we may wish to deny the validity of such a question (which would provide a severe challenge to conventional views of *Knights*). If the parabatic advice of the chorus of *Frogs* is taken seriously, one might wonder at the apparently positive response of the *demos* to its palpably aristocratic ideology (the civic crown and right of reperformance awarded to the poet).[2] But since we can only conjecture about the date of this award of the crown (and do so on the basis of the assumption that the advice in the parabasis was offered directly and seriously on the poet's behalf),[3] even this palpably external piece of evidence cannot be used as a solid basis for assessing political intent. Heath himself chooses to focus on the contradiction between the interpretation of *Clouds* as an attack on Socrates and the fact that Plato has Aristophanes on such apparently friendly terms with his victim in *Symposium* as external evidence for a sceptical treatment of Aristophanic political intent. To do so, of course, also involves a basic assumption, that we really do know what is going on in Plato, that we can judge *his* tone accurately, and also that we can trust the historical accuracy of his representation (as though he might not have had some motive for inventing this encounter).[4]

---

[2] Dover 1993, 114, Hypothesis 1(c); *Life of Aristophanes* (*PCG* T1) 35–9.   [3] Sommerstein 1996a, 21.
[4] Ancient commentators were more willing than are modern to suggest that the portrait of Aristophanes is satirical (Olymp. *Vit. Pl.* 3, Ath. 187c). The poet is, however, addicted to wine and sex (177d–e)

In the absence of any unequivocal external evidence, we might be tempted to begin our enquiries by looking at the parabases. After all, these interruptions of the play's plot often purport to present authorial perspectives directly to their audience (e.g. *Wasps* 1016, *Peace* 738). But this direct approach is confined to *Acharnians, Knights, Clouds, Wasps* and *Peace* and the results from such an enquiry are not generally thought satisfactory. What are we to make, for example, of the contradiction between *Acharnians* 629 and *Knights* 513, from the first of which it appears the poet is a long-standing and experienced *didaskalos* and from the second is taking his first solo plunge into comic production? Or of the critique of the circumcised phallus (*Clouds* 538–9) versus its use at *Acharnians* 158f.? Or that of the cry ἰοὺ ἰοὺ at *Clouds* 543 with its use at line 1 of the same play? Indeed, so problematic do these utterances appear to Silk that in his recent monograph he even asserts that the parabases are not in any way helpful to our quest for a true understanding of Aristophanes' art: 'Aristophanes' characterisation of his comic practice or his comic ideals are in the end calculated to frustrate us: they are uncommunicative, almost as repeated instances of a conventional formula are uncommunicative.'[5]

This judgement does seem unduly pessimistic. Just because the instances of this group of texts do not appear to communicate anything substantive and coherent to us, this is no guarantee that they did not do so for the audiences for whom they were designed and who would have been possessed by their historical position of everything we lack through ours, an instinctive knowledge of the context of the drama (in every sense) and an awareness of the nuances of the contemporary language and its references. And Silk does not take into account similar material from other comic poets (e.g. Cratin. fr. 213, Eup. fr. 89) where the poet apparently made comments (sometimes in the first person) about his own and his rivals' work. We might, in fact, get somewhere by taking as our primary assumption the exact opposite of Silk's finding, namely that authorial statements were intended to be – and actually *were* – coherent and informative at some level, and our impression that they produce at best inconsistent and at worst downright self-contradictory impressions of the dramatist's understanding of his art and its social role and aesthetic standards suggests rather that we are missing something pretty crucial which the original audience would have known

---

and overindulges in food at the party (185 c–e), neither positive traits for an ancient audience (see Davidson 1997 *passim*). Moreover, his defence of homosexual intercourse (192a) reflects not only the view of his own Unjust Argument (*Clouds* 1084–1104), but also that of Prodicus' Kakia (D-K fr. 7 = Xen. *Mem.* 2.1.24).

[5] Silk 2000, 47–8.

without being told. But in order to approach the question of what sort of information we might glean from them, we must be slightly more circumspect than is usual in our primary analysis of their role and function.

For example, quite apart from the problem of poetic voice already mentioned between the parabasis of *Acharnians* and *Knights* (which MacDowell sensibly resolves by attributing the overt authorship of *Acharnians* to Callistratus),[6] it is important to note some crucial differences between the parabases. First of all, only five parabases (those of *Ach.*, *Knights*, *Clouds*, *Wasps* and *Peace*) purport to be representing – directly or indirectly – the author's own views. The parabases of *Birds*, *Thesmophoriazusai*, and *Frogs* are all made in the persona of the chorus (*Birds* 688, *Thesm.* 786, *Frogs* 686).[7] More importantly, there is no reference in them to the poet or his views, in complete contrast to the parabases of *Acharnians*, *Knights*, *Clouds*, *Wasps* and *Peace*, which might be characterised as quite specifically defences of the author's comedy (often in contrast to that of his rivals). However, even these five parabases are not on all fours with each other. We have already mentioned the distinction in voice between that of *Acharnians* and the rest. What is not usually noticed is that four of the five (*Ach.*, *Knights*, *Wasps* and *Peace*) belong to plays which were produced at a major festival (three Lenaea and one Dionysia), while that of *Clouds* is a revised version made for a performance which is generally agreed not to have occurred at a major festival (if it was performed at all). Moreover, and this substantiates the reality of this distinction, although each of the five parabases contains allusions to rival comic poets and attacks on politicians, the specificity of reference is much more pronounced in the *Clouds* parabasis. Only *Acharnians* apart from *Clouds* gives the name of a politician (Cleon at 659) and then not as someone attacked in a comedy. Only *Knights* apart from *Clouds* actually names contemporary rivals (Cratinus 526, Crates 537 – with the earlier poet Magnes mentioned at 520) and then in what on the surface at least is not an absolutely negative manner (unlike the attacks on unnamed rivals at *Ach.* 657–8 and *Peace* 739f.). In *Clouds*, however, we hear the names of Cleon and Hyperbolus (549, 551, 557, 558), and of Eupolis (553), Phrynichus (556) and Hermippus (557). Finally, we may point out that the poet's individual voice is heard only briefly in the other parabases (*Ach.* 659–64, *Peace* 754–74), but the whole of the *Clouds* parabasis is in the first

---

[6] MacDowell 1982, 1995, 39. See further below pp. 14, 111 for a slightly different solution.
[7] The arguments rehearsed by Dover 1993 68–9 (cf. Sommerstein 1996, 215–16) denying that the words χορῶν ἱερῶν at *Frogs* 674 and τὸν ἱερὸν χορόν at 686 are a 'deliberate reminder of the chorus' role as initiates' are weak, as is tacitly admitted when he remarks of this sobriquet's use for a chorus that '[i]t happens not to be called so elsewhere in comedy'.

person. It may be, then, that our at least quasi-external point of departure might be the one parabasis which is unequivocally personal, contains detailed information about political and poetic targets and may not have been designed for production before a major festival audience. Let us turn, then, to the question of the audience and occasion for which the revised *Clouds* parabasis was produced.

I shall deal with the passage under a number of headings, which in each case are in the form of an important question which can be answered by interrogating the parabasis in the context of external information. These headings correspond with a section-by-section analysis of the text. I shall begin each of these with a complete text of the part of the parabasis to be examined, accompanied by my translation, which inevitably will point up some of my interpretative emphases.

FOR WHAT AUDIENCE WAS THE REVISED PARABASIS DESIGNED? CLOUDS 518–36

ὦ θεώμενοι, κατερῶ πρὸς ὑμᾶς ἐλευθέρως
τἀληθῆ, νὴ τὸν Διόνυσον τὸν ἐκθρέψαντά με.
οὕτω νικήσαιμί τ' ἐγὼ καὶ νομιζοίμην σοφός, 520
ὡς ὑμᾶς ἡγούμενος εἶναι θεατὰς δεξιοὺς
καὶ ταύτην σοφώτατ' ἔχειν τῶν ἐμῶν κωμῳδιῶν
πρώτους ἠξίωσ' ἀναγεῦσ' ὑμᾶς, ἣ παρέσχε μοι
ἔργον πλεῖστον· εἶτ' ἀνεχώρουν ὑπ' ἀνδρῶν φορτικῶν
ἡττηθείς, οὐκ ἄξιος ὤν. ταῦτ' οὖν ὑμῖν μέμφομαι 525
τοῖς σοφοῖς, ὧν οὕνεκ' ἐγὼ ταῦτ' ἐπραγματευόμην.
ἀλλ' οὐδὲ ὡς ὑμῶν ποθ' ἑκὼν προδώσω τοὺς δεξίους.
ἐξ ὅτου γὰρ ἐνθάδ' ὑπ' ἀνδρῶν, οὓς ἡδὺ καὶ λέγειν,
ὁ σώφρων χὠ καταπύγων ἄριστ' ἠκουσάτην,
κἀγὼ - παρθένος γὰρ ἔτ' ἦν, κοὐκ ἐξῆν πώ μοι τεκεῖν - 530
ἐξέθηκα, παῖς δ' ἑτέρα τις λαβοῦσ' ἀνείλετο,
ὑμεῖς δ' ἐξεθρέψατε γενναίως κἀπαιδεύσατε,
ἐκ τούτου μοι πιστὰ παρ' ὑμῶν γνώμης ἔσθ' ὅρκια.
νῦν οὖν Ἠλέκτραν κατ' ἐκείνην ἥδ' ἡ κωμῳδία
ζητοῦσ' ἦλθ', ἤν που 'πιτύχῃ θεαταῖς οὕτω σοφοῖς· 535
γνώσεται γάρ, ἤνπερ ἴδῃ, τἀδέλφου τὸν βόστρυχον.

Members of the audience, I shall tell you the truth freely, by Dionysus who raised me. Cross my heart and hope I win and be reckoned *sophos* (clever; intellectual; artistic?), it was because I thought you theatre-buffs and this to be the cleverest (most intellectual?) of my comedies that I thought you should have the *first* taste of it, since it cost me an enormous amount of labour. And *then* I had to retreat, defeated by vulgar men, although I did not deserve it. So for this I blame you *sophoi* (intellectuals?), for whose sake I was taking such trouble. But even so I shall not willingly betray the theatre-buffs among you. For ever since in this place my 'chaste and buggered boys' were praised by men whose names it is a pleasure even to pronounce, and I – since I was still unmarried and not yet allowed to give birth – exposed the child, and another girl took it and claimed it as her own, and you gave her a noble upbringing and education, since then I have oaths from you staking your good opinion of me. So now, just like that Electra, this comedy has come looking to see if she can chance upon spectators as clever as those were. I can tell you, she will recognise her brother's lock of hair, if she sees it.

The *Clouds* parabasis stands out from the other known examples of the form in two important respects: (1) it comes from a revision, perhaps in its surviving form one not amenable to what we envisage as the production values of the state festivals; (2) this revised version was never produced at a state festival. These pieces of information, though they amount only to inferences, in the first case from the mention by the parabasis of the play's first production (522–3) and from the absence of a crucial choral ode (after 888) and the retention of an (apparently) out-of-date attack on Cleon (575–94), in the second from the criticism by Eratosthenes of Callimachus' inference that the didaskalic records were wrong to place *Clouds* before *Marikas*, are generally accepted and seem to me to be incontrovertible points of departure.[8] And yet, even if the play was not in a condition to be produced at a state festival and was not so produced, nonetheless the revision had reached a stage at which Aristophanes could envisage an audience to whom he wished to show it (ὦ θεώμενοι 'members of the audience' 518) well enough for him to write a parabasis that is at once the most personal and the most theatrically and politically explicit (in terms of the naming of names) of all those in the surviving plays and the one in which he appears close enough to his projected spectators (521, 535) to mark out groups among them (525–7). We must surely infer from this that the play in its surviving form was at least *near* to some form of production and that the poet had remodelled the play with an audience in mind.[9]

The problem comes at the next step. Despite the fact that the play was never produced at a state festival, scholars tend to assume (though with some discomfort, given the actual language of the text) that the audience envisaged would nonetheless have been the audience of a Lenaea

---

[8] Dover 1968, lxxx–lxxxi. The only possible objection might be that the revision appeared under a different title, but that, since its *contents* appeared to be the same as those of *Clouds*, the Alexandrian scholars chose to call the revised play by the title *Clouds*. However, that would in its turn require that the play had come down without a title (not impossible, but perhaps unlikely?).

[9] See also Revermann 2006, 326–32 (Appendix C).

Getting to grips with the politics of Old Comedy 9

or Dionysia.[10] Here we must attend to the detail, with the crucial words italicised (521–5):

ὡς ὑμᾶς ἡγούμενος εἶναι θεατὰς δεξιοὺς
καὶ ταύτην σοφώτατ' ἔχειν τῶν ἐμῶν κωμῳδιῶν
πρώτους ἠξίωσ' ἀναγεῦσ' ὑμᾶς ἣ παρέσχε μοι
ἔργον πλεῖστον· *εἶτ'* ἀνεχώρουν ὑπ' ἀνδρῶν φορτικῶν
ἡττηθείς, οὐκ ἄξιος ὤν.

It was because I thought you theatre-buffs and this to be the cleverest (most intellectual?) of my comedies that I thought you should have the *first* taste of it, since it cost me an enormous amount of labour. And *then* I had to retreat, defeated by vulgar men, although I did not deserve it.

Commentators have noticed the problem that is created, on the assumption of an Athenian festival audience, of the claim 'first' to have given the audience a taste and 'then' to have been defeated by 'vulgar men'. This looks like a *temporal* progression (as the use of πρώτιστον 'very first' and εἶθ' 'then' at 553 and 557 below certainly is). The explanation favoured by both Dover and Sommerstein is that Aristophanes is implying that, like some tragic poets, he might have put his play on first in some other state and so is making a joke about his international reputation.[11] But this manifestly skews the detail of the text, since what happened is represented as *fact* and there is not the slightest hint (though one must obviously be careful about such claims) of anything amusing given the context of defeat and complaint that encompasses the lines. In particular, though, this explanation appears to elide the obvious chronological significance of πρώτους 'first' and εἶτ' 'then': *Clouds* was seen by *this* audience first, then produced at the state festival and defeated.[12] There is, then, a clear historical sequence expressed here of which we may be able to make sense, and which we should attend to before assuming that it is only part of an elaborate joke which scarcely fits the linguistic data.

---

[10] See Dover 1968 on 523: 'We may well ask how Ar. could speak of giving his audience the first taste of the play..., as if it had been open to him to put on in some other state a comedy about contemporary Athenian life.' Sommerstein 1982 on 521–3: '**you** seems to mean here "you Athenians". The only plausible alternative would be that it meant "the international audience at the City Dionysia" as opposed to the more homogeneous public who attended the Lenaea...; but it would then be impossible to explain "in this place" (528), since Dionysian and Lenaean audiences were alike only to be found in one place, the Theatre of Dionysus. Ar. must therefore be claiming to have done the Athenians a favour by producing *Clouds* first at Athens rather than abroad ("this place" in 528 will then mean "Athens").'
[11] *Loc. cit.* previous note.
[12] As Dover points out (*loc. cit.* n. 10), we do not know what ἀναγεῦσαι really means. However, the temporal sequence appears to rule out 'taste for a second time', since the point of reference here must be *Clouds I* (524) and not the new version.

Given that the revised play was not ever performed at a state festival in Athens, and that we know absolutely nothing about the process by which tragedies or comedies made their way from the dramatist's imagination and pen to that stage, it does not seem unreasonable (especially since there are other problematic things about the relationship implied between poet and *this* audience which never occur in other parabases) to suggest that Aristophanes may have had a quite different audience in mind from the one at the Lenaea or Dionysia when he wrote this parabasis. If so, it is an audience to whom Aristophanes presented a version of *Clouds I before* it was seen by the festival audience who voted it down at Dionysia 423. In any case, it is difficult to interpret ἐνθάδ' 'here' in 528 as 'at the Lenaea/Dionysia', since logically it must be the same place in which the 'taster' of *Clouds I* was presented *before* its defeat at the festival. It will imply, then, 'the same place in which the current revision of *Clouds* and the *Banqueters* were produced *before* entering the state competitions'. The identity of this location, and its theatrical resources, will remain obscure to *us*, but the text does tell us that such a place existed and remained a fixture for such pre-festival performances over a period extending from 427 to (at least) 417, or whenever the second *Clouds* was revised.[13]

Now I can see no reason at all to deny that there might be opportunities for the performance of plays prior to their entry into competition. Indeed, at the very least rehearsals would have been necessary. But comparative evidence would suggest that the production of plays, with their costumes, music, masks and props, required financial assistance and though in Athens such funding was given to a few chosen ones by the state for the festival (through the *choregia*), that does not explain how the play and its playwright got to the stage of being chosen, unless we wish to rely on the assumption that the archon sat down with fifty manuscripts which he whittled down to three (or five).[14]

Once we have adumbrated this more literal interpretation of the lines, it at once becomes clear that some other things in the parabasis not only fit in with it, but also add to our understanding of precisely what the audience was there *for*. Halliwell has noted that 528–31 appears to refer to a specific group of Aristophanes' patrons, who had supported *Banqueters*.[15] The language allows us to go further, though. The play, like the revised *Clouds*, was first produced 'here' (i.e. before this audience, in this – perhaps

---

[13] Set by most scholars between 419 and 417. See further Kopff 1990 and Storey 1993b, and chapter six below for a different solution.
[14] See Luppe 1972 for discussion of the number of plays produced at each festival.
[15] Halliwell 1980, 42–3.

private – theatrical space), *before* it was shown and judged at the state festival. This can be inferred both from the way in which the earlier play is brought into the discussion immediately after the first *Clouds* and from the fact that the audience is said to have 'brought it up and educated it', a process which surely looks forward to the consummation of marriage (i.e. metaphorically, production at the festival). The audience of which Aristophanes was thinking, then, when he revised the play and wrote the parabasis was the same group of patrons who had seen *Banqueters* through from its first rough draft presentation in a private theatrical space, and this applies whether or not the play as we have it represents that rehearsal production.

Another Aristophanic comedy is actually named at 554: ἐκστρέψας τοὺς ἡμετέρους Ἱππέας κακὸς κακῶς 'a wicked refurbishment of our *Knights* by a wicked man'. A peculiar, and hitherto barely explained, aspect of this statement, the use of the plural form ἡμετέρους, can now be aligned with the newly won insight. Halliwell has commented, albeit somewhat reservedly, on the peculiarity of the plural possessive adjective and wondered whether it might not allude to Eupolis' claim (*Baptai* fr. 89) to have co-written this play with Aristophanes.[16] Given the deeply critical language used of his rival in the same line (κακὸς κακῶς), this seems unlikely. Halliwell is correct, however, to claim that the word cannot be assumed to mean simply 'mine', since this does not accord with general Aristophanic practice. Moreover, it is specifically against the way he expresses himself later on in this parabasis when he wants to focus on the comic material from his pen. At 559 (τὰς εἰκοὺς... τὰς ἐμάς), 560 (τοῖς ἐμοῖς) and 561 (ἐμοὶ καὶ τοῖσιν ἐμοῖς... εὑρήμασιν), he use the singular. It is therefore difficult to deny ἡμετέρους a literal significance. Now that we have hypothesised a quite specific audience for the parabasis, however, it is possible for us to see what that is. Aristophanes is surely reminding the group he is addressing as a fundraising base for *Clouds II* that they had also been of material assistance in bringing the *Knights* to its state festival success. It is in this sense that *Knights* is not just 'mine', but 'ours'. All sorts of inferences might flow from this, of course, not least (given the reference to the attack on Cleon in the play at 549) that the group from whom Aristophanes drew financial support had some sort of political agenda. I shall return to this issue in due course.

If the audience (or envisaged audience) of the revised parabasis is a cohesive and identifiable group, rather than a vast and undifferentiated

---

[16] Halliwell 1989, 524 n. 17. See Storey 2003, 287 for approval of this interpretation.

one, as at the state festivals, this will also help us to tie down the other groups referred to by the poet in his address. First of all, before the defeat of *Clouds* proved that some of them (specified at 525–6) did not understand the popular taste and/or the prevailing mood in 423, the whole audience had been considered by the poet to be θεατὰς δεξιούς ('theatre-buffs' 521). This phrase makes it clear once more (cf. 535) that we are here speaking of the pre-festival *Clouds* as a *performance* before an audience (cf. 518), albeit a selected and restricted one. Secondly, the audience contains a specific group who are called τοῖς σοφοῖς ('the wise' 526), who are the ones blamed both for the poet's failure and for his composition of the play (ὧν οὕνεκ᾽ ἐγὼ ταῦτ᾽ ἐπραγματευόμην 'for whose sake I was taking such trouble'). Given the intellectual theme of *Clouds*, specifically its attack on Socrates, and the contemporary association of the term οἱ σοφοί ('the wise') with Socrates' intellectual opponents, the sophists (Pl. *Apol.* 20a, *Prt.* 309b, Xen. *Mem.* 2.1.21), it is surely right to identify the particular group addressed here with them, though naturally there is no indication who they were individually. They must also be the same group mentioned in the discussion of the failure of *Clouds I* in the parabasis of *Wasps* (1049 ὁ δὲ ποιητὴς οὐδὲν χείρων παρὰ τοῖσι σοφοῖς νενόμισται 'the poet is no less well regarded by the wise'), where, significantly (this *is* addressed to the whole festival audience) they are *not* blamed. This insight has, of course, very important consequences for the general interpretation of the play, not the least of them that the attack on Socrates was intended to contrast him with the sophists, not to present him as one of them, and that Aristophanes may have aspired to become one of their number (520).[17] Moreover, it strongly suggests that his anti-Cleonian agenda was fuelled both by intellectual backers (whom Cleon despised: see Thuc. 3.37.3–5; cf. *Knights* 986 and 191–3 for his lack of education) and perhaps by Aristophanes' own intellectual pretensions (520). Thirdly, having singled out the intellectuals, he returns once more to the whole audience and once again casts them, excluding those who have already shown their fallibility (525–6), as τοὺς δεξίους ('theatre-buffs' 527) before once more picking out the specific, but unnamed, individuals who supported *Banqueters* when it was shown in this venue (ἐξ ὅτου γὰρ ἐνθάδ᾽, ὑπ᾽ ἀνδρῶν οὓς ἡδὺ καὶ λέγειν, | ὁ σώφρων τε χὠ καταπύγων ἄριστ᾽ ἠκουσάτην 'For ever since in this place my "chaste and buggered boys"

---

[17] Thus the suggestion of Willink 1983 that Socrates' non-Socratic features in *Clouds* (cf. the argument by Socrates at Pl. *Apol.* 19c that he has nothing to do with the 'Socrates' of Aristophanes) reflect a deliberate assimilation to the popular prejudicial image of Prodicus, which in turn probably depends upon comedy, is extremely helpful in unravelling the difficulties associated with the chorus' praise of Prodicus (at *Clouds* 361). See further chapter 5, p. 174.

were praised by men whose names it is a pleasure even to pronounce'), and who presumably persuaded the rest of this audience (ὑμεῖς 'you' 532) to lend (again presumably) financial assistance to bring the play to its competitive production. The purpose of the current (or envisaged) production is to replicate the discovery of 'spectators as clever as those' (θεαταῖς οὕτω σοφοῖς 535) to help (presumably by defraying costs) to bring the *Clouds* revision to the state festival, or at least the stage where the archon made his selection.

This brings us to the problem of 534. Sommerstein thinks the phrase Ἠλέκτραν κατ' ἐκείνην means 'like Electra of old', that is, like the Electra in tragedy. The difficulty with this interpretation is that the character in the surviving drama where she recognised her brother's lock of hair (Aeschylus' *Choephoroi*) did not come with the intention of searching, (ζητοῦσ'), and especially not for 'spectators as clever as those were'.[18] The Electra in 534 must surely, then, *be Banqueters*, partly because this removes the need to accuse Aristophanes of making a basic mistake about Aeschylus, partly because the play *did* come before this audience, as *Clouds II* now does, *looking for* people like those praised at 528–9. Hence, 'that Electra' is *Banqueters*, versus 'this comedy' *Clouds II*, rather than 'the Electra in so-and-so's tragedy'. The comparison operates fully between the two plays because both have come before their potential sponsors to seek spectators intelligent enough to take them on. Calling *Banqueters* 'that Electra' then allows Aristophanes an amusing cross-reference to Aeschylus' *Choephoroi* without any erroneous additions. *Banqueters* could be said to be like Electra in the first place because comedy is feminine (cf. Comedy's appearance as the wife of the poet in Cratinus' *Pytine*), and the analogy at 530–2 develops the play into a girl of marriageable age. Like Electra/*Banqueters*, then, *Clouds II* will also recognise her brother's hair when she sees it, which, translated, means that the play will at once divine the presence of men who will protect her, as Orestes would protect his sister.

This raises another question, however. Why does Aristophanes need to remind his audience about the fact that *Banqueters* was picked up and claimed for herself by another girl, presumably, as Sommerstein argues ad loc., a young married woman (530–1)? After all, he assumes that they will know the very individuals who recommended that play (529–30) and it is the rest of that very same audience he envisages addressing (ὑμεῖς 'you' 532, ὑμῶν 'of you' 533) who provided the necessary environment for its

---

[18] Both Sommerstein (1982 ad loc.) and Dover (1968 ad loc.) suggest that Aristophanes has made a mistake in his reference to Aeschylus' *Choephoroi*.

nurture and production (translating κἀπαιδεύσατε 'you gave her an education' into the cognate theatrical language of διδάσκειν 'to produce' and διδάσκαλος 'producer'). Of course, 530–1 are usually taken to mean that the play was, for whatever reason (perhaps because Aristophanes really was below the minimum age to compete) given to a producer, Callistratus, in whose name it appeared at the state festival. There is a problem with this, though: the audience addressed here certainly are meant to know that it had been a subterfuge and that Aristophanes was the real mother (author) since the parabasis we have is clearly in the voice of the dramatist Aristophanes (witness the references to his baldness at 540 and 545). Moreover, the arguments of Mastromarco, Halliwell and Brockmann have shown that it is highly unlikely that Aristophanes was not known as the author of all his plays at their time of production at the state festivals.[19] Besides, the very specific detail at 530, παρθένος γὰρ ἔτ' ἦν κοὐκ ἐξῆν πώ μοι τεκεῖν ('since I was still unmarried and not yet allowed to give birth') is part of Aristophanes' *captatio benevolentiae* of an audience that is *not* that of the state festivals. It must, therefore, have both a function within the parabasis and an external point of reference that relates somehow to the *pre-festival* performance which gained the play sponsorship. The reason this fact is mentioned, then, is probably because it reflects well on this specific audience and is the basis of the πιστὰ ... ὅρκια ('oaths ... staking your good opinion') that exist between Aristophanes and them. The implications of this passage for the conduct of matters at the state festival itself depend once more upon the *sequence* of the narrative. A closer reading of the text suggests that events unfolded in this order: (1) Aristophanes brought *Banqueters* before this audience and gained the approval of specific, but unspecified, men (528–9); (2) he then exposed it (i.e. *after* its 'taster' performance), because he was too young (or inexperienced? Cf. *Knights* 541–4) to enter the state festival (531); (3) it was put on at the festival under the name of another (already experienced) poet (531); (4) it was prepared for the selection process with the financial support of this group (532). On this interpretation, then, it is not possible that the παῖς ... ἑτέρα ('another girl') of 530 alludes to Callistratus, since according to the terms of the metaphor, he did not simply produce the pre-festival comedy, he actually had to pretend for the time being that it was his. Callistratus, however, was not a poet (see *PCG* IV s.v.) and his claim would not have been plausible. My guess is that a more experienced poet belonging to this group (Philonides, perhaps?) was the front-man. If that is what happened, then we can see

---

[19] Mastromarco 1979, Halliwell 1980, Brockmann 2003, 316–46.

exactly why Aristophanes sees fit to recall the strange circumstances of his first play's first performance: the anecdote confers great credit on the vision of a small group of people – including an experienced comic poet who realised what the group had in Aristophanes – and the lengths they were prepared to go to to launch a talented youngster's career, and Aristophanes owes his success entirely to the faith they showed in him at that point.

This reading of the opening of the parabasis, then, opens up a new vista in respect of the social context of Old Comedy, one in which a poet might look for financial support for his work with an established group, with intellectual interests and political coherence, which supported, perhaps even invited (526), attacks upon individuals, whether in the intellectual sphere (Socrates) or in politics (Cleon, 549, 555). The appeal for patronage would in these circumstances naturally contain elements of appeal to shared experience (plays *we* have done together) and praise of specific individuals for having shown their confidence in the poet's skills.

WHY DOES ARISTOPHANES ATTACK COMIC NONSENSE AND COMIC POETS SO VIGOROUSLY IN THIS PARABASIS? *CLOUDS* 537–50

ὡς δὲ σώφρων ἐστὶ φύσει σκέψασθ᾽· ἥτις πρῶτα μὲν
οὐδὲν ἦλθε ῥαψαμένη σκυτίον καθειμένον,
ἐρυθρὸν ἐξ ἄκρου, παχύ, τοῖς παιδίοις ἵν᾽ ᾖ γέλως·
οὐδ᾽ ἔσκωψεν τοὺς φαλακροὺς, οὐδὲ κόρδαχ᾽ εἵλκυσεν·   540
οὐδὲ πρεσβύτης ὁ λέγων τἄπη τῇ βακτηρίᾳ
τύπτει τὸν παρόντ᾽, ἀφανίζων πονηρὰ σκώμματα·
οὐδ᾽ εἰσῇξε δᾷδας ἔχουσ᾽, οὐδ᾽ 'ἰοὺ ἰού' βοᾷ·
ἀλλ᾽ αὑτῇ καὶ τοῖς ἔπεσιν πιστεύουσ᾽ ἐλήλυθεν.
κἀγὼ μὲν τοιοῦτος ἀνὴρ ὢν ποιητὴς οὐ κομῶ,   545
οὐδ᾽ ὑμᾶς ζητῶ ᾽ξαπατᾶν δὶς καὶ τρὶς ταὔτ᾽ εἰσάγων,
ἀλλ᾽ ἀεὶ καινὰς ἰδέας εἰσφέρων σοφίζομαι,
οὐδὲν ἀλλήλαισιν ὁμοίας καὶ πάσας δεξιάς·
ὃς μέγιστον ὄντα Κλέων᾽ ἔπαισ᾽ εἰς τὴν γαστέρα,
κοὔκ ἐτόλμησ᾽ αὖθις ἐπεμπηδῆσ᾽ αὐτῷ κειμένῳ.   550

Consider how chaste (*sophron*) she naturally is. In the first place she hasn't come here with any dangling leather appendage stitched on, red at the end and thick, to give the young lads a laugh. Nor has she made fun of bald men, nor dragged on stage a vulgar dance (*kordax*). Nor does the old man speaking the lines hit the other character on stage with his stick, as a cover for bad punch-lines. Nor has she rushed on stage with torches, nor shouted 'ooh ooh'. Instead she has come relying upon herself and her words. I myself, because I am a poet of this sort too, am not a member of the long-haired brigade, nor do I look to deceive you by bringing on the same play two and three times, but I play my tricks by always presenting new plots, completely different from each other and all clever. When Cleon was at the height of his power, I hit him in the stomach. But I did not have the audacity to jump on him again when he was laid low.

In attempting to answer this question, it is of particular importance to note (a) that the parabasis early on speaks in a highly derogatory manner of the poetic rivals who defeated *Clouds* in 423 (ὑπ' ἀνδρῶν φορτικῶν 'by vulgar men' 524), (b) that the central section, to which I now move, has so much to say about comic motifs of which the author disapproves (537–43) and of contrasts between his own practice and that of his rivals (545–52), and (c) that the penultimate part speaks in very specific and again deeply critical terms of specific poets and specific problems with their work (553–9). Although other parabases criticise poetic motifs (e.g. *Ach.* 657–8, *Peace* 739f.), only in *Knights* is there a specific mention of any individual rival (526, 537). We may now reasonably suspect that the difference is made by the particularity of the audience to which Aristophanes addresses himself.[20] In that case, it is also important for us to re-examine our general interpretations of 537–43, since its address to an audience whose members Aristophanes knew, who knew and had supported his earlier comedies, and who might be expected to support his current endeavour implies that they might be expected *not* to support other comic poets, especially those whose work is implicitly criticised here and explicitly in 553–6 (see below).

That Aristophanes is serious about his differences with at the least Cratinus and Ameipsias is clear from line 524, taken together with the didaskalic record of the comic competition at Dionysia 423 recorded in *Clouds*, Hypothesis II (Dover).[21] He calls the men who defeated him φορτικοί, ('vulgar') a word associated with vulgar comedy also at *Wasps* 66 and *Lysistrata* 1217 (cf. Plato *Phdr.* 236c; note φόρτον 'rubbish' at *Peace* 748). It seems unlikely *a priori*, then, that when Aristophanes begins to complain about low-grade comic techniques on returning to the claim of the current play upon his patrons he is not also serious, even if his tone is ironic and his language – and the image of the play as a well-bred Athenian girl ready for marriage, chastity intact (σώφρων φύσει 537) – comic. However,

---

[20] It is difficult to make proper comparisons with the practice of other poets, because no surviving fragment unequivocally contains the name of a rival. It is true that it is not clear that Cratin. fr. 213 *Pytine* is actually a paraphrase, rather than a quotation, and there has to have been some way for the scholiasts to have known that the poet was speaking of Aristophanes and Eupolis. Aristophanes might have been called ὁ φαλακρός, as he is at Eup. *Baptai* fr. 89, or his name may have been given (it fits the anapaestic metre perfectly), but we know of no parallel nickname for Eupolis. Other references to Aristophanes, specifically to *Peace*, in Pl. *Nikai* (fr. 86) and Eup. *Autolycus* (fr. 62), are subject to the same analysis.

[21] Dover 1968, 1 = *PCG* Cratin. *Pytine* T1.

the two contending available interpretations both in different ways deny the passage's underlying seriousness. The traditional one, articulated by Sommerstein, is that Aristophanes is merely being self-ironic here, since at least one of the motifs mentioned is found in earlier Aristophanes (the circumcised phallus of 538 at *Ach.* 158–61) and three more are, arguably, used in *Clouds* itself (old man beating with a stick 541, cf. 1297–1300; rushing on stage with torches 543, cf. 1490f.; cries of ἰού ἰού 543, cf. 1, 1321 and 1493).[22] This may be partly true, in that the audience may have gained a humorous frisson from the bold way the poet states the differences between his comedy and that of his rivals. But it is not a sufficient explanation because of the earlier involvement of the issue of comic rivalry (524), and because the complaints are embedded in a contrast with what the poet claims is his own practice, reliance on the dramatic vehicle and its lines, or language (544). The more radical explanation, first voiced by Hubbard in 1986 and defended in 1991, contends that Aristophanes is saying that his original *Clouds* did not have these motifs, but the new one does, for reasons pertaining to the need to achieve popular success. This view depends on demonstrating that *all* the motifs criticised belong to *Clouds II*, but his evidence for the circumcised phallus, the *kordax* and the critique of bald men falls short of proof.[23] More importantly, he needs to interpret the aorist tenses of 538, 540 and 543 as referring to *Clouds I*, which is difficult in light of the occurrence at 541 and 543 of the present tense and at 544 of the perfect. On the contrary, since the poet has just been speaking of the way in which *Banqueters* was received by *this* audience, it is quite clear that it is *Clouds II* which now comes before that same discriminating assembly at 537f. and contains none of the motifs so roundly abused.

Except, of course, that it does contain at least three. Hence the Sommerstein line. But self-irony about the use of bad comic techniques in the context of the attempt to get support (in the form of money?) from your patrons seems a perverse ploy, especially when you have begun with the description of those who defeated the play in 423 as 'vulgar', a category into which it seems relatively easy to put these motifs. We need to pay

---

[22] Sommerstein 1992, 21. See also Murray 1987, Hubbard 1991, 99–100, 146.
[23] Hubbard 1991, 91–2. There is no textual evidence to compel us to believe that the *circumcised* phallus (alluded to at 538–9) was worn by any character in *Clouds*, though it might, of course have been used as a merely visual device. The play may have represented Socrates as bald, but we do not know the state of his hairline in the 420s or 410s, and nothing verbal is made of this, if it was so, while the references to his head (cf. 146–7, 171–3) do not become obviously more hilarious if we envisage him thus. That Strepsiades dances at 439–56 is not a necessary inference and even were it so, there is no indication that the dance is a *kordax*, though, again, it might be.

further attention to the claims Aristophanes is making about his own comedy here. The explicit contrast with the vulgar techniques listed at 537–43 is with a comedy 'reliant only upon herself and her words' (αὐτῇ καὶ τοῖς ἔπεσιν πιστεύουσα 544). 'Relying upon herself' seems to suggest an implicit rebuttal of claims that he had copied from – or collaborated with – another poet, such as those made in reference to *Knights* at Cratin. *Pytine* fr. 213 and Eup. *Baptai* fr. 89. The fact that he will make this type of attack upon Eupolis at 553–5 tends to support this interpretation (see further below). 'Relying upon its words' can be related to Aristophanes' claim in the parabasis of *Peace* (749–50) that he has built up a great art with, among other things, ἔπεσιν μεγάλοις 'great words'. His use (presumably in relation to the 'plots', ἰδέαι, of his comedies) of the term σοφίζομαι ('I play my tricks' 547), as of the earlier wish to be considered σοφός ('wise' 520), also suggests a contrast between the subtlety of his own comedy and the rumbustious visual and vocal effects of that of his rivals (537–43). However, the term σοφίζομαι also seems very often to carry the undercurrent of trickery (*Knights* 299; Dem. 18.227; Eur. *IA* 744, *Bacch.* 200), so that Aristophanes may well be intimating to his knowing and sympathetic audience that his play-writing is not entirely straightforward.

But if Aristophanes is *serious* in his criticisms of other comic poets, while using these motifs himself, does not that still constitute a self-contradiction? Not necessarily. The context of this parabasis is not just defence, but also self-promotion. It is entirely possible, then, that we must think of another explanation, which would rely upon the familiarity of this audience with his earlier work and their taste for a type of comedy which plays verbal tricks (544 with 547) while at the same time apparently giving those rivals cause to complain of his reliance upon their work (544, with Cratin. fr. 213 and Eup. fr. 89). Fortunately, there is one to hand. Several years ago, I suggested that the business of Aristophanes, Eupolis and *Knights* and the accusations of plagiarism (voiced by Cratin. fr. 213), collaboration (Eup. fr. 89), and annoyed rebuttal (*Clouds* 554, see pp. 24–6 below) could be understood if Aristophanes had been *parodying* Eupolis in that play. The suggestion has not met with much approval, partly because it is not readily demonstrable in the state of our evidence for the plays of Eupolis.[24] But it is nonetheless a reasonable alternative, precisely because in parody we have all the necessary terms to fit the self-portrait Aristophanes offers in this parabasis. Parody does involve trickery and it can be reliant upon language.

---

[24] See Sidwell 1993. Storey 2003, 297–300, Kyriakidi 2007, 91, 132–4 contain a critique of my earlier work.

Moreover, it depends fundamentally upon the preservation of similarities with its vehicle (sometimes even upon the usurpation of its *voice*). Thus if Aristophanes does parody the material and style of his rivals, this might easily extend to critical imitation of their visual and vocal motifs. If so, this is what we are seeing in the apparent self-contradiction between 537–43 and the play within which it is set. That is to say, the cry of ἰοὺ ἰού ('ooh ooh') which begins the play also establishes for the audience an immediate point of parodic reference in the comedy of a rival, who is thus being satirised.

The interpretation offered here of 537–43, then, assumes first that Aristophanes was serious in his attacks on the use of these motifs, and secondly, therefore, that his audience would recognise them as associated with the work of specific rival poets. It may even be, given their specificity, that they belonged to a single play, by an individual poet, which his audience would be expected immediately to recognise – and which was being parodied in its turn at certain points in the new *Clouds* (specifically at 1, 1321, and 1493: cries of ἰοὺ ἰού ('ooh ooh'); 1297–1300 leading old man hitting someone with a stick; 1490f. rushing on stage with torches). If so, what clues do we have about the identity of the comic poet and the comedy that forms the target of these verses? At least three of the motifs can be tied, in one way or another, to Eupolis, the poet most roundly lambasted later in the parabasis (553–5). The scholium (ε) on 541 reads: οὐδὲ πρεβύτης ὁ λέγων· ὡς Εὔπολις ἐν τοῖς Προσπαλτίοις 'Nor the old man who speaks: as Eupolis in the *Prospaltioi*'. This is not necessarily unequivocal evidence, since the ancient scholia are notoriously unreliable. Nonetheless, it does betoken a search for the motif and, thus, it is reasonable to believe, the discovery of a really obvious example of it (though it does not tell us anything about Eupolis' objectives in presenting it, which may not have been straightforward either). As to joking at bald men (540), Eupolis had included someone called τὸν φαλακρόν ('the bald man') in a list in his *Chrysoun Genos* (fr. 298.5) which some have interpreted as identifying members of the play's chorus. One might hesitate to describe this mention as satirical (ἔσκωψεν 'he joked at') were it not for the fact that most of those listed are also classified by peculiarities of physique or dress (ὁ τυφλός 'the blind man'; ὁ τὴν κάλην ἔχων 'the hunchback' 1; ὁ στιγματίας 'the branded slave' 2; ὁ πυργός 'the tower';[25] ὁ διεστραμμένος 'the squinty-eyed man' 3; ὁ τὸν τρίβων' ἔχων 'the man with the old cloak' 6) and are pretty obviously real individuals (like Archestratos at line 4). It is too much of a coincidence that Aristophanes later claims this sobriquet, φαλακρός ('baldy': cf. *Peace*

---

[25] Storey 2003, 26 reads πυρρός 'redhead'.

767f.) – and that Eupolis uses it, clearly referring to Aristophanes (*Baptai* fr. 89), for us to believe that we are dealing with two different Athenians known publicly by the same nickname. Finally, we know that Eupolis introduced a *kordax*, criticised at 540, into his *Marikas* of 421, because Aristophanes tells us so specifically further on in this parabasis (555). If we are to suggest a single play which might have accommodated all these motifs, then, the evidence might points us towards *Marikas*, produced in 421, the most recent of the three possible Eupolidean referents and the one most manifestly in Aristophanes' mind as he wrote this parabasis, since it is mentioned at 553 and its *kordax* is brought in at 555.

This cannot, unfortunately, be demonstrated independently. Nonetheless, it is worth pausing for a moment to reflect upon the major inference we might make if it were true. Since Aristophanes was bald (*Peace* 767–73, *Knights* 550), and makes play with the fact here at 545, we might infer (if the motifs criticised at 537–43 are from *Marikas*) that *Marikas* had for some reason satirised him (and that he had been attacked much earlier, before *Knights*, in Eupolis' *Chrysoun Genos*). We know *Marikas* satirised Hyperbolus as the main character (553 below with Quintilian 1.10.18), and the scholium on 555 suggests that the drunken old woman who danced the *kordax* represented Hyperbolus' mother. The fact that Aristophanes will shortly attack in particular Eupolis' assault on Hyperbolus (553–5), in part because his play turned *Knights* inside out, like a piece of clothing being prepared for reuse, looks, in the context of a friendly and limited audience of potential patrons, very like a political defence of the politician and *Marikas* like an attack upon someone who was associated with him. I shall say more about this when I turn to the next section of the parabasis.

Lines 537–43 are not the only point at which Aristophanes has appeared to commentators to be contradicting himself egregiously. At 546, he implicitly accuses his rivals of presenting the same things two and three times, and this in a play which Hypothesis 1 (Dover) assures us is substantially the same as the 423 version! Moreover, at 549–50, he claims not to have attacked Cleon after his death, an assertion contradicted by *Peace* 47–8, 269–72, 313–20, 647–56 and 752–60, not to mention the retention (as most scholars think) of the first epirrheme from the first version (575–94).[26] If the interpretation offered of 537–43 is correct and if this parabasis is, as I have argued, an appeal for patronage to a sympathetic audience which had supported at least three of his earlier productions (*Banqueters*, *Clouds I*, and *Knights*), then we are obliged here too to seek an alternative explanation,

---

[26] Dover 1968, lxxx–lxxxi. Sommerstein 1982, 2 n. 2.

since it appears to be inherently self-defeating to lie directly to potential sponsors who are already very familiar with your oeuvre.

Some scholars have associated the attack at 546 with a fragment from the parabasis of Aristophanes' *Anagyros* (K-A fr. 58) which attacks a rival for 'making three thin cloaks out of one of my luxury overcoats' (ἐκ δὲ τῆς χλανίδος τρεῖς ἀπληγίδας ποιῶν) and linked it with *Clouds* 553 to suggest that it is Eupolis who is being accused in both places of reusing Aristophanic material with repetitious tedium.[27] This is a perfectly logical explanation, even if we can not identify the three Eupolidean plays and can only surmise that the Aristophanic play in question is *Knights*. It also leaves us with the question of whether Aristophanes is speaking accurately or not in saying 'twice and three times'. Was there some doubt as to the third remake's relationship with the original? Or is he just speaking vaguely? Whatever the answer to this puzzle, though, we are still left with the apparent self-contradiction of *Clouds II* as an example of 'the same thing a second time'. One answer is to say, with Dover, that what follows shows that 'he is criticising his rivals for writing ostensibly different plays on the same themes'. This is partly true, at least, and the observation clearly has something to contribute to resolution of the conundrum. However, the explanation evades the fact that line 546 looks more like an attack upon individual poets for rewriting the *same* play, not upon different poets for attacking the same target. This is backed up by the personalised claim of Aristophanes in 547–8 that *his* plays are always different from each other. We still need, therefore, to find a way in which Aristophanes could claim before his patrons that in revising *Clouds* he was not producing the same play.

The key is in Dover's already quoted observation. What we should note, however, is that 'theme' is not at the centre of Aristophanes' complaint. It is quite specifically the *individuals* attacked by a play that he focuses on. This is why, as a preamble to his assault on Eupolis, Hermippus and other unnamed comic poets (conducted at 551f.), he stresses that he only produced *one* play which centred around an attack on Cleon (an argumentative ploy which perhaps implies an established enmity between Eupolis and Cleon which had been expressed in multiple comic assaults upon the politician by Eupolis). The assumption underlying this complaint, then, is that the focus of what we call Old Comedy was not the plot *per se*, but the individual(s) whom it attacked. We can go further, because we know for certain that Cleon was represented on stage (as Paphlagon) in *Knights*, the referent of 549, and Hyperbolus as Marikas in *Marikas* (Quint. 1.10.18). And we may,

[27] E.g. Storey 1990, 22, 2003, 108.

following the thrust of Aristophanes' argument here, infer that Hermippus' *Artopolides* (named by the scholion on this line) and Plato's *Hyperbolus* (of which six fragments remain, K-A frr. 182–7) also presented Hyperbolus on stage as their butt. This observation has wider ramifications, of course, some of which I shall pursue when I deal with the next section of the parabasis. Here, however, it can help us understand why *Clouds II* could be regarded as substantially different from *Clouds I*, even while substantially retaining the plot-line and language of the first version: the individuals targeted through the play's characters had changed.

Now, of course, we are accustomed to thinking of only one 'target' who can be identified in the play, Socrates, and it is clear that he had not changed between the two versions (Pl. *Apol.* 19c taken with Socrates' role in the revised text makes this clear). But the defeat of *Clouds I* is referred to in the parabasis of *Wasps*, certainly at 1043f. and less certainly, because the outline does not appear to fit our play, at 1037–42. If that passage *does* refer to *Clouds*, however, – and the silence of the ancient commentators might be for once interpreted as an indication that *Clouds* was the only 423 play of Aristophanes in the didaskalic record – then it provides good evidence that the original play constituted an attack not just upon Socrates, but also on members of his circle, as the scholia suggest (Σ^{VAAld} *Wasps* 1038c).[28] I shall deal with the detail of this passage later (see chapter five). For now it is enough to say that the only way to bring the two sets of data into harmony will be to assume that for some reason it was permissible to name Socrates, but not the other targets, who consequently appeared in disguise. That is not especially problematic: Cleon appears under the disguise of Paphlagon in *Knights* and Hyperbolus as Marikas in Eupolis' *Marikas*. My suggestion, then, is that Aristophanes could make the claim of 546 without irony because this audience had seen and approved of (and even suggested the attack strategy of? 525–6) *Clouds I* before it reached the state festival (523–4) and will have been able to identify the new targets of *Clouds II* (i.e. who the individuals were who were represented on stage by Strepsiades and Pheidippides) before the parabasis was spoken by the poet.

We still have to deal with the claim of 550 not to have attacked Cleon κειμένῳ ('lying down'). Commentators assume without discussion that this refers to Cleon's death, rather than to the effect of Aristophanes' assault upon him in *Knights*.[29] This is reasonable, since manifestly the comic attack did not prevent him from remaining a general until his death in 422, so

---

[28] πέρυσιν· πέρυσι γὰρ τὰς Νεφέλας ἐδίδαξεν, ἐν αἷς τοὺς περὶ Σωκράτην ἐκωμῴδησεν. 'Last year: because the previous year he produced *Clouds*, in which he satirised the Socratic circle.'

[29] E.g. Sommerstein 1982 on 550.

that it is unlikely to be metaphorical of the effect of Aristophanes' punch in the stomach (549). In the light of the above discussion, however, it is much easier to see what this means. The major attack in *Knights* (and the minor one in the trial scene at *Wasps* 894f.) brought Cleon on stage as a *character*, while the attacks in *Peace* are only verbal. This may seem at first sight to be a mere quibble. It is interesting to note, however, that while Paphlagon is never called Cleon, Cleon is *named* in a choral passage of *Knights* (976). If we are to absolve Aristophanes of self-contradiction – as we must before his audience of long-established patrons – we should accept that this distinction, between attacking an individual by on-stage caricature and merely by naming him – is one to which the poet himself subscribes. It is, in fact, a vital insight and it will help us to understand another apparent contradiction, how it can be that Aristophanes is so annoyed with the attacks on Hyperbolus (on-stage caricature attacks), while allowing characters or choruses in his own plays to make verbal attacks on the politician.[30]

If the interpretation of 537–43 is correct (that Aristophanes is attacking work by his rivals, possibly a quite specific work, which he also makes fun of in his comedies by parodying), we may formulate a new theorem about parabatic attacks on rival comic rubbish: if such a motif occurs in Aristophanes, it is being used to attack a rival, and very probably has a quite specific point of departure – an intertext – recognisable (or potentially recognisable) to the audiences of his plays. We know that audiences would have seen at least three comedies at each festival. And the other parabases besides *Clouds* confirm that Aristophanes and his rivals expected their audiences to recall not only their own earlier plays (*Ach.* 633f., *Wasps* 1038, 1044, Eup. fr. 89), but also those of their rivals (Cratin. fr. 213, Eup. fr. 89, Plato fr. 86). Even though we lack almost any clue about the nature and content of almost all the plays against which Aristophanes competed, nonetheless, it is a premiss which we can work with, precisely because it locates quite specific material from which we can begin to test it. It does, of course, have repercussions for our understanding of other plays besides *Clouds*. It predicts, for example, that the Thracian scene in *Acharnians*, with its use of the circumcised phallus (158f), will be a parody of something in Eupolis. I shall return to this issue later.

[30] It also obliges us to find a situation corresponding to Cleon's death which allows Aristophanes to attack the multiple comic assaults on Hyperbolus in contrast to his *single* assault on Cleon 'when he was down'. It seems obvious enough to me, though this is a minority position, that it must be Hyperbolus' ostracism that is in the background, his death occurring only in 411. This would move the revision of *Clouds* to 416 or 415. I deal more fully with this issue and its consequences in chapter six below.

WHY IS ARISTOPHANES SO ANGRY ABOUT ATTACKS ON HYPERBOLUS AND EUPOLIS' REUSE OF *KNIGHTS*? *CLOUDS* 551–9

οὗτοι δ', ὡς ἅπαξ παρέδωκεν λαβὴν Ὑπέρβολος,
τοῦτον δείλαιον κολετρῶσ' ἀεὶ καὶ τὴν μητέρα.
Εὔπολις μὲν τὸν Μαρικᾶν πρώτιστον παρείλκυσεν
ἐκστρέψας τοὺς ἡμετέρους Ἱππέας κακὸς κακῶς,
προσθεὶς αὐτῷ γραῦν μεθύσην τοῦ κόρδακος οὕνεχ', ἣν   555
Φρύνιχος πάλαι πεποίηχ', ἣν τὸ κῆτος ἤσθιεν.
εἶθ' Ἕρμιππος αὖθις ἐποίησεν εἰς Ὑπέρβολον,
ἄλλοι τε πάντες ἐρείδουσιν εἰς Ὑπέρβολον,
τὰς εἰκοὺς τῶν ἐγχελέων τὰς ἐμὰς μιμούμενοι.

But ever since Hyperbolus gave them something to grab hold of, they have been continuously trampling the poor fellow and his mother. First of all Eupolis dragged him on stage as Marikas, a wicked refurbishment of our *Knights* by a wicked man, giving him as a sidekick a drunken old woman, just to get in a *kordax*, the very woman invented ages ago by Phrynichus, the one being eaten by the sea-monster. Then Hermippus made another play attacking Hyperbolus, and now everyone is leaning on Hyperbolus, imitating my eel images.

But if there was a 'poets' war' involving widespread parodic use of rival material, what context would explain it? It has been the default position that competition between the comic poets is not especially acrimonious (despite *Clouds* 553) and that they all fish in a generic pool of material.[31] This latter view, however, is held against very strong evidence: *Clouds* 547 and *Peace* 748–50, both claims of Aristophanic originality, the indication of Phrynichus' copyright on the old woman eaten by the sea-monster and its usurpation by Eupolis at *Clouds* 555–6, Aristophanes' claim to the eel image at 559, and the whole business of whose intellectual property *Knights* was (Cratin. fr. 213, Eup. fr. 89). However, we can now say that since Aristophanes was prepared to associate with a group with a specific agenda (attacking Socrates and Cleon), then it is highly likely that his rivals were also supported in the same way, but by opposing interests. Thus we have immediately a context which would explain just *why* the poets might attack each other: their agenda was political and associated with specific political groupings.

That this is so is confirmed by consideration of the sympathetic treatment of Hyperbolus in 551–9. Aristophanes specifically complains about the number of separate attacks on Hyperbolus (ἀεὶ 'continuously' 552, πάντες 'everyone' 558). It has usually been interpreted as a general plea for

---

[31] Storey 2003, 299–300, Parker 1991, 204, Heath 1990, 152.

satirical fair play. But the word δειλαῖον ('the poor fellow') at 552 belies such an interpretation, even it were believable in the context of a genre whose essential business was to say nasty things about individuals ([Xen.] *Ath. Pol.* 2.18). It is not credible in the context of an appeal for patronage before a limited group of Aristophanic afficionados. More plausible, though still not without its own problems (which I alluded to above and shall address below), is the proposition that the audience of patrons here addressed by Aristophanes consists of *supporters* of Hyperbolus. That Aristophanes has been helped in his dramatic career by this group, and that they have apparently sanctioned attacks on Socrates (525–6) and Cleon (554), places the poet at the least at no very great distance from their political sympathies. However, the central point of appeal to their patronage used in this argument does appear to be the need to redress the imbalance caused by this string of attacks on Hyperbolus. If I am correct in seeing the special focus of counter-attack as Eupolis (in 537–43 and at 546–8), then the audience will already have spotted the parodic cross-references (e.g. in line 1) to his work. If it is to *Marikas* in particular that 537–43 refer, then Aristophanes' emphasis upon the treatment of Hyperbolus in particular is designed to promote in his erstwhile and, he trusts, future patrons – supporters of the radical democrat – a feeling that what he is doing in his *Clouds* revision is timely and will be an effective riposte.

Aristophanes in fact gives an earlier signal of his radical democratic credentials, which may also serve as a description of his main comic adversary's political leanings. Line 545 is usually seen simply as a joke at his own baldness: κἀγὼ μὲν τοιοῦτος ἀνὴρ ὢν ποιητὴς οὐ κομῶ ('I myself, because I am a poet of this sort too, am not a member of the long-haired brigade'). However, it is actually formulated negatively in terms which relate to a fashion associated with Spartans (Herod. 1.82.8; Xen. *Lac.* 7.3) and the Knights (Lysias 16.18, cf. *Knights* 580 and 1121), the wearing of long hair. The implication is surely that an opponent he does not need to name (but probably Eupolis) wears his hair long, which not only means that he gives himself airs, but that his political sympathies lie with the very wealthy and/or with the values of Sparta. But it also suggests that Aristophanes does *not* belong to this political persuasion, which makes him a democrat.

The central problem with this reading, alluded to above, is that elsewhere in Aristophanes' plays Hyperbolus is attacked by name twelve times.[32]

---

[32] *Ach.* 846–7, *Knights* 739, 1302f., 1362–3, *Clouds* 623f., 876, 1065, *Wasps* 1007, *Peace* 921, 1321, *Thesm.* 839f., *Frogs* 570.

But this undoubted fact needs to be reconsidered within the context of my earlier analysis of the central focus of Old Comedy's attacks, as it emerges from Aristophanes' way of speaking about his – and his rivals' – plays in this parabasis. It appears that on-stage caricature of recognisable individuals, whether named (Socrates) or in disguise (Paphlagon/Cleon, Marikas/Hyperbolus), is the basis of reference and *named attacks* (like those upon Cleon in *Peace*) do not count as the same thing at all. When we consider that Aristophanes can never be shown to have put Hyperbolus on stage in any of his plays, the issue becomes more focused. If we propose that recognisable individuals underlie its (to us) apparently fictitious characters, then it becomes clear why there could be a fundamental distinction between the evaluation of on-stage caricature as against verbal assault: naming always occurs on the lips of a character (or chorus) *within the play* (the only exception being in parabatic anapaests or Eupolideans). The mention of Hyperbolus (or any other individual), then, is always focalised upon the character who speaks and the attack – which is presumably there to appeal to the non-converts in the audience, as opposed to the ideologically committed author and promoters of the comedy – can be regarded by the poet (and his ideologically committed patrons) as a device to characterise and sometimes, no doubt, ironically to devalue the on-stage individual who is under attack. Later on (chapter three) I shall deal with the specific references to Hyperbolus and demonstrate how they operate within the wider reinterpretation of Aristophanic and other Old Comedy that this reorientation of basic perspectives calls for.

HOW DOES ARISTOPHANES' CODA RELATE TO HIS EARLIER REMARKS? CLOUDS 560–62

ὅστις οὖν τούτοισι γελᾷ, τοῖς ἐμοῖς μὴ χαιρέτω·
ἢν δ' ἐμοὶ καὶ τοῖς ἐμοῖς εὐφραίνησθ' εὑρήμασιν,   560
εἰς τὰς ὥρας τὰς ἑτέρας εὖ φρονεῖν δοκήσετε.

So whoever laughs at them ought not to enjoy my work. But if you delight in me and my inventions, you will in the future gain a reputation for sensible judgement.

Aristophanes ends his parabatic plea with a firmly disjunctive view of his own comedy versus that of those who have attacked Hyperbolus (560–2). People should not like his comedies if they are amused by those of the anti-Hyperbolean rivals he has just lambasted. If, on the other hand, his present audience likes him and his inventions (as very likely they do and will, given their past track record in this regard), then they will receive the accolade of history for their excellent sense (562).³³ What is constantly at stake in this parabasis, then, and is made explicit at the end, is the idea that there is a special bond between this audience and Aristophanes, which operates at the level of both comic taste and intellectual and political allegiance.

CONCLUSIONS AND CONSEQUENCES

This reading of the *Clouds* parabasis creates a new starting point for a study of the plays which arguably relies on categories of intention formulated by the poet himself. These involve (1) intellectual orientation (against Socrates and towards the 'sophists'); (2) poetic rivalry (which is essentially political); (3) political stance (on the side of one radical democrat, Hyperbolus, against another, Cleon, and opposed to the conservatism of such groups as the Knights); (4) the use of disguised caricature. Each of these categories has a consequence for our approach to reading Aristophanic (and probably therefore other) Old Comedy.

The consequence of the first category of intention is specifically that we are obliged to see *Clouds* as an attack on Socrates and his circle motivated by a philosophical and political position shared with οἱ σοφοί ('the sophists'), and more generally that his comedy must have satisfied some intellectual as well as comedic criteria to keep them on board. The discovery that Aristophanes was a card-carrying member of a philosophical circle has no obvious specifically methodological consequences.³⁴ It might perhaps lead us to a rather different view from normal about the role of vulgarity in the comedies (cf. *Peace* 750), unless we can assume that ancient intellectuals were as prone to laugh at a dirty word as are we modern students of Old Comedy. In any case, however, the establishment from the *Clouds* parabasis of obscene costuming (the circumcised phallus), as an element from rival comedy to be attacked and probably parodied, suggests that

---

³³ In Sidwell 1995, 68 I proposed that the final line meant 'you will think it right to look kindly upon my second version of *Horai*', on the grounds that (a) it was rhetorically stronger (b) there is no good parallel for ἕτερος meaning 'future' (c) there are visible links with Prodicus' *Horai* in (i) the behaviour of the Clouds as though goddesses of justice (i.e. like the Horai – Eunomie, Dike and Eirene, Hes. *Theog.* 901f.), (ii) in the parodic version of his 'Choice of Heracles' in the scene with the *Logoi* (see also Papageorgiou 2004). However, the current audience will not have known yet in this version that this misnomer reflected the play's use of Prodicus' *Horai* for the confrontation of the *Logoi*, unless it was also there in the first version (in which case it is only the preamble to their debate 889–948, as Sommerstein 1982, 4 n. 9 suggests, which was new), and the same goes for the behaviour of the Cloud chorus. Thus, if my interpretation were correct, it would imply that among members of *this* audience, at least, *Clouds I* had also been known as *Horai*. For the current argument I accept the conventional view.

³⁴ Cf. Heath 1987, 10 who uses Alcibiades' comment at *Symp.* 218a7–b4, where he names Aristophanes, as evidence for his interest in philosophy.

there is a sophistication in the deployment of such motifs in Aristophanes which might have suited the highbrows he was trying to please more than we allow when we interpret them as material pandering to the popular taste.

Certainly, the second proposal, that Aristophanes is engaged in a battle with his rivals which is both political and aesthetic, has profound consequences for our methodology. If we can trust the inference that parabatic criticism versus the occurrence of the motif in Aristophanes implies that the occurrence is parodic of something in a rival's work, then in the first instance a catalogue of those contradictions will allow us a way of tracking where parody of comedy is operating (though it will not be comprehensive and it may not lead to specific plays, let alone specific playwrights).

The third category brings us face to face with even more serious problems. First of all, as I have already noted, Hyperbolus is satirised by name no fewer than twelve times in Aristophanic comedy. Since we are accustomed to regarding such attacks as indices of the author's political stance (if anything is), the direct contradiction between the positive authorial evaluation of him in the *Clouds* parabasis and these passages forces us to reassess the nature of named attack. Secondly, while we do not have a very good idea of Hyperbolus' policies in detail, his (comic?) association with an enterprise such as the putative attack on Carthage (*Knights* 1300–4) seems to guarantee his radical democratic credentials, while the attitude of Peace towards him (*Peace* 682–4) suggests that he wished to continue the war even in 421. Since one conventional view of *Acharnians* and *Peace* has them supporting the ending of war, our inference from the authorial intention suggests that they cannot have done so. When surface is opposed to intent, we are dealing with irony, a mode which can only be spotted when the underlying intention is known (as it might have been by the original audience, but cannot be by us unless we have external evidence). It will be reasonable to suppose that such irony will have been carried and conveyed to the audience partly by the parodies of comic rivals' material (including characters) and partly by the audience's recognition of the individuals targeted by the play's disguised caricatures.

This brings us to the final category, which drives a wedge between the two modes of satire, naming and representing, and suggests the priority of the latter as the true satirical focus. This inference is especially difficult to accept, since (like the apparent criticisms of Hyperbolus and the apparent support of the poet for peace) it cuts across our current modes of interpretation. We need to ask why poets would have worked thus and why our instinctive feeling that 'Aristophanes was never coy about his caricatures' may be wrong.[35] Methodologically, of course, this inference has major implications. If characters were textually disguised, then we must find new ways of detecting the targets of these plays. Certainty will in these circumstances be at best difficult, at worst impossible.

The contrast between the specificity of the *Clouds* parabasis and the deviousness of the other early examples complained of by Silk can now be explained by the necessity for the poet – who after all was aiming for the prize, which though to some extent a lottery, nonetheless required a broad consensus among the judges and could not be fixed[36] – to keep his festival audience on board. In contrast to the private motivation of the *Clouds* itself mentioned at 526, the other parabases cast the poet as public benefactor, sometimes teaching altruistically lessons which benefit the whole city (*Ach.* 633f., 656), sometimes as an *alter* Heracles, cleansing the land of monsters (*Wasps* 1029f., *Peace* 752f.), sometimes as sharing a political enmity with a quite different group from his usual (contrast *Knights* 510–11 with *Clouds* 545). On the whole, his poetic rivalries are understated, with the persons attacked left unspecified (*Ach.* 656f., *Wasps* 1024–9, *Peace* 734–51), except where he is prepared to mix faint praise with his sardony (*Knights* 520f.) and this too suggests the desire to explain his own position without giving direct offence to supporters of his rivals. The political thrust of the comedy would in any case be carried largely by the caricature targets, and these too would mostly be disguised (or, perhaps like Socrates in Aelian's anecdote *VH* 2.13, unknown to some members of the audience) and would usually have had to do *something* to bring them into the comic poet's snare (cf. *Clouds* 551, Lysias fr. 53). The author could in any case easily disguise his private intent, most noticeably for us by introducing named jokes (in Aristophanes' case wrapped in the cocoon of caricature and cross-references to other comedies) against his own favourites. Still, the *Clouds* parabasis shows that over a period of some ten years a poet could have the consistent sponsorship of private individuals (*Clouds* 528) and a wider group with private intellectual and political preferences, and for their benefit use his publicly-funded comedy to further his and their political goals.

I propose, then, to begin testing these inferences by looking first at 'meta-comedy', as I shall call the deliberate reuse of material from rival comedy,

[35] Moorton 1988, 346.   [36] *DFA*² 95–8.

as a way of locating what must now be seen as a political battle between Aristophanes and Eupolis. From there, I shall examine the issues and then the particularities surrounding the interaction between metacomedy and disguised caricature. Finally, in part two, I shall begin a chronological survey of Aristophanic and, where possible, his rivals', comedies with a view to demonstrating how the inferences we have drawn from the *Clouds* parabasis reveal a consistent political viewpoint in Aristophanes and his rivals during the Peloponnesian War, and a particular rivalry with Eupolis which culminated in the radically democratic *Frogs*.

CHAPTER 2

Metacomedy and politics

INTRODUCTION

The analysis of the *Clouds* parabasis offered in the previous chapter delineates a politicised comedy, which Aristophanes treats as deeply polarised both on the level of the targets chosen, and of dramatic technique. If it is correct to see the critique of comic motifs as part and parcel of this ideological battle, then it is possible to utilise the so-called self-contradictions between such critiques and Aristophanes' own use of them in his plays to discover more about the scope and parameters of the contest. For this purpose we must primarily use the material which appears to undercut the critiques of the *Clouds* parabasis (537–543: the circumcised phallus, the *kordax*, the leading old man beating people with a stick to hide bad jokes, bringing torches on stage, cries of ἰού ἰού 'ooh ooh') and motifs from the *Peace* parabasis (740–7: making fun of rags, waging war on lice, Heracleses kneading dough and going hungry, slaves who run away, practise deceit or get beaten, jokes by fellow-slaves about such beatings; 751: attacking private individuals, male and female). Some other material, however, may be considered *prima facie* relevant: close textual or thematic parallels with the surviving fragments of the comedies of rival poets; naming of rival poets; parabatic concern with comedy; metatheatrical reference to comedy. With this template in mind, we can proceed to examine each of the wartime comedies to see whether or not it contains metacomic material.

METACOMEDY FROM *ACHARNIANS* TO *FROGS*

Acharnians

Acharnians was produced at Lenaea 425 and won first prize. It contains two of the pieces of comic business which are criticised in the *Clouds* parabasis. The circumcised phallus is worn by the Odomantian Thracians at 158f.

And the 'leading male character beating others' motif is used at 824f. and 864f. (though in the first scene at least the implement is a set of leather straps).[1] The play also manifests at least one feature criticised in the *Peace* parabasis, that is vulgar jokes (750), jokes literally of the marketplace. A whole scene is made on this template at *Acharnians* 769f., the famous 'Megarian piggies' episode.

It is worth noting the following features, which might indicate that the play has more to do with other comedy than we might have thought. It contains two passages which provide close echoes of surviving fragments of Cratinus (580f., cf. Cratin. *Horai* fr. 271; 933f., cf. Cratin. *Horai* fr. 273). Moreover, the use of the nickname οὐλύμπιος 'the Olympian' for Pericles at 530 and the theme of a critical stance on a Periclean-inspired war both bring to mind Cratinus (cf. frr. 73, 118, 258 for Pericles as Zeus and *Dionysalexandros PCG* Ti 44f. for Pericles and war). Cratinus is mentioned twice by name (848 and 1173). The parabasis focuses on comic poetry, mostly defence of the author's political position as misrepresented by other poets in the theatre of Dionysus (*Ach.* 630–2: see further chapter 4, pp. 119–20 below). The main character alludes to comedy at 378 and claims to be producing one at 499. The chorus at 1154f. identifies itself with an earlier comic chorus. There is metatheatrical reference to comedy also at 886.

Knights

Knights was produced at Lenaea 424 and also won first prize. The play contains one motif criticised by Aristophanes in the *Clouds* parabasis, the use of ἰοὺ ἰού ('ooh ooh': *Knights* 451, 1096; cf. *Clouds* 543). It also utilises one of the scene-types attacked as low-grade rubbish in the *Peace* parabasis, runaway slaves who have been beaten (*Knights* 1–10, cf. *Peace* 743f.).

The following features also connect the play with rival comedy. First, there is the evidence about the supposed collaboration of Eupolis and Aristophanes (Eup. *Baptai* fr. 89), otherwise interpreted as Aristophanes' plagiarism of Eupolis (Cratin. *Pytine* fr. 213). Secondly, the ancient scholars seem to have had access to information which made them regard specifically the second parabasis as composed *in toto* by Eupolis. Sommerstein's view, that it was the similarity of 1288 to *Demoi* fr. 99.33 which induced them to form this conclusion, seems too restricted.[2] It is unlike the scholiasts to infer anything so large from so distant a similarity: there are many other places

---

[1] Olson 2002 on 864 suggests that the main character is 'probably still armed with his whip'.
[2] Sommerstein 1980b, 51–3.

where texts are closer and they make no comment (e.g. the passages from Cratinus' *Horai* mentioned above in relation to *Acharnians*). Hubbard's view, that the line is an actual quotation from a Eupolis play, seems more likely to have prompted this view, given the claim of collaboration in fr. 89 (*Baptai*).[3] Hubbard's conclusion, that '[b]y quoting Eupolis here, Aristophanes manages to place the most savage invective of the play onto another poet's shoulders', is not far from saying that the second parabasis is presented in Eupolis' voice (see further chapter 5, pp. 164–5 below). Thirdly, line 1225 is also the object of a garbled report from scholia that seems to imply the line was taken from another play. Incidentally, this shows clearly that the ancient scholars could spot a match when they saw one. Sommerstein traces it to Eupolis' *Heilotes*,[4] but it might equally come from one of Cratinus' plays (*Lacones*, for example). Fourthly, as in *Acharnians*, the parabasis (507–50) focuses on comic poetry, both that of Aristophanes and of his rivals.

Wasps

Wasps was produced at Lenaea 422, and came second. The play contains a large number of the motifs specifically criticised by Aristophanes in parabatic statements. 'Slaves discussing a beating' opens the play (1f.; cf. *Peace* 743f.). Philocleon rushes on stage with a torch at 1326.(cf. *Clouds* 543). He shouts ἰοὺ ἰού ('ooh ooh') at 931 (cf. *Clouds* 543). The vulgar dance he performs at 1484f. may have been a *kordax* (cf. *Clouds* 540). The 'leading old man beating someone with a stick' motif is also associated with Philocleon (1307 and 1326f.; cf. *Clouds* 541), though in the latter case it is a torch that he uses as his weapon. It is also possible that the Myrtia scene could be classified as 'satirising women in their private capacity' (1388ff.; cf. *Peace* 751), since her name and those of her parents are 'ordinary Athenian names'[5] and she appears with a person who turns out to be the well-known Chaerephon (1408).

The following features also connect the play's concerns with comedy. The parabasis (1015–59) concentrates once more entirely upon comic poetry – both that of Aristophanes and of his rivals. Bdelycleon's metatheatrical statement at 650–1 refers to comedy: χαλεπὸν μὲν καὶ δεινῆς γνώμης καὶ μείζονος ἢ 'πὶ τρυγῳδοῖς | ἰάσασθαι νόσον ἀρχαίαν ἐν τῇ πόλει ἐντετοκυῖαν ('It's a hard task, requiring a cleverer mind than the comic poets manifest, to heal a chronic disease endemic to this city').

---

[3] Hubbard 1991, 86. [4] Sommerstein 1980b, 51–3. [5] MacDowell 1971 on 1397.

Peace

Peace was produced at the Dionysia of 421, and came second. It contains at least two, and possibly three, comic features criticised by the *Clouds* parabasis. The 'leading old man beating someone with a stick' motif appears at 1121f., when Trygaeus is given the job of beating Hierocles by his own slave (cf. *Clouds* 541–2). Cries of ἰοὺ ἰού ('ooh ooh') are heard on Trygaeus' lips at 345 and 1191 (cf. *Clouds* 543). The chorus' dance at 321f. is possibly a *kordax* (cf. *Clouds* 540).

The following features also connect it with other comedy. It has a parabasis which deals directly with the contrast between Aristophanes' own comedy and that of his rivals (729–74). The figure called Trygaeus has a name the root of which is not only pertinent to his claimed expertise as a vine-grower (190), but also to comedy (cf. the use of the τρυγ- root at *Ach.* 499–500).

Clouds

The text we have is a revision of the play which came third at Dionysia 423. Despite the detailed list of despised comic techniques at 537f., the play itself contravenes several. The 'leading old man beating someone with a stick' motif is played out by Strepsiades at 1297–1300 (but with a goad, not a stick), *contra* 541–2. Strepsiades commands a slave to bring a torch on stage at 1490f., *contra* 543. Characters cry ἰοὺ ἰού ('ooh ooh') at 1 and 1321 (Strepsiades), and 1493 (someone inside the burning *phrontisterion*), *contra* 543. A motif criticised in *Peace* (740 waging war with lice) appears at *Clouds* 634 and 707f.

The following features also connect it with other comedy. Its parabasis (discussed in detail in chapter one) once more focuses upon comic poetry and this time includes very specific attacks on rivals, named (Eupolis and Hermippus, 553, 557) and unnamed (537f., 551–2, 558f.). There is metatheatrical reference to comedy in Socrates' mention of οἱ τρυγοδαίμονες οὗτοι 'those blasted comic poets' at 296 to criticise Strepsiades' use of vulgar language.

Birds

In *Birds*, produced in 414, there are three major – and in two cases multiple – contradictions of the criticisms of the *Peace* and *Clouds* parabases. First, the poet has a 'hungry Heracles' scene (1583f.) of the type rubbished at *Peace* 741. Secondly, he has five or six scenes where the leading old man character, Peisetairus (called πρεσβύτης at 320 and 1401, and γέρων at 1256), beats τὸν παρόντα ('the other character on stage') with something to hand (999f., a scroll, 1017–18, 1029f., possibly 1207, 1397f., 1464f.), against the strictures of *Clouds* 541–2. Thirdly, the play is absolutely rife with the cries of ἰοὺ ἰού reprehended at *Clouds* 543, at 194 (Tereus), 295 (Euelpides), 305 (Peiseteirus), 819 (Chorus), 889 (Peisetairus), 1170 (Second Messenger, three times in one line) 1510 (Peisetairus). If, as one might expect, the wedding procession at 1720f. was accompanied by torches, then there will be a fourth contradiction, this time of *Clouds* 543.

Lysistrata

Lysistrata was produced in 411 through Callistratus, according to the first ancient hypothesis. Although no further details are given, it is now generally agreed that it was a Lenaea play (see further chapter five). This play also has examples – two certain, one possible – of scenes which cut across the criticisms of the *Clouds* parabasis. First, we hear the cry ἰοὺ ἰού ('ooh ooh'), criticised at *Clouds* 543 as one of several markers of bad comedy, on the lips of several participants. At 67 it is uttered by Calonice, at 295 and 305 by the Men's semi-chorus, and at 829 by Lysistrata herself. Secondly, at 1217f., the Athenian ambassadors re-enter with torches. The first threatens to burn the Spartan slaves with his, then remarks φορτικὸν τὸ χωρίον ('Low-grade piece of business, though'). The critical stance towards torch-business is similar to that adopted at *Clouds* 543. Thirdly, there is a possibility that some of the phalli worn by male characters were shown displaying the ψωλή ('glans'). This is implied, at any rate, by Cinesias at 979. If this costuming was used, then it cuts across yet another criticism of comic business in *Clouds*, where at 539 the poet attacks the use of the red-tipped phallus.

Thesmophoriazusai

There is no direct evidence for the date of *Thesmophoriazusai*, but arguments for City Dionysia 411 are cogent.[6] There are two contradictions of the criticisms of the *Clouds* parabasis. First, at 101, 230, 280, and 917 torches appear on stage (cf. *Clouds* 543). Secondly, in the final one of those

---

[6] See Sommerstein 1994, 1–3. See Prato and Del Corno 2001, xi–xvii for arguments locating the play at Lenaea 411.

appearances, the torch is brandished by an old woman, threatening Euripides, in a variation of the 'old man beating with a stick' routine reprehended at *Clouds* 541–2.

Two further considerations link the play with other comedy. First, the scholion on line 215 tells us that it was lifted wholesale from Cratinus (fr. 90 *Idaioi*). Secondly, there are some clear correspondences between *Thesmophoriazusai* and *Acharnians*. At 39 begins the scene in which the tragic poet Agathon's servant performs a prayer and is insulted by the *kedestes*. Next Agathon plays the part of a tragic heroine and chorus. He is then asked for help by Euripides, but refuses, all the same, however, lending various parts of his kit to Euripides before asking to be rolled back in (265 εἴσω τις ὡς τάχιστα μ' εἰσκυκλησάτω 'will someone wheel me in as quickly as possible'; cf. 96 οὑκκυκλούμενος 'the man who's being wheeled out now'). The following strong resemblances with the Euripides scene in *Acharnians* (393f.) can be noticed: (a) Dicaeopolis goes for help to Euripides in respect of a lawsuit in which he could lose his life (as Euripides goes to Agathon for help with the women's capital case against him); (b) the servant in both cases shares the style of his master; (c) both Euripides and Agathon appear on the *ekkyklema* (cf. *Acharnians* 408–9, 479); (d) both poets lend items despite being insulted. It has often been noted that the speech of the *kedestes* at the Thesmophoria (468ff.) contains some verbal reminiscences of Dicaeopolis' defence speech in *Acharnians* (cf. 469–70 with *Ach.* 509–12; 471–2 with *Ach.* 502–8; 473 with *Ach.* 514; and 517–9 with *Ach.* 555–6).[7] It is usually thought that the similarities are due to common utilisation of Euripides' *Telephus*, which is parodied both in *Thesmophoriazusai* 688ff. and *Acharnians* 325ff.[8] But MacDowell notes that, in contradistinction to *Acharnians*, no explicit mention is made of the play, which was in any case now twenty-seven years in the past.[9] However, part of the problem with rejecting *Telephus* as an intertext designed to be noticed by the audience is that that play's actual structure is (it is generally agreed) quite closely followed in *Thesmophoriazusai* in a way it is not in *Acharnians*, and this probably does imply – given that Euripides is a central character – that the audience were supposed to notice the structural similarities. It will no doubt be part of the satirical structure that the comic play depends so heavily upon Euripidean tragedy.[10] The structural

---

[7] See MacDowell 1995, 61, Sommerstein 1994 ad loc., Austin and Olson 2004 ad loc.
[8] So Sommerstein 1994 on *Thesmophoriazusai* 466–519. [9] MacDowell 1995, 266–7.
[10] This is in opposition to MacDowell 1995, 61, who claims that 'similarity of the situations and arguments in the two speeches... could have led Aristophanes to use similar wording without [sc. in *Thesmophoriazusai*] even realising he was doing so'.

similarity of the two 'poet-visiting' scenes rather suggests that it was the desire to have the audience recall *Acharnians*.

Frogs

Frogs was produced in 405 at the Lenaea through Philonides and won first prize.[11] Dicaearchus reported that it was given a second production (because of its parabasis).[12] The play has two features criticised by the *Clouds* parabasis. First is the use of torches as part of a comic scene (313, 340, 1525; cf. *Clouds* 543). Second is the cry ἰοὺ ἰού ('ooh ooh', used by Dionysus at 653; cf. *Clouds* 543). A possible third is an old man beating someone (605ff.; cf. *Clouds* 541–2).

There are three further features of the play which connect it with other comedy. First, the chorus at 357 claim comedy to be 'the tongue rites of bull-eating Cratinus' (Κρατίνου τοῦ ταυροφάγου γλώττης Βακχεῖα). Secondly, the formulation Λάμαχος ἥρως ('heroic Lamachus') at 1039 echoes across twenty years the address by Dicaeopolis to Lamachus at *Acharnians* 575, 578, ὦ Λάμαχ' ἥρως ('O heroic Lamachus'). Thirdly, there are several specifically Eupolidean cross-references to be noted. (a) Scholars accept that the scene in which Dionysus is taught how to row Charon's boat (197f.) is calqued on the rowing-scene in Eupolis' *Taxiarchoi*.[13] (b) The resurrection of dead Athenians in an attempt to save the city was the central theme of Eupolis' *Demes*.[14] (c) There is a correlation between line 734 (in the parabasis) and Eup. fr. 392, the phrase μεταβαλόντες τοὺς τρόπους ('changing your ways'), also found in slightly different form at *Wasps* 1461 (with μετεβάλοντο indicative, instead of the participle). (d) Line 1400 and Eup. fr. 372 both contain the phrase δύο κύβω καὶ τέτταρα 'a pair of one-spots and a four' (tr. Sommerstein).[15] (e) Line 1036 (Παντακλέα... τὸν σκαιότατον 'completely stupid Pantacles') shares

---

[11] Hypothesis 1(c) in Dover 1993, 114: ἐδιδάχθη ἐπὶ Καλλίου ἄρχοντος τοῦ μετὰ Ἀντιγένη διὰ Φιλωνίδου εἰς Λήναια. πρῶτος ἦν· Φρύνιχος β Μούσαις, Πλάτων τρίτος Κλεοφῶντι. 'It was produced in the archonship of the Callias who followed Antigenes through Philonides at the Lenaea. It was first. Phrynichus was second with *The Muses*, Plato third with *Cleophon*.'

[12] Hypothesis 1(c), Dover 1993, 114: οὕτω δὲ ἐθαυμάσθη τὸ δρᾶμα διὰ τὴν ἐν αὐτῷ παράβασιν ὥστε καὶ ἀνεδιδάχθη, ὥς φησι Δικαίαρχος 'The play was so admired that it was actually accorded a second showing because of its parabasis, as Dicaearchus reports.'

[13] Wilson 1974, Dover 1993, 39, Sommerstein 1994, 11 and on 197f.

[14] See Storey 2003, 111–74, Sommerstein 1994, 9.

[15] On this passage, Dover 1993 states unequivocally ad loc.: 'The phrase 'two ones and a four' is from Eupolis', though he does not explore the ramifications of this quotation. Sommerstein also comes close to suggesting that Aristophanes is quoting Eupolis here: "Achilles has hit'... are the beginning of a Euripidean line, whose second half Dionysus has replaced with a piece of comic triviality.' But why?

an otherwise unknown named target and epithet with Eup. fr. 318 from *Chrysoun Genos* (Παντακλέης σκαιός 'Pantacles is stupid').

ARISTOPHANES' METACOMIC TARGETS

Aristophanes, then, continued to pursue for twenty years a style of attack upon certain types of comic device (shouts of ἰοὺ ἰού 'ooh ooh', the leading old man beating people with a stick, torches on stage are the most important). He also for some reason reflected material from *Acharnians* in both *Thesmophoriazusai* and *Frogs*. Furthermore, his quasi-parabatic chorus of *mystai* in *Frogs* (357) virtually identifies the type of comedy being presented as Cratinean in style. There must be a reason for this and it is unlikely to be that he had a merely general distaste for the comedy of anyone but himself. The agenda seems focused and personalised. The best explanation is surely that he is attacking an individual poet, whom he accuses of constructing his comic technique in close imitation of Cratinus and whose political views and alliances he regarded as threatening to the *demos*. If my analysis of the criticisms of the *Clouds* parabasis is correct, then the obvious candidate will be Eupolis, who can definitely be tied to three of them (the leading old man character hitting someone with a stick; attacking bald men; using the *kordax*). It was he, and no other poet of his time, who was described by one ancient critic as ζηλῶν Κρατῖνον ('an admirer/imitator of Cratinus').[16]

As I have shown, the heavy intimation of *Clouds* 545 is that Eupolis is anti-democratic, and that of 551f. that Aristophanes was a radical democrat, so that a conflict between Aristophanes and this particular rival over a period of twenty years in a city at war and subject to all sorts of political crises is not inherently incredible. The presumptive background of this metacomic evidence, however, must be that Eupolis was still around to be attacked. What is problematic, however, is that he drops out of our record after about 411.[17] What happened to him? And under what circumstances would it make any sense at all for Aristophanes to write *Frogs* as an attack upon him in 405? Let us first examine the reports of his death.

THE FATE OF EUPOLIS

The evidence presents us with four radically different scenarios. One has him drowned by Alcibiades on the way to Sicily in 415, but, as Eratosthenes

---

[16] Koster, *Prolegomena* p. 9 (Anon. *De Comoedia* III.34 = K-A Eupolis T2a.7).
[17] Storey 2003, 59 'no allusion in Eupolis demands a date after 410'. See most recently Kyriakidi 2007, 10–11.

had already noted (Cic. *Att.* 6.1.18), it was palpably false, since Eupolis had produced plays after that date. A second has him dying on Aegina (Ael. *NA* 10.41), but as part of an anecdote which involves a faithful dog and a comedy-stealing slave called Ephialtes. Storey has plausibly suggested that the anecdote was lifted from Eupolis' *Autolycus*, where he thinks Eupolis was a character.[18] A third, the one argued for recently by Storey, and generally accepted, is the report by the Suda (ε 3657) that the poet died in a shipwreck in the Hellespont during the war against the Spartans. This has been expanded by identification of the poet with the Eupolis mentioned on the naval casualty list *c.* 411 in *IG* I[3].1190.52 and the conjecture of Körte that he died at the battle of Cynossema.[19] The fourth is that reported by Pausanias (2.7.3), that on the left as one goes from Sicyon and across the Asopos is to be found τάφος Εὐπόλιδι Ἀθηναίῳ ποιήσαντι κωμῳδίαν 'the grave of the Athenian comic poet Eupolis'.

Storey does not attempt to reconcile the evidence of the Suda and Pausanias, except to report the suggestion of Kinzl that Eupolis may have had relatives at Sicyon.[20] However, if the evidence of the Suda is correct, Kinzl's explanation would not suit the established Athenian procedures for burial of war dead (Thuc. 2.34.5), for even those not recovered from a sea-battle would be commemorated by the inscription placed on the communal tomb, which is where the name of the Eupolis who did die – possibly at sea – would have been permanently visible, even if his bones and ashes were not actually within.[21] Moreover, Sicyon was Athens' enemy, consistently on the Spartan side during the war (Thuc. 2.9.3; 2.80.3; 4.70.1; 4.101.3–4; 5.52.3; 5.58–60; 5.81.2; 7.19.4 and 58.3; 8.3.2), and it does not seem at all likely that the ashes of an Athenian who had fallen fighting *against* the alliance to which Sicyon belonged would be sent there, even if there had been no Athenian tradition of communal burial for the war dead. This makes it possible to explain the tradition reported by the Suda, of course, since anyone might have seen the name on the casualty list, noted the battle in which the entombed had fallen, and then put two and two together (in this case making five). As Storey admits, the name Eupolis was not unusual and just because we want to make the connection – as perhaps did the ancient scholars on whom the Suda is ultimately dependent – it does not mean that it is correct. However, nothing explains away Pausanias' report

---

[18] Storey 2003, 57.   [19] Storey 2003, 56–60.
[20] Storey 2003, 57 with note 14. See Telò 2007, 23–4, n.49 for the conjecture that the Suda's evidence might be nothing but a variant of the other version of the poet's death at sea at the hands of Alcibiades, and the contention that, since scholars cannot agree on the date of the inscription, there is no firm ground for assuming that it records Cynossema rather than Arginusae or Aegospotamoi.
[21] Wees 2004, 145–6.

of Eupolis' burial at Sicyon except the hypothesis that someone added Eupolis' name to the monument later. In recent years, archaeologists have found more and more reason to trust Pausanias,[22] so that it does seem likely that he really did see this tomb and inscription. The possibility that the tomb was a later fabrication has nothing at all to support it. Indeed, it is hard even to imagine a scenario which might explain it. It is therefore worth considering the inference that Eupolis the Athenian comic poet was buried at Sicyon, because he had died there.

But why would Eupolis have been at Sicyon, a city which was on the Spartan side throughout the war and had been an enemy of Athens even earlier (Thuc. 1.108.5, 111.2 and 114.1)? Only one plausible explanation springs to mind: he was in exile. Moreover, his choice of refuge must in some way have reflected a perceived level of enmity such that a neutral location was rejected, and a place within the Athenian sphere of influence out of the question.[23] There were, of course, always individual cases of exile for specific offences against the *demos* (one thinks of Thucydides after Amphipolis in 424, Alcibiades in 415 and later Xenophon, who ends up in the enemy camp). But it is difficult to avoid thinking of the oligarchic revolution of 411 or the final showdown with the Thirty in 404–3 (or both) as possible reasons for his absence from the later record. In the aftermath of the first, members of the Four Hundred had been disenfranchised and many had fled.[24] After the second, though members of the Thirty and their close supporters were included in the amnesty (Arist. *Ath. Pol.* 39), the events of 401/400, when some of the generals based at Eleusis were killed (Xen. *Hell.* 2.4.43), cannot have been encouraging for them and some were certainly in exile around this time (Lysias 25.24).[25] If I am correct to see *Frogs* as having Eupolis once more as a focus of attack, then he will not have been exiled following 411. Rather, he will have been τις... σφαλείς τι Φρυνίχου παλαίσμασιν 'someone a bit tripped up by Phrynichus' wrestling-throws' (*Frogs* 689) – that is by the oligarchic activities of one of the 411 revolution's leaders (Thuc. 8.68.3). The point of the *Frogs* parabasis (though if it is satire of Eupolis, it must be ironic) is to persuade the Athenians to restore the franchise to these former citizens, who in any case are obliged to fight for the city in the fleet (*Frogs* 693–702). It follows that Eupolis had been disenfranchised after 411, but had remained in the city, constrained to

---

[22] Habicht 1985, 3–4: 'Comparison of Pausanias' narrative and the fragments of earlier periegetic literature, added to the evidence of excavations in numerous places, has proven conclusively that Pausanias, as he claims, wrote from personal observation.'
[23] E.g. Hyperbolus went to Samos after his ostracism, Thuc. 8.73.3.
[24] Andocides 1. 78, the decree of Patrocleides.   [25] Krentz 1982, 102f., 123f.

fight with the fleet. Though obliged to defend the *polis*, he would not, of course, have been allowed to participate in such activities as the comic competitions, and this will explain how it could be that he was still able to be a target for Aristophanes. His death in the enemy city of Sicyon, however, means we will have to align him in 404/3 with the Thirty (and we shall see some reason to do this when we look at the satirical purpose of *Birds*) and conjecture that he was too nervous to attempt to take advantage of the amnesty.

ARISTOPHANES' POLITICS

In these circumstances Dicaearchus' report of a public crown and a second production of *Frogs* should not be dismissed as baseless. If Eupolis, a comic poet whose role was supposed to be defence of the *demos*, had been involved in the oligarchic plots of 411 and then had used his reinstatement under the decree of Patrocleides to assist those who later usurped the democracy (the Thirty) and to defend their position against the men from Piraeus, then it would have seemed quite right for the *demos* to regard Aristophanes as a hero, who in his own sophisticated and long-established ironic manner had persuaded the Athenians that re-enfranchisement of such as his old enemy was a bridge too far. However, the idea that it was the advice in the parabasis that had made the Athenians honour Aristophanes is quite palpably not feasible, given this interpretation of the play's meaning. We must look again, therefore, at the evidence for Aristophanes' civic crown, for the unusual honour of a re-performance and in particular for its date.

Uniquely in the case of *Frogs* we have ancient external evidence which tends to support the idea that Aristophanes had sought to give advice in the play. Hypothesis 1 (c) (Dover 1993) reports: οὕτω δὲ ἐθαυμάσθη τὸ δρᾶμα διὰ τὴν ἐν αὐτῷ παράβασιν ὥστε καὶ ἀνεδιδάχθη, ὥς φησι Δικαίαρχος 'The play was so admired because of its parabasis that it was actually put on for a second time, as Dicaearchus reports.' And the *Life of Aristophanes* (*PCG* Aristophanes Testimonium 1.35–9) reports: ἐστεφανώθη θαλλῷ τῆς ἱερᾶς ἐλαίας, ὃς νενόμισται ἰσότιμος χρυσῷ στεφάνῳ, εἰπὼν ἐκεῖνα τὰ ἐν τοῖς Βατράχοις περὶ τῶν ἀτίμων 'he was crowned with a wreath of sacred olive, which is deemed equal in honour to a golden crown, for having said in the *Frogs* the following words about the disenfranchised' (lines 686–7 follow). Sommerstein argues: '[I]t is overwhelmingly probable that these two testimonies go back to a common source (very likely Dicaearchus), and that the source was citing an actual state decree passed in Aristophanes' honour'.[26] This is almost certainly correct. But the current argument makes it hard to believe that the decree mentioned the 'advice' of the parabasis. Why would Aristophanes have wished Eupolis to be reinstated? This would have cut across a political posture Aristophanes apparently held consistently for over twenty years.

It is easy to see why later scholars may have assumed that the parabasis was meant, however, if the decree named the play and praised Aristophanes for services – perhaps even his advice – to Athens: ancient scholars (like their modern counterparts) regarded the parabasis as always the site of the 'advice' given by the poet.[27] But there is some evidence that has been overlooked. Sommerstein has in fact quoted selectively from the *Life*. The immediately preceding portion of the text (32–5) reads as follows:

μάλιστα δὲ ἐπῃνέθη καὶ ἀγαπήθη ὑπὸ τῶν πολιτῶν σφόδρα, ἐπειδὴ διὰ τῶν αὐτοῦ δραμάτων ἐσπούδασε δεῖξαι τὴν τῶν Ἀθηναίων πολιτείαν, ὡς ἐλευθέρα τὲ ἐστι καὶ ὑπ' οὐδενὸς τυράννου δουλαγωγουμένη, ἀλλ' ὅτι δημοκρατία ἐστι καὶ ἐλεύθερος ὢν ὁ δῆμος ἄρχει ἑαυτοῦ. τούτου οὖν χάριν ἐπῃνέθη καὶ . . .

He was very much praised and especially loved by the citizens since through his plays he strove to show that the Athenians' constitution was free and subject to no tyrant's slavery, but that it was a democracy and the *demos* was free and ruled itself. *Therefore because of this* he was praised and [he was crowned . . .].

Since ancient readings, like modern, tended to focus most upon Aristophanes' *criticisms* of the *demos* and its institutions (e.g. Σ *Ach.* 378, Dio Chrys. 16.9), and advice to recall oligarchs (*Frogs* 687–737) may not immediately seem the best way of showing one's democratic credentials, it is certainly surprising to find so positive a spin put on Aristophanes' support for the *demos*. I suggest, therefore, that the words italicised in my translation ('Therefore because of this . . . ') show that it was the commitment to the *demos* shown by Aristophanes' plays, and not a specific reference to the parabasis, that was recorded in the decree. These words certainly imply that Aristophanes' plays contained a message and this might have been articulated in general terms in the decree. Some such phrasing as '[the *demos* resolved] to restage at the next Lenaea the *Frogs* in which he gave sound advice to the *demos*' could easily have spawned later guesses about the message of *Frogs*, since Sommerstein is almost certainly correct to suggest that along with the wreath the decree also mentioned the play and its re-performance.[28] Dicaearchus' reading of the decree, then, will have

---

[26] Sommerstein 1996a, 21. See also Sommerstein 1993.
[27] E.g. Koster, *Prolegomena* p. 4, Platonius *On Differences* I.35–7. [28] Sommerstein 1996a, 21.

been an interpretation based on current ancient readings of the parabases of Old Comedy.[29]

However, a *Frogs* which vindicated Aristophanes' democratic stance – especially in the face of tyranny – could hardly have been given a re-performance before the re-establishment of the democracy after the defeat of the Thirty in 403. It was at that time, and not before, that the *demos* would have been able to recall that Aristophanes' particular service in the *Frogs* had been to attack with his inimitable ironic and metacomic satire the whole idea that non-democrats deserved to be re-enfranchised and to reassure the *demos* that their present policies would work, if pursued with more diligence and the right military leadership. For the advice given on policy at 1463–5 amounts, as Sommerstein has argued, to concentration of Athenian resources on the fleet, and mounting of attacks on enemy territory while regarding enemy control of Attica as understood and not challenging it.[30] Since this pretty much represented current *demos* policy, Sommerstein concludes, 'Aeschylus' message is... (a) that the current Athenian strategy is essentially right, (b) that it must, however, be pursued with more single-mindedness, and, above all, (c) that the way to save Athens is by fighting, not by talking.'[31] As the scholiast notes, this is, *mutatis mutandis*, the strategy advocated by Pericles in the early years of the war (Thuc. 1.141–3). If Aristophanes had been a supporter of Hyperbolus, he will probably have always believed that fighting on against the Spartans was the correct course. Not only are both pieces of advice given by Aeschylus plausible as strategic policy, but they are also plausible as *Aristophanic* advice. It is not, then, absurd to read this final scene as simultaneously suggesting that Aeschylus' true political position when he returns from the dead will be to stand side by side with his former *choregos*, Pericles. It is worth reflecting too that Xenophon will not have been the only person to have known that Alcibiades' advice might have saved the Athenians from disaster at Aegospotamoi in the summer of 405 (Xen. *Hell.* 2.1.25–6), so that the Periclean view articulated by Aeschylus might have stood the test of that defeat and not appeared absurd when the play was produced again. If Sommerstein is correct in regarding 1437–41 and 1451–3 as the original (406) script and 1442–50 as a revision for the second performance,[32] then, assuming that he is also correct in assigning lines 1445–7 to Euripides, the purpose of the change can only have been to emphasise the losing tragedian's agreement with the parabasis and its anti-democratic agenda.

---

[29] See Goldhill 1991, 203.   [30] Sommerstein 1996a, 291 on 1463–5.
[31] Sommerstein 1996a, 291–2.   [32] Sommerstein 1996a on 1435–66.

The original version served merely to produce a greater contrast between the foolishness of Euripides' strategy and the sense of Aeschylus'.

I conclude, then, that Aristophanes was honoured in 403 – in like manner to the democrats who had resisted the oligarchs at Phyle[33] – for having sided with the *demos*, as well as for having given important political advice in *Frogs*. My reconstruction of the lost decree would run somewhat as follows:

The *demos* resolved to honour Aristophanes, son of Philippus of Kydathenaion, with a wreath of sacred olive because through his plays he has striven to show that the Athenians' constitution is free and subject to no tyrant's slavery, but that it is a democracy and the *demos* is free and rules itself, and to restage at the next Lenaea the *Frogs* in which he gave sound advice to the *demos*.[34]

This 'sound advice', however, had been offered not in the parabasis, as later commentators assumed, but rather in the final scene through Aeschylus.

---

[33] Krentz 1982, 112: 'Those who had been at Phyle... were each given a crown of olive... Their names were inscribed with an honorary decree on a stele set up in the Metroon, part of which has been found; it also contained the following epigram: "The ancient people of Athens rewarded these men with crowns for excellence, because they first began to stop those ruling the city with unjust statutes, risking bodily danger"'.

[34] Contrast Sommerstein's version 1996a, 21.

CHAPTER 3

Metacomedy and caricature

HOW COULD METACOMEDY HAVE WORKED IN PRACTICE?

The preceding chapter argued on the basis of a positive evaluation of the dissonances between parabatic critique of certain motifs and their appearance in Aristophanic drama that Aristophanes used metacomedy to conduct a politically motivated comedic campaign against one particular rival, whom I identified as Eupolis, over a period of twenty years. The suggestion that at least Aristophanes systematically parodied his rivals' work instantly raises two major questions. First, what level of cross-reference are we talking about? Was it merely visual? Or did the poet attempt to parody language as well? And did he appropriate plots or elements of plot and character as well? Secondly, if the poet really did operate in this mode, how did he suppose the audience would understand what was going on and at what level of detail? Since these questions more or less mirror those asked in the familiar area of paratragedy, we might take our cue from that field in attempting answers.

Aristophanes' parody of tragedy operates at every level: plot elements (e.g. the use of Euripides' *Telephus* in *Acharnians* and *Thesmophoriazusai*), characters (e.g. Euripides as Helen and Echo in *Thesmophoriazusai*), visual motifs (e.g. Bellerophon's ascent on Pegasus in *Peace*), and language – from direct citation to close stylistic parody (see *Frogs passim*). It is usually argued that the close correlation between many passages of Aristophanes and the tragic texts must mean that copies were in circulation.[1] But it is equally possible that the author took notes during performances, and indeed this explanation works better for parodies of very recent productions (like those of *Helen* and *Andromeda* in *Thesmophoriazusai*). In any case, whatever the audience may have made of the intertextual references, there can be no doubt that the *author* had a very detailed knowledge of tragedy.

[1] Most recently Revermann 2006, 16 with n. 24.

The assumptions the author made about his audience that underlie this depth of cross-reference surely are, (a) some pretty close correlation between the groups who watched tragedy and comedy (which were, after all, presented at the same festivals) and (b) at least the presumption that some of the audience paid close attention to – and would recall much of – what they had seen. Of course, studies of this phenomenon rightly stress that as far as the audience is concerned, there will certainly have been many different levels of appreciation of this deep parodic range: some (perhaps a very few) will have got all or nearly all the jokes, while at the other end of the spectrum there may have been people who only got the general stylistic and visual references.[2]

The same conditions certainly apply to the use of metacomedy. To take the author first, it is clear from the early parabases that Aristophanes paid very close attention to the sort of things his rivals were presenting on stage (e.g. *Knights* 520f., *Clouds* 553, *Peace* 739f.). This evidence demonstrates that he could quote verbatim (*Knights* 529–30 from Cratinus; *Peace* 746–7, possibly also from Cratinus), had an eye for visual business (*Clouds* 538, 540–3, 555–6, *Peace* 740f.), an ear for their language (*Clouds* 542–3, *Peace* 746–7) and paid close attention to their targets (*Clouds* 551–9). It seems unlikely that he would not have been able, if he wished, to mock rival comic techniques, language, characters and plots in precisely the sort of detail with which we know he mocked tragedy and its producers. After all, he claims twice that *language* is the crowning glory of his work (*Peace* 750, *Clouds* 544). There is no evidence for the circulation of full comic texts.[3] But *Knights* 529–30 shows that choral songs (in this case those of Cratinus' *Eumenides*) were known and sung at symposia. This is not surprising. Every year at least twenty-four choreuts will have known the choral words and music of one of the comedies. It is also the case that three or four actors will have been *au fait* with the dialogue (and may even have possessed

---

[2] See Harriott 1962, Rau 1967, Revermann 2006, 40. Exactly the same might be said of audiences of 'The Simpsons', where film cross-references are often very densely superimposed onto the narrative. I recall showing to one academic audience a clip about a male and female greyhound wandering around Springfield and ending up at an Italian restaurant, where they eat spaghetti, but snarl at each other when they find they have hold of the same strand. Everyone found this amusing, but it turned out that only one member of the seminar knew that this was a parody of a scene from Disney's famous cartoon *Lady and the Tramp*.

[3] *A fortiori* there is absolutely no reason to believe, with Brockmann 2003, 160 n. 40, that texts came equipped with notes. Halliwell 1984, 83–4 demonstrates clearly the way scholiasts often simply used inference from the text to construct their glosses. The Alexandrians and their successors had to make do, as do we, with the texts, the *didaskaliai* and such titbits as were preserved in other sources about comedy.

written-out parts.)⁴ Since the chorus certainly and the actors probably were assigned by the *archon*, the poet would have had no control over the political views of his performers and details – sometimes even perhaps complete scripts – might have been passed to rivals. At any rate, the theme of Eupolis' *Autolycus* may have been script-stealing (if Storey is right to accept Kaibel's linking of Aelian's anecdote at *NA* 10.41 with this play)⁵ and this presupposes both the existence of full scripts and the opportunity to get hold of them – if only from the *author*. The same might be said for the accusations of plagiarism so rife in Old Comedy.⁶ But apart from these acts of comedic espionage, we can assume that Aristophanes could also gather material for his parodies at the festival performances he clearly attended (see *Ach.* 630f., *Clouds* 553f.). As I argued in chapter one, the correlation between the motifs criticised in the *Clouds* parabasis and their appearance in Aristophanes might be taken to demonstrate that he was capable of operating parody at all these levels, especially the visual and verbal, and the business of *Knights* and Eupolis, which I shall re-examine in detail in a moment, seems to show that there was a broader level at which his use of rival material might operate, covering a whole play (whatever the actual relation was). In this context, the discovery of close verbal echoes even between the fragmentary material and Aristophanes, such as those between Eupolis fr. 316 (*Chrysoun Genos*, possibly 426) and *Knights* 75 (424), Eupolis fr. 302 (*Chrysoun Genos*) and *Knights* 162f., suggests that Aristophanes did pay very close attention to the actual words of his rivals' comedies.⁷

Whether or not he could expect his audience to recognise such details is subject to the same sort of speculation as for tragedy. Certainly the parabases show that he expected them to know not only his own earlier plays (*Ach.* 636f., *Knights* 513, *Wasps* 1018f., *Peace* 748f., *Clouds* 529, 549–50, 554), but also those of his rivals (*Knights* 520f., *Clouds* 546). His rivals' parabases show the same thing (e.g. Cratin. fr. 213, *Pytine*, Eup. fr. 89, *Baptai*, both referring to *Knights*). We tend to underestimate just how memorable some scenes might have been. Plato certainly expected the target audience of his *Apology* to remember the *mechane* entrance of Socrates in *Clouds* more than a quarter of a century after its performance as well as some of the scene's dialogue (*Apol.* 18c–d: note especially φάσκοντά τε ἀεροβατεῖν 'claiming to be walking on air' – *Clouds* 225). Scenes from comedy might (however rarely)

---

[4] See Revermann 2006, 88f. for a discussion of the evidence for actors' scripts.
[5] Storey 2003, 87 citing Kaibel 1889, 40–2.   [6] See Halliwell 1989 and Sidwell 1993.
[7] Sidwell 1993, 381–4.

appear on Attic vases (the Getty 'Birds' is the best example).[8] And whatever we make of Taplin's arguments for revival performances of Old Comedies in South Italy, he has clearly demonstrated that the so-called 'phlyax-vases' very often recall specific scenes from Athenian plays.[9] In particular, we should note in the current context that the famous *Thesmophoriazusai* painting replicates exactly details of the *text* and that the New York Goose vase incorporates lines of dialogue.[10] Since the audience for Aristophanic comedy was, in the context of the festival competition, also the audience for the comedy of Cratinus, Eupolis, Phrynichus, Plato, Ameipsias and others, the conditions clearly existed for metacomedy to operate in precisely the same manner as we know paratragedy did.

A TEST CASE: *KNIGHTS*

In *Baptai* fr. 89, Eupolis claims: †κἀκεῖνος† τοὺς Ἱππέας | ξυνεποίησα τῷ φαλακρῷ... κἀδωρησάμην, 'I co-wrote *Knights* with the bald fellow and gave it as a gift.' In an article published in 1993, I argued that the conventional view which read this as evidence of collaboration between Eupolis and Aristophanes on *Knights* was mistaken (because collaboration was generally regarded as a sign of *weakness*) and that in fact Aristophanes had been parodying something by Eupolis in this play.[11] More than a decade later, Storey has nuanced the conventional view in favour of seeing the debate between the two poets as deriving from the desire of each to denigrate his rival's originality and praise his own, rather than as a real collaboration.[12] But he does not rule out collaboration (citing the ἡμετέρους of *Clouds* 554 and the fact that Eupolis did not compete at Lenaea 424 as evidence) and as yet no one has taken really seriously the idea of metacomic appropriation.[13] Now that we have direct and indirect evidence of a comedically articulated political conflict between the two poets, it is time to re-examine what is gained in explanatory power by doing so.

If my analysis of the *Clouds* parabasis is broadly correct and in particular if ἡμετέρους at 554 does not refer to collaboration with Eupolis, but to sponsorship by a political/intellectual group opposed ideologically

---

[8] Green 1985, Csapo 1993, Taplin 1993, 101–4.
[9] Taplin 1993, 38–40. See Rusten 2006, 556 n. 27 for a sceptical view of the evidence of vase-painting for the re-performance of Old Comedy in South Italy.
[10] Taplin 1993, 41–2.   [11] Sidwell 1993.
[12] Storey 2003, 281–8, especially 287. See Kyriakidi 2007, 154–71 for the most recent discussion, concluding that there is no good evidence for the practice of collaborative writing in comedy.
[13] Partial exceptions are Ruffell 2002 and Biles 2002 and Kyriakidi 2007, 90–3, 137–54.

to Eupolis, then friendly co-authorship can be ruled out definitively. This will be all the more so if Storey's dating of *Chrysoun Genos* to 426 is accepted and τὸν φαλακρὸν ('baldy') at fr. 298.5 both refers to Aristophanes and is taken as satirical.[14] Moreover, the twenty-year battle evidenced by the metacomic material in Aristophanes shows that the enmity between the poets both was real and predated *Knights*. In such circumstances, the interpretative choice of what is happening in *Knights* is between two models: imitation and parody.

It is certainly true that imitation is a possible explanation, given the evidence to hand. There are, as I have shown, detailed verbal correspondences between *Knights* and *Chrysoun Genos*.[15] And Storey tabulates thirteen correspondences between *Marikas* (of 421) and *Knights* (of 424) which he classifies as 'the most extensively documented use of one comedian's material by another outside Roman comedy'.[16] But this list does not tell us what had gone on with *Knights*, which must surely be part of the same story, given the riposte of Eupolis (presumably to something like *Clouds* 553–5) at fr. 89. Moreover, Cratinus fr. 213 reports the parabasis of *Pytine* (423) in which Cratinus lambasted Aristophanes for τὰ Εὐπόλιδος λέγοντα ('speaking Eupolis' words', 'saying what Eupolis said') in *Knights*, and this guarantees that there was something obviously Eupolidean about the play.

If, however, as I have argued, there was long-standing antagonism between Aristophanes and Eupolis, and if the remarks in the *Clouds* parabasis reflect that enmity (as they seem to, given the ten-year period of reference within it to his sponsors), then imitation is a poor explanation of the relationships between *Knights* and earlier Eupolis and between *Marikas* and *Knights*. The basis of their mutual disrespect is, rather, political (see chapter two). There *is* a political distinction to be drawn between *Knights* and *Marikas*: the first plays attacks Cleon and the second Hyperbolus. It appears from my analysis of the *Clouds* parabasis that Aristophanes was a supporter of Hyperbolus (or at the least was prepared to write plays sponsored by his supporters), while Eupolis was an enemy of Hyperbolus. In such circumstances it is difficult to believe that Aristophanes simply 'imitated' Eupolis, and that behind the construction of these plays there does not lie a clear and personal political motive.

If I am right in inferring that the attack on Hyperbolus in *Marikas* also involved an attack on the bald poet (as it will have if *Clouds* 537–43 refers specifically to *Marikas*), who is appealing in the *Clouds* parabasis to Hyperbolus' supporters for patronage, and that *Clouds* 545 is jokingly

---

[14] Storey 2003, 266–7.   [15] Above n. 7.   [16] Storey 2003, 202–3.

hinting at a fundamental political division between himself and Eupolis, then Eupolis' remark in *Baptai* fr. 89 cannot be read straightforwardly. What it tells us, stripping aside the top layer of humour, is that *Knights* was quite recognisably Eupolidean, something echoed by Cratinus' accusation of plagiarism in the parabasis of *Pytine* (fr. 213). Aristophanes, then, was doing something in *Knights* which borrowed Eupolidean material. In the light of my analysis of *Clouds* 537–43, however, it would not be reasonable to accept Cratinus' judgement on the matter (his comment was meant to sting both Aristophanes and Eupolis): Aristophanes *intended* that his Eupolideanism be recognised, because it was meant to satirise Eupolis and his work, and presumably, his political stance. The counterblast by Aristophanes at *Clouds* 553 shows that Eupolis hit back in *Marikas*, by somehow recognisably using the structure of *Knights*, which he would claim later was his in the first place, to get back at Aristophanes and *his* political base.

Unfortunately, despite the best efforts of scholars, it is impossible to reconstruct the plot of *Marikas* from its fragments, though Storey's reliance on our knowledge of the plot of *Knights* leads him to the sensible conclusion that 'we may conjecture an introduction of Marikas/Hyperbolus, an initial confrontation..., the involvement of the *despotes* and a resolution of the conflict, very likely to the detriment of Marikas'.[17] Following the same train of thought, but paying more attention to the *characters* (that is, the real individuals satirised on stage), we can infer from *Clouds* 553 that Hyperbolus took the place of Cleon, this time represented as a Persian, rather than a Paphlagonian slave.[18] Since Paphlagon/Cleon answers to Demos and his position is usurped by Sausage-Seller, we can infer a similar structure for *Marikas*. Thus Hyperbolus in *Marikas* will have begun the play as the *despotes'* favourite, but will have lost that position to the Sausage-Seller's equivalent by the end. There is, in fact, an unassigned fragment of Eupolis which indicates the presence in one of his plays of a character Demos (fr. 346): καὶ μὴ πονηρούς, ὦ πονηρά, προξένει ... τῶν μὲν γὰρ τοὺς τρόπους ὁριζόμενος ὁ δῆμος, τῆς δὲ αἰτιᾶται ('And don't recommend low-lifes, you ugly woman' ... The People defining the character of the

---

[17] Storey 2003, 206.
[18] This change, I guess, is associated with whatever the λαβή 'hold' was of which Aristophanes speaks at 551. It is a reasonable conjecture that it has something to do with a flip-flop in Hyperbolus' position concerning Athenian relations with Persia. Thus Eup. *Marikas* fr. 207, a parody of Aeschylus *Persians* 65, might suggest that Hyperbolus actually travelled (on an embassy?) there. The significance of his being *Persian* rather than Paphlagonian emerges more clearly if we accept Braund's recent insight (2005, 94–5) that the choice of the sobriquet for Cleon may be related rather to the export market in hides from that region than the verb παφλάζω 'I bluster'.

men, while he accuses the woman). Storey thinks that this fragment is likely to belong to *Marikas*.[19] If correct, this would certainly help us to understand better why that play was perceived as a rerun of *Knights* – it would, just like its 'model', have both a slave-politician and Demos at its core.

But this tentative reconstruction leaves us with a problem. If both Aristophanes and Eupolis put Demos on stage, how can we avoid the inference that both were critical of the *demos* itself? Aristophanes certainly pulls no punches in the first part of *Knights* and as Sommerstein acutely observes: 'The claim of Demos (1111–50) that he is not really being gullible but rather acting on a crude calculation of self-interest is one that offers little comfort even if we believe it.'[20] We cannot really save Aristophanes from accusations of harsh criticism of the *demos* as it currently is, either, by looking to the play's rejuvenation of Demos, since even if we take this at face value rather than ironically, the play would still satirise the contemporary *demos* and suggest how it might be cured of its despicable traits *in the future*. The evidence of the Old Oligarch ([Xen.] *Ath. Pol.* 2.18) might, of course, be pertinent: κωμῳδεῖν δ'αὖ καὶ κακῶς λέγειν τὸν μὲν δῆμον οὐκ ἐῶσιν, ἵνα μὴ αὐτοὶ ἀκούωσι κακῶς ('Making fun and insulting of the *demos* they do not allow, so that they do not get a bad reputation.'). If it does articulate the legal situation at the time of *Knights*, it tells us that Demos cannot have been intended to represent the *demos*. But even if we set this aside, because we are unsure of his date,[21] the account we have now given of the fundamental ideological division between the two poets ought to give us pause. Aristophanes' commitment to the political supporters of the radical democrat Hyperbolus (*Clouds* 551f. with chapter one above) makes it unthinkable that he would want to attack the very *demos* which gave him his power base. We might not be able to say the same of Eupolis, at least as Aristophanes represents him (*Clouds* 545). But if *Knights* and *Marikas* are as closely linked in structure as I have argued above, Eupolis must to a recognisable extent have been following his bald rival's lead. I conclude that the Demos in *Knights*, and *a fortiori* the one (if he existed) in *Marikas*, were not meant as personifications of the *demos*, but were caricatures of recognisable individuals. The claim implicit in the name Demos of their direct association with the *demos* would on this scenario operate satirically

---

[19] Storey 1995–6, 143–4.   [20] Sommerstein 1981, 2.
[21] There is currently no agreement among scholars on a date (and no sign of this emerging any time soon). Guesses range across the 420s (e.g. Atkinson 1992, 58, Mariotta 2001, 116–17), the 410s (e.g. Lapini 1997, 1998, Mattingly 1997), after 411 (Sordi 2002) and the fourth century (Roscalla 1995; Hornblower 2000 – but ironic and referring to the fifth).

to challenge some perception in the *polis* that they were people who could or did presume to speak on the *demos'* behalf in some capacity. This will help us when we attempt later to make identifications. But first we must face up to some dramatic problems which this hypothesis raises in respect of the presentation of Demos in *Knights*.

DEMOS IN *KNIGHTS*

In *Knights* the appearance of Demos himself on stage is delayed until line 728, but the audience must, on the hypothesis now constructed, somehow have been aware of his identity from the beginning of the play for the satirical point to be understood. The only way this could work in practice is, in fact, if the plot of *Knights* took its starting point from a comedy already in the public domain, in which Paphlagon/Cleon and Demos/X had been characters. Given the public discourse about Eupolis' collaboration, it makes sense to imagine that this will have been a play by Eupolis.

There are certainly signs from the opening of *Knights* that could be used to support this hypothesis. Demos is introduced and strongly characterised at line 42 long before his entry. But Paphlagon is mentioned already in line 2: κακῶς Παφλαγόνα τὸν νεώνητον κακόν ('[May the gods destroy, schemes and all,] miserably that miserable newly-bought Paphlagon!'). On the conventional view, this is merely a type of audience-teasing (cf. *Peace* 43f.) or 'warm-up'. But it is entirely possible that the opening rather depends upon the fact that Cleon's nickname Paphlagon was already known to the audience from an earlier comedy, in which it had perhaps been used for the first time. The mention of his sobriquet would therefore immediately indicate to them that what was going on was a misappropriation of this earlier comedy. The clue (for us) may be contained in the explanation given at 43–4: οὗτος τῇ προτέρᾳ νουμηνίᾳ ἐπρίατο δοῦλον, βυρσοδέψην Παφλαγόνα ('Last market day he bought a slave, the tanner, Paphlagon'). Eupolis' Lenaea play of the previous year, 425, which came a poor third behind Aristophanes' *Acharnians* and Cratinus' *Cheimazomenoi*, was called *Noumeniai* 'Market Days' ('New Moon Days'). This play seems already to have been lost in antiquity, so that ancient commentators were not in a position to read and excerpt it. However, it is certainly reasonable to conjecture that Aristophanes may have been crowing about his success with *Acharnians* by immediately subverting a recent Eupolidean failure in *Knights*. If this is right, it is probable that lines 50–2 will have been direct quotations from a scene in which Demos was fed titbits and mollycoddled by Paphlagon. In such circumstances, the domestic allegory in *Noumeniai* would have been more sustained and its incompleteness and inconsistency in *Knights* would have had a parodic and subversive intent. The central effect, though, would certainly have been that from the very start the audience would have known who at least two of the central figures would be, and doubtless the identity of the slaves – already obvious to them, whether from mask, gesture, vocal imitation or language (see further below pp. 155–7) – would have added a further comic frisson to that knowledge.

It should by now be clear that the result of the foregoing analysis is to refocus attention in respect of this issue not only on comic borrowings (for which read ideologically motivated parody), but also on the role of on-stage satire of individuals, who stand behind the major characters in these plays. Aristophanes' focus in the *Clouds* parabasis upon this is the key to understanding how the comedy of others could be satirically subverted. His disgust at the treatment of Hyperbolus by other poets guarantees that in Eupolis' 'recasting' of *Knights* in *Marikas* the substitution of Hyperbolus for Cleon as the focus of attack matters crucially. That is, for the politically motivated subversion of earlier comedies to work effectively, there must be not merely comic motifs and *plots*, but also recognisable targets which can be substituted for each other in the subverted version. On this reading, then, not only does Demos represent a real and identifiable individual, but the Sausage-Seller – the new factor introduced to subvert the original Eupolidean point of attack– does too. It will be the identification of the real individual behind him that drives the play in new directions.

THE EUPOLIDEAN *KNIGHTS*

If it is correct to focus on structure as the common factor, we can do the same exercise for the Eupolidean play which was being subverted by *Knights* as we have done already for *Marikas*. It too will have centred round two politicians, their service to Demos (a caricature of some individual), and the replacement of the first as *prostates* of the satirised individual by an even worse one. It must again be emphasised that such a structure would only have lent itself to parodic subversion if it dealt with real politicians throughout, not (as is the commonest understanding of *Knights*) with the replacement of a real politician by a fictional one. The structure is essentially ironic, because its central premiss is that the replacement is a *worse* individual than the original (*Knights* 328f.). Thus an original play which began with a bad *prostates* of Demos and a plot to replace him with a *worse* one would have lent itself very easily to subversion, and then re-appropriation, thus producing the series X-*Knights*-*Marikas* (and perhaps even one or two more: cf. Ari. *Anagyros* fr. 58, *Clouds* 546, Eup. *Baptai* fr. 89).[22]

There is another important consideration. The analysis of the *Clouds* parabasis in chapter one has brought out the way in which comic poets align themselves with political groupings. Since Aristophanes' alignment appears to be with Hyperbolus, and Eupolis attacked Hyperbolus in *Marikas*, it seems quite likely that the comedic tit-for-tat between himself and Eupolis also involved attacks and counter-attacks upon the political favourites of the other comic poet. In other words, we can, for example, infer that Sausage-Seller in *Knights* was substituted for the worse *prostates* in Eupolis' X (*Noumeniai?*) because Eupolis belonged to his support group.

In the battle between Eupolis and Aristophanes, then, some of the blanks in the series can now be filled out with a degree of confidence. If we can say that *Knights* shows the pattern 'Cleon replaced by Y (Eupolis' man)', we can infer that *Marikas* has 'Hyperbolus (Aristophanes' man) replaced by Z (someone with an embarrassing association with Aristophanes)'. The original Eupolidean play must by the same token have replaced a bad politician with someone supported by Aristophanes. If *Marikas* takes over from where this play ended (thus by-passing *Knights*), it is reasonable to conclude that the worse *prostates* in the original will have been Hyperbolus. This is not contradicted by *Clouds* 553, since the series of attacks complained about by Aristophanes occurs in the wake of the λαβή ('hold') mentioned at 551, a reference ignored by commentators, but very clearly the immediate catalyst for Eupolis' belated response to *Knights* (three years afterwards, in 421).[23] The claim that Eupolis made in *Baptai* fr. 89 draws the *Knights* very close to its original, however, otherwise it would not have been funny. This helps confirm that what Aristophanes borrowed from Eupolis, apart from this basic plot structure (the function of which was to satirise *individuals*, not just to make generic points about political life in Athens), were Eupolis' main characters, Paphlagon and Demos. Thus the first play in the series (Eupolis' X) cast Paphlagon the leather-seller as the chief slave of the elderly curmudgeon Demos, and the plot eventually removed him in favour of the even worse *prostates* Hyperbolus, whose characterisation as a lamp-maker/seller must surely have originated, or at least gained its most

---

[22] The fact that Eupolis chose *Baptai* as his vehicle for claiming the original idea behind *Knights* as his own might indicate that it is this play that could be counted as the third rerun of the same material (*Clouds* 546), though we would still need yet another rerun (the fourth) if *Knights* is the referent of *Anagyros* fr. 58.

[23] See n. 18 above.

memorable staging, in this Eupolis comedy.²⁴ Thus the absurd figure of the Sausage-Seller would be a direct response to Eupolis' market-oriented political allegory in *Noumeniai*.

Knights now subverts the Eupolis play by reworking its beginning and immediately substituting for the lamp-maker a new merchant, the Sausage-Seller, who must, by analogy, have represented a young politician who (at the time) had close links with Eupolis. Given that the group called in to support the usurper are Knights, who, like Aristophanes' unnamed comic rival at *Clouds* 545, also wore their hair long, it is highly likely that the real individual behind Sausage-Seller either belonged to or was closely associated with them (see further chapter five).

In 421, following a golden opportunity provided by some unknown action of Hyperbolus' (see n. 18 above), Eupolis reused his original schema to take a vengeful shot back at Aristophanes. Casting Hyperbolus as *Marikas*, presumably now the *prostates* of Demos, he again has him replaced (apparently this time after his death: fr. 209), presumably by a worse politician who also has ties to Aristophanes. I will leave for later (chapter five, pp. 157f., p. 201) the identification of Sausage-Seller and the adversary of *Marikas*.²⁵ But it is important to emphasise once more that this exchange centrally implicates the comic poets who support the politicians satirised: otherwise it would be difficult to see why the exchanges between them are so acerbic (Cratin. fr. 213; Eup. fr. 89; Ar. *Clouds* 553f. and *Anagyros* fr. 58).

DEMOS

This analysis also tends to confirm that we can only make sense of the political nexus of X (*Noumeniai?*)-*Knights*-*Marikas* if in each case Demos does not represent the actual Athenian people, but someone closely associated with the politician ousted. So in Eupolis' *X* (*Noumeniai?*) and *Knights*, Demos represents someone who has close ties to Cleon, though his rejuvenation in *Knights* may transform him into someone else who has ties with

---

²⁴ The information at *Peace* 681f. that Hyperbolus is the current *prostates* has nothing in reality to support it and has against it the high probability that he was against the Peace of Nicias. It is noteworthy in the current context, however, that he is characterised here as a lamp-maker and that the comment at 692 can (like *Clouds* 876) be seen as a *positive* endorsement of his political effect. I suggest below (pp. 95–6) that this is a cross-reference to comedy, more likely Eupolis *X* (*Noumeniai?*), since there is no evidence that Marikas was presented as a lamp-maker.

²⁵ If my earlier suggestion that *Baptai* is another of the '*prostates* usurped' series, then it is a very good bet, given the association with that play of Alcibiades (*PCG Baptia* Tiii-vi), that Alcibiades was at the very least the 'worse *prostates*' in *Marikas*. I deal with the complexities of this issue in chapter five.

the individual caricatured as the Sausage-Seller (and this may also be a motif taken, *mutatis mutandis*, from Eupolis' original play). In *Marikas*, by contrast, Demos represents someone who is associated with Hyperbolus. In each case, then, the satirical plot structure serves ironically to discomfort a supporter of someone branded 'worse' than the original bugbear. Though this mode does involve direct political attack, through on-stage caricature of the individuals behind Paphlagon, Sausage-Seller and Marikas, it is satire focused through their spokespersons, who can be caricatured as Demos for reasons somehow relating to their status.

Who, then, might adequately be satirised in these circumstances as Demos? There is one group of individuals, employed by the *demos* to speak on their behalf about, among others, politicians, precisely to protect their interests against the elite *rhetores* they were constrained to employ to lead their business.[26] They are the comic poets, whose pronouncements on their value to the *demos* are well known, even if the interpretation of them is controversial. Take, for example, Cratinus fr. 52 (*Dionysoi*): νικῷ μὲν ὁ τῇδε πόλει λέγων τὸ λῷστον ('May the poet win who gives the city the most useful advice'), or Aristophanes, *Acharnians* 656f.: φησὶν δ' ὑμᾶς πολλὰ διδάξειν ἀγάθ' ('He says he will teach you many good things'). If Demos represented a comic poet, the comedy would centre on a desire to satirise him by making him the focus of a contest for his favour on the part of recognisable politicians of the day. As we have seen, this fits not only the inferences drawn from the *Clouds* parabasis in the preceding chapter, that comic poets were associated with political groups (as well as serving as teachers of the *demos* at festival time), but it also explains very simply how comic misappropriation could work hand in hand with political attack: Demos in *Marikas* will have represented Aristophanes, while in Eupolis' *Noumeniai* and Aristophanes' *Knights* he will have represented a third comic poet who was known to support Cleon and who was also an enemy of both Aristophanes and Eupolis. Who Demos might be in *Noumeniai* (?) and *Knights* will become clearer in the exposition which follows.

COMIC POETS ON STAGE

Still, the only comic poet we have firm evidence of having been a character in comic drama appeared in Cratinus' *Pytine*, at Dionysia 423, the year after *Knights* (Σ *Knights* 400a = *PCG* Testimonia on *Pytine* ii). But other examples are not unlikely. For instance, Storey has recently argued

[26] Edwards 1993.

(from Apsines, *Rhet.* 3 and Ael. *NA* 10.41) that Eupolis put himself and Aristophanes on stage in his *Autolycus*. In Cratinus fr. 342.2, it is usual to see the words ὑπολεπτολόγος, γνωμιδιώκτης, εὐριπιδαριστοφανίζων ('A subtle sophist, a chaser of tropes, a Euripidaristophaniser') as referring to Aristophanes.[27] If the words are presented as answers to the clever spectator's question in line 1 τίς δὲ σύ; ('Who are you?'), this implies in addition the attempt to identify a comic poet on stage. Pieters thought that the comedy-writing scene in Cratinus' *Pytine* (fr. 208–9) involved another comic poet besides the main character.[28] Ancient commentators seem to have thought it clear that Aristophanes spoke directly at fr. 488 (Σ Pl. *Apol.* 19c: καὶ αὐτὸς δ' ὁμολογεῖται Σκηνὰς καταλαμβανούσαις 'and he himself admits in the *Women Pitching Tents*') and also at fr. 604 (*loc. incert.*: *Life of Aristophanes* = PCG Aristophanes T1, 55: ὧν καὶ αὐτὸς ἐμνήσθη 'which he himself mentioned'), even though both these fragments are in iambic trimeters, not a metre associated with the parabasis. And it is all too well known that Aristophanes' characters Dicaeopolis in *Acharnians* (377–82 and 496–556) and Bdelycleon in *Wasps* (650–1) seem to equate themselves with the (or rather 'a') comic poet (again in iambic trimeters).

In fact, there is good evidence to suggest that in antiquity the self-representation of comic poets in their own works was a prominent feature in the theories espoused by commentators. First of all, it seems clear from Lucian, whose inspiration for his hybrid comic dialogue came largely from Old Comedy. For example, Dialogue says in his prosecution speech at *Bis Accusatus* 33: εἶτά μοι εἰς τὸ αὐτὸ φέρων συγκαθεῖρξεν τὸ σκῶμμα καὶ τὸν ἴαμβον καὶ κυνισμὸν καὶ τὸν Εὔπολιν καὶ τὸν Ἀριστοφάνη ('Then he brought together and shut up with me joking, iambus, Cynicism, Eupolis and Aristophanes'). Actually, it seems clear that in this particular work Lucian expected his audience to see in his own satirical self-representation here a strong echo of that of Cratinus. At any rate, the personification of Rhetoric as his wife and her charge against him of κάκωσις 'mistreatment' (*Bis Accusatus* 14) both suggest that Cratinus' *Pytine* lies silently behind the fabric of this particular dialogue. Plutarch – no lover of Old Comedy (*Mor.* 853a–854d) – provides good evidence that the use by Old Comedy of self-satire was thought a way of taking the sharp edge off invective (*Quaestiones Conviviales, Mor.* 634d): τῶν κωμικῶν ἔνιοι τὴν πικρίαν ἀφαιρεῖν δοκοῦσι τῷ σκώπτειν ἑαυτούς ('Some of the comic poets reckoned to take away the bitterness [sc. of comic invective] by satirising themselves').

---

[27] Sommerstein 1992, 22, Storey 2003, 327. *Contra* Olson 2007, 110, who without argument takes the adjectives to agree with the *spectator*.
[28] Pieters 1946, 151.

And one of his examples is Cratinus' *Pytine*. But Lucian also knew – and appears to have expected his audience of *pepaideumenoi* to know – the scholarship on Old Comedy. This much is clear from the way in which he speaks of his hidden comic allusions at the opening of *Verae Historiae* (1.2):

καὶ τῶν ἱστορουμένων ἕκαστον οὐκ ἀκωμῳδήτως ᾔνικται πρός τινας τῶν παλαιῶν ποιητῶν τε καὶ συγγραφέων καὶ φιλοσόφων πολλὰ τεράστια καὶ μυθώδη συγγεγραφότων, οὓς καὶ ὀνομαστὶ ἂν ἔγραφον, εἰ μὴ καὶ αὐτῷ σοι ἐκ τῆς ἀναγνώσεως φανεῖσθαι ἔμελλον

I have also in a manner not unconnected with comedy framed each element of my tales as an enigmatic allusion to some of the ancient poets, historians and philosophers who wrote much of mythical monsters. I would give you their names, if they were not going to be obvious to you from your reading.

The language deliberately appropriates the terms of a well-represented ancient account of the history of Old Comedy, according to which the genre went through a stage where enigma was central and names were suppressed.[29] It is of some importance to note that in this work, too, Lucian is satirically centre-stage as the narrator of his own fantastic voyages.[30] Beyond the instances already noted above where scholia directly identify the comic poet as a stage-character or where we can see indirect evidence that this was a normal view (as in the case of the anecdotes in Apsines and Aelian), a misunderstood passage in Platonius (Koster, *Prolegomena* p. 6, II.8–12) can be argued to support the notion that this phenomenon was reckoned especially notable in Eupolis.

Εὔπολις δὲ εὐφάνταστος μὲν εἰς ὑπερβολήν ἐστι κατὰ τὰς ὑποθέσεις. τὰς γὰρ εἰσηγήσεις μεγάλας τῶν δραμάτων ποιεῖται, καὶ ἥνπερ ἐν τῇ παραβάσει φαντασίαν κινοῦσιν οἱ λοιποί, ταύτην ἐκεῖνος ἐν τοῖς δράμασιν, ἀναγαγεῖν

---

[29] Ancient scholars characteristically divided the history of invective comedy into three stages, according to the way their attacks were made. These were (1) open attack against anyone, (2) enigmatic attack against anyone and (3) attack only against slaves and foreigners. Stage (2) is here the point of reference for Lucian, the 'enigmatic' or 'symbolic' moment in Old Comedy's development, variously called ψόγος κεκρυμμένος ('hidden invective'), κωμῳδεῖν ἐσχηματισμένως ('satirizing figuratively'), συμβολικὰ σκώμματα ('allegorical jokes'), ἐλέγχουσα αἰνιγματωδῶς ('attacking enigmatically'). The first three are Tzetzes' formulations (*PCG* Aristophanes T83a and b), the last of the scholium on Dionysius Thrax (*PCG* Aristophanes T84). In some accounts, this 'enigmatic turn' is associated with the abandonment of ὀνομαστὶ κωμῳδεῖν ('satirising by name'), e.g. the *Anonymus Cranmeri* (Koster, *Prolegomena* p. 40, xIb 49) and the scholia to Dionysius Thrax (Koster, *Prolegomena* p. 71 xvIIIa 31–2), where, however, the term ὀνομαστὶ ἐλέγχειν ('to criticise by name') is employed instead. It is to this concatenation of terms that Lucian alludes here. See von Möllendorf 2000, 50–1, for a different account.

[30] I owe this point to Karen Ní Mheallaigh.

Metacomedy and caricature 59

ἱκανὸς ὢν ἐξ Ἅιδου νομοθετῶν πρόσωπα καὶ δι' αὐτῶν εἰσηγούμενος ἢ περὶ θέσεως νόμων ἢ καταλύσεως

Eupolis is excessively imaginative in his plots. For he makes his *mises en scène* grand and the imagination which the others bring to bear in the parabasis, this he uses in the dramas, being capable of bringing back from Hades the personages of law-givers and through them giving advice about the making or repealing of laws.

Telò has recently re-examined this passage, focusing attention on the interpretation of the dichotomy between 'in the parabasis' and 'in the dramas'.[31] He points to evidence which assimilates the notion of φαντασία 'imagination' to εἰδωλοποιία 'making images' ([Longinus] *Subl.* 15.1), that is giving speeches to recognisable individuals, and notes further that Hermogenes (*Prog.* 9 R.) and Aphthonius (*Prog.* 11) both define εἰδωλοποιία as specifically related to the *dead*. Aphthonius even cites the *Demoi* as an example. This brings Telò to the conclusion that the ambivalence of the term εἰδωλοποιία has led Platonius 'to unify under one label two conceptually distinct entities, purely verbal evocativeness (φαντασία in its strict sense) and a specific type of dramatic action (bringing people back to life)'.[32] However, he still has some difficulty understanding 'the distinctive 'eidetic' peculiarities of the parabasis alluded to by Platonius'.[33] The problem with the argument is that while pseudo-Longinus gives evidence that some people call εἰδωλοποιία φαντασία, he does not imply that the terms are necessarily coterminous. That Platonius is not here using φαντασία as a synonym for εἰδωλοποιία is clearly demonstrated by the fact that there is no way to claim a relevance to the parabasis of εἰδωλοποιία in the sense used by Hermogenes and Aphthonius. As Platonius tells us elsewhere (Koster *Prolegomena* 1.36–7), in the parabasis οἱ ποιηταὶ διὰ τοῦ χοροῦ ἢ ὑπὲρ ἑαυτῶν ἀπελογοῦντο ἢ περὶ δημοσίων πραγμάτων εἰσηγοῦντο ('the poets either defended themselves or gave advice about public affairs'). Given that both passages are ascribed to Platonius, we are probably looking here at a single theory. The φαντασία employed in the parabasis, then, must be something to do with the manner in which the poet presents his own views. Platonius is making it clear that there is something different

---

[31] Telò 2007, 46–8.
[32] Telò 2007, 48: 'L'ambivalenza funzionale (estetica e retorica) di εἰδωλοποιία porta... Platonio a unificare sotto un'unica etichetta due entità concettuali, l'evocatività puramente verbale (cioè la φαντασία *stricto sensu*) e un particolare tipo di azione scenic (l' ἀνάστασις appunto), nettamente disomogenee.'
[33] Telò 2007, 48 n. 153: 'Difficile stabilire univocamente le peculiarità 'eidetiche' parabatiche cui allude Platonio'.

about the 'in your face' way Eupolis does this *in the plays* as opposed to *in the parabasis*. And since Platonius does not appear to confine himself to the example of the *Demoi* in making this claim – rather it is something generally true of the author, which can be exemplified by the specific example of the resuscitation of the leaders – we need to ask what kind of φαντασία could possibly have justified such a statement. The answer must, I think, be that, just as what was placed 'before the eyes' of the audience in the parabasis was, via the chorus, *the poet himself*, so Eupolis had a habit of putting himself on stage *in the dramas* to get his views over. This interpretation is confirmed in turn by the manner in which Lucian utilises Eupolis' *Demoi* as an intertext in his *Piscator*, where the ancient philosophers emerge from Hades with the intention of having their revenge upon the writer, who once more appears as a central figure in his own work.[34] In other words, Lucian can rely on his audience's understanding of his satirical self-representation precisely because it was regarded as a crucial ploy in his models. Below I shall be arguing that the whole business of charges of *xenia* against Aristophanes was elicited from plays where, as in *Acharnians* (377f. and 499f.), the author appeared to ancient scholars to be coterminous with the stage-character. Lucian is probably taking advantage of this model when he allows Rhetoric to describe him as a *barbaros* at *Bis Accusatus* 27. And it is certainly possible to argue that the currency in the ancient scholarship of the theory that comic poets appeared in their own plays is what underlies Lucian's ironic comment on Nephelococcygia in *Verae Historiae* 1.29: καὶ ἐγὼ ἐμνήσθην Ἀριστοφάνους τοῦ ποιητοῦ, ἀνδρὸς σοφοῦ καὶ ἀληθοῦς καὶ μάτην ἐφ' οἷς ἔγραψεν ἀπιστουμένου 'For my part, I thought of the poet Aristophanes, a wise and truthful man whose portrait of the place had been wrongly disbelieved.' But it is another question entirely whether the ancients were *correct* in their identification of first person self-satire as a normal mode of Old Comedy, even if it led to the creation of genres in which this was the norm.[35]

CRATINUS' *PYTINE*

As it happens, a crucial piece of evidence, already mentioned above, links *Pytine* with critique of Aristophanes (and possibly *Knights*), namely Cratinus fr. 213 (=Σ *Knights* 531a), which coincidentally also involves Eupolis:

---

[34] For the ramifications of this finding for our understanding of *Demoi*, see chapter six pp. 276f.
[35] I refer both to Lucian and to Roman Satire; the dependence of the latter upon Old Comedy may also, I suspect, be as much a matter of imitation of the apparent stance of Old Comic poets as appropriation of named invective.

Metacomedy and caricature 61

ταῦτα ἀκούσας ὁ Κρατῖνος ἔγραψε τὴν Πυτίνην, δεικνὺς ὅτι οὐκ ἐλήρησεν· ἐν ᾗ κακῶς λέγει τὸν Ἀριστοφάνην ὡς τὰ Εὐπόλιδος λέγοντα.

When he heard this (viz. the charge of talking nonsense), Cratinus wrote *Pytine*, showing that he had not talked nonsense. In this play, he abuses Aristophanes for saying the words of Eupolis.

It is not quite clear whether the scholiast was theorising in the first of his statements (that *Pytine* was Cratinus' *response* to *Knights*). However, it must have been clear from the context (this is almost certainly the parabasis) (a) that Cratinus was here referring specifically to *Knights*, and (b) that he was accusing Aristophanes of in some way using material known to have derived from Eupolis. In any case, then, the scholiast had reason to connect *Pytine* and its criticisms of Aristophanes back to *Knights*. Eupolis fr. 89 and *Clouds* 553f. guarantee that whatever Cratinus meant by 'speaking the words of Eupolis', the dispute was in the public domain.

What is not at all obvious is why Cratinus would have thought it a good riposte to Aristophanes' criticisms of him to present a caricature of himself on stage. It would seem much more logical to attack in this manner either his young rival Aristophanes or the other equally young comic poet he accuses him of copying, Eupolis, though on the surface this seems to be ruled out by the age of the central character (fr. 193.4). This inference would also suit the view of Old Comedy which has now emerged from consideration of the *Clouds* parabasis and the satirical structure of the *X* (*Noumeniai?*)–*Knights*–*Marikas* series. If the point of the genre was to show up on stage the vices of specific individuals, with the intention of alerting the *demos* to them and bringing them down a few pegs in public estimation, it seems difficult to imagine that any poet would ever use the weapon on himself. In fact, though there has been no investigation to date of the possibility that Cratinus' comic poet was not himself, but a rival, several considerations combine to support such a case. The next step is to look more closely at the comic poet of *Pytine*.

The only evidence identifying the central character of *Pytine* as its author, Cratinus, comes in the scholium vetus on *Knights* 400a, the relevant portion of which reads:

τὴν Κωμῳδίαν ὁ Κρατῖνος ἐπλάσατο αὐτοῦ εἶναι γυναῖκα καὶ ἀφίστασθαι τοῦ συνοικεσίου σὺν αὐτῷ θέλειν, καὶ κακώσεως αὐτῷ δίκην λαγχάνειν, φίλους δὲ παρατυχόντας τοῦ Κρατίνου δεῖσθαι μηδὲν προπετὲς ποιῆσαι, καὶ τῆς ἔχθρας ἀνερωτᾶν τὴν αἰτίαν, τὴν δὲ μέμφεσθαι αὐτῷ ὅτι μὴ κωμῳδοίη μηκέτι, σχολάζοι δὲ τῇ μέθῃ.

Cratinus made Comedy his wife and portrayed her as wishing to end her cohabitation with him and taking against him a suit for mistreatment. Some friends arrive by chance and ask Cratinus not to do anything hasty. They ask the reason for the dispute and she criticizes him for not writing comedy any more but instead spending his time on drink.

Although this seems quite cut and dried as it stands, it is not clear that the character was actually named Cratinus. Indirect confirmation of this can be found in Lucian's *Bis Accusatus*, argued above to rely on Cratinus' *Pytine* and his audience's knowledge of that play. Lucian himself appears in the piece, but he is not named, and a point is made of this at 14: Δίκη: τίς δὲ οὗτός ἐστιν; οὐ γὰρ ἐγγέγραπται τοὔνομα. (Justice: 'Who is he? His name is not recorded'). Hermes replies: οὕτως ἀποκλήρου, τῷ ῥήτορι τῷ Σύρῳ· κωλύσει γὰρ οὐδὲν καὶ ἄνευ τοῦ ὀνόματος ('Allot the case to him as the Syrian orator. There's nothing to stop him being tried, even without his name.') The same strategy is used in another piece which draws inspiration from Old Comedy, *Piscator*, where Lucian, when asked his name, replies (19) Παρρησιάδης Ἀληθίωνος Ἐλεγξικλέους ('Parrhesiades, the son of Truthteller, the son of Famed-Examiner'). It seems reasonable to infer that Lucian is deliberately imitating what was perceived as an authorial strategy for self-presentation in Old Comedy.[36] That being so, we must conclude that (a) the central character of *Pytine* was not given his real name but (b) that his status as a comic poet was made clear rather from the text, especially the character's first-person utterances (c) that ancient Alexandrian readers (and those, like Lucian, who learned from their commentaries) easily made the leap from the first-person statements of a comic poet to the assumption that the character represented the author, particularly because the character was old (fr. 193.4).

Once this last step had been taken, the general view of Cratinus as a hopeless drunk had its firmest foundation. The scholia were now free to load onto other references in Aristophanes the full interpretative force which the identification of Cratinus as the drunken poet of his own *Pytine* allowed. For example, *Knights* 400 γενοίμην ἐν Κρατίνου κῳδίον ('May I become a blanket in Cratinus' house') is interpreted by the scholium vetus on this line as follows: ὡς ἐνουρητὴν δὲ καὶ μέθυσον διαβάλλει τὸν Κρατῖνον ('He attacks Cratinus as an incontinent drunkard'), and specifically adduces the evidence of *Pytine* to support the contention (the passage has already been quoted above). The lines might, however, simply allude to Cratinus' old age and incontinence, without any implication that he is a boozer. Another passage where over-interpretation is normal, because of the assumption that the central character of *Pytine* is Cratinus,

---

[36] Compare the way in which he articulates his method in *Verae Historiae* 1.2, p. 58 above.

is *Knights* 535: ὃν χρῆν διὰ τὰς προτέρας νίκας πίνειν ἐν τῷ πρυτανείῳ ('When because of his earlier victories he ought to be having a drink in the Prytaneum'). While it is true that πίνειν is a surprise for σιτεῖσθαι, this word picks up the theme of thirst from the previous line's allusion to Connas (δίψη δ' ἀπολωλώς 'dying of thirst'). Without the immediate assumption – based on *Pytine* – that Cratinus is a drunkard, commentators both ancient and modern might have drawn the conclusion that like Connus, despite his Olympic victories, Cratinus also was too poor to provide the wine which would be essential to the proper celebration of his successful career. The passage in *Peace* (700–3) where Cratinus' death is reported is also, of course, interpreted in terms of the assumed identification of Cratinus as the drunken poet. Hence 702–3 οὐ γὰρ ἠνέσχετο | ἰδὼν πίθον καταγνύμενον οἴνου πλέων ('Because he couldn't bear seeing a vat full of wine being broken') receives notes such as ὅτι φίλοινος ὁ Κρατῖνος, καὶ αὐτὸς ἐν τῇ Πυτίνῃ σαφῶς λέγει ('That Cratinus likes wine he himself also says clearly in the *Pytine*'). Love of wine, evidenced apparently in the *Peace* passage, is not equivalent to overindulgence in it and without *Pytine*, interpreters might have seen in these lines as much the response of the Attic farmer protective of his produce and his winter enjoyment (cf. *Ach.* 512, 979–87), comically expressed, as that of the alcoholic. For elsewhere in Aristophanes, the image of Cratinus is rather of the smelly, geriatric has-been comic (*Ach.* 849f., *Knights* 400, 531f.).

Another important caveat comes from examination of the fragments themselves. As Rosen has recently remarked, the comic poet character is actually treated very critically.[37] For example, it appears to be considerably beyond friendly self-mockery to represent oneself as so prolific that one's mouth has to be stopped before everything is flooded with one's verses (fr. 198) or (if this does belong to *Pytine*) to have a character speak of one's love of wine in imagery taken from boy-chasing (fr. 195, cf. Lysias 3 for expression of a shamefaced attitude to public knowledge of this proclivity). Moreover, we do not know how the play ended. The trials in Lucian's *Bis Accusatus* end favourably for the Syrian orator, but for all we know this may be a deliberate reversal of the outcome of *Pytine*. Moreover, apart from *Pytine*, Cratinus has in antiquity a reputation for the severity of his personal attacks (Platonius Koster *Prolegomena* p. 6, II. 1–5: ἅτε δὴ κατὰ τὰς Ἀρχιλόχου ζηλώσεις, αὐστηρὸς μὲν ταῖς λοιδορίαις ἐστίν... ἁπλῶς κατὰ τὴν παροιμίαν γυμνῇ τῇ κεφαλῇ τίθησι τὰς βλασφημίας κατὰ τῶν ἁμαρτανόντων 'as an imitator of Archilochus he is harsh in his ridicule... as the proverb has

---

[37] Rosen 2000, 32.

it, he simply sets out his insults against those who do wrong with his head bare'). This sits oddly beside a sudden urge for self-satire.

If these arguments are sound, then Cratinus was most likely satirising one of his younger rivals, even though on the surface it looks unlikely because of the character's age (the explanation for this is complex and will emerge later). The play is, thus, possibly, as the scholiast knew or surmised, a response to *Knights*, and hence attacking either Aristophanes or Eupolis.

We do at least have ancient evidence which brands Aristophanes as a seasoned drinker (Pl. *Symp.* 176b and 177e; Athen. 10.429a). In the first *Symposium* passage, Aristophanes admits to having been drunk the day before, while in the second Socrates avers that Aristophanes' whole time is spent with 'Dionysus and Aphrodite'. Athenaeus tells us that both Alcaeus and Aristophanes wrote while drunk. The source of this anecdote is unknown. It could have been an accusation made by another comic poet, however, perhaps even Cratinus.[38]

We know nothing of Eupolis' proclivities, but this does not mean that we can dismiss him from consideration, precisely because of Cratinus' implicit criticism of him in *Pytine* (fr. 213) and the evidence for his role in the composition of *Knights*. We have no direct route into this area. However, we can get further by looking at the play Aristophanes chose to produce at the very next festival after the defeat of his *Clouds* by Cratinus' *Pytine* at Dionysia 423, *Wasps*.

ON-STAGE CARICATURE

First, however, we must pause briefly to consider the position we find ourselves in when we try to follow up the implication of the *Clouds* parabasis that characters such as Strepsiades and Pheidippides stood for real individuals in disguise, which we have now found is also the best explanation for the representations of Demos and Sausage-Seller in *Knights*. For it

---

[38] We might add here that if Panofka 1849 was correct to see in Fig. 1, the scene depicted on the Apulian bell-krater formerly Berlin, Staatliche Museen F3047 (lost during World War II), a representation of Cratinus' *Pytine*, then the baldness of the drunken figure on the left would naturally make us think of Aristophanes (*Clouds* 545, *Peace* 771–4) rather than Cratinus, who had enough hair for its style to be satirised (*Ach.* 848–9, with Olson 2002 ad loc.). However, we have no idea whether the painting will have had any connection with the original performance. It may simply reflect Sicilian or South Italian re-performance (Taplin 1993). But it may have been recreated from the reminiscence of an expatriate Athenian ordering some reminder of home from an Apulian potter. If the latter, then it is possible that it reflects the original performance, since the baldness of the leading actor will surely have been memorable. It is also possible, of course, that the character's baldness was mentioned in the text, and was ignored by ancient scholiasts as a clue to his identity since one might have expected an old man to have no hair. See further Harvey and Wilkins 2000, 21.

Figure 1 Mid-fourth century Apulian bell-crater, perhaps illustrating Cratinus' *Pytine*.

does seem from this argument likely enough that this is a much more widespread phenomenon than we have hitherto believed and ought to be taken into consideration as quite possibly a normal 'filter' through which Athenians interpreted Old Comedy. Three crucial questions obtrude. First of all, why did poets obfuscate in this way? Secondly, why have modern scholars ignored or downplayed the possibility that disguised caricature was normal? Thirdly, if it was normal and the text was apparently in most cases constructed not to reveal the identities of the κωμῳδούμενος, how are we to approach the task of tearing away the veils?

The first question might be answered with reference to the battle between a poet and Cleon evidenced by *Acharnians* (377f., 502f.). Whether this refers to a real incident or a fictitious one (as Rosen suggests),[39] one may accept Sommerstein's recent negative reassessment of the evidence for the right of the comic poet to immunity against prosecution for slander[40] and conclude that in certain instances it could be positively dangerous for a comedian to attack a politician. Subterfuge may therefore have been necessary and the fact that most of the characters in Aristophanes do not seem to be obvious caricatures of individuals will point rather to a desire to keep what was *written*, at least, from being used in a law-court

---

[39] Rosen 1988, 62–4. [40] Sommerstein 2004.

as evidence than to an avoidance of political caricature *tout court*. It follows that where a comic poet makes his caricatures obvious, either by naming them (Socrates, Euripides, Lamachus) or in some other way (e.g. Paphlagon/Cleon, Slave/Demosthenes, Labes/Laches), either he felt he had nothing to fear from them or he was doing something more sophisticated. In the latter case, it may well be that parody of his rivals enters into the equation, especially since for *Knights* in particular we have several pieces of evidence to suggest that the play had something to do with Eupolis, and have now concluded that it involved deliberate misappropriation of Eupolidean material for political ends. It would have been a clever ploy, in circumstances where Cleon was known to be especially averse to caricature attack, for Aristophanes to 'borrow' a Eupolis plot and some of his characters (who would not have been so obvious in his text: cf. *Knights* 230f.), and to make them absolutely blatant (as they are in *Knights*), thus not only ridiculing his rival's play, but also exposing him to public danger through association.[41]

The second question can be answered with reference to the standard textually based approach to Old Comedy. If we begin from the text and assume that it is our best guide to what is going on in the plays, then it is quite natural to conclude that except where a character is named or is very obviously disguised (e.g. Paphlagon), caricature of individuals is not in play. Scholars of the nineteenth century such as Süvern and Cobet, however, were much less inclined to dismiss the possibility of disguised caricature than their more recent successors.[42] In particular, Dover has been in the forefront of an assault on what he terms 'allegorical' interpretation.[43] It should be stated clearly, however, that 'allegory' – saying something else – is not usefully equated with disguised on-stage caricature. In allegory, the terms of discourse are deliberately altered so that a complete frame of reference is substituted for the literal meaning. This can happen in comedy, as apparently it does in Cratinus' *Dionysalexandros*, where the Trojan War is substituted for the Samian War.[44] But on-stage disguised caricature merely makes the identity of the satirised individual obscure from the textual standpoint (unless the desire is to satirise a rival: see above). If the poet's reason for doing this was self-protection, he would nonetheless have wished the *audience* to see who he was getting at (cf. *Knights* 230f.). And he could have used all sort of non-textual means of communicating this, including

---

[41] Naturally, this argument brings *Wasps* also firmly into the metacomic category, since Kuon/Cleon and Labes/Laches are blatantly identifiable. See below and chapter five, pp. 188–91.
[42] E.g. Süvern 1826, Cobet 1840.
[43] See Dover 2004 for a recent review of the issue on traditional lines.   [44] See Storey 2006.

the mask, the actor's gait and posture, costume, props, gesture, and vocal caricature.[45]

I will deal here, *exempli gratia*, with only the most often discussed of these aspects, the so-called 'portrait-mask'. Scholars have tended to accept Dover's sceptical view of the practicality of such masking more than the good evidence for its practice.[46] Yet it is a fair inference, as Dover (2004, 268) admits, from *Knights* 230f., that εἰκάζειν ('making a recognisable image') was a customary aspect of comedy. His challenge to its widespread use for purposes of identifying individuals portrayed on stage is based on two criteria: (a) the severely limited number of physical and cultural differences available to caricaturists in Athens (as opposed to twentieth-century Britain), and (b) the problems faced by modern cartoonists in drawing readily identifiable caricatures of ordinary-looking individuals. To the possible objection that the analogy is flawed because the cartoonist works in two dimensions, whereas the audience-member would use other clues (movements, gestures and voice) to recognise any given individual, he responds with a number of points, which include the limited acquaintance of 'the average Attic farmer' with even major politicians and refutation of the notion that Athens was like a village and everyone knew everyone else. Practical difficulties in his view also supervene in mimicry, since 'recognition by movement and voice is possible only in so far as the behaviour and speech of the person recognised fall within that person's normal range' and because lack of electronic amplification would have limited the range of vocal mimicry, which is difficult enough anyway. Thus, because real people are often put in unreal situations in comedy, 'the actor has to imagine how Nikias would move if he were a slave and how he would howl if he were beaten.'(271) The need for eye and mouth holes is another limiting factor, conflicting with the importance to recognition of 'the most important of all means of facial expression, the set and interrelation of the eyes and mouth – facial expression, in fact.'(272)

But, if the customary use of the 'portrait-mask' (which I would in any case prefer to call 'caricature-mask') is a 'fair inference' from *Knights* 230f.,

---

[45] All these means of conveying a character's identity as a real individual were at play in the Irish satirical musical *I Keano*, which dealt with the famous incident at the Soccer World Cup in 2002 when the Irish Manager Mick McCarthy sent home the captain Roy Keane. At one point Keano, apparently alone on stage, is approached by a female nymph, who offers him help and consolation. Long before the nymph gives her name ('Dunpheia'), the audience was seized by gleeful and long-lasting laughter: the voice of the 'nymph' was recognisably that of Eamon Dunphy, a soccer commentator well known for his strong support of Keane's side of the story and the female costume and wide-eyed hero worship were an effective mode of personal ridicule.

[46] Exceptions are, significantly, historians of performance such as Dearden 1976, Stone 1981, and Revermann 1997, 2006.

then none of these arguments can possibly be persuasive. The Athenian comic dramatists, their σκευοποιοί and their actors will have to have made it work somehow, despite the limitations. We should not suppose that, when individual soldiers in uniform in the Spartan army were recognisable to their officers (Xen. *Lac.* 11.6), Athenians would have thought they all looked too similar to be distinguished by physical criteria (even if the Old Oligarch was able to claim that in terms of dress it was impossible to tell the *status* of someone in the streets: [Xen.] *Ath. Pol.* 1.10). Moreover, there are certainly places in Aristophanes where a real individual must be recognised long before he is named (e.g. Cleisthenes who enters at *Thesmophoriazusai* 574, but is not named until 635), which shows that such recognition was possible. And the art of caricature did exist, as we know from the example of Pauson, whose portraits made people look worse than they actually were (Arist. *Poetics* 1448a6, cf. *Ach.* 854; Eup. fr. 99.5 *Demoi*). It must also be true that, while evidence shows that not all Athenians knew each other, there was a presumption that individuals *named* in comedy must be familiar in some respects to the audience at large, otherwise there is simply too much 'white noise' for the actual state of our surviving comedies to be explicable at all. Besides all of this, recent work on the theatre of Dionysus shows that in the fifth century it was much smaller than we have tended to think. Its back rows were no further back than the obtruding wall of the Odeon and the seating is now estimated at more like 5,000 than 15,000. Visual and vocal imitation could have been managed much more easily in such a space than in that envisaged by Pickard-Cambridge.[47]

The third question is this: deprived of the visual and aural clues available to the original audience, and shut out by deliberate textual obfuscation from direct identifications, how are we to proceed? One might expect to find some help from those few scholars who have suggested identifications of characters with real individuals (e.g. Katz 1976), or even made 'political allegory' the cornerstone of their interpretation (Vickers 1997). But studies which offer only one or two identifications do not attempt to formulate any general principles or methods and necessarily therefore do not offer any broader view of the role of on-stage caricature in the corpus. Vickers does begin his book with a defence of the tradition of what he still calls 'allegorical' interpretation and pays some attention to the evidence for ambiguity in Greek literature. But he covers only six Aristophanic plays (*Acharnians* to *Birds*), plus the *Dionysalexandros* of Cratinus, and the method he develops for penetrating disguised on-stage caricatures is hit and miss. For example,

---

[47] Pickard-Cambridge 1956. Recent work on the Theatre of Dionysus in Whitley 2001, 336–40.

in his eagerness to see Pericles almost everywhere, he ignores the apparent fact that the representation of the deceased on stage is always established in our surviving material within the framework of either a descent to Hades (as in *Frogs*) or a raising of the dead (as perhaps in Eupolis' *Demes*).[48]

The best place to begin is from an inference we can draw once we see how Aristophanes, at *Clouds* 549f., describes the focus of plays (both his and his rivals') as attacks on individuals (cf. Arist. *Poetics* 1451b with Appendix 1). If the satirised individual is the focus of satirical comedy, it follows that the *plot*'s function is to carry satire of the individuals who are caricatured on stage. The methodological inference we should in turn draw from this is that the themes and dynamics of these plots are our best guide to the individuals we are searching for.

To give a negative example, *Birds* focuses on a movement by its main characters away from the *polypragmosyne* ('busybodiness') of Athens towards a *topon apragmona* ('unbusybody place': 44). Since Thucydides (6.18.6) has Alcibiades tag Nicias with the label *apragmosyne* ('unbusibodiness'), it follows that whatever *Birds* is doing, it is *not* attacking those involved in the Sicilian expedition.[49] Once a preliminary analysis of the plot has been made from this perspective, the parameters of the search can usually be restricted (at least for the central characters). It is then that cross-references within the corpus and indications of identity (e.g. of comic poets: *Ach.* 499f., *Wasps* 650–1, Cratin. *Pytine* Tii *PCG*) can be brought to bear. All of the above, however, are required to fit within a larger structure which is self-consistent: this may be comedy, but the poets attacked each other nonetheless for the level and targets of their plays (e.g. Cratin. fr. 213, *Clouds* 551f., Eup. fr. 89) and it is therefore reasonable to assume that they attempted not to be caught out in inconsistencies.

PYTINE AND WASPS

Recently Biles has noted very strong thematic links between *Pytine* and *Wasps*, produced at Lenaea 422.[50] Both plays deal, it seems, with an attempted change of behaviour (cf. *Pytine* fr. 199, *Wasps* 1459–61). Both involve the law-courts (cf. *Pytine* Tii = Σ *Knights* 400a, *Wasps* 891f. and *passim*), though whether the case brought by Comedy actually came to court is not known. Drinking to excess and its consequences are important in both (cf. *Pytine* Tii and fr.199, *Wasps* 1252f., 1299f.). The parabases of

---

[48] See Sidwell 1997.   [49] Contrast e.g. Vickers 1997, 160f.
[50] Biles 2002. Cf. Sidwell 1995.

both contain criticism of rival comic poets (*Pytine* fr. 213, *Wasps* 1025f. with scholia). If in addition to these thematic similarities we now investigate *Wasps* as caricature drama, we will be able to gain a much clearer idea of why Aristophanes appears to pick up Cratinus' themes and run with them.

When we ask, as we did above for *Birds*, what the plot implies about the real individuals it is constructed to satirise, it becomes clear that politicians are not central. For the plot centres on individuals who are in the camp of, or opposed to, a specific politician, Cleon. This brings up a family resemblance to *Knights*, where the caricature hypothesis reveals for the first time – if we accept that Demos most likely caricatures a comic poet – that the notion of politicians competing for the favour of comic poets (as opposed to being prosecuted by them, *Ach.* 378f., *Wasps* 1284f.) was in the Athenian imaginary. If the thematic closeness between *Wasps* and *Pytine* now makes it appear to belong in a series of satire and counter-satire (*Knights*, responded to by *Pytine*, responded to by *Wasps*), it looks possible that the satirical point made in *Knights* – that politicians need comic poets because of their status with the *demos*, and that some comic poets are corrupt enough to use this power (the implication of *Knights* 1111–50 if Demos represents a comic poet) – is now viewed from the other side, that comic poets also do actually support politicians. As it happens, there is evidence that at least one of the characters of *Wasps* was meant to represent a comic poet.

Scholars have often noted the close association of Bdelycleon with comic poetry (650–1): χαλεπὸν μὲν καὶ δεινῆς γνώμης καὶ μείζονος ἢ 'πὶ τρυγῳδοῖς | ἰάσασθαι νόσον ἀρχαίαν ('It is difficult, and requires daunting intelligence, greater than that found among comic poets, to cure an old disease . . .'). Some have gone so far as to suggest that this virtually identifies Aristophanes with Bdelycleon.[51] On the caricature hypothesis, then, there is a strong sign that Bdelycleon might represent a comic poet. But just as in *Pytine* it makes more sense to see the main character as the focus of invective attack, so it does in *Wasps*. Bdelycleon is wedded to luxurious excess in clothes, food and drink (*Wasps* 1003f., 1122f. *passim*) and is into group sex at symposia (*Wasps* 1345–6). These vices ought to make him a negative figure.[52] He also, apparently, fails to achieve his reform objective, since at 1482 Philocleon emerges once more from the house into which Bdelycleon has carried him at 1444f. to conduct his drunken dance contest with the sons of Carcinus. This would be a strange way for Aristophanes

---

[51] Biles 2002, 198f., Storey 2003, 87, 346, 371.   [52] Davidson, 1997, Dover, 1974, 206.

Metacomedy and caricature

to represent himself, but would make perfect sense if he were attacking a rival.

If we are looking for a comic poet behind Bdelycleon's character, the chorus' formulation of a message to Cleon at 410f. might help us with identification, even though it was intended to interact with the original audience's *prior* recognition of the real target:

> καὶ κελεύετ' αὐτὸν ἥκειν
> ὡς ἐπ' ἄνδρα μισόπολιν
> ὄντα κἀπολούμενον, ὅτι
> τόνδε λόγον εἰσφέρει
> μὴ δικάζειν δίκας.

And tell him to come here, as to a man who hates the *polis* (lit: 'is *misopolis*') and who will die, because he's bringing in this idea of not judging lawsuits!

Two aspects of this passage might point towards Aristophanes' rival – and supposed co-author of *Knights* – Eupolis. First the formulation ὡς ἐπ' ἄνδρα μισόπολιν ὄντα could react very amusingly with the name of Eupolis, if the audience had already recognised the satire's intended target. Secondly, because the play involves on my argument politically motivated parody of Eupolis, it may be significant for the identification just proposed that after the rejuvenation of Demos, the law-courts are closed (1317) (whether temporarily or not is not clear), and Demos is seen as οὐ χοιρινῶν ὄζων 'not smelling of mussel-shells', that is, not interested in judging lawsuits.

We might add to this argument the support of fr. 392.7 of Eupolis, from a play not named in the source that quotes it (Stobaeus 3.4.32), where the chorus, after accusing the audience of a prejudice towards foreign poets, concludes:

ἀλλ' ἐμοὶ πείθεσθε, πάντως μεταβαλόντες τοὺς τρόπους

But obey me, changing your ways completely

The 'change of behaviour' theme is central to *Wasps,* as noted above, and words very similar to Eupolis' appear in the chorus' reflection at 1459–61 on the question of whether or not Philocleon really has changed:

> καίτοι πολλοὶ ταῦτ' ἔπαθον·
> ξυνόντες γνώμαις ἑτέρων
> μετεβάλοντο τοὺς τρόπους.

Still, many people have had this experience, and by contact with others' views have changed their ways.

Again, the basis for an intertextual joke here rests on prior identification by the audience of Eupolis behind Bdelycleon. But if this phrase predated *Wasps* (which cannot be certain), then the resonance established between the character identification and the origin of the catchphrase would certainly have caused a laugh.[53] The recurrence of this phrase in the parabasis of *Frogs* (734) will hark back to the Eupolidean intertext and will make a substantial difference to our interpretation of the seriousness of that passage.

If *Wasps* was in some way a response to Cratinus' criticism of Aristophanes in *Pytine*, and Bdelycleon represents a comic poet (say Eupolis), it is very likely that precisely the same is true of Philocleon. In other words, the comedy targets two rivals whom Aristophanes has already had a run-in with and does so by imagining that they are father and son, that the father is addicted to judging lawsuits, while his son is a snob who is intimately involved in the symposium circuit and eager to change his father's ways to match his own (a theme associated with Eupolis through his fr. 392.7). It is difficult to avoid the conjecture that Philocleon represents the older rival Cratinus, whose criticisms in *Pytine* and victory over *Clouds* at the previous festival have rankled with his younger rival, especially if it had been Aristophanes who had been caricatured as the drunken, old, and no-longer comic poet in that play.

There is, once more, other evidence to suggest that Cratinus would be a suitable target, besides the parabatic attack on Aristophanes in Cratinus, *Pytine* fr. 213, but for reasons already articulated it is necessarily only circumstantial.

First, it would be appropriate to attach to him the disease of jury-addiction. He had produced a play *Nomoi*, which Meineke and Kaibel saw announced as a chorus of decrepit old men in fr. 133: ἢ πρεσβῦται πάνυ γηραλέοι σκήπτροισιν ἄκασκα προβῶντες ('Yes, really old seniors approaching gently with sticks'). The play's theme will have been grafted directly onto its author to make fun of him.

Secondly, the chorus' inference that Bdelycleon's actions are a response to something Philocleon said (343–4): ὅτι λέγεις τι | περὶ τῶν νεῶν ἄληθες; 'Because you say something true about the ships?') seems to respond to something outside the bounds of the play. It could be a reference to the parabasis of *Pytine*, where fr. 210 probably came from: οὐ δύνανται

---

[53] See below chapter four, p. 116 for a positive ascription to *Autolycus I* and chapter six, p. 220 for the dating of that play before *Wasps*, at Lenaea 423.

πάντα ποιοῦσαι νεωσοίκων λαχεῖν | οὐδὲ κάννης 'Whatever they do, (the triremes) can't get ship-sheds or reed-matting.'

Thirdly, the appropriateness of using a dance at the finale of *Wasps* to satirise Cratinus is made clear by the following passage of Athenaeus 1.22a:

φασὶ δὲ καὶ ὅτι οἱ ἀρχαῖοι ποιηταί, Θέσπις, Πρατίνας, Κρατῖνος, Φρύνιχος ὀρχησταὶ ἐκαλοῦντο διὰ τὸ μὴ μόνον τὰ ἑαυτῶν δράματα ἀναφέρειν εἰς ὄρχησιν τοῦ χοροῦ, ἀλλὰ καὶ ἔξω τῶν ἰδίων ποιημάτων διδάσκειν τοὺς βουλομένους ὀρχεῖσθαι

They also say that the ancient poets, Thespis, Pratinas, Cratinus and Phrynichus, were called dancers because they not only made the dancing of the chorus an essential component of their plays, but also quite apart from their own works they taught dancing to anyone who wanted to learn.[54]

If Cratinus is the individual represented as Philocleon, it looks as though *Wasps* constitutes a direct reply to *Pytine* and its criticisms of Aristophanes and his use of Eupolidean material – but also an attack upon Eupolis and his relationship with Cratinus. If *Pytine* itself had in turn been constructed as a response to *Knights*, which had contained obvious use of Eupolis and had caricatured a comic poet as Demos, it is difficult to see how anyone other than Cratinus could underlie that figure either. We must now turn to correspondences between *Knights* and *Wasps*, especially on those between the figures of Demos and Philocleon, to see whether they are significant enough to substantiate the conjecture.

DEMOS AND PHILOCLEON

There are several major and many minor correlations between the two figures. The major ones are:

(1) Both are foolish old men, easily gulled by politicians (e.g. *Knights* 754–5, 1336f.; *Wasps* 515f., 695, 720f.).
(2) Both have a very close connection with Cleon (*Knights* 2f., 730f.; *Wasps* 133).
(3) Both are keen and harsh jurors (*Knights* 808, 1332; *Wasps* 88f. and then to 1008 *passim*); cf. *Knights* 1317 and *Wasps* 412–14 for the theme of closing the law-courts; cf. *Knights* 1332 and *Wasps* 333, 349 for the unusual word χοιρίνη 'mussel-shell' used for a voting-pebble).
(4) Both show concern for the navy (*Knights* 1065, cf. 1366–7; *Wasps* 343–4).

---

[54] See also Sidwell 1995 73–7 for possible references to Cratinus' *Odysses* in the escape-scene and other jokes which may work on the basis of audience recognition of him as the target.

If the arguments offered above are correct, these are likely to be material for satire of individuals, so that numbers (2), (3) and (4) are not explained in the case of Demos by his status as an allegorical figure. The minor correlations (though no less significant) are:

(1) The rejuvenation theme is applied to both (*Knights* 908, 1321f.; *Wasps* 1333, 1352–5).
(2) Comic business is made in the case of each figure with an εἰρεσιώνη 'harvest-wreath' (*Knights* 729; *Wasps* 398–9).
(3) Oracles about fantastic developments in jury-service appear in both plays (*Knights* 797f., 1089; *Wasps* 798–804).
(4) The theme of caring for the old is found in respect of both figures (*Knights* 799, 1261; *Wasps* 1003f.). The language used in each case is very similar.
(5) In the case of both characters, re-clothing is made into comic business (*Knights* 881f. a tunic; *Wasps* 1122f. a Persian cloak). Note especially the close correspondence between *Knights* 893 and *Wasps* 1134 (the new clothes are said to be given with the intention of suffocating their wearer: in both cases the word ἀποπνίγω is used).
(6) Lentil-soup (φακῆ) is mentioned to both figures by their would-be helpers (*Knights* 1006; *Wasps* 811, cf. 814, 984).
(7) There is a family similarity between the preparation scenes in each play (*Knights* 997f. the oracle contest; *Wasps* 798f. the trial).
(8) The characters are addicted to (weak) puns (e.g. *Knights* 899; *Wasps* 1148).
(9) There is a family resemblance between the exchange of Paphlagon and Demos (*Knights* 1110f.) and that between Bdelycleon and Philocleon (*Wasps* 715f.) over barley distribution.
(10) There is close thematic and linguistic correspondence between *Knights* 1334 and *Wasps* 711 (both have ἄξια... τοῦ 'ν Μαραθῶνι τροπαίου 'worthy of the trophy at Marathon'), lines spoken in each case to the old-man character.

In all these cases, a single explanation will cover the similarities: there is a point of reference which the passages share and that point of reference was originally related in some way to the individual who is represented by both characters.

There is, then, a clear basis on which to suspect that the same individual is being attacked as Demos in *Knights* and as Philocleon in *Wasps*. If it is Cratinus, then the points of reference which connect the thematically and linguistically similar passages in the two plays are quite likely to be scenes in comedy, either that of Cratinus, or, if Aristophanes' use of Eupolidean material includes satire of Cratinus, of Eupolis. For if Aristophanes did caricature Cratinus as Demos in *Knights*, Cratinus would certainly have had something to complain about in *Pytine*, but we would still have to explain why Eupolis comes into it. And it does seem as though in criticising Aristophanes' attack in *Knights*, Cratinus is actually just as annoyed with Eupolis, because it was somehow perceivedly Eupolidean to do what was done in *Knights*. Thus, if it correct to conjecture that Demos appeared in Eupolis' *X (Noumeniai?)*, then he will also have represented Cratinus. This still does not make it seem as likely that Eupolis is the target of *Pytine* as Aristophanes, because it is easier to explain a continuation of the attack on Cratinus as the Cleon-lover in *Wasps* if Aristophanes himself had been the main focus of attack in *Pytine*. In *Wasps*, as I have now reinterpreted it, Aristophanes subverts the plot and attack point of *Pytine* by substituting for himself the author of the play, and law-court obsession for drunkenness, and perhaps recycling a Cratinean Eupolis from that play (one of the 'friends' trying to save the career of the drunken poet?), who now attempts to turn the poet he obviously admires (because he imitates him so much...), satirically represented as his father, from his law-court obsession to his own – drinking and whoring.

EARLIER CARICATURES OF COMIC POETS?

If that is so, then it is worth searching for earlier manifestations of the caricaturing of comic poets on stage, since it seems unlikely that the caricature series I have now reconstructed will have sprung from nowhere. And this series may help explain why the rival attacked in *Pytine* (Aristophanes?) though actually young, could intelligibly and humorously be satirised as *old*.

We find a less hypothetical, though highly controversial, example of a comic poet on stage in the egregious case of the self-representation of the poet as character in *Acharnians* 377f. and 496f. The two passages are different from one another. In the first, the character brings as an example illustrating his fears the experience related to 'last year's comedy' of being dragged into the *bouleuterion* by Cleon and almost perishing as a result of the attack. In the second, he addresses the chorus and audience (ἄνδρες οἱ θεώμενοι 496) dressed as Euripides' Telephus and actually proclaims that he is 'producing a comedy' (τρυγῳδίαν ποιῶν 499), and humorously argues that Cleon will not be able to attack him in this instance for slandering the city in front of foreigners, since it is the Lenaea, and not the Dionysia, and there are none present (except metics). The traditional interpretation of these lines, recently defended once more by Sommerstein,[55] is that the audience is to understand these words as applying not to the character, but to the author or producer of the play (thus, Aristophanes or Callistratus), and that these temporary metatheatrical intrusions into the play's fabric have no implications at all for the identification of the character 'Dicaeopolis'. However, the examples from Menander's practice which Sommerstein gives to support the idea that the author can introduce his own voice into the mouth of a character without being misunderstood are all from the *end* of plays, where the prayer for victory itself already moves the dialogue onto a metatheatrical level. In any case, the formulaic nature of this type of ending is in no way parallel to the apparent sudden intrusion of the authorial voice and then the just as sudden refocusing (but when precisely?) upon the character *per se* which scholars see in the *Acharnians* passages. It seems to me, then, that we would be looking at something quite without parallel on this interpretation and that we are obliged instead first of all to see what are the consequences of trying to understand the passages as comments of the play's central character, conceived (within the limits of Aristophanic comedy) as a consistent voice within the play.

The obvious inference from the first passage is that the audience must recognise the character as an individual whose experiences outside the play are so well known to them that they can be alluded to not only without causing problems, but presumably in such a way that they actually add to the humour. In the second passage, the character's claim to be 'composing a comedy' (and the quasi parabatic form of this speech, addressed as it is to 'the audience', cf. e.g. *Clouds* 518) has to mean that he is a poet. If the argument so far is sound, then this rules out the actual poet, since he is unlikely to have subjected himself to critical representation of the sort involved in the final scenes or in the places where he criticises democracy and seeks to speak on behalf of the Spartans.

Who is the comic poet behind the 'old man'? We must, as in the other plays, be guided by the theme of the plot, which will have been chosen with the express purpose of satirising the individual under attack. No one will deny that the focus of *Acharnians* is the acquisition of peace in the Archidamian War. The comic poet behind the 'old man', then, must have produced a play which could be interpreted as having advocated peace. The obvious candidate, then, is Cratinus.[56] Whenever we place

---

[55] Sommerstein, 2004, 209–10.

[56] His career dates from the mid-450s. See *PCG* IV T2a, where his first victory is put after 437/6. Meineke emended the date to 453/2, because the Dionysian victor lists show Cratinus' name between Ecphantides and Diopeithes. If the later date has any validity, it may be his first victory at the Lenaea, where his name occurs between Aristomenes and Pherecrates (*IG* II^2 2325, most accessible in *DFA*^{2}, 112–13).

his *Dionysalexandros*, soon after the beginning of the Archidamian War, possibly in 430, or (more likely given the Trojan War allegory) after the Samian War, he is the one 'older' poet for whom we have unequivocal evidence of criticism of Pericles for involving Athens in conflict.[57] The hypothesis (*PCG* IV, 140, lines 44–8) tells us: κωμῳδεῖται δ' ἐν τῷ δράματι Περικλῆς μάλα πιθανῶς δι' ἐμφάσεως ὡς ἐπαγηγοχὼς τοῖς Ἀθηναίοις τὸν πόλεμον ('In the play, Pericles is very well satirised, though covertly, for having brought the war upon the Athenians'). An attack on Pericles of an exactly similar kind is made by 'Dicaeopolis' at 530f., where it is he, Περικλέης οὐλύμπιος ('Pericles the Olympian'), whose reactions to the whore-stealing incidents actually cause the war. It is significant that it was Cratinus who had elsewhere identified Pericles with Zeus (*Nemesis* fr. 118; *Thraittai* fr. 73; *Cheirones* fr. 258).

Once this identification has been made, strong similarities and even verbal correspondences with the figure of Demos in *Knights* will tend to support the identification already made between Demos and Cratinus:

(1) Both are old men (*Ach.* 387, 1130, cf. 1228; *Knights* 42).
(2) Both are portrayed as 'gaping' (κέχην-) while attending the assembly on the Pnyx (*Ach.* 30; *Knights* 755).
(3) Both are said to be living in bad conditions during the war (*Ach.* 71–2; *Knights* 792–6).
(4) Both are essentially rustics (*Ach.* 32f.; *Knights* 805f., cf. 40), even though in the case of Demos this contradicts his demotic (Πυκνίτης 42), and both would therefore benefit from peace by return to their country demes (*Ach.* 32f.; *Knights* 805f.).
(5) Both use strikingly similar language in relation to the way courts force recompense from thieving politicians (*Ach.* 5–8; *Knights* 1145–50). Note especially the use of ἐξεμέω in both.

The characterisation varies in each play because the line of attack is different. But the family resemblance between these details suggests that they were designed to be read against a common reference point within the audience's knowledge of Cratinus and his comedies.

We can now go a little further back from *Acharnians*. What the character (not yet named as Dicaeopolis) says at 377f. will not after all now refer to Aristophanes' problems with Cleon after *Babylonians*, because the comic poet character does not represent him, but his rival Cratinus, and the audience will recognise from their background knowledge that this constitutes a reference to something they will know from outside the play about the central 'old man' character. Sommerstein has recently asserted

---

[57] For the date, see *PCG* IV, p. 141, Geissler 1925, 24–5. Storey 2006, 124.

that 'The speaker of these lines, Dikaiopolis of Cholleidai (though this piece of metatheatre is not brought to the fore until 406), cannot conceivably be imagined as having anything to do with the production of a comedy in 426 except as a spectator, let alone as having been attacked by Kleon because of it.'[58] This is not true, if the character is recognised by the audience as a rival comic poet. In that case, they will have known instantly what was being referred to, unless we conceive the passage to be providing new information, rather than making a joke. We, however, are completely in the dark and have to rely on the text for guidance, a fallible approach in the case of comedy, especially knowing now that such extra-textual references as it contains are deliberately enigmatic and may have their basis in other comedies now irretrievably lost to us.

Lines 377–8 read:

αὐτός τ' ἐμαυτὸν ὑπὸ Κλέωνος ἅπαθον
ἐπίσταμαι διὰ τὴν πέρυσι κωμῳδίαν.

Myself I know what I personally suffered at Cleon's hands because of last year's comedy.

Two distinct interpretations of 377–8 have been offered. The traditional explanation attaches διὰ τὴν πέρυσι κωμῳδίαν ('because of last year's comedy') to ἅπαθον ('what I suffered'). This has the effect of making the charge in the *boule* an event (not necessarily a *real* event) which was the *result* of a comic production by the comic poet character in the previous year. Most commentators take it as alluding to a real indictment by Cleon against Aristophanes. Within the hypothesis under investigation, however, it would have to refer to one based on a production by Cratinus at the Lenaea or Dionysia of 426 and subsequently enough of a *cause célèbre* to be able to be referred to by his caricature here.

It is also possible, however (as Riu has argued)[59] that διὰ τὴν πέρυσι κωμῳδίαν ('because of last year's comedy') relates syntactically rather to ἐπίσταμαι ('I know'). What is referred to here, then, would be a scene in last year's play in which Cratinus saw himself represented at loggerheads with Cleon ('I know because of last year's comedy' not 'what I suffered because of last year's comedy'). Even understanding the syntax in the traditional way, however, the passage could refer to a scene in a Dionysia comedy by a rival responding to a Cratinus Lenaea comedy. The jokes on this interpretation have the advantage of referring to 'events' completely in the domain of the public to whom *Acharnians* is addressed – the comic theatre audience.

---

[58] Sommerstein 2004, 209.   [59] Riu 1992, 1999, 5, 27–8, 32–3.

Metacomedy and caricature

In that case, it is worth considering Riu's further hypothesis that the scene referred to could have been in Aristophanes' *Babylonians*. The scholion on 378 tells us: τοὺς Βαβυλωνίους λέγει. τούτους γὰρ πρὸ τῶν Ἀχαρνέων Ἀριστοφάνης ἐδίδαξεν ('He means *Babylonians* because this was the play Aristophanes produced before *Acharnians*'). It is generally accepted that the information given here was based on consultation of the *didaskaliai*. That makes *Babylonians* a play of 426. As Riu points out, fr. 75 implies that the central character, Dionysus, had been involved in some kind of trial:

κἂν τοῖς Βαβυλωνίοις... ἀκούσομεθα ποτήριον τὸ ὀξύβαφον, ὅταν ὁ Διόνυσος λέγῃ περὶ τῶν Ἀθήνησι δημαγωγῶν ὡς αὐτὸν ᾔτουν ἐπὶ τὴν δίκην ἀπελθόντα ὀξυβάφω δύο

Also in the Babylonians... we will hear of the *oxybaphon* as a cup, when Dionysus says about the Athenian demagogues that they asked him when he came to answer the charges against him to bring two *oxybapha*.

It is, unfortunately, not absolutely clear from this that a trial scene occurred, since Dionysus is reported as narrating the incident. Nonetheless, Cratinus is identified with Dionysus at *Frogs* 357: Κρατίνου τοῦ ταυροφάγου ('bull-devouring Cratinus'). So it is possible that Cratinus was represented on stage as Dionysus in *Babylonians* and that 377f. is a humorous cross-reference to a *boule* trial in that play.

On the surface, then, the obvious identification of the central figure of *Acharnians* is with the comic poet Cratinus. However, things are not quite so straightforward, for two reasons. First, Cratinus is mentioned twice, at 850 and 1173. The later instance occurs in the punch line of a choral attack upon the choregos Antimachus (1150–73), and is not problematic, since in *Knights* too Cleon is mentioned by name at 976, even though his caricature has been on stage in disguise for hundreds of lines. The first passage, however, is addressed by the chorus directly to the central character, indicating various individuals who will not run into him in his market:

οὐδ ἐντυχὼν ἐν τἀγορᾷ
  πρόσεισί σοι βαδίζων
Κρατῖνος ἀεὶ κεκαρμένος
  μοιχὸν μιᾷ μαχαίρᾳ,
ὁ περιπόνηρος Ἀρτέμων,
  ταχὺς ἄγαν τὴν μουσικήν,
ὄζων κακὸν τῶν μασχαλῶν
  πατρὸς Τραγασαίου.

Nor will Cratinus on his walk approach and bump into you, the man always coiffeured with a single blade in the adulterer's fashion, 'Artemon the super-wicked', too fast in his music, his armpits giving off an appalling smell of his Tragasaian father.

Secondly, the name given by the character as he approaches Euripides' house at 406 is Δικαιόπολις ('Dicaeopolis'), and this is used throughout the rest of the play whenever the central character is directly addressed or alluded to (748–9, 823, 959, 1048, 1085). Not only does this not immediately appear to evoke Cratinus (though we might be missing vital information, of course), but, as Ewen Bowie pointed out in 1988, it might rather might remind theatregoers of the younger poet Eupolis (cf. the suggested joke in *Wasps* with *misopolis*).[60] As to the demotic given, Χολλῄδης 'from Cholleidai', the first thing to note is that we do not know Eupolis' deme affiliation. The second is that there may be some kind of a joke involved (cf. chapter six on *Birds* 645), since there is a contradiction between 32–3 and 266–7 (which make it clear Dicaeopolis is from the country) and the fact that Cholleidai is a city deme.[61] Aristophanes' deme was, we know, Kydathenaion.

There is only one way in which these counter-indications might be made to yield dramatic and satirical sense. We know from *Pytine* fr. 213 that whatever Aristophanes was doing in *Knights* to annoy Cratinus was apparently seen by him as simply repeating something originating from Eupolis. I have suggested that what may really have bothered Cratinus about *Knights* was his representation on stage as Demos and that it was this (among other things perhaps) that Aristophanes was being accused of having plagiarised from Eupolis (possibly from the lost *Noumeniai*). There would in those circumstances, then, be a quite specific satirical point in presenting a Cratinus on stage in *Acharnians* who was being *acted* by Eupolis (see further below chapter four, pp. 133f.). For such a move would reformulate Eupolis' attack on Cratinus as *support* and serve to implicate him in unacceptable criticism of the *demos*. It will be the voice of Cratinus, then, which we hear at 377f. recalling his battle with Cleon, and claiming to be involved in writing/producing a comedy at 499f.[62] But it will be

---

[60] Bowie, 1988. See *contra* Parker 1991, Kyriakidi 2007, 130–6 (suggesting the name Dicaeopolis may refer to one of the cities of this name). In support Sidwell 1994.

[61] See Olson 2002, 180 with bibliography. He also cites the scholium in REΓ, which suggests a pun on χωλός 'lame', but in advance of mention of Euripides' penchant for crippled characters.

[62] It is just possible that Diodorus 12.40.6 (= Ephorus 70 F 196 *FrGrH*), where *Acharnians* 530–1 is ascribed to *Eupolis*, reflects a genuine tradition about the 'voice' behind this quasi-parabasis. See Telò 2007, 144 for defence of the paradosis in Diodorus (Cicero had Atticus change the text of *Orator* 29 to reflect the Aristophanic authorship, *Att.* 12.6.3, but he had clearly read 'Eupolis' in his copy of Ephorus).

the voice of the *actor* behind the Cratinus mask, Eupolis, whom we hear giving his name to Euripides (for reasons which I will deal with below) in order to secure his help in putting his case to the *chorus* at 405f. (cf. 443) as the Cratinus character (441, which will, because of the superimposition of Cratinus upon Eupolis, have an extra layer of humour).

For the audience, I suggest, this type of disguise would have been easy to penetrate. First, the overlaying of one character upon another appears to be a central ploy of Old Comedy. In *Acharnians*, the Telephus disguise adopted by Dicaeopolis is an obvious example (cf. 440–4 for the principles involved). But Dionysus as Heracles in *Frogs* and in the same play Xanthias as Dionysus playing Heracles (Ἡρακλειοξανθίαν 500) show how far the ploy can be taken. Secondly, and inaccessibly to us, the way in which the character was presented and costumed, his gait, mask and voice, will immediately, upon his appearance, have told an audience which had seen Eupolis' Cratinus what was going on. It is possible that even the actor's build might have been a crucial factor (if the producer had any control over which parts he assigned). For if *Wasps* really does satirise Cratinus and Eupolis, the former will have been tiny (cf. 105, 107, 129, 140, 206, 207–9, 363, 366, where he is likened to various small creatures and 126–7, 140–1, 142–3, 205, where he is imagined as trying to slip out through impossibly small holes), while the latter will have been big (fat) or tall (68 ὁ μέγας). Thus the textual indicators of Eupolidean (and Cratinean) parody, which begin in line 3 with ψαμμακοσιογάργαρα ('teeming with sand-hundreds': cf. Eupolis fr. 308 *Chrysoun Genos* ψαμμακοσίους 'sand-hundreds', but also note Cratinus' use of γαργαίρω 'teem', fr. 321 ἀνδρῶν ἀρίστων πᾶσα γαργαίρει πόλις 'the whole city teems with really noble men'), will already have had a clear basis for the original audience – one to which we have lost the code because we are not contemporary *viewers* of the play with access to essential points of reference from earlier comedy. The direct address of Dicaeopolis in the choral interlude at 836–9 will thus most likely gain its humorous frisson through interaction with the audience's knowledge of a scene from Eupolis in which Cratinus was put on stage in a market scene and bothered by the *other* individuals mentioned here.

Now if this complex scenario, in which Eupolis is represented on stage playing his rival Cratinus as he produces a play in defence of making peace with Sparta, is indeed what was happening, then it behoves us to search further for evidence that caricature abuse of his older rival Cratinus was characteristically Eupolidean. There is, of course, no *direct* evidence. But we might suspect from Cratinus' criticism of Aristophanes (*Pytine* fr. 213) that Eupolis had attacked Cratinus before the *Knights*.

And, as we have seen, there was a stylistic relationship which was something visible to later readers. Anon. *De comoedia*[63] tells us: Εὔπολις Ἀθηναῖος... γεγονὼς δυνατὸς τῇ λέξει καὶ ζηλῶν Κρατῖνον ('Eupolis the Athenian had a powerful style and imitated Cratinus'). As we can now see, no doubt this was because he was parodying the older rival's style.[64] If so, Aristophanes ignores Eupolis' satiric intent and to all intents and purposes treats Eupolis almost as though he were a collaborator of Cratinus.

A suggestive piece of information is offered to us by late encyclopaedic and paroemiographic sources. *PCG* T15, reported from Zenobius, Hesychius, Photius, the Suda and Apostolius, tells us:

Ἐπειοῦ δειλότερος· οὕτως ἐλέγετο Κρατῖνος ὁ κωμικός, ἴσως διὰ τὸ ταξιαρχῆσαι τῆς Οἰνῇδος φυλῆς καὶ δειλότερος φανῆναι. καὶ γὰρ ὁ Ἐπειὸς δειλὸς ἦν

More cowardly than Epeios. This is what was said of the comic poet Cratinus, perhaps because he had been taxiarch of the Oeneis tribe and had been revealed as cowardly. For Epeios was also a coward.

Another version says: Ἐπειοῦ δειλότερος· οὐ τὸν ἀρχαῖον λέγει, ἀλλὰ Κρατῖνον τὸν κωμικόν ('More cowardly than Epeios. He does not mean the ancient individual, but Cratinus the comic poet'). Kaibel rightly saw the suspiciousness of Cratinus as taxiarch of a tribe whose name had something to do with *wine* (though it may relate, as I have suggested, not to his bibulousness, but to a connection with wine – perhaps an identification with the interests of grape-farmers: cf. *Ach.* 512) and thought that its source was very likely a comedy. Kock printed this as fr. adespot. 31. (= *PCG* VIII fr. 952). Eupolis' *Taxiarchoi*, however, did have Dionysus as a character (Σ *Peace* 348e, see fr. 274 *PCG*), learning naval skills from Phormio. As we have seen, Cratinus is identified with Dionysus at *Frogs* 357 and this suggests that Cratinus may have been represented on stage as Dionysus. What better taxiarch of the tribe Oeneis, then, than Dionysus himself? As it happens, Eupolis fr. 269 from this play is one of a very small group of instances where the citation identifies the poet as one of the characters. Pollux 9. 102 quotes as follows: ἐν γοῦν Ταξιάρχοις Εὔπολις τοῦ Φορμίωνος εἰπόντος οὐκοῦν... κύκλον, ἀποκρίνεται τί... ὄρτυγα 'In *Taxiarchoi*, when Phormio has said the line 'Therefore... circle', Eupolis replies 'What.... quail'. Others are Hermippus fr. 36, *Demoi* fr. 102 and

---

[63] Koster, *Prolegomena* p. 9 (Anon. *De Comoedia* III.34 = K-A Eupolis T2a.7).
[64] There are many instances of close verbal correspondence between the two poets. E.g. Cratin. fr. 363 (*loc. incert.*) and Eup. fr. 13 (*Aiges*).

115. Though it is usual to regard such instances as simply mistakes, they do in fact appear quite clearly to identify the poet as a character rather than as the author. If the current analysis is broadly correct, this will have been because in those instances the character spoke, like Dicaeopolis in *Acharnians*, as though he were the poet, and naturally enough, the ancient scholars took the apparent self-reference at face-value. These 'mistakes' are in fact very good evidence that a character in the play was identified in antiquity with the author. Actually, however, the on-stage comic poet will, according to our current argument, always have been a rival, subjected to satire through on-stage caricature.

Such a portrayal of Cratinus, deriving in the first place from an association between the god of comedy and wine and the old and successful poet, who also had a connection with viticulture, might even be the basis for the joke about his love of wine in *Peace* 703 (if my earlier explanation is not correct pp. 62–3), though it is much more likely to have *followed* an already established connection. His mission to Phormio to learn the arts of war is thus explained. Dionysus/Cratinus has been elected as the taxiarch of the Oeneis tribe and needs to learn how to do his stuff. If, however, Cratinus was represented in Eupolis' play as the taxiarch of Oeneis, it will likely not have been obvious from the text itself, given what I have just argued.

Cratinus may, then, have been represented by Eupolis as Dionysus in *Taxiarchs*. Though the play's date is disputed, and Storey has recently argued forcefully for *c.* 415, other scholars date the play *c.* 427.[65] And it is scarcely likely that Eupolis would be bothering to attack in 415 a comic poet whose last production appears to have been the *Pytine* of 423. If the earlier date is correct, Aristophanes could have been responding to Eupolis' *Taxiarchs* in representing his Cratinus caricature in the guise of Dionysus in *Babylonians*. It is certainly the case that Eupolis' *Prospaltioi* (probably his first production, in 429) contained an old man (scholion on *Clouds* 541a) and if he is the stubborn figure in fr. 260, then he has something clearly in common with Philocleon. But there is another individual who appears in Eupolis characterised by a feature which is prominent in Philocleon also. At fr. 298.6, the last in a list of what has plausibly been thought to be the chorus of *Chrysoun Genos*, comes ὁ τὸν τρίβων' ἔχων 'the one who wears the homespun cloak'. Just such a cloak is the focus of *Wasps* 1122f. (though the garment is named only at 1131) and it appears to be so characteristic of

---

[65] Storey 1990, 22–4 and 2003, 246–8 (cf. Handley 1982, 24–5), Kyriakidi 2007, 24–5 argue for 415, E. L. Bowie 1988, 185 for 427. For a full discussion see Appendix 4.

Philocleon that much comedy is had at his (and Bdelycleon's) expense when he is forced to relinquish it in the process of changing his ways. If, as I have argued, Philocleon represents Cratinus, then so will Eupolis' homespun-cloak wearer. It will strengthen this interpretation if the immediately preceding individual (fr. 298.5), τὸν φαλακρὸν 'the bald fellow', represented Aristophanes. Thus a play now dated by Storey to 426 would already display Eupolis' satirical engagement with both Cratinus and Aristophanes.[66]

'Cratinus' on my argument was represented as virulently *anti*-Cleonian in *Babylonians*, but other indications point to his being the pro-Cleonian Demos in *Knights* (and also in Eupolis' *Noumeniai*?) and *Philo*cleon in *Wasps*. Something must have triggered this and it may perhaps have been that Cratinus had not always been in Cleon's camp, but had moved over to support him only after having attacked him virulently in his own comedies. See Cratinus, *Seriphioi* fr. 228, where Cleon's eyebrows were made fun of and he was accused of μανία 'madness', though this is a named attack and obviously might have appeared in the mouth of a satirised character, rather than directly in the poet's – or his chorus' – parabatic statement. If in *Knights* Demos does represent Cratinus, then the passage already alluded to where Demos cynically speaks of his exploitation of politicians (1121f.) may refer to his perceived political changeability, especially since the language and the theme of 1141f. (ἐξεμεῖν and the mention of theft) may recall another comic scene, the conviction of Cleon for theft (evoked at *Ach.* 5–8: see below, chapter four, pp. 127–8). The parabasis of *Wasps*, a play which we have already seen reason to classify as a response to *Pytine* (obvious enough anyway from the space given in the parabasis to complaints about the defeat of *Clouds* in 423), also perhaps alludes to this inconsistency at 1036: τοιοῦτον ἰδὼν τέρας οὔ φησιν δείσας καταδωροδοκῆσαι ('when he saw a monster like this, he claims not to have allowed fear to make him take a bribe to betray you [sc. as some other poet did]'). Interestingly, though, the monster imagery used of Cleon in this passage is only partially based on the Cerberus figure used in *Knights* (1017). Most of it evokes rather Typhoeus (cf. Hes. *Theog.* 824–30), apparently in the form Typhon,

---

[66] Perhaps the earliest indication in Cratinus that this contest was going on is to be seen in *Cheirones* fr. 255, which was probably produced during Pericles' lifetime (fr. 258–9). At the end of the play (an odd place for a parabatic statement, one might think), Aelius Aristides tells us (28.91), Cratinus wrote ταῦτα δυοῖν ἐτέοιν ἡμῖν μόλις ἐξεπονήθη ('I only just managed to write this after two years of hard labour'). He then paraphrases what followed: τοῖς δ' ἄλλοις ἐν ἅπαντι βίῳ προτιθέναι φησὶ ποιηταῖς μιμεῖσθαι ('And he says that he sets it forth for the other poets to imitate in the rest of their lives'). It is unlikely that Cratinus is seriously proposing his work as a model. It seems better to read this as an ironic reflection upon its likely reception by Eupolis and others.

also an alias of Cleon (*Knights* 511). It is certainly possible that the sobriquet had an origin in comedy. Among Cratinus' plays, the best bet is *Ploutoi*.

Cratinus *Ploutoi* fr. 171.22 refers to the end of Pericles' tyranny and this is probably not his death, but his removal from the generalship (Plut. *Per.* 35.3–4). The play had a chorus of Titans (fr. 170.11–12) and this must have been related allegorically to Cratinus' penchant for portraying Pericles as Zeus (frr. 73, 118, 258, 259), since their arrival is linked firmly to the re-establishment of the democracy (fr. 170.22–4). Presumably, it also signals the return of the reign of Kronos (fr. 170.12 and 18). But their motivation is to seek out their brother (fr. 170.25–6). Several suggestions have been made as to his identity: Prometheus, Saturn, Plutus, a personified Demos (see references in *PCG* ad loc.) But we are surely looking for someone to match on the Titans' side the allegorical antagonism that their battle with the Olympians brings to mind (Hes. *Theog.* 624f., 711f.). Plutarch (*Per.* 35.4) tells us that his sources (whom he names) give three different reports of the prosecutor in Pericles' trial – Cleon Simmias and Lacrateides. Of these, Cleon is known from Aristophanic comedy to have borne the epithet Typhon (*Knights* 511; cf. *Wasps* 1033, *Peace* 755f.). Like the Titans, Typhon or Tyhoeus was a child of Gaia (Hes. *Theog.* 824–30), though not by the same father. One version of the myth has Zeus tackling him and coming off worse (Apollod. *Library* 1.6.3). He suits both the mythology, then, and the political allegory.[67] If Cleon had been represented as Typhon in Cratinus' *Ploutoi* as well, then this will also be part of the metacomic humour in the *Knights* passage (230f.) which alludes to the mask-makers' fear of Cleon's appearance.

I conclude, then, that once Cratinus had made the move to support Cleon (probably by the time of *Nomoi*?), his rivals could make comic capital out of his former opposition to him in just the way evoked by the Cratinus figure at *Acharnians* 377f. and 499f. As I shall argue later, Eupolis did precisely the same thing in his *Chrysoun Genos* (see chapter four, p. 130).

On this reconstruction, Eupolis' *Prospaltioi* might have been the beginning of a series of metacomic caricatures which stretch with blow and counter-blow from Eupolis' earliest play via *Taxiarchoi* and *Chrysoun Genos* to Aristophanes' *Acharnians* and *Knights* and Cratinus' *Pytine* to (at least) Aristophanes' *Wasps*. The ploy of *Acharnians* in making the *young* Eupolis play the old Cratinus will also explain how the comic poet in *Pytine* (probably Aristophanes) can be represented as *old*, though in reality he was a young man (though his baldness may also have had something to do with

---

[67] I owe this theory to Keith Cooke.

this) and why the audience of *Acharnians* might not have been puzzled by the overlapping identities of Cratinus and Eupolis: his on-stage attacks on Cratinus were an integral datum of his comedy and it is to this known fact that the chorus will be alluding at *Frogs* 357 when they identify comedy as 'the rites of bull-eating Cratinus'.

But the general principle now established, that a comic poet will not satirise himself, also compels us to reconsider the 'voice' of two Aristophanes fragments, fr. 604 (*loc. incert.*) and fr. 488 (*Skenas Katalambanousai* ['*Women Pitching Tents*']). The first of these has the comic poet speaker (according to the writer of the *Life*) claim: τὴν γυναῖκα δὲ | αἰσχύνομαι τώ τ' οὐ φρονοῦντε παιδίω ('I am ashamed before my wife and my two senseless children'). The second has the comic poet speaker (according to the scholiast who quotes it) say: χρῶμαι γὰρ αὐτοῦ τοῦ στόματος τῷ στρογγύλῳ | τοὺς νοῦς δ' ἀγοραίους ἧττον ἢ 'κεῖνος ποιῶ ('For I utilise his [i.e. Euripides'] terseness of expression, but I make my ideas less vulgar than he does'). It seems very likely, since ancient scholars quote passages from the plays ascribed directly to the poet very seldom, that (as at *Ach.* 377f. and 499f.) the character who was given these lines was palpably a comic poet, but not Aristophanes. This observation has a number of important consequences. Fr. 604 was used by some ancient biographers (*PCG* II.56–7) to suggest that the tradition attested elsewhere that Aristophanes had three sons (Philippus, Nicostratus or Philetairus and Araros) was wrong and he had only two. There is one play of Aristophanes where the central character has two sons, *Daitales* (cf. *Clouds* 529 and fr. 205). It is true that the father here is an old man (fr. 205), but then, so is Dicaeopolis and ancient scholars took *Acharnians* 378 as expressing something about *Aristophanes* (as many scholars still do). I conclude that it is not impossible that the very first play of Aristophanes also had an old man/comic poet at its heart. In respect of fr. 488, it suggests that, since *Skenas Katalambanousai* is generally dated to after 420, on-stage attacks on rival poets continued into the 410s. It also divorces Aristophanes from the charge of using Euripides, foists it upon a rival, and brings with it the referent of Cratinus fr. 342 (εὐριπιδαριστοφανίζων 'Euripidaristophanizing'). We must now turn to examine this idea further.

CARICATURES OF EURIPIDES

It will help substantiate this analysis if we recognise an element which ties together plays from each of the three decades in which Aristophanes was apparently squared up against a specific comic antagonist. In *Acharnians*,

Thesmophoriazusai and *Frogs* Euripides plays an important role, one which, moreover, is closely connected with that of the protagonist in each comedy (Dicaeopolis, *kedestes* and Dionysus).

It has not been noticed just how peculiar the transition to the Euripides scene in *Acharnians* is, nor have scholars asked precisely why it is that it is only here (406) that the character gives his full name, or why Euripides responds by changing his mind, seeing Dicaeopolis and, despite all the insults, lending him items of his trade. Obviously, Dicaeopolis must know who Euripides is, otherwise he could not have the idea to visit him. But Dicaeopolis' use of his own name in a direct appeal to the tragedian when refused entry by the servant and the way he makes his address suggest that Euripides has some obligation to speak to *him*. This comes across in the use of the diminutive (Εὐριπίδιον 405), a form used familiarly to his son by Strepsiades at *Clouds* 80,[68] and in the phrase εἴπερ πώποτ' ἀνθρώπων τινί ('if ever [you answered] any man'), but most especially in the formulation of 406: Δικαιόπολις καλεῖ σε Χολλῄδης, ἐγώ, where instead of Sommerstein's 'It's Dicaeopolis of Cholleidae calling you – that's me' the emphasis appears to require 'It's Dicaeopolis calling you – of Cholleidai – me', where the rhetoric, with Χολλῄδης and ἐγώ as the climactic words, implies that Euripides will recognise who it is when he hears the name – since the tragedian is still inside the house there has been as yet no visual contact – and realise then that he really will have to speak to him. This he indeed eventually does, without any further explanation being given as to why he gives in.[69] There is also here possibly a humorous signal to the audience (441) that he really *is* Eupolis, despite his Cratinus costume. In its turn, this reading offers a reason to accept that Cholleidai may be the real deme of Eupolis, rather than a joke. The comic poet needs help and the only way he can get in to see Euripides, it seems, is to make him aware of his *real* identity (since he will still look like Cratinus, when Euripides eventually sees him). This drives a wedge, of course, between the character he is playing (a countryman 32–3, 266–7) and himself as poet/actor, as

---

[68] The norm, I suggest, even though Strepsiades' use of it to address Socrates at 222 may begin to suggest that this is metacomic or may reveal a similarly close relationship in real life between the person Strepsiades represents and Socrates.

[69] Storey 1993a, 388f. argued that the name was revealed because this is a door-knocking scene. But in *Clouds* 134, the closest parallel, it is the student who asks for the name of the person knocking and not Strepsiades who volunteers the information, while in the door-knocking scene in *Frogs* 35f. Heracles asks who is knocking, but Dionysus does not have to answer, since Heracles recognises him as soon as he opens the door. Cf. *Knights* 1257 and *Birds* 643–5, where the names are also given at the request of another character. In this scene, Dicaeopolis has already been refused access to Euripides and he announces his name without being asked.

also between the role of countryman and the fact that Cholleidae is a *city* deme (see chapter 5, pp. 206–7 with n. 113). That will not come as a surprise to the audience: but the sudden casting off of the mask would surely create intense amusement.

But what underlies the satire of this scene is not just a presumption of intimacy in the real world between the two individuals, let us say Eupolis and Euripides, but something about the comic poet's propensity to utilise Euripidean tragic language and motifs. Here we can get some help by re-examining the famous Cratinus fragment already mentioned above (fr. 342), in which a comic poet is said to be a 'Euripidaristophaniser'.

The fragment reads:

τίς δὲ σύ; κομψός τις ἔροιτο θεάτης.
ὑπολεπτολόγος, γνωμιδιώκτης, εὐριπιδαριστοφανίζων

'Who are you?' a clever spectator will ask.
'A subtle sophist, a chaser of tropes, a Euripidaristophaniser'

There is, unfortunately, no agreement about how to read this fragment. If a full stop is read at the end of line 1 (as in K-A), then the series of compound adjectives likely represents an answer (perhaps that of the clever audience member, perhaps that of the character) to the question 'Who are you?' Remove the full stop after line 1 and the compound adjectives will refer to the clever spectator.[70] We should concentrate, however, on what the spectator is asking. Clearly, if he is defined specifically as a theatregoer, he must be directing his question towards what is going on on stage (cf. *Peace* 43–9). Whatever we do with the punctuation at line 1, then, he is asking about a character on stage whose identity is not obvious (otherwise, why would the spectator be described as *clever*?). Moreover, it is difficult to see why a spectator should be called a 'Euripidaristophaniser', and the scholia (not always to be trusted, of course, but here with access to the whole passage and not just the fragment) read it as referring to a comic poet (Aristophanes).[71] If, as I believe, the K-A punctuation is correct, then this line identifies a comic poet on stage, either recognised through his disguise by the clever spectator[72] or revealing his identity with hints (depending on whether the second line is spoken by the spectator or the character). Is he in someone else's comedy, or Cratinus', though? If this is from a parabasis (so e.g. Lübke),[73] it is possible that Cratinus is explaining his target in the play from which the passage comes.

[70] The preference of Olson 2007, 110.   [71] Σ Plato, *Apol.* 19c, quoted below.
[72] For 'clever' spectators see *Peace* 43–8, *Knights* 228, 233, *Clouds* 521, 527, 535.
[73] See references in *PCG* on this fragment.

Who was the poet? The scholiast who quotes the lines was in no doubt (Schol. Areth. (B) Pl. *Apol.* 19c [p. 421 Gr.]): Ἀριστοφάνης ὁ κωμῳδοποιός... ἐκωμῳδεῖτο δ' ἐπὶ τῷ σκώπτειν μὲν Εὐριπίδην, μιμεῖσθαι δ' αὐτόν ('Aristophanes the comic poet... was satirised for making fun of Euripides, even though he imitated him'). However, the spectator does not have to be especially clever if the poet basically tells him in εὐριπιδαριστοφανίζων that he is Aristophanes. If the line is the clever spectator's answer, then much the same applies: there is nothing clever in giving the answer rather than hinting at it. In any case, although compound nouns may be used to imply a relationship of the sort 'part B acts as part A' (e.g. Ἡρακλειοξανθίαν at *Frogs* 499, 'Xanthias playing Heracles') or indeed 'part A plays part B' (e.g. Διονυσαλέξανδρος 'Dionysus plays Paris' in the title of Cratinus' play), non-compound *verbs* of this type would not be used of the person or group from which they take their root. For example, σωκρατέω/σωκρατίζω 'I Socratise', σικελίζω 'I act like a Sicilian', λακωνίζω/λακεδαιμονιάζω 'I imitate Laconian ways'. On both counts, then, it is possible that the word εὐριπιδαριστοφανίζων means 'a poet who mixes Euripides and Aristophanes'.[74] Cratinus, then, in all likelihood, is not attacking Aristophanes here, but another poet who has connections of some kind with Euripides and Aristophanes, such that the neologism can act as an effective dig at him. This reading is confirmed by my earlier argument that fr. 488, where ancient scholars heard Aristophanes' voice (scholium on Pl. *Apol.* 19c), must in fact represent satire of a comic poet rival.[75]

We know that Eupolis allegedly used Aristophanes (albeit later, in *Marikas* of 421), from the accusation at *Clouds* 553f.[76] If τὸν φαλακρὸν ('the bald fellow') at Eupolis *Chrysoun Genos* 298.5 referred to Aristophanes, on stage as part of a chorus, their 'war' was already in progress only a year after Aristophanes' hidden debut. However, parody of Euripides is not marked in Eupolis' fragments. Rather, in the very few places where Euripidean reference is suspected (fr. 99.35 and 102 and fr. 106), there seems only to be heightened tone.[77] But we can see that the claim to give political advice to the city, voiced by Dicaeopolis/Eupolis at *Acharnians* in the famous line

---

[74] See references in *PCG* on this fragment, especially Baker 1904, 144 n. 1: 'εὐριπιδαριστοφανίζων *significat imitans tam Euripidem quam Aristophanem... Aristophanes igitur non ipse... in his verbis appellari videtur sed tantum alio nescio quo appellato ita circuitione quadam vituperari*.' Even the verb μελλονικιᾶν 'to delay like Nicias' at *Birds* 640, does not refer to the action of Nicias, but of those who would behave like him.
[75] Above p. 86.   [76] See Storey 2003, 202–4 for points of similarity between the two plays.
[77] Storey 2003, 329. See also Telò 2007, 106–21.

500, τὸ γὰρ δίκαιον οἶδε καὶ τρυγῳδία ('for trygedy also knows what justice is'), is based on the premise that *tragedy* has this role: and the Euripides of *Frogs* concurs (e.g. 1009–10).

The possible relationship between *Taxiarchoi* fr. 280 and *Electra* 184–5 argued for by Storey[78] might imply parody, but it is probably significant that this is a play which may also have involved caricature of Cratinus, since he must also in some way be involved in the fabric of the *Acharnians* scene, given that Eupolis is (if my arguments are correct) playing him.[79]

The connection between Euripides and Eupolis, then, may have been personal, as the announcement of his name at *Acharnians* 406, I have argued, implies.[80] They might, for example, have been related in some way. If this is the case, then it is unlikely that Eupolis will have put Euripides on stage, even to attack Cratinus, though he might have allowed a Euripidean parody to slip from the lips of his Cratinus character, as I have suggested. The humour of the *Acharnians* scene on this hypothesis, then, would operate on the pretence that Eupolis was both using his personal connection to help him defend his character's politically dangerous position and grossly insulting Euripides in the process, in Cratinean mould. The scene gains particular piquancy from falling within types of humorous criticism which we can clearly see Cratinus himself making in fr. 342, where he attacks (on my interpretation) Eupolis for utilising a comic poet (Aristophanes) and a tragic poet (Euripides) to make his verse, and in fr. 213, where he criticises Aristophanes for using a comic poet (Eupolis).

Furthermore, the conjecture that a close family connection with Euripides helps fuel the satire at *Acharnians* 393f. and that it is Eupolis whom Cratinus labels the 'Euripidaristophanizer' (fr. 342), makes the continuation of an attack upon Eupolis into Aristophanes' *Skenas Katalambanousai* (fr. 488, see above, pp. 57, 86), *Thesmophoriazusai* and *Frogs* much more understandable. In fr. 488, the comic poet character who claims to use Euripides will not be Aristophanes, but Eupolis. And the possibility of a close personal or family connection would also make it clear why the role of *kedestes* in *Thesmophoriazusai* might make a good cover for Eupolis, and would explain the close connections between *Acharnians* (where on my argument, Eupolis had also been satirised on stage) and this play (his age would simply be a function of an established caricature, already used in *Acharnians* and possibly *Peace*, see below, which satirised his on-stage attacks

---

[78] Storey 2003, 247–8. [79] See chapter four for arguments about this.
[80] On the other hand, there may be the implication that Eupolis also imitated Euripidean tragedy's didactic stance (though the poet in *Skenas Katalambanousai* is claiming a linguistic, rather than an ideological influence).

on Cratinus). The desire of Dionysus for the dead Euripides as well as the cross-references to Eupolidean comedy (and that of Cratinus at *Frogs* 357) would also be well explained if this were another caricature of Eupolis. The surprising fact that Dionysus is an *epibates* on a trireme (*Frogs* 48f.) and that re-enfranchisement of former fighting in the navy is a central theme of the parabasis (*Frogs* 697f.) makes best sense in terms of an ironic on-stage attack on Eupolis as Dionysus, the Cratinus disguise *par excellence*.

CARICATURE AND NAMED ATTACK: THE CASE OF HYPERBOLUS

The one type of satire which does appear to be open and accessible to direct political analysis is that involving attacks on named individuals. However, the uncovering of two other important satirical structures, disguised caricature and metacomedy, obliges us to re-evaluate the role of named satire. It will be best to do this within what has been argued above from *Clouds* 545f. to be the real ideological framework for Aristophanes' plays, his support for the radical democrat Hyperbolus.

I also argued earlier that at *Clouds* 545f. Aristophanes himself assumes a fundamental distinction between the two forms of satirical assault, and that it is caricature attack which has priority in determining the true political polarity of a comedy. It helps to substantiate this proposition that there is nowhere any sign that Aristophanes ever put Hyperbolus on stage as a character in any of his many plays. Moreover, his complaint against Eupolis for the travesty of *Knights* (*Clouds* 553–6) focuses attention quite specifically upon the on-stage caricature of Hyperbolus as Marikas (553), and of his mother (551, 555 with scholium).

Nonetheless, it is also the case that Hyperbolus is ridiculed by name many times in Aristophanes' plays and this needs to be explained if we are to justify taking at face value the remarks in the *Clouds* parabasis. However, if on-stage caricature of individuals is at the centre of iambic comedy, then from this it follows that the vast majority of invective attacks will come in the speeches given to these figures. In a very high proportion of instances, then, such attacks will be part of the comedy made from the on-stage characters and *their* social and political attitudes. The metacomic texture of the plays will also contribute to the effect of distancing invective attack from the author. At this point, therefore, it is important to review the Aristophanic passages in which Hyperbolus is named in an attempt to establish where the focus of satire lies. It needs to be said that in order to do this ahead of detailed analysis of the plays, I must take some short-cuts and suggest what these named invective attacks upon Hyperbolus look like when read with caricature identifications which will be more fully justified later.

NAMED ATTACKS ON HYPERBOLUS IN ARISTOPHANES

Aristophanes' 'named' attacks on Hyperbolus can be divided up into three categories: (a) those spoken by characters already identified or now identifiable as on-stage caricatures of Eupolis: *Wasps* 1007, Bdelycleon; *Knights* 1362–3, rejuvenated Demos (see further below); *Clouds* 1065, Unjust Argument (see further below); *Peace* 921, 1321, Trygaeus (see further below); (b) those spoken by the chorus: *Acharnians* 846–7; *Knights* 1300–15; *Clouds* 623f.; *Thesmophoriazusai* 839f.; (c) those spoken by other characters: *Knights* 738–40 Sausage-Seller; *Clouds* 876 Socrates; *Frogs* 570 Plathane.

(a) Passages put in the mouth of Eupolis caricatures

(i) As I argued above, pp. 70f., *Wasps* 650–1 seem to require a comic poet to speak them and, since this cannot be Aristophanes, it is likely to be a rival. Close thematic connections with Cratinus' *Pytine*, and the ongoing battle over *Knights* and a joke on his name (411) make Eupolis a good bet. It is Eupolis, then, who speaks 1007: κοὐκ ἐγχανεῖται σ' ἐξαπατῶν Ὑπέρβολος ('and Hyperbolus will not deceive and laugh openly at you'). The line is spoken to Philocleon, whom I have identified as Cratinus. The implication is, then, that somehow and somewhere, Cratinus has been seen being deceived and made a fool of by Hyperbolus. I suggest this reflects a Eupolis play in which Cratinus was shown in such a scene. See further on *Ach.* 846–7 below.

(ii) I argued in chapter one that *Clouds* 545, coming directly after criticism of Eupolidean themes (537–43) and directly before an open attack on him for his treatment of Hyperbolus in *Marikas* (551f.), contains in the jest about Aristophanes' baldness the implication that Eupolis wore his hair long (οὐ κομῶ 'I do not have long hair'). Thus it is significant that in *Knights*, a play now identified as a metacomic attack on Eupolis, the rejuvenated Demos should have long hair (1331) and share Bdelycleon's distaste for law-courts (1332; cf. *Wasps* 414). The satirical point of the play would certainly have been enhanced by turning Demos/Cratinus into Demos/Eupolis, and if this is what happens, then *Knights* 1362–3 are also spoken by Eupolis. They are an answer to the Sausage-Seller's enquiry about what Demos will do if an

Metacomedy and caricature

advocate threatens the jurors with no pay unless they convict (1357–61): ἄρας μετέωρον εἰς τὸ βάραθρον ἐμβαλῶ, | ἐκ τοῦ λάρυγγος ἐκκρεμάσας Ὑπέρβολον ('I'll lift him up and throw him into the chasm, hanging Hyperbolus from his neck.'). Once more, a hostile attitude towards Hyperbolus helps characterise the response.

(iii) It will not be immediately clear why Unjust Argument in *Clouds* should be identified with Eupolis. The matter is complex and depends on the argument for a cross-reference between *Clouds* 920f. and *Acharnians*. The *Clouds* passage is as follows:

> Ἥττων Λόγος· αὐχμεῖς αἰσχρῶς.
> Κρείττων Λόγος· σὺ δέ γ᾽ εὖ πράττεις·
> καίτοι πρότερον γ᾽ ἐπτώχευες,
> Τήλεφος εἶναι Μυσὸς φάσκων,
> ἐκ πηριδίου
> γνώμας τρώγων Πανδελετείους.

Unjust Argument: You're awfully dirty. Just Argument: But you're in the pink, though before you were a beggar, pretending to be Mysian Telephus, and eating Pandeletean ideas from a little pouch.

Sommerstein comments:[81] 'The relevance of mentioning Telephus here is not clear: possibly the point is that the Worse Argument, when he was a 'beggar', with typical impudence pretended to be a king in disguise.' The *aporia* is honestly admitted. But it is worth noting that Sommerstein is obliged to accept some point outside the current drama as a reference-point. The conversation does not end here, it continues:

> Ἥττ. Λ᾽ ὤμοι σοφίας –
> Κρέττ. Λ ὤμοι μανίας –
> ἧς ἐμνήσθης.

Sommerstein translates: 'Lesser Logos: Oh the cleverness. Greater Logos: – Oh the lunacy – of what you have mentioned.' But the last phrase more likely means 'which you have mentioned'.[82] This underlines the particularity of the incident involving being Telephus and being a beggar, and makes it more difficult not to regard it as something the audience already knows specifically from outside the play in relation to the Lesser Logos. As Sommerstein notes, there is a problem with the reference to Telephus. But Dover remarks:[83]

---

[81] Sommerstein 1982 on *Clouds* 922.   [82] For the genitive object of μιμνήσκομαι, see LSJ s.v. B.II.
[83] Dover 1968, on *Clouds* 922.

Euripides' *Telephus* represented the Mysian king as appearing disguised as a beggar at Agamemnon's court. The play, produced in 438, seems to have made a great impression, perhaps because the audience liked to see splendid costumes in tragedy and were shocked by a realistic portrayal of beggar's rags; Ar. exploits the play very fully in *Acharnians* and *Thesmophoriazusae*.

This avoids the issue. At least Sommerstein, though he does not clearly state what the problem is, recognises that the reference cannot be unequivocally and directly linked to Euripides' play, as Dover seems to think, since there Telephus was pretending to be a beggar. Here, however, it is Unjust Argument who *was* a beggar, pretending to be *Telephus*.

We do know a scene from drama which answers this description. It is in Aristophanes' *Acharnians*. At 496f., the main character, Dicaeopolis, having borrowed the ragged costume of Telephus and other props from Euripides' play from the author himself, stands before the audience pretending to be Telephus.[84] His opening words make clear that he is a beggar (498 πτωχὸς ὤν).

This interpretation by cross-reference within Aristophanes, however, could only have worked if the audience could recognise that 'Dicaeopolis' in *Acharnians* and 'Unjust Argument' in *Clouds* were representing the same individual in different disguises. Since we have identified the figure at the centre of *Acharnians* as a comic poet, Unjust Argument must by the same token also represent a comic poet. But the caricature was *double*, Eupolis playing Cratinus. So this might mean that he represents either Cratinus or Eupolis. However, Cratinus' career appears to have been over after his success with *Pytine* in 423, so that it makes more sense to see the allusion as being to Eupolis.

Thus Eupolis speaks *Clouds* 1065: Ὑπέρβολος δ' οὐκ τῶν λύχνων πλεῖν ἢ τάλαντα πολλὰ | εἴληφε διὰ πονηρίαν, ἀλλ' οὐ μὰ Δι' οὐ μάχαιραν ('Hyperbolus from the lamp-market has got hold of loads of talents through wickedness, but, by Zeus, not of a dagger'). This neatly encapsulates the inimical attitude towards Hyperbolus which is evident in his 421 play *Marikas*. It also seems directly to link Eupolis with satire of Hyperbolus as a lamp merchant. This is possibly, then, a cross-reference to Eupolis' lost *Noumeniai*.

---

[84] It is true, as Alan Sommerstein argues in correspondence, that a beggar's pouch is not among the props given to Dicaeopolis by Euripides (or, more strictly, not among those mentioned). However, the words before this are clearly metaphorical. The Unjust Argument is envisaged as having made his beggar's meal (or a speech?) out of scraps from Pandeletus. So it is not an impediment to the cross-reference that the πηρίδιον does not feature in *Acharnians*. By the time of this coda, the cross-reference will already have been recognised.

(iv) I have argued above (chapter two, p. 34) that Trygaeus' name in *Peace* evokes comic poetry as much as viticulture. It does not seem unlikely, then, that he also represents a comic poet rival. At 921 and 1321, the central figure rejoices at Ὑπέρβολον... παύσας ('having put a stop to Hyperbolus'), and in the second at Ὑπέρβολον ἐξελάσαντας 'having driven Hyperbolus out'. Earlier, however, he has spoken a quite contradictory passage at 680f. There Peace, through Hermes, asks who is in charge of the Pnyx, receives the reply 'Hyperbolus', and turns away in disgust. Once Trygaeus has assured Peace that this situation will not continue (685), and has explained how the temporary aberration occurred (686–8), he is asked what benefit the *demos* will receive from his *prostasia* (688). The reply (689) is (unusually) positive: εὐβουλότεροι γενησόμεθα 'We shall be better counsellors'. Asked to explain further, Trygaeus responds (690–2): ὅτι τυγχάνει λυχνοποιὸς ὤν. πρὸ τοῦ μὲν οὖν | ἐψηλαφῶμεν ἐν σκότῳ τὰ πράγματα, | νυνὶ δ' ἅπαντα πρὸς λύχνον βουλεύσομεν. ('Because he is a lamp-maker. Before, we had to feel our way in the dark at our difficulties. But now we can plan by lamplight!'). A very similar political self-contradiction also occurs in *Wasps*, between the eponymous Philocleon's devotion to Cleon and his membership of a jury that convicts Cleon of theft (757–9). The jokes will work here too if the central character is well known personally for opposition to Hyperbolus, and is the poet most closely connected with his representation on stage as a lamp merchant (as *Clouds* 1065 implies). The claim to have 'stopped Hyperbolus' would sit well on the lips of the author of *Marikas*. I propose, then, that these considerations suggest we are seeing a caricature of Eupolis as Trygaeus in *Peace* (I shall return to this identification and the problem of the demotic Athmoneus at 190 and 918–19 in chapter five). What the unusually positive portrayal of Hyperbolus at 690–2 implies, however, is the same as *Clouds* 551–2, that Aristophanes was an ardent supporter and found it amusing to have this articulated by Hyperbolus' – and his – arch enemy. But there is more. Hyperbolus' *prostasia* is certainly not evidenced in our other sources. Thucydides (5.16.1) identifies Nicias as the most influential politician of the period after Cleon's death and since Hyperbolus was probably still against peace (*Peace* 682–4), he cannot really be said to have influenced affairs in the year of the Peace of Nicias. A better explanation, then, for the counter-factual *prostasia* of Hyperbolus is that it was a fabrication of Eupolidean comedy. Since *Knights* is, as I have argued, a parody of Eupolis and has as a central theme the *prostasia* (won from Paphlagon/Cleon by the Sausage-Seller), this substantiates the solution offered earlier to the problem of *Knights* and Eupolis. Like *Clouds* 1065 ((iii) above), this could be a cross-reference to Eupolis' lost *Noumeniai*.

(b) Passages spoken by the chorus

(i) *Acharnians* 846–7 is addressed to Dicaeopolis/Eupolis costumed as and acting Cratinus: κοὐ ξυντυχών σ' Ὑπέρβολος | δικῶν ἀναπλήσει ('and Hyperbolus will not run into you and fill you full of lawsuits'). It seems probable that behind this ode lies an intertextual reference to Eupolidean comedy. The reference must be to a market play, possibly one in which his caricature of Cratinus (mentioned in the ode at 848) was confronted with various nuisances, Ctesias, Prepis, Cleonymus, Hyperbolus, Pauson and Lysistratus (*Ach.* 839f.). Two of these appear also in incidents referred to elsewhere in contexts where, on my identifications, the Cratinus caricature is speaking or being addressed: Lysistratus at *Wasps* 787f., and Hyperbolus at *Wasps* 1007 (see (a)(i) above). The humour in the Hyperbolus references at *Ach.* 846–7 and *Wasps* 1007, then, has the same basis, possibly a single comic scene in Eupolis.

(ii) Similarly, the epirrheme at *Knights* 1300–15, where the personified triremes complain about Hyperbolus' plan to attack Carthage by sea, is associated with Eupolis both generally because of the satire of his comedy the play has been shown to contain and because ancient scholars saw something specifically Eupolidean about the second parabasis (Σ *Knights* 1288), of which this epirrheme forms part. We can now add the Hyperbolus/lamp merchant motif, which occurs at *Knights* 1314–15, and with which, as I have argued above ((a)(iii)), the on-stage caricature figure of Eupolis is associated: ἀλλὰ πλείτω χωρὶς αὑτὸς ἐς κόρακας, εἰ βούλεται | τὰς σκάφας, ἐν αἷς ἐπώλει τοὺς λύχνους, καθελκύσας ('let him launch the tubs in which he used to display the lamps he sold, and sail off all by himself – all the way to blazes, if that's where he wants to go!' tr. Sommerstein). Like *Clouds* 1065 and *Peace* 690–2 ((a)(iii) and (a)(iv) above), this could be a cross-reference to Eupolis' lost *Noumeniai*.

(iii) The epirrhemes of the *Clouds* parabasis (575–94 and 607–26) follow from a critique of Eupolis which is both direct and, I have argued, indirect. The play itself contains an on-stage caricature of the poet (as Unjust Argument), and since it has several of the motifs complained about by Aristophanes in the parabasis, it must be construed as having him as a prime target. Besides, the two political points of attack in them, Cleon (581f.) and Hyperbolus (623f.), can now be argued to be central to the satirical agenda of Eupolis. Eupolis as Dicaeopolis has a fundamentally anti-Cleonian agenda (which can be located also in his 'collaboration' over *Knights*) and is, I have argued, even caricatured on stage as *Bdely*cleon, so implacable is his hatred (and this implacability probably also underlies Aristophanes' claim at *Clouds* 549–50 only to have attacked Cleon once). It is not unlikely, then, that the humorous point of both these epirrhemes is to be found in cross-references to scenes in Eupolidean or Cratinean comedy, and very possibly both. The attack on Cleon will have belonged to Eupolis, but that on Hyperbolus might have belonged to either. The epirrhemes are at any rate connected by the motif of the celestial bodies (sun and moon in the first, the moon in the second) criticising the Athenians' behaviour. In that case, 623–6, where Hyperbolus is chosen as ἱερομνήμων '*hieromnemon*' (representative at the meeting of the Delphic Amphictyony) and then has his garland removed by the gods for messing around with the calendar, will not be a direct reflection of reality, but recall a humorous incident in a Eupolidean or Cratinean play which dealt with Hyperbolus.[85]

(iv) The final choral passage to mention Hyperbolus is in the parabasis of *Thesmophoriazusai* and is linked to an attack on Hyperbolus' mother (839f.):

> τῷ γὰρ εἰκός, ὦ πόλις,
> τὴν Ὑπερβόλου καθῆσθαι μήτερ' ἠμφιεσμένην
> λευκὰ καὶ κόμας καθεῖσαν πλησίον τῆς Λαμάχου,
> καὶ δανείζειν χρήματ'; ᾗ χρῆν, εἰ δανείσειέν τινι
> καὶ τόκον πράττοιτο, διδόναι μηδέν' ἀνθρώπων τόκον,
> ἀλλ' ἀφαιρεῖσθαι βίᾳ τὰ χρήματ' εἰπόντας τοδί·
> 'ἀξία γοῦν εἶ τόκου τεκοῦσα τοιοῦτον τόκον'

How can it be right, city of Athens, that Hyperbolus' mother can sit here, dressed in white clothing and with her hair loose, close by Lamachus' mother, and be a money-lender too? What should happen to her is if she dared make a loan to anyone and ask for interest, no one should pay her any, but they should take away her money by force saying this: 'Well now you're worth paying interest to, when the only interest you've paid is that worthless son of yours!'

---

[85] Sommerstein 1982 ad loc. treats it as a real incident which had possibly occurred in autumn 424.

Eupolis had attacked Hyperbolus' mother, in *Marikas* of 421, as the scholium on *Clouds* 555 informs us. Even if the figure was derived, as Aristophanes complains it was, from Phrynichus (*Clouds* 555–6), nonetheless the evidence presented above strongly suggests that the audience is invited here to see a pro-Eupolidean stance taken up by the chorus, since Aristophanes had strenuously objected to Eupolis' ridicule of her to his private audience of potential and past sponsors (*Clouds* 552). This choral critique, then, will have been part and parcel of the ironic metacomic attack upon Eupolis constituted by *Thesmophoriazusai* as a whole. Moreover, it would also be reasonable to infer that, since Hyperbolus' mother had been caricatured at least once on stage, the whole business of her as a money-lender recalls another such comic attack.[86]

(c) Attacks in the mouth of other characters

(i) At *Knights* 738–40, Sausage-Seller attacks Demos for the company he keeps:

> τοὺς μὲν καλούς τε κἀγαθοὺς οὐ προσδέχει,
> σαυτὸν δὲ λυχνοπώλαισι καὶ νευρορράφοις
> καὶ σκυτοτόμοις καὶ βυρσοπώλαισιν δίδως

You don't take up those who are fine and noble, but give yourself instead to lamp merchants and cobblers and shoemakers and leather-sellers.

If Demos here represents Cratinus, then we have a scenario in which Cratinus is associated with both Hyperbolus, through the lamp merchant motif, and Cleon through the leather-selling theme (and possibly also through shoemaking, cf. *Knights* 315–21). The lamp merchant motif has already been associated directly with Eupolis (at *Clouds* 1065), and both Eupolis and Cratinus have been associated directly with Hyperbolus (*Ach.* 846–7, *Wasps* 1007) and Cleon (as *Bdely*cleon and *Philo*cleon in *Wasps*). It looks as though here Sausage-Seller is alluding to a comic scene in which Cratinus was shown with Hyperbolus and Cleon, possibly in a market context (cf. *Knights* 1315–16, where Hyperbolus sells lamps, and 315–21, where Cleon sells shoes,

---

[86] Contrast Austin and Olson 2004 on 842–5: 'the attack must have some basis in reality'. In 'Spitting Image' for a long period John Major was shown at table with his wife Norma. He always commented on how good the peas were. It perhaps needs to be said that if we applied the methodology of assuming a basis in reality to that incident, we would be a long way off the mark in understanding the humour of the sketch!

and *Ach.* 836f., with *Wasps* 787–93). This will probably have been in the play *Knights* subverts, possibly *Noumeniai* of Lenaea 425, as I argued above. If so, this confirms something crucial about the play's structure hypothesised earlier: it had as a character a Demos who 'gave himself' to Cleon *and* Hyperbolus (just as Demos in *Knights* gives himself to Cleon and Sausage-Seller).

(ii) The mention by Socrates at *Clouds* 876 may open up another possible on-stage satire of Hyperbolus. At the end of a speech ridiculing Pheidippides for his pronunciation and suggesting that he will never be able to learn ἀπόφευξιν δίκης | ἢ κλῆσιν ἢ χαύνωσιν ἀναπειστηρίαν ('acquittal from a private suit, the summons, or making something out of nothing to win over the jury'), Socrates appears to jettison his objection with a final throw away line: καίτοι ταλάντου γ' αὔτ' ἔμαθεν Ὑπέρβολος ('And yet for a talent Hyperbolus learned them!'). Sommerstein interprets this as suggesting (a) that Hyperbolus had no 'natural oratorical ability', (b) that the training is nonetheless valuable, because Hyperbolus was prepared to pay so much for it and it has made him successful, (c) that it was Socrates who taught him.[87] The first inference is probably correct: it certainly suits the situation in the play at this point and since, as I shall argue in the next two chapters, Aristophanes had in mind for both versions a specific individual representing Pheidippides, this jibe would be funny (for a different reason in each case) as an *ad hominem* joke. The second inference is also reasonable, but the logical extension of the point, as Sommerstein sees, that Hyperbolus emerges as a '*successful* prosecutor and politician' undercuts the implied criticism in exactly the same way as Trygaeus' answer to Peace at *Peace* 689f., where I have suggested that Aristophanes takes delight in attributing his own positive assessment of Hyperbolus to his arch-rival Eupolis. The third inference is not essential and one might have expected, if this is what Socrates was meant to be understood as saying, some indication such as 'from me' in the text. Yet there must be a point in the fact that it is *Socrates* who mentions it.

The answer to this conundrum, however, is complex, and lies in the identification made above at (a)(iii) of Unjust Argument as Eupolis. The Unjust Argument is fundamental to the satire of Socrates, since it underlies the subversion of traditional moral values (*Clouds* 116,

---

[87] Sommerstein 1982 on 876.

1336f.). Behind this quasi-allegorical cover, then, there must lie a publicly known friendly relationship between the poet and the philosopher (for despite Lucian, *Piscator* 25, there is evidence in Eupolis only for invective attacks, and not for on-stage caricature attacks on Socrates: frs. 386 and 392).[88] It could, it is true, make comic sense for Socrates to be made to claim to have taught his friend Eupolis' arch-enemy his political skills. But since the upshot is a *positive* view of Hyperbolus, it seems more likely, in the context of Aristophanes' implied attitude at *Clouds* 551–2, that Socrates is referring to someone else as Hyperbolus' teacher. If so, the reference must be to something well-known. Sommerstein notes that the charge for Hyperbolus' lessons is ludicrous: it is twelve times higher than the highest sophist's fee reliably recorded (five minas, Pl. *Apol.* 20b; cf. *Cra.* 384b).[89] It does seem possible, then, that Socrates' remark is meant to evoke a quite specific scenario in which this exaggerated fee is charged for a lesson in rhetoric. This could well have been in a comedy. A scene where a sophist took Hyperbolus in hand would have been comparable to those in *Clouds* where Socrates teaches Strepsiades, and we might glimpse here another battleground between Aristophanes and Eupolis. For if Eupolis was in the Socratic circle, Aristophanes clearly was not (despite the apparent evidence of Plato's *Symposium*; contrast *Apol.* 18a f., 19c). In chapter five I shall follow Willink[90] in suggesting that the un-Socratic aspects of the Socrates of *Clouds* have been appropriated from the on-stage caricature of a sophist, namely Prodicus. I suspect, then, that *Clouds* 876 is a cross-reference to a comedy, which gains its humorous *frisson* from the fact that Socrates inadvertently praises the sophist (Prodicus?) who taught Hyperbolus so well. In fact it is a Cratinus play, *Horai*, which has the closest obvious connection to Prodicus, who wrote a work of this title, which, as I shall argue later in detail, has strong links with *Clouds* (chapter six, pp. 173–5). It could be, then, that the humour of Socrates' remark is also linked to the fact that the scenario he recalls as a serious proof of the validity of sophistic teaching is from a comedy by Eupolis' arch-rival, Cratinus.

(iii) The reference to Hyperbolus at *Frogs* 570 σὺ δ' ἔμοιγ' ἐάνπερ ἐπιτύχῃς, Ὑπέρβολον 'And you call Hyperbolus for me, if you run into him' is spoken by Plathane, who is associated, by her name ('kneading-tray') and by the female innkeeper's comment at 550–1

---

[88] See Braun 2000, 193 for the argument that εἰσάγει does not necessarily mean 'bring on stage'.
[89] Sommerstein 1982 ad loc. See also Dover 1968 ad loc.   [90] Willink 1983.

about Heracles' having eaten up sixteen of their loaves, with bread. It is unlikely to be a coincidence that Hyperbolus' mother may have been associated with bread-selling in Eupolis' *Marikas* (fr. 209) and that in any case Hermippus' anti-Hyperbolean play *Artopolides* ('Female Bread-Sellers') apparently centred around this theme.[91] Moreover, the reference comes within what must be a parody of one of the 'hungry Heracles' scenes criticised at *Peace* 741 (and also by Cratin. fr. 346). The scholiasts on *Peace* 741 (see below, p. 204) tell us that the jibe is aimed at Eupolis or Cratinus, both of whom had apparently introduced such scenes (Eupolis probably to attack Cratinus). Given that *Frogs* contains, as I have shown, a large number of Eupolidean elements, it seems likely that Eupolis is the direct target of this misappropriation. Once more, then, the mention of Hyperbolus is bracketed within a meta-comic sequence relating to Eupolidean comedy, but most probably via Cratinean comedy.

CONCLUSION

If Aristophanes intended, then, on each occasion that Hyperbolus was mentioned to have the attack associated with Eupolis or Cratinus and their comedies, we must conjecture that both Eupolis and Cratinus had caricatured him earlier than the *Marikas* of 421. The formulation Εὔπολις... πρώτιστον ('Eupolis was the very first') at *Clouds* 553 does not disallow this. Hyperbolus was certainly already well enough known by 425 for his involvement in the law-courts on any reading of *Acharnians* 846–7. And Cratinus had mentioned Hyperbolus' early entry into public life (fr. 283) in *Horai*, a play which must, I think, belong before *Acharnians*, because of the verbal echoes already mentioned.[92]

In any case, he is mentioned in fr. 209 of *Pytine*, in a section where someone – possibly Comedy, more probably (given the marital difficulties involved) another poet – is giving advice on writing a comedy, almost certainly to the central comic poet character (on my interpretation, Aristophanes): Ὑπέρβολον δ' ἀποσβέσας ἐν τοῖς λύχνοισι γράψον ('Put Hyperbolus out and write him at the lamp-market'). The word γράψον ('write') is potentially ambiguous, since it might imply 'write his name and

---

[91] Storey 2003, 204–5. Was Plathane, then, Hyperbolus' mother?
[92] This motif was then possibly reused by Eupolis (no doubt with some satirical twist against Cratinus) in *Poleis*, fr. 252 (Lenaea 422 or 423?). 'Possibly', because the reference to Eupolis comes after a reference to *Wasps*, where mention of Hyperbolus does not involve Hyperbolus' arrival at the speaker's platform young, as it does in the case of the Cratinus fr.

associate it with the lamp-market' and thus refer merely to an invective attack rather than on-stage caricature. But the preceding fragment (208.1–2), which must belong in the same context, also uses this term: γράφ' αὐτὸν | ἐν ἐπεισοδίῳ. γελοῖος ἔσται Κλεισθένης κυβεύων ('Write him in the episode. Cleisthenes will raise a laugh dicing...'). This does not sound like the composition of an invective attack, but of an on-stage caricature, since it seems to be linked to a section of the play itself ('the episode'). Hence we should probably interpret the verb γράφω here as 'represent on stage'. Thus in 423, Hyperbolus could already be envisaged as a caricature target.

The argument that Eupolis had already in *Noumeniai* (425) portrayed Hyperbolus as a lamp-merchant – something which immediately set off a whole nexus of metacomic references in Aristophanic comedy (*Knights* 738–40, 1314–15; cf. *Peace* 690–2) – helps to substantiate another conjecture. In *Pytine*, I have argued, the comic poet character was not the author Cratinus, but his younger rival Aristophanes. Since the recipient of the advice of fr. 208–9 is probably the central comic poet figure, the reference to Hyperbolus in fr. 209 by a metaphor from oil-lamps (ἀποσβέσας 'extinguishing') and located in the lamp-market associates the speaker of the lines with these motifs. Since, as Pieters long ago conjectured, advice on writing comedy is most likely to have come from another comic poet, it looks as though it is Eupolis who appears to fit the bill. The joke is that the arch-enemy of Hyperbolus advises the faithful friend of Hyperbolus, the poet Aristophanes, on how to write an anti-Hyperbolus scene.

The named references to Hyperbolus, then, can all be explained as in some way connected to Eupolis or Cratinus, as attitudes typical of the individual satirised and speaking and as cross-references to earlier on-stage caricature attacks, and in two cases as paradoxical positives in the mouth of an enemy. Eupolis had been the first to take advantage of some quite specific (but unknown) circumstance to attack Hyperbolus on stage in the post-421 period, but, I have argued, Eupolis had probably already caricatured him as a lamp-maker and seller, and as a (successful) antagonist to Cleon for the *prostasia* of the *demos* in the lost *Noumeniai* of 425, the model for *Knights*. We do not know how many of these early plays there were or by whom, but we can conclude that Hyperbolus was not a negligible figure on the comic stage even before *Marikas*.

This brief investigation has produced a picture radically different from the traditional one which emerges from a reading of the plays *per se*. It shows the Peloponnesian War as a period in which comic poets attacked each other by on-stage caricature, making play in the process with political attitudes, alliances and hatreds. Aristophanes and Eupolis were at opposing ends of the Athenian democratic spectrum, the former at the radical and the latter at the conservative – one which might always threaten to become oligarchic in either more or less restrictive ways. Aristophanes' reaction to Eupolis' perversion of *Knights* in his *Marikas* (*Clouds* 551f.) is especially severe, saying it was done by a κακὸς κακῶς ('a vile fellow, vilely'), words which bespeak the level of enmity whose roots we have now uncovered.[93] Sandwiched uncomfortably between them was Cratinus, who had a predilection for Cleon, we can now suggest, basing this view upon his role as Demos in *Knights* (and possibly in Eupolis' lost *Noumeniai*) and as *Philo*cleon in *Wasps*, though he had come to this political accommodation after a period in which he had also attacked the leather-seller (possibly as Typhon in *Ploutoi*). This new-found affection for Cleon was not shared by either Aristophanes or Eupolis.

If one's first reaction is to regard the scenario as a bizarre fantasy, it is worth recalling here that precisely the same one also occurred to Plato when he was composing his legislation for invective comedy at *Laws* 936a:

οἷς δ' εἴρηται πρότερον ἐξουσίαν εἶναι περί του ποιεῖν, εἰς ἀλλήλους τούτοις ἄνευ θυμοῦ μὲν μετὰ παιδιᾶς ἐξέστω, σπουδῇ δὲ ἅμα καὶ θυμουμένοισιν μὴ ἐξέστω.

The persons to whom permission has already been granted by an earlier arrangement to compose personal satire shall be free to satirise each other dispassionately and in jest, but not in earnest or with angry feeling.

One might in fact be inclined to draw the inference from this passage that Plato was only reflecting what he knew to have occurred in reality, except that in real life the war between the poets had actually been conducted in complete earnest and with the bitterest of anger.[94]

---

[93] Cf. Demosthenes 21.204.
[94] Contrast Storey 2003, 300: 'The atmosphere is not antagonistic: competitive, yes, and even combative, but there is no need to see borrowing or imitation as necessarily hostile.'

PART II

The poets' war

The first part of this book has proposed a hypothesis about the way Old Comedy operated in the political arena. Essentially, this has involved so far following a number of inferences from the discovery that the *Clouds* parabasis was addressed to an audience of past Aristophanic sponsors, whose political and intellectual interests the poet both shared and served, within the tightly circumscribed goal of also achieving success in the comic competition. Without this success, it stands to reason, there could be no possibility of serving these private interests. And so, although there is now no doubt that the attacks on individuals such as Socrates and Cleon were serving a private agenda (*Clouds* 526, 554), the poet always presented his comedy as though it was designed impartially to teach the *demos*. It will be important at some stage to enquire into the way in which the *archon* chose plays, if only by looking at the pattern of production and success of the major playwrights whose political agendas we now have some grip upon, since in the circumstances now outlined, there is no way of claiming that the poets' political agendas would not be pretty generally known. Indeed, in the argument which precedes, it has become clear that plays could be made precisely out of the assumption of audience knowledge of those agendas (*Noumeniai, Knights, Wasps, Marikas*). Nonetheless, a consequence of the need to *appear* impartial is the way in which even the poet's true political allies might be lampooned, as we have seen in Hyperbolus' case. However, this compromise, no doubt adopted so as not to alienate important elements of the judging audience, did not at all affect the poet's ability to attack his true targets. As I have tried to demonstrate, in the first place these were *characters* in the comedy. In the second, the poet could always distance himself from responsibility for named invectives by placing them on the lips of those characters, or of the chorus (which, as we shall see, might itself have metacomic origins).

In this second part I shall attempt to demonstrate, in more detail and chronologically, how Aristophanes communicated his political agenda and managed the battle with his rivals over the period of the war. In this account I shall also be trying to incorporate as much as possible some indications, necessarily conjectural, given the state of the evidence, about what he was responding to and how his rivals responded to him. In the end, the hypothesis will stand or fall on its ability to shed new light on old problems, so it will be necessary to dig over much-ploughed soil in the course of this reinterpretation of the phenomenon.

CHAPTER 4

Acharnians: *Parabasis versus play*

We are now in a better position to deal with two serious difficulties related to the parabasis of *Acharnians*. Who is the poet represented? Is it Aristophanes or is it someone else, the same poet, perhaps, who had been the cover for *Banqueters* (*Clouds* 530–1)? And, whichever of these it is, how could the audience cope with the disjunction proposed by Bowie 1988 and supported by my analysis in chapter three above between the parabatic poet and the comic poet character, Dicaeopolis?

WHO IS THE POET OF THE *ACHARNIANS* PARABASIS?

The parabasis is spoken on behalf of the poet (*Acharnians* 628 ὁ διδάσκαλος ἡμῶν 'our *didaskalos*'). But which poet? Here we must consider briefly the problem about the relationship between the parabases of *Acharnians* and *Knights*, which arises because the role of διδάσκαλος is ascribed to the poet in *Acharnians* 628, while *Knights* 513f. clearly indicates that Aristophanes' debut as διδάσκαλος was at Lenaea 424, with *Knights*. Some scholars have tried to explain this problem by suggesting that *Knights* refers back to Aristophanes' practice of using a producer (in the case of *Acharnians* Callistratus).[1] Sommerstein's note on *Knights* 507 neatly illustrates the principal difficulty with this interpretation: '**producer:** as is usual (cf. *Ach.* 628, 633), 'producer' and 'poet' are interchangeable terms *except when the discussion is specifically about the practice of authors producing their own plays*' (my italics).[2] In other words, in order to make the argument that Callistratus is meant at *Acharnians* 628f., we must assume that it is the *context* of *Knights* 513f., and not its vocabulary, that alerts the audience to Aristophanes' meaning. Indeed, the original audience will not have needed to tackle the matter as we do, since they will have been *au fait* with theatrical events and the procedures for

[1] Sommerstein 1981 on *Knights* 513, MacDowell 1982, 24, 1995, 38–9. Callistratus as producer, Olson 2002, Hypothesis to *Ach.* line 32.
[2] Sommerstein 1981 *loc. cit.*

staging them. But it does seem strange – and potentially confusing – that exactly the same words should be used for what we would call the director and the dramatist.[3] That this is not the correct explanation can be argued on three further sets of grounds. First, Aristophanes continued to use 'directors' for later plays (e.g. Philonides for *Wasps*, Callistratus for *Birds* and *Lysistrata*),[4] there is no evidence that Callistratus was ever a ποιητής 'poet' in the attested sense of the word in literary and dramatic contexts,[5] and there was at least only a little later a perfectly serviceable word for 'director', ὑποδιδάσκαλος (Pl. *Ion* 536a), which distinguished that role from the composer's. Secondly, it cannot be demonstrated independently that the *didaskaliai* did *not* contain Aristophanes' name, and this suggests (though it cannot prove conclusively, since we do not know precisely how and when these records were compiled) that the audiences of *Daitales*, *Babylonians* and *Acharnians* will have known who *really* composed these plays, as well as who was supposed to have written them and who directed them.[6] Finally, *Wasps* 1022, the last line in a passage describing Aristophanes' early career, whose meaning has been the subject of recent scholarly contention, certainly claims *control* over the composition of the early 'secret' plays (which would, on MacDowell's interpretation, include *Daitales*, *Babylonians* and *Acharnians*): οὐκ ἀλλοτρίων ἀλλ' οἰκείων Μουσῶν στόμαθ' ἡνιοχήσας 'managing the reins not of someone else's but of his own Muses'.[7] The metaphor of driving a chariot applies equally to both limbs of the line and this fits perfectly with the notion that the poet was the writer of the early comedies, but that they appeared under the names of more experienced poetic colleagues (i.e. their 'Muses'). Likewise, the charioteers who drove at Olympia and other games were not the entrants in the contest and it was not their names that appeared on the victory roster, but those of

---

[3] Essentially MacDowell's argument 1982, 25 and 1995, 39, which relies, like Sommerstein's, entirely on explaining this context, and is thus circular. See Perusino 1982, 137–45 (following E. Hiller, *Philol. Anz.* 17 (1887), 362–4).
[4] *Wasps* Hypothesis I, *Birds* Hypothesis I and II, *Lysistrata* Hypothesis I.
[5] See *PCG* IV, where the testimonia are scholia on *Wasps* 1018a and a supplement to *IG* II[2] 2325.60 Κα[, which is now generally believed to hide the name of Cantharus.
[6] Note the wording in the Anon. *De Comoedia* (= Koster, *Protegomena* p. 9, III.38) ἐδίδαξε δὲ πρῶτος ἐπὶ ἄρχοντος Διοτίμου διὰ Καλλιστράτου 'he first produced in the archonship of Diotimos (427) through Callistratus' referring to *Banqueters* and Σ *Ach*. 378 τοὺς Βαβυλωνίους λέγει. τούτους γὰρ πρὸ τῶν Ἀχαρνέων Ἀριστοφάνης ἐδίδαξεν 'he means the *Babylonians*, because this was the play Aristophanes produced before the *Acharnians*'. In both places, it looks as though the *didaskaliai* have been consulted. See now Brockmann 2003, 344–6.
[7] MacDowell 1982, 24 n. 4, writes: 'οὐκ ἀλλοτρίων in *Wasps* 1022 is a negative phrase inserted to emphasise οἰκείων. It is not permissible to extract from it a positive statement that Aristophanes did, at an earlier date, control other men's muses; such a statement would, in fact, be incompatible with ἐπικουρῶν.' See also Totaro 1999, 205–7.

Acharnians: *parabasis versus play* 109

their chariot-team's rich and distinguished owner. As I have shown (p. 14), Aristophanes in fact claimed authorship of *Daitales* and tells us clearly that its first audience had known its true origin, even though the author had somehow transferred it to another poet (*Clouds* 528–33).

The upshot of this is that while MacDowell is surely correct to insist that there is a fundamental distinction between the voice of the *Knights* parabasis, where Aristophanes emerges from the shadows for his first production (*Knights* 513f.), and that of *Acharnians*, where the chorus' poet has already had long experience in charge (*Acharnians* 628–9), nonetheless the individual represented in the parabasis must have been regarded as the poet composer and not merely the director of the play. This tells against Callistratus, on grounds already stated above. However, this analysis tends to confirm that MacDowell's view of *Wasps* 1018f., the famous account of Aristophanes' career, is otherwise substantially sound. It is important to review the passage briefly, along with the diverse interpretations offered by MacDowell on one side and Halliwell and Mastromarco on the other.

> ἀδικεῖσθαι γάρ φησιν πρότερος πόλλ' αὐτοὺς εὖ πεποιηκώς
> τὰ μὲν οὐ φανερῶς ἀλλ' ἐπικουρῶν κρύβδην ἑτέροισι ποιηταῖς,
> μιμησάμενος τὴν Εὐρυκλέους μαντείαν καὶ διάνοιαν,
> εἰς ἀλλοτρίας γαστέρας ἐνδὺς κωμῳδικὰ πολλὰ χέασθαι,
> μετὰ τοῦτο δὲ καὶ φανερῶς ἤδη κινδυνεύων καθ' ἑαυτόν,
> οὐκ ἀλλοτρίων ἀλλ' οἰκείων Μουσῶν στόμαθ' ἡνιοχήσας.

He says that they have wronged him without justification, when he had done them many favours. At first not openly, but in secret, assisting to other poets, inveigling himself into the bellies of others, mimicking the prophetic method of Eurycles, he poured out a stream of satire; after that he did actually take a gamble on his own, openly, guiding the mouths of Muses that were his, not someone else's.

MacDowell interprets ἑτέροισι ποιηταῖς as Aristophanes' director(s) Callistratus (and Philonides?), κρύβδην as implying that the audience would have thought the plays in question to be by their directors, and the passage as a whole to be referring to first the plays *Banqueters*, *Babylonians* and *Acharnians* (1018–20), then those from *Knights* onwards (1021–22).[8] Mastromarco and Halliwell see ἑτέροισι ποιηταῖς as other comic poets, κρύβδην as indicating a period before Aristophanes' entry into the official competition, and so 1018–20 as a stage of apprenticeship prior to 427, and

---

[8] MacDowell's views were first articulated in his edition of *Wasps*, Oxford 1971 on 1018. For the reply, see Mastromarco 1979 and Halliwell 1980. MacDowell 1982 replied to Halliwell and Halliwell 1989 extrapolated from his 1980 article. For more recent assessments of the discussion, see Hubbard 1991, 227f., Totaro 1999, 202–7, Brockmann 2003, 240f.

1020–2 as the period between 427–425. This conjecture is necessitated, in their view, by the lack of evidence for Callistratus as a poet and the difficulty of showing that Aristophanes' name was not known to the audiences of his first three productions.[9] This is a fair criticism of MacDowell's position. However, it means only that he is wrong to assign *Acharnians* (and the other early plays) to *directors* rather than poets. The Mastromarco/Halliwell view of the sequence of Aristophanes' career is otherwise, in fact, difficult to sustain, for two reasons. First, there is no syntactical room to differentiate what is said in 1018 from what follows.: 'secretly helping' is expanded by 'through imitation of Eurycles' method': there is no chronological sequence here. Secondly, the correspondence between *Wasps* 1029f., where his first effort at διδάσκειν ('production') indicates an attack on Cleon (which must, therefore, be *Knights*, even though the imagery here portrays Cleon as Cerberus or Typhoeus, and not as a slave), the parabatic claim of *Knights* 513 that it was the first play for which he asked for a chorus in his own name (καθ' ἑαυτὸν) and the use of the term καθ' ἑαυτὸν in *Wasps* 1021 describing the second of the phases of the poet's career shows that 1020–2 refer to the period from *Knights* onwards. MacDowell, then, is correct both to separate the poetic voice of the *Acharnians* parabasis from that of the *Knights* and to see the career of Aristophanes falling into only two phases, a secret and an open, the second beginning with *Knights*.

Before *Knights*, then, Aristophanes was in the background, actually writing plays which were produced in the names of other poets. The image of Eurycles (*Wasps* 1019–20) makes it clear that Aristophanes was responsible for the material being uttered, but using another body and voice to project it (Plut. *Mor*. 414e).[10] There is a hint, though, because Eurycles' presence could be detected only by the contrast between what he says and what the real individual would have said (cf. Pl. *Sophist* 252c), that the subterfuge will have been palpable – which also tends to confirm Halliwell, Mastromarco and Brockmann's view of public knowledge of Aristophanes' role well ahead of *Knights*.[11] But even if that were not the case, *Wasps* 1017 clearly

[9] See now also Brockmann 2003, 344–6. The argument of Perusino 1982 is pertinent here. If the terms ποιητής and διδάσκαλος are interchangeable, then neither is what the person 'through' (διά) whom a poet produced was called.
[10] Plut. *Mor*. 414e: εὔηθες γάρ ἐστι τὸ οἴεσθαι τὸν θεόν ὥσπερ τοὺς ἐγγαστριμύθους Εὐρυκλέας ἐνδυόμενον εἰς τὰ σώματα τῶν προφητῶν ὑποφθέγγεσθαι τοῖς ἐκείνων στόμασι καὶ φωναῖς χρώμενον ὀργάνοις 'It is simple-minded to think that the god enters the bodies of prophets and surreptitiously speaks using their mouths and their voices as his tools, like the belly-speaking Eurycleses.' This does not tell us, however, how you could tell that it was *Eurycles* who was speaking, and not the person whose voice he was appropriating.
[11] Pl. *Soph*. 252c gives clear evidence that Eurycles said noticeably different things from those the person affected would normally say: οἴκοθεν τὸν πολέμιον καὶ ἐναντιωσόμενον ἔχοντες ἐντός

Acharnians: parabasis versus play

implies that the festival audience of Lenaea 422 have by now have access to this information, otherwise they could not be expected to accept reproof for having betrayed him on the grounds mentioned (πόλλ' αὐτοὺς εὖ πεποιηκώς 'when he had done them a lot of favours'). Moreover, as I have already argued above, at least the original sponsoring audience of *Banqueters* are assumed to have known this from the start: otherwise the narrative line at *Clouds* 529–31, namely that *Banqueters* was recommended by certain men, Aristophanes exposed the baby play, and another poet pretended it was his, makes little sense. In addition, the mention of 'the bald man' in Eupolis' *Chrysoun Genos* (probably in 426) is, as I have argued above, a clear indication that the subterfuge was known publicly and seen through.

AEGINA AND CHARGES OF *XENIA* AGAINST COMIC POETS

MacDowell is also correct, then, to claim that it was not Aristophanes that had a connection with Aegina, but the poet who was notionally its *didaskalos*.[12] This appears to be confirmed by a review of the ancient evidence for Aristophanes' background. The full details of his Athenian identity seem to have been known to the ancient commentators. The *Life* for example reports *PCG* T1.1–2: πατρὸς μὲν ἦν Φιλίππου, τὸ δὲ γένος Ἀθηναῖος, τῶν δήμων Κυδαθηναιεύς, Πανδιονίδος φυλῆς 'His father was Philippos, he was Athenian born, his deme was Kydathenaion and his tribe Pandionis', although an inscription (*IG* XIV 1140) reports his father as Philippides. His sons Philippus, Nicostratus and Araros were also, apparently, Athenian citizens (Suda α 3737, ψ 308, *Life* 1.55–6), which should have guaranteed that their father and mother were native-born Athenians also. Yet the ancient scholars had also to deal with another uncomfortable and contradictory 'fact', that Aristophanes had been indicted for ξενία 'being a foreigner falsely claiming the rights of an Athenian citizen' by Cleon three times (*Life* 19; cf. Σ *Ach.* 378). This seems to have led to the conjecture

---

ὑποφθεγγόμενον ὥσπερ τὸν ἄτοπον Εὐρυκλέα περιφέροντες πορεύονται 'They go about always with an enemy inside their house speaking surreptitiously to oppose them, as though they were carrying the amazing Eurycles around with them.' This is partly because the adjective ἄτοπον is used of Eurycles, but more importantly because the example of Eurycles comes in a discussion of *self-refutation*. People who deny predication must use predicates in their arguments and so they risk being refuted out of their own mouths Thus it is the fact that a person is refuted out of his own mouth that marks the presence of Eurycles. In Sidwell 1993, I explained this allusion differently, arguing that Aristophanes' role was parodic and satirical of rival poets. I now withdraw this view, though there is still room in metacomedy for a sort of ventriloquial satire, as *Ach.* 499f. shows, on the interpretation offered in chapter three above.

[12] MacDowell 1982, though it will not have been Callistratus, as I have argued above, unless Κα[in *IG* II² 2325.60 were to turn out to be Κα[λλίστρατος, despite the lack of evidence for his being a poet.

that he was made a citizen.[13] In turn, this conjecture seems to have led to attempts to identify his true place of origin. Hence, we read that he was from Lindos, Aegina, Camirus on Rhodes, or even from Naucratis (*Life* 21–2; Koster, *Prolegomena* p. 141, xxxa.1; Athenaeus 6. 229). Kassel–Austin rightly dismiss the Naucratis connection as 'deriving from a stupid explanation of *Clouds* 272, where the Nile is mentioned' (Aristophanes *PCG* T12). Theogenes (Jacoby 300 fr. 2) is reported by the scholium on Plato, *Apology* 19c to have said in his work *On Aegina* that Aristophanes was a cleruch on the island. But since another ancient scholar (Σ *Ach.* 654b) tells us equally that οὐδεὶς ἱστόρηκεν ὡς ἐν Αἰγίνῃ κέκτηταί τι Ἀριστοφάνης ('No one has recorded that Aristophanes held property on Aegina'), it looks as though Theogenes was relying, like everyone else, on the mention of Aegina in *Acharnians*.

It seems equally likely that it was something else from Aristophanes' plays which led ancient scholars to believe that the poet had faced several charges of *xenia* at Cleon's hands. It can only have been a passage such as *Acharnians* 377f., where the character speaks unmistakably as though he is a/the poet. It is possible that it was in the *Babylonians* that such a speech was to be found, since Σ *Ach.* 378 is speaking precisely about that play when it mentions καὶ ξενίας δὲ αὐτὸν ἐγράψατο καὶ εἰς ἀγῶνα ἐνέβαλεν ('and [Cleon] also indicted him for *xenia* and brought him to trial') and that the character who spoke about his indictment, Dionysus (fr. 75), did represent a comic poet, but that it was Cratinus and not Aristophanes.

There is some indirect evidence which connects Cratinus with a charge of *xenia*. The one made against the poet figure in *Babylonians* (Σ *Acharnians* 378), whom I identified with Cratinus in the previous chapter, will correspond in terms of the person attacked to the indictment for *xenia* found at *Wasps* 715–21, which is voiced, if the identification is correct, by an on-stage caricature of Eupolis to the on-stage caricature of Cratinus. Right at the end of his refutation of Philocleon's claims for the comforts and power of the juror's lot, Bdelycleon says of the *rhetores*:

ἀλλ' ὁπόταν μὲν δείσωσ' αὐτοί, τὴν Εὔβοιαν διδόασιν
ὑμῖν καὶ σῖτον ὑφίστανται κατὰ πεντήκοντα μεδίμνους
ποριεῖν· ἔδοσαν δ' οὐπώποτέ σοι· πλὴν πρώην πέντε μεδίμνους,
καὶ ταῦτα μόλις ξενίας φεύγων, ἔλαβες κατὰ χοίνικα κριθῶν.
ὧν οὕνεκ' ἐγώ σ' ἀπέκλῃον ἀεὶ
βόσκειν ἐθέλων καὶ μὴ τούτους
ἐγχάσκειν σοι στομφάζοντας·

---

[13] Compare Koster, *Prolegomena* p. 141, xxxa.2 ἐπολιτογραφήθη 'was admitted to citizenship' with *Life* 27 οὕτω φανερὸς κατασταθεὶς πολίτης 'thus (i.e. as a result of being acquitted in three separate trials on this charge by Cleon) clearly established as a citizen'.

But when the politicians themselves are scared, they start to hold out Euboea to you and promise to provide corn in fifty-bushel handouts. They've never given it to you, though. Except the other day you got *choinix*-sized instalments of barley, and at that after only just being acquitted on a charge of *xenia*. This is the reason *I* kept locking you up all the time. I was willing to give you your victuals and I didn't want these fellows ranting and making fun of you.

However, it may not refer precisely to the same incident, since Cleon is not mentioned.

But there is also some evidence which connects Eupolis with a charge of *xenia*. Its interpretation is not straightforward, for the same reason as in the case of the evidence connecting Aristophanes with the same sort of indictment: two crucial layers – caricature and metacomedy – lie between it and our access to the original meaning. A passage of Apsines (=*PCG* Eupolis, *Autolycus* Tiii) tells us that Eupolis was said to have been accused of *xenia* and sold into slavery when found guilty: Εὔπολις ἁλοὺς ξενίας δημοσίᾳ ἐπράθη. πριάμενος αὐτὸν ὁ Λύκων ἐγχειρίζει τὸν παῖδα ('Eupolis was convicted of *xenia* and sold publicly. Lycon bought him and put him in charge of his son.') I suggest, following Storey,[14] that this anecdote was an extrapolation of a passage in Eupolis' *Autolycus* in which a character was manifestly speaking *qua* comic poet (and was thus, as in the *Acharnians* passage, automatically identified by ancient readers with the author). Storey has also recently suggested that an anecdote in Aelian (*Nature of Animals* 10.41) concerning Eupolis (represented as a slave), his fellow-slave Ephialtes and a dog named Augeas, who belonged to Eupolis and prevented Ephialtes from stealing some of his master's plays, may have been derived from *Autolycus* too.[15] The passage reads as follows:

Εὐπόλιδι τῷ τῆς κωμῳδίας ποιητῇ δίδωσι δῶρον Αὐγέας ὁ Ἐλευσίνιος σκύλακα ἰδεῖν ὡραῖον, Μολοττὸν τὸ γένος, καὶ καλεῖ τοῦτον ὁ Εὔπολις ὁμωνύμως τῷ δωρησαμένῳ αὐτόν. κολακευθεὶς οὖν ταῖς τροφαῖς, καὶ ἐκ τῆς συνηθείας ὑπαχθεὶς τῆς μακροτέρας, ἐφίλει τὸν δεσπότην ὁ Αὐγέας ὁ κύων. καί ποτε ὁμόδουλος αὐτῷ νεανίας, ὄνομα Ἐφιάλτης, ὑφαιρεῖται δράματά τινα τοῦ Εὐπόλιδος· ἀ᾽ οὐκ ἔλαθε κλέπτων, ἀλλὰ εἶδεν αὐτὸν ὁ κύων, καὶ ἐμπεσὼν ἀφειδέστατα δάκνων ἀπέκτεινεν. χρόνῳ δὲ ὕστερον ἐν Αἰγίνῃ τὸν βίον ὁ Εὔπολις κατέστρεψε, καὶ ἐτάφη ἐνταῦθα· ὁ δὲ κύων ὠρυόμενός τε καὶ θρηνῶν τὸν τῶν κυνῶν θρῆνον, εἶτα μέντοι λύπῃ καὶ λιμῷ ἑαυτὸν ἐκτήξας ἀπέθανεν ἐπὶ τῷ τροφεῖ καὶ δεσπότῃ, μισήσας τὸν βίον ὁ κύων. καὶ ὅ γε τόπος καλεῖται μνήμῃ τοῦ τότε πάθους Κυνὸς Θρῆνος.

Augeas of Eleusis gave as a gift to Eupolis the comic poet a nice-looking puppy, of the Molossian breed, and Eupolis called it by the same name as the man who had

---

[14] Storey 2003, 87.   [15] Storey 2003, 57. Kyriakìdi 2007, 137–49 is sceptical.

given him. Spoilt by good feeding and brought to heel by their long-established cohabitation, the dog Augeas began to grow fond of its master. Now a young man named Ephialtes, who was a fellow-slave of Eupolis', at some point stole some of his plays. But the theft was detected, because the dog saw him, attacked, and gave him such a bite that he killed him. Later on, Eupolis completed his life on Aegina and was buried there. But the dog howled and mourned the doggy lament. Then, however, it wasted away of grief and hunger over the grave of the master who had cared for it, conceiving a hatred for life. And actually, the place is still called 'Doggy Lament' in remembrance of its suffering.

If we accept that *Autolycus* had a comic poet as a central character, Storey may well be correct to locate the material concerning Ephialtes and the dog Augeas in that play. Storey's imaginative take on the plot is that Ephialtes represented Aristophanes (an excellent cover for a radical democrat), and the other slave the poet himself. It may well be significant that Apsines clearly indicates that Ephialtes was a young man (νεανίας), which would suit Aristophanes.

However, the terms of this discussion oblige us to exclude Storey's idea that Eupolis represented himself negatively either in *Autolycus* or in any other comedy and this forces us to drive a wedge between the scholiast's interpretation of the *xenia* episode and Eupolis: if it was (as must have seemed obvious) a comic poet who was arraigned, then it must have been a *rival* (as with the figure in *Babylonians*). The way Apsines expresses the relationship between the two characters in the anecdote, ὁμόδουλος αὐτῷ νεανίας ('a young fellow-slave of his') could be taken to imply that there was in fact an age difference between them, which with the exclusion of Eupolis (who in any event would not have wished to perpetuate Aristophanes' and Cratinus' vision of himself) probably pushes us towards an older comic poet. Ephialtes turns up again in the only testimonium to Eupolis' *Hybristodikai*: τοὺς δ' Ὑβριστοδίκας Εὐπόλιδος πρὸς τῇ Ἐφιάλτου (κεφαλῇ εὑρεθῆναί φασι)' 'They say Eupolis' *Hybristodikai* was found under Ephialtes' pillow.' Doubts have been cast upon the authenticity of this play, of which no fragments survive and Storey suggests that it may have been an alternative title for another play (possibly *Chrysoun Genos*).[16] I suspect, however, that this anecdote was also excerpted from one of the two versions of the comedy in which Ephialtes the slave stole comedies from the comic poet character. Hence, the *Hybristodikai* may have been a satirical name ('abusers in the court', as Storey translates) for a comedy by

---

[16] Kaibel, 1907, 1231.12. Storey 2003, 262.

whoever the other comic poet target of Eupolis' comedy was.[17] If Storey is right, as seems reasonable, to identify Ephialtes as Aristophanes, then the play found under his pillow, stolen from the other poet, will have had a legal theme which Aristophanes might have been generally thought to have plagiarised from another poet. But since there were two versions of *Autolycus*, it is not quite clear to which this belongs (see further chapter 6, pp. 218–20).

The Aelian anecdote also contains puzzling information about Eupolis' death and burial on Aegina, which I have touched on in chapter two above. One might suppose that this could not possibly belong to the plot of *Autolycus*, on the grounds that not even the crassest ancient scholiast could have identified Eupolis as both the author and central character of a play in which his own death was described. However, although there are two realistic accounts of Eupolis' death and burial, one where he dies at sea (Suda ε 3657), one where he is buried in Sicyon (Pausanias 2.7.3), there is a third, according to which he was drowned by Alcibiades on the way to Sicily (e.g. Platonius 1.18–19). This had circulated widely in antiquity, but had already then been shown to be false (Eratosthenes in Cicero *ad Atticum* 6.1.18).[18] It seems quite possible that this information had, like the *xenia* material, also been drawn from comedy. There is, however, a clear temporal distance between the play and the drowning and this means that the drowning story, if from comedy, was not from *Baptai*, but from a *later* play (see further chapter six for the implications of this).[19] In that case, since the tale of the dog and the death of the poet in this anecdote are integrally connected, we should probably infer that the play (*Autolycus*?) did include the death of the comic poet on Aegina. There is a good parallel for reference (comic and probably false) to the death of a rival at *Peace* 700–3, where Cratinus' demise is described. I propose, then, that Aelian's material derived ultimately from a play (probably Eupolis' *Autolycus*) in which the comic poet character who owned the dog Augeas was said to have died on the island of Aegina. The play, though, must also have contained an account – or a dramatisation – of the death of Ephialtes, if the anecdote does come lock stock and barrel from *Autolycus*. Like the association between Cratinus and wine-production in *Peace* (700f.), the comic poet's death on Aegina

---

[17] Storey 2003, 262. An alternative translation is 'Vigilantes' (*id.* 261). Storey thus suggests it refers either to those who by-pass the courts altogether, or to those who employ violent tactics in courts, or to the *sykophantai* (id. 262). It is possible that the joke refers to *Babylonians*, which, as I have already argued in chapter two, may have had a trial scene and showed Cleon using violent and abusive methods in the *boule*. For a different suggestion, see chapter six below.

[18] See Storey 2003, 379–81 for the evidence in full, 56–9 and 101–3 for discussion.

[19] Cf. Storey 1990, 5.

will have been based on some perceived connection. It is the only evidence we have outside *Acharnians* for a comic poet's link with Aegina. It is very likely, then, that the referent was the (older?) poet who had fronted for Aristophanes in *Acharnians*. The comedy is made, paradoxically from our viewpoint, from the notion that it was *Aristophanes* who had stolen *this* poet's comedies. One can see how this might have been amusing at the time when it was being widely rumoured in public that Aristophanes ('the bald guy') was the author of the Aeginetan poet's plays. Since the island had not been fully Athenian until soon after 431 (Thucydides 2.27), the comic charge could then be made that the 'Aeginetan' poet was a *xenos*, hence the charge made within the play.

There are signs in one extended Eupolis fragment (392, *loc. incert.*) of a battle with 'foreign poets', which has been read in the context of a fight between Eupolis and Aristophanes in the light of (a) public knowledge of his association with Aegina (b) comic misinterpretation of that association as evidence of being non-Athenian. It reads:

ὅ τι μαθόντες τοὺς ξένους μὲν λέγετε ποιητὰς σοφούς·
ἢν δέ τις τῶν ἐνθάδ' αὐτοῦ, μηδὲ ἓν χεῖρον φρονῶν,
ἐπιτίθηται τῇ ποιήσει, πάνυ δοκεῖ κακῶς φρονεῖν,
μαίνεταί τε καὶ παραρρεῖ τῶν φρενῶν τῷ σῷ λόγῳ.
ἀλλ' ἐμοὶ πείθεσθε, πάντως μεταβαλόντες τοὺς τρόπους,
μὴ φθονεῖθ' ὅταν τις ἡμῶν μουσικῇ χαίρῃ νέων.

Why do you call foreign poets wise, but if someone from here puts his mind to poetry, with no wit worse intellectual capacities, you really think he is a terrible thinker, mad and out of his mind, in your opinion? But take my advice, alter your ways completely, and don't show your annoyance when one of us enjoys the artistry of the young (or 'when one of us youngsters enjoys... *mousike*' Storey).

On Storey's interpretation, the fragment might be from an *agon* or an *epirrhema*, and possibly belongs within the metatheatrical context of *Autolycus*. If it is from the *agon* of *Autolycus*, it is a chorus speech attacking a position taken up in defence of the Aeginetan poet, possibly by Ephialtes/Aristophanes (note the singular possessive σῷ at line 4). If it is from a parabatic *epirrhema*, then the chorus are directly addressing an audience which has voted the prize to the Aeginetan. This interpretation, however, since it involves envisaging a moment when the issue of Aristophanes' relationship with his older cover from Aegina was current, has probable consequences for the dating of *Autolycus I*, which I shall deal with in chapter six, p. 220.

THE COMIC POET CHARACTER, DICAEOPOLIS AND THE AEGINETAN POET OF THE PARABASIS

I now turn to the problem that exercised Parker in her response to Bowie's identification of Eupolis as the poet behind Dicaeopolis, namely the similarity of the language and centrality of Cleon between 377–80 and 501–3 on the one hand (in the speeches of 'Dicaeopolis') and 630–1, 645 and 659–62 in the parabasis on the other.[20] Let us re-examine the relevant passages, in the light of the third chapter's argument about the centrality of on-stage caricature in disguise to Old Comedy and the location of the 'poets' war' in a real political contest.

αὐτός τ' ἐμαυτὸν ὑπὸ Κλέωνος ἅπαθον   377–80
ἐπίσταμαι διὰ τὴν πέρυσι κωμῳδίαν.
εἰσελκύσας γάρ μ' ἐς τὸ βουλευτήριον
διέβαλλε καὶ ψευδῆ κατεγλώττιζέ μου

What I myself suffered at Cleon's hands I know because of last year's comedy. He dragged me into the council-chamber and began slandering me and glibly lying about me...

ἐγὼ δὲ λέξω δεινὰ μέν δίκαια δέ.   501–3
οὐ γάρ με νῦν γε διαβαλεῖ Κλέων ὅτι
ξένων παρόντων τὴν πόλιν κακῶς λέγω

I shall be saying some things that are terrible, but right. For at least now Cleon will not be casting the slander that I insult the city while foreigners are present...

διαβαλλόμενος δ' ὑπὸ τῶν ἐχθρῶν ἐν Ἀθηναίοις ταχυβούλοις   630–1
ὡς κωμῳδεῖ τὴν πόλιν ἡμῶν καὶ τὸν δῆμον καθυβρίζει

Because he is being slandered by his enemies before the Athenians who make their minds up quickly on the charge that he satirises our city and insults the *demos*...

ὅστις παρεκινδύνευσ' εἰπεῖν ἐν Ἀθηναίοις τὰ δίκαια   645
who took the risk of saying what was right before the Athenians...

πρὸς ταῦτα Κλέων καὶ παλαμάσθω   659–62
καὶ πᾶν ἐπ' ἐμοὶ τεκταινέσθω.
τὸ γὰρ εὖ μετ' ἐμοῦ καὶ τὸ δίκαιον
ξύμμαχον ἔσται, κοὔ μή ποθ' ἁλῶ
περὶ τὴν πόλιν ὢν ὥσπερ ἐκεῖνος
δειλὸς καὶ λακαταπύγων.

In the face of this let Cleon make cunning plots and cobble all he can together against me. For the good and right will be in alliance with me and I shall never be

---
[20] Parker 1991, 206–7.

found guilty, as he has been, of being a coward and a truly buggerable one at that in matters relating to the city.

Parker puts her conclusion strongly: 'it is not merely implausible that an audience should be expected to take the first two passages as referring to one person and the second three to another: the idea destroys the coherence of the play'.[21] The case is very much overstated, as we can now see from the fact that the audience will have been able to see what was going on visually and will also have been *au fait* with the political stance of the comic poet represented as Dicaeopolis and of the Aeginetan poet. But evidence can be brought to bear to support a version of Bowie's original contention that both Eupolis and Aristophanes (and thus also the Aeginetan poet whose voice this parabasis represents) were opponents of Cleon[22] and that the parabatic voice is distinct from that of the character Dicaeopolis. I will deal with the latter point first.

There is one crucial basis for differentiating the claims to speak δίκαια 'just things' within the play (501) and within the parabasis (645). In Dicaeopolis' speech, this claim is followed by the argument that it was not the Spartans, but Pericles and his private interests, that were responsible for the war (509f.), which Dicaeopolis has now brought to an end *for himself and his family alone* (*Acharnians* 131–2). By contrast, the statements on behalf of – and then by (659f.) – the parabatic poet are embedded in a comic discourse which, albeit humorously, *supports* the continuation of the war. Not only is the poet said by the Persian King to be an asset in the war to the side he most abuses (649–51), but the poet advises the Athenian audience *not* to make peace, though the Spartans are asking for it, because this will mean, on the terms offered, losing Aegina (the poet's home) and thus the poet to the enemy (655). What the comic poet *character* Dicaeopolis thinks is just, then, is exactly the opposite of what the Aeginetan poet represented in the parabasis considers just. The audience, who unlike us had the advantage of knowing the plays alluded to at 633f. and from them (and from general knowledge of the political landscape), presumably, the Aeginetan poet's posture on various issues, are very unlikely to have seen anything other in the repetition of the justice theme than a desire to contrast the comic poet character's (Dicaeopolis/Eupolis') claims with those of the Aeginetan poet, given that the idea that the poet 'teaches' was a topos general to comic poetry (cf. Cratinus, *Dionysoi* fr. 52 νικῶ μὲν ὁ τῇδε πόλει λέγων τὸ λῷστον 'May the person win who says what is best for this city'). Since Dicaeopolis' private peace is also against the will not only

---

[21] Parker 1991, 203.   [22] Bowie 1988, 184.

of the *demos* of the play (37f.), but also of the actual *demos* in 425, one might conclude that the poet-character's initial position is being none-too-subtly undermined here.

The similarity of language, then, must be addressed within the disjunction between a poet who supports the continuation of the war and a comic poet character who is being satirised for wishing to end it. The remaining congruences, then, involve two further items, the verb διαβάλλειν ('to slander'), and the accusation that the poet mistreats the city.

In the case of the first word, there is evidence to suggest that it was widely used by Cleon's opponents to characterise his political style. Diodotus, in his reply to Cleon's speech in favour of carrying out the death sentence on the Mytilineans (Thuc. 3.42), is made to attack a certain type of *rhetor* as follows:

διαφέρει δ' αὐτῷ, εἰ βουλόμενός τι αἰσχρὸν πεῖσαι εὖ μὲν εἰπεῖν οὐκ ἂν ἡγεῖται περὶ τοῦ μὴ καλοῦ δυνάσθαι, εὖ δὲ *διαβαλὼν* ἐκπλῆξαι ἂν τούς τε ἀντεροῦντας καὶ τοὺς ἀκουσομένους. χαλεπώτατοι δὲ καὶ οἱ ἐπὶ χρήμασι προκατηγοροῦντες ἐπίδειξίν τινα.

Self-interested, if, wishing to put through a discreditable measure, he realises that while he cannot speak well in a bad cause, he can at least *slander* well and thus intimidate both his opponents and his hearers. Most dangerous of all, however, are precisely those who charge a speaker beforehand with being bribed to make a display of rhetoric. (Tr. C.F. Smith.)

Since Cleon is the speaker Diodotus is replying to, it seems reasonable to suggest that this is a generalised portrait of Cleon's political style. That would mean that any adversary might use the term διαβάλλειν of his political techniques, as Bdelycleon/Eupolis does at *Wasps* 950. We would still have to show that both Eupolis and Aristophanes (or the front for him at this time) opposed Cleon (and I shall come back to this point). But the audience would not respond as Parker suggests to the use of similar vocabulary, both because it was in the current discourse of the *polis*, and because they will have understood what the poet had been doing before the parabasis (putting a rival on stage, playing another rival), and in particular who his main on stage target was.

The accusation that the poet mistreats the city may be the same in both cases (even though the words used are not), but the person who delivers the attack at 502 is Cleon in person, while the assailants are plural at 630 (ὑπὸ τῶν ἐχθρῶν), even if Cleon is somehow involved in the *machinations* and *planning* (659f.). It is, thus, not necessarily the case, even if the word διαβάλλειν was regularly used of Cleon in the political discourse of the *polis*, that lines 630–1 refer to an attack by Cleon himself. The words ὑπὸ τῶν ἐχθρῶν 'by my enemies' seem in fact a little vague if they refer specifically to Cleon and the *pnigos* makes it clear that the poet could have come out and said this, had it been the point. The chorus also mention, however, (630) the *place* where this slander has been uttered ἐν Ἀθηναίοις ταχυβούλοις 'among the Athenians who make quick decisions', and this can be identified from the parallel statement (632), πρὸς Ἀθηναίους μεταβούλους 'to the Athenians who change their decisions quickly', as the theatre of Dionysus (cf. 645, which must also refer to this venue). The attack on the poet, then, which the chorus is now answering on his behalf was made *in a comedy* (or in more than one, if the plural is a real one), in the very arena where *Acharnians* is now being played, by rival *poets*. Of course, the comic poet of 497f. also purports to speak before the Athenians in a comedy and his insults against the city (according to Cleon, 502–3) were, naturally, made in comedy. But if, as I have suggested in chapter two and the analysis of the *Clouds* parabasis in chapter one confirms, there was a genuine political battle between the comic poets, then this is exactly what we would expect. The scene of Cleon in the *boule* with 'Dicaeopolis' (378f.) may also, I have argued (with Riu: chapter three, p. 79), have been from a comedy. This scene and whatever is referred to at 631 are not from the same play, however, because, as I have pointed out above, the parabasis seems to suggest only that Cleon has had a background role in the plan, not that he actually delivered the attack. It stands to reason – and here Bowie was also correct – that more than one comic poet may have been an adversary of Cleon, just as more than one was an adversary of Hyperbolus (where we can name Eupolis and Hermippus because of Aristophanes' own statements at *Clouds* 553 and 557, and Plato from other evidence, the fragments of his *Hyperbolus*). Thus there is every reason why accusations against two different comic poet enemies which were made by or at the behest of Cleon might look similar.

We may, I think, even be seeing in the anecdote about the Spartan embassy to the Great King a small slice of one of the plays that had attacked the poet of *Acharnians* on Cleon's behalf. It is notable that it is in fact for insulting the *demos* (the very accusation made against the poet by his enemies in the comic theatre 631) that the Persian King praises him (649). Why should he have specific information about an Athenian comic poet, when literary Persians are usually ignorant about Greek affairs (see especially the representation of the Persian Queen in Aeschylus' *Persians*)? What the poet may be doing here is turning a comic motif designed to blacken his character to his advantage. Persians, like other 'orientals' are likely to interpret Greek norms in an unusual way. So the insult against the *demos* that for free Athenians is deleterious (and banned, according to [Xenophon] *Ath. Pol.* 2.18) is for the Persian King a galvanising force which the Spartans would do well to obtain, if they wish to win the war. Paradoxically, of course, they will have to *end* the war to gain the means of their victory in it. This may have been part of the original as well, since there is no external evidence for Spartan peace offers between 430 (Thuc. 2.59.2; 2.65.2) and 424 (Thuc. 4.41.3–4), and it would have been a good hit at the Aeginetan poet of *Acharnians* – whose support for war and antagonism towards the Spartans was presumably known – to make him both the cause of the peace and to hand him over to the Spartans to boot. This scenario, then, the Aeginetan poet of the parabasis turns round, by pretending that the Spartan offer is real and then urging the Athenians to reject it (652–5).

As I have already argued, nothing forbids the notion that both Eupolis and Aristophanes (and his early Aeginetan cover) were opponents of Cleon. It appears, however, as we have seen, that there is also evidence to support the contention that they were nonetheless also enemies of each other. On the first point, the closeness of *Knights* to Eupolis is claimed both by Eupolis himself at *Baptai* fr. 89 and by Cratinus at fr. 213 of *Pytine*. It is clear that one aspect of that closeness, given the play is characterised by Aristophanes at *Clouds* 449–50, *Wasps* 1037f. and *Peace* 752f. as an attack upon Cleon, may have been enmity towards Cleon (Eupolis mentions Cleon at *Chrysoun Genos* fr. 316.1 ὦ καλλίστη πόλι πασῶν ὅσας Κλέων ἐφορᾷ 'O most beautiful of all the cities Cleon watches over' and we find an exactly parallel claim at *Knights* 75: ἐφορᾷ γὰρ αὐτὸς πάντ' 'For he [Cleon] watches over everything'.) And we can now add the evidence of *Wasps*: for if Bdelycleon is in fact representing Eupolis (as I argued in chapter three), then he can only do so because he is *famous* for his hatred towards Cleon. On the second issue, I have already argued above that politically motivated parody and not collaboration is the best explanation of the relationships between the two poets over *Knights*. And Eupolis (as I have also argued above) may already have attacked Aristophanes in his own *Chrysoun Genos* (fr. 298.5), produced, if Storey's new dating is correct, in 426.[23] Moreover, if Eupolis is the butt of satire under the guise of Bdelycleon in *Wasps*, as I have argued in chapter three, then this of itself shows not only that Eupolis was well known for his hatred of Cleon, but that he was an enemy of Aristophanes.

---

[23] Storey 2003, 267.

If, then, Aristophanes and Eupolis were both inimical to Cleon, but opposed to each other, their attacks on Cleon will have had different motivations. Since Eupolis is being satirised under the guise 'Dicaeopolis', and the play's central idea is the notion of making peace with Sparta even against the wishes of the *demos*, it can be inferred that the poet attacked Cleon because Cleon was a supporter of the war and could be represented as having actively prevented the acceptance by the Athenians of peace-terms (cf. *Knights* 1392–3). On the other hand, the Aeginetan poet of *Acharnians* was, as the parabasis shows, opposed to making peace with Sparta (*Acharnians* 655). The enmity between himself and Cleon was, therefore, based on different grounds from that between Eupolis and Cleon. It is possible to see what these were from the *pnigos* (659f.). There Cleon is labelled δειλὸς καὶ λακαταπύγων 'a coward and a pathic'. Olson's note brings out the significance of δειλὸς clearly: 'i.e. the sort of man who avoids military service if possible... and then, if forced to participate, runs away from battle... Perhaps an allusion to the fact that Kleon, despite his political prominence, had at this point never served as a general.'[24] For a supporter of the war, a hatred of Cleon could certainly have been rhetorically focused upon his undistinguished military record. Thucydides perhaps hints at a public belief that Cleon avoided military action in his description of the assembly-meeting where Nicias offers to relinquish his command at Pylos in favour of Cleon (Thucydides 4.28). The reactions of Cleon (reluctance, Thuc. 4.28.2) and the Athenian assembly (vocal encouragement to accept, 4.28.3) certainly fit this reading. It is worth noting, however, that a charge for evasion of military service looks more like an expression of political distaste than the true basis for attacking Cleon. That might have lain rather in the locus of his support – the old countryman type satirised as the chorus of *Wasps*, perhaps (*Wasps* 230f.)[25] – or his antagonism towards intellectuals (Thuc. 3.37.3–5; cf. *Knights* 986 and 191–3 for Cleon's lack of education).

Parker's analysis of the links between play and parabasis, then, is not convincing. We can see a clear distinction between the satirical treatment of the central character, Dicaeopolis/ Cratinus/ Eupolis, and the chorus' defence of the Aeginetan poet that revolves around completely opposed attitudes to the war and within this the outlines of a dispute between comic poets that also involves politicians.

---

[24] Olson 2003 on 659–64. Cf. his note on 79 for the implications of λακαταπύγων.
[25] Note that the two demes mentioned in this passage, Konthyleus (233) and Phlya (234), are both rural.

CLEON'S ATTACKS ON THE COMIC POET CHARACTER

The logic of the argument that in *Acharnians* the conflict between the character poet (377f., 496f.) and Cleon is completely different from that mentioned by the parabatic poet (628f.), demands that similar poet-versus-Cleon incidents throughout the Aristophanic corpus be ascribed to the representation of Cratinus on stage, probably in *Babylonians*. This, then, is the referent of *Acharnians* 377f. and 496f., but not of 630–1 and 659f., which, as I have shown, deal with attacks by a poet or poets supported by Cleon (probably therefore Cratinus at any rate) on the Aeginetan poet of *Acharnians*. It is also, then, the necessary background also of *Wasps* 1284–91, the second epirrheme of the second parabasis:

> εἰσί τινες οἵ μ' ἔλεγον ὡς καταδιηλλάγην,
> ἡνίκα Κλέων μ' ὑπετάραττεν ἐπικείμενος
> καί με κακίσας ἔκνισε· κᾆθ', ὅτ' ἀπεδειρόμην,
> οἱ 'κτὸς ἐγέλων μέγα κεκραγότα θεώμενοι,
> οὐδὲν ἄρ' ἐμοῦ μέλον, ὅσον δὲ μόνον εἰδέναι
> σκωμμάτιον εἴ ποτέ τι θλιβόμενος ἐκβαλῶ.
> ταῦτα κατιδὼν ὑπό τι μικρὸν ἐπιθήκισα·
> εἶτα νῦν ἐξηπάτηκεν ἡ χάραξ τὴν ἄμπελον.

There are some who said I made a deal, when Cleon attacked me, hassled me somewhat and stung me with abuse. And then, when I was being flayed, those outside watching as I howled loudly laughed, not a bit bothered about me, but only about if as I was being squeezed I might toss out a little joke. When I saw this, I played the monkey for a while. Now the prop has deceived the vine.

This must now be interpreted as being spoken in the voice of Cratinus, dropping for a few moments the dramatic pretence that he is to be distinguished in any way from the character Philocleon. The sudden intrusion of the poet's voice into the fabric of the play is exactly parallel to what we have seen at *Acharnians* 377f. and more spectacularly in the quasi-parabasis at *Acharnians* 499, where the phrase τρυγῳδίαν ποιῶν 'while composing a comedy' clearly ties a comic poet (now identified as Dicaeopolis/Eupolis playing Cratinus) into the plot. Unlike the anapaestic and Eupolidean parabases, then, a so-called 'second parabasis' may, it seems, take up a parodic posture which implies that the material of the play actually belongs to the satirised poet. This is another confirmation that *Wasps* was intended primarily as a reply to *Pytine*. I shall come back to this later, in respect of both *Knights* and *Wasps*. For now it is important to note that the scenario envisaged in the *Wasps* eppirrhema tells us (a) (once more) that Cratinus could be satirised as being in violent opposition to Cleon (probably because of his attack on Cleon as Typhoeus, possibly in *Ploutoi*) (b) that the way Cratinus escaped the attack by Cleon (in *Babylonians*?) was by making a deal with Cleon (κατεδιηλλάγην 1284), which figures and explains his current portrayal as *Philocleon* (and is alluded to in the parabasis at 1036) (c) that he has now reneged on the deal, which in any case was just a front (ὑπό τι μικρὸν ἐπιθήκισα 1290), and this will be the central point of the satire in *Wasps*. As at *Knights* 1145f., then, Aristophanes is making play with Cratinus' political *inconsistency*.

THE ROLE OF THE CHORUS

The argument so far should have made it clear that textual analysis *per se* and following the drama as it unfolds do not necessarily prove the best way to understand what is going on in Aristophanic plays. This preamble applies to the chorus of *Acharnians*. For although for the modern *reader* there is no indication early on that the chorus has been 'borrowed' from elsewhere (and is thus fundamentally metacomic), when we arrive at the lyric interlude, 1150–73, we are given a textual hint which suggests this clearly. Here the chorus attacks one Antimachus, a *choregos* at the Lenaea ὅς γ' ἐμὲ τὸν τλήμονα Λήναια χορηγῶν ἀπέλυσ' ἄδειπνον ('who let poor me go off without my dinner when he was choregos at the Lenaea'). They wish upon him an appropriate punishment, having his hot fish dinner stolen by a dog, and then a further one, that he be attacked by Orestes the mad, and, when intending to pick up a stone with which to drive him off, he grab instead a fresh turd, with which he misses his aim and hits Cratinus.

Although there is a long-running dispute about how to interpret the chorus' association of itself with a previous comic chorus, I need cite here only Halliwell's reason for reformulating Russo's view that Aristophanes had competed at the Lenaea of 427/6: 'there are no grounds for supposing that without warning or explanation an Aristophanic chorus could speak for a particular chorus belonging to a different poet.'[26] In fact, in the metacomic atmosphere already established for *Acharnians* in this discussion, it is quite clear that there is a particular reason to believe that what Halliwell rejects is happening here. The lack of warning or explanation is merely a feature of the modern *reader's* distance from the cultural climate of the comedy. The chorus calls attention to its previous existence because it creates humour

---

[26] Russo, 1962 26f. This view was contested by Dover, 1963, 23, but reformulated by Halliwell, 1980, 44–5.

Acharnians: parabasis versus play

for an audience which has recognised it already from a previous encounter (or previous encounters) in a play (or plays) by a rival (or rivals). It is worth mentioning that long ago J. van Leeuwen suggested, with appropriate reservations, that the connection between Antimachus and Cratinus was that it was a Cratinus play of which he had been *choregos*.[27] In the context of the current discussion, this makes good sense. The point of the chorus' desire for revenge is seen more clearly, and the humour of the punch-line is the more pointed, if they are recognisable to the audience already as the chorus of a previous Cratinus play. In addition, the misappropriation of a whole Cratinean chorus makes sense in terms of the satirical targets of *Acharnians*, as they emerge from this discussion, namely Eupolis imitating Cratinus.

It is worth noting that the metre of the ode (iambo-choriambic, with some paratragic aspects), is also used at Cratinus fr. 184 (*Pylaia*).[28] Note also that the dimissal to the actors sounds very like the introduction used elsewhere for the parabasis (1143; cf. *Knights* 498, *Clouds* 510, 1113, *Peace* 729), where metacomic reference becomes open. One detail in the second strophe, the role of 'mad Orestes', might be connected directly to Cratinus. The scholia tell us that he was a λωποδύτης ('a mugger'). But this looks like an inference from the text. Σ 1167c: Ὀρέστης τὴν μανίαν ὑποκρινόμενος ἀπέδυε τοὺς παρίοντας. λωποδύτης γὰρ ἦν. 'Orestes pretended madness while he robbed passers-by. For he was a mugger.' The following sentence of the scholium suggests the alternative that the mugger was called mad because he shared the name of Orestes son of Agamemnon. There

---

[27] Van Leeuwen, 1901 on 1163–73: '*Fortasse autem praeterea hinc efficere licet Cratini choregum fuisse Antimachum, sed nimis incertam esse hanc suspicionem sponte concedo; comicus vero poeta quin sit Cratinus ille, cuius iterum nunc fit mentio . . . , non dubito*'. Sommerstein (Warminster 1980) speaks with approval of this view (ad 1173).

[28] See Parker 1997, 148–51, where there is no mention of the Cratinus passage. Much remains problematic, of course. One wonders whether the ancient scholiasts found Antimachus' name in the *didaskaliai*. If they had, one might have expected them to have wondered why a man connected with the limiting of comic licence to satirise (Σ*Ach.* 1150a) became a comic *choregos* at all. The absence of comment suggests rather that he did not feature in the lists and this makes it more likely that his *choregia* was confined to the comic stage. An Antimachus who wrote laughable poetry was satirised by Cratinus (fr. 355, cf. *Ach.* 1151), though we have no way of knowing whether it is the same individual or if the satire is direct or indirect. Antimachus could have been *choregos* within a Cratinus play in which there was a scene where the chorus were denied a dinner (much the same as what happens in *Ach.*, cf. 1044–6). In support, we might offer the following: in Cratinus' *Pytine*, a play is shown being composed on stage (fr. 208–9); it is possible to mention the *choregos* in a play (*Peace* 1022, Eup. fr. 329 – in both of which places the *choregos*' parsimony seems to be the issue); and even to base a play around the *choregia*: Nikochares, a contemporary of Aristophanes, put on a play called *Herakles Choregos* and we now have the New York vase which labels each of two *komoidoi* ΧΟΡΕΓΟΣ (first published in Trendall 1991), though debate still goes on about whether these are simply the leaders of two semi-choruses (Trendall 1991), or the representatives of two rival semi-choruses of choregoi (Taplin 1993, 55–66), or choregoi in the sense of 'wardrobe-masters' (Gilula 1995, 9–10). See now Wilson 2000, 259–62. It is also possible to mention the festival at which a play is (supposedly) being presented within the play itself (as *Acharnians* 504 shows).

is clearly reason to think of the mythical individual of this name, since he did go mad after killing his mother. Cratinus' *Eumenides* (before 424, because fr. 70 from *Eum.* is from *Knights* 529–30) might well, therefore, have had a mad Orestes as a character: a reference to bribery in the lawcourts would certainly suit a play which is likely to have contained, like Aeschylus' *Eumenides*, a trial scene.

The audience, then, will have to have recognised the chorus at least as soon as it came on, if it had not guessed what was going to happen from hearing the title at the *Proagon* and Amphitheus' preparation at 177f. We can now see that the remarks about the chorus' identity in Amphitheus' speeches at 177 and 179–81, and the manner in which the chorus seems to be able to recognise the traitor from his voice alone at 238–9, may also suggest not only that the audience ought already to be familiar with this group, but also that the chorus appears already to know the protagonist.

If this analysis is correct, we would have to posit a Cratinus play with a chorus resembling that of *Acharnians*. At 375–6 there is an implication that this chorus, as well as being old Acharnians are also *jurors* (cf. their concern with lawcourts at 676f.), and this may also be the basis of the joke at 299–302, where the chorus threaten the protagonist in a context where their punishment of Cleon can only be as jurors. And they are *very* old indeed: cf. 676 οἱ γέροντες οἱ παλαιοί 'we old men, we ancients'. In their youth they could keep up with the famous Crotonian pentathlete and runner Phayllus (*Acharnians* 214) who, Herodotus 8.47 tells us, commanded a ship at Salamis (cf. *Wasps* 1206). At 220, the chorus-leader seems to refer to himself as Lacrateides, a name known to be that of an archon from the period of Darius' rule (Philochorus *FGrH* 328F 202).[29] In the light of this, combined with Amphitheus' description of the Acharnians at 181 as Μαραθωνομάχαι ('men who fought at Marathon'), it is tempting to take the phrase οἱ γέροντες οἱ παλαιοί at 676 as meaning 'we old men from a bygone era' (rather than simply as intensive). If these interpretations are right, then we might connect the chorus with Cratinus' *Nomoi*, in which it seems likely that the chorus were also *very* old men as well as laws: fr. 133 *PCG* ἦ πρεσβῦται πάνυ γηραλέοι σκήπτροισιν ἄκασκα προβῶντες 'Really aged old men, advancing gently with the help of their sticks'. The inference that they were jurors is tempting, though it is possible that making laws into jurors is a subversive step taken by a parodist between Cratinus and Aristophanes. It is also possible that Cratinus' chorus of laws are the old

---

[29] Sommerstein ad loc. suggests that the name is used because it sounds old-fashioned. This may be true, but since it was the name of a known historical figure, a direct association cannot be ruled out in the fantastic satire of comedy.

Acharnians: parabasis versus play

men spoken about as supporters of Cleon at *Knights* 977f.: πρεσβυτέρων τινῶν… ἐν τῷ δείγματι τῶν δικῶν 'old men in the case-market', who will thus also be the model for the chorus of *Wasps*.

If, however, the play's central joke is the subversion of Eupolis' satire of Cratinus, then it is possible that the Acharnians are meant to recall a Eupolidean chorus which had in turn been misappropriated from Cratinus. The notion of a demesman chorus is on our surviving evidence more likely to be derived from Eupolis than Cratinus. There are no Cratinus plays with names indicating such a chorus, whereas Eupolis' *Prospaltioi* did have a demesman chorus, and is only four years earlier than *Acharnians*.[30] Moreover, it has several points of contact with Aristophanes' play.[31] It is possible, of course, that the chorus of *Prospaltioi* was also parodying Cratinus' chorus of *Nomoi*, but there is no way to be certain. At least one other comic Acharnian is certainly attested (though in an unnamed play, by an unnamed poet) by the vocative Δρυαχαρνεῦ 'oak-Acharnian' (*PCG* VIII *Adespota* fr. 498), which might have been addressed to a chorus-leader or a character.

There is, it happens, another route into the prehistory of this chorus, afforded us by their remarks at 299f., the connection of these with those of the central figure at 5–8 and some cross-references in *Wasps* and *Knights* which only come into play once we have on other grounds accepted that Dicaeopolis, Demos and Philocleon all caricature the same individual, a mode of interpretation which would have been, on my argument, second nature to the original audiences of Old Comedy.

Let us begin with 299–302. There are difficulties with the paradosis, so I offer Sommerstein's text, recently adopted also by Olson:

ὡς μεμίσηκά σε Κλέ-
ωνος ἔτι μᾶλλον, ὅν ἐ-
γὼ τεμῶ τοῖσιν ἱπ-
πεῦσι καττύματα

301 κατατεμῶ codd. and Suda τεμῶ Elmsley ’ταμον Sidwell   302 καττύματα Dindorf: εἰς καττύματα Suda ποτ’ ἐς καττύματα codd.

For I hate you even more than Cleon, whom I shall cut into soles for the Knights.

---

[30] It has to be admitted, though, that we do not have from our scholiastic sources a complete list of even Aristophanes' plays. Only on the damaged inscription *IG* II² 2321, 87f. do we have the title *Odom]antopres[beis*. There could have been a play called *Thumoitadai* (*PCG* VIII, Tituli 8) and if so, it could have been by Cratinus.
[31] *Ach*. 162, Eup. fr. 260.30; *Ach*. 375–6, Eup. τii (both Acharnians and Prospaltians dikastically disposed); *Ach*. 128f., Eup. fr. 260 (central character in opposition to the *demos*); *Ach*. 426–9, Eup. fr. 262 (Eur. *Beller*.); *Ach*. 524f., Eup. fr. 267 (Aspasia as a catalyst for war); *Ach*. 824f., 864f., 924f., Σ *Clouds* 541 (an old man beating someone); *Ach*. 1149, Eup. fr. 260.19, 261.1 (τὸ δεῖνα 'thingumajig').

Sommerstein comments: 'there is no particular reason why the Acharnians should be hostile to Cleon; rather, the chorus here (in the middle of a sentence) shift to speaking in their capacity as a comic, and specifically an Aristophanic, chorus... Here the chorus foreshadow the violent attack on Cleon delivered in *Knights* the following year.'[32] This is an unsatisfactory explanation, for at least two reasons. First, the audience could not understand such foreshadowing, since *Knights* was a year away. And if I am correct to see the play as a parody of *Noumeniai*, since this was competing against *Acharnians* there is no way in which *Knights* could have been even conceived yet. Secondly, the abrupt transition to the poet's voice is quite unlike anything we find elsewhere. But how else are we to explain why the chorus should hate Cleon? The present discussion provides an alternative and less problematic explanation: the audience knows the chorus from a previous dramatic existence, in which, presumably, they had something to do with a conflict with Cleon. Whatever the solution to the textual problem here (and I have already suggested a new one in an earlier article),[33] the close proximity of Cleon and the Knights recalls the passage at 5–8 where the central character had already mentioned these two together in the context of what must have been a trial for misappropriation. This is too much of a coincidence for there not to be some connection between the two mentions.[34] The metacomic context points towards the probability that both rest on the same comic intertext, though the point of the joke created by the reference will probably be different in each case. So, as Lübke long ago suspected, there had been a play, produced at one of the earlier festivals, in which Cleon was arraigned by the Knights for misappropriation and forced to repay the money.[35] We can go further. The chorus of *Acharnians* must have somehow been involved in that scene, otherwise the personal nature of their comment makes no sense (as Sommerstein saw). That involvement can only have been as jurors.

Once we have reached this point, we notice that at *Knights* 1145f. (already mentioned above at p. 70, p. 77 and p. 84) we have three of the same elements: prosecution for theft, the Knights (to whom the passage is

---

[32] In his edition (Warminster, 1980) on 299–302. Hubbard 1991, 34 says the passage contains 'a hint about his next play'. Olson 2002 on 299–302 concurs with Sommerstein's views both on the intrusion of the poet's voice and (but less firmly) on the 'proleptic reference' to *Knights*.
[33] Sidwell 1994, 110–11, reported in my apparatus here. See below for an alternative explanation.
[34] As Olson agrees (2002 on 299–302). [35] Lübke 1883, 17–18.

addressed), and punishment by jurors. Moreover, the word ἐξεμεῖν 'to vomit up' used of the punishment by Demos at *Knights* 1148 mirrors ἐξήμεσεν 'vomited up' used by 'Dicaeopolis' at *Acharnians* 6 of precisely the same activity. This passage in *Knights* too, then, was very likely designed to create laughter on the basis of interaction between it and the scene (wherever in comedy it had occurred) in which Cleon was forced to vomit up five talents by a jury convinced by the arguments of the prosecuting Knights. When we stop for a moment to ask how such humour might be created, by the central character of *Acharnians*, the chorus of *Acharnians* and Demos in *Knights*, it becomes obvious that there is only one reasonable answer. The chorus and the individual satirised (on the surface) by 'Dicaeopolis' and Demos were all involved in that scene.

This analysis receives confirmation from two further passages. At *Knights* 805–8, Sausage-Seller tells Paphlagon that if this Demos ever returns to the countryside and lives in peace (a scenario, note, that is also envisaged more generally in *Peace*) εἶθ᾽ ἥξει σοι δριμὺς ἄγροικος, κατὰ σοῦ τὸν ψῆφον ἰχνεύων ('then he'll return, you'll see, as a harsh countryman, looking for a voting-pebble against you'). Once again, we have two elements of the scenario, this time the rustic juror (as in *Acharnians*) and a vote against Cleon. But as with the passages already discussed, there is also a third dimension, the creation of humour by a cross-reference involving the individual satirised as Demos. In other words, this reference confirms that whoever Demos represents was also involved in the original scene (and must, therefore, be identical – on one level – to the figure represented on stage in *Acharnians*).

The final piece of this reconstruction is provided by *Wasps* 758–9, where Philocleon, after failing to dispatch himself with his sword, cries out μή νυν ἔτ᾽ ἐγώ 'ν τοῖσι δικασταῖς κλέπτοντα Κλέωνα λάβοιμι ('may I never again be among the jurors and find Cleon guilty of theft'). This is surely the same scenario, though the elements mentioned here are Cleon, theft and acting as a juryman in his trial. As with the other passages, humour must be generated by the fact that it is *this* person (and not anyone else) who makes the reference to the comic scene. Again, the inferences we should make are first that Philocleon represents the same individual as Dicaeopolis and Demos (already argued on quite different grounds: see 000 above) and secondly that this individual had been put on stage as a member of the jury (a chorus, then?) in the play referred to. The familiarity between Dicaeopolis and chorus in Acharnians, then, is explained by the fact that they had been part of the same team and this also explains part of the humour of 5–8 and of 299–302.

Let us assume for a moment that my earlier arguments for identifying these figures as caricatures of Cratinus are correct. The consequence will be that he is very likely to be the homespun-cloak wearer of Eupolis fr. 298.6 *Chrysoun Genos*, given that the scene at *Wasps* 1122f. focuses attention upon precisely this garment as an essential badge of Philocleon's character. Eupolis' *Chrysoun Genos*, then, where Cleon is mentioned at fr. 316.1, will very probably be the play in which this scene was located and the references, which ignore the fact that Aristophanes was also caricatured there (fr. 298.5), are Aristophanes' way of getting back at both Cratinus and Eupolis for their attitude to him. The humour of 5–8 depends upon a double recognition – of the poet Eupolis behind the character Cratinus – since it would as naturally delight the one (Eupolis) to recall the scene, since he had written it, as it would pain the other (Cratinus), since he had been satirised in it.

It is now possible to suggest an alternative explanation of both syntax and reference at *Acharnians* 299f.: because chorus and central character are already acquainted with each other (and their identities known to the audience), it is perfectly understandable for the threat to be taken as *personal*. Thus ὅν 'whom' will refer not to Κλέωνος 'Cleon' but to σε 'you'. The passage thus implies 'and I shall cut *you* (Dicaeopolis/Cratinus/Eupolis) up into soles for the Knights, just as I did to Cleon himself in the play'. The intertextual reference is still, as at *Acharnians* 5–8, to *Chrysoun Genos*, but the joke (for the audience) is different.

Indirectly, then, this argument also suggests that Eupolis' *Chrysoun Genos* utilised Cratinus' *Nomoi* to satirise Cratinus himself and to parody his play. This conclusion can be reinforced by consideration of the epirrhemes of the parabasis. In the epirrhemes, the chorus slips back fully into its Cratinean persona, as evidenced by several verbal reminiscences. For example, the opening δεῦρο Μοῦσ' ἐλθέ... Ἀχαρνική 'Come here, Muse... of Acharnae' (665–7) has analogues in a Cratinus chorus fr. 237 (*Trophonius*) ἔγειρε δὴ νῦν, Μοῦσα, Κρήτικον μέλος 'Arouse now, Muse, a Cretan melody' and χαῖρε δή, Μοῦσα, χρονία μὲν ἥκεις... 'Greetings, Muse, and about time too...', where the metre is also parallel with the *Acharnians* passage.[36] The phrase Θασίαν... λιπαράμπυκα 'the Thasian brine with its sleek rim' (672–3) is reminiscent of Cratinus fr. 6 (*Archilochoi*) εἶδες τὴν Θασίαν ἅλμην... 'you saw the Thasian brine...'. Euathlus (710) is also mentioned in Cratinus' *Thraittai* fr. 82 and Thucydides son of Melesias (703f.) was

---

[36] Aristophanes and Cratinus both use a cretic-paeonic metre. The parody would have been even more palpable if a Cratinus tune had been used for the lyric sections.

ostracised in 443 and is unlikely to have been a political force on his return ten years later.[37] Thucydides had been the main opponent of Pericles in the period before his exile and Cratinus had attacked Pericles and his mistress Aspasia virulently. The trial reference is thus unlikely to be to anything recent in the real world, if it is to the real world at all.

The judicial theme of the epirrhemes involves a reversal from the posited dikastic activity of this chorus in its earlier manifestations. Old jurors become old defendants. But the (over) lengthy protestations of 676–702 may stem from and be leading up to the single example of Thucydides and his prosecution by Euathlus, son of Cephisodemus:

τῷ γὰρ εἰκὸς ἄνδρα κυφόν, ἡλίκον Θουκυδίδην,
ἐξολέσθαι συμπλακέντα τῷ Σκυθῶν ἐρημίᾳ;
τῷδε τῷ Κηφισοδήμου,[38] τῷ λαλῷ ξυνηγόρῳ;
ὥστ' ἐγὼ μὲν ἠλέησα κἀπεμορξάμην ἰδὼν
ἄνδρα πρεσβύτην ὑπ' ἀνδρὸς τοξότου κυκώμενον·

For how can it be right for a bent old chap like Thucydides to perish, after tangling with the 'Scythian desert', this fellow, the son of Cephisodemus, the chattering barrister? I felt pity and had to wipe my eyes dry, seeing an old man troubled by an archer.

It seems entirely possible that this trial was a scene in a comedy, rather than a real one. This is made more likely when we consider that it is also mentioned by Bdelycleon/Eupolis at *Wasps* 946–8, with the additional information that Thucydides could not even speak. If the identification argued for earlier is correct, then that occurrence has a metacomic context in which Cratinus is surprised by Labes' inability to speak and then informed by Eupolis that this also happened to Thucydides. Cross-reference to a comic scene thus again brings humour from two different angles in the two places where it is recalled. But who was the author, Cratinus or Eupolis? It makes comic sense that the Cratinean chorus should protest against the triumph of Euathlus and the worsting of Thucydides if they had actually themselves been the ones who convicted Thucydides: then the humour will lie in their protestation here that they actually pitied him. The mention of young prosecutors specifically includes Alcibiades in 716. This might identify the prosecutors as Knights, since Alcibiades belonged to this body early in his career (Pl. *Symp.* 221a, Plut. *Alc.* 7). This tends to suggest that

---

[37] Sommerstein, relying on Satyrus in Diog. Laert. 2.12, suggests that Thucydides prosecuted Anaxagoras for impiety on his return in 433. But Mansfield 1979 and 1980 dates the trial and exile to 437/6. From then on, Anaxagoras lived at Lampsacus.
[38] I adopt Hamaker's conjecture in 705, Κηφισοδήμου for MSS. Κηφισοδήμῳ.

the Thucydides scene was in Eupolis' *Chrysoun Genos*, a companion to the Cleon scene. The chorus, having actually condemned Thucydides there (as Labes will be acquitted in *Wasps* despite the trialomanic proclivities of Philocleon/Cratinus) now show sympathy with him, as apparently now does Eupolis/Bdelycleon in *Wasps*, and this is the source of the humour in both places.

Two other choral interludes seem to take us into different metacomic references. The choral interlude at 836–59, which I have already examined briefly (see pp. 79–80 above), will direct the audience's attention to a Eupolidean parody of a market scene, in which I have conjectured that he put Cratinus on stage with the individuals mentioned here. But the chorus is here merely narrating and not giving any hint of its own involvement (if any) in that scene. The matter is different with the second parabasis (971–99). Here the chorus recalls an incident involving personifications of War (979–87) and Reconciliation (989–99). Note how the chorus suddenly mutate here from charcoal-burning Acharnians to farmers, principally harvesting grapes (986–7, 995–9; cf. the claim in the defence speech that Dicaeopolis also has had vines cut down: 512). It seems very likely that once again we have humorous use made of a comic scenario, featuring War as an individual who refuses to accept symposiastic norms and Reconciliation as a rejected lover (both figures presumably based on real persons whose attitudes to the conflict were well known).[39] The play must have been set in the Attic countryside and its main character may have been a grape-farmer, backed up by a chorus of farmer friends, as represented here (shades of *Peace*, then). War will have burst in like a komast and made a mess of their farms. Perhaps Reconciliation offered to restore their lives to normality, but they refused.

None of the surviving titles of Cratinus' plays leads us directly to this scenario. However, Reconciliation is addressed at 987–9 as Κύπριδι τῇ καλῇ καὶ Χάρισι ταῖς φίλαις ξύντροφε 'foster-sister to Cypris the fair and the beloved Graces'. These same divinities are associated at *Peace* 356 with Hermes, Desire and the Horae.[40] One of the Horae, according to Hesiod (*Theogony* 901), was Peace. Since the contrast in this ode is essentially between War and Peace (of which Reconciliation is a mode), it is open to us to conjecture that the Cratinus comedy being played with here is

---

[39] For further discussion of War see below on Lamachus. For Reconciliation, see chapter six on *Lysistrata*. Presumably, her original would not have been as desirable as she appears to the old men of the chorus (990, 994).

[40] See also *Homeric Hymn to Aphrodite* 6.5f. for the association between Aphrodite and Horae. Pausanias 9.35.2 is testimony to confusion between Graces and Seasons.

his *Horai*. The close connections we can still see between some of the fragments of that play and the *Acharnians* (fr. 297 cf. *Ach*. 273; fr. 277 cf. *Ach*. 350; fr. 271 cf. *Ach*. 582f.; fr. 273 cf. *Ach*. 935), then, gain an added significance.[41] It is perhaps not too much to conjecture that *Horai* was Cratinus' response to yet another war brought upon Athens by Pericles (cf. the hypothesis of *Dionysalexandros PCG* ΤΙ 44f. with Storey's dating of 437 or 436). In that case, the overlaying of Eupolis as antagonistic to the war upon his caricature of Cratinus would have had a solid recent basis in the comic theatre.

The chorus of *Acharnians*, then, seems to have been recycled by Aristophanes from Cratinus (*Nomoi?*) via Eupolis (the *Chrysoun Genos* in particular). They have good reason to know their (original) maker and fellow juryman in Eupolis' play and much humour is derived at various points from their references to the *Chrysoun Genos* scenario (299f., 665f.), to at least one other Eupolidean satire of Cratinus (834f.), and to Cratinus' own *Horai*. One can only guess how much the music, dance and costumes (cf. *Peace* 729–31 for theft of comic paraphernalia) will have contributed to the inherently amusing scenario of a Eupolidean parody of Cratinus which serves to undermine the standing of the satirist who misappropriated them in the first place.

DICAEOPOLIS WITH AMPHITHEUS, EURIPIDES AND LAMACHUS

Central to any Old Comedy, according to the inference made from the *Clouds* parabasis in chapter one, was on-stage caricature. The plot was really only a vehicle for attacks on individuals presented in a manner designed to make them look as foolish – and wicked – as possible. It follows, then, that although in the case of a comic poet κωμῳδούμενος a great deal of the humour of a play will depend on cross-references to his plays and in putting him in situations where he plays out or refers to his own scenes, the relationship of the main target character with other characters in the drama is in a way more central. Here, then, I will make a few remarks designed to help us to understand why some of these individuals have been chosen to play scenes with Dicaeopolis/Eupolis and how the comedy operates in these cases.

First, a few general considerations. In a straightforward satire, the targets would simply be persons chosen because they represented individuals

---

[41] Less convincing parallels are also found between fr. 278 and *Ach*. 254, fr. 291 and *Ach*. 255.

whom the poet felt ought to be attacked for various vices. However, in a metacomic satire – in this instance a double one – we need to pay attention to relationships that might exist – either in comedy or in real life – between the satirised poet(s) and the individuals chosen for attack. The simplest model for *Acharnians* would be one in which all the individuals caricatured had been objects of Cratinus' satire, but were associated in some way personally – as friends, political associates or relations, perhaps sometimes even as enemies – with Eupolis. For in this way the use of Cratinus by Eupolis will be brought most sharply to bear against the younger poet: his imitation of Cratinus brings with it, logically, Aristophanes seems to say, a willingness to satirise the same individuals as Cratinus, who are, however, actually in Eupolis' own circle.

In a number of instances, in fact, we can see that Dicaeopolis is represented as already familiar with the individuals he encounters. While the herald of the assembly does not know Amphitheus, Dicaeopolis appears to know enough about him to wish to support him and the fact that he calls him τὸν ἄνδρα 'the man' (57) seems to confirm at least that for him he is not an immortal. When Theorus is announced, the comment ἕτερος ἀλάζων οὗτος εἰσκηρύττεται (135) 'Here's a second pseudo being announced' might also suggest familiarity. Obviously, he must know who Euripides is, otherwise he could not have the idea to visit him, but as I have argued above, there is much more to it than that: he is probably both a relative and an admirer and, in some senses, an imitator of the tragedian. When Lamachus enters (at 572), he has been summoned by name, but still there is an addendum to the publicly available information about him in Dicaeopolis' first address to him: ὦ Λάμαχ' ἥρως 'Heroic Lamachus' which suggests again that he knows him well enough already to mock him thus (and the fact that this same formulation recurs in *Frogs* 1039 in the mouth of Aeschylus without any contextual reason for its use should probably alert us to its origin in a comic text). By the same token, the Megarian and the Boeotian know rather quickly that Dicaeopolis has opened a market, and the Megarian even knows his name (748), so that satirical fun must here too derive from a public association of markets with Eupolis (and Cratinus), even if these 'foreigner' characters are not attacking real individuals. Dicaeopolis does not seem to know the first informer (824), but he recognises Nicarchus (908). In the scene with Dercetes, the opening suggests that Dicaeopolis does not recognise the man (1019 τίς οὑτοσί; 'Who's this?'), but the revelation of the man's name at 1027 is accompanied by the phrase ἀλλ' εἴ τι κήδει ('If you care at all for . . .' tr. Sommerstein), a very strange verb to use and a strange formulation if there is no familial relationship between the characters.[42]

Out of these characters, I choose here to investigate Amphitheus, Lamachus and Euripides once more not because I think they are necessarily more important than say Theorus or Dercetes, but because I think that there is enough ancillary evidence to be able to say something useful about them.

Amphitheus

Amphitheus was a real Athenian name,[43] so the joke here might be based on what Athenians would know about the individual who bore it.[44] However, since the name Amphitheus supports a joke about the character's divinity, we cannot be completely sure whether the name has been chosen to support the joke, or the joke rests on the identification by the audience of the character as a real Amphitheus.[45] At any rate, the name is not given right at the beginning of the scene,[46] but *after* the entry and first speech of the character at 46. So for maximum comic impact, it would be best to assume that he is instantly recognisable.

The inscriptional evidence which assures us of the currency of the name has also been used to support the suggestion of an association between

---

[42] There was a fifth-century Derketes of Phyle (*IG* II² 75.7 and 1698.6), as Sommerstein first noted (1980, on 1028). He thought it merely 'curious' and it was left to MacDowell and Parker to draw the conclusion that this was a caricature either of the individual whose name is recorded in the surviving inscriptions or of his son or grandson. (MacDowell 1983, 159, Parker 1983, 11). The word κήδομαι ('I care for') tends in Homer to be connected with the verb φιλέω ('I love') (e.g. *Il.* 1.196, 7.204). Thus κήδομαι is used of people who would be in the ambit of your φιλία ('close relationships'). Homeric and later examples which do not have φιλέω also nonetheless show that care is related to persons or communities which have a special meaning for the carer (e.g. *Il.* 1.56, Hera caring for the Danaans; *Od.* 22.358 Telemachus asking Odysseus to spare the herald Medon because he had cared for him as a child; Herod. 9.45, care for the whole of Greece; Thuc. 6.14, care of the prytaneis for the city of Athens; Pl. *Charm.* 173a, care for oneself). The obverse, that to show care in this way for strangers is odd, emerges from *Il.* 6.55–6, where Agamemnon, having come upon Menelaus with a prisoner (Adrestos), berates him with the words: τίη δὲ σὺ κήδεαι οὕτως ἀνδρῶν ('why are you so concerned for the welfare of men (sc. who have no call on your special care)?'). In *Ach.* 1028, then, the joke should rest upon something known to the audience already about the attitude of Eupolis to this person.

[43] *IG* II² 2343. The inscription is from the late fifth or early fourth century.

[44] *Pace* Sommerstein 1980.

[45] Anthropos (46) was also an Athenian name and Griffith 1974, 367–9 argues that the joke is something to do with the two real bearers of these names. However, given that Amphitheus' response to the herald picks up this paradoxical situation and confirms it, it is better to read the herald's οὐκ ἄνθρωπος 'Not human?' as sarcastic and leading up to Amphitheus' claim. Such textual explanations pay no attention to the costume of Amphitheus, for which see below.

[46] See Olson 1992.

Amphitheus and Aristophanes. *IG* II² 2343 lists the sixteen members of a *thiasos* of Heracles. Among them are several names also found in Aristophanes (though none of the identifications is absolutely secure): Simon of Kydathenaion (cf. *Knights* 242); Amphitheus (cf. *Acharnians* 46); Antitheus (cf. *Thesmophoriazusai* 898); possibly also Lysanias (cf. *Clouds* 1163).[47] We know that Aristophanes' first play, *Daitales*, had a chorus composed of ἐν ἱερῷ Ἡρακλέους δειπνοῦντες ('men dining in Heracles' temple').[48] This was what made Dow think that Amphitheus might have been among Aristophanes' circle.[49] However, Welsh argues of the persons named on the inscription: (1) that Simon is the man mentioned at *Knights* 242; (2) Amphitheus is the original of the character in *Acharnians* and (3) Antitheus is the man mentioned at *Thesmophoriazusai* 898. If this is so, the satirical intent shown especially in the two on-stage caricatures (Simon and Amphitheus) rules out his identification of the Philonides listed in the inscription with Philonides of Kydathenaion, the poet and producer of Aristophanes' plays, unless we wish to assert (against the run of this argument and much other evidence) that people were happy to consort with their enemies in the course of such activities, and it also strongly suggests that the *thiasos* was made up of *enemies* not friends of Aristophanes.[50] As I have shown (above, pp. 19–20, 25), it is Eupolis who gets the sharpest and most sustained criticism in the parabasis of *Clouds*, where *Banqueters* is recalled. And I have suggested (chapter three, p. 86) that the play may have satirised an old comic poet, as I think Eupolis had done earlier (and one might wonder whether Eupolis had also been satirised as one of the old poet's sons in this play). In these circumstances, the suggestion that the chorus might have contained friends of Eupolis is not untoward, given the intention to attack him in *Acharnians*. The play will have had a chorus of individuals identifiable as members of the Heraclean *thiasos*, with the hint, perhaps, that it was in fact a political *hetaireia*. The inscription – which may be twenty years or more after *Daitales* – may only record a son or grandson of our Amphitheus, but this would surely be indicative that membership of the *thiasos* had been a family tradition and should bring us back to the Amphitheus of *Acharnians*.[51]

---

[47] See Dow 1969, Welsh 1983b.
[48] *PCG* Ari. *Daitales*, Test. iii (Orionis Thebani Etymologicum, ed. Fr. G. Sturz, Leipzig 1820, p. 49, 8).
[49] Dow 1969, 234–5. See *contra* MacDowell 1995, 52. [50] Welsh 1983b.
[51] For the introduction of a son by a father into Heraclean *thiasoi*, see Isaeus 9.30. For possible connections of *thiasoi* with phratry organisation, see Lambert 1993, 81–93.

Acharnians: parabasis versus play

However, as MacDowell writes (1995, 52): 'we never hear elsewhere of a god called Amphitheos; one would expect the gods' messenger to be Hermes or Iris (both of whom appear in other plays of Aristophanes).' Amphitheus does indeed behave precisely as Hermes or Iris would have been able to. His journey from Athens to Sparta and back, including negotiations, is made in the space of the scene with Theorus and the Odomantians (sent off at 129–32, he is back at 175). It happens that we know Hermes was a character in Cratinus' *Dionysalexandros*. The hypothesis (*PCG* IV, p. 140, lines 5–6) reads (with Körte's supplement): Ἑρμῆς ἀπέρχ]εται ('Hermes leaves'). The scene which follows the parodos there has Dionysus as Paris judging the goddesses (hypothesis lines 6–12).[52] It seems likely that the opening either showed Zeus giving Hermes orders to set up the contest or Hermes actually setting it up.[53] As we have seen, the hypothesis also tells us that the whole play satirised Pericles covertly for bringing the war on Athens (lines 44–8) – even if it is the Samian War and not the Peloponnesian War which is the referent. Hermes' role in the play, then, could have been as intermediary for Zeus in *starting* the war (in Euripides' *Trojan Women*, Paris is seen by Helen at 919f. as its ultimate cause, via the judgement of the goddesses). The role given to Amphitheus here, then, could on this basis be a metacomic subversion of Cratinus' drama. It is entirely possible that the costuming of Amphitheus would have underpinned this metacomic joke. Was he accoutred like Hermes, with winged sandals, *petasos* and *kerykeion*?[54]

Given that the overall satirical schema requires a Cratinus character now subverted for the purpose of making fun of Eupolis, it seems likeliest that Amphitheus is the same person represented as Hermes in *Dionysalexandros*. However, in the real world, Amphitheus will also presumably have been known as a friend of Eupolis. This would explain the satire both of Cratinus (he is now relying on someone he satirised) and Eupolis (like him, his friend is prepared to act against the will of the *demos* in securing peace for Dicaeopolis alone).

There is a humorous paradox, then, in the role of Amphitheus. If in Cratinus' *Dionysalexandros* he was Hermes, the messenger whose actions heralded (the Samian) war, in *Acharnians*, by contrast, he is the messenger who instigates peace, ostensibly for the Cratinus figure, but actually for

---

[52] See Heath 1990.
[53] Cf. Lucian, *Dearum Iudicium*, which could have drawn its inspiration from Cratinus, given Lucian's boast that he mixed dialogue with comedy (*Bis Accusatus* 33).
[54] The connection between Hermes and a comic account of the way the war began is clearly marked in *Peace* (603f.), a passage which I shall examine at the end of this chapter.

the Eupolis who controls him. Here the top layer of humour rests in the volte-face of Cratinus, but the satire must subsist in the conspiracy of two friends, Eupolis and Amphitheus, to subvert the settled will of the *demos* by making a private treaty with Sparta.

Euripides

In chapter three (pp. 88–90), I argued that Cratinus' 'Euripidaristophaniser' should be identified as Eupolis. In a play which we can now see attacks this young rival of Aristophanes, it is now clear why Euripides is chosen to play the role he does. But where does Cratinus come in? It seems likely that the answer is that Euripides had been a favourite target for his on-stage satire.

It is possible, in fact, that Cratinus had Euripides as a character in *Idaioi*, a play of which we have only two fragments, neither of them helpful in dating. Fr. 90 of this play is essentially the scholion on *Thesmophoriazusai* 215:

ΚΗΔΕΣΤΗΣ· ἀτὰρ τί μέλλεις δρᾶν μ'; ΕΥΡΙΠΙΔΗΣ· ἀποξυρεῖν ταδί, τὰ κάτω δ' ἀφεύειν.

Relative: 'What are you going to do to me?' Euripides: 'Shave this off, and singe the bits below the plimsol line'.

The scholiast writes: τὰ γένεια. ταῦτα δὲ ἔλαβεν ἐκ τῶν Ἰδαίων Κρατίνου ('The beard. This he took from the *Idaioi* of Cratinus').[55]

Van Leeuwen was right to suggest that the scholion means that this whole section was taken from Cratinus. But was he correct in adding the rider: 'It would be safer to assume that Cratinus' play had something *similar*'?[56] The scholiasts were pretty good at spotting quotations (especially from

---

[55] Other scholars have questioned the location of this fragment, for two reasons. First, Clement of Alexandria (*Strom.* VI, 26.4) tells us: Ἀριστοφάνης δὲ ὁ κωμικὸς ἐν ταῖς πρώταις Θεσμοφοριαζούσαις τὰ ἐκ Κρατίνου Ἐμπιμπραμένων μετήνεγκεν ἔπη ('The comic poet Aristophanes in the first *Thesmophoriazusai* transferred the words from Cratinus' *Empimpramenoi* (*Men Inflamed*)'). Dindorf 1829 p. 94ᵃ (= Dindorf 1835 p. 574ᵃ) put this together with the scholion on *Thesm.* 215 already cited and suggested that the play alluded to was in fact called Ἐμπιμπράμενοι ἢ Ἰδαῖοι '*Men Inflamed* or *Idaioi*'). Bergk 1838, 109f. added the conjecture that the chorus of this play were devotees of Cybele. However Luppe (1966, 187) inferred from Cratinus fr. 91 'καὶ ὁ Κρατῖνος ἐν τοῖς ἰδίοις [Bergk Ἰδαίοις] τὰς θείας μορφὰς ἐν ἀρχῇ 'Cratinus also in his own work < Bergk *Idaioi*> [put] the forms of gods at the beginning') and from the gap in the papyrus hypothesis of *Dionysalexandros* (*PCG* IV, 140 Ti, line 27) following the letter h, that *Idaioi* was an alternative title to *Dionysalexandros*.

[56] Leeuwen, 1904 ad loc.: '*quamquam tutius fuerit statuere* **simile quid** *habuisse quondam Cratini fabulam*'. Austin and Olson 2004 are also sceptical: 'whether he borrowed whole lines or parts of lines or (more likely) simply took over the idea of a scene in which a male characters is shaved, depilated, and dressed like a woman is impossible to say'.

tragedy and other genres).⁵⁷ When they merely record similarities, whether of language, syntax or substance, their method is to quote the various examples.⁵⁸ It is thus more in line with normal scholiastic procedure to infer that the scholiast meant Cratinus had written these specific lines in *Idaioi*. The further inference is then possible that Euripides was a character in the play. For if Aristophanes was quoting lines from Cratinus, then there was a humorous point behind the misappropriation. This could lie either in the fact that the whole scene, characters and all was transferred to a different plot, or that in the Cratinus play the person shaved and singed was Euripides.⁵⁹ A connection of *Idaioi* with Euripides is not unreasonable, given that he had written a play called Κρῆτες, in fr. 472 (Nauck) of which a character (Minos?) addresses the chorus: ὦ Κρῆτες, Ἴδας τέκνα 'Cretans, children of Ida'.⁶⁰

The double joke of the Euripides scene in *Acharnians*, then, lies in the fact that Eupolis goes to ask for help from his relation (?), but treats him exactly as he would have been treated in one of his older rival's satires.

Lamachus

The conflict and contrast between Dicaeopolis and Lamachus forms the focus of much of the play. If my hypothesis is sound, the scenes with Lamachus will recall a play by Cratinus in which Lamachus was satirised, and rest on some known relationship between Lamachus and Eupolis.

Certainly the most significant aspect of the presentation of Lamachus in *Acharnians* is his warlike disposition. His first words (572–4) find him eager for the fray and he is clearly dressed in full fighting kit (575), which is subsequently made fun of (581f.). We are reminded of this characterisation again in the exchange between Lamachus' servant and Dicaeopolis at 959f. Then from 1071f. Lamachus presents a foil to Dicaeopolis, representing the trials of war, just as his adversary represents the joys of peace. He was, it is true, a soldier. Son of Xenophanes probably of the deme of Oe (*PA* 8981),

---

⁵⁷ See e.g. Σ *Acharnians* 8a (a half-line from Euripides' *Telephus* identified).
⁵⁸ For possible identification of a comic quotation see Σ *Knights* 1225 with Sommerstein 1980b, 51–3. For identification of similar language, see e.g. Σ *Acharnians* 933a on πυρορραγές ('cracked in the firing').
⁵⁹ It is worth noting that Callias' *Pedetai* had Euripides as a character dressed up as a woman (Diog. Laert. 2.18). See Callias fr. 15 *PCG*. If this argument is correct, then Luppe is unlikely to be right, since the hypothesis to *Dionysalexandros* would have mentioned Euripides if he had been – as seems usual – a named character. More likely, the opening of *Idaioi* may have shown a group of gods, as Bergk suggested (cf. the opening of Eur. *Tro.*).
⁶⁰ In fact, this fragment is cited by Σ *Frogs* 1356a in a parody of Euripidean monody.

he had led a military force to help the *demos* of Sinope against their tyrant Timesileos (Plut. *Pericles* 20), was elected general for 425/4 and again led a naval force to the Black Sea in 424 (Thuc. 4.75), and was one of the three commanders of the Sicilian expedition in 415 (see Plut. *Alcibiades* 18.2 for his advancing years), where he died (Thuc. 6.101.6). But he was also to be one of the signatories of the Peace of Nicias (Thuc. 5.19.2). And the details of his characterisation in Aristophanes take us far beyond a mere soldier.

At 964, when the servant of Lamachus enters the market to buy some thrushes and a Copaic eel for his master, Dicaeopolis does not seem to know who he is (963: ὁ ποῖος οὗτος Λάμαχος τὴν ἔγχελυν; 'What Lamachus is it who wants the eel?'). The servant replies with a description which begins: ὁ δεινός, ὁ ταλαύρινος ('the terrible, the redoubtable...'). These are precisely the words used by Trygaeus in describing the personified War at *Peace* 241.[61] At *Acharnians* 1080, as Lamachus laments his expedition at festival time, Dicaeopolis responds: ἰὼ στράτευμα πολεμολαμαχαϊκόν ('Yo for the polemico-Lamachan army!'). The compound adjective seems to identify War with Lamachus, in the way that such compound substantives tend to do (cf. Ἡρακλειοξανθίαν 'Xanthias plays Heracles' at *Frogs* 499). It is unlikely to be fortuitous that the semi-chorus which summons Lamachus at 566f. does so in terms which would normally be used to invoke the help of a god or goddess: ἰὼ Λάμαχ᾽, ὦ βλέπων ἀστραπάς,| βοήθησον ὦ γοργολόφα, φανείς 'O Lamachus with the lightning look, appear and help us, thou of the gorgon-crest!'.[62] Πόλεμος ('War') is personified by the Cratinean chorus later at *Acharnians* 978f.[63] Furthermore, there is more than a passing resemblance between the words of Trygaeus just before War's entry (*Peace* 234–5: καὶ γὰρ ὥσπερ ᾐσθόμην | καὐτὸς θυείας φθέγμα πολεμιστηρίας 'For I too have heard the voice of a martial mortar') and the opening words of Lamachus (*Acharnians* 572: πόθεν βοῆς ἤκουσα πολεμιστηρίας; 'From where did I hear a martial shout?').[64]

The best explanation of all these phenomena is that Cratinus had presented Lamachus as War (Πόλεμος) in a comedy (perhaps *Horai*? See above, pp. 132–3 on the choral interlude 978f.) from which various elements are parodied both in *Acharnians* and in *Peace*. The fact that Lamachus appears

---

[61] It is also worth noting that Lamachus uses the word κυδοιμός ('turmoil') at *Ach.* 573 and that precisely this term appears as a personification at *Peace* 255f. We also learn at Plut. *Nic.* 15.1 and *Alc.* 21.9 that Lamachus was still a poor man in 415, which seems to contrast with the attack made at 619 that his main focus is upon getting paid posts.
[62] Sommerstein 1980 on 567 comments: 'the epithet *gorgolopha*... is a title of Athena... and the phraseology of this line is that of a prayer to a deity...'.
[63] See also *Clouds* 6, and *Peace* 205 and 236f.
[64] Cf. 1132, where Lamachus again uses the word πολεμιστήριος.

Acharnians: *parabasis versus play* 141

on stage at *Peace* 473–4, when we have already seen War, may, rather than confirming a disjunction between the Cratinean allegory and Aristophanes' appropriation of it in *Acharnians*, in fact play on his identification by Cratinus as War.

Within a complex of cross-references to a Cratinus play where Lamachus was presented as War, two more possibilities crop up. (a) Lamachus is first mentioned at 270, in Dicaeopolis' hymn to Phales, where his name, in the plural, comes as the climax to three things from which the character will be freed, having made peace: πραγμάτων τε καὶ μαχῶν καὶ Λαμάχων ἀπαλλαγείς ('from troubles, battles, and Lamachuses freed'). Sommerstein comments: 'He is mentioned here mainly because of his name ('great fighter'), which is suggested by *makhon* 'from battles' directly preceding'. But the repetition of exactly the same series at 1071 is suspicious in a metacomic text. Is this also a cross-reference to something in Cratinus? This conjecture might be confirmed by the repetition of similar phrases in *Peace*.[65] (b) At 575 and again at 579, Dicaeopolis addresses Lamachus as ὦ Λάμαχ' ἥρως ('O heroic Lamachus!'). This is precisely the designation Aeschylus uses of Lamachus at *Frogs* 1039. It is not enough to say, as Dover does, that this is like the treatment of Brasidas after his death (Thuc. 5.11.1).[66] This does not explain the invocation in *Acharnians*. It is possible, as I have already argued, that for some reason the *Frogs* passage is deliberately recalling *Acharnians*. But *Acharnians* is already likely to be recalling a comic intertext in Cratinus. But whatever underlies these references, there is surely also parody of Aeschylus here too. It is Aeschylus who picks out Lamachus as one of those who learned the military lessons taught by Homer (*Frogs* 1039) and at *Frogs* 1016f. Aeschylus' tragedy is equated with the inculcation of warlike spirit and the presentation of brave warriors as characters. Lamachus is certainly presented with all the bombast and hyperbole associated with Aeschylean characters in the discussion about his art in *Frogs*. The use by Lamachus' servant of the phrase τρεῖς κατασκίους λόφους ('three shadowy crests') at 965 specifically equates him with Tydeus from Aeschylus' *Seven against Thebes* 384.[67] Given the prominence of Aeschylus in the theatrical

---

[65] 293 ἀπαλλαγεῖσι πραγμάτων τε καὶ μαχῶν 'released from troubles and battles'; 303 τάξεων ἀπαλλαγέντες καὶ καλῶν φοινικίδων 'released from battle-lines and fine purple cloaks'; 352–3 ἀπαλλαγέντα πραγμάτων 'released from troubles'; 1128–9 κράνους ἀπηλλαγμένος | τυροῦ τε καὶ κρομμύων 'released from the helmet, and from cheese and onions'.
[66] Dover 1993 on *Frogs* 1039.
[67] There may be further layers here. (1) Lamachus' son was called Tydeus (Sommerstein 1978, 383: Lamachus is 'like Tydeus'?); (2) the proximity to the evocation of Lamachus as War (964) may suggest that Cratinus' War was based on use of Aeschylus (cf. Kratos and Bia in the probably *c.* 430 *Prometheus Bound*).

reminiscences of Dicaeopolis at *Acharnians* 9–11, and the title of Cratinus' play *Eumenides*,[68] it would be surprising if Cratinus' use of Aeschylus was not part of the underlying metacomedy surrounding Lamachus.

But where does Eupolis come in? The one individual who we actually know was associated with War personified in comedy was Phormio, in Eupolis' *Taxiarchoi*. In the commentary on that play fr. 268.13–16 reads: οὐκ οἶσθ' Ἄρη μοι τοὔνομα· Ἄρης ὁ Φορμίων ἐπεκαλεῖτο ('Don't you know my name is Ares? Ares was the nickname of Phormio'). And at *Peace* 348–9, we read: πολλὰ γὰρ ἀνεσχόμην πράγματα καὶ στιβάδας ἃς ἔλαχε Φορμίων ('I have endured many trials and palliasses, which are in the lot of Phormio'.). Sommerstein comments ad loc., 'Phormio is humorously spoken of as if he were a god who had palliasses (i.e. campaigning and its discomforts) under his special protection.'[69] It looks as though Eupolis satirised the general Phormio as the god of war (and the passage in *Peace* recalls his *Taxiarchoi* for some humorous purpose). Aristophanes now, it seems, superimposes Lamachus as Cratinus' War onto Eupolis' Ares/Phormio, and this will explain why Lamachus is portrayed as a general in the first scene in which he appears (593), while his inferior position later (1073), perhaps as taxiarch, might also be a metacomic reference to Eupolis' *Taxiarchoi*.[70] Note 569–71, where the chorus, directly after calling for Lamachus, cry: εἴτ' ἐστι ταξίαρχος ἢ στρατηγὸς ἢ τειχομάχας ἀνήρ, βοηθησάτω ἀνύσας ('Or any taxiarch or general or man who fights on the walls, let him make haste to help us'), where the term 'taxiarch' might be deliberately reminding the audience of Eupolis' play. Compare *Thesmophoriazusai* 832–3, which contextualises the praise of Lamachus via his

---

[68] Note also the mention of Cratinus in *Frogs* 357 as Dionysus and the way comedy is assimilated by the chorus to Cratinus' comedy.

[69] Sommerstein 1985. He cites parallels from Pindar (*Nem.* 11.1) and Plato (*Ti.* 23d).

[70] To get over the inconsistency (denied *tout court* by Dunbar 1970, 269–70), it has been suggested that he was a taxiarch at the time of the writing of *Acharnians*, but had been elected a general shortly before the performance. Aristophanes managed to rewrite 593 to take advantage of the topicality, but could not do the same at 1073–83. MacDowell, 1995, 68. Cf. Lewis 1961, 120 and Molitor 1969, 141 (426/5 was an extraordinary year and the elections for 425/4 were held before the Lenaea. Thus Lamachus is a *strategos*-elect in *Ach*.). The conjecture is based on two dubious assumptions: (a) that the text is related directly to historical reality, and therefore that historical reality can be recovered from the text; (b) that contradictions in the text are based on the desire to keep that historical reality in close contact with the text. In any case, as Wilamowitz inferred correctly long ago, because of sensitivity to criticism of the *demos* in its officials, since Lamachus is named, he cannot have been a general in 426/5 (von Wilamowitz-Moellendorff 1935, 287 n.3). The position of taxiarch was, however, also an office elected by the *demos* (Arist. *Ath. Pol.* 61.3). Demosthenes 25.50 suggests great sensitivity to attacks on such χειροτονία ('election by show of hands'). Whatever position Lamachus is given in the play, then, does not correspond with a position which he actually held in 426/5. The satire is not topical, and we are likelier to find its basis in metacomedy than in reality.

mother (841 χρῆν γάρ, εἰ τέκοι τις ἄνδρα χρηστὸν τῇ πόλει ταξίαρχον ἢ στρατηγόν, λαμβάνειν τιμήν τινα ('If a woman bore a man the city profits from, a taxiarch or a general, she ought to receive some honour'). I have already suggested in chapter three (above, pp. 82–3) that Cratinus may have been put on stage as Dionysus in that play, as taxiarch of the tribe Oeneis, learning military skills from Phormio. If this is so, then it is likely that in *Taxiarchoi* Eupolis was parodying Cratinus. It could be, then, that Ewen Bowie was correct about the attribution of some facets of Eupolis' Dionysus to Dicaeopolis and Handley and Storey will be wrong to try to move *Taxiarchoi* to the 410s.[71]

But there is a further thing which connects the satire of Cratinus as taxiarch in Eupolis' *Taxiarchoi* with Lamachus. If he was ever a taxiarch, he would (if the ascription to him of the deme Oe is correct) have been taxiarch of the tribe of Oeneis, to which the deme of Acharnae also belonged.[72] The satire of Cratinus in *Taxiarchoi*, then, may rest on Eupolis' substitution of Cratinus for the real Oeneis taxiarch whom Cratinus had earlier satirised as War. Given Cratinus' established connection with wine (though probably, I have argued, with growing it, rather than with drinking it to excess), it was the oeonological etymology of the name that carried the sting. If it was *Horai* in which Cratinus had urged peace, it makes sense to place this caricature of Lamachus as War in that play.

We are still, however, some way from seeing a clear connection between Lamachus and Eupolis, though the hypothesis just aired would suggest a desire to *defend* him. It is interesting that beyond the plays of this period Lamachus is mentioned quite positively elsewhere in Aristophanes at *Thesmophoriazusai* 841, where his mother is praised by the chorus of women in contrast with the mother of Hyperbolus, and at *Frogs* 575 and 579 by Aeschylus. Just as in *Frogs* it must be significant that it is Aeschylus who calls Lamachus a hero, in *Thesmophoriazusai* it may be that it is *women* who indirectly praise Lamachus. Elsewhere in Aristophanes, women are desperate for peace (*Ach.* 1058, *Peace* 992, *Lys.*). The centrality of Euripides to *Thesmophoriazusai* does, as I argued earlier, suggest another hit at Eupolis, possibly in reality a relation (κηδεστής), though if so it is also done by presenting him on stage via the by now long-established caricature of Cratinus. This could imply that the positive evaluation of Lamachus is part of a much larger satirical structure in which attack on Eupolis is the central point. An underlying assumption, then, would have to be

---

[71] See chapter three n. 65, and Appendix 4 for a detailed discussion of the dating.
[72] MacDowell 1995, 70.

that there had been a close connexion between Eupolis and Lamachus. This view is supported by the fact that in the same passage, Hyperbolus' mother is attacked (839–41), something done by Eupolis and criticised by Aristophanes (*Clouds* 551f.).

Perhaps, then, as I have suggested with Amphitheus and Euripides, there was a known personal connection between Eupolis and Lamachus and what is amusing is the combination of Eupolis' apparent admiration for an imitation of Cratinus' comic techniques with the logical – but absurd – consequence of his adoption also of Cratinus' satiric *targets*, even when those are close personal friends or relations.

METACOMEDY IN ACTION

The larger structures which carry the personal attacks against not only Cratinus and Eupolis, but also Amphitheus, Theoros, Euripides, Lamachus, Nicarchus, Dercetes and others, are on my argument linked also to smaller ones which take their material from and parody plays by Cratinus and Eupolis. There are two primary ways of identifying such scenes, I have argued: one by comparing what we have with what is criticised in parabases, a second by direct comparison with surviving fragments. We may now add a third, which we have encountered incidentally while tracking cross-references such as the cluster Cleon/Knights/theft. Passages which display close similarities of theme (for example, dancing against Carcinus' sons, *Wasps* 1498f., *Peace* 781f.) are very likely to be utilising as their base a comic intertext. This will especially be the case in plays which have comic poet characters, but may apply anywhere. The traditional explanation, that such 'repetition' is 'self-imitation' is obviously not impossible, but rather less likely where the general context is metacomic. There is certainly one example of the first type in *Acharnians* (circumcised phalloi in the Thracian episode at 155f.) and a possible second (an old man, with the leading part, beating – or threatening to beat – people in the market scene at 824f., 864f. and 924–5), two of the second (the vomiting scene at 585f. and the packaging of the sycophant at 933f.), and at least one of the third (markets involving Megarians and Boeotians, *Acharnians* 515f., 719f., *Peace* 999f.). Close scrutiny of all these scenes would help us to come to terms with the notion of parodying comedy and bring to light certain subversive techniques which are characteristic of the mode. Here, however, because my focus is on the political battle between the poets, I shall look only at the Megarian/Boeotian material and use this to attempt an analysis of the comedy (and satirical targets) of the famous 'defence-speech'.

Megarians and Boeotians at market (719–970)

The market scenes fall into the category of passages having themes which are also adumbrated elsewhere in a passage of 'self-imitation' – in this case *Peace* 999f. – which itself occurs in a play which can be counted as metacomic since it contains elements criticised elsewhere in parabatic statements (e.g. the shout ἰοὺ ἰού at 317, 345 etc.; cf. *Clouds* 543), besides the fact that its parabasis focuses on the contest between comic rivals (729–74), and its central character, Trygaeus, very likely represents a comic poet (note the particular association of the root τρυγ- with comedy).

In the course of a prayer to the newly unearthed Peace, Trygaeus asks: καὶ τὴν ἀγορὰν ἡμῶν ἀγαθῶν | ἐμπλησθῆναι 'And may our Agora be filled with nice things' (999–1000). This is followed by two lists of goods, the first from Megara (1000–2), the second from Boeotia (1002–5). The Megarian list begins with garlic, which is mentioned not only in the market scene at *Acharnians* 761, but also in the poet character's quasi-parabatic defence speech at 521, where we also hear of cucumbers (*Ach.* 520, *Peace* 1001) and cloaks (*Ach.* 519, *Peace* 1002). In terms of Megarian goods, there is actually considerably fuller correspondence between the *Acharnians* defence-speech and the *Peace* list than between the *Peace* list and the *Acharnians* market-scene. The Boeotian list, however, corresponds in every item with the goods mentioned in the *Acharnians* market-scene (though there are more in *Acharnians*): ducks (*Ach.* 875, *Peace* 1004), geese (*Ach.* 878, *Peace* 1004), wrens (*Ach.* 875, *Peace* 1004), Copaic eels (*Ach.* 880, *Peace* 1005). One further correspondence emerges at *Acharnians* 1104, where while cooking Dicaeopolis asks for τὰς φάττας 'the pigeons', which are listed as Boeotian goods at *Peace* 1004.

However, what is striking is the complete lack of correspondence between the lists of market customers in *Peace* and in the choral interlude at *Acharnians* 836–59. In *Acharnians*, the people who will *not* be seen at Dicaeopolis' market are: Prepis, Cleonymus, Hyperbolus, Cratinus, Pauson and Lysistratus. In *Peace*, the customers are: Morychus, Teleas, Glaucetes and Melanthius. I have already suggested (above, pp. 79–80) that the purpose of the references in the *Acharnians* passage is to call attention to a Eupolis play in which Cratinus was put on stage interacting with precisely these individuals in a market. If the identification of Philocleon with Cratinus is accepted, this conjecture can be supported by reference to two passages in *Wasps*. At *Wasps* 787f., Philocleon relates an incident at the fish-market in which Lysistratus gave him fish-scales instead of obols as change (note the correspondence between σκώψεται 'will make fun of' at *Acharnians* 852 and σκωπτόλης 'buffoon' at *Wasps* 788). At *Wasps* 1007, after Philocleon has acquitted Labes, Bdelycleon/Eupolis tells his father that he will never again be tricked and made a fool of by Hyperbolus (though here there is no mention of the market context). A third passage may also be relevant, if Bdelycleon is representing Eupolis, because Cleonymus (another of the non-customers at Dicaeopolis' market) is mentioned satirically by him to Philocleon/Cratinus at *Wasps* 822.

The *Peace* list seems to suggest a completely different set of characters for what is essentially the same scenario. However, there is in fact one correspondence between the *Peace* list and *Acharnians*. At *Acharnians* 887, the Copaic eel is mentioned as φίλη δὲ Μορύχῳ 'and dear to Morychus'. Given that the preceding line is metatheatrical (ποθεινὴ μὲν τρυγῳδικοῖς χοροῖς 'desired by comic choruses'), it is possible to infer that there had been a Cratinus play in which Boeotian goods – especially eels – played an important role. The announcement of the eels' arrival on stage at 883 with a line parodied from Aeschylus' *Award of the Arms* (fr. 174 Nauck) fits within a complex already adumbrated within which Aeschylus appears to be connected with Cratinus. What we may be seeing here, then, are the vague outlines of two market plays, one by Cratinus involving Megarians and Boeotians, and featuring the individuals mentioned at *Peace* 1007–8, the other by Eupolis satirising Cratinus in a market setting which starred the denizens listed at *Acharnians* 842f. Of the Eupolis plays already listed as possible satires of Cratinus, *Prospaltioi* seems the most likely candidate (cf. the pipers of *Acharnians* 862f. with those of *Prospaltioi* fr. 259.116–17). As for the Cratinus play, it seems reasonable to suggest that it either preceded the war or came early in it, if the account given by the poet character at 499f. is meant, at least in part, to recall comedy, as has already been argued in the case of the Cleon/Knights reference (above, p. 128). It is worth recalling once more that it was Cratinus who had attacked Pericles as Zeus (frr. 258, 118, 73; cf. *Ach.* 530) and who is reported to have used his *Dionysalexandros* to blame him for bringing the war on the Athenians (Cratinus, *Dionysalexandros* Ti, 45f), even if it now seems more likely to have been the Samian than the Archidamian War. It would follow, then, if 499f. were to turn out to be evoking comedy, that the 'piggy' scene (*Ach.* 764f.) and the sycophant scene (*Ach.* 818f.) are directly parodied from the Cratinus play (cf. *Ach.* 521 for the Megarian piggy and 519f. for the sycophants denouncing Megarian goods). Since the purport of the 'defence speech' is to criticise Pericles for bringing the war on Athens, the comedy is likely enough to be Cratinus' Archidamian peace play, probably *Horai*, as I suggested above. The central joke, then, is that Eupolis constructs his defence of peace play out of material from Cratinus, while being revealed as the actor behind his own Cratinus satire.

One thing which probably marks off Aristophanes' treatment of the Megarians and Boeotians is the use he makes of their dialects. As Colvin has recently shown, though there are a few invented and Attic forms in the dialect sections, comparative evidence suggests that 'there are no grounds... for describing the Aristophanic rendering as parody or pastiche'.[73] Moreover, there is no evidence that earlier poets had done the same thing.[74] The primary motivation that suggests itself here is the satirical one that accurate knowledge and use by the poet (Eupolis) of the language of the enemy during a period of war condemns him as a traitor. However, one can not discount, in a writer to whom language was crucial (*Peace* 749–50, *Clouds* 544), the inherent joy felt by Aristophanes in mimicking the speech of other Greeks.

THE CAUSES OF THE WAR AND DEFENCE OF THE SPARTANS

This analysis of metacomic references at the beginning of the crucial 'causes of war' speech leads inexorably to an examination of the content of the rest of that passage. For if the 'self-imitation' between the Megarian and Boeotian scenes of *Acharnians* and *Peace* 999f. implies, on my hypothesis, that these passages share a common comic intertext, it follows that the place where Megarian goods are first mentioned (519) may also be evoking the same comedy. However this may be, MacDowell has noted that the account of Dicaeopolis 'though expressed in a manner suitable to comedy, is not inconsistent with the account given by Thucydides; it is not illogical or incredible'.[75] What we may have here, then, with metacomic references to spice the mixture, is, rather than a recycled comedy, a politically slanted account of the war's causes which will provoke laughter because of the way it plays with the double-identity of the comic-poet character and the opposed political views of the *surface* poet (Cratinus) and the *controlling* poet (Eupolis).

As we have learned from earlier chapters (and especially from chapter three), the securest way to tie down such political satire is to begin from known positions held by those involved. Cratinus' view of Pericles is not in doubt: we have several fragments of plays which appear to have

---

[73] Colvin 1999, 298. See also Kloss 2001, 53–4.
[74] No other poets use Megarian and only Strattis (in *Phoinissae* after 409) and Aristonymus (late fifth, early fourth century) use Boeotian (Colvin 1999, 276–8, 282).
[75] MacDowell 1995, 66.

been aimed at him, but it seems likely that at least in two, *Thraittai* and *Dionysalexandros*, he was an on stage caricature.[76] It is likely that this persona in *Thraittai* was that of Zeus (fr. 73 K–A), the guise in which he is presented at *Acharnians* 530. For Eupolis, the picture is not so straightforward. He featured Pericles on stage in his *Demes* (K–A *Demoi* τι), which could mean that he was presented as a figure of fun. However, given that he is there in the company of three *positive* figures (Solon, Aristides and Miltiades), it seems more likely that Eupolis regarded him in a similar way.[77] And if it is correct (see chapter two, p. 43) to see Aeschylus' Periclean advice in *Frogs* as the key moment in a satire of Eupolis, it would explain why Dionysus is so caught between Aeschylus and Euripides, but eventually chooses Aeschylus. It would also enhance the humour of the denouement, since if Eupolis had been a defender of Pericles at the start of his career (in opposition to Cratinus), then he would presumably have had to defend his role in starting the war and his policy in conducting it. What appears to lie behind the double metacomic satire of *Acharnians*, then, would have to be a reversal of positions on the war by *both* Cratinus *and* Eupolis between Pericles' death and 425. We have already seen how a Cratinus play (*Horai?*) may have attacked the war (aligning itself with the interests of the farming community). If the identifications of Demos and Philocleon as Cratinus are correct, we can infer that when Cratinus changed his allegiance to Cleon, he also adopted an aggressively supportive attitude towards the war. If Eupolis began the war in the Periclean camp (perhaps by attacking Cratinus in his *Prospaltioi?*), the anti-Eupolidean *Knights* certainly appears to portray his position as now totally behind peace (cf. *Knights* 1388f.). This reconstruction would give the right satiric structure for the speech (and the comedy as a whole): Eupolis speaks through a Cratinus-costume articulating a position on the war which Cratinus once held, but no longer holds, just as Eupolis' commitment to peace is the exact opposite of what he began the war with.

As MacDowell has shown, the account appears to mirror the way Thucydides relates the war's causes. Since he does not lay upon Pericles the responsibility for starting the war (and does not even mention that the Megarian decree was his proposal, as appears from the *Acharnians* passage, 530f.), it looks as though the outline of what Dicaeopolis says might have formed the basis of a *defence* of Pericles, were it not for two moves: (1) Pericles' response to the Aspasia incident portrays him as the Cratinean Pericles-Zeus (530–1)

[76] See K–A fr. 73 for Pericles in *Thraittai* and Revermann 1997 for Pericles in *Dionysalexandros*.
[77] See Telò 2007, 67–125 and further chapter six, p. 280. Eupolis had satirised Δία μοιχὸν 'an adulterous Zeus' Σ *Peace* 741b (see chapter five, p. 204), but this may have been a metacomic reference to Cratinus.

Acharnians: *parabasis versus play*

and (2) the ἀληθεστάτη πρόφασις ('the *real* reason') – the Spartan fear of Athenian power encroaching on their sphere of influence[78] – is turned into a sympathetic reading of Spartan aggression. The humour here may be generated from the way in which an account which Eupolis might have used originally to *support* a pro-Periclean interpretation of the war's origins (possibly in a comedy) is undercut by the superimposition of Cratinus' perspective on Pericles ('the Olympian') and by the use of its main background argument as a pointer to Eupolis' present position on the war. This is sophisticated, intertextual satire of real individuals.

We may apply the same type of analysis to the other account in *Peace* 603–48, since this is also a metacomic play, with a comic poet at its centre – and probably (as I have argued in chapter three, p. 95) replicating the satirical ploy of *Acharnians*, namely Eupolis playing Cratinus. Here Hermes explains to Trygaeus that it was Pericles' fright when Pheidias the sculptor got into trouble that caused him to enact the Megarian decree and fan the flames of war. The Athenian allies then began to turn towards the Spartans, who threw out Peace and embraced War. The Athenians began reprisals against Spartan territory, while at home the country folk flocked into the city. There they looked for help towards the politicians, who instead took advantage of the situation by rejecting Peace, and starting a series of attacks on rich men among the allies. The allies in turn started to bribe the Athenian politicians to leave them alone. Cleon was the man chiefly responsible for this.

Once more, MacDowell's analysis suggests that here too we are seeing an actual account of the causes of the war which was being offered by 'individuals who were opposed to the war'.[79] For one part of it, at any rate (the connection between Pheidias' prosecution and the start of the war), there is also good ancient evidence (Diodorus 12.39–40, following Ephorus; Plut. *Per.* 31).[80] It is important to note that this account is fundamentally different from that of *Acharnians*. First of all, Pericles is *directly* responsible in *Peace* (606f.), because he fears the indictment of his friend Pheidias will quickly lead to his own demise, while in *Acharnians* he is responding to a series of incidents which culminate in something close to home, the Megarian theft of Aspasia's whores (526f.), but which are actually started by ἀνδράρια μοχθηρά 'worthless little men' (517) and νεανίαι... μεθυσοκότταβοι 'drunken young cottabus-players' (525), who are the real culprits (515). Secondly, the Spartans in *Acharnians* begin the

---

[78] MacDowell 1995, 66.   [79] MacDowell 1995, 186–92. The quotation is from 188.
[80] See MacDowell 1995, 187.

war because of Athens' refusal to rescind the Megarian decree (535–9), while in *Peace* it is the subject-states, fearing increases in tribute, whose realisation of the opportunity offered by internal Athenian political dissension is what leads to their bribery of the Spartan nobles and the ejection of Peace from Sparta (619–24). Thirdly, *Peace* outlines a scenario involving the country-folk of Attica within the city, duped by the politicians into ejecting Peace whenever she appeared, and fooled by them into many condemnations of metics, whose response was to bribe the orators, which has no counterpart in the *Acharnians* 'causes of war' speech, though it provides many points of contact with both this play and *Knights*. The crucial thing to note here is that, again unlike in the *Acharnians* account, Cleon plays an important part (*Peace* 647–8). In the ideological struggle between Eupolis and Cratinus, it is Eupolis who attacks Cleon. However, the ascription to Pericles of a *personal* and *private* reason for beginning the war looks very much more like what Cratinus might have been inclined to argue. That this scenario does have something to do with the central character is confirmed comically by Trygaeus' astonished claim at 615–16 that he had never heard this account before from anyone (which might be funny if the audience recognised him as – on one level – the author of this very account) and by the chorus' use of Peace at 617 of an adjective (εὐπρόσωπος 'fair of face') which recalls the chorus' description of Diallage at *Acharnians* 990 (ὡς καλὸν ἔχουσα τὸ πρόσωπον ἄρ' ἐλάνθανες 'I didn't notice how fair a face you had'). As in *Acharnians*, then, satirical comedy is built from having Trygaeus (Eupolis acting Cratinus) offered a basically Cratinean view of the war's origins, which he rejects as soon as Cleon's name comes up (648f.). If my analysis of *Acharnians* 978f. is correct, the personification of Peace and War at *Peace* 624 and of Peace at 637–8 might also depend for its humour on a cross-reference to Cratinus' *Horai*.

A possible confirmation of the Cratinean origin of the political analysis of the *Peace* passage may be found, following the argument about Aristophanes' parodic use of Eupolis' attack (in *Noumeniai?*) on Cratinus in *Knights*, in the very close parallels between it and *Knights* 792f., where Sausage-Seller mentions (a) the country people in the city (792–4); (b) the rejection of peace-terms offered by the Spartans (794–6) (c) bribe-taking from the subject-states (801–2); (d) the war as a mist (803, cf. *Peace* 610–11), (e) the dependence of the country-folk upon the orators (804).[81] The humour of the passage will be constructed, as in the *Acharnians* and *Peace*

---

[81] Note also the Archilochean tag τἀμὰ δὴ ξυνίετε | ῥήματ' 'understand my words' at *Peace* 603–4 which is also found at Eup. fr. 392 and also in Cratin. *Pytine* fr. 211.

passages, by having something which belongs to a discourse *supporting* Cleon (thus either from Cratinus or from the rhetoric of the Cleonian circle he supported) used to *attack* him (he is the recipient of this barrage in the guise of Paphlagon). But it will also be crucial who Sausage-Seller represents, because the humour may actually have come from a Cratinean scenario specifically designed to attack *him*.

Perhaps this difference in the thrust of the two accounts helps us to locate where Eupolis attacked Cratinus' account of the war's origins in his 'Megarian play' (*Horai*?). All the signs are that Cratinus had continued his battle against the war-mongering Pericles from *Dionysalexandros* into the Archidamian War (see in particular *Ploutoi* fr. 171.22f.) and I have conjectured above that his *Horai* was a peace-play (given the parody of its details in *Acharnians* and the fact that Eirene was one of the Horae). The play involved an erotic liaison between Dionysus and his concubine (K-A fr. 278: τῆς παλλακῆς ἀποδημοῦντος τοῦ Διονῦσου ἐρώσης 'when the concubine has the hots for the absent Dionysus'). Who then were Dionysus and his concubine in *Horai*? The clue to her identity may be given by *Acharnians* 524, that is Simaitha. The clue to Dionysus', then, will be given in the scholion which says that Alcibiades was Simaitha's lover. Cratinus might have cast Alcibiades as Dionysus (in every respect a brilliant comic and satirical choice, if so), and in this play he will have ascribed to Alcibiades' activities the blame for Pericles' extravagant response (the Megarian decree) to the provocations mentioned. If this is so, then in this reference we may have incidentally located another source of humour in the speech which depends upon ascribing to Eupolis something which originated in Cratinus.

If my reconstructions are correct, in *Prospaltioi* Eupolis made two fundamental corrections to Cratinus' attack on Pericles in *Horai* for bringing the war on Athens: Pericles was not to blame and Alcibiades was not involved. I conclude that, at least at this early stage of the war, Eupolis had close enough personal, political or intellectual connections with Pericles and his ward to make it important that he divert opprobrium from him, and attack Cleon for his current activities. His attack in *Prospaltioi*, then, will have brought Cratinus on stage, as Aristophanes does with Eupolis in *Acharnians*, to give the Spartans support.

Prospaltioi probably belongs in 429.[82] If it responds to *Horai*, then it makes sense to place this in 430, an apt moment to attack Pericles for

---

[82] Storey 2003, 230–1. Note his arguments *ibid.* 335–6 against the view of Bowie 1988 that *Prospaltioi* was an anti-war play.

bringing yet another war on Athens for entirely personal reasons. These datings bring their problems, however. Hyperbolus' early entry onto the *bema* was mentioned in *Horai* (fr. 283), which would push his notoriety back into the Periclean period. But since he had become a major figure – at least as far as comedy was concerned – by 425 (*Ach.* 846–7), this is not perhaps difficult to accept.[83] Fr. 259.1–5 appears to give some account of the young Eupolis' being requested, for some reason, to write this play and perhaps this was because they needed a swift riposte to Cratinus' version of events as political spin. More difficult, perhaps, is that Storey rejects the notion of Goossens that fr. 260 has as its theme a debate over the evacuation of the Attic population into the city, which would fit squarely with the general interpretation offered here.[84] Storey argues against it that (1) the interpretation relies too much on supplements and assumptions related to the possible date; (2) such a debate does not suit 429, since it will actually have occurred earlier (in 431/0); (3) Pericles' unpopularity (and removal from office) belongs in late 430, so that he may not have been in office in 429, therefore an unlikely target for comedy, and if he were, Thucydides implies (2.65.4) the animus against him was largely spent by the time of the festivals. Argument (1) can be aimed against large-scale interpretation of any fragment. As for (2), if *Prospaltioi* were designed as an attack upon Cratinus' *Horai* and that had featured (as seems likely from the metacomic references I have conjectured in *Acharnians* and *Peace*) such a debate, then topicality will not have been an issue (any more than it is with Labes/Laches' trial in *Wasps*). Moreover, the dikastic nature shared by the metacomic choruses of the two Aristophanic 'peace' plays is mirrored by that of the Prospaltians (Suda δ 1515) and this may suggest that, like Aristophanes later, Eupolis was aping Cratinus' chorus in order to mock him and his political stance. Argument (3) assumes also that targeting of individuals was direct and topical. But if Eupolis' beef was really Cratinus and his group's spin on the origins of the war and the blame for its outbreak, then Goossens' reading would still make perfect sense even in 429.

Why, then, did Aristophanes choose to wait till 425 to reuse the material and political attitudes from these comedies of the early war years? Presumably, as with Eupolis' three-year wait to respond to *Knights* with *Marikas*, it was a matter of political expediency and the seizing of opportunities provided by individuals and events (cf. *Clouds* 551 for the λαβή 'hold' Hyperbolus allowed the comic poets to get on him). While there

---

[83] Storey 2003, 200–1 lists the Hyperbolus references in comedy and notes that they cover more than twenty years, more than fifteen plays and at least eight playwrights.
[84] Goossens 1935, Storey 2003, 341–2.

is no external evidence of formal peace-talks or offers at this time, Olson is prepared to take the reference in the parabasis (*Ach.* 652–3) as proof of some sort of rapprochement.[85] Even if this is not the case (as I have argued above), it does seem that something happened in the period 427–5, when there were no Spartan invasions of Attica, to bring the idea of peace – along with the no-doubt vitriolic debates on its appropriateness – back into the public arena. It must have been well known where various politicians – and their associated artistic coteries – stood on the issue. Undoubtedly, if my analysis of the play is correct, Eupolis now stood with the peace party and Cratinus with the war party. Only in such circumstances does it make sense that Aristophanes would have tried to tar Eupolis with the anti-Periclean brush of Cratinus' early anti-war comedy.

CONCLUSION

The hypothesis that *Acharnians* is a fundamentally metacomic satire of Eupolis' use of Cratinus (and also of Cratinus' plays) and that the humour of its key scene – the defence of the Spartans – may rest upon a well-rehearsed ideologically slanted view of the war's origins similar to that found in Thucydides and designed to exonerate Pericles, a view with which in essence Eupolis would have concurred (and which he may have used in *Prospaltioi*) has more than merely literary implications. It would not have been possible to align Eupolis artistically with Cratinus as is done here had there been no connection between them, and I have shown here, as far as the evidence will allow it, some of the ways their antagonism was managed by both. But by the same token, it seems unlikely that the central political point of the play – the ascription to Eupolis of the same attitude to the war as Cratinus manifestly had shown in his earlier plays – would have served its purpose had the poet not belonged to a political group which did see peace with Sparta as a more reasonable goal than consistent enmity. This does not mean, however, that the groups that Cratinus and Eupolis belonged to were the same, any more than Aristophanes' and Eupolis' shared opposition to Cleon had the same ideological basis. Cratinus' opposition to the war arose in the first place from a long-term opposition to Pericles as a political leader, and probably not from Laconophilia, if his caricature as Philocleon replicates a real-life affiliation (cf. especially *Wasps* 1161–5).[86] He also may

---

[85] Olson 2002, xxxviii.
[86] Despite fr. 228 *Seriphioi*, where the accusation may in any case belong to a *character*. On this issue, see above, pp. 84–5 and chapter five below, especially pp. 182–3.

have been antagonistic towards Alcibiades. Eupolis may have begun his career defending Pericles' role in starting the war, and he featured him in his *Demes* (Ti), which, as I have suggested above and shall investigate further below (chapter six, p. 280) is a *positive* portrait. But he could easily have begun, after Pericles' death, to hold the view that peace was preferable to war because he did have strong ties to the Spartan aristocracy. And, as I have suggested (above, p. 151), he may have wished specifically to answer criticisms of Alcibiades, because Alcibiades was close to both the pro-peace party and to the Spartans at this time.

The very fact that Aristophanes' attack is framed around a political question – one on which his attitude is that it makes sense to continue the war and not to make peace with Sparta (*Ach.* 652–5) – makes it as clear as it could be that real political questions were the business of Old Comedy. What has proved problematic both for ancient and for modern readers is the level of intertextual reference between plays and the assumption of the playwrights that the political landscape of the city, including the predilections of the combatants in the comic competitions, was a known quantity to the audiences of the festivals. For us, neither pole is at all obvious. However, now that the role of metacomedy and caricature can be seen at work in *Acharnians*, a process becomes visible which may help to recapture at least the major structures upon which both surviving and lost Old Comedies rest.

CHAPTER 5

Metacomedy, caricature and politics from Knights *to* Peace

KNIGHTS

We have already dealt in chapter three with the evidence for Eupolis' involvement in the composition of *Knights*. To recap, the conclusion was that the play borrows the overall schema of Eupolis' *Noumeniai* of Lenaea 425, in which a wicked *prostates* of Demos is replaced by an even worse one, plus at least two major characters. One is Paphlagon (a name chosen possibly because of the connection of this Black Sea territory with the export of hides and Cleon's involvement in that trade),[1] possibly represented in Eupolis' play as a tanner, shoemaker and shoe-salesman (cf. *Knights* 315–21), and a recently acquired slave of Demos (cf. *Knights* 2). The other is Demos/Cratinus. The market-trader theme will have been calqued on *Noumeniai* too, with the strong possibility that Hyperbolus was represented there as a lamp-manufacturer and seller (*Knights* 738–40). A final point of appropriation may be the rejuvenation of Demos. However, far from being an imitation or even a rip-off, Aristophanes' play in fact subverts the earlier comedy's political thrust (the replacement of Cleon by Hyperbolus and possibly the change of Demos from the old Cratinus to the young Aristophanes) by altering the person who gains the *prostasia* to someone in Eupolis' political circle and probably by throwing in a few other surprises designed to pour scorn upon his rival. The task here will be to deal with these changes as far as possible, placing particular emphasis upon the identification of the slaves and Sausage-Seller, the role of the chorus, and the implications of the rejuvenation of Demos.

The caricatures of *Knights* are all disguised, but few dispute the identification of Slave 1 with the general Demosthenes,[2] and many would also

---

[1] Braund 2005, 94–5.
[2] See Handley, 1993, 100–1 for dissent about identification prior to this moment. The scholia speak with some uncertainty about this character. On the one hand, the *Dramatis Personae* have Δημοσθένης, rather than 'Slave' (see Mervyn Jones and Wilson, *Schol.Ar*. 1.2 p. 4 for the MSS which contain the

follow the ancient scholiasts in seeing Nicias in Slave 2.[3] Sommerstein, for example, has given as reasons for sustaining this latter identification the correspondence between the characteristics attributed to Slave 2 and those for which Nicias was noted (timidity, strong religiosity, pessimism, and dislike of over-indulgence).[4] These identifications make good sense within the general political objectives of the play. Demosthenes' plan to land on Sphacteria was, Thucydides tells us, known to Cleon before he chose him as his fellow general on the Pylos expedition (4.29). The historian's view of Cleon is well known (4.28.5) and may have skewed his objectivity here.[5] Very likely, the information had been vouchsafed voluntarily to Cleon by Demosthenes because he was politically close to him. The humour of the satire in Aristophanes makes better sense on this reading, because it is a man the audience knows to be an ally of Cleon who is making the charge. If metacomic cross-reference is at work, one possible implication of Demosthenes' speech at 319–21 is that he also was a character in Eupolis' *Noumeniai*, a booby sold a bad pair of shoes by his political friend Cleon. As for Nicias, he was of course Cleon's principal political opponent at the time of Pylos (Plut. *Nic.* 2; Thuc. 4.27f.). He was a member of the group who wanted peace (Thuc. 5.16, Plut. *Nic.* 9) – an essential element in Sausage-Seller's platform (794–6, 1388–9) – and was responsible for the success of negotiations in the winter of 422/1 which led to the treaty which bears his name (Thuc. 5.19). Apart from this amusing alliance of opposites and the amusement value of lining up an ally of Cleon *against* him, though, it seems likely that Aristophanes is also exploiting here a

---

list). And Triclinius wrote on 1[d]: ἔστι δὲ εἷς τῶν οἰκετῶν Δημοσθένης ὁ προκαμὼν ἐν Πύλῳ ἀποδυρόμενος πρὸς τὸν ἕτερον ('One of the slaves is Demosthenes, who did the ground-work at Pylos, complaining to the other [slave]'). But on the other, the scholia vetera write: ἔοικε δὲ ὁ προλογίζων εἶναι Δημοσθένης ('The presenter of the prologue *appears* to be Demosthenes...'). And hypothesis A3 (*Scholia* p. 2) has the same formulation at the start, while later we read (lines 6–7): λέγουσι δὲ τῶν οἰκετῶν τὸν μὲν εἶναι Δημοσθένην ('They say that one of the slaves is Demosthenes'). There are signs that, as with the identification made by modern scholars, the ancient view was an inference from line 55. Σ 1c adds διὰ τοῦτο ('because of this'), after the identification and the mention of Pylos. And Σ 55b reads: ὁ Κλέων ἔδοξεν κατορθοῦν πλέον τοῦ Δημοσθένους ἐφαρπάσας τὸ τέλος τῶν ἐκείνου πόνων ('Cleon appeared to be more successful than Demosthenes, after stealing the *coup de grace* of his labours'). It does not look as though, then, in this case the identification was something handed down with the text. See below for the suggestion that in any case Demosthenes was a character in Eupolis' *Noumeniai*.

[3] The *Dramatis Personae* call this character Νικίας. Hypothesis A3 (lines 6–7) tells us: λέγουσι δὲ τῶν οἰκετῶν τὸν μὲν εἶναι Δημοσθένην, τὸν δὲ Νικίαν, ἵνα ὦσι δημηγόροι οἱ δύο ('They say that one of the slaves is Demosthenes, and the other Nicias, so that both should be political leaders'). It is likely from this formulation and *a fortiori* from the previous indications about the identification of Slave 1 as Demosthenes that no ancient evidence had survived which identified the character with the general. It was, however, an intelligent inference, whoever made it, that if Slave 1 was Demosthenes, Slave 2 should also be a general and a political leader.

[4] 1980b, 46–7.   [5] See Hornblower 1996 on this passage and on 4.29.2 and 4.30.4.

known political predilection of Eupolis. There is no evidence that Nicias was ever caricatured in his comedies and of the only two mentions of him (fr. 193 and 351) one is certainly from *Marikas* and belongs to a conversation in which Marikas/Hyperbolus is making an absurd accusation involving Nicias, while the second may also be from the same play, and focalised in a similar way.

The fundamental question about *Knights* on this interpretation, however, is the identity of Sausage-Seller. To fit the plot, he must be be an individual who was already in the public arena, perhaps even in an official capacity, and, probably, a leading light in a circle of which Eupolis was a member. Given that the plot involves the *prostasia* of the *demos*, this individual must have had at least a political profile, and certainly political pretensions. One needs only to contemplate the topsy-turviness of satire, however, to recognise that there may be no correlation at all between either the family and educational profile of Sausage-Seller's original or his proposed accession – for the first time – to the *prostasia*. Indeed, it is quite possible that the vileness of Sausage-Seller and the *prostasia* motif were both taken from *Noumeniai* (cf. *Knights* 738–40), where they had been related to Hyperbolus, whose family origins may actually have been lowly and who was certainly spoken of as though they were (cf. Thucydides' language at 8.73.3 μοχθηρὸν ἄνθρωπον 'a vile fellow', which may mirror that which lies behind *Knights* 1304 μοχθηρὸν πολίτην 'a vile citizen'; Andocides fr. 5: περὶ Ὑπερβόλου τοίνυν λέγειν αἰσχύνομαι, οὗ ὁ μὲν πατὴρ ἐστιγμένος ἔτι καὶ νῦν ἐν τῷ ἀργυροκοπείῳ δουλεύει τῷ δημοσίῳ, αὐτὸς (MSS. ὡς) δὲ ξένος ὢν καὶ βάρβαρος λυχνοποιεῖ, 'I am ashamed to speak about Hyperbolus, whose father bears a brand and is still a state slave in the mint, while his son makes lamps, though a barbarian foreigner').[6] Hence, Sausage-Seller's objection to Demos' current choice (738) τοὺς μὲν καλούς τε κἀγαθοὺς οὐ προσδέχει ('you don't accept the fine and noble individuals') may ironically reflect the substitution by Aristophanes of an aristocrat to play the role assigned to Hyperbolus in Eupolis' play. It therefore seems likely that Sausage-Seller's original was an aristocrat with a conservative agenda which could always be presented as having its roots in a 'back to basics' movement to re-establish the values of the early democracy, before the opening up of the franchise to all and sundry and when all Greeks fought together against the Persian menace (an ideology which would naturally have rested on the necessity of achieving peace with

---

[6] Since Hyperbolus could not have had a political career had his father been a slave, this picture sounds very much as though it derives from comedy, perhaps, given the reference to lamp-making, even from Eupolis' lost *Noumeniai*.

Sparta and her allies and which continued to surface from time to time, as it does in *Peace* and *Lysistrata*).

Solomos rejects the idea that 'the sausage-seller is the theatrical disguise of a real political personality'[7] mainly because 'no political personality mentioned by history could in those days be considered as an outstanding figure in the People's Assembly, or even in Attic Comedy. Alcibiades had, of course, begun his career; but this up-and-coming politician, so typical of the depraved youth that Aristophanes loathed, could by no means typify the comic poet's vision of the State's savior. Besides, nothing alluding to Alcibiades' precious personality can be traced in the role.'[8] Solomos' argument is flawed since the structure of the play is satirical and ironic. Vickers has in fact ventured to identify the Sausage-Seller as a caricature of Alcibiades.[9] Of his thirty-seven arguments, however, none is compelling, and, since I shall argue that he is, nonetheless, correct, this is a good demonstration of how difficult it is to pry from the text what it was not meant to reveal *per se*. Alcibiades probably did not advocate the ending of the war in 422/1 and certainly tried to wreck the peace in the ensuing years, but that might have been one of many shifts he would make in his career.[10] It also seems quite likely that he was the central figure in Eupolis' *Baptai*, which suggests he was by then a political opponent. However, we have seen that Cratinus may have attacked Alcibiades (as Dionysus) in *Horai* and Eupolis may have defended him (in *Prospaltioi?*). Eupolis could, therefore, have supported Alcibiades up till 422/1, but then undergone a change of heart and political allegiance, since he kept his original position in favour of peace in 421 when Alcibiades altered his (as the satire of Eupolis as Trygaeus in *Peace* shows).

One place to start is, however, helpfully examined by Vickers.[11] It is the insight that *Knights* 511 may refer to *both* the caricature targets of the play. The line reads: καὶ γενναίως πρὸς τὸν Τυφῶ χωρεῖ καὶ τὴν ἐριώλην 'and marches nobly against Typhoon and whirlwind'. It is quite right to

---

[7] Solomos 1974, 97–8. One of his arguments is that 'If it were so, the ancient scholiasts, who tell us who the 'rope-seller' and the 'sheep-seller' were, would have deciphered the sausage-seller's identity as well.' His confidence in the ancient scholiasts is misplaced. They only identified slave 1 as Demosthenes because of line 55, and slave 2 as Nicias because if one of the two was a political leader, it made sense for both to be, and they used the same procedure for the 'sellers' only as far as logic necessitated. That is, the 'leather-seller' was clearly Cleon, and it made no sense for his predecessors to be fictitious. Since his supplanting was a fiction, however, it made sense (to them) that the supplanter should be fictional. If they had possessed *Noumeniai*, all this might have been different.

[8] Solomos 1974, p.97. His argument for a sort of allegory, in which 'Agoracritus is Aristophanes himself' (id., p. 99.) is refuted by the evidence presented in chapter three.

[9] Vickers 1997, 100f.   [10] *CAH*[2] v, 441f.   [11] Vickers 1997, 110.

see two targets here, rather than one. And so the ἐριώλη 'whirlwind' ought logically to be another politician. Though it is not logically *necessary* in the context that the line speaks of the targets of *this* play, rather than of earlier plays, it does nonetheless seem quite likely. The rest of Vickers' argument here depends, however, on the correlation of Alcibiades' known penchant for extraordinary clothes with the assumption that Bdelycleon represents Alcibiades, which on my arguments can not be correct.[12] Yet the punch-line of *Wasps* 1147–8 would be explicable in terms of Alcibiades for another reason. For it is the *extravagance* of the garment which leads to its description as ἐριώλη (1146–7: αὕτη γέ τοι | ἐρίων τάλαντον καταπέπωκε ῥᾳδίως 'This drank down a talent of wool easily'). Extravagance and a high consumption of alcohol were associated with Alcibiades.[13] The resulting joke could be translated thus: 'Bdel: This is an extravagant garment, which has drunk an enormous amount of wool. Phil: Well better call it an Alcibiades, then!' This would serve both to link with Cratinus' attacks on Alcibiades and with the hypothesised political agreement between Eupolis and Alcibiades at this time. It would also be amusing in the context of an Aristophanic parabasis for the Knights to attack one of their own. Insofar as we know about Alcibiades at this time, he seems to have been close enough to Cleon on financial issues relating to the allies and in enmity to the Spartans to make representation of him as Sausage-Seller a good way to satirise him (and through him, his at the time close ally Eupolis).[14]

We can go further. The garment out of which such fun is made in the *Wasps* passage is a Persian cloak called a *kaunakes*. Among the characteristics which strike Philocleon are the tufts of wool which cover it, which he likens to woollen sausages (κρόκης χόλιξ 1144). The laboured joke which follows has Philocleon punning weakly on the word for wool (ἔριον) in order to get the word ἐριώλη in as his preferred name for the garment. If, as seems likely from *Knights* 511, the word ἐριώλη 'whirlwind' was the sobriquet of a politician, and he is the other focus of attack in this play, then it was someone also renowned for wearing what looks like a garment covered with strings of sausages. If my identifications are correct, this scene has another point of contact with *Knights*: Bdelycleon/Eupolis is the one who by asking his father to wear the sausage-like garment associates himself closely with the Sausage-Seller – the ἐριώλη 'whirlwind'. The wind imagery used of Sausage-Seller by the chorus at 760 would also fit with the proposition that his original – like Cleon as Typhon (cf. *Wasps* 1033) – was known by a wind sobriquet.

---

[12] Vickers 1997, pp. 121–2.   [13] Thuc. 6.15.3, Pl. *Symp.* 212df.   [14] Ostwald 1986, 293.

I conclude that Sausage-Seller might be a cover for Alcibiades (a) because he was known for his extravagant clothing (Plut. *Alc.* 16.1); (b) because he may at this time have been politically close to Eupolis; (c) because he was a Knight (Pl. *Symp.* 221a; Plut. *Alc.* 7) and it would be natural for him to find support from this group, as he does in this play (see further below); (d) because we know that he was involved in court advocacy at an early date (*Daitales* fr. 205.6, *Acharnians* 716), which suits *Knights* 346–50; (e) he had a reputation for sexual profligacy, both hetero- and homosexual (*Daitales* fr. 244; Pherecrates fr. 164), which fits with his characterisation at e.g. *Knights* 167, 423–6, 721.[15]

Further, if Aristophanes was deliberately calquing Sausage-Seller on the lamp-seller Hyperbolus in *Noumeniai*, then a large part of the humour is being made just through this transfer. I shall argue below (p. 174) that exactly this manoeuvre accounts for the non-Socratean appearance of Socrates in *Clouds*. If this was the case, all the more reason for Eupolis to have made his claim in *Baptai* in the way that he did (fr. 89). As to Eupolis' change of attitude to Alcibiades, if Alcibiades does speak the response to Ἀλκιβιάδης ἐκ τῶν γυναικῶν ἐξίτω ('Alcibiades is to come out of the womens' quarters') at fr. 171 of Eupolis' *Kolakes*, this on-stage caricature will quite reasonably mark the point at which the poet turned away from him, since the play was produced in the year of the Peace of Nicias, which, I have argued, Eupolis will have fervently supported.

One of the most paradoxical aspects of the play has always seemed to be the political alliance between the Knights, representing the richest Athenian class, and the low-born and scoundrelly Sausage-Seller. However, the difficulties can now be resolved by the proposal that Sausage-Seller represents Alcibiades, a knight himself and also a political ally of Eupolis, who may also have been connected with the Knights (*Clouds* 545 with chapter one, p. 25). Eupolis' close association with the Knights may be evidenced also if *Acharnians* 5–8 and 299f. both refer to a trial-scene in *Chrysoun Genos*. I suggested earlier that the Knights themselves may have had as their proxy on stage there Alcibiades (*Ach.* 716, *Ach.* 301–2 τοῖσιν ἱππεῦσι 'for the Knights'). Though this does imply that (apparently unlike Aristophanes) Eupolis sometimes had *positive* characters, this is not a problem, as his Solon, Aristides, Miltiades and Pericles in *Demoi* do also appear to be non-satirical figures.[16]

---

[15] We may now thus give this as a reasonable reply to Solomos' problem that 'nothing alluding to Alcibiades' precious personality can be traced in the role.' (Solomos 1974, p. 97).
[16] See Telò 2007, 102f.

From Knights *to* Peace

But Eupolis may be satirised by another device which appears only vestigially in *Knights*, the double chorus. We have no solid evidence from his own plays of his having used this before *Marikas*, where fr. 192.98–9, 117, 118, 121, 186 with fr. 193 show that there were two semi-choruses, one of poor men, the other of rich men. However, the split chorus of *Acharnians* (557f.) may be taken, given the anti-Eupolidean metacomic context of the play, to be an indication that it was already associated with his work. In an article published in 2000, I pointed out that the staging of the *Knights* parodos is problematic and Cleon's call for his own old-juror supporters at 255f. may well be answered by their appearance and paradoxical rejection of their patron at 258f. At least it is very difficult to explain why in Paphlagon's reply at 266 he uses the verb ξυνεπίκεισθε 'join in attacking' and the emphatic pronoun ὑμεῖς '*you*', which ought to imply that a *new* group has joined the fray, one he would have expected to get *support* from and not opposition.[17] But how this semi-chorus was represented on stage and whether they remained and joined the Knights or departed after the affray is impossible to say from textual indications.[18] If, however, the old juror semi-chorus formed part of the greater Knights chorus, then *Knights* 507–9 may gain added humorous depth. Their statement that they would never have come forward to speak for a comic poet of the old school must in the circumstances be an allusion to Cratinus, the originator, on my argument, of the old juror who supports Cleon (in *Nomoi*?). The allusion will only be apt, however, because in the play as a whole Eupolis is being satirised as the imitator of Cratinus. Although it has proved possible, then, for Ste Croix to regard the treatment of the horsemen of Athens in *Knights* as favourable, Gomme's assessment is more accurate: the chorus 'in effect only propose to get rid of Cleon by putting Athens... in the power of a similar demogogue'.[19]

But the difficulty of understanding the relationship between Sausage-Seller and Knights is joined as a problem by its apparent dissonance with the *katastrophe* in which Demos appears reborn in pre-Persian War guise (1325) and Sausage-Seller appears to lose his vileness as they discuss future policy (mostly dictated by Demos). Thus, Ste Croix objects to Gomme's assessment of the Knights by saying that it ignores the rejuvenation of Demos as well as the removal of Sausage-Seller's 'demagogy and all his

---

[17] Sidwell 2000c, 45–8.
[18] See Sidwell 2000c, 47–50 for some speculations. I now withdraw the explanations of poetic voice offered on page 50 of this article.
[19] Ste Croix 1972, 360f. Gomme 1938, 106.

unpleasant characteristics' after 1316.[20] However, the satire does not stop once Paphlagon/Cleon is defeated: the reference to the Peace-Terms is a good index of this (1388–9), since peace with Sparta was not a current goal of Hyperbolus, and thus the apparently positive use of the motif ought to be taken ironically in the work of one of his supporters (*Clouds* 554). The attack merely changes focus, presumably by making fun of political attitudes displayed in Eupolis' plays and shared by the Sausage-Seller's original, but not by Aristophanes. In the context of a representation of Demos as a Cratinus who changes his support from Cleon to a young man whom he had possibly attacked in *Horai* as a ne'er-do-well ultimately responsible for the outbreak of the war, the rejuvenation, the 'pre-Persian War' Athens, and the Sausage-Seller's new demeanour will only be further aspects of the satire. And the ironic ending would, of course, have been expected if Hyperbolus' takeover of the *prostasia* in *Noumeniai* ended Eupolis' play, since the audience will have been well aware of where that comic poet stood politically also.

The rejuvenation of Demos at *Knights* 1321 is calqued on that of Aeson, Jason's father, performed by Medea. The scholium on 1321 and comparison with a passage from *Nostoi* (fr. 6 Allen) make it clear that this is not just a case of making him καλὸν ἐξ αἰσχροῦ ('handsome instead of ugly'), but of making him young again.[21] The focus on his former ugliness must surely be a hit at the looks of Cratinus. The rejuvenation theme occurs twice more in Aristophanes, each time in relation to what I have argued are comic poet figures, Philocleon at *Wasps* 1333 and 1355, and Trygaeus at *Peace* 860–1. It is likely, then, that they are underpinned by a metacomic reference. That could be either to an unknown passage in Cratinus, which *Knights* is satirising by inserting the author into his own scenario, or to Eupolis' prior use of a Demos rejuvenation in the lost *Noumeniai* (as I suggested above), or to the *Knights* passage itself, or both. If Philocleon represents Cratinus, then the *Wasps* passage need look back only to *Knights*, since that is where his rejuvenation occurred. And if Trygaeus represents Eupolis, dressed up still as his old comic poet figure Cratinus (as in *Acharnians*), then the *Peace* joke too would work with the same intertext. However, both jokes might be funnier if what happened in *Knights* was that Cratinus was transformed into his younger rival, Eupolis, and if that in turn had been a subversion of Eupolis' rejuvenation of Demos/Cratinus into Demos/Aristophanes in *Noumeniai*. Demos certainly changes his hairstyle, possibly from short

---

[20] 1972, 361. See also Sommerstein 1981, 2–3.
[21] Edmunds 1987, 43 argues otherwise, focusing on his mistaken interpretation of γέρων at 1349 as 'though I was an old man'.

to long (*Knights* 1331), and this would suit a change from Cratinus' style (*Acharnians* 849)[22] to Eupolis' (*Clouds* 545 with my gloss, above, p. 25). He abandons the χοιρίνη 'mussel-shell' (*Knights* 1332) which marks out Philocleon/Cratinus at *Wasps* 349. He also (*Knights* 1331) jettisons the poor clothing (cf. 881f.) that also characterised Philocleon/Cratinus in *Wasps* (1122f.) and, I have argued, Eupolis' Cratinus in *Chrysoun Genos* (fr. 298.6), for garments that would be more suitable for the Bdelycleon/Eupolis figure whose extravagant – and Persophilic – sartorial tastes are pilloried at *Wasps* 1122f.

The ideology that accompanies this transformation from old to young poet will also satirise something known about Eupolis' political proclivities. The era to which the rejuvenated Demos belongs is that of Aristides and Miltiades (1325), later protagonists of Eupolis' *Demes* (where with Solon and Pericles they played a positive role: see below chapter six, p. 280). This was a period before the radical democracy and a perfectly respectable rallying-cry for opponents of radical democracy who wished to claim the potency of an earlier, still democratic, constitution, since it could be represented as having won the ultimate battle against the Persians, Marathon (1334). That the appeal to Marathon was attached somehow to Eupolis can be argued by the coincidence of phrasing in 1334 (τῆς γὰρ πόλεως ἄξια πράττεις καὶ τοῦ 'ν Μαραθῶνι τροπαίου 'You are faring worthily of the city and of the trophy at Marathon') and that of *Wasps* 711, in the speech of Bdelycleon/Eupolis (ἄξια τῆς γῆς ἀπολαύοντες καὶ τοῦ 'ν Μαραθῶνι τροπαίου 'profiting worthily of the land and of the trophy at Marathon').[23]

If the rejuvenated Demos is now a figure of fun for his adherence to a conservative, if still quasi-democratic, ideology possibly shared by many Knights (who were certainly anti-democratic in 411, Thuc. 8.92.6, and who as a body later served the Thirty, Xen. *Hell.* 2.4. 2, 4, 7, 8, 24, 31, 3.1.4, Lysias 16.6), the relationship with him of the apparently altered Sausage-Seller also has satirical purpose. While Sausage-Seller criticises other demagogues for their controlling tactics (1340–4, 1350–4, 1356–61) and appears to cede the primacy of Demos in decision-making (1359–82), it is nonetheless he who rewards Demos for his new policies (1384 ἔχε νῦν ἐπὶ τούτοις... 'Then on those terms you can have...'; 1388–9 ἐπειδὰν παραδῶ σοι... 'When I hand over to you...'; νῦν οὖν ἐγώ σοι παραδίδωμ' 'Now I present (them) to you...') and who will punish Paphlagon (1395–1403).

---

[22] With the comments of Olson 2002 ad loc.
[23] It will also be significant that the *Acharnians* chorus are Μαραθωνομάχαι 181, cf. 696f., and that the *Wasps* chorus were also involved in the fight against the barbarian Persians (1078f.).

In fact, he will be taking Paphlagon's place (1404–5) and there is certainly not a complete discontinuity between the ideas of the old Demos and the rejuvenated model (compare 1065–6, 1078–9 with 1366–7, full pay for rowers on arrival in port). An Athenian audience would be attuned to the general irony implicit in the soft-centred approach of the Sausage-Seller as he promises Demos control while deftly retaining it himself. But if the identification with Alcibiades is correct, they would also laugh uproariously at the conflict between the chorus' address to the victorious Sausage-Seller at 1319 and their knowledge of his original's political record in this regard. The chorus says: ὦ ταῖς ἱεραῖς φέγγος Ἀθήναις καὶ ταῖς νήσοις ἐπίκουρε 'O thou beam of light to sacred Athens and helpmeet to the islands'. Develin accepts the historical accuracy of the reference at [Andocides] 4.11 to Alcibiades' role, probably as *taktes*, in the virtual doubling of the tribute in 425, certainly a move instigated by Cleon (*IG* i¹.63).[24] If he is correct, then a further running joke in the play will be furnished by the closeness of Alcibiades to Cleon in policy towards the allies (as noted above). That the harsh treatment of the allies can be exploited humorously in relation to Eupolis is clear from the way in which he is made to present his own policy for redistribution of those funds as Bdelycleon at *Wasps* 706f. (for which see further below, pp. 194–5).

I suggested earlier (chapter three) that the ancient claim that the second parabasis was written by Eupolis may have had some basis in reality – at least to the extent that a real Eupolidean line was detectable in it. I cited there Hubbard's conclusion, that '[b]y quoting Eupolis here, Aristophanes manages to place the most savage invective of the play onto another poet's shoulders' and remarked that this is not far from saying that the second parabasis is presented in Eupolis' voice. In that case, what happens here is exactly like the metacomic quasi-parabasis of *Acharnians* 496f. If this is so, then we can draw two further conclusions. First, as in the epirrhemes of the parabasis of *Acharnians*, the chorus' effusions are ironical and aimed at subversion of Eupolidean ideas and political friends (possibly via reference to Cratinean comedy: cf. *Knights* 1309 and Cratinus fr. 512). Secondly, the play itself – as opposed to the parabasis (507–50) which alludes to its central targets and humorously explains the poet's own career – is made to look, and sound, like one of Eupolis' own productions. Such a ploy is not unusual in parody, of course, and appears to be what is also happening in *Acharnians* and *Wasps*. What is more, this conclusion may help add an extra layer of meaning to Cratinus' complaint (fr. 213) against Aristophanes

---

[24] Develin 1989, 131.

for τὰ Εὐπόλιδος λέγοντα: the play was quite literally using Eupolis' voice in subversively recycling his *Noumeniai*.

The reading of *Knights* as a comedy as much – if not more – focused upon satire of Eupolis and the new Cleon, that is the Sausage-Seller/Alcibiades, somewhat reduces any surprise that despite Aristophanes' first prize, Cleon was elected to the generalship only a few weeks later. Public opinion was still very much in favour of prosecuting the war and Cleon had given the Athenians a major new bargaining counter as well in the prisoners from Pylos. In any case, as I have argued, Aristophanes was not averse to this policy, even if he found Cleon unacceptable as a political personality (perhaps because he represented a rustic and uneducated (cf. *Knights* 986 and Thuc. 3.37.3) strand of radical democracy rather than the educated (cf. *Clouds* 876) and city-based type of Hyperbolus?). Indeed, his case in *Knights* amounted to saying that although Cleon was appalling, the alternative offered by the peace party (to which Alcibiades still belonged at this point) was even worse and the ideology of a return to proto-democracy merely pandered to another unacceptable political force.

CLOUDS I

The first *Clouds* was produced at the Dionysia in the archonship of Isarchus (423) and came third, behind Cratinus' *Pytine* ('Wine-Flask') and Ameipsias' *Konnos*.[25] However, we possess only a few fragments of the play produced in 423 and the version of *Clouds* we have is a revised one. Independent evidence for the places revised comes from the first hypothesis, whose information Dover has shown convincingly derives from a copy of the first version which survived into Hellenistic times:[26]

τοῦτο ταὐτόν ἐστι τῷ προτέρῳ, διεσκεύασται δὲ ἐπὶ μέρους, ὡς ἂν δὴ ἀναδιδάξαι μὲν αὐτὸ τοῦ ποιητοῦ προθυμηθέντος, οὐκέτι δὲ τοῦτο δι' ἥνποτε αἰτίαν ποιήσαντος. Καθόλου μὲν οὖν σχεδὸν παρὰ πᾶν μέρος γεγενημένη <ἡ> διόρθωσις <. . .> τὰ μὲν γὰρ περιῄρηται, τὰ δὲ παραπέπλεκται καὶ ἐν τῇ τάξει καὶ ἐν τῇ τῶν προσώπων διαλλαγῇ μετεσχημάτισται, ἃ δὲ ὁλοσχερῆ τῆς διασκευῆς τοιαῦτα ὄντα τετύχηκεν. Αὐτίκα ἡ παράβασις τοῦ χοροῦ

---

[25] Hypothesis II (Dover): αἱ πρῶται Νεφέλαι ἐδιδάχθησαν ἐν ἄστει ἐπὶ ἄρχοντος Ἰσάρχου, ὅτε Κρατῖνος μὲν ἐνίκα Πυτίνῃ, Ἀμειψίας δὲ Κόννῳ. 'The first *Clouds* was produced in the city in Isarchus' archonship, when Cratinus won with *Pytine*, and Ameipsias <took second prize> with *Konnos*.'
[26] His edition lxxx–xcviii.

ἤμειπται καὶ ὅπου ὁ δίκαιος λόγος πρὸς τὸν ἄδικον λαλεῖ, καὶ τελευταῖον ὅπου καίεται ἡ διατριβὴ Σωκράτους.

This is the same play as the earlier one, but it has been revised partially, as though the poet had actually wanted to put it on again but for whatever reason did not. In general, the text has been altered in almost every section . . . Some things have been deleted, some have been worked in and remodelling has taken place both in the arrangement and the change (?) of speaking parts (characters?), others have been revised entirely, such as the following: for instance, the parabasis of the chorus has been replaced, as has the passage where the just argument chatters with the unjust one, and finally the passage where the school of Socrates is burned down.

The writer of this hypothesis may give us some hint in the phrase ἐν τῇ τῶν προσώπων διαλλαγῇ μετεσχημάτισται, as Dover notes, 'that characters found in one version are not to be found at all in the other'.[27] Even if it seems unlikely that he would not have alerted us to a change in the central characters, especially since he asserts at the outset that this play is the same as the first *Clouds*, this does not mean that the targets behind those characters necessarily stayed the same. And I have argued above in chapter one that Aristophanes rewrote the play to attack two different individuals for whom he judged the play's plot was equally relevant as satire and that this is why he could think of putting on again what looked to the hypothesis writer to be the same play even while he was claiming he never did such a thing (*Clouds* 546–7).

The only evidence we might have comes in the parabasis of *Wasps* (1037–45).

> φησίν τε μετ' αὐτὸν
> τοῖς ἠπιάλοις ἐπιχειρῆσαι πέρυσιν καὶ τοῖς πυρετοῖσιν
> οἳ τοὺς πατέρας ἦγχον νύκτωρ καὶ τοὺς πάππους ἀπέπνιγον,
> κατακλινόμενοί τ' ἐπὶ ταῖς κοίταις ἐπὶ τοῖσιν ἀπράγμοσιν ὑμῶν
> ἀντωμοσίας καὶ προσκλήσεις καὶ μαρτυρίας συνεκόλλων,
> ὥστ' ἀναπηδᾶν δειμαίνοντας πολλοὺς ὡς τὸν πολέμαρχον.
> τοιόνδ' εὑρόντες ἀλεξίκακον, τῆς χώρας τῆσδε καθαρτήν,
> πέρυσιν καταπρούδοτε καινοτάτας σπείραντ' αὐτὸν διανοίας,
> ἃς ὑπὸ τοῦ μὴ γνῶναι καθαρῶς ὑμεῖς ἐποιήσατ' ἀναλδεῖς.

And he says after him, he tackled the shivers and the fevers, who throttled fathers and strangled grandfathers by night, lying down on the beds of those of you who don't like getting involved, and pieced together affidavits, summonses and depositions, so that lots of you in fear leaped up and went to the polemarch. Such was the warder off of ill, the purifier of this land, that you had found; but last year

---

[27] Dover lxxxiii.

you betrayed him, when he had sowed a fieldful of spanking-new ideas which you cast a blight on by not understanding them clearly.

The one thing of which we can be reasonably certain is that we are looking for a play belonging to 423. But is it *Clouds* or another, of which there is no independent record? And if it is not *Clouds*, does the word πέρυσιν at 1044 refer to *Clouds* or the unknown play?

The more general modern view is that 1037–42 relates to an unrecorded Lenaea play of 423, possibly *Holkades*, while 1043f. refers to *Clouds*.[28] This is presumably because the subject matter alluded to in the first part of the passage (young men using the law-courts for personal and corrupt motives) does not seem congruent with the play we now possess.[29] As we shall see, however, when *Clouds* is read as caricature comedy, and the allusion in *Wasps* to its targets and not to its plot, the matter will appear differently. As to the apparent transition at 1043, Hubbard is right when he remarks that 'the reference to the *Clouds* in vv. 1044–5 as last year's comedy... would be too confusing and abrupt if it were not the same as the play referred to as last year's comedy in vv. 1037–43'.[30]

There are in fact two further arguments to support the view that Aristophanes' chorus is only alluding to one play, *Clouds*, in this passage of *Wasps*.

(1) Σ^{VΓAld} *Wasps* 1038c reads: πέρυσιν· πέρυσι γὰρ τὰς Νεφέλας ἐδίδαξεν, ἐν αἷς τοὺς περὶ Σωκράτην ἐκωμῴδησεν. ἠπιάλους δὲ αὐτοὺς ὠνόμασεν εἰς ὠχρότητα παρασκώπτων. ('Last year: because the previous year he produced *Clouds*, in which he satirised the Socratic circle. He called them 'shivers', joking about their paleness'). Σ^{VÃ} *Wasps* 1038a (= Ari. fr. 399 PCG, from *Clouds* I) reads: ἠπίαλος τὸ πρὸ τοῦ πυρετοῦ κρύος. Ἀριστοφάνης Νεφέλαις ('Shiver: the coldness before a fever. Aristophanes *Clouds*').

---

[28] See Hubbard 1991, 119 with n. 14 for a conspectus of views. Of more recent scholars, Platnauer 1949, 7 opts for *Holkades* as the referent of 1037f. MacDowell 1971 ad loc. cites Platnauer (*loc. cit.*), and after giving various objections to his view, suggests that the play may have been *Georgoi*.

[29] However, since neither MacDowell 1971 nor Sommerstein 1983 thinks that there is any doubt that the first play is different from *Clouds*, and thus neither argues the case at all, this is merely an inference.

[30] Hubbard 1991, 119. Of course, this is not cut and dried. It is really an argument for us rather than the original audience, who would already have identified 'last year's play' before the second πέρυσιν because of the description given of it. But an analysis of the parabasis makes it clear that the two occurrences of πέρυσιν belong to different sections of the argument. In the first it is the points of attack in the plays which are central ('immortal monsters', including Cleon at 1029–37 and then the ἠπίαλοι καὶ πυρετοί 'the agues and the fevers' at 1037–42). In the second (1043f.) the emphasis is upon the audience's response ('you didn't understand the play and so didn't award it the prize'). So even on general grounds it is possible to defend a reference to *Clouds* here.

There are two points to make about the evidence of these scholia. First, the positive way the note is formulated might be taken to indicate that the scholiasts did not know of another play by Aristophanes produced in 423, since the ancient scholars regularly consulted the *didaskaliai*. It seems most unlikely that had there been a record of a Lenaea play for 423 we would not either hear of it in our sources or at least see its shadow in a *zetema*. Callimachus' problems with the text of *Clouds* vis à vis the *didaskaliai*, and Eratosthenes' answer are a good example of the way these scholars investigated the plays, as of the attention which was paid to the *didaskaliai* in the specific case of *Clouds*.³¹ Secondly, the information that τοὺς περὶ Σωκράτην... ἠπιάλους... ὠνόμασεν ('he called the Socratic group "shivers"') is not directly accessible from the *Wasps* passage. It is possible that it was a conjecture based on the assumption that the play referred to was *Clouds*. But the citation of ἠπίαλος from *Clouds*, which must mean the first version, suggests that it might have been taken from there. It is tempting to conjecture that as in *Wasps*, so in the first *Clouds*, the parabasis mentioned the targets of the play by this name. This conclusion seems the more cogent when one compares the statement of the *Life* (Koster, *Prolegomena* p. 134, XXVIII.33–5): φασὶ δὲ αὐτὸν εὐδοκιμῆσαι συκοφάντας καταλύσαντα οὓς ὠνόμασεν ἠπιάλους ἐν Σφηξίν (followed by the citation of *Wasps* 1039) ('they say he won popularity by getting rid of the sycophants, whom he called "shivers" in *Wasps*'). This coincides with modern views (e.g. Hubbard's) of the purport of *Wasps* 1037–42.³² Like the modern view, it is based solely on an attempt to interpret the passage without recourse to external evidence (and even the implication that he may have won a prize can be interpreted thus). Its existence suggests that without external evidence, ancient scholars too were inclined to see the targets as sycophants. It thereby leaves open a reasonable possibility that the identification of the targets as Socrates' circle does depend on external evidence. However, we should be cautious here, since just as in *Wasps* the targets are left vague – for the audience to identify – so the reference to ἠπίαλος in the parabasis of *Clouds I* might not have specified the targets. The scholiasts might then have identified them as τοὺς περὶ Σωκράτην since, of course, the central characters of the play are pupils of Socrates in the play.

The possibility that the identification of these denizens with the Socratic group goes back to the first *Clouds*, however, is further enhanced by consideration of the syntax and background of 1039. Sommerstein translates 'that

---

³¹ See Dover 1968 lxxxi.
³² Hubbard 1991, 119: 'Last year... Aristophanes presented a play attacking sycophants.'

by night throttled fathers and grandfathers', treating the definite articles as generic. MacDowell, however, seems to imply that the article suggests these are *their own* fathers and grandfathers.[33] This understanding is reflected in the intrusion of αὐτῶν ('their') into the citation of the line in the *Vita* (Koster, *Prolegomena* p. 134, XXVIII.35).

MacDowell's inference is surely correct. In Xenophon *Memorabilia* 1.2.49f. we read several reports of accusations made against Socrates. They centre upon the charge that he taught his pupils to insult their fathers and to think themselves wiser than them, and even to take them to court for παράνοια ('madness') if necessary. This contempt was also to be extended to other relatives, according to one accuser.[34] In *Clouds*, the central characters *are* pupils of Socrates. The possibility that the formulation in *Wasps* could apply to their originals is enhanced by the fact that at 844–6 Pheidippides turns to the audience and asks if he should indict his father for παράνοια ('madness').

(2) Σ^LhAld *Wasps* 1039a reads: τὸ δὲ 'τοὺς πατέρας ἦγχον' λέγει διὰ τὸν ὑπ'αὐτοῦ, ὥς φησιν, πέρυσιν εἰσαχθέντα ἐν Νεφέλαις τύπτοντα τὸν πατέρα αὐτοῦ ('He says 'they strangled their fathers' because of the person, as he says, last year brought on stage in *Clouds* beating his father'). The scholion thus points out a thematic connection between the formulation of the *Wasps* parabasis and the episode in *Clouds* 1321f. where Pheidippides chases Strepsiades out of the house, where he has been beating him. In the course of the ensuing discussion, Strepsiades at 1385–90 specifically says that his son throttled him and choked him. The words are ἀπάγχων ('throttling') and πνιγόμενος ('being choked'), with which one should compare ἦγχον ('they throttled') and ἀπέπνιγον ('they choked') in *Wasps* 1039. That such coincidences of textual detail may indeed link the allusions of this parabasis to the plays from which they come is suggested by the use of the epithet καρχαρόδοντι ('jag-toothed') in *Clouds* 1031 to refer to Cleon. In *Knights* (the play alluded to in the *Clouds* passage) he is called κύνα καρχαρόδοντα ('the jag-toothed hound') at 1017.

Another clear connection emerges on re-examination of the syntax of 1040–1: κατακλινόμενοί τ' ἐπὶ ταῖς κοίταις ἐπὶ τοῖσιν ἀπράγμοσιν ὑμῶν | ἀντωμοσίας καὶ προσκλήσεις καὶ μαρτυρίας συνεκόλλων. MacDowell comments: ' ἐπὶ ταῖς κοίταις is 'on the beds', but the following

---

[33] MacDowell 1971 on 1039: '1039 is simply a way of saying 'were utter scoundrels', since attacking one's parents... is a cliché for the worst kind of crime.' Hubbard 1991, 115 translates it with the pronominal adjective 'their'.

[34] Note the way in which Plato's *Euthyphro* implicitly refutes the charge that Socrates approved of or encouraged taking one's father to court.

ἐπί is more vaguely 'in relation to'. Sommerstein's translation, 'lying down on the beds of those among you who keep out of politics', also interprets thus. However, such an odd construction, the addition of a prepositional phrase onto another with the same preposition in a different meaning, seems unlikely in itself and is not necessary. There is a forward point of reference in the verb συνεκόλλων ('they stuck together'), with which the preposition will mean 'against'. The phrasing is thus more natural rhetorically, since there is a pause after the first item at mid-line before the second section begins. The sentence thus means 'and lying on their beds concocted affidavits, summonses and depositions against the *apragmones* among you'. The allusion in the first phrase will be to a connection between proponents of the new learning and beds which is much utilized in *Clouds*. At the beginning of the play Strepsiades and Pheidippides are both seen in bed. Strepsiades, however, is not asleep, but working out his problems. This is precisely what he is made to do later on in the play, in the *phrontisterion* (694f.), as part of his training as a speaker. Moreover, that the bed had some already established part in the public's perception of sophistic method before *Clouds* can be inferred from Strepsiades' response to the Clouds at 420. They have just asked him if he has a whole list of qualities which he will need if he is to be a successful student and one of the things claims is δυσκολοκοίτου . . . μερίμνης ('thought on a bed which disallows sleep'). It is interesting to note that in Plato's *Protagoras* 315d, Prodicus is depicted in bed wrapped up in several blankets (like Pheidippides at *Clouds* 10), surrounded by his pupils, who are also on couches. This picture is usually taken at face-value, but one may wonder whether in fact Plato did not borrow this along with other motifs from comedy (for example the door-knocking scene 314c–e, and the description of Protagoras' χορός ['chorus'] 315b).[35]

The standard explanation of the passage is that these are *xenoi*, who bring indictments against peaceable Athenians, who then go to the polemarch to ask for his protection against these meddlesome foreigners (perhaps by making them post bail with him).[36] As Sommerstein notes, however, we know of no instance in which a case was brought by an alien which did not involve himself as victim. This rather suggests that the so-called *sykophantai*

---

[35] On Plato and comedy, see Brock 1990. The question of a prior comic portrayal will be investigated under *Clouds II*. See further Sidwell 2005a.

[36] So MacDowell 1971 ad loc.: 'Ar's statement that Athenians afflicted by συκοφάνται rush to the polemarkhos is evidence that many συκοφάνται were not citizens but metics.' Sommerstein enters a caveat, 'The insinuation is not necessarily or even probably true', because accusations of foreign birth were a commonplace of comic or oratorical abuse, used even when demonstrably false (on this see now MacDowell 1993).

attacked in this play could not have been aliens, asked to post bail by their victims. Instead, it is the victims of these 'sycophants' who are *xenoi* and must go to the polemarch when accused by these monsters.[37] Precisely this scenario, a would-be politician taking steps against a metic, is envisaged by Paphlagon at *Knights* 346–50 (cf. 326, 1408, *Peace* 635–48).[38] Hence a third point of contact with *Clouds* emerges, since the whole purpose of Strepsiades' (and then Pheidippides') education is to win lawsuits unjustly for private gain (99, 112f., 239f., 433–4, 739, 758f., 1209–11 etc.). Note the rejection *en passant* by Strepsiades of what would in reality have been the aim of such politicians (431–2), namely to gain influence in the assembly. Once more there is telling coincidence of detail between *Wasps* 1041 συνεκόλλων ('stuck together') and *Clouds* 446 ψευδῶν συγκολλητής ('a sticker-together of falsehoods').

On the argument so far, whichever play is referred to in *Wasps* 1037–42, its central characters will have been 'the shivers and fevers who throttled their fathers by night and choked their grandfathers, and lying down on their couches concocted affidavits, summonses and depositions against the *apragmones* among you'. Cleon has been referred to in the immediately preceding passage of the *Wasps* parabasis (1031–5) as a monster, one of the immortals; these satiric targets are also referred to as monsters (ἠπίαλος is a 'nightmare-demon'),[39] and the poet has had the chorus make the claim that at least after his début as a *didaskalos* he did not attack mere ἀνθρώποις ('human beings' 1029). If it is correct to interpret this disjunction as a differentiation between ordinary human beings and politicians (a position which is substantiated by recalling Cratinus' presentation of Pericles as Zeus[40] and Aristophanes' rejection at *Peace* 751 of satire of private individuals), then it follows that the targets of this play ('those around Socrates') were not 'sycophants', as is usually said,[41] but politicians using the law-courts to aid their careers.

The play described in *Wasps* 1037–42, then, was not an attack on sycophants, but on Socrates and associates of his who tried to make their political reputations by attacking metics in the courts. Line 1039, taken at face-value, might imply that the targets of *Clouds* were in fact *young* men, since otherwise they would not be able to prosecute their fathers, let alone their grandfathers. This interpretation is given support by the

---

[37] For the demanding of bail from *xenoi* see, for example, Isoc. 17.12, Dem. 32.29.
[38] And perhaps it is significant that it is the Sausage-Seller (i.e. on my identification, pp. 157–60 above, Alcibiades) to whom Cleon's accusation refers.
[39] Sophron fr. 68 (Kaibel) calls it the 'father-choker'.   [40] See e.g. fr. 73, *Thraittai*.
[41] MacDowell 1971 on 1038.

foregoing analysis. If it is correct, we will identify them as members of the Socratic circle. Though the Socratic circle did, it seems, include some older members, it attracted the young rather more (Pl. *Apol.* 23c). This certainly seems to be the case also for the adherents of the other sophists, who were after all mostly in search of training.

The final part of the *Wasps* parabasis (1042–59) berates the audience once more for their lack of support for the Heracles who sowed new ideas in his previous year's play and for their misunderstanding of the concepts in it, though the satire was his best ever. The poet claims to have lost thereby, however, none of his *kudos* with the *sophoi*, even though his ambitious driving (cf. 1022 for the image) led him to wreck his chariot. The *pnigos* (1052–9) advises the public to admire novelty in future in comic poetry: its ideas will be useful to give an odour of cleverness to their cloaks if stored with them for a year. This cannot be other than a reference to the ignominious defeat of *Clouds*. It is interesting, however, that Aristophanes' target audience here and in the revised parabasis of *Clouds* is a group called οἱ σοφοί ('the wise': *Wasps* 1049, *Clouds* 526) and his own wish is to share this appellation (*Clouds* 520 νομιζοίμην σοφός 'may I be considered wise'). Commentators say little or nothing about this coincidence. Yet in this period, as I have argued in chapter one, the word σοφός was strongly associated with practitioners of the new learning (e.g. Pl. *Apol.* 20a, referring to Evenus of Paros; *Prt.* 309b etc., referring to Protagoras; Xen. *Mem.* 2.1.21, referring to Prodicus). It may be, then, that the attack on Socrates and his circle which *Clouds* attempted has to be set within a context in which it is also a *defence* of the sophistic learning Socrates and his circle (according to Plato) opposed. It is possible to go further. The greeting given by the Clouds at 358f. differentiates Socrates specifically from one of those practitioners, Prodicus of Ceos, σοφίας καὶ γνώμης οὕνεκα 'because of his (Prodicus') wisdom and intelligence'. Of this passage Dover writes '*Nu.* 358ff. are intelligible as comedy only if we believe that Ar. shared the popular esteem of Prodikos as an artist, and regarded Socrates, by contrast, as a pretentious parasite who inexplicably fascinated some wealthy young men but had nothing coherent to say and produced nothing of any artistic merit'.[42] Of other mentions of Prodicus in Aristophanes' plays (*Birds* 688f. and fr. 506 *Tagenistai*), he comments that 'neither of these two passages expresses hostility on the part of Ar. himself

---

[42] Dover 1968, lv–lvi. Of course, this would not be true if Aristophanes' Cloud chorus were to be construed – like the Acharnians and Knights on my interpretation – as themselves objects of satire. However, as I shall show below, their behaviour also sets them on the side of the angels, against the dishonest practices not only of Socrates but also of Strepsiades.

towards Prodikos'. The hostility, as I have demonstrated in Hyperbolus' case earlier, is ascribed to characters in the play. In the case of *Birds*, if I am right in supposing that Eupolis is once more in the satirical foreground there, the rejection of Prodicus will be an established part of that poet's known intellectual persona. As is the case also with Hyperbolus, then, there is an argument for suggesting that Aristophanes was actively sympathetic towards Prodicus, as opposed to Socrates, whom he satirised mercilessly (if, to our mind, unfairly).

Four further aspects of *Clouds* and one of Aristophanes' speech in Plato's *Symposium* can be adduced as reasons to link Aristophanes with Prodicus.

First, though the exchange between the *Logoi* possibly belongs in its entirety to the second version, it is worth noting that there are strong resemblances between the arguments used there and the outline of Prodicus' 'Choice of Heracles' found in Xenophon *Memorabilia* 2.1.21f., where two personified figures, Arete and Eudaimonia (or Kakia, as her enemies call her) each try to persuade Heracles to choose her path in life. Similarly in *Clouds*, each of the two *Logoi*, representing respectively justice and injustice, attempts to persuade young Pheidippides to choose *his* style of education and life (886–1111; note especially the choice at 1105f.). The passage therefore presents Strepsiades and Pheidippides in a comic rerun of Prodicus' Heracles motif, making the *wrong* choice (pointed up immediately by the Clouds at 1113–14).[43] The general parallelism could not be clearer, and becomes compelling when one considers the detail: (a) Arete argues for a tough life, with no avoidance of hard graft (Xen. *Mem.* 2.1. 28, 30–3), and berates the adherents of Kakia for having weak bodies as young men (31). *Greater Logos* has σωφροσύνη as his watchword (962, 1067) and expects his boys to be made tough by their hard training (965); (b) Arete argues that under her regime the old are honoured by the young (33). *Greater Logos* requires his boys to give up their seats for older men (993), to respect their parents (994), not to contradict their fathers (998–9), and not to take food from their elders (982); (c) Arete attacks lewd sexual practices (homosexual intercourse especially 30) and the disregard for a good reputation (31). *Greater Logos* combines these two themes at 996–7 and (albeit his interest is part of the ironic humour) castigates homosexual titillation among his boys (973–80) and attacks the καταπυγοσύνη of Antimachos (1022–3);(d) Kakia on the other hand offers a life devoted to pleasure and

---

[43] See Sommerstein 1997a for the suggestion that Strepsiades stays on stage for the debate in the revised version.

free from hard work (23–5). *Lesser Logos* gives a comprehensive list (1072–3) of what the boy will lose if he agrees to go with *Greater Logos*; (e) Kakia pays particular attention to the pleasures of homosexual intercourse (24), just as Arete castigates them (30). *Lesser Logos* includes in his list of pleasures παίδων (1073) and defends anal intercourse (1085–1100).[44]

Secondly, there may be a link with Prodicus arising from consideration of the differences between the Platonic and Xenophontic picture of Socrates (not a teacher, not interested in the workings of the *kosmos* or in philological niceties, never receiving fees, a pious believer in the gods and practitioner of ritual) and the Aristophanic (the opposite of all the above). In an interesting piece on the presentation of the sophist Prodicus in Plato's *Protagoras*, Willink opined that 'Prodikos had already said and done enough to establish for himself a reputation in the eyes of the ordinary Athenian as another pernicious 'atheist' after the pattern of Anaxagoras and Protagoras'.[45] In relation to *Clouds* he comments: 'the *arch-sophistic* 'Sokrates' satirised in the play is in several features (e.g. fee-taking, philological quibbling, heretical cosmology) specifically modelled on what we may take to have been the popular view of the arch-sophist Prodikos'.[46] Willink suggests comedy as a source for the formulation of such prejudicial attacks.[47] It is certainly possible that Aristophanes is in *Clouds* grafting onto Socrates the satirical attack made upon Prodicus by a rival. I have conjectured above that this was precisely what he had done with Sausage-Seller/Alcibiades in *Knights*, utilising the matrix of Eupolis' Hyperbolus as lamp-seller/manufacturer in the lost *Noumeniai*. And, as I have already argued at pp. 99–100, *Clouds* 876 may be evidence of Hyperbolus being taught rhetoric by a sophist in comedy, possibly Prodicus. That the play could have been by Eupolis is possible. It may have been *Aiges* (fr. 17 with Bergk's *Prodicus* for the unknown *Prodamus*, or assuming that *Prodamus* stood for *Prodicus*). *Clouds* 988–9, where a bad version of the Pyrrhic dance is mentioned, might be a cross-reference to the scene recalled at Eupolis fr. 18 *Aiges*, and the κάρδοπος ('kneading-tray') jokes at 669f. and 1248f. could be picking up fr. 21 of *Aiges*.[48]

Thirdly, a puzzling feature of the play is the way in which the chorus gradually shows itself more and more concerned with justice (810–11, 1113–14, 1303–20, 1458–61). In their lyric invocations at 563–74 and 595–606, Sommerstein notes, 'all but one of the deities summoned are traditional

---

[44] See also Papageorgiou 2004.   [45] Willink 1983, 28.   [46] Willink 1983, 26.
[47] Willink 1983, 33 for the conjecture that Anaxagoras was a target for comic satire.
[48] Note too verbal correspondence between *Ach.* 34, 35 and fr. 1 (πρίω 'buy') and 188, 191 and fr. 10 (γεῦσαι λαβών 'Take and taste') where the repetition in *Acharnians* may signal parody and thus help date *Aiges* before *Clouds*.

ones, and right at the start Zeus is emphatically called king of the gods, contrary to the belief of Socrates'.[49] If the comedy is deliberately transferring a prior on-stage caricature of Prodicus onto Socrates in order to attack Socrates and his circle, however, this can be explained on the basis that beneath the surface the 'Clouds' are actually Prodicus' goddesses of justice, the Horai, who were, according to Hesiod (*Theogony* 901f.), Eunomie, Dike and Eirene, the daughters of Zeus and Themis. This would, of course, give extra point to their praise of Prodicus at 361. It seems likely, on this reading, that Aristophanes was utilising and rebutting a chorus from Cratinus' *Horai* and consequently that that play may have contained the scene I suggested lies behind *Clouds* 876 (Hyperbolus learning rhetoric, possibly from Prodicus).[50] Unlike some of his earlier choruses, then, Aristophanes may have been using his Clouds as a sympathetic foil against his main on-stage caricature targets.

Fourthly, Aristophanes' speech in Plato's *Symposium* seems to have common ground with the argument of Kakia in Prodikos' *Horai* as well as with that of Unjust Argument in *Clouds*. The dialogue has strong links with the play: Alcibiades quotes from it at 221b and Agathon is made to exclaim ἰοὺ ἰού in addressing him at 223a. Aristophanes was, according to some ancient scholars, satirised (Olymp. *Vit. Pl.* 3, Athenaeus 5.187c) and this can certainly be seen from the way he is said to be addicted to wine and sex at 177d–e, as well as by his hiccoughs, caused by overeating (πλησμονή) at 185c–e. At 192a his strong support of homosexual intercourse recalls not only the remarks of Unjust Argument at *Clouds* 1084–1104, but also Prodicus' Kakia (DK fr. 7 = Xen. *Mem.* 2.1.24).[51]

But whether or not *Clouds* implicitly mounts a strong defence by Aristophanes of Prodicus, by bringing his goddesses of justice, the *Horai*, to bear on the perpetrators of a plot to subvert justice, it does explicitly involve a violent attack upon Socrates (Pl. *Apol.* 18d, 19c; cf. Xen. *Symp.* 6.6–8)[52] and even in its altered form was still marked, on my argument, by direct and metacomic targeting of Eupolis (*Clouds* 551f., the cross-reference to *Acharnians* at 920f. and the attacks on his comic techniques at 537f.). Given that (see above at pp. 93–4) in the version we have the role of Unjust Argument

---

[49] Sommerstein 1982 on 563–74.
[50] See above chapter one, n.33 for the linguistic arguments I made in Sidwell 1995, 68 that *Clouds* 560–3 may comically allude in εἰς τὰς ὥρας τὰς ἑτέρας to *Clouds II* as a 'second version of *Horai*'.
[51] A further point may lie in the self-portrait of the poet which likens his spirit to that of Heracles at *Wasps* 1030f. This coheres with Prodicus' promotion of Heracles in his *Horai* (Xen. *Mem.* 2.1.21f.). The repetition of the attack two years later at *Peace* 752f. perhaps underlines the importance and deliberateness of the self-image.
[52] See also Revermann 2006, 235.

is given to Eupolis, it seems that the best explanation for this is that Eupolis was among the adherents of Socrates in the 420s. There are, however, some difficulties attached to this conjecture. First, there are two named attacks on Socrates in Eupolis, in fr. 386 (μισῶ δὲ καὶ Σωκράτην | τὸν πτωχὸν ἀδολέσχην 'I hate Socrates too, the beggarly chatterer') and 395 (δεξάμενος δὲ Σωκράτης τὴν ἐπιδέξι'... | ... οἰνοχόην ἔκλεψεν 'Socrates took up the 'right'... and stole a wine decanter'), from plays whose title is not given. Bergk may be right to think they belong to *Kolakes* (421), one of the caricature targets of which, along with Callias, may have been Protagoras (cf. fr. 157, 158, though they do not prove that he was). Secondly, Lucian (*Piscator* 25) has Diogenes say in his speech against Parrhesiades: καὶ πάλαι ἔχαιρον Ἀριστοφάνει καὶ Εὐπόλιδι Σωκράτην ἐπὶ χλευασίᾳ παράγουσιν ἐπὶ τὴν σκηνήν 'and the audience used to enjoy Aristophanes and Eupolis bringing Socrates onto the stage to make fun of him'. However, we have seen above (pp. 91–102) that named references are not to be taken as a guide to the author's own predilections, but often occur as part of the satire of someone else. Here, then, it will be the speakers that are made fun of by the attacks on Socrates. As for Lucian, it is a moot point whether writers of his period actually understood or could articulate effectively the difference between a named and a caricature attack. Athenaeus, who uses *Kolakes* to prove that Protagoras was in Athens in 421 (5.218b–c), uses the verb εἰσάγει 'brings on' (cf. παράγουσιν in Lucian). But in both cases, had the name not been used, the writers would scarcely have been able to make their points or to have them understood by their readers. I conclude, then, that Lucian, like Athenaeus with Protagoras, evidences the *naming* of Socrates, which, as I have shown, is not the same as putting him into a play as a character.[53] As to the frequency of attack, a scholium on *Clouds* 96 tells us: Εὔπολις, εἰ καὶ δι' ὀλίγων ἐμνήσθη Σωκράτους, μᾶλλον ἢ Ἀριστοφάνης ἐν ὅλαις ταῖς Νεφέλαις αὐτοῦ καθήψατο. 'Eupolis may not have mentioned Socrates much, but he attacked him more than Aristophanes did in the whole of *Clouds*', and then quotes fr. 395. Given that this fragment is also noted by a scholium at 179e as a direct parallel for Socrates' inclination to theft there, it is also possible to see here a misappropriation of Aristophanic material which would have been palpable in context for the original audience and easily interpreted as a hit rather at Aristophanes than at Socrates. If Eupolis did actually put Protagoras on stage in *Kolakes*, this would allow us to draw in another detail of his intellectual *parti pris*: as a member of the Socratic circle, Eupolis was antipathetic to sophists. As

---

[53] *Contra* Storey 2003, 323–4.

a person close to Euripides, as I have conjectured he was, the hypothesised adherence to Socrates also makes sense (*Frogs* 1491f.).

The targets of *Clouds I*, then, were young members of Socrates' circle, actively involved in court advocacy, and Socrates himself. Eupolis, the comic poet, an opponent of the sophists and, presumably, a friend of Socrates, may have been counted among the ἠπίαλοι. If the *Logoi* were inserted wholesale into the second version, and if the identification of Unjust Argument as Eupolis (made above, pp. 93–4 via the cross-reference at 920f. to *Acharnians*) is sound, it is possible that the poet played a greater role in the original, perhaps even as Strepsiades. The 'old man' disguise will already have become semi-naturalised to him because of the way he played Cratinus in *Acharnians*.[54] For the plot to work satirically, we would probably have to assume that the poet had loaned money to the real person being caricatured as Pheidippides. Whether he was or was not widely known to have done so could well have affected the effectiveness of this satire, and the old-man disguise, if detached from the specific Cratinus context of *Acharnians*, could easily have caused the audience μὴ γνῶναι καθαρῶς 'not to understand clearly' the whole scenario, as Aristophanes has his chorus berate the audience in *Wasps* (1045). The *Wasps* parabasis may simply overstate and only one of the central caricature targets was involved in advocacy, unless there were other characters who do not appear in the later version because its satirical point and its targets had altered dramatically (as I think is probably the case: see chapter six), or incidental figures (e.g. the student who answers the door and the debtors) were also members of the Socratic circle (a real possibility).

It is impossible, in fact, in the absence of really clear information about the first version of the play, to be sure of any identification of the original play's on-stage caricatures. However, it is certainly not outside the bounds of reason to suggest that Pheidippides was originally modelled on Alcibiades:[55] in the version we still have, he is obsessed with chariot-racing (25, 28, 32, 124–5, cf. Davies *APF* 20–1), he manifests contempt for the laws (1321f., cf. Plut. *Alc.* 8, [Andocides] 4.10f.), he has a lisp (868–73, cf. *Wasps* 44–6),[56] he belongs to the Knights (120, cf. Pl. *Symp.* 221a, Plut. *Alc.* 7). He certainly became deeply embroiled in debt in the 410s (Thucydides 6.15.3).

---

[54] It is also possible (as Sommerstein argues, 1982, 4 n. 9), that it is only the opening of the *Logoi* scene which has been altered, the part, in fact, which contains the cross-reference to *Acharnians* and it does seem that the *Wasps* parabasis suggests the targets to be advocates, which does not, as far as we know anything solid about him, especially suit Eupolis.

[55] Vickers 1997, 22–58.

[56] The word τραυλίζω is used in relation to Pheidippides as a child (862, 1381), though not at 868–73. See Appendix 5.

If indeed he had been attacked the year before in *Knights* and was still part of the pro-Laconian peace party, then it makes sense to associate him with Eupolis in 423. The tale of his quick absorption of the lessons of villainy would have been extremely funny.[57] On this interpretation, the recasting (in both senses) of the play in the 410s will have retained certain Alcibidean traits in Pheidippides for a satiric purpose which I will deal with at the appropriate chronological moment, and will have moved Eupolis from central character to bit part because there was a new target Aristophanes wanted to hit.[58]

PYTINE AND WASPS

Clouds I failed, miserably, coming in a poor third to Cratinus' *Pytine* and Ameipsias' *Konnos*, another play which may have had Socrates as a character, albeit among the chorus of *phrontistai* (if fr. 9 is actually from that play). I have argued above (pp. 61–4) that Cratinus' *Pytine*, which is traditionally thought to have had the poet himself as the central character, having marital problems with his wife Comedy because of his drunkenness, was in fact an attack on Aristophanes, and not self-directed. The reason for this assault will not have been aesthetic, but political. If I am right in seeing the ideological differences between Cratinus and Eupolis played out in Aristophanes' response to *Pytine* at the next Lenaea, *Wasps*, then the attack on Aristophanes in *Pytine* will have been prompted by his outspoken satire of Cleon in 424, since among other things *Knights* was

---

[57] Plato's *Symposium* looks now like a direct answer in kind to *Clouds* (*mutatis mutandis* for the Platonic philosophical agenda and his view of comedy), since one of the central caricatures from that play, Alcibiades, is presented in *Symposium* with many of the (exaggerated?) vices ascribed to him in comedy and *defends* Socrates, whose reputation has been compromised by the play (*Apol.* 19c). At the same time, the philosopher implies by the scenario that men who think take no notice of the prejudicial power of comic satire, but can even *drink* together with their apparent enemies and swap theories with them. According to this picture, it is not the followers of Socrates who are making themselves look stupid, but the comic poet who satirises them. The playing down of enmity is an important aspect of Plato's own legislation on comedy (*Laws* 935d–36b). Note the remark of Gorgias upon reading Plato's dialogue *Gorgias* reported by Athenaeus (11.505d): ὡς καλῶς οἶδε Πλάτων ἰαμβίζειν 'What a fine talent Plato has for satire!', which suggests a strong connection in Gorgias' mind between Old Comedy and Platonic dialogue.

[58] If the figure of the father (Strepsiades in our version) did not represent Eupolis, then perhaps, if it was targeting the guarantor of Alcibiades' debts in the late 420s, that may have been Hipponicus, his father-in-law, given that both his father Cleinias and his guardian Pericles were now dead. Hipponicus, if he was still alive in 423, as some scholars believe (see Davies *APF* 262, commenting on [Andocides] 4.13, which says Hipponicus died at Delium in 424, probably a mistake for Hippocrates (Thuc. 4.101.2); see also Storey 2003, 67), might be the target for Strepsiades, since at some stage Alcibiades married his daughter Hipparete (see further p. 227 below), and along with her came a substantial dowry. However, we do not know whether he was an intimate of Socrates or not.

certainly a frontal assault upon Cleon (*Wasps* 1029f., *Peace* 754f., *Clouds* 449–50) and, I have argued, upon Cratinus as his creature in the persona of Demos. Cratinus' annoyance towards the bald poet, probably in respect of *Knights*, is palpable in fr. 213. But *Pytine* may also have included a bit-part for Eupolis, if Pieters' reading of frr. 208 and 209 is correct (and as I have accepted and expanded above, pp. 101–2).[59] Certainly if Eupolis was included alongside Aristophanes in the attack, it makes it much easier to see why Aristophanes' response involves both Cratinus *and* Eupolis as characters: he wanted to make it clear that the poetic collaboration between Eupolis and himself shown in *Pytine* (probably a hit at the way Aristophanes had used Eupolis' *Noumeniai* in *Knights*) was the reverse of the truth.

That his rivals are once more the focus of his attention in the play is clear from the parabasis, where, apart from a direct mention at 1050, he accuses one or more of them of (a) using his success as an excuse to try to pick up boys at the wrestling-schools (1025) (b) allowing their comedy to be used for *lovers'* quarrels, (c) to attack *private* individuals (1026–9); (d) taking fright at Cleon and accepting a bribe from him, presumably to go over to his side (1036). Each of the first three charges might fit Eupolis, (a) if rejuvenated Demos represents Eupolis at *Knights* 1384–6 (where Sausage-Seller offers him a slave-boy for sex); (b) if this is a reference to *Autolycus*, which attacked Callias' lover (though we would have to revise our current view of its date: see further chapter six, p. 220), (c) because we know he later attacked Hyperbolus' mother in *Marikas* (*Clouds* 555 with scholium; cf. *Peace* 753). But (d) does not, because, as I have conjectured, it was Cratinus represented as Dionysus in *Babylonians* who had made a deal with Cleon (*Acharnians* 377f., *Wasps* 1284f., *Babylonians* fr. 75). I am inclined to think that because *Wasps* is focused principally on the defeat by *Pytine* (1044f.), his more likely target here is Cratinus, whose association with Cleon is figured by his representation as Demos in *Knights* and as Philocleon in *Wasps*. This judgement is reinforced by Biles' recent demonstration of the closeness between the scenic development (insofar as one can tell this from our meagre information about *Pytine*) between Cratinus' winning play and *Wasps*.[60] It would be rendered still more reasonable if, as I have argued above, Aristophanes had, as well as being lambasted in the parabasis of *Pytine* (fr. 213), been given a major satirical role on stage as the central character. This does not by any means imply that the attack upon Bdelycleon/Eupolis is any the less serious or

---

[59] Pieters 1946, 151.   [60] Biles 2002, 192.

cutting. It does, however, explain why the focus of two thirds of the play is upon the political conversion of the Cleon-loving comedian, Cratinus.

This view may be substantiated by tackling the issue of the 'voice' of the play, which, aside from the parabasis proper, may, like *Knights* (and *Acharnians* before it: cf. 499f.), satirically adopt the pretence that it actually *is* by another poet. If so, then the identification of the referent of the conflict with Cleon in the second parabasis (1284f.) with the tribulations of the Cratinus character in *Acharnians* 377f. suggests that Aristophanes was usurping Cratinus' poetic persona. Further support for this proposition can be gained through close examination of the metatheatrical speech of Xanthias at 55–66. This contains references which can now be tied to Cratinus. The passage reads:

Ξανθίας: φέρε νυν κατείπω τοῖς θεαταῖς τὸν λόγον,
            ὀλίγ' ἄτθ' ὑπειπὼν πρῶτον αὐτοῖσιν ταδί,
            μηδὲν παρ' ἡμῶν προσδοκᾶν λίαν μέγα,
            μηδ' αὖ γέλωτα Μεγαρόθεν κεκλεμμένον.
            ἡμῖν γὰρ οὐκ ἔστ' οὔτε κάρυ' ἐκ φορμίδος
            δούλω διαρριπτοῦντε τοῖς θεωμένοις,
            οὔθ' Ἡρακλῆς τὸ δεῖπνον ἐξαπατώμενος,
            οὐδ' αὖθις ἀνασελγαινόμενος Εὐριπίδης·
            οὐδ' εἰ Κλέων γ' ἔλαμψε τῆς τύχης χάριν,
            αὖθις τὸν αὐτὸν ἄνδρα μυττωτεύσομεν.
            ἀλλ' ἔστιν ἡμῖν λογίδιον γνώμην ἔχον,
            ὑμῶν μὲν αὐτῶν οὐχὶ δεξιώτερον,
            κωμῳδίας δὲ φορτικῆς σοφώτερον.

Well now, let me tell the audience the plot, first just slipping in the following few remarks, that they shouldn't expect anything too grandiose from us, but on the other hand not comedy stolen from Megara either. *We* don't have a pair of slaves sharing out nuts from a basket to the spectators, nor Heracles cheated of his dinner, nor Euripides being roughly treated again. And if Cleon has gone supernova again through luck, we aren't going to make a Caesar Salad of the same guy a second time. What we do have is a little tale with a moral, not too smart for *you*, but cleverer than low comedy.

Criticism of Megarian comedy is found in Eupolis' earliest play, *Prospaltioi*, fr. 261. In a conversation between two unidentified characters, the first asks τὸ δεῖν', ἀκούεις; ('Did you hear that?'). The second replies, irritatedly: Ἡράκλεις, τοῦτ' ἔστι σοι | τὸ σκῶμμ' ἀσελγὲς καὶ Μεγαρικὸν καὶ σφόδρα | ψυχρόν. †γελᾶς† ὁρᾷς τὰ παιδία ('By Heracles, that is your usual vulgar, Megarian and absolutely frigid joke. You see, it's the boys [who are laughing]'). The closeness of the last line to Aristophanes' criticism of bad comedy at *Clouds* 539 (τοῖς παιδίοις ἵν' ᾗ γέλως 'so as to give the boys a laugh') suggests that its context is also criticism of comedy. The motif of an old man, the central character, beating someone with a stick to cover up bad jokes (*Clouds* 541–2) also appeared in *Prospaltioi*, as the scholiast on *Clouds* tells us. Aristophanes' criticism of Eupolis' use of it (if he is the referent) is disingenuous: Eupolis will probably have been attacking Cratinus, who, I have conjectured, may have been represented by the old man character in this play and whose Megarian humour is being attacked (possibly because he had Megarians in his *Horai*: see chapter four, pp. 146–7). In any case, the vulgar scene in *Acharnians* where Dicaeopolis/Eupolis playing Cratinus is involved in low sexual humour with a Megarian must rest, as I have argued in chapter four, on some such metacomic reference to Cratinus.

The motif of slaves throwing things to the audience occurs in *Peace* (962–7). The scholia are of no help here, but the self-contradiction between it and the *Wasps* rebuttal makes it clear that the *Peace* passage must be satirising something by another comic poet. If, as I have argued above, the audience is supposed to recognise in Trygaeus a re-run of the Cratinus/Eupolis figure of *Acharnians*, then it is probable the primary referent is Cratinus.

The motif of Heracles deprived of his dinner (60) also occurs at *Peace* 741:

τούς θ' Ἡρακλέας τοὺς μάττοντας καὶ τοὺς πεινῶντας ἐκείνους

Those famous kneading and starving Heracleses...

One scholium (741c) says τινὲς δέ φασιν εἰς Κρατῖνον αἰνίττεσθαι, ὡς τοιαῦτα ποιοῦντα δράματα 'Some scholars say that this is a covert hit at Cratinus for producing plays like this.'[61] But there is also a reference to Eupolis' use of this motif in 741b: αἰνίττεται ταῦτα εἰς Εὔπολιν, ὃς ἐποίησε τὸν Ἡρακλέα πεινῶντα 'This alludes covertly to Eupolis, who put on stage the hungry Heracles.' Here we have an instance in which the motif is evidenced for both comic poets. It is certainly possible to construe Eupolis' use of the motif as an attack on Cratinus (to which perhaps Cratinus fr. 346 was an answer), just as Aristophanes' later 'hungry Heracles' in *Birds* must now be understood as an attack on a rival poet.

Concerning the rough treatment of Euripides, Sommerstein notes that the strong word ἀνασελγαινόμενος 'is not a word that one applies to one's own actions, and therefore Ar. cannot be referring to his own earlier

---

[61] I note that among the titles we have of Cratinus' plays there is a *Bousiris*, which must have featured Heracles. The title *Horai*, which coincides with that of Prodicus the sophist's work in which the famous 'Choice of Heracles' occurs, is another possibility.

satires on Euripides and his tragedies... We know of two other plays earlier than *Wasps* in which Euripides was satirised by other comic dramatists – Callias' *Men in Fetters (Pedetai)* fr. 12 (= *PCG* fr. 15) and a play of unknown title by Telecleides (fr. 39, 40 = *PCG* fr. 41, 42) – but at least one and probably both of these belong before 429 or earlier, and it is likely that Ar. is alluding rather to a more recent play or plays that we cannot identify.'[62] Sommerstein's logic works here only if there is no metacomic irony present, which now seems unlikely. This will refer, then, to the previous satires of Euripides produced by the putative 'author' of the *Wasps* whose voice Aristophanes has borrowed for satirical purposes. Only Callias' play certainly presented Euripides on stage. But, as I mentioned in chapter three, Cratinus (fr. 342) criticised a rival for addiction to Euripides, as did Aristophanes (fr. 488 *Skenas Katalambanousai*), which suggests that Cratinus might have been capable also of an on-stage attack on the tragedian. I argued earlier that this rival was Eupolis. I also showed that it is possible that Cratinus had Euripides as a character in *Idaioi*, a play of which fr. 90 (the scholion on *Thesm.* 215) suggests was copied by Aristophanes and that this Cratinean attack on Euripides may also be the basis of the satire of Eupolis in *Acharnians*.

The use of τὸν αὐτὸν ἄνδρα ('the same man') and the first person plural at 63 suggest that this is also a reference to something the putative poet himself has produced. Of course, Aristophanes had attacked Cleon in *Knights* (cf. *Wasps* 1029f., *Peace* 752f., *Clouds* 549–50). And on my earlier interpretation, the metacomic references at *Acharnians* 5–8 and 299f. strongly suggest that Eupolis had already attacked Cleon. The metacomic texture of *Knights* is also deeply implicated with Eupolis (witness the whole issue of his collaboration with Aristophanes). The chorus refers to Cleon in Eupolis' *Chrysoun Genos* (fr. 316.1), dated by Storey to 426.[63] And if we follow one possible implication of *Clouds* 549–50, this will have been only one of many attacks made by him on the leather-seller, which will probably have included *Noumeniai*. And finally the identification of Bdelycleon as Eupolis might focus attention on this feud, rather than on that of Aristophanes. However, it is perhaps not so amusing to stress the enmity of a person really well known for opposition to Cleon as that of someone who has – embarrassingly – changed sides after making comic attacks in the past. If the material about the poet and Cleon relayed in *Acharnians* and revisited in *Wasps* (1284f.) actually does refer to Cratinus, then, we must read Xanthias' statement as a further reference to an earlier play or

---

[62] Sommerstein 1983 on line 61.   [63] Storey 2003, 267.

From Knights to Peace

plays in which Cratinus had satirised Cleon (perhaps *Seriphioi* and *Ploutoi*: see above, p. 85).

There is a case, then, for regarding *Wasps* (apart from its anapaests) as a deliberate misappropriation of *Cratinus*' comic voice, designed to repay the old poet for his attack on Aristophanes in *Pytine*. It is in a sense, then, a *remake* of *Pytine* (shades of *Knights* and *Noumeniai*), with Cratinus and his mania (jury-service and support for Cleon) substituted for Aristophanes' alcoholism and prurience, and the helpful poetic 'friends' (probably Eupolis at least, as I have argued above in chapter three, p. 102) being replaced by a loving 'son' (his 'imitator' Eupolis), whose only desire is to cure and rehabilitate his 'father' (but who signally fails to do so).

I now turn to the more specifically political themes: the pro-Cleonian chorus, the trial of Labes and the way in which Bdelycleon/Eupolis' counter-Cleonian ideology is satirised.

The Wasp chorus

At 197, Philocleon calls upon his fellow-jurors and Cleon: ὦ ξυνδικασταὶ καὶ Κλέων, ἀμύνατε ('My fellow jurors! Cleon! Protect me!'). This shout for help is parallel to that of Paphlagon/Cleon at *Knights* 255–7: ὦ γέροντες ἡλιασταί, φράτερες Τριωβόλου | οὓς ἐγὼ βόσκω κεκραγὼς καὶ δίκαια κἄδικα | παραβοηθεῖθ᾽ ('O aged heliasts, phratry-members of the Three Obol clan, whom I keep in fodder with my loud shouts, just and unjust! Come to help me...').[64] This is not the only indication in *Knights* that a group of elderly pro-Cleonian jurors predates *Wasps*. At 977f., after the chorus has suggested that it would be better if Cleon were done for, they note:

> καίτοι πρεσβυτέρων τινῶν
> οἵων ἀργαλεωτάτων
> ἐν τῷ δείγματι τῶν δικῶν
> ἤκουσ᾽ ἀντιλεγόντων,
> ὡς εἰ μὴ ᾽γένεθ᾽ οὗτος ἐν
> τῇ πόλει μέγας, οὐκ ἂν ἤ-
> στην σκεύει δύο χρησίμω,
> δοῖδυξ οὐδὲ τορύνη.

('And yet there were some older, really harsh, men at the market of lawsuits whom I heard making the contrary case, namely that if he hadn't become

---

[64] See Sidwell 2000c and above, p. 161 for interpretation of this passage as evidence for a double chorus in *Knights* (like that of *Marikas*), one Knights, the other old jurors.

a grandee in the city, we wouldn't have had those two useful pieces of equipment, a pestle and a ladle'). The *Acharnians* chorus too are tough jurors (375–6) and the mention of Cleon right next to them (377) is unlikely to be coincidence. The neatest explanation for these overlaps is not that most jurors were elderly and naturally supported Cleon,[65] but rather, as I have already argued (pp. 126–7), that the elderly Cleon-supporting juror is an invention of a specific comedy, one which predates *Acharnians*, *Knights* and *Wasps* and is utilised in turn to satirise its inventor. This analysis is confirmed by otherwise dislocated correspondences of detail (e.g. the πρινώδη θυμὸν 'oak-like spirit' of the wasp-chorus 408, cf. the oak charcoal of the Acharnians at *Ach.* 668; the use of the rare word φέψαλοι at 227, cf. *Ach.* 668 of the charcoal; the naming of the same individual, Strymodorus 233, cf. *Ach.* 273). And, although there is nothing as clear as *Acharnians* 1153f. to equate the chorus with an earlier comic manifestation, the phrase τῶν τριχοινικῶν ἐπῶν ('from our three-choinix word pile') at *Wasps* 481 could very well imply a prior existence for the chorus with an established poetic language of its own.

In the context of a satirical attack upon a poet who was known to be a supporter of Cleon, it seems likely enough that such a group, here subverted by being persuaded of the validity of the arguments of Cleon's most virulent comic opponent Eupolis (650–1), belonged originally in Cratinus. I have suggested earlier that his *Nomoi* might have been their first home (cf. fr. 133) and that Eupolis had already utilised them to satirise both Aristophanes and Cratinus in a scene where Cleon was convicted of theft (*Ach.* 5–8, 299f., *Wasps* 757–9) in his *Chrysoun Genos* (fr. 298.5–6). But how does having a *wasp* chorus help this subversion and what does the suggestion that passages such as *Knights* 977f. relay an unironic view directly from *Nomoi* tell us about Cratinus' comedy?

The metacomic aspect of the play certainly helps explain the peculiarities of the short passage which links the escape scene with the parodos and which first introduces us to the waspish characteristics of the chorus. Xanthias suggests a drop of shuteye (211–13), but Bdelycleon rejects this

---

[65] Commentators tend to reason as follows: the Acharnians are old, 'Athenian juries were disproportionately composed of elderly men whose working lives were over' (Sommerstein 1980a, on *Acharnians* 376), because court service was not compulsory and remuneration was below the standard working wage, therefore the Acharnians are also jurors. However, this line of inference has been challenged by Todd 1990. The jury pay was set where it was to act as an attractive bonus to farmers. Nothing can be inferred from this about the actual composition of juries by age and it is dangerous to use comedy as grist to the mill precisely because it operates on the basis of distortion and exaggeration. Todd's argument does not prove that juries did not tend to attract the old. However, it does impel us to question whether we can assume *tout court* that any comic motif is a direct reflection of reality.

From Knights to Peace

by saying that Philocleon's fellow-jurors will soon be there, even though it is still quite dark (214–6, 217–21). Xanthias replies (221–2) by saying they can ward them off with the stones (piled in front of the door at 199). Bdelycleon responds by revealing their waspish tendencies, including their stings (223–7), only to be reassured by Xanthias that the stones will do the job against wasp jurors (228–9). Yet when the chorus reveal their stings, Xanthias is astonished (420). Bdelycleon's sanguine response, that these were the ones they used to destroy Philippus son of Gorgias (421), seems only to be amusing if it refers across to an event known to the audience in which such stings were employed. To a scene in comedy, then, and not to a real trial. In fact, the idea that old jurors can *sting* probably already underlies *Acharnians* 375–6:

τῶν τ' αὖ γερόντων οἶδα τὰς ψυχὰς ὅτι
οὐδὲν βλέπουσιν ἄλλο πλὴν ψήφῳ δακεῖν

What's more, I know the old men's souls have no other goal than biting with their ballots.

The word δακεῖν 'bite' is used of insects (*Iliad* 17.572, Ar. *Clouds* 710, Lucian *Muscae Encomium* 6) and in any case it is difficult to see to what, apart from an insect's sting, the formulation 'bite with the ballot' could be analogous. It is not normal to add 'with the teeth' when speaking of the mouth as the site of the biting action (cf. *Wasps* 972, Lucian *Bis Accusatus* 33.21), while it is the natural way to express the use of the sting (cf. *Wasps* 225–6: ἔχουσι γὰρ καὶ κέντρον... ᾧ κεντοῦσι 'they have a sting... with which they stab'). In the context of this book's argument, the inference we can draw from this is that the pre-existing comic model portrayed old jurors/farmers as stinging insects.

If this is so, then the satirical purpose of Aristophanes will hardly have been served by presenting his old jurors in the guise of the same insects. Perhaps, then, the originals were represented as *bees*, since there was a well-established contrast between bees and wasps relating to their comparative usefulness, as well as to their relative pleasantness.[66] We can confirm this

---

[66] Bees make honey, while wasps have no such useful product, and so are universally presented as merely dangerous. The representation of bees in ancient literature is, consequently, universally positive (with negativity confined to an internal contrast between workers and drones: cf. Plato's long analogy of the money-makers with drones in *Republic* 8.555d–e, 564a–f.). That of wasps is entirely negative. For bees, see e.g. Ael. *VH* 10.21, 12.45, *NA* 1.9–11, 58–60, 5.13. The contrast between bees and wasps can be readily seen in Plut. *Mor.* 96b (*On having many friends*): ὥσπερ οὖν ὁ τῷ Τιμησίᾳ περὶ τῆς ἀποικίας δοθεὶς χρησμὸς προηγόρευσε σμῆνα μελισσάων τάχα τοι καὶ σφῆκες ἔσονται, οὕτως οἱ φίλων ζητοῦντες ἑσμὸν ἔλαθον ἐχθρῶν σφηκίαις περιπεσόντες ('As the oracles given to Timesias about his colony prophesied: "Soon shall your swarms of honey-bees turn out to be

conjecture by noting also that the word ἑσμός 'swarm' is used of *Wasps* at 1107, although neither wasps nor *anthrenai* ('hornets') swarm (Arist. *HA* 8.629a). Moreover, at 107 Xanthias compares Philocleon to a μέλιττ' ἢ βομβύλιος 'a honeybee or a bumblebee' and at 366, the Chorus address Philocleon as ὦ μελίττιον 'my little honeybee' (Sommerstein). The latter is very difficult to explain, since the term is elsewhere not used as a form of endearment (despite the suggestion of one of the scholiasts, who glosses it ὦ προσφιλέστατον 'my dearest').[67] It is perhaps also significant in the context of the identification of Philocleon as Cratinus that μέλιττα 'bee' *is* a term often used to describe poets (*Birds* 748 of Phrynichus, Σ *Wasps* 462b of Sophocles, Cratinus *Archilochoi* fr. 2). If the *Nomoi* chorus were dressed as bees, and this is still in the metacomic background in *Ach.*, then the fact that the Acharnians have been able to *smell* Amphitheus' wine-samples (*Ach.* 179), may be associated with the heightened sense of smell which made bees dislike strong odours, whether good or bad (Aelian, *NA* 1.58, 5.11), and their response to Dicaeopolis is similar to that of productive honey-makers to drones (Ael. *NA* 1.9).

Further support for the idea that Cratinus' *Nomoi* were represented as bees may in fact be sought from the only other place where we get personified Laws in ancient Greek literature: at the end of Plato's *Crito* (50a f.). Given Plato's abundant use of comedy and its techniques (despite his condemnation of it), it would not be ridiculous to suggest that he took this idea from Cratinus.[68] Indeed, though what the laws say is entirely serious, Plato may give a hint of his inspiration when he makes Socrates ironically undercut his own solemnity by portraying himself as a Corybant at the end of his long dramatisation of the speech of the Laws (54d). Socrates says: καὶ ἐν ἐμοὶ αὕτη ἡ ἠχὴ τούτων τῶν λόγων βομβεῖ 'and the echoes of these words *buzzes* inside me'. The word βομβέω can be used of any booming sound, but is generally used to describe the sound made by insects (cf. Pl. *Rep.* 564d) and bees in particular (Ael. *NA* 5.11). It is certainly possible that this is a playful reference to Cratinus' play, which would be doubly amusing, first because it would remind the reader of the representation of the Laws as bees, and secondly because it would equate the Laws with jurors, whose verdict Socrates is arguing he should accept.

---

wasps", so in like manner, men who seek for a swarm of friends unwittingly run afoul of a wasps' nest of enemies', tr. adapted from Babbitt Loeb vol. II, 63). Cf. also Lucian, *Muscae Encomium* 2 for the contrast in sound.

[67] See MacDowell ad loc., who notes 'it is unlikely to have any connection with the insect guise of the chorus, since they are not bees but wasps.'

[68] See Brock 1990.

This proposed subversion of a Cratinean bee-chorus helps us to understand what Aristophanes is doing in the epirrhematic sequence of the parabasis (1060–1121). The burden of the strophe, epirrhema, antistrophe and antepirrhema is the chorus' nature as wasps, the contrast of their current condition with their former prowess in battle, the way they swarm when they gather as jurors and use their sting to procure a livelihood, and finally the way young stingless drones live off the tribute that in their military days they themselves had been responsible for gathering in. The details of waspishness set out by the chorus at 1102ff. are in fact based largely upon bees, and not upon wasps.[69] First, at *Wasps* 1062, the chorus wanly point out how they once were καὶ κατ' αὐτὸ τοῦτο μόνον ἄνδρες ἀλκιμώτατοι 'very brave in just *this*'. This could be intertextual humour generated by the difference between their anatomy in Cratinus and what they have here, because bees had their sting attached to the stomach (Plin. *NH* 11.19.60), while wasps had theirs attached to the rump, rather than simply a sexual joke based on their withered phalluses. Secondly, as I have mentioned above, wasps do not swarm (Arist. *HA* 8.629a, Plin. *NH* 11.24.74), and do not appear to have drones (Arist. *HA* 8.627b–628b, cf. Plin. *NH*11.24.74, where only some species of hornet are said to have drones). Thirdly, the bee uses its sting to protect itself as it goes about its useful duties of honey-gathering (cf. Plin. *NH* 11.19.60), while the wasp-juror is simply a predator, gaining his livelihood by condemning all and sundry (1112–13). In this respect, the wasp-jurors are simply an aggressive, human-unfriendly counterpart to the friendly bee, whose work benefits humanity, even if he is armed for self-protection. Thus, there is probably specific point in the way that the chorus criticise the ἀστράτευτοι ('evaders of military service') in contrast with the original bee-jurors' ideas about drones. It might be significant that Cratinus produced a play called Μάλθακοι 'Softies' and Eupolis an Ἀστράτευτοι 'Evaders of military service' (which Geissler assigned to Lenaea 423).[70] And there might also be point in the fact that the tribute seems to have been an important aspect of Eupolis' *Poleis* (it is mentioned at fr. 254: see below for the argument that this play underlies the speeches of Bdelycleon at 655f.).

What would Cratinus have been doing, representing the Laws as very old men dressed as bees? If the *Acharnians* passage and *Wasps* do refer back to this representation, then they cannot have been stingless drones. Moreover, the principle of satirical subversion suggests rather that, though comically

---

[69] And this may also be true of the image of the behaviour of the wasp-jurors in their courts (1107–11), cf. Plin. *NH* 11.16.46–9.
[70] Storey 1990, 15–17, 29 disputes this and prefers a date of *c.* 414.

presented, Cratinus' Laws were intended as a chorus with *positive* value (rather like *Clouds*, then). One of the anonymous lives records of Cratinus that τῷ χαρίεντι τὸ ὠφέλιμον προσέθηκε ('to the grace of comedy he added usefulness') and this could well refer to his claim that comedy could teach positive lessons (which was not the general view among those who discussed the genre – see Appendix 1 – and which I have argued was not the way Aristophanes approached his art).[71] As I noted before, there is one fragment of Cratinus which might confirm this, from the *Dionysoi* of uncertain date. Fr. 52 reads νικῷ μὲν ὁ τῇδε πόλει λέγων τὸ λῷστον 'May the victor be the one who says what's best for this city.' If this is so, then part of Aristophanes' purpose in *Wasps* is to subvert this positive model of comic satire by reversing the image of the chorus. *Nomoi* may, then, have been a play whose chorus supported Cleon (cf. what the Knights say about old men at the lawsuit bazaar, *Knights* 977f.), a position reinforced by the picture of Cleon's *nomos*-bound ideology at Thucydides 3.37.3–5.[72]

The trial of Labes

If there was a trial of Cleon for theft in Eupolis' *Chrysoun Genos*, as I have argued, and Cratinus was a member of the jury who convicted him and forced him to vomit up the five talents (*Chrysoun Genos* fr. 298.6, *Ach.* 5–8, *Wasps* 757–9), then it is easy to see what the metacomic background of the trial of Labes/Laches is. There is certainly no strong argument for regarding the scene as topical, given that Laches' tenure of command in Sicily (Thuc. 3.90.2), which is hinted at as the background for the charge (838, 911, cf. 924–5), ended in 425 (Thuc. 3.115.2). Here Labes/Laches is indicted by Dog/Cleon for the same offence as Cleon was in Eupolis' play (896, 900, 933, 953, 958). Note that Cleon is still branded a thief too by his own admission (927–8). One of the same jurors, Philocleon/Cratinus, is

---

[71] Koster, *Prolegomena* p. 14 (Anon. *De Comoedia* v.17 = *PCG* Cratinus T19).
[72] On which, see Hornblower 1991. Another reference to buzzing might also refer to Cratinus' *Nomoi*. As Socrates passes by the treasury in which the sophist Prodicus is lodging at Callias' house, he tries to hear what he is saying to his pupils, but despite his strong desire to partake of his wisdom διὰ τὴν βαρύτητα τῆς φωνῆς βόμβος τις ἐν τῷ οἰκήματι γιγνόμενος ἀσαφῆ ἐποίει τὰ λεγόμενα 'because his voice was so deep, a buzzing which arose in the room made what he said unclear' (Pl. *Prt.* 316e). If Plato knew the chorus of *Nomoi* had been represented as bees, he might have been told also that Prodicus had also appeared, possibly costumed as a drone, a figure of satirical attack. I have argued above that behind the atheistic and sophistic Socrates of *Clouds* lies a similar attack on Prodicus and that *Clouds* 876 points to a scene in which Hyperbolus was taught by a sophist, possibly Prodicus. If that attack had been launched by Cratinus, it would then be much more pointed for him to be ridiculed as the *Logos* who was supposed to represent justice in the Prodicean scheme used by Aristophanes in *Clouds* as a counterpoint to Eupolis' Unjust Argument (see further chapter six).

now involved in achieving the opposite result, acquittal, which presumably is just as surprising in the circumstances as was Cleon's conviction in *Chrysoun Genos*. The reversal must operate through the presumption that, just as Cratinus is well-disposed towards Cleon, he is ill-disposed towards Laches. It is likely enough that this also implies that Eupolis was well-disposed politically towards Laches. This would make sense in that he was involved in both the truce with Sparta of spring 423 and the peace negotiation of 422/1 (Thuc. 5.43.2) and was a signatory of the treaty (Thuc. 5.19.2, 5.24.1). He also appears in Plato's *Laches* as an admirer of Socrates. These are both postures I have argued can be ascribed to Eupolis. Laches is patently guilty, however, and while Eupolis remakes his own trial-scene to favour his man, he is nonetheless shown to care nothing for the facts so long as he defeats Philocleon/Cratinus' obsession with Cleon.

There are in fact some indications of more detailed debts to *Chrysoun Genos* here.[73] At *Wasps* 836–8, the charge against Labes is set up when Xanthias complains οὐ γὰρ ὁ Λάβης ἀρτίως, | ὁ κύων, παράξας εἰς τὸν ἰπνὸν ἁρπάσας | τροφαλίδα τυροῦ Σικελικὴν κατεδήδοκεν; ('That dog Labes! He just ran by into the kitchen, snatched a Sicilian *trophalis* cheese, and has gobbled it up!'). It is unlikely to be a coincidence that at Eupolis *Chrysoun Genos* fr. 299 we also meet that rare cheese, the τροφαλίς: λοιπὸς γὰρ οὐδείς· <ἡ> τροφαλὶς ἐκεινηὶ | ἐφ' ὕδωρ βαδίζει σκῖρον ἠμφιεσμένη ('There's no one left. That *trophalis* is going for water, dressed in her rind.'). In Eupolis, the *trophalis* has human characteristics, while in Aristophanes it merely becomes Labes' meal. Human characteristics for inanimate objects do appear in Aristophanes' version, however, when the witnesses for Labes are called at 937–9, and then at 963–6, where the Cheese-grater gives evidence.

It is useful here to recall my earlier argument that *Knights* reflected not only the lost *Noumeniai*, from which it probably took the idea of the rule of Cleon usurped, but also *Chrysoun Genos* (cf. fr. 316.1, where Cleon watches over Athens and the other cities). The oracle of Sausage-Seller at *Knights* 1030–4 has Cleon behaving like a dog and, just like Labes in *Wasps*, εἰσφοιτῶν τ' εἰς τοὐπτάνιον... κυνηδὸν | νύκτωρ τὰς λοπάδας καὶ τὰς νήσους διαλείχων 'going into the kitchen... in doggy fashion licking the platters and the islands clean'. It is not only dogginess, secret entry to the kitchen and food-stealing that Cleon and Labes have in common. At *Wasps* 924–5, Cleon's prosecution speech produces an exact parallel for

---

[73] Note also Thucydides son of Melesias' silence and *Ach.* 703f., which I have argued on different grounds might also come from *Chrysoun Genos*, above, pp. 130–2.

the combination of the charge of the theft of food and money from the allied states: ὅστις περιπλεύσας τὴν θυείαν ἐν κύκλῳ | ἐκ τῶν πόλεων τὸ σκῖρον ἐξεδήδοκεν 'for he sailed in a circuit around the mortar and has eaten the rind off the cities'. In both places, the charge of theft of money originally made against Cleon (*Ach.* 5–8), which alludes, I have conjectured, to Eupolis' *Chrysoun Genos*, is made in terms of food. Aristophanes' parodic point may be precisely the revelation by his combination of metaphor and clear statement that in the original Eupolis was allegorising. It may also be uncoincidental, though the point is harder to grasp here, that at *Wasps* 925 the σκῖρον 'rind' of a cheese is mentioned by Dog/Cleon in connection with the accusation of theft and that the same word occurs in fragment 299 of Eupolis' *Chrysoun Genos* cited above. The conclusion that Aristophanes is parodying Eupolis' earlier Cleon court-scene would also be supported by the way Aristophanes makes the identities of the dogs absolutely transparent. It will not have been so in the original – or at least, the dramatist will (implies Aristophanes) have *thought* he was being clever, but actually was being completely obvious (and stupidly so: cf. Cratinus fr. 342).

It is only a half-step from here to the suggestion that Cleon was represented in *Chrysoun Genos* as a dog stealing food, which stood for a sum of five talents (presumably an amount he was rumoured to have misappropriated). The metaphor of vomiting, found at *Acharnians* 6 and *Knights* 1148 in the context of juridical restitution, may therefore derive from the original trial scene, in which the dog-character was made to spew back what he had consumed. How such a scene might be shown it is not especially hard to imagine, and that there was something like this in Old Comedy may emerge from the existence of an exact parallel in the *Lexiphanes* of Lucian, that arch-recycler of Aristophanic and Eupolidean comedy (*Bis Accusatus* 33). The doctor Sopolis (possibly a significant name)[74] gives the bombastic Lexiphanes a medicine and this makes him vomit up all his excessive Atticising vocabulary (*Lexiphanes* 20–1). It seems worth suggesting further that *Knights* 1030–4, Sausage-Seller's oracle, is based as a whole on crossreference to *Chrysoun Genos*. The opening lines read: φράζευ Ἐρεχθείδη, κύνα Κέρβερον ἀνδραποδιστήν, | ὅς κέρκῳ σαίνων σ', ὁπόταν δείπνῃς, ἐπιτηρῶν | ἐξέδεταί σου τοὔψον, ὅταν σύ που ἄλλοσε χάσκῃς 'Take note, scion of Erechtheus, of Cerberus, the dog who kidnaps men, who brushes you with his tail while you are dining, watching for when you are

---

[74] Because in antiquity this was the reported name of Eupolis' father (Suda ε 3657 = *PCG* Eupolis T1, as corrected by Meineke).

perchance gawping in some other direction to eat up your savouries.' It is possible, then, that the likeness to Cerberus, found elsewhere in *Peace* 313 in the mouth of Trygaeus/Eupolis, and probably evoked by the adjective καραχαρόδους 'jag-toothed' used by Paphlagon in his oracle (*Knights* 1017) and in the parabases of *Wasps* (1031) and *Peace* (754), is derived from Cleon's representation as Cerberus in *Chrysoun Genos*. This in turn makes it much easier to understand the joke at *Knights* 230f.: καὶ μὴ δέδιθ'· οὐ γάρ ἐστιν ἐξῃκασμένος· 'Don't be afraid: he's not cast in his own image'. After so recent an appearance as the monstrous Cerberus, the audience is told that Cleon won't appear in his proper guise (that frightened the prop-makers too much).[75] I guess Paphlagon then walks on with a caricature mask of Cleon's real features. This volte-face, of course, is also, like the whole trial-scene, a hit at Eupolis' way of making comedy: even when they choose the same target, Aristophanes implies, he himself is far cleverer and much funnier.

Political satire of Bdelycleon/Eupolis

I have suggested that the reason for the focus upon the Cleon issue in the first half of *Wasps* is because Aristophanes wanted especially to hit back at Cratinus after the defeat of *Clouds* and especially because he himself had been attacked in it, directly in the parabasis (Cratinus fr. 213), but also as the central drunken, played-out old comic poet character. And there is no way of denying that the play continues to focus upon Philocleon as its main character even in the final third. The comedy after all ends with his drunken dance-contest. But the manner in which Aristophanes chose to do this involved the amusing pretence that Eupolis, Cratinus' arch-imitator, was the one who could perform best the task of weaning him away from his unhealthy addictions to jury-courts and Cleon. The play was always designed to be, then, also an attack upon his younger rival, with whom, I have argued, he had been in conflict since the start of his career, and who had possibly put him on stage at least once, in *Chrysoun Genos* along with Cratinus (fr. 298.5). I have already suggested one way in which Bdelycleon's original is ridiculed politically, namely by his unprincipled support for the guilty Labes/Laches in the trial-scene (875f.). Here I want to add another five: his personal appearance, his arguments against jury-service,

---

[75] If Cleon had been represented as Typhon in Cratinus' *Ploutoi* as well, then this will also be part of the metacomic humour in the *Knights* passage. See above, p. 85.

his imaginary symposium, the associations at the reported symposium (1299f.) and his inclinations towards drunkenness and sex.

1 Personal appearance

Bdelycleon wears his hair long, as emerges from the chorus' insult at 466 κομηταμυνία 'long-haired Amynias'. It is the style with which the rejuvenated Demos appears at the end of *Knights* (1331). It aligns him with the Knights (*Knights* 580), but also with Laconophiles and followers of Socrates (Herod. 1.82.8, Xen. *Lac.* 7.3, *Birds* 1281f.). After the end of the war, it could be a sufficient motive in itself for suspicions of oligarchic tendencies (Lysias 16.18).[76] The same is true of dress in general (Lysias 16.19), so that the wearing of the simple τρίβων ('cloak') and ἐμβάδες ('shoes') can stand for poverty and thus democratic leanings (the cloak: *Wasps* 34, 1131–2, *Eccl.* 850, *Wealth* 714, 842–6, 882, Lysias 32.16; shoes: *Knights* 316–21, 868–70, *Wasps* 1157), but, paradoxically, also for the asceticism associated with pro-Spartan leanings (*Lys.* 278; Dem. 54.34).[77] Undoubtedly, in the scene at 1122f. where Philocleon is made by Bdelycleon to divest himself of the homespun cloak and the workaday leather shoes he has hitherto been wearing, the joke is that he is being physically mutated from a radical Cleonian democrat into something of a different order. It is not clear what Bdelycleon is wearing, but it would be logical to suggest that he dresses Philocleon up in the same type of clothes he affects himself, i.e. Persian, even though he probably cannot be wearing the καυνάκης (a Persian garment), since the garment is a complete novelty to Philocleon and has to be explained (1136f.).[78] However, as I suggested earlier, the joke about the ἐριώλη ('whirlwind') at 1148 may refer to the original of the Sausage-Seller in *Knights* (cf. *Knights* 511). If so, then the political joke here is about making Cratinus look like his hated foe – and still at this time Eupolis' friend – Alcibiades. At any event, Bdelycleon's apparently first-hand knowledge of Persia is not mentioned to his credit, so that we may infer that Eupolis is being attacked for pro-Persian leanings which Aristophanes would have reckoned unacceptable (and this must also be the point of the Persian embassy scene in *Acharnians*, if I am correct in my contention that the play principally satirises Eupolis). The imposition of Laconian shoes on Philocleon (1158f.) taps another area

---

[76] For contemptuous treatment of the Spartan hairstyle in tragedy, see Poole 1994, 22. For Spartan long hair in Aristophanes see Harvey 1994, 37.
[77] On Demosthenes 54.33–4, see Fisher 1994, 358.
[78] MacDowell 1971 ad loc. suggests that Bdelycleon's reference to visiting Sardis at 1139f. may relate to a recent embassy (424/3), from which some individual such as Epilycus had brought back one of these garments.

of the political spectrum. Cratinus/Philocleon must be regarded as anti-Spartan, Eupolis/Bdelycleon pro-Spartan. This posture would fit what I have so far conjectured about their respective political and intellectual leanings.

2 Arguments against jury-service
The agon proper begins once Bdelycleon has convinced Philocleon and his fellow-jurors to enter a formal arbitration process (521), to decide whether he is correct or not in saying that Philocleon's position is nothing less than slavery (517). Philocleon speaks first (548–630), while Bdelycleon takes notes (559, 576, 587), perhaps another hit at Eupolis' close observation and reuse of Cratinean comedy. The chorus congratulate Philocleon in extravagant terms (631–3, 636–41) and warn Bdelycleon to think of a good response (644–9). Bdelycleon's arguments (650–724) are punctuated by comments from Philocleon which gradually show their effect (especially 696–7 and 713–4). At 724–7, the chorus announces that Bdelycleon is the victor.

Keeping in mind the identifications already suggested, it will be clear that the humour of the agon will derive primarily from the ascription to each of the main characters either of political positions they are generally thought to have held or their opposites (cf. 757–9 versus the name *Philo*cleon). Hence, while Philocleon/Cratinus is represented as a supporter of the jury-court system which is widely regarded as keeping Cleon in such a powerful position (cf. *Knights* 255f.), Bdelycleon/Eupolis' annoyance at Philocleon's trialophilia arises from a general aversion to the law-courts (412–4, cf. 505, 517), which can be compared to the attitude of the rejuvenated Demos (possibly representing Eupolis) as expressed by Sausage-Seller/Alcibiades at *Knights* 1317 and 1332. However, within this basic set of divergent political postures, each of the characters is made fun of, very probably through metacomic use of material associated with each of them, but *not* from their own comedies. The chorus, deriving initially from Cratinean comedy, adds piquancy through changing its allegiance to Bdelycleon/Eupolis. Within this comic structure, there are many individual places where contacts with the fragments can be made. However, it is most important to note that there may be two main single sources for the parodies.

One may strongly suspect that much of the humour of Philocleon's defence speeches (548–58, 560–75, 578–87, 590–602 and 605–30) derives from material which they share with Eupolis' *Chrysoun Genos*. I suggested earlier that the trial of Thucydides son of Melesias mentioned at *Acharnians*

703 and *Wasps* 947 may go back to a scene in that Eupolis play. If so, then it is worth noting that the prosecutor there, Euathlus,[79] also features at *Wasps* 592. Philocleon's comment at 643 ἦ μὴν ἐγώ σε τήμερον σκύτη βλέπειν ποιήσω 'By God I'll make you wear a leather-whipped look today' replicates part of a line from Eupolis' play (fr. 304): ἀτεχνῶς μὲν οὖν τὸ λεγόμενον σκύτη βλέπει 'No, he really does, as the saying goes, have a whipped look on his face.' Thus for all his pretension to be making a solid defence of the juror's position, Philocleon/Cratinus is actually shown recycling for his case material originally intended to satirise it.

The same will probably be true of the arguments put by Bdelycleon at *Wasps* 655–724. The speeches contain details, probably exaggerated, but close enough to figures we can verify from non-comic sources, for the finances of Athens during the Archidamian War and an argument which proposes that the city ought to use this money to provide direct support for the poor citizens of Athens.[80] It is difficult to see how such logic could be associated with anything but a radical democratic ideology. Compare *Knights* 1350–5, where the rejuvenated Demos/Eupolis is shocked by his former (pro-Cleonian) attitude (as Demos/Cratinus) to state-pay. I take it, then, that just as Philocleon is satirised by being given arguments from Eupolidean satire to bolster his position, Bdelycleon is being given quasi-Cleonian arguments about the proper distribution of the state revenues. These arguments are also likely to rest on scenes from earlier comedy. Part of the attack is focused upon politicians (666f.) and highly-paid office-holders (682f.), a theme Aristophanes had already used, probably metacomically, in *Babylonians* (Σ *Ach.* 378) and *Acharnians* 595f. If attacking the *demos* was forbidden ([Xen.] *Ath. Pol.* 2.18), then ascribing anti-democratic sentiments such as *Wasps* 682f. to one's rivals was an excellent means of satirical attack. The attack on politicians for extracting bribes from the allies (666f.) looks very close to what Hermes says at *Peace* 635f., in a series of speeches I have already argued might be traced back to attitudes expressed in Eupolis' *Prospaltioi*. If such arguments were originally exercised in a satirical treatment of Cratinus, this is now being offered by Bdelycleon/Eupolis, i.e. its original author, as a straightforward political position.

The rest of the argument is made up of references to the tribute and the treatment of the allied states, including the response of the cities to the realities of political power in Athens (655–63, 669–79, 698–712). Here too we can find a Eupolidean play which might be germane. His *Poleis*

---

[79] *Ach.* 705 with Hamaker's emendation and 710 with Sommerstein and Olson's notes.
[80] See MacDowell 1971 ad loc., 1995, 160–5, and Sommerstein 1983 ad loc.

dealt with the tribute and the allied states. We have some 41 fragments of it (218–58 in *PCG* v). Its date is unknown, but Storey puts it at Dionysia 422.[81] There are no especially strong arguments, however, for not dating it before *Wasps*, say at Lenaea 423. Fr. 254 tells us that Eupolis mentions the bringing of the tribute to Athens from the cities at the Dionysia. The chorus consisted of the allied cities dressed as women and named individually (fr. 244–7). The plot may have envisaged marriage between individual Athenians and the woman representing the state (fr. 243). It seems unlikely to be coincidental that these two themes of tribute and allied states as marriageable women occurred together in the same play. Perhaps the scenario envisaged is one in which a particular political policy was being satirised by the normal Eupolidean (and Cratinean) technique of allegorical fantasy. That policy may have been that the tribute from the allied states should be used to support members of the Athenian state who had no other means of support. This is transmogrified by fantasy into the notion of the states bringing the tribute (as dowry?) to marry individual Athenians who are satirised by their collocation with the policy. The passage in *Wasps*, then, might be an 'unmasked' version of the play's plot. Two things, though, are to be noted. First, the presentation in *Poleis* was ironical, but this is ignored in the misappropriation of the plot into an argument put seriously in the mouth of the author of that play. This may mean, if we follow the trail logically, that Eupolis' *Poleis* was a satire (of Cratinus?). Thus the humour of the misappropriation of the argument of *Poleis* into the mouth of the Eupolis-caricature in *Wasps* is fundamentally to do with the inversion whereby Eupolis agrees with the arguments of a comic poet whom he was satirising in that play (as a character?) – the same ploy used in *Acharnians*. The second point is that the argument given to Bdelycleon/Eupolis has been virtually stripped of its comic exaggeration. In this case, then, the close approximation to reality which appears from comparison between actual tribute records and the figures here is another deliberate satirical ploy. The argument as it appears here (at 653–63 and 706–11) is probably very close to the original argument as it would have been put by whichever demagogue proposed it (Cleon?). The humour comes (as possibly also in the 'causes of war' speeches in *Acharnians* and *Peace*) from the ascription to a comic poet of an actual policy which he satirised by fantasy in the play upon which this scene relies for its comic structure.[82]

---

[81] I now withdraw the argument in Sidwell 1994 for Dionysia 426.

[82] Supporting this last point, perhaps, is a correspondence between *Wasps* 709–10 (ἐν πᾶσι λαγῴοις | καὶ στεφάνοισι παντοδαποῖσιν καὶ πυῷ καὶ πυριάτῃ 'in oodles of hare cutlets, wreaths of all

3 The imaginary symposium

MacDowell says of the mock symposium with Cleon and his cronies (1219–48): 'It is a little surprising that Bdelycleon names Cleon and his friends as the guests at a typical high-class party.'[83] He rationalises thus: 'As for Bdelycleon's name, that is now forgotten... Since he won the debate in the agon, he and his father no longer hold different views about Cleon; the contrast now is between a son familiar with wealthy society, such as Cleon, and a father ignorant of it.'[84] Under the current theory this can not be so, since (a) the names of the characters are jokes based on prior audience identification of the individuals they satirise, so that (b) the opposition expressed in their names is never lost sight of in the play. The humour of this scenario lies, rather, in two interlocking frames of reference based on reality: (1) Eupolis' intensely vitriolic campaign against Cleon in his comedies; (2) Cratinus' friendly relations with Cleon. Thus, Bdelycleon's line at 1224 καὶ δὴ γάρ εἰμ' ἐγὼ Κλέων 'OK, so I'm Cleon', is funny simply because of the absurdity of the idea that Cleon's greatest opponent impersonates him. And Philocleon's satirical replies derive humour from the precise opposite, the attack upon people known to be his associates.[85]

4 The reported symposium (1299f.)

At 1299f., Xanthias reports on the symposium to which Bdelycleon had taken Philocleon. Various attempts have been made to identify the individuals mentioned, who are Hippyllos, Antiphon, Lycon, Lysistratus, Thouphrastus, and (unless the phrase is meant to encompass the preceding individuals) οἱ περὶ Φρυνίχου ('the Phrynichus group').[86] As I have said, at the earlier, imagined, symposium at 1219f., the satire appears to be based on subversion of known political attitudes: Philocleon/Cratinus attacks his political favourite, and Bdelycleon/Eupolis uses his arch-enemy

---

sorts, fresh beestings and boiled beestings'), *Peace* 1150 (ἦν δὲ καὶ πυός τις ἔνδον καὶ λαγῷα τέτταρα 'There was also beestings inside and four lots of hare') and Cratin. fr. 149 *Odysses* (ἦσθε πανημέριοι χορταζόμενοι γάλα λευκόν, | πυὸν δαινύμενοι κἀμπιμπλάμενοι πυριάτῃ 'Ye sit all day long, feeding upon white milk, dining upon fresh beestings and filling yourselves up with boiled beestings'). This allusion operates differently. Though the particular point of the appropriation is unclear, here we see two Aristophanic instances of reflections of Cratinus which must be being used satirically.

[83] MacDowell 1971, on 1220.
[84] MacDowell 1995, 172–3, largely repeating his note on 1220 in MacDowell 1971.
[85] It would have been logical for MacDowell to sustain his position by insisting that the pro- and anti-Cleon opposition was still valid, for then he could have argued that the humour derived from this opposition. However, it is very hard to see what the basis of the humour is if it is not this opposition and difficult to see how, if it is in this opposition, it is not based in the personalities of the characters caricatured.
[86] See MacDowell 1971 and Sommerstein 1983 ad loc, and Storey 1985.

Cleon as a social model. The group described here seems at first sight to be rather more mixed. However, there are some signs that the same sort of humour is being attempted here also. We know nothing independently about Hippyllos and Thouphrastus, but Lysistratus and Lycon occur in places which might suggest they had been Eupolidean targets. Lysistratus makes fun of the Cratinus figure at *Wasps* 787f., and Dicaeopolis/Eupolis is congratulated at *Acharnians* 854 that he will not have to deal with him in *his* market (see above, pp. 79–80), while Lycon was a target – mostly in the person of his son Autolycus – in Eupolis' two *Autolycus* plays (fr. 61).[87] If the humour here is being made in much the same way as in the fictive symposium, by representing Bdelycleon/Eupolis associating with people he has *satirised* in his plays, then even if MacDowell is correct to understand the phrase οἱ περὶ Φρυνίχου as *descriptive* of the men named, rather than a separate set, Aristophanes seems also to be linking Eupolis here with Phrynichus.[88] MacDowell quite rightly points out that there is no evidence to connect the famous politician Phrynichus at this stage in his career with the oligarchic views he put into action in 411. Indeed, Thucydides, who seems to have been an admirer (8.27.5 and 8.68.3), tells us that he opposed oligarchy as late as 412/11 (8.48.4–7). Nor, as Storey points out, can we be absolutely certain that this is the same Phrynichus.[89] Nonetheless, it is reasonable to understand the satire here as based on Bdelycleon/Eupolis' association with people whose politics he detests, since such a clash of political allegiance is central to the plot, and so by my argument to the point of attack upon the targets underlying Philocleon and Bdelycleon. Hence, it makes most sense to identify this Phrynichus with the politician, who at this time will have been firmly in the radical democratic camp and thus utterly anathema to Eupolis. Cratinus will presumably be satirised not only in the same way he presumably was by Eupolis in the original scenes to which *Wasps* 878f. and *Acharnians* 854 refer, but also because *his* radical democratic politics are centred around Cleon and not Phrynichus.

5 Drunkenness and sex

At 1251, Bdelycleon asks the slave Chrysus to pack up the dinner for himself and Philocleon ἵνα καὶ μεθυσθῶμεν διὰ χρόνου ('so that we can really get drunk at last'). Philocleon's reply (1252–5) seems to be quite serious, even moralistic.

---

[87] If it is the same person, and not, for example, the one mentioned at Ctesias *Pers.* 52 (*PAA* 611745=*PA*9267).
[88] I doubt this, even if the count for each symposium would then amount to seven, supposing Philocleon to be the seventh in the first case and both Philocleon and Bdelycleon at the second.
[89] Storey 1985, 328–30.

μηδαμῶς.
κακὸν τὸ πίνειν. ἀπὸ γὰρ οἴνου γίγνεται
καὶ θυροκοπῆσαι καὶ πατάξαι καὶ βαλεῖν,
κἄπειτ' ἀποτίνειν ἀργύριον ἐκ κραιπάλης.

No! It's a bad idea, drinking. Wine is the cause of door-breaking, fisticuffs and stone-throwing, and then paying up after the drinking-session.

This appears to be a contradiction within the plot, of course, since Philocleon brandished a wine-flask at 616–18 and made it clear that he expected to drink and had his own source of supply if Bdelycleon's steward did not serve him. The contradiction is explained perfectly well if Philocleon is representing Cratinus, because the first passage is a passing parody of the πυτίνη 'wine-flask' of his own play,[90] while such a serious note is struck here because alcoholism and its consequences were the basis of his attack on Aristophanes in *Pytine*, the previous year's comedy. As for Eupolis, the double satire of *Acharnians* suggests that he was also satirised as a heavy drinker in the guise of Dicaeopolis at *Acharnians* 1202f.

The same can be said for his sexual appetite. At *Acharnians* 1197f., Dicaeopolis/Eupolis was shown fondling dancing-girls and here Bdelycleon/Eupolis attends a party where the pipe-girl is hired to fellate the whole group (1346). The contrast between the public taboo upon the expression of sexual matters in anything but indirect ways, even where they might be central to the point of a lawsuit[91] and the unabashed way in which Philocleon/Cratinus says what he wants from Dardanis would, of course, also arouse much laughter at the expense of Cratinus. But Eupolis is also under attack. As Aeschines tells us (1.42), appealing no doubt to a prejudice general in the public consciousness, consorting with an αὐλητρίς 'pipe-girl' was one of those αἰσχίσται ἡδοναί ('most shameful pleasures') which the free and well-born man ought to be able to resist.[92] Hence the humour of Philocleon's encounter – and of Bdelycleon's involvement with the pipe-girl – is exactly the opposite of what is assumed by modern commentators, for whom it is the expression of deep-rooted desires shared by the audience

---

[90] Does the donkey shape play on the *hybristic* qualities of the donkey, later attributed to Philocleon/Cratinus by Xanthias at 1306 and 1310? For the *hybris* of donkeys, cf. e.g. Xen. *An.* 5.8.3, and for an elucidation of *Wasps* passages see Fisher 1992, 120.

[91] See for example the way that anal intercourse is never mentioned in Aeschines' case against Timarchus except by periphrases such as 'shaming his body' (40). The ideology of restraint is articulated by Aeschines in 37–8. See Fisher 2001 on this passage.

[92] ὑφ' ὧν οὐδενὸς χρὴ κρατεῖσθαι τὸν γενναῖον καὶ ἐλεύθερον 'by none of which the well-born and free man ought to be conquered'.

that is the point.[93] It would be all of a piece with this reputation if, as I have suggested, the rejuvenated Demos in *Knights* represented Eupolis. He can not wait to bed the *Spondai* (1391) and happily accepts the possibility of doing the same with the slave-boy at 1386–7. There is more of the same to come in *Peace* (e.g. 709f., 862).

MARIKAS AND PEACE

Cratinus seems to have been content to rest on the laurels he gained with *Pytine*. At least, we have no evidence that he produced another play after Dionysia 423. Perhaps he felt no need to respond to *Wasps*. Perhaps he was dead, though the evidence of *Peace* 700f., where Trygaeus tells Peace that Cratinus died during a Spartan invasion, cannot be taken seriously, since Spartan invasions of Attica had ceased after 425: hence (see above, p. 115) this may be a cross-reference to a scene from a Eupolis play, as I have argued is Hyperbolus' *prostasia* in the same scene (from *Noumeniai*). By the same token, the report of [Lucian] *Longaevi* 25 that Cratinus lived to ninety-four and died soon after producing *Pytine* may partially depend on the evidence of *Peace* (as does that of the Anonymous *De Comoedia* = Koster, *Prolegomena* p. 8, III.20.3). However, one may suspect that later scholars were bolstered in their speculations by the silence of the *didaskaliai* about later productions, so that we have no real reason to doubt that *Pytine* was Cratinus' last play, even if we cannot say whether or not he had died soon after its production. The reason he stopped producing, though, may be rather that after Cleon's death in 422, Cratinus' political base was no longer available and he may have felt, if he was getting on a bit by now (though the evidence for his first victory might put him only in his fifties by this time) that it was time to quit.

The case with Eupolis is, as I have already argued, quite different. *Marikas*, produced at Lenaea 421, the year after *Wasps*, provoked a counter-attack which helps us to understand more clearly another stage in the poets' war. Aristophanes' complaints in the parabasis of *Clouds II* (553–6) are part of a series of exchanges between the two poets over the *Knights* (Eup. *Baptai* fr. 89) and plagiarism (Ar. *Anagyros* fr. 58) which make it clear that something substantive was at issue.[94] My earlier analysis shows what it was. In *Knights*, Aristophanes developed from Eupolis' *Chrysoun*

---

[93] E.g. Sommerstein 1983, xviii: 'for though Bdelykleon no doubt represents what we all ought to seek to be, it is Philokleon who represents what most of us would wish to be like if we dared'. This does not relate specifically to the Dardanis scene, but it must be held to include it.

[94] *Pace* Heath 1990, 152, with whom Storey 2003, 202 is in agreement.

Genos (426), but more specifically from the *Noumeniai* (Lenaea 425), an attack which combined vilification of Cleon with an assault upon the military-political group with which Eupolis was associated, the Knights, an up-and-coming young politician from that group with whom Eupolis at the time made common cause, Alcibiades, and, finally, upon Eupolis as (a) a plagiariser of Cratinean comic style and (b) in the guise of the rejuvenated Demos as a *laudator temporis acti* and as such an enemy of the current radical democratic system. When Eupolis' response came, it focused on Aristophanes' political favourite, Hyperbolus (*Clouds* 552). The moment was propitious for this attack, since Aristophanes tells us that Hyperbolus had recently παρέδωκεν λαβὴν, 'given (his opponents) a handle' (*Clouds* 551), though it is not clear what that was, nor do commentators appear to have felt the need to explain. However, I think we should expect it to be something to do with Persia, since the name Marikas is now generally agreed to be of Persian origin.[95] We may add to this the parody of the *parodos* of Aeschylus' *Persians* (65) in fr. 207: πεπέρακεν μὲν ὁ περσέπτολις ἤδη Μαρικᾶς 'The city-sacker Marikas has already crossed'. One may conjecture that the point of choosing a Persian name and parodying a line from *Persians* in which Xerxes' army's crossing of the Hellespont was evoked was to make fun of some connection between Hyperbolus and Persia. The Athenians had from time to time negotiated with the Persians, just before the start of the war (Thuc. 2.7.1), and then in 424, though the mission was aborted (Thuc. 4.50.3). The satirical treatment of Persians on stage by Aristophanes, as chorus in *Babylonians* and as an entourage from the Great King at *Acharnians* (61f.), strongly suggests an antipathy on his part towards any accommodation with them. If this reflected Hyperbolus' own position, then the λαβή of which Aristophanes speaks in *Clouds* 551 could very well have been either his suggestion – a volte-face for him – of an accommodation with Persia or even personal involvement in an embassy there (cf. πεπέρακεν 'he has crossed' in Eup. fr. 207). The portrayal of Hyperbolus as actually Persian, and therefore an enemy of Athens (as Sommerstein acutely observes)[96] certainly goes a step beyond the satire of Bdelycleon/Eupolis at *Wasps* 1137f. for his first-hand knowledge of the Persian rag-trade.[97]

Aristophanes does not in the *Clouds* parabasis focus upon the specific elements which made *Marikas* appear to be a 'turning-inside out' of *Knights*

---

[95] Cassio 1985, Morgan 1986. Cf. Lewis 1977, 20–1. For Cleon as Paphlagonian, see Braund 2005, 94–5.
[96] Sommerstein 2000, 441.
[97] Though, as I have already suggested, that may well also have had a political basis in Eupolis' support for political accommodation with Persia (of a kind quite against the underlying ideology of Aeschylus' *Persians* as expressed by Aeschylus at *Frogs* 1025–7: see further chapter six, p. 296).

(an image from the reuse of clothing to secure longer wear),[98] since his outrage is concentrated on the treatment of Hyperbolus. However, as I mentioned in chapter 3, pp. 50–1, Storey has made a good argument for the *despotes* of *Marikas* being (once again, picking up his own *Noumeniai* and Aristophanes' *Knights*) Demos.[99] This conjecture would, as I have said, be immensely strengthened were he correct to assign to that play fr. 346, a line we are told was spoken by that character.[100] I think by now I have said enough to make it clear that Eupolis' reuse of *Knights* will not have been innocent, especially so if he and his political allies were the central target of that satire (a fact Aristophanes avoids mentioning presumably since it would damage his case against Eupolis), and the more so if *Knights* was already a malicious reworking of Eupolis' *Noumeniai*. The list of detailed correspondences between *Knights* and *Marikas* constructed by Storey is, of course, impressive, and shows beyond doubt that there was substance in Aristophanes' charge (though like Aristophanes, Eupolis will have been imitating merely to attack).[101] But given that the focus of these plays was caricature by characterisation *on stage*, the plays would have looked much more comparable if (a) Demos in *Marikas* represented Aristophanes (as Eupolis had presumably represented Cratinus in *Noumeniai* and Aristophanes the same older rival in the pre-rejuvenation part of *Knights*) and (b) Marikas was opposed by an individual recognisably allied to Aristophanes (just as Hyperbolus had been used to subvert Cleon's rule ironically, I have conjectured, in *Noumeniai*). If, as has been suggested, the change of attitude towards the war by Alcibiades in 422 had indeed brought him into alliance – however uncomfortable – with Hyperbolus over this issue, then Eupolis could have signalled his abandonment of the rising young star by casting Alcibiades in exactly the same role vis à vis Aristophanes/Demos as he had been cast in by Aristophanes in *Knights*.[102] Eupolis will in this way have been able to kill two birds with one stone, taking revenge for *Knights* and *Wasps* simultaneously. And Aristophanes' image in ἐκστρέψας 'turning inside out' (*Clouds* 554), as well as his annoyance, would have a real point of reference for his audience. He might have added that although

---

[98] Σ *Clouds* 88 and Dover 1968 ad loc.   [99] Storey 2003, 209–10.
[100] Storey 1995–6, 143–4.   [101] Storey 2003, 202–3.
[102] Storey 2003, 210 suggests the antagonist may have been Nicias. This reading, however, rests on the assumption that the ending of *Knights* is positive. If, however, Hyperbolus' *prostasia* in *Peace* (681f.) was, as I have suggested, a Eupolidean invention for the ending of his *Noumeniai* and this was the model for *Knights*, then the two plays up to *Marikas* will both have closed ironically. Hence, it seems to me less likely that we should look for a positive outcome in *Marikas*. Moreover, to have produced a resolution with Nicias emerging triumphant would not have been the best way to satirise Aristophanes' political position, which the current hypothesis suggests is the real reason for the reuse and subversion of Aristophanes' *Knights*.

Hyperbolus' mother had been taken from Phrynichus (*Clouds* 555–6),[103] the *kordax* she dances at the end of the play was probably meant as a hit at the final scene of *Wasps*, substituting for a Philocleon/Cratinus drunkenly triumphant over Bdelycleon/Eupolis the mother of Aristophanes' political ally drunkenly triumphant with the bones of her son on a baker's tray.

It is not clear whether or not in Eupolis' next play, *Kolakes*, produced at the City Dionysia alongside *Peace*, and which carried off the first prize, there was any continuation of the feud. However, it is entirely possible that in a play about Callias and his sponging entourage there could have been a place for Aristophanes, if, as I have suggested earlier, he was an admirer of Prodicus. It is precisely in the house of Callias that we find the sophist in Plato's *Protagoras*, 315cf. (though, as I have said above, pp. 4, 175, 178, caution is required in using the evidence of these dialogues, given Plato's penchant for satire).

There is ample reason, however, to see *Peace* as Aristophanes' response to some recent attack, one which reprises the central theme of *Acharnians* – the making of peace – and uses some of the same basic material for its intertextual humour, as in *Acharnians*, from rival comedy. For the focus of the attack in the parabasis is once more on rival poets' rubbish. It is worth looking at the accusations in some detail, in order to gain some idea of their possible target or targets.

At *Peace* 739–53, the chorus lists a series of their poet's triumphs against the bad comedy of his rivals:[104]

πρῶτον μὲν γὰρ τοὺς ἀντιπάλους μόνος ἀνθρώπων κατέπαυσεν
εἰς τὰ ῥάκια σκώπτοντας ἀεὶ καὶ τοῖς φθειρσὶν πολεμοῦντας·
τούς θ' Ἡρακλέας τοὺς μάττοντας καὶ τοὺς πεινῶντας ἐκείνους
τοὺς φεύγοντας κἀξαπατῶντας καὶ τυπτομένους, ἐπίτηδες
ἐξήλασ' ἀτιμώσας πρῶτος, καὶ τοὺς δούλους παρέλυσεν
οὓς ἐξῆγον κλάοντας ἀεί, καὶ τούτους οὕνεκα τουδί,
ἵν' ὁ σύνδουλος σκώψας αὐτοῦ τὰς πληγὰς εἶτ' ἀνέροιτο·
'ὦ κακόδαιμον, τί τὸ δέρμ' ἔπαθες; μῶν ὑστριχὶς εἰσέβαλέν σοι
εἰς τὰς πλευρὰς πολλῇ στρατιᾷ κἀδενδροτόμησε τὸ νῶτον;'
τοιαῦτ' ἀφελὼν κακὰ καὶ φόρτον καὶ βωμολοχεύματ' ἀγεννῆ
ἐποίησε τέχνην μεγάλην ἡμῖν κἀπύργωσ' οἰκοδομήσας
ἔπεσιν μεγάλοις καὶ διανοίαις καὶ σκώμμασιν οὐκ ἀγοραίοις,
οὐκ ἰδιώτας ἀνθρωπίσκους κωμῳδῶν οὐδὲ γυναῖκας...

First of all, he alone of all men, stopped his rivals always making fun of rags and waging war on lice; then he was the first to outlaw and expel from the stage those

---

[103] Storey 2003, 205 rightly identifies him as the comic poet.
[104] Problems have been long mooted with the text of 742–4, but I follow here the text of one papyrus and all the MSS, as defended by Olson 1998 ad loc.

Heracleses who kneaded dough or went hungry; who were always running away from someone, and deceiving someone, and getting beaten, and he released from their duties the slaves they used to bring out, always wailing just in order that a fellow-slave might make fun of his bruises and ask him: 'Poor devil, what have you done to your skin? It's not a bristle-whip, is it, that's invaded your sides in great strength and laid waste your back?' Such poor stuff, such rubbish, such ignoble buffoonery, he has removed; he has created a great art for us, and built it up to towering dimensions with mighty words and ideas and with jokes that are not vulgar. Nor has he satirized the little man or woman in private life... (tr. adapted from Sommerstein)

Commentators note that jokes against poor people, scenes involving a gluttonous Heracles, and slaves lamenting over beatings are all features of Aristophanic comedy.[105] The conventional interpretation of this and other parabatic passages is that Aristophanes is indulging in a little self-irony.[106] We can now reformulate thus: Aristophanes constructed such scenes as direct parodies of his rival comic poets' material, which he claims has pushed them in a different direction, since motifs of this kind are reviled, now they have been parodied mercilessly, often by making their originators play out the parody on stage, as with *Acharnians* 412f. (where Dicaeopolis/Eupolis playing Cratinus borrows and then speaks in the rags of Telephus from Euripides). Hence, passages such as *Acharnians* 857–9, *Knights* 1268–73, *Wasps* 1267–74 (introducing the first person epirrhemes of which the second, 1284–91, has now been identified as spoken in the voice of Cratinus), and *Thesmophoriazusai* 948–52 (to mention only Sommerstein's list of contra-indicators) as well as scenes like *Clouds* 698f. (where Strepsiades fights with bed-bugs) and *Birds* 1583f. (a hungry Heracles), will all have been recognisably take-offs of the material, style and techniques of his rivals.

The identity of the rivals attacked here exercised ancient scholars, however, and continues to tax moderns. Olson suggests that ἀντιπάλους ('rivals') means '[m]en like Kratinos..., Aristomenes, and Amipsias, although these barbs are presumably directed in the first instance against Eupolis and Leukon..., whom Ar. had defeated in the past... and clearly hoped to defeat again'.[107] However, the ancient scholia, derived from scholars who were able to look for material of this sort in the surviving plays, to which we no longer have the same access, tell a different story. Σ^{RVΓ}740 tells us αἰνίττεται καὶ εἰς Εὔπολιν ('he is hinting also at Eupolis') and ΣLh

---

[105] Sommerstein on 740, 741, 743–2, 742/5.
[106] See Hubbard 1991, 146 ('he may be technically correct in saying that he has avoided the particular things mentioned here'), though he admits that the passage contains 'self-undercutting irony'.
[107] Olson 1998, on 739–40.

word their remark τὸν Εὔπολιν αἰνίττεται ὡς εἰσάγοντα ῥακοφοροῦντας ('he is hinting at Eupolis for bringing on stage characters wearing rags'). In relation to the 'kneading Heracleses', at 741, Lh repeats the allegation that αἰνίττεται ταῦτα εἰς Εὔπολιν, ὃς ἐποίησε (ΣVÄLh continue) τὸν Ἡρακλέα πεινῶντα καὶ Διόνυσον δειλὸν καὶ Δία μοιχὸν καὶ δοῦλον κλαίοντα ('he is hinting at Eupolis, who produced a starving Heracles, a cowardly Dionysus, an adulterous Zeus and a slave being punished'). Of great interest here is the specifying of comic scenes which are *not* mentioned by Aristophanes ('cowardly Dionysus' and 'adulterous Zeus'). Dionysus is certainly attested for Eupolis' *Taxiarchoi* (Σ *Peace* 348e = *PCG* fr. 274), and a situation in which the god learns τὰ πολεμικά ('the arts of war') would give plenty of scope to show his cowardice (cf. *Frogs* passim, where the rowing-scene is probably based on that in Eupolis' *Taxiarchoi*). For an adulterous Zeus there is no direct evidence, though indicative of the probability that there was a play of this sort are: (1) the fourth-century South Italian vase with a comic scene which shows Zeus aided by Hermes attempting to climb up to Semele's window;[108] (2) the ubiquity of the 'Zeus adulterer' motif in Lucian, e.g. *Dialogues of the Gods* 8 (5).2. Since Lucian himself claims to have been inspired by Old Comedy (e.g. *Bis Accusatus* 33) this could be an example of that influence. One might, however, also point to the identification of Zeus with Pericles in Cratinean comedy (e.g. *Cheirones* fr. 258–9) and surmise that Eupolis had misappropriated this for his own satirical purposes. The only other comic poet they mention is Cratinus, interestingly enough directly after Eupolis in ΣVΓLh: καὶ εἰς Κρατῖνον αἰνίττεσθαι ὡς τοιαῦτα ποιοῦντα δράματα ('and at Cratinus for composing plays like these'). As we have seen (above, p. 82), a fundamental similarity was perceived in antiquity between Eupolis and Cratinus, and was interpreted as imitation driven by admiration. Olson's other candidates, Leucon, Aristomenes and Ameipsias are mentioned by name nowhere in the scholia.[109] It is possible, then, that the satiric humour created here is directed quite specifically against Eupolis and his 'model', Cratinus, though the probability that in staging such scenes Eupolis was satirising Cratinus is ignored by Aristophanes, to denigrate Eupolis further.

To turn to specifics, in respect of the slave conversation criticised here, it is worth asking whether the quoted lines in the *Peace* parabasis are

---

[108] *DFA²* 217, with figure 106. Taplin 1993 has shown convincingly that many of these scenes refer back to fifth-century Athenian comedy.

[109] Leucon's name only appears in Hypothesis III in a report of the *didaskaliai*. Olson's formulation here is, therefore, misleading ('cf. ΣRVÄ 740…741…763') since, as we have seen, only Eupolis and Cratinus are mentioned there.

meant to be the work of an actual rival or not. Compare the metaphor of invasion in the *Peace* passage (εἰσέβαλεν 'invaded'... στρατιᾷ 'in great strength'... κἀδενδροτόμησε 'laid waste')[110] with *Wasps* 11–12, since, in general terms, the conversation in the opening of *Wasps* recalls the motif of the beaten slave. We find an exact parallel:

κἀμοὶ γὰρ ἀρτίως ἐπεστρατεύσατο
Μῆδός τις ἐπὶ τὰ βλέφαρα νυστακτὴς ὕπνος

Against my eyelids too just now an attack was made by a sort of Persian... drowsy sleep.

Here the metaphor is contained in the conceit ἐπεστρατεύσατο Μῆδός τις... ὕπνος ('an attack was made by a sort of Persian... sleep'). At *Wasps* 3, moreover, we have a statement not altogether different from the question criticised in *Peace* and involving a joke (according to MacDowell), which has a slave σκώψας ('jesting') over the prospect of a fellow-slave's beating. The argument that the scholia would have spotted such a thing does not negate the possibility: by no means all of the plays by Aristophanes' rivals survived even to the Alexandrian period. In chapter three, I suggested that *Knights* began from a scenario and characters appropriated from Eupolis' *Noumeniai*. If that play centred on slaves, then not only would it have been a suitable place for the lines quoted here to be spoken, but it would relate the openings of *Knights*, *Wasps* and *Peace* to a single comic intertext in Eupolis.[111]

At *Peace* 751, the chorus claim their poet did not attack men and women who were ἰδιῶται, i.e. individuals who did not meddle in affairs of the *polis* (note the implication that women might, if they did so involve themselves, attract satire and cf. *Peace* 992). If passages such as *Acharnians* 1056f. and *Wasps* 1388f. did contain recognisable individual women in caricature, then Aristophanes' motive will have been to satirise his rivals' practice. Olson makes the perceptive point that the accusation fits well with what the scholion at *Clouds* 555–6 tells us about the woman added by Eupolis

---

[110] As Platnauer noted (1964, ad 747): 'The humour lies in the sustained (too sustained) metaphor of invasion'.
[111] Certainly, such borrowing is not unknown. Sommerstein 1980b, 51f. has argued convincingly that *Knights* 1225 was identified by the scholiasts as a line from a rival's work. (I have questioned whether it was in fact not by Cratinus rather than Eupolis: Sidwell 1993, 371). And Hubbard 1991, 86 gave the same explanation for the scholiasts' view that the second parabasis of that play was Eupolis' work.

(imitating Phrynichus) to his new version of *Knights*, *Marikas*, namely that she was a caricature of Hyperbolus' mother.[112]

The main butt of the play's parabasis is likely, then, to be Eupolis (via his appropriations of Cratinus once more) and the use of the *tryg-* root for comedy helps us to identify the central figure, Trygaeus, as a comic poet. By this stage, through the fantastical transmogrifications of Old Comedy, the representation of the old grape-farmer of *Acharnians* (512) as Cratinus (possibly derived from Eupolis' *Prospaltioi* or Cratinus' *Horai*) played by his arch-imitator Eupolis will easily have allowed the audience to recognise the designated target as Eupolis right from the start, especially if Cratinus had now hung up his comic *kothornoi*. In any case, the passage at 700f., where Peace asks after Cratinus (because, of course, he has always been – or at least is ironically being represented as always having been – an advocate of peace), shows (in a way like *Acharnians* 848f.) that despite appearances Trygaeus is not Cratinus. Moreover, by identifying him as Eupolis it is easier to explain why Trygaeus should be so proud of personally Ὑπέρβολον... παύσας ('having put a stop to Hyperbolus' 921, cf. 1319 Ὑπέρβολον ἐξελάσαντας 'after driving out Hyperbolus'), since he had just produced *Marikas* as an attack on Hyperbolus at the Lenaea of 421. The one difficulty that remains is to explain why, in contrast to what I have argued in chapter four is the use of his real demotic at *Acharnians* 406, Cholleidai, here Eupolis/Trygaeus gives Athmonum as his deme (190,

---

[112] Olson 1998, on *Peace* 751. One more possible parabatic self-contradiction needs to be examined. At *Peace* 734–5, after warning the stewards to guard their gear against the thieves who skulk around (very probably a reference to the intertextual games which now appear to be a central aspect of the comedy of this period), the chorus make the following apparently unequivocal statement: χρῆν μὲν τύπτειν τοὺς ῥαβδούχους, εἴ τις κωμῳδοποιητὴς | αὑτὸν ἐπῄνει πρὸς τὸ θέατρον παραβὰς ἐν τοῖς ἀναπαίστοις. ('The Rod-Bearers should beat a comic poet who comes forward towards the audience and praises himself').They then proceed to report their own poet's (i.e. Aristophanes') view that if anyone deserves great praise for comic poetry it is he, and his grounds for making this statement (736–53). The poet then joins in in the first person (754–74), thus making the self-contradiction complete. Aristophanes, as has been often noted, does not elsewhere seem shy of blowing his own trumpet in parabases (e.g. *Knights* 544f., *Wasps* 1018f., *Clouds* 561–2), e.g. by Olson 1998, on *Peace* 734–5. It may be, then, that this is, rather than a self-contradiction of the types noted above, an allusion to an incident in a comedy in which a boastful poet was portrayed suffering this indignity. Aristophanes' ironic cross-reference serves thus to undercut his rival. We do now know of a comedy by Plato called *Rhabdouchoi* ('Stewards'). *P. Oxy.* 2737 = Plato T7 PCG: Ἐρατοσθένης περὶ Πλάτωνος ὅτι ἕως μὲν [ἄλ]λοις ἐδίδου τὰς κωμῳδίας εὐδοκίμει, δι' αὐτοῦ δὲ πρῶτον διδάξας τοὺς Ῥαβδούχους καὶ γενόμενος τέταρτος ἀπεώσθη πάλιν εἰς τοὺς Ληναικούς 'Eratosthenes says of Plato that while he gave his comedies to others he gained great success, but that when he for the first time produced on his own he was fourth with the *Rhabdouchoi* ("Stewards") and was forced back to the Lenaea festival.' Given that Plato also satirised his rivals it is possible that this was the source (cf. *Nikai* fr. 86, where he makes fun of the statue of Peace in Aristophanes' play). I do not discount the idea that Aristophanes himself was the butt of the on-stage caricature: the deliberate flouting of the criticism would be a delicious touch.

918–19). The obvious answer seems to me to be that here the deme given corresponds in reality with that of Cratinus (whose affiliation we do not know: cf. *LGPN* II s.v. Καλλιμήδης and Κρατῖνος). Dicaeopolis gives his real affiliation, Cholleidai, a city deme, at *Acharnians* 406 because he has to persuade Euripides, who cannot see him, to give him an audience and can only do this by stressing his identity – note the stressed ἐγώ 'It's me (sc. whom you know)' – and with it familial ties (?), thus amusingly breaking the dramatic illusion. But actually, as I have argued, the character Dicaeopolis is representing the old grape-farmer and countryman, his rival poet Cratinus (*Ach*. 512; cf. *Peace* 700f.). In *Peace* his outward aspect is the same (190). Here there is no reason for him to break the illusion (he is not visiting Euripides) and in any case Aristophanes has by now through his earlier plays fully established the identification between the younger and the older poet. Hence, the affiliation given, which is that of a deme of the inland trittys of Kekropis, belongs to the character he is playing rather than to the author whose identity can still be seen peeping through the parody.[113]

On the other side, the structure of the plot itself makes it unlikely that we should look for a political figure as the main target. One might surmise that someone at the centre of the process of negotiation with the Spartans, such as Laches or Nicias, might fit the bill, but this would make it hard to see why Lamachus, an important butt of *Acharnians* for his addiction to war, is again employed in the satire (in the rescue scene, 473, and, through his son, at the wedding, 1291) on exactly the same basis, as a war-monger, when it must have been known by this time that he was among the group negotiating the treaty. Besides there is no line we can trace which would explain the casting of one of these men as a grape-grower (contrast the argument about the *kaunakes* and Sausage-Seller in *Knights*). The emphasis too upon peace and Trygaeus' private pleasure recalls *Acharnians* and the attitude of rejuvenated Demos in *Knights* rather than the predilections of Paphlagon or Sausage-Seller. The personification of War (*Peace* 236f., 520f.) has its analogue at *Acharnians* (979f.), as do the evocation of a market for Megarians and Boeotians (*Peace* 1000f., *Ach.* 719f.), an explanation of the war's cause which puts the blame on Pericles' personal circumstances (*Peace* 605f., *Ach.* 515f.), the parodic use of Euripides (*Peace* 76f., *Ach.* 426–9), and a chorus which is closely linked with over-harsh judgements in the jury-courts (*Peace* 348–53, *Ach.* 375–6, cf. *Ach.* 299–302). This final overlap also brings into play connections with *Wasps*. Apart from the harshness as jurors

---

[113] Olson 1998, 105 regards Cholleidai as an inland deme, but corrects this in 2002, 180.

which the chorus of *Peace* has in common with the *Wasps* chorus, they have Charinades in common (*Peace* 1155, *Wasps* 232), and they enter dancing vigorously (300f.) just as they had left the stage in *Wasps* (1516–37).[114] But *Peace* has a number of other features in common with *Wasps* also: the fable of the dung-beetle used in the opening is mentioned by Philocleon (*Wasps* 1448), the kitchen-implements allegory used in the War scene (*Peace* 236–88) bears a close family resemblance to the use of cheese-grater, brazier, pots and pestle as witnesses in the trial-scene at *Wasps* 936–9,[115] and dancing with Carcinus' sons occurs in both plays (*Peace* 775–818, *Wasps* 1474f.). All this suggests that we are, once more, in the realm of metacomedy and that the audience is expected to see very clearly the intertextual references to rival comedy which bind together elements which until now have looked like 'self-imitation'.

If *Peace* has the same target as *Acharnians*, it is possible to see in it both a strong political purpose – opposition to the treaty – and a metacomic method which explains the apparent weakness of its plot.[116] Since, as I showed above, metacomedy is the vehicle for the expression of the political content of the comedy, I shall deal first with the way the plot utilises the comedy of Eupolis (and his 'model' Cratinus) to satirise Trygaeus/Eupolis and then move on to a more detailed examination of the other political targets and themes.

The play falls naturally into two halves. In the first, the plot centres upon the journey of Trygaeus to heaven (1–288), the rescue of Peace from her prison (289–600), and the explanation by Hermes of the war's causes and his mediation of Peace's questions (601–728). In the second, which follows the parabasis, the focus shifts to the consequences of Peace's rescue, Trygaeus' return with Theoria and Opora (819–921), the ritual of installation (922–1126), which includes the discomfiture of Hierocles (1043–1126), and the wedding of Trygaeus to Opora (1191–1359), which includes the scenes with the sickle-maker (1197–1209), the arms-dealer and his companions (1210–64), and the sons of Lamachus and Cleonymus (1265–1304).

If my analysis of *Acharnians* as a reflection of earlier comedies is correct, then the personification of War belongs in two earlier comedies, one by Eupolis (*Taxiarchoi* fr. 268.14–15), where Phormio was Ares, and the other by Cratinus (his *Horai*?), where Lamachus played the part (a caricature which is then taken over by Aristophanes into *Acharnians* to make fun

---

[114] For this final point, see Hubbard 1991, 151.
[115] See Hubbard 1991, 151–2, who argues that these allusions 'contextualise the present play as... a continuation of last year's comedy, but with more harmonious results'.
[116] For weakness of plot see Murray 1933, 57.

of Dicaeopolis/Eupolis). Moreover, Peace was, according to Hesiod, one of the *Horai* (*Theog.* 901–2), so that it is likely that the second parabasis at *Acharnians* 974–99, with its references to Polemos and Diallage, and where the chorus suddenly become grape-farmers (986–7, 995–9), parodies something from this play. The general similarity of the second parabasis of *Peace* (1127–90), with its focus on homely rustic feasting, encourages the proposition that their invocation of Ὧραι φίλαι ('Beloved Seasons') at 1168 is meant to be amusing because it evokes Cratinus' play of that name (cf. also Hermes' libation at 455, which includes the Horae). Given the close linguistic links between *Horai* and *Acharnians*, I have argued that *Horai* probably belongs earlier than *Acharnians*, and, if it is the play to which Eupolis' *Prospaltioi* responded, probably to one of the festivals of 430. Satire of Euripides, I have argued, also belongs in Cratinus, while Eupolis had a close connection with the poet (of friendship or family). Hence the use of the Pegasus sequence from his *Bellerophon* (76f., 154f., cf. frr. 306, 307) and a lyric exchange from his *Aeolus* (114–23, cf. fr. 17, 18) ridicules Eupolis in a similar way to the Telephus scene in *Acharnians*, by having him dependent upon Euripidean tragedy in precisely the way I have argued Cratinus portrayed him in fr. 342. The posture of Trygaeus as described by one of the slaves at 56f., looking at the heavens and accusing Zeus of wishing to sweep away Greece, may even be borrowed from Cratinus' *Boukoloi*, where fr. 19 reads: καὶ πρὸς τὸν οὐρανὸν σκια- | μαχῶν ἀπο- | κτίννυσι ταῖς ἀπειλαῖς ('And shadow-boxing with the heavens he kills with threats'). If so, then the satire is double: Eupolis the arch-imitator of Cratinus is cast as a combination of two Cratinean characters himself.

If Cratinus' 'Megarian play' (*Horai?*) and his anti-Euripidean satires constitute the main intertext of the first half of *Peace*, then the joke will presumably be that now Eupolis himself is being portrayed as the reverser of the outcome there – the eviction of Peace by War – through motifs from this and others of his plays. However, the use of this metacomic device only has bite if it is being used to ridicule both Eupolis' political position on the war and at the same time his pretensions to having played a personal part in the change in public opinion through his satire of Hyperbolus (and Alcibiades, if I am correct, the really important pro-war politician of the time) in *Marikas* (cf. 921). It may also be that his initial position, that Zeus was responsible for the war (56–63, 102–8) is to be read through Cratinean lenses as satire of Eupolis' attitude to Pericles, who was often 'the Olympian' in the older poet's oeuvre (e.g. fr. 73). By the time we get to Hermes' explanation of Pericles' role (605f.), the focus of the satire has altered and, if my analysis is correct, the humour here is that a Cratinean political position is being explained to Trygaeus/Eupolis by someone whom the audience will recognise as having prior comic associations with the war's beginnings and with Eupolis (see below, p. 211 for a suggestion of who this might be).

Three further political themes which emerge during the first half of the play and a fourth, the only one, which emerges briefly in the second, may also have satirical force in respect of Eupolis. First is the focus on the rescue as a Panhellenic venture (292, 302), which founders as the Boeotians (466), Lamachus (473), the Spartans (478–80), Megarians (481–2, 500f.), Argives (493), and Athenians (503f.) are all berated for lack of effort and the farmers (probably just the Attic farmers they were at 349–57) finish the job by themselves (508, 511). Second is the mention of the Persians as a threat to Greece and its gods (108, 406f.). In ideological terms, Panhellenism and anti-Persian sentiment could have the same locus, that is the idea that internecine warfare among the Hellenes could induce another Persian assault (cf. *Lys.* 1133). Reference to the historical parallel of Panhellenic cooperation during the Persian Wars (as evinced in Aeschylus' *Persians*) could substantiate this posture (as it did for Isocrates and Alexander in the fourth century). However, in 411 the oligarchs could hold a position in which they would *both* make peace with Sparta (Thuc. 8.70.2) *and* with Persia (Thuc. 8.6). I suspect, then, that what is being made fun of here is an attitude which was circulating already in the proto-oligarchic *hetaireiai* that Panhellenisim plus pro-Persianism would bring the greatest prospect of lasting peace, and I have already shown (pp. 192–3) that it is likely that Eupolis' pro-Persian and pro-Spartan tendencies were both ridiculed in *Acharnians* and *Wasps*. The force of the allusion to the Sun and Moon's pro-Persian plot will very probably have been enhanced by the audience's recognition in it of reference to a comedy that also involved the calendar (cf. *Clouds* 607f.; Cratinus' *Horai*?). Third is the attack upon the *demos*, made here not by Trygaeus (contrast Dicaeopolis' refusal to abide by the *demos'* decision and his treatment of Lamachus in *Acharnians*), but by Peace herself at 664–7 and 683–4. The first passage recalls their refusal to make peace after Pylos and the second their choice of Hyperbolus as their *prostates*. It is worth noting that on my earlier argument, in reality Aristophanes would have supported the *demos* on both counts. This, then, is a way of emphasising the correctness of the *demos'* vision.

In the second half of the play at 931–6, Trygaeus' slave, after making what could be considered a laboured pun with the word οἴ ('with a sheep' or 'yow!'), remarks that this cry will be part of a refusal to make war again on the assembly's part and also of a change of behaviour towards each other and, more specifically, the allies: καὶ τοῖσι συμμάχοισι πραότεροι πολύ ('[so that we shall be] . . . much kinder towards the allies'). If my analysis of *Wasps* is correct, then Eupolis had been associated with some sort of policy towards the allies (698f.). But if it was that Athens should treat them better, then his view is controverted in the *Acharnians* parabasis by the attribution to the allies of a desire to deceive the Athenians (634f.) and subverted by the speech given to Bdelycleon/Eupolis at *Wasps* 698f. (see above, pp. 194–5). If Eupolis' *Poleis*, a play which certainly dealt with the allies, who form its chorus, belongs before *Wasps*, this speech may satirise Eupolis by having him articulate its satirical plot with a radical democratic twist. It may be, then, that what is amusing about *Peace* 931–6 is (1) Trygaeus/Eupolis' ready acquiescence in any statement which would advocate lenient treatment of the allies, though it might be (2) that Eupolis actually did advocate such treatment and Aristophanes regarded it as risible.

As to the individuals who are satirised in the first part of the play, in Hermes we may have a rerun of Amphitheus, who is prominent in the first scenes of *Acharnians*, and who, I argued (pp. 137–8), may already have been satirised by Cratinus as someone who had played a role in beginning the Samian War (perhaps by helping establish Pericles' relationship with Aspasia?). In *Dionysalexandros*, then, he will have been the lackey who as Hermes made arrangements to put Paris in the way of his Helen (and thus an indirect causer of the war). He was probably, having been attacked by Cratinus and then hi-jacked to satirise Eupolis by Aristophanes, a friend of Eupolis, and presumably – despite his involvement in the Samian War's beginnings – by 425 professed an attachment to peace. Hence his ambivalent position in respect of the war would be well satirised, as would his venality (192f., 378f.) by the initial refusal to help Trygaeus/Eupolis, followed by his collaboration and then his Cratinean explanation of the roots of the conflict (605f.). It also seems likely enough that Polemos once more evokes the (Cratinean) Lamachus, another friend of Eupolis (if my analysis of *Acharnians* is correct), whose absolute commitment to war in Aristophanic comedy (cf. 304, 473) is contradicted by his signature on the peace of Nicias (Thuc. 5. 19.2). A brief reappearance of Polemos/Lamachus at 473 would provide a neat follow-up to this joke. Kudoimos, the belaboured underling of Polemos (255f.), is likely enough also a product of metacomic reference (cf. *Peace* 742 for complaints about 'beaten slaves' in comedy) and will perhaps have represented another individual in the circle of Eupolis and Lamachus (maybe even the same person represented as Lamachus' slave in *Acharnians*). But there are no clues which would help us to identify him.

As for Peace herself, she was a statue (Pl. fr. 81 *Nikai*, Eup. fr. 62, *Autolycus*), not necessarily excessively large – she had, after all, to be able to emerge from the *skene* doors, and, as Olson argues, Hermes has to be able to put his ear to her lips (661f.). So the suggestion of the scholium on Plato, *Apology* 19c that Eupolis' criticism was made because he brought on κολοσσικὸν ... ἄγαλμα ('a colossal image') has no value as evidence.[117] I wonder whether the source of the criticism by his rivals may have been that Peace was made to resemble an individual well-known in the city for her views about the war. In that case, line 992 will be a clue for us (and a good joke for the original audience): ἵνα Λυσιμάχην σε καλῶμεν 'in order that we may call thee Lysimache'. Lysimache daughter of Dracontides of Bate (*PA* 9470) was the incumbent priestess of Athena Polias in 421. A further reference at *Lysistrata* 554 also implies that Lysimache may have supported making peace with Sparta for some time. For this reason, she is associated by some scholars with Aristophanes' peace-maker extraordinaire, Lysistrata (correctly, I think, but with the unwarranted assumption that she is a *positive* figure there: see chapter six).[118] Perhaps, then, the statue of Peace was equipped with a caricature mask of Lysimache. This might have been criticised by Eupolis because it annoyed him (as also Plato *comicus*), since Lysimache's support was an important part of the case he and his friends were making for the cessation of hostilities, but it could be that both poets nonetheless simply attacked the use of the statue as a piece of low-grade comic business (as Aristophanes does things which may well have been sophisticated satire or parody in Eupolis).

The second half of the play, with its strong focus on Trygaeus, is also likely to have important links with Eupolidean and Cratinean comedy, but as in *Acharnians*, its foci of attack are probably mostly individuals Eupolis would in reality be unlikely to satirise, because they were his friends and political associates. It is funny to have people caricaturing recognisable individuals on stage saying things they would never say, and this includes making gross attacks on their known friends or making common cause with their known enemies.

The cast of characters who interact with Trygaeus includes Hierocles, the oracle expert, an unnamed sickle-merchant, an arms-dealer with his two companions, and the sons of Lamachus and Cleonymus. In each case, the scene has two satiric components, the behaviour of Trygaeus and that of the other character. Just in case there are lingering doubts

---

[117] Olson 1998 ad loc. and xliv.
[118] Lewis 1955, 1–12, Dunbar 1970, 270–2, Sommerstein 1990, 5–6. *Contra* Henderson 1987, xxxviii–xl.

about the intention to satirise the central character (for the second half of this play is usually read as justified celebration by a culture hero),[119] I shall briefly list some examples of Trygaeus' actions, attitude and language which conform to those of figures satirised in plays already discussed. (1) Arrogant self-praise (865f., 912, 916, 918f., 1026; cf. Strepsiades at *Clouds* 1206f.); (2) Mocking and hybristic treatment of others (1119f. Hierocles is beaten after being mocked; the arms-dealer leaves with the word ὑβριζόμεθα 'Trygaeus is treating us hybristically' 1264; cf. Philocleon at *Wasps* 1417f., *hybris* followed by mockery); (3) Open expression of his sexual desires, explicit description of sexual activity and use of sexual vocabulary (862, 885f., 894f.; cf. Dicaeopolis at *Ach.* 1199, 1216, 1220); (4) Scatology (1228f. crapping in a cuirass, cf. the opening scene, 1266, cf. *Wasps* 940–1). We should add to these his involvement in several comic motifs criticised by Aristophanes: (1) Throwing things to the audience (Trygaeus gives the order at 962f., cf. *Wasps* 58–9, *Wealth* 794–801); (2) The leading old man hitting someone with a stick (Trygaeus beats Hierocles at 1119f., cf. *Clouds* 541–2); (3) Cries of ἰοὺ ἰού (Trygaeus does so at 1191, cf. *Clouds* 542); (4) Rushing on stage with torches (Trygaeus orders torches for the wedding procession to be brought on at 1317, cf. *Clouds* 543).[120] Moreover, the chorus engage in overblown praise of Trygaeus (856f., 860f., 909f., 913f., 938f., 1027f., 1033f.) which is exactly comparable to that of the ironic choral contributions in *Acharnians* (836f., 971f., 1008f., 1015f., 1037f.) and *Wasps* (1450f.).

Of Trygaeus' interlocutors, we do not need to deal with Lamachus' son in detail. If my analysis of *Acharnians* is correct, Lamachus will have been not only a proponent of peace but also a friend of Eupolis. The introduction of his son is a clever variation on the Lamachus-as-War theme. The sickle-maker is – uniquely – treated well and this induces me to suspect that in the real world he was an enemy of Eupolis or perhaps a figure from one of his own plays (or both). By the same token, I surmise that the arms-dealer and his friends represent known friends of Eupolis, and perhaps targets in Cratinus' *Horai*. Hierocles, who is first ignored (1051f.), then mocked (1058f.), then beaten off the stage (1119f.), must, one would have thought on this argument, have been a close friend of Eupolis. However, this may not be so. What happens here may be the first concrete example we have seen of a poet being mocked by his representation on stage with one of his own targets (though that is what the hypothesised clash of Dionysus/Cratinus

---

[119] E.g. Platnauer 1964, viii–ix, Sommerstein 1985, xvi–xvii. Cf. Olson 1998, xlii.
[120] We might add to this 'drenching', which is done to the chorus at 969 and made explicit at 971–2 (cf. *Lys.* 384f.), since at *Ach.* 658 the chorus mentions καταρδων as one of the things their poet promises never to do.

and Cleon in *Babylonians* would have amounted to). For Hierocles is named in the vocative in fr. 231 of Eupolis' *Poleis*: Ἱερόκλεες, βέλτιστε χρησμῳδῶν ἄναξ 'O Hierocles, most excellent king of soothsayers' and this may mean that he was a character in the play. It might be argued that the rather positive greeting indicates a favourable presentation of Hierocles in the play (and this, as we have seen, is not out of the question for Eupolis). But it only means that whoever was addressing him had a favourable view and in any case the line constitutes a parody of Aeschylus, *Seven* 39, which, when compared with fr. 207 *Marikas* (aimed at Hyperbolus) does not suggest friendly intent. It is likelier that his pro-war views (mentioned by Trygaeus at 1049–50) made him a satiric butt for Eupolis (unless this is a case of comic reversal: cf. *Wasps* 757–9). All we can say about him is that, if he was in favour of the war, then despite his views, Aristophanes did not like him any more than Eupolis (and this would not be the only target they shared: Cleon is another example). Possibly it is simply the fact that he deals in oracles at all that puts him beyond the pale (for oracles get a pretty unsympathetic treatment in Aristophanes: cf. *Knights passim*, *Birds* 959f.). However, it is for his greed and dishonesty that he is satirised here (1050, 1111, 1117–18, 1120, 1122f.). In this instance, the satiric humour may be being made first of all by substituting Eupolis for the other character in his own Hierocles scene from *Poleis* (if Storey is right, as I now think he is, to date it before *Peace*),[121] then from superimposing on that character's positive attitude the negative one displayed by Trygaeus here. We could only see precisely how this inversion operates if we could read the original scene.

A few words need also to be said about the treatment of Cleonymus' son at 1296–1304. Cleonymus is also treated as a friend of Peace earlier, at 673–8, and is mentioned during the prayer for peace at 446. In all three passages the point of the joke lies in the well-known incident in which this minor politician is said to have fled from battle and abandoned his shield (*Clouds* 353–4; *Wasps* 15–27, 592, 822–3; *Birds* 290, 1473–81). MacDowell argues (rightly) that it is improbable that Cleonymus actually threw away his shield and fled from battle: 'that was an offence for which a man could be prosecuted and the penalty was disenfranchisement. Kleonymus was a politician... yet he seems not to have been disfranchised, for he continued to take part in public affairs.'[122] The dilemma would be well explained by

---

[121] Storey 2003, 216–17.
[122] MacDowell 1995, 24, referring to MacDowell 1978, 160. See also Storey 1989, Degani 1993, 423, Dunbar 1995, 238, Olson 1998, 167, Sommerstein 2001, 230. The other Cleonymus references in Aristophanes relate to his size and gluttony: *Ach.* 88, *Knights* 958, 1290–9.

supposing that this incident occurred not in real life but in *comedy*. To be sure, there would still have to have been a general feeling in the city that he was a coward, but that falls a long way short of any actual proof and could have been all that was needed to motivate an attack of this kind (cf. the attack on Cleon for cowardice at *Acharnians* 659f.). Cleonymus' shield-dropping is mentioned by Eupolis (fr. 352, from an unknown play): ῥιψάσπιδόν τε χεῖρα τὴν Κλεωνύμου 'and the shield-throwing hand of Cleonymus'.[123] Trygaeus/Eupolis' treatment of Cleonymus in *Peace* might be amusing because he was the one who had written the shield-dropping scene. In that case, it is ironic that he appears now to think his cowardice is a positive thing. It could be, however, that he was a friend and that the scene belongs in a rival's comedy, perhaps Cratinus' – and this is the more likely of the two proposals, judging by what I shall be saying in the next chapter, pp. 272–3 about the part played by Cleonymus' wife in *Thesmophoriazusai*. In that case, the known connection between the two will be what fuels the humour here and fr. 352 will be in the voice of an opponent who is characterised by the attack (as I have argued earlier that Cratinus and Eupolis may be by their articulation of prejudice against Hyperbolus).

It is worth, finally, considering the exodus briefly. The wedding-scene (which actually occurs in Aristophanes only here and in *Birds*) was, for Cornford, part of a ritual pattern underlying Old Comedy.[124] Recent scholars are generally more reticent about such extrapolations.[125] I note here merely that the criticism of *Clouds* 543 (rushing on stage with torches) is quite likely to denote a wedding-scene. In that case, the weddings in *Peace* and *Birds* are very probably mocking a specific scene from Eupolidean comedy. Perhaps it was at the end of *Poleis*, as Norwood thought.[126] At any rate, the metacomic texture of the play as a whole makes it unlikely that the scene could be read 'straight' by its original audience, as it usually is today. Rather, like the ending of *Acharnians*, it ridicules the political views of the central character (Trygaeus/Eupolis) by placing him in a parodic version of one of his own most memorable scenes.

CONCLUSION

If we regard the Archidamian War as round one in a prize fight between Eupolis and Aristophanes (Cratinus having ruled himself out after his

---

[123] Austin 1973, 83–119, 236–7 for discussion. It is possible (though by no means proven) that the mention in *P. Oxy.* 4301.5 = *PCG* VIII.1151.5 might also be attributable to Eupolis.
[124] Cornford 1961, 56–66. [125] See further Hofmann, 1976, 138–60.
[126] Norwood 1931, 96. See also Sidwell 1994, 102.

victory wth *Pytine* in 423), there can be no doubt at all that the bald fellow was beaten on points, if not by a knockout. After those glorious wins with *Acharnians* and *Knights* in the successive Lenaea festivals of 425 and 424, his record from 423 until the peace of Nicias looks mediocre. A bad third in 423 with *Clouds* was followed by second place for *Wasps* (though it is true some scholars believe the winning play, *Proagon*, was actually by Aristophanes and not Philonides).[127] Then came the *coup de grace*, the defeat of *Peace* by the poet whom, on my hypothesis, it was designed to attack. For whatever success Eupolis had with *Marikas* at the Lenaea (we simply do not know), his *Kolakes* won the first prize at the Dionysia. In the light of my political reading of the antagonism between these poets, it is worth reflecting on whether the turnaround in their respective fortunes in 421 might not mirror the altered atmosphere created especially by the death of Cleon, which led to the conditions in which the peace party could once again make their voices heard. If there is such a correlation, then it goes some way to confirming that however much Aristophanes charged his rival with a propensity for Laconism, treachery and tyranny (*Ach*. 499f., *Wasps* 410f., 466f.), neither Eupolis nor any of his political set had moved in the 420s in their political theory much beyond vague expressions of the need to reclaim a proto-democratic polity such as that exemplified by the pre-Periclean constitution (*Knights* 1325f.). As I have argued above, things were to change in the 410s and it will be the business of the next chapter to track through the two poets' continuing hostilities the way this move occurred and what its consequences were, both for Eupolis and for Aristophanes.

[127] E.g. Sommerstein 1983, xv. See MacDowell 1971 on hypothesis 1 line 34, for a more neutral view.

CHAPTER 6

Metacomedy, caricature and politics from Autolycus *to* Frogs

THE *ARCHON* AND POLITICAL COMEDY

The records of comic production for the years between the beginning of the Archidamian War and the renewal of the conflict prompt the question, how did the *archon* make his selections of what would go on at the festivals, especially in the light of his knowledge of the seriously political nature of the genre? It is clear from the productions of the 420s that competing political interests were pretty well represented, if the argument so far is accepted. Both anti- and pro-war poets were able to get their comedies into the major festivals, and supporters of Cleon, Hyperbolus and Alcibiades managed to have their respective say. The ebb and flow of judgement is another matter, of course, and Aristophanes' lack of success after 424 may suggest, as I have noted above, a political shift towards the peace-party. Things are more difficult to judge between 420 and 414, because our records are lacunose. However, we have no firm date of production for an Aristophanes play between Dionysia 421 and *Birds* in 414. For Eupolis, on the other hand, 421 was a bumper year, in which he competed with *Marikas* at the Lenaea and won with *Kolakes* at the Dionysia. In 420 came one of the versions of *Autolykos*. His *Baptai* must also belong to this period, since it appears to have attacked Alcibiades and he was off the scene by summer 415. Can it be, then, that the *archon* made – or was induced to make – a decision not to allow the plays of the pro-war radical democrat onto the public stage between the Peace of Nicias and the Sicilian expedition's departure? On the other hand, however, the fact that the arch-democratic poet was allowed to produce *twice* in 411, the year of the oligarchic revolution, suggests along with the evidence for the 420s that such obvious political interference was not the norm.

It seems in fact more likely that the (projected?) private audience of the *Clouds* revision guides us to a more pragmatic explanation of the *archon's* choices. Since the *archon* could never be presumed to have any theatrical expertise, the procedure was perhaps for the *poet* to secure choregic sponsorship (and this system might help to explain also the modus operandi of the close working relationship between Aeschylus and Pericles). Since the *choregia* was an expensive liturgy, it would in all likelihood not often be the case that too many poets could find their financier. When it did happen, as in the case lamented by the chorus of Cratinus *Boukoloi* (K-A fr. 17), where Gnesippus was given a chorus over Sophocles, it was noteworthy. In such a case we may indeed be looking at a *political* choice.

AUTOLYCUS, THE DATE OF *CLOUDS II* AND *BAPTAI*

Hostilities between Sparta and Athens may have ceased and Aristophanes may for the moment have been *hors de combat*. But Eupolis did not scruple to take advantage of his rival's political indisposition (if this is what it was). For him, it was business as usual. In fr. 62 of *Autolycus* Eupolis satirised Aristophanes' statue of Peace. He may also have been attacking the bald poet in fr. 65, where the issue of misuse of comic victory to pick up boys in the palaestra arises. But since this was placed at someone else's door by Aristophanes at *Wasps* 1023f. and *Peace* 762–3, the point of attack is more difficult to pin down. I have argued above (chapter five, p. 179) that the parabasis of *Wasps* is quite specifically targeted at Cratinus (victor over *Clouds* in 423 with a vicious satire of Aristophanes in his *Pytine*). But the scholium on *Wasps* 1025b suggests that it refers to Eupolis: δι' Εὔπολιν ἐν Αὐτολύκῳ δὲ τοιαῦτά φησιν ὅτι περιήει τὰς παλαίστρας σεμνυνόμενος καὶ τοῖς παισὶν ἑαυτὸν δῆλον ποιῶν τῆς νίκης ἕνεκα ('Because of Eupolis. He makes a claim like this in his *Autolycus*, namely that he went haughtily round the wrestling grounds showing himself off to the boys because of his victory').[1] How are we to reconcile these contradictory indications?

Part of our problem is created by the existence of two versions of the play, a fact we know from a number of citations (e.g. Σ *Clouds* 109 = Eup. *Autolycus* fr. 50 ἐν Ἀυτολύκῳ β' 'in *Autolycus II*').[2] Athenaeus 216c-d gives 421/20 (the archonship of Aristion) as the date of one of the two versions. Since the point of the citation is to criticise the inaccuracy of Xenophon's claim in *Symposium* 1.2 to have attended the party thrown by Callias for his

---

[1] Σ *Wasps* 1025c says δι' Εὔπολιν ταῦτά φησιν· ἐκεῖνος γὰρ ἐν ταῖς παλαίστραις περιιὼν τοιαῦτα ἐσεμνύνετο 'He says this because of Eupolis; for he [Eupolis] used to cruise the wrestling grounds and was very full of himself'. There are no linguistic grounds for Storey's interpretation of the 1025b scholium as referring to Aristophanes (2003, 100), though he is right to feel that it would be a little odd for the *author* to boast of this himself. See Sidwell 1994, 85–6.
[2] Storey 2003, 82–3 lists the other evidence in full and discusses the issues arising from it.

lover Autolycus' Panathenaic *pankration* victory, we can be pretty certain (a) that this reflects Athenaeus' (or his source's) consultation not only of the *didaskaliai*, but also of the list of Panathenaic victories and (b) therefore that this victory occurred at the games of 422.[3] But this does not tell us which of the two versions this was, since the boy's victory may have simply added an extra frisson for a satire of him which predated his athletic success and in any case, it is probable that this information was gleaned from a *named* attack in the text and not a caricature, because of the method of study common to ancient readers of comedy. It is clear at any rate from the attack on Callias in *Kolakes* of Dionysia 421 that Eupolis might easily have vented his spleen against this enemy earlier than 420 for his political and intellectual views and that Callias' relationship with Autolycus could easily have formed the focus of this satire even before the *pankration* victory.

We must also consider what basis there will have been for Eupolis' revival of what Galen assures us was essentially the same play (*Commentary on Hippocrates' On Regimen in Acute Diseases* 1.4). The discussion of the *Clouds* revision in chapter one will help here. There it was argued that since comedies were designated by their *caricature targets* rather than by their plots, the likeliest explanation for Aristophanes' apparently illogical complaint against other poets (Eupolis in particular, probably) for putting the same play on time and time again when he was doing exactly this with *Clouds* was that he had changed his targets, that is the individuals represented in the main roles, for the second version. I have argued above (pp. 56–7, 113–16, following Storey's reconstruction of the plot from Aelian *NA* 10.41),[4] that one version of *Autolycus* satirised Aristophanes as Ephialtes the slave stealing comedies from an older poet, who must have been the 'Aeginetan' under whose more experienced cover the *Acharnians* (652f.) was produced. Such a play would have been well past its sell-by date by 420, though it might well fit as a swift riposte to the successful attack of *Knights* in 424 at Lenaea 423. The scholiast on *Wasps* 1025b, on the other hand, appears to be reporting a boastful statement made by the poet himself in *Autolycus* which replicates the accusation made by Aristophanes against a poet I have argued above (pp. 179–83) was probably Cratinus. Given the argument that such self-satire as is read here into the comedy will not represent the original intention of the poet, it is very likely that the older comic poet figure in this version – the second, then – was in

---

[3] Storey 2003, 81–2. At 82 he admits that the first version could be earlier, offering as an argument for 420 Lenaea only that 'it is much more likely that the boy's victory belongs to the summer of 422', citing the inference of Kirchner in *PA 2748* as his evidence. But the date of the first version does not depend upon the date of Autolycus' victory.

[4] Storey 2003, 86–9.

fact Cratinus. The charge against Aristophanes/Ephialtes for play-stealing remains the same, but his comedies are now stolen from a different poet. As I conjectured earlier, the unique citation of a play called *Hybristodikai* from Eupolis' pen (Ptol. Chenn. *apud* Photius *Bibliotheca* 190 = *PCG* IV, 466), said to have been found under the pillow of Ephialtes, is very likely to have derived ultimately from *Autolycus*. It may be a reference to one of Cratinus' 'jury' plays, perhaps *Nomoi* or *Euneidae* or even *Eumenides*, which was parodied by Aristophanes in *Wasps*.

I conjecture, then, that *Autolycus I* was produced at the Lenaea of 423, the contestants of which we do not know, thus making the 421/420 version whose date is given by Athenaeus the second one. The first play was revenge for the blistering attack on Eupolis in *Knights* and a first – and entirely appropriate – response to the insolent reuse of his own *Noumeniai*: Aristophanes was not original, but stole his material from other poets. It might also help us to see why Eupolis should have wanted to revive the play in 421/420, since, if my analysis is correct, he had been the prime target of *Peace* at the preceding year's Dionysia. Most immediately, this will represent Eupolis' revenge for the hammering he had received both in *Wasps* and in *Peace*, and it will help us to understand why, although *Wasps* was mainly a response to Cratinus' attack upon him in *Pytine*, Eupolis also features so prominently as Bdelycleon: *Wasps* is also a response to *Autolycus I*. It will have been at one of the festivals of 421/420, then, that Eupolis chose to reiterate the attack on Cratinus for cruising the *palaistrai* which Aristophanes had mentioned in both plays (*Wasps* 1023f., *Peace* 762–3; cf. *Wasps* 1301 for Lycon, Autolycus' father). If this is correct, it is easier to see grounds for Aristophanes' accusation at *Clouds* 546 that another poet presented the same things for a second and a third time (a charge that would apply also to Eupolis' *Noumeniai* and *Marikas*), but less easy to forgive him the specious argumentation.

As I mentioned in chapter three, Aristophanes is generally thought to have been attacking Eupolis in *Anagyros* fr. 58: ἐκ δὲ τῆς ἐμῆς χλανίδος τρεῖς ἀπληγίδας ποιῶν ('making three tunics out of my one cloak'), in eupolideans, though it is difficult to know which play he designates as his cloak and which of Eupolis' three plays as tunics, since the play's date is unknown.[5] Storey argues that it is to this attack, and not to the revised *Clouds*, that Eupolis was replying in *Baptai* fr. 89, where he famously claims to have been the co-writer of *Knights*: †κἀκεῖνος †τοὺς Ἱππέας |

---

[5] Storey 2003, 293 opts for *Knights* as the cloak and *Poleis, Marikas* and *Demoi* as the tunics. See chapter three n. 22 for the suggestion that *Baptai* might be added to the Eupolidean list.

ξυνεποίησα τῷ φαλακρῷ < – x> κἀδωρησάμην 'I co-wrote the *Knights* with baldilocks and gave him the play as a gift'.[6] He speculates that Aristophanes may have composed for *Anagyros* a eupolidean parabasis accusing Eupolis of using his material and that much of the same matter was used for the revised parabasis of *Clouds II*. Accepting Sommerstein's argument that *Anagyros* must postdate *Clouds II* because it mentions a threefold plagiarism, whereas *Clouds II* mentions only *Marikas*, Storey dates *Clouds II* to 419 or 418, *Anagyros* to *c.* 417 and *Baptai* to 416.[7] There are two problems with these conclusions. First, it does not seem very likely that the scholia to *Clouds* would have overlooked such a substantial overlap between the *Anagyros* parabasis and that of *Clouds*. Secondly, the contrast made by Aristophanes at *Clouds* 550–1 on his lack of attacks on Cleon after he was thrown (κειμένῳ) with those now being made upon Hyperbolus must have some understandable point of reference. Does the throw refer to Cleon's death?[8] On my earlier argument, it cannot refer to Aristophanes' having refrained from other on-stage caricature attacks on Cleon after *Knights*, since he did this in *Wasps* 902f. But if the reference is to Cleon's death, then the corresponding 'throw' required by the rhetoric – inevitable once the λαβή 'hold' had been conceded – must refer to something equivalent. This cannot be Hyperbolus' death (which occurred in 411, Thuc. 8.73.3), but might very well be his ostracism, the exact date of which is unknown (though the consensus now is for a choice between 416 and 415).[9] This focus upon continuing attacks after Hyperbolus' ostracism does not necessarily undermine the use made by Sommerstein of the difference between *Anagyros*' accusation of threefold versus *Clouds*' of a single plagiarism to date the plays, though it may weaken it slightly (the accusation of bringing on the same thing two or three times at 546 may be parallel). The upshot of this discussion is that (a) *Clouds II* postdates Hyperbolus' ostracism (so, depending on where that is placed, it could belong to the period between spring 417/416 and the festivals of 416/415, or between those of 416/415 and those of 415/414); (b) *Anagyros* may still be later than *Clouds II*; (c) there must have been a response from Aristophanes after *Marikas* which did not survive into the post-classical period to which *Baptai* fr. 89 replies (we know of one such play, conjecturally restored as *Odomantopresbeis*, recorded on *IG* II[2] .2321, the name of which is not given by Alexandrian or Pergamene scholars). This revised timetable stretches the unenigmatic evidence for

---

[6] Storey 1990, 22 and 2003, 293.   [7] Sommerstein 2001, 220, Storey 2003, 108.
[8] As Sommerstein 1982 infers ad loc.
[9] Rhodes 1994, 91 n. 36. Rhodes argues for 415, *ibid.* 86–91. Bianchetti 1979 and Kopff 1990 also date *Clouds* after the ostracism. See *contra* Storey 1993b.

the conflict between the poets into the mid-410s, possibly down as far as 415/414.

But even if *Anagyros* belongs to the later 410s, Eupolis was clearly still in conflict with his bald rival in the period between 420 and 415, as the citation from *Baptai* fr. 89 shows. Given the plethora of anecdotes which have some reference to the play, it must have involved Alcibiades in some way, if only perhaps as a character in the 'dyeing' or 'dipping' scene.[10] Storey reasonably enough, then, dates the play to Lenaea 415, when Alcibiades was at the height of his influence, but before he sailed to Sicily.[11] It is worth asking, however, where the anecdote could possibly have arisen from. The most detailed version is in fact in Tzetzes (Koster, *Prolegomena* p. 27, XIa 1, 88–95):

ἐπεὶ δὲ οὗτος εἰς Ἀλκιβιάδην τὸν στρατηγὸν ἀπέρριψε σκῶμμα καὶ φανερῶς τὴν τραυλότητα τούτου διελοιδόρησεν – ἔτυχον δὲ τότε καὶ ταῖς τριήρεσιν ὄντες ὡς ναυμαχίας προσδοκωμένης – κελεύει τοῖς στρατιώταις, καὶ ἢ ἅπαξ ἐκβράττουσιν αὐτὸν εἰς τὴν θάλατταν καὶ ἀπώλετο, ἢ σχοινῷ δεδεμένον ἀνάγοντες καὶ κατάγοντες ἦσαν εἰς θάλατταν καὶ τέλος περιέσωσαν τοῦτον τοῦ Ἀλκιβιάδου εἰπόντος αὐτῷ· βάπτε με σὺ θυμέλαις, ἐγὼ δὲ σε κατακλύσω ὕδασιν ἁλμυρωτάτοις.

When Eupolis had satirised Alcibiades the general and openly mocked his lisp – they happened to be on board triremes, expecting a sea-battle – Alcibiades gave orders to his soldiers and either they tossed him into the sea immediately and he died or they tied a rope around him and pulled him in and out of the sea, eventually saving his life when Alcibiades declared: 'Dip me on the stage, and I will drench you in the bitterest of waters.'

West suggested that the couplet which underlies Tzetzes' final sentence was genuine and represents some response made publicly.[12] Storey asks in response, 'in what public context could one respond to a comic poet?'[13] The answer surely is 'in a comedy' (cf. *Ach.* 630f.), but not necessarily only in a parabasis.[14] What we have here looks very much as though it was derived at an early stage from a play which mocked Eupolis' *Baptai* and had a scene set on board ship on the way to Sicily in which the 'dyeing' or 'dipping' scene was subverted by being transferred to a naval context and Alcibiades was able to take his revenge in person on stage. I guess, however, that such a play will have to have been staged *after* Alcibiades' rehabilitation in *c.* 411 and *after* Eupolis' disenfranchisement in 410 (when the naval context will

---

[10] Storey 2003, 101–5.   [11] Storey 2003, 110.   [12] West 1989–92: II.29.
[13] Storey 2003, 103.   [14] The conjecture of Storey 2003, 103.

have become appropriate enough, if my conjecture at pp. 41, 91 above is correct that Eupolis was an *epibates* in this period).

Earlier (p. 54 n. 22) I ventured the suggestion that, because Eupolis chose the parabasis of this play to defend his intellectual property claim to *Knights* in the parabasis (fr. 89), *Baptai* may have been another in the series of ironic *prostasia*-changing plays which began, on my conjecture, with Eupolis' *Noumeniai*. If so, then it will have attacked both Alcibiades and Aristophanes, who was probably still supporting a man who had wished to prolong the war, may have made common cause with Hyperbolus on the matter, and now had been one of the main proponents of the radical democratic expansionist project in Sicily. This will not, unfortunately, tell us anything about how the plot was managed: there is no evidence for a Demos character nor for an antagonist for Alcibiades. But we may still see the cross-dressing theme as one which would be picked up only a few years later by Aristophanes in yet another counter-attack on Eupolis, the *Thesmophoriazusai*.

DEMOI

There is another play, possibly of this period, which may have been part of this ongoing battle, Eupolis' *Demoi*. Storey argues for a date of 417 or 416, as opposed to the 'traditional' one of *c.* 412.[15] But since, more recently still, Telò has argued (convincingly in my view) for Lenaea 410, and especially because his redating is accompanied by a major shift in suggested political orientation of the comedy, from essentially conservative to radically democratic, I will reserve analysis of the issues until the appropriate chronological point, after *Thesmophoriazusai* and before *Frogs*.[16]

CLOUDS II

Clouds II, on the arguments brought above, belongs after the ostracism of Hyperbolus, since there must be something corresponding to Cleon's death (*Clouds* 550) with which the multiple attacks on Hyperbolus can be parallel. Since this cannot be his death (which happened in 411), it must be his ostracism. We can go further. If the parabasis is any guide to the motivation which guided the play's revision, as I have argued earlier that it

---

[15] For agreement, see Braun 2000, 192.
[16] See Telò 2007, 16–24 on the date, 73–80 on the political colour of the play. See further below, pp. 276–83.

ought to be, then it tells us two things: first, that rivalry with his peers was an important factor, since the theme covers the entire set of eupolideans (518–62), and, secondly, that his rivals' treatment of Hyperbolus is unacceptable to him (551–9). I have argued that these concerns are connected: most of his irritation in the parabasis is felt against Eupolis, even before his naming at 553 (and he puts him on stage in the guise of Unjust Argument (920f.)), and Hyperbolus, whose political λαβή ('hold') had been taken advantage of first by Eupolis (553) is the political leader with whom Aristophanes felt most in tune (552). Hence, the ostracism is crucial in tracking Aristophanes' reason for reworking the play. This will have taken place in the eighth prytany (Philochorus, *FGrH* 328 F 30). It is not possible to be certain what relationship there was between dates for ostracism and the Dionysia festival. All one can say is that in most years the eighth prytany and Elaphebolion will have had significant overlap. Aristophanes' fury at the performance of comedies attacking Hyperbolus after his ostracism may be explained if we posit a date for the ostracism *preceding* the festival.[17] The comedies will already have been given choruses and rehearsed and if, as it seems we must also presume, these did contain on-stage attacks on Hyperbolus, they would certainly have irritated a supporter into retaliation. That retaliation will most obviously have been targeted on individuals who were *both* connected with the Socratic circle, since Socrates remains a central satirical figure in the revision, *and* involved in Hyperbolus' ostracism, the focus, on my analysis, of the parabasis.

The ostracism became famous for three connected reasons: (1) because Hyperbolus proposed it and became its victim; (2) because it was the last time the law was used; (3) because the politicians between which the bill's proposer saw the *demos* having to choose, Nicias and Alcibiades (Plut. *Nic.* 11, *Arist.* 7.3–4), or Nicias, Alcibiades and Phaeax (Plut. *Alc.* 13), joined forces somehow to bring this unexpected result.[18] Of these three political figures, Alcibiades was certainly connected with Socrates and, I have argued, had been the target behind the Pheidippides of the first *Clouds*. In the case of Nicias, however, we have absolutely no information connecting him with any intellectual sphere at all. Phaeax is not a well-known figure.

---

[17] In an ordinary year, Elaphebolion will have begun around day 240 and ended around day 270. The eighth prytany will have begun around day 245 and ended around day 280. Since the festival seems to have taken place between the 10th and the 14th Elaphebolion (*DFA*² 65–6), my conjecture assumes that the ostracism would have been held between the 5th and 9th Elaphebolion. We know from Aeschines 3.67 that in 346 an assembly was held on the 8th Elaphebolion. Since the decision to hold an ostracism must have been made already in the sixth prytany (Arist. *Ath. Pol.* 43.5), such timing certainly seems possible.

[18] See Rhodes 1994 for an excellent survey of the evidence. I follow his conclusions here.

Nonetheless, he is mentioned at *Knights* 1377 as the object of admiration of τὰ μειράκια... τὰν τῷ μύρῳ ('the youths in the perfume-market'), who call him σοφός ('clever') in terms (a string of adjectives ending in -ικος) which suggest *their* adherence to intellectual circles, at any rate, and may imply his too.[19]

This argument from plot and parabatic focus to individual targets appears to leave us with two possible sets of identifications: (1) Strepsiades represents Alcibiades, Pheidippides Phaeax; (2) Strepsiades represents Phaeax, Pheidippides Alcibiades. But if (2) were the case, the target behind Pheidippides would stay the same, which would contradict what is said in the parabasis (546f.). This consideration casts Alcibiades as Strepsiades (suitable as far as the creation of a comic name goes, at any rate), and leaves Phaeax as our choice for Pheidippides. One of the three major changes to the play was, according to Hypothesis I, the ending, where Strepsiades burns down the *phrontisterion*. This would make the sharpest satire against an individual who has known connections to Socrates. There is nothing to stop the fantasy of satire from ageing or rejuvenating individuals to suit its purposes, as we have seen with the transmogrification of Eupolis into the old man Cratinus in *Acharnians* and Trygaeus in *Peace* in one direction, and that of Demos in *Knights* in the other.

Close examination of the text tends to confirm this reasoning. First, a real clue to Strepsiades' original (for *us*) may be offered by the passages in which he complains about his wife, Μεγακλέους τοῦ Μεγακλέους | ἀδελφιδῆν 'the niece of Megacles son of Megacles' (45–6) and their conflict over naming their son (60f.). The Athenian audience, used to the system wherein a woman is named by her association with her kinsmen, could certainly have recognised the woman in question if she was real, and it is in fact very odd that Strepsiades, who is after all speaking of a woman who would normally be known as 'the wife of Strepsiades' or 'the daughter of X (father)', is made to describe her rather in relation to her mother's side of the family and in such specific terms.[20] And if she is real, presumably there is something amusing not just about what Strepsiades says about her, but also about the very fact that he formulates her identity as he does. However, the humour of this passage will depend primarily upon prior recognition by the audience of Strespiades' true identity.

---

[19] These adjectives were not confined to the sophistic milieu (Dover 1970, and 1987, 229 with n. 11). However, in Aristophanes, especially in *Clouds*, they are associated with Socrates and his school (e.g. 483, 728, 747).

[20] For the naming of women see generally Schaps 1977. For naming of women in Aristophanes see Sommerstein 1980c. The implication of the results of these researches is that 'the niece of Megacles son of Megacles' is still alive, if she is real.

Dover and Sommerstein both accept the possibility that Megacles son of Megacles refers to *PA* 9697 (= Davies *APF* 9688.xi), but they both also underplay the textual evidence.[21] On the other hand, as Dover has pointed out (p.xxvii), the attendant circumstance alluded to in 41–2 of a προμνήστρια ('matchmaker') inducing Strepsiades to marry and the inference that Strepsiades owns land worth a good deal of money might be taken to imply that there is nothing surprising about the match *per se*. If we look at this within the framework of caricature, the scenario could be funny because the person being represented as Strepsiades was a landowner and had been approached by the family of Megacles to marry the ἀδελφιδῆς ('niece') in question (or the reverse, because it was *he* who had made the move, on account of the family's status and wealth). In other words, the joke rests on the presentation of an individual whose circumstances are well known to the audience, in a guise (the boorish rustic) designed to ridicule him.

The other information given about the ἀδελφιδῆς ('niece') is consistent with one of the accounts we can give about the family of Megacles son of Megacles (Davies *APF* 9688.x). The younger Megacles' mother was Coisyra (*Ach.* 614 with scholium). The niece of *Clouds* would have to be the daughter of his brother or sister (48, 70, 124, 800), though the stress on the female side at 48 and 800 makes a sister more likely. The family had close connections with Pericles' family, because Megacles' father Megacles (IV) was the brother of Pericles' mother Agariste (their father was Hippocrates (I)). It is worth noting that when Strepsiades describes the argument about names, the first example of a ἱππο- ('horse') name chosen by his wife is Xanthippos (64), the name of Pericles' father and of his first-born son. Thus a real family-tree can be drawn up on the basis of the references in *Clouds*, which connects consistently with information from other sources. This seems difficult to account for except on the assumption that it reflects reality. This genealogy reads as follows:

---

[21] Dover 1968 in particular is adamant that this is not the point: 'it is most unlikely that Ar. means us to think of his fictitious hero as married to the niece of an actual person. The whole point is that "Megakles" is in itself a grandiloquent name...' (on 46). In other words, Dover doubts even the intention to attack a real person. Dover ad loc: 'A real Megakles son of Megakles was one of the treasurers of Athena in 428/7..., but... [t]he whole point is that "Megakles"' is itself a grandiloquent name... and in particular is a name borne in earlier days by several members of the wealthy and distinguished Alkmeonidai.' Sommerstein 1982: 'That the fictitious Strepsiades should be related by marriage to the real Megacles need be no more surprising than that the fictitious hero of *Thesm.* is related to Euripides.' Van Leeuwen (1898 on 46) already noted that Pheidippides was being made by this connection a relative of Alcibiades. But for him the name Megacles is fictitious.

From Autolycus to Frogs

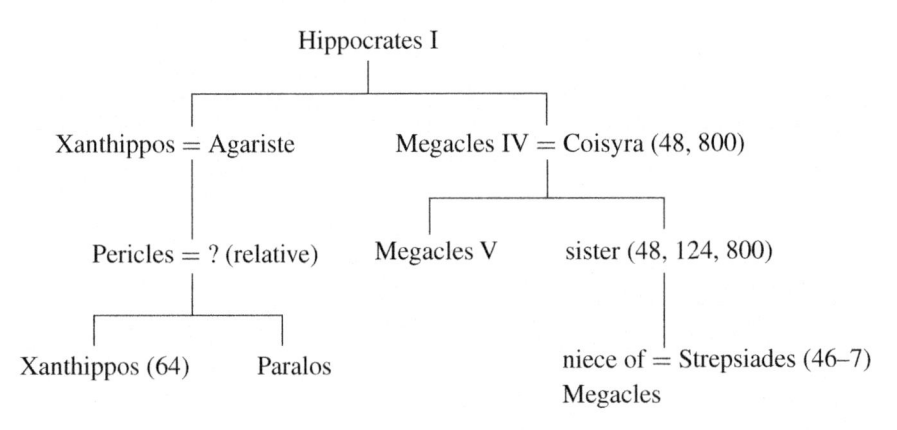

```
                    Hippocrates I
                         |
         ┌───────────────┴───────────────┐
   Xanthippos = Agariste          Megacles IV = Coisyra (48, 800)
         |                                |
         |                    ┌───────────┴───────────┐
   Pericles = ? (relative)   Megacles V        sister (48, 124, 800)
         |                                            |
    ┌────┴────┐                                       |
Xanthippos (64)  Paralos                    niece of = Strepsiades (46–7)
                                            Megacles
```

We can get further with this by following the discussion about the identity of Pericles' first wife. She was a close relative (Plut., *Per.* 24.5: προσήκουσα κατὰ γένος). After bearing him Xanthippos and Paralos, she was married to Hipponicos, to whom she bore Callias and Hipparete. Scholars have considered it likely that the woman was a sister of Megacles.[22] The only known sister of Megacles (V) is Deinomache, mother of Alcibiades and Cleinias, and if we accepted Nepos' statement which explains Pericles' wardship of Cleinias' children on the basis that he was their stepfather (*Alc.* 2.1) she would indeed be the first wife of Pericles. In that case her daughter Hipparete would be the only known candidate for the ἀδελφιδῆς of *Clouds*. This would be very suitable to the humour of 63–4, since the woman who is trying to get ἱππ- into the name is not only from a family which prided itself on victories at the Isthmian and Pythian games (Davies *APF* 371), but has herself a name which starts with ἱππ-, and a father and a stepbrother whose name involved this root (Hipponicus and Xanthippos), the latter of whom is the first example given by Strepsiades. In this context, it is crucial to note that Alcibiades son of Cleinias married this Hipparete in the late 420s (Isoc. 16.31; [Andoc.] 4.13; Plut. *Alc.* 8.1–3). If she is the ἀδελφιδῆς ('niece') of Megacles (V) at *Clouds* 46–7, and the humour of the passage is based on the audience's recognition of reality, this supports the identification of Strepsiades as Alcibiades. Further, if Deinomache was Pericles' first wife, as Nepos *Alc.* 2.1 implies, then Alcibiades and Hipparete would be brother and sister by the same mother. On this reconstruction, in which they are homometrial siblings, another important detail of Alcibiades' family history

[22] See Thompson 1967, 1970, Podlecki 1987, 111.

is reflected comically in *Clouds*. For Strepsiades' shock at the Euripidean passage (probably from *Aeolus*) quoted by Pheidippides about the incest of a brother and sister ὁμομητριάν ('with the same mother': 1371–2: note the detail) would ironically relate to this fact.[23]

Nonetheless, if Deinomache is rejected,[24] then it is still possible that Pericles was married to an unknown sister of Deinomache,[25] whose daughter Hipparete remains the only known ἀδελφιδῆς ('niece') of Megacles (V). On this reconstruction, Strepsiades is still most probably married to the woman who in reality was Alcibiades' wife.

If this identification is correct, then the actual familial association and deme mentioned by Strepsiades at 134 (cf. 65) must be jokes. The father's name, Φείδων, could allude *per ironiam* to Alcibiades' well-known extravagance (see [Andoc.] 4.32, where Phaeax contrasts Alcibiades' spendthrift habits with those of his own family). The deme is certainly chosen, as against his real one, Skambonidai (in the city trittys of the Leontis tribe), at least partly because Kikynna is from an inland trittys (of the Akamantis tribe), and the whole point of the satire is to make the individual caricatured into a bumpkin.[26]

What will be funny about the passage? First is the humour of Alcibiades describing his own wife by such a strange periphrasis – incidentally focusing

---

[23] Davies has two worries about the reconstruction: (i) Deinomache's marital career would be 'impossibly complicated' (*APF* 18 n. 1); (ii) we would need to explain why we lack evidence for this in Plutarch and more seriously Plato *Alcibiades I*. However, on (i), if she divorced Pericles in *c.* 455 and married Cleinias rather than Hipponicos, then married Hipponicos after Cleinias' death at Coroneia in 448/7, the relative ages of her children, Xanthippos, Paralos, Alcibiades, Cleinias, Callias and Hipparete can be well explained, as can the political implications of the last marriage and Pericles' guardianship of Cleinias' sons. As for point (ii), this might be explained by deliberate suppression, since, if the reconstruction is correct, the marriage of Alcibiades and Hipparete attracted the satirical attention of comedy (*Clouds* 1371–2). The evidence of Nepos must have come from somewhere (perhaps comedy?). Thompson's attempt to ascribe it to a double misunderstanding of Greek kinship terms by Diodorus and Nepos is not wholly convincing, since such details were grist to the mill of ancient scholarship (Thompson 1970, 33). But Plato's bias towards Socrates can very well account for the suppression of a detail which might well read badly when seen in the context of an undeniable relationship between Socrates and Alcibiades. A further advantage of this reconstruction will be that Antisthenes' statement (Ath. 5.220c) that Alcibiades committed incest with his mother, his daughter and his sister can be given some sort of context. It is not, as Davies assumes, that one would have to postulate a daughter for Cleinias and Deinomache, for she would have a daughter from Hipponicos, Hipparete, who married Alcibiades her homometrial brother. The other parts of the calumny might be the sorts of thing which could have an origin in comedy (especially one which parodied Euripidean tragedy). And, as I have shown, the joke at 1371–2 has much more punch if the reconstruction is correct.

[24] As for example by Davies *APF* 18 n.1, on the grounds that Deinomache's marital history would be 'impossibly complicated'.

[25] Thompson 1970.

[26] See Olson 1998, 105 on *Peace* 190. This is not to say that there is not some other, more specific, joke hiding beneath the surface.

attention on his own status as an ἀδελφιδοῦς ('nephew') of the same man. Secondly, there is the fun gained by hearing him attack his wife on stage, in a way which would recall to the audience's minds the well-known difficulties in their marriage (see Davies *APF* 19, and especially Plut. *Alc.* 8.4–5).[27] Third is the amusement offered by the counter-factual: if Alcibiades the younger had been born by now (and there is a chance he might very well have been born by 415),[28] he could not be grown up. In any case, the audience ought already to have seen whom Pheidippides represented during the preceding scene (he speaks in his sleep at 25, 28, 32, and awake – and sitting up? – at 35–6 and 38). Fourth is, probably, the intertextuality with the first *Clouds*, where, I have surmised, Pheidippides represented Alcibiades: the specificity of the reference will perhaps explain for the dim-witted (cf. *Wasps* 1045) how the targets have changed and why it is that Pheidippides seems so much like Alcibiades: (i) he is obsessively involved in chariot-racing (25, 28, 32, 124–5);[29] (ii) he eventually manifests a contempt for the laws (1321f.) which matches the accusations often made against Alcibiades (e.g. Plut. *Alc.* 8, striking a man of his father's generation purely for a laugh; [Andoc.] 4.10f., acts of adultery and violence); (iii) he has a lisp (868–73); cf. *Wasps* 44–6;[30] (iv) he belongs to the ἱππεῖς (120; for Alcibiades as Knight see Pl. *Symp.* 221a; Plut. *Alc.* 7).[31] He is, in short, his father's son and the character is taken over wholesale from *Clouds I* to ridicule someone else (see further below).

There are four more respects in which the identification of Strepsiades as Alcibiades fits reality: (1) Alcibiades was an associate of Socrates;[32]

---

[27] She died relatively young, though the evidence (Isoc. 16.45, Plut. *Alc.* 8.4) is too vague to tie down, but was probably still alive at this time, since there is a chance that if she had been dead, her real name would have been used (see Sommerstein above n. 20) and there would be little point in the satire if she were.
[28] It depends upon the dating of Isoc. 16, since Teisias' suit cannot have been brought until the younger Alcibiades reached his majority.
[29] Cf. Davies *APF* 20–1.   [30] See chapter five, n. 56 and Appendix 5.
[31] It is very tempting to associate with this characterisation the lines of Archippus (fr. 48 *PCG*) quoted by Plut. *Alc.* 1.7 in which he speaks of Alcibiades' son's attempts to imitate his father in dress, head posture and lisp. Archippus won his only Dionysia prize between 415 and 412 (*PCG* T2) and Geissler dates other plays before the end of the century (Geissler 1925, 8, 11, 62–3, 66–7, 80). We do not know the precise date of the birth of Alcibiades' son Alcibiades IV (perhaps 417/16 or 416/15), but the information we have about him suggests that he was still a boy when he was expelled by the Thirty (Isoc. 16.46; see Davies *APF* 19 for discussion). These two points taken together might lead to the conclusion that Alcibiades IV is unlikely to have been attacked by Archippus, but that the portrait of Pheidippides in *Clouds II* could have been misappropriated to attack Aristophanes. This would depend, however, on *some* public performance and consequent public knowledge of the revised play.
[32] For example, Pl. *Prt.* 309a–c, *Symp.* 212d f. See also Ath. 5. 219e (verses ascribed to Aspasia). See further Nails 2002, 10f.

(2) Alcibiades was heavily in debt by 415 (Thuc. 6.15.3).³³ (3) The Panhellenic fame which Alcibiades aimed at and eventually achieved is ironically mirrored at lines 412–13 and 429–30;³⁴ (4) The training sought by Strepsiades is not as a political orator, persuading the demos to adopt his motions (431–2), but as a wily and unscrupulous pleader in the courts serving his own crooked interests (433–4, 443–51, 468–75, 791–3), and this suits early references to Alcibiades (Ar. fr. 205.6 and *Ach.* 716; cf. *Wasps* 1037–42 with my interpretation).

There are a number of other places where we might at once perceive jokes resting on the audience's recognition of Alcibiades as Strepsiades. Some of the evidence comes in the anecdotal tradition, whose veracity is of no concern to my argument: a joke based on an apocryphal story will still be an effective joke.³⁵ And some anecdotes may themselves stem ultimately from comedy, read with the enigmatic surface unmasked. I will take them in the order they come in the play.

1 The humour of Alcibiades' debts is made from transference of the cause from himself to his 'son'. But it seems likely that the basis of the plot, the plan to get out of paying his dues (see 112–18), may depend on an anecdote about Alcibiades' advice to Pericles. At Plutarch *Alcibiades* 7.2–3 and Diodorus 12.38, we hear that he visited Pericles when he was busy working out how to present his accounts to the Athenians. Alcibiades' response was: εἶτα... βέλτιον οὐκ ἦν σκοπεῖν αὐτὸν ὅπως οὐκ ἀποδώσει λόγον Ἀθηναίοις; ('Then wouldn't it be better for him to see how he can avoid giving his accounts to the Athenians?'). In *Clouds I*, the humour will have lain in old man/Eupolis' attempt to practise what his friend Alcibiades had preached.³⁶

2 At 206–17, the Student shows Strepsiades a map of the whole world. Aelian, *Varia Historia* 3.28 reports that once Socrates showed Alcibiades a map of the world, because he saw that he was proud of the land he possessed. He told Alcibiades to find Attica, which he did. Then he asked him to find his own estates. Alcibiades replied: 'They aren't marked.' At which Socrates said: 'And yet you give yourself airs on account of possessions which don't make a mark on the surface of the earth!' Clearly, if this anecdotal tradition was available in 423, or even by the date of the revision, the scene as we now read it, with a student of Socrates (presumably identifiable by the audience as someone significantly ridiculed

---

³³ For Alcibiades' property, see the account in Davies *APF* 20–1.
³⁴ On this issue, see also Vickers 1997, 32–3.   ³⁵ On this issue, see Vickers, 1997, xxiv–xxv.
³⁶ Alternatively (see chapter five, n. 58), if the old man represented Hipponicus, then the humour will have lain in his attempt to follow his prospective son-in-law's advice.

by this association) showing the map, and Strepsiades/Alcibiades being rustically incapable of understanding even the concept of a map, then wanting to know why he can't see the jurors sitting if it really is Athens, is in some significant relationship with it. Indeed, it would not be surprising if the original anecdote was itself based on a scene from comedy.[37] Both comic scenes would have the aim of ridiculing Alcibiades. But the *Clouds* scene remakes the incident metacomically, with Alcibiades more deeply ridiculed, not just for pretension because of wealth, but for intellectual ignorance. And the cross-reference may have been supported by exaggerated props, which recalled and mocked the comic style of the original.

3 In Athenaeus 9.407 b-c there is an anecdote about Alcibiades rubbing out an indictment against Hegemon in the Metroon by wetting his finger. The climax is at 407c:

ὁ δὲ θαρρεῖν παρακελευσάμενος εἰπών τε πᾶσιν ἕπεσθαι ἧκεν εἰς τὸ Μητρῷον, ὅπου τῶν δικῶν ἦσαν αἱ γραφαί, καὶ βρέξας τὸν δάκτυλον ἐκ τοῦ στόματος διήλειψε τὴν δίκην τοῦ Ἡγήμονος.

Alcibiades told them to be upbeat about it and said they should all follow him. He went into the Metroion, where the records of indictments were kept, put his finger in his mouth and wet it, then rubbed out the case against Hegemon.

At *Clouds* 757–74, Strepsiades finds a novel solution to the problem of evading a five talent lawsuit, namely to erase it with a magnifying glass to concentrate the sun's rays on the wax tablet. If the Athenaeus anecdote was already well known by the time of the second *Clouds*, then the passage in the play just cited is a ridiculous version of it, created to poke fun at Alcibiades.

4 A similar relationship might exist between the anecdote told by Xenophon in *Memorabilia* 1.2.40–6 and *Clouds* 1171f. The story of Alcibiades running argumentative rings around Pericles in a discussion of νόμος ('law, custom') must belong before 428, and so could have been well known already in 423. It is striking that the same subject is chosen for discussion between Strepsiades and Pheidippides. The humour once more arises from irony. The audience recognises Strepsiades as Alcibiades, knows the anecdote about Pericles, and sees Alcibiades ridiculed in a rerun of the same argument with a less successful political opponent

---

[37] It may be obliquely used by Lucian at *Icaromenippus* 18, given that one of Lucian's main sources for his fantasy material was Old Comedy (see e.g. *Bis Accusatus* 33). As Menippus flies between earth and heaven, he laughs to think people should take pride in land, when even the largest estate is not equal to one of Epicurus' atoms.

who now runs rings round *him*. (In the first version, the joke will have been that Eupolis replaced Pericles).[38]

5 The scene which follows Pheidippides' return from the *phrontisterion* and his lessons to Strepsiades (1214–1302) shows Strepsiades himself using the 'weaker argument', in his usual unlearned way, to dispatch two creditors, insolently and violently. Certainly, the scene well ridicules a man noted in anecdote for having beaten his future father-in-law for a joke (Plut. *Alc.* 8.1), killed a slave with a club (*ibid.* 3.1) and bought a chariot for a friend then raced it under his own name (*ibid.* 12.2f.). [39]

The pretence in *Clouds II* that Alcibiades is a dimwitted yokel (e.g. 398) incapable of learning what he has to from the master (789–90), who has eventually to rely on the intelligence of his son (whose original is an enemy with whom he has formed a temporary alliance), and who finally burns down the school of his master, produces piquant amusement at the expense of a person who was in fact not only the smartest young politician around, but very close to Socrates and highly valued by him. The humour lies in casting Alcibiades the waster as the father who must control his spendthrift 'son'.

The humour of the caricature of Pheidippides/Phaeax, on the other hand, rests partly, as I have said above, upon the ascription to him of characteristics which in reality belong to Alcibiades (chariot-racing, lisp, membership of the Knights, contempt for law). But there are two aspects of his characterisation in *Clouds* which most likely recall his own image and reputation, rather than his conflict with Alcibiades; (i) antagonism towards Socrates, and (ii) his movement from being unable to put two words together to being a much better speaker than his 'father' (1401–2).

(i) Pheidippides' opposition to associating with the teachers in the *phrontisterion* is marked. He knows the names of Socrates and Chaerephon, their ascetic habits of dress and their pallid complexions, but calls them ἀλαζόνας ('frauds', 102–4). He thinks his father mad because of his desire to have him taught by them (844–6), asking if he should indict him for παρανοία ('madness'), a procedure which Socrates is said to have induced his young associates to bring against their parents and other relatives (Xen. *Mem.* 1.2.49). He insults them by the obscure epithet γηγενεῖς ('earthborn', 853),[40] warns Strepsiades he will be sorry later (865), and then as he embarks

---

[38] Or Hipponicus, if the old man represented him. See chapter five, n. 58.
[39] For a consideration of coincidences between Strepsiades and Pericles in Vickers 1997 see Appendix 6.
[40] It is possible that Socrates and Chaerephon were called γηγενεῖς for two reasons: (i) they, unlike the sophists, were natives of Attica, whose citizens were reputed to have emerged from the earth

upon his training reflects that he will lose his racing-tan (1112). Yet once he emerges from the school (1167), he shows himself not only absolutely equipped with the required skills of rhetoric associated with the Lesser Argument and Socrates (1178–1200, 1321–1475), but manifests a total loyalty to his teachers (1432, 1467), especially in refusing to aid Strepsiades in his burning of the *phrontisterion*. It would make satirical sense if Pheidippides' original was attached to some other sophistic teacher, and this is a possible inference, as I have already argued, from *Knights* 1375–80 (see pp. 224–5 above). One might note that as the son of Eresistratos, he would certainly have been wealthy enough to afford a sophistic education as well as pursue a career in politics.[41] Early on the amusement will be based on the audience's recognition of his actual repugnance for Socrates and Chaerephon, and the absurdity of asking *him* in particular to go to Socrates. (ii) Later the point is that despite Strepsiades/Alcibiades' attempts to learn the rhetorical skills, Pheidippides/Phaeax outdoes his rival in this respect and is able, as he is not in life, to outsmart his cleverer rival by exploiting a teacher who in life is repugnant to him.[42] At 1401–2, Pheidippides' contrast of his former inability to speak with his facility after the lessons taught him by Socrates can be correlated with his rivalry with Alcibiades and his lesser ability as a speaker (Plut. *Alc.* 13.1): [Φαιάκα]... γνωρίμων ὄντα πατέρων, ἐλαττούμενον δὲ τοῖς τε ἄλλοις καὶ περὶ τὸν λόγον ('[Phaeax]... did come from a well-known family, but was a less talented man than Alcibiades, especially in regard to public speaking'). This view of Phaeax' relative weakness as a speaker seems to be the basis of Eupolis fr. 116 *PCG*: λαλεῖν ἄριστος, ἀδυνατώτατος λέγειν ('The best prattler, the worst speaker').[43] There is, in fact, a passing reference to this motif at 1077, where the Unjust Argument addressing Pheidippides tells him why he cannot beat a (justified) charge of adultery: ἀδύνατος γὰρ εἶ λέγειν 'because you're unable to make speeches'. Once more, this jest would interact with prior audience

---

(Erichthonios); (ii) the Giants were the standard paradigm of people who attacked the gods of Olympus. This looks like a portrait that has comic predecessors.

[41] Davies *APF* 521.

[42] The principle behind such humour is well highlighted by Vickers (1997, 14), though Dover (2004, 244) has refuted his citation of the second-century AD rhetorician Hermogenes (*Meth.* 34), 'by means of parody, by means of the unexpected, and by means of images that were diametrically opposed to what was being represented', to support it. As Vickers correctly notes, though: 'The 'Hermogenes principle' only works... if the characterization has been firmly established already.' Once a specific real individual is known to be the target of ridicule, humour may be created both out of what is known to be true and what is known to be false about that person.

[43] The use of the word λαλητικός 'bletherative' (Sommerstein) at *Knights* 1381 suggests a connection of the term λαλεῖν with intellectuals. See Telò 2007, 207–9 for an unimpeachable argument in favour of assigning this fragment to *Demoi*.

recognition to produce laughter – but only if Pheidippides represented Phaeax. None of this lets Pheidippides off the satiric hook, of course, since his portrayal as a πατραλοίας ('father-beater', 1321f.) is designed to ridicule him quite as much as the 'old rustic' guise is meant to ridicule Alcibiades.

If this identification is right,[44] then there should be some point in his case to the comic name Pheidippides (as there certainly was for Alcibiades in *Clouds I* – he did not spare the horses!). Phaeax or his father may, for example, have had a reputation for stinginess, and perhaps even one or the other carried the sobriquet Φείδων ('Pheidon'). [Andocides] 4 (a speech that does seem quite close to genuine biographical information about both Phaeax and Alcibiades which we might feel able to utilise)[45] contains a passage which might relate to this. At 32, Phaeax argues as follows:

ὑμεῖς δὲ νομίζετε τοὺς φειδομένους καὶ τοὺς ἀκριβῶς διαιτωμένους φιλοχρημάτους εἶναι, οὐκ ὀρθῶς γιγνώσκοντες· οἱ γὰρ μεγάλα δαπανώμενοι πολλῶν δεόμενοι αἰσχροκερδέστατοί εἰσιν.

You regard the sparing and those who live parsimoniously as avaricious, wrongly. It is those who spend great sums of money and beg from many who are the real money-grubbers.

The context is the public support for the extravagance of Alcibiades. The undercurrent suits very well the ironic framework of *Clouds II*, as I have analysed it, with the vices of the extravagant politician, Alcibiades, visited upon the φειδόμενος, Phaeax, in a context where the unhealthy alliance of opposite interests has combined with the deleterious influence of Socrates to conspire to overturn justice – for which read the underlying circumstances and causes of the ostracism of Hyperbolus.

On my earlier argument, however, *Clouds II* (and probably also its earlier version) implicated the comic poet Eupolis in this politically motivated attack. I have already argued that the conversation between the *Logoi* at 920f. gives a cross-reference to *Acharnians* which compels identification of the target of that play, Eupolis, with Unjust Argument. Note that Unjust Argument shares with Dicaeopolis a penchant for quoting

---

[44] I do not consider viable the identification with the Pheidon who was later one of the Thirty Tyrants (Lysias 12.54f.; Xen. *Hell.* 2.3.2), which would be made on the assumption that Strepsiades' father's name and demotic are designed to point to him. His membership of the Thirty might (but might not) point towards an association with Socrates. The main difficulty with this identification would be that we have no information at any point connecting Pheidon with Alcibiades, nor for any outstanding political activity of his before 404–3.

[45] See Rhodes 1994, who argues for a later date for the ostracism on the basis that the information in the ps.-Andokides speech is reliable.

Euripides' *Telephus*.[46] The clear implication of this characterisation is that the poet is an agent of Socrates, an active participant in the subversion of virtue, and politically in the pay of the 'right'. But this does not mean that Just Argument is not also a caricature. I suspect that this crusty old supporter of *Nomos* represents another comic poet, Eupolis' and Aristophanes' rival Cratinus. His reference to Pandeletus is appropriate (this figure is found only at Cratin. fr. 260 *Cheirones*). He is probably retired (above p. 199), and Unjust Argument's reference to him as 'repulsively dry-skinned' (αὐχμεῖς αἰσχρῶς) might tally with this and the description of him at *Knights* 534, where he is parched with thirst and his garland is withered, implying that he cannot get an invitation to a symposium and is neglecting his appearance (cf. his filthy smell at *Ach.* 852–3 and his incontinence at *Knights* 400). Finally, he is a *didaskalos*, in two senses, as a *Logos* and as a producer of plays. His portrayal as a *laudator temporis acti* may have resonance with his *Nomoi* and the support I have argued he gave to Cleon. But he is an incompetent representative of Prodicus' *Arete*, since he does not argue his case either effectively or without an undercurrent of homoeroticism (e.g. 978) and eventually admits defeat (1102f.).[47]

The above discussion helps to resolve the problem of the date and purpose of the play's revision. It was written with a view to performance at a festival after Hyperbolus' ostracism to attack two –unlikely – allies, whose collaboration had ensured his removal, Alcibiades and Phaeax.[48] The play did not find its way into the *didaskaliai*, however, because it was not performed at a state festival. A date soon after the ostracism of Hyperbolus, if this is placed in spring 415, falls just before the setting out of the Sicilian expedition. The moment for satire of Alcibiades for involvement in the ostracism therefore did not last long. By August of 415, he had set sail for Sicily, been recalled and defected to Sparta. This allows us to conjecture that Aristophanes got the idea of reviving the play directly after the Dionysia of 416/15. He worked on the revision and perhaps even gave the play a dry run

---

[46] *Clouds* 891–2, Unjust Argument's first words = *Telephus* fr. 722 N; cf. *Ach.* 8, 430f., 497–8, 541, 543 etc.

[47] Hence this is not a criticism of Prodicus, as Papageorgiou 2004 seems to suggest, but utilises Prodicus to undermine the *Logoi*, which are ultimately a Protagorean invention. It is therefore criticism of Protagoras' views which may be the basis of both Aristophanes' use of them here and Prodicus' presentation of their opposition with an ethical outcome in his *Horai*.

[48] Recently Kopff, 1990 argues for a date after 414. Storey, 1993b rejects this, as does Henderson 1993. It must be said that while none of Kopff's arguments is absolutely convincing, his opponents have only shown that he has not proven his case and not that a later date is not possible. See Rhodes 1994, 96, n. 58: 'Dover dates the revision of the play between [420] and Hyperbolus' ostracism... That is probably right, but interest in Hyperbolus will not have been immediately extinguished by his ostracism, and a slightly later date for the revision of *Clouds* ought not to be ruled out.'

before a selected audience of backers (*Clouds* 520–36), who would have seen the company through to the application for a chorus in the following year (415/14). But by the time the moment for asking for the chorus had arrived in the early prytanies of 415/14, Alcibiades was with the Spartans and satire of his part in the Hyperbolus ostracism would have passed its sell-by date, if there were not measures in place to restrict references to those implicated in the affairs of the Herms and Mysteries.[49] On this account, the play as it stands might well have been performed,[50] though not yet in a state ready for being acted at one of the major festivals. But it could not hope to gain a chorus, given the unforeseen change in political circumstances.

BIRDS

If my dating of the *Clouds* revision and explanation for its failure to receive a chorus are correct, then Aristophanes had to go back to the drawing board. He came up with two plays for 414: *Amphiaraus*, produced through Philonides at the Lenaea, and *Birds*, produced through Callistratus at the Dionysia and gaining second prize.[51] Sommerstein writes that '*Birds*

---

[49] See Byl 1994 on possible references to the Eleusinian mysteries in the play. It is possible, if Sommerstein's 1986 view of the decree of Syrakosius is accepted, that there was legislation banning plays about those convicted in the mysteries case. But see Halliwell 1991b *contra*. Henderson 1993 points out that general references could be made to the events and those involved (*Lys.* 1093–4 and *Birds* 145–7).

[50] The evidence for lack of complete revision (for which see Dover 1968, xcii and Sommerstein 1982, 2) consists of : (i) the absence of a theatrically indispensable choral ode at 888; (ii) the inclusion of passages such as 575–94 (Cleon's generalship) 'closely tied to the ephemeral circumstances of the year 423' (Sommerstein *loc. cit.*). To (i) one might reply (a) that circumstances in a pre-festival patronage performance need not have been the same as those for a festival (so that the *Logoi* could have been played by new actors – where did actors learn their craft and rise up the ladder which led to their employment by the state at festivals?); (b) that there is a theatrically essential choral ode missing at *Wasps* 1283, but no one uses this as evidence of incomplete revision; (c) the lack of a choral ode is normal (since choral odes were often omitted and marked merely by the sign χοροῦ). To (ii) the answer must be once more to note that the mention of Cleon relates to a trial for theft (and bribery), which in the metacomic context of this play is surely best interpreted as yet another reference across to the famous scene in which Cleon was convicted (see *Ach.* 5–8; cf. *Knights* 1125–30 and 1145–50, *Wasps* 757–9). The future tense possibly marks the supposed temporal priority of *this comedy* over the one referred to. There is every reason in the state of the parabasis and its very specific ideas about its audience to believe that the play either was performed (not at a festival) or was very close to being performed when it was left aside. See also Revermann 2006, 326–32.

[51] Hypothesis II 32–3: ἐπὶ Χαρίου τὸ δρᾶμα καθῆκεν εἰς ἄστυ διὰ Καλλιστράτου, εἰς δὲ Λήναια τὸν Ἀμφιάραον διὰ Φιλωνίδου, 'In the archonship of Charias he put on the play through Callistratus, and at the Lenaia the *Amphiaraos* through Philonides'. Hypothesis I, 8–10: ἐδιδάχθη ἐπὶ Χαρίου ἄρχοντος διὰ Καλλιστράτου ἐν ἄστει, ὃς ἦν δεύτερος τοῖς Ὄρνισι, πρῶτος Ἀμειψίας Κωμασταῖς, τρίτος Φρύνιχος Μονοτρόπῳ 'It was produced in the archonship of Charias through Callistratus in the city. Aristophanes was second with *Birds*, Ameipsias first with *Komastai* and Phrynichus third with *Monotropos*.'

differs from all the other fifth-century plays of Aristophanes that survive in having no strong and obvious connection with a topical question of public interest, whether political..., literary-theatrical..., or intellectual-educational.'[52] And Dunbar remarks 'no play of Aristophanes has aroused more controversy over its interpretation'.[53] Neither scholar investigates the possibility that *Birds* makes its satire through on-stage caricature attack, though Dunbar does mention the allegorising theories of Süvern, Katz and Vickers, for all of whom in various ways the comedy plays out aspects of the Sicilian expedition.[54]

It needs to be said at the outset (as I have briefly indicated earlier) that there is no sensible way of making the plot of *Birds* fit the Sicilian situation. The central characters are not conquerors (cf. Thuc. 6.15), but (voluntary) fugitives from a legal system in Athens which they dislike (33f., 110), in search of a city to settle in (48, 121f.), though the equipment they carry suggests they may be looking for a place to colonise, not one already inhabited (43–5). Their success in founding a new city in the air and eventually even using the strategic strength of their colony to take control from the gods follows from this premiss and is thus connected with the motives of the Sicilian expedition only by stark antithesis, since this involved precisely an abandonment of the policy of ἡσυχία 'peace and quiet' and ἀπραγμοσύνη 'non-interference' (Thuc. 6.18.3–7) which Peisetairus states as the objective of their flight (τόπον ἀπράγμονα 'a trouble-free place', 44).[55] Besides, on my argument, Aristophanes was a supporter of the radical democrats, whose project the Sicilian expedition was, and opposed to those like Nicias who wished to keep Athens out of conflict. Even though his loyalty had lain with Hyperbolus, I do not think his bitterness over the ostracism and his annoyance at Alcibiades in particular could possibly have brought him over to the conservative side, especially when the expedition was committed and Alcibiades was out of the picture.[56] The evidence of the honorific decree (see chapter two, pp. 41–3) in any case suggests Aristophanes' consistency in the radical democratic cause right to the end of the war. If there were any connection with the Sicilian adventure (which was in Aristophanes' mind, as 145–7, 363–4, 639 seem

---

[52] Sommerstein 1987, 1.
[53] Dunbar 1995, 1.
[54] Dunbar 1995, 4 n. 8, citing Süvern 1835, Katz 1976, and Vickers 1989.
[55] In fact, as is often pointed out, the anti-Athens established by the pair of discontented Athenians abandons its vaunted ἡσυχία 'peace and quiet' (1321) in its quest for supremacy over the Olympians (554f.).
[56] See also Dunbar 1995, 5 'Aristophanes may have fully approved of the expedition'.

to show), then it would be to *satirise* those who rejected the expedition as typical of Athenian πολυπραγμοσύνη 'interference'.

Before leaping to that conclusion, however, we need to look at the key elements of the plot and the characteristics these imply of the individuals caricatured in the central roles of Peisetairus and Euelpides. Crucial are: (a) the desire for a utopia, which is *not* Athens (123–4); (b) the introduction of new gods (the birds: 465f., cf. 848, 862); (c) negotiation of power from Zeus through the embassy of Poseidon, Heracles and the Triballian (1596f.,1632f.).[57] It will be immediately apparent that two of these are intellectual themes, the first relating to the design of a model *apragmon* city which is to be the antithesis of Athens (though, as is often noted, it turns out to be all too like it), the second to a discussion about the nature and origin of the universe (set up in specific opposition to Prodicus, 692). The third theme, which leads directly to Peisetairus' acquisition of a tyranny, looks more like an attack on personal ambition than anything else.

Though the philosopher most often mentioned in respect of the central character's utopian ideas is Gorgias,[58] and the concatenation of the themes of scepticism about the gods and practical and theoretical political wisdom might rather suggest Protagoras,[59] we should probably not look for Gorgianic or Protagorean influence on Peisetairus' political utopianism for three reasons: the metacomic signals in the play once again suggest Eupolis as the target of the comic style of the play (see chapter 2, pp. 34–5, 38); Eupolis had satirised Protagoras (possibly on stage) in *Kolakes* of 421 (frr. 157–8); I have located Eupolis' intellectual position as within Socrates' circle, which (if Plato is to be believed) was in opposition to both of these sophists' ideas. There are in fact a number of aspects in which the intellectual content of *Birds* parallels Socratic ideas or their Aristophanic satirical versions. (a) The city's name, *Nephelococcygia*, agreed on at 820f. (and which it appears from 821 may have already existed, perhaps in popular speech),[60] has strong resonances with the area governed by the Socratic deities of the *Clouds* (252, 269f.). (b) The introduction of new deities is strongly marked as part of the Socratic agenda (*Clouds* 247–8, 252–3, 264f., 365, 367; cf. Pl. *Apol.* 24b). (c) The best example of a utopian polity is found in Plato's *Republic* (369c f.), where it is ascribed to Socrates. It may very well have had its origin, therefore, in well-known discussions going

---

[57] See Dunbar 1995, 13–14 on the limits of Peisetairus' triumph over the gods.
[58] See Süvern 1927, Vickers 1997, 155ff.
[59] His association with Pericles and the invitation to write the constitution of the Athenian colony at Thurii would fit, as would his famous agnosticism.
[60] See Sommerstein 1987 on 821, but Dunbar 1995 *contra*.

From Autolycus *to* Frogs 239

back into the fifth century of Socrates and his acolytes, where the dramatic date of many pieces set them (see further Appendix 2 on *Eccl.*). (d) In the developed Platonic analysis, the ideal city has a tendency eventually to fall away, via a series of less and less desirable polities (timocracy *Rep.* 545c f., oligarchy 550c–f., 551c, democracy 557b–e) into tyranny (565a–576), exactly the end-point reached in *Birds* (though the other stages are by-passed).[61] (e) As in *Clouds* the ethereal deities support dithyrambic poets (333–4), so the city of the birds is attractive to the same group (*Birds* 904f., 1377f.). (f) At *Birds* 1000–1 the idea of the sky as a πνιγεύς 'baking-cover' recurs, marked as a Socratic notion at *Clouds* 96f. Given the strong affinity, it does not seem to me to be coincidental that in Timaeus' discourse about the origins of the universe we read the following statement about birds (Pl. *Ti.* 90d):

τὸ δὲ τῶν ὀρνέων φῦλον μετερρυθμίζετο ἀντὶ τριχῶν πτερὰ φῦον, ἐκ τῶν ἀκάκων ἀνδρῶν, κούφων δέ

The race of birds arose out of a change from men, harmless, but light-headed, growing wings instead of hair.

This is precisely the metamorphosis already effected for Tereus and his servant in *Birds* (71–3, 96f.), managed during the play's action for Peisetairus and Euelpides (654–5, 801f.) and in store for thousands of new recruits to the colony (1304f.). It seems possible, then, that the opposition of the play's new cosmogony to that of Prodicus (692) deliberately mirrors the antithesis expressed at *Clouds* 360–2 by the Clouds between Prodicus and Socrates (as μετεωροσοφισταί 'experts on the heavens'). In other words, the whole idea of the birds as originators of the universe and the proper gods is a parody of ideas widely known to have been discussed by the Socratic circle in the 410s (probably, for what it is worth, around the dramatic date for *Republic* and, thus, *Timaeus*, which is supposed to follow on on the next day).[62] It is worth mentioning also that Socrates and Chaerephon, who is prominent in *Clouds* (104, 144f., 156f., 501f., 1465), are mentioned by the chorus at 1555 and 1564 and that Socrates acquires his own verb at 1282.[63]

---

[61] The 'triumph' of Peisetairus involves his becoming a τύραννος 'tyrant' (1708), a word which seems to have been regaining political currency during this period (cf. *Wasps* 417, 463, 490f., *Lys.* 619, *Thesm.* 338; Thucydides 6. 15.4) and which was associated in the real world with real and severe penalties (Arist. *Ath. Pol.* 16.10; Andoc. 1.96–8). It is hard to see how in these circumstances the ending could be regarded as positive (cf. Dunbar 1995, 11–14).

[62] Dramatic dates for Platonic dialogues, like their dates of composition, are the subject of scholarly dispute. However, anywhere between the late 420s and 415 would do perfectly well for my thesis. See Taylor 1926, 263 for 421.

[63] I strongly suspect that the Chaerephon references in *Clouds* are metacomic (see Dover 1968 xcv f. on the problem). That will, if so, also be the case in *Birds*.

There are clear signs that the two central characters (and especially Peisetairus) are supposed to be recognised as having intellectual credentials, some specifically Socratic. First of all, Tereus introduces them to the birds at 318 as λεπτώ λογιστά 'subtle arguers'. The word λεπτός 'subtle' is, as Dunbar remarks, almost a badge of the Socratic party in *Clouds* (153, 230f., 320, 359).[64] Secondly, Tereus at 409 says they come σοφῆς ἀφ' Ἑλλάδος 'from wise Greece'. While this may simply recall Herodotus' description (1.60.3),[65] the σοφ- root is associated with intellectual activity (e.g. Xen. *Mem.* 2.1.21; *Clouds* 361). The chorus soon afterwards ask of Peisetairus ἔνι σοφόν τι φρενί; 'Has he any cleverness in his mind?' (428), and eventually accept his mental capacity (γνώμη) as superior (637). Thirdly, Tereus' answer to the chorus' question at 428, that Peisetairus is πυκνότατον κίναδος, | σόφισμα, κύρμα, τρῖμμα, παιπάλημ' ὅλον 'A very sharp fox, an ingenious device, a true shot, an old hand, experience on wheels' (429–30) has very strong resonances with the language of Socratic aspiration at *Clouds* 260 (Socrates) and 445–51 (Strepsiades). Finally, when Peisetairus is about to reveal his great plan, he uses very rich metaphorical language and exhibits a real desire (and capacity) for intellectual discourse (462–3, 465–6).

It seems, then, that we are dealing, in Peisetairus at least, with a prominent member of the Socratic circle (and therefore, on my earlier argument, an associate also of Eupolis). But while this helps to fix the intellectual milieu and explain the basic plot-device, it does not help with the jumping-off point for the satire. This must lie, I think, in the motivation of the principal characters in leaving Athens to find – or, as it turns out, found – their utopia. The stress here is quite specifically upon the law-courts (36f., 109–10) and equally upon discovering a spot where the *Salaminia* can not turn up to bring them back to Athens for trial (145–7). Given that this last is bound to remind us of the most famous incident of this sort, the attempt to bring Alcibiades back to Athens for trial in the previous summer (Thuc. 6.61), we perhaps ought to direct our attention to the internal situation in the city at this time. There had been two major scares on the eve of the Sicilian expedition, the Mutilation of the Herms and the Profanation of the Mysteries, which were widely believed to be signals for an oligarchic coup against the democracy (Thuc. 6.27–9). Many arrests were made and eventually one of those arrested and thrown into prison in connection with the

---

[64] Dunbar 1995 on 318, where she notes that the word is 'first found of intellectual refinement' in Euripides' *Medea* (529). Dover 1968 on *Clouds* 153. Note especially *Clouds* 320 λεπτολογεῖν 'to reason subtly', the verb equivalent of the formulation at *Birds* 318.
[65] As Dunbar 1995 suggests ad loc.

Mutilation, Andocides, confessed under a promise of immunity. Whether or not the right people were indicted, the Athenians put on trial and then executed the people implicated by this testimony (Thuc. 6.60) and then went after Alcibiades, who escaped via Thurii, to the Peloponnese (Thuc. 6.61). What made the evidence of Andocides acceptable, seemingly, was the fact that it did seem to reveal the activities of a clearly anti-democratic group.[66] Andocides himself wrote *To His Comrades*, in which Plutarch describes him as ἐπὶ τὸν δῆμον παροξύνων τοὺς ὀλιγαρχικούς ('inciting the oligarchs against the *demos*') and the suspicion remained in antiquity that his confession had condemned some innocent men, but also exonerated some of the guilty (Thuc. 6.61.4–5; Plut. *Alc.* 21.2–4).

Now Peisetairus and Euelpides are not on the run: they tell us this explicitly, and in rhetorically pointed fashion (by means of the contrast with Sacas at 31) at 30–8. Note especially 33–5:

ἡμεῖς δὲ, φυλῇ καὶ γένει τιμώμενοι,
ἀστοὶ μετ' ἀστῶν, οὐ σοβοῦντος οὐδενὸς
ἀνεπτόμεσθ' ἐκ τῆς πατρίδος ἀμφοῖν ποδοῖν.

But we, with full rights of tribe and clan membership, citizens among citizens, with no one attempting to shoo us off, have got up and flown out of our homeland with both feet.

The reason, which follows, concerns their dislike of lawsuits (39–41) and they make it abundantly clear that it is *this* that has driven them out (διὰ ταῦτα 'it is because of this' 42). If they are free and have not been deprived of their citizen rights, but nonetheless have had problems with lawsuits, the implication must be that they have had a close call with justice from which they deem themselves lucky to have escaped. The lawcourt-hating theme comes up again when Tereus asks them where they are from (108) and when they reply asks μῶν ἡλιαστά; 'Not jurors, are you?' (109), to which the swift answer comes μάλλὰ θατέρου τρόπου, | ἀπηλιαστά. 'No, the other type, misodicasts.' (109–10). Their horror of the idea of living in a city by the sea suggests a very specific field of reference (145–8): they are thinking of the events of the previous summer. It seems very possible, then, that the two individuals being attacked in this play are men who had been implicated in the Mutilation of the Herms, but then released through the evidence of Andocides. Aristophanes has the chorus joke at *Lysistrata* 1093–4: εἰ σωφρονεῖτε, θαἰμάτια λήψεσθ', ὅπως | τῶν Ἑρμοκοπιδῶν μή τις ὑμᾶς ὄψεται 'If you have sense, you'll

---

[66] MacDowell 1962, 191–2.

pick up your cloaks, in case one of the Hermcutter family sees you.' As Sommerstein notes: 'it is assumed that some of them, having escaped detection, are still in Athens... Ar. coins for the mutilators the appellation *Hermokopidai*, formed with a patronymic suffix as if they constituted a kingroup, perhaps with an allusion to the fact that many of them had been members of aristocratic clans (*gene*) which usually had names ending in *–idai*.'[67] For 'having escaped detection', however, one ought to say 'having got out of gaol free', because of Andocides' evidence, despite being guilty.[68] In *Birds*, then, Aristophanes is using what we would now call the 'tabloid court' to intimate that these two aristocrats[69] were, after all, guilty at least of holding anti-democratic opinions, since their intellectual ties are to Socrates. It may be symptomatic (though it is obviously satirical) that the new city replaces with bird-fever specifically Laconophilia and Socratism (1281–3).

Peisetairus, at any rate, is portrayed as a Laconophile, as emerges from the opening of the conversation on naming the city. First it is agreed that they must find a great and noble name for the city (Peisetairus at 809–11, Euelpides at 811 and the chorus at 812). Then Peisetairus offers his first thought (813–14): βούλεσθε τὸ μέγα τοῦτο τοὐκ Λακεδαίμονος | Σπάρτην ὄνομα καλῶμεν αὐτήν; 'Do you want us to call it by that great name from Lacedaimon, Sparta?'. 'This improbable suggestion', as Dunbar calls it,[70] makes sense when attached to the individual who is being attacked in the play. If the audience already knows him as a person who favours Spartan ways, it is obvious that 'Sparta' will be the first name he thinks of.

A list of those released on Andocides' testimony is given at Andocides 1.47. It includes one well-known member of the Socratic circle, Critias. That he fits the satirical framework will be immediately obvious. An associate of Socrates (see Pl. *Charm.*, *Ti.*, *Criti.*, *Prt.* 316a, 336d, Xen. *Mem.* 2.12–39), he is reported by him at *Timaeus* 20a to be adept at all the areas of philosophy currently under consideration (that is, the construction of ideal constitutions and cosmology, the topic of *Timaeus*).[71] He was specifically known as an admirer of Sparta (cf. Xen., *Hell.* 2.3.34) and wrote accounts of the Spartan constitution in both prose and verse (Jacoby *FGrH* fr. 6–9, 32–7). He is portrayed in Plato as sceptical about man's knowledge

---

[67] Sommerstein 1990 ad loc.
[68] Hence I am inclined to think that Henderson 1987 ad loc. is quite mistaken to comment 'the tone is jocular: no doubt the Athenians were satisfied that they had found and punished the culprits' and 'Ar. has no one particular in mind here'.
[69] Cf. the word γένει 'clan' at 33 with Dunbar 1995 ad loc.   [70] Dunbar 1995 on 813–14.
[71] Κριτίαν δέ που πάντες οἱ τῇδ' ἴσμεν οὐδενὸς ἰδιώτην ὄντα ὧν λέγομεν. 'As far as Critias is concerned, all of us here know that he is no layman in any of the areas of our current discourse.'

of the gods (*Ti.* 107b), a position at the heart of Peisetairus' new order. His favourite aphorism appears to have been that σωφροσύνη ἂν εἴη τὸ τὰ ἑαυτοῦ πράττειν 'self-restraint would be doing one's own business' (Pl. *Charm.* 161b, cf. 162c f.). That this comes down to the opposite of πολυπραγμοσύνη ('being a busybody') is clear from Pl. *Rep.* 433a: τὸ τὰ αὑτοῦ πράττειν καὶ μὴ πολυπραγμονεῖν δικαιοσύνη ἐστιν ('doing one's own business and not being a busybody is what we mean by justice'). Thus the idea ascribed to Peisetairus at *Birds* 44 of the search for a τόπον ἀπράγμονα ('an unbusybody place') is a precise hit at Critias' known views. If we can take it that his account of Atlantis (advertised in *Timaeus* 25f. and related at more length in *Critias*) was already well known, even his propensity towards mythical polities and the precise detail of their physical make-up may be the object of parody in the play (cf. Pl. *Criti.* 115f. with *Birds* 1130f. and note the encounter with the planner Meton at 992f.). As far as the implication that Peisetairus is a would-be tyrant, Xenophon tells us (*Mem.* 2.14) that both Alcibiades and Critias were ambitious above all else for power (βουλομένω τὰ πάντα δι' ἑαυτῶν πράττεσθαι καὶ πάντων ὀνομαστοτάτω γενέσθαι 'the two of them wished everything to be done through them and to gain the greatest name of all'). The joke in his comic name, then, will surely be based partly on a resemblance with Peisistratus, the sixth-century tyrant, giving more than a hint of the eventual (satiric) outcome, partly to associate him with the ἑταιρεῖαι 'political clubs', which were to be so deeply involved in the establishment of the oligarchy in 411 (Thuc. 8.48.3), and partly on his apparent capacity to bring along with him a not entirely sympathetic partner (cf. the slight scratchiness of the exchanges in the opening scene, e.g. 12, 54–5, 87–8; Euelpides' response to the suggestion they call the new city Sparta, 814–16,[72] and his reaction

---

[72] The response by Euelpides is hostile (814–16): Ἡράκλεις | Σπάρτην γὰρ ἂν θείμην ἐγὼ τἠμῇ πόλει; | οὐδ' ἂν χαμεύνῃ πάνυ γε, κειρίαν γ' ἔχων ('By Heracles! Would I put the name Sparta on my city? I wouldn't even use it for a bed, not even if I had *keiriai*'). The humour of this will also be primarily at the expense of the individual targeted by the character of Euelpides. However, understanding how it operates is also complicated by the difficulty of explaining precisely the joke in 816. It is certainly a pun on Σπάρτη 'Sparta' and σπάρτον or σπαρτίον 'esparto rope' (it is not clear whether there was a feminine form σπάρτη. See Dunbar 1995 ad loc.). Sommerstein could be correct to interpret κειρίαν γ' ἔχων ('not if I had linen girths') as an anti-climax: 'It was a mark of luxury to use these broad girths, instead of esparto cords, to stretch over one's bed-frame as supports for the mattress; cf. Plut. *Alc.* 16.1... Euelpides is thus unlikely ever to have *keiria* – and whatever he may think of esparto, in practice he will go on using it.' (Sommerstein 1987 on 816). On the other hand, Dunbar may be right to see here a quite specific reference to Alcibiades' behaviour (reported in Plut. *Alc.* 16) in cutting away parts of trireme decks in order to get a better night's sleep and using κειρίαι. But there is a third level at which the joke may operate, which can only be seen if we accept my identification of Eupolis as the metacomic target of the play and the thesis that Aristophanes continually portrays him as an imitator of Cratinus. For the only other place where we get this pun is in Cratin. fr. 117 (*Nemesis*): Σπάρτην λέγω γε σπαρτίδα τὴν σπάρτινον 'I mean

when given the job of building-superintendent 845–6). One consequence of seeing Peisetairus as Critias in a play which also attacks Eupolis is, of course, that already in the mid-410s Aristophanes was grouping the poet with a Laconophile who would later be one of the most notorious of the Thirty Tyrants. It would certainly help us to understand why he ended his days in Sicyon and was not able to take advantage of the amnesty of 403 if he was in fact a close associate of Critias and had got involved with him in 404.

Euelpides might on this argument also be someone in the same position as Critias, that is put into prison on the information of Diocleides and released on that of Andocides, but perhaps not entirely of his political stamp. The only handles we have upon his identity are his name, given at 645 as Εὐελπίδης Κριῶθεν 'Euelpides of Crioa', and Tereus' statement at 368 that Peisetairus and his companion are τῆς ἐμῆς γυναικός . . . ξυγγενεῖ καὶ φυλέτα 'relatives and fellow-tribesmen of my wife'. The name by itself does not help. It might be a parody of the original (and there are two *eu-* names on Andocides' list, Euphemus and Eucrates, the first from Pandionis, the second from Aigeis). But, as Dunbar points out, it may just be literally 'person of good hopes', and thus mean 'typical confident Athenian'.[73] She points as a key to his characterisation to a passage in Thucydides (1.70.3) where the Corinthian envoy at Sparta describes the Athenians: οἱ μὲν καὶ παρὰ δύναμιν τολμηταὶ καὶ παρὰ γνώμην κινδυνευταὶ καὶ ἐν τοῖς δεινοῖς εὐέλπιδες ('They take risks beyond their capacities, endanger themselves beyond rationality and are optimistic in the midst of misfortune'). It also turns out to be problematic in terms of Tereus' statement, which implies that both Peisetairus and Euelpides share the same tribe and that of Procne (presumably, as Sommerstein suggests,[74] Pandionis, her father's tribe). The deme Crioa, however, is in Antiochis. Moreover, if Peisetairus represents Critias, his real tribe was Erechtheis (not unconnected with Procne, of course, since Erechtheus was her brother).[75] Sommerstein urges a less-than-literal interpretation, since Tereus can not know this: 'Either . . . *phuleta* "fellow-tribesmen" is used here loosely for "compatriots", or else it is comically and inappropriately tacked on after "relations" because under *normal* circumstances two Athenians

---

Sparta . . . the place made of *esparto*'. The other figure in Aristophanes who makes his opposition to Sparta as openly as this is Philocleon (*Wasps* 1159–65), where he rejects even Laconian shoes. On my identification, Philocleon represents Cratinus. The joke here, then, is that Euelpides is made to appropriate a well-known (bad?) pun from Cratinus in order to focus the audience's attention upon his attitude to Alcibiades.

[73] Dunbar 1995 on 645–6.   [74] Sommerstein 1987 on 368.   [75] Apollodorus 3.14.8.

who were blood relations usually did belong to the same *phule*.'[76] However, even this implies that ξυγγενεῖ 'blood-relations' must be taken to mean something and Dunbar acutely remarks: 'The phrase "kinsmen and fellow-tribesmen" suggests a much closer relationship than "fellow-Athenians"', even though she ends by saying 'but in this crisis Ter. diplomatically exaggerates'.[77] In caricature comedy, however, the jokes will operate on a different basis, namely the audience's recognition of the on-stage targets. Thus Tereus will have been recognised, immediately he appeared, as an individual appropriate to the main characters and their situation (perhaps as one of those denounced by Teucrus who escaped from Athens before they could be apprehended? Cf. Andoc. 1.34). Hence the amusement here will be provided at two levels: (1) within the plot Tereus should not recognise the new arrivals, but breaks the illusion by admitting an acquaintance which the audience already knows about; (2) he points very clearly to their actual identities by a genealogy easily reconstructable by the Athenians in the theatre (cf. *Clouds* 46, with my argument above, pp. 226–7). If this is correct, we can say a number of things. First, Peisetairus and Euelpides are relatives and fellow-tribesmen of the wife of the man represented on stage as Tereus (and not of the mythological figure Procne, though there might be a secondary joke here). Secondly, as Dunbar suspected, the deme given by Euelpides at 645 must be a joke (on κρίος 'ram'?) and is therefore entirely dependent upon the audience's prior association of the word with the target behind Euelpides (cf. my arguments about the demotics in *Ach.* 406 and *Peace* 918, pp. 87–8 and 206–7). Thirdly, if the identification of Peisetairus as Critias is correct, then since we know his tribe (Erechtheis),[78] it may be possible to make a guess at the identities of Euelpides and Tereus.

For example, Euphemus the blacksmith from Andocides 1.40 and 47 was from Pandionis (*IG* II² 3018), so might fit the bill for Euelpides, if φυλέτα is taken less than literally (though it is difficult to say why he might have been picked and some indications in the text suggest Euelpides is a countryman (e.g. 494–6, 585). However, as I have argued earlier, the metacomic signals provided by the appearance of scenes criticised by Aristophanes in the parabases of *Peace* and *Clouds* (a hungry Heracles, cries of ἰοὺ ἰού, an old man striking someone, torches on stage), as well as a number of other family resemblances to scenes in his other plays, strongly suggest a continued battle with a specific rival. This, I have argued, was Eupolis. Storey has recently

---

[76] Sommerstein 1987 on 368.
[77] Dunbar 1995 on 368. Cf. her note on 33, where she stresses the importance of the γένος, which indicates that these men belong to the old Athenian aristocracy.
[78] *LGPN* 2 s.v. Κριτίας no. (7).

pointed to several possible detailed links between *Birds* and Eupolis' *Demoi*: the openings (in *Demoi* he imagines that Pyronides and his companion set out 'with the accoutrements for a sacrifice and a soul-raising'); the parallels between the Phrynis/Pyronides and the Cinesias/Peisetairus scenes (Paestan Bell Krater *c*. 350[79] and fr. 326,[80] *Birds* 1372–1409, cf. 851–8) and the Aristeides/sycophant and Peisetairus/sycophant scenes (*Demoi* fr. 99.78–120, *Birds* 1410–69). And he concludes his study with a stronger statement still 'that *Demoi* resembled *Birds* in both idea and structure'.[81] But if we accept, as I think we should, Telò's new date of 410 for *Demoi*, then the relationship will be the other way round and the probability is that Eupolis will have been getting his own back in this play for the earlier attack on him in *Birds*. I shall argue below that *Demoi* included Aristophanes as a character, and if this is correct, then it is reasonable to suppose that this was Eupolis' response to yet another on-stage attack upon him, possibly, given these apparent similarities, the one in *Birds*. If so, the figure of Euelpides, Peisetairus' companion and helper, is the likeliest cover, though he would not then be precisely in the same boat as Peisetairus. The name (like Dicaeopolis) could easily be a sardonic version of Eupolis, with which it would interact meaningfully in the context of a plot where a *polis* was founded, ridiculing him for his absurdly optimistic – and dangerous – ideas about the possibility of political reform, already satirised at the end of *Knights*. Specific hits at Eupolis would include: his antagonism to the law-courts (*Birds* 40–1, 109f.; cf. *Wasps* 411f., *Knights* 1316–17, 1332); the implication of his addiction to pederasty at 137f. (cf. the play with this at *Knights* 1384–7); the anecdote about losing a Phrygian wool cloak at 492f. (cf. the Persian cloak he, as Bdelycleon, makes Philocleon put on at *Wasps* 1137f.); and perhaps the list technique at 302f (cf. *Aiges* fr. 13.3f. and Aristophanic parodies at *Ach.* 546f. and *Peace* 1000f.), though this operates anyway within the overall parody of Eupolis' style. One nagging problem, however, if I am correct (chapter four, pp. 87–8) in seeing Cholleidai at *Acharnians* 406 as Eupolis' real deme, since this belongs to the Leontis tribe, is that there will be a conflict with *Birds* 368.

Turning to Tereus, Phaedrus son of Pythocles from Myrrhinous, also in Pandionis, (*SEG* XIII 12–22, cf. *SEG* XVI 13) went into exile after being denounced by Teucrus (Andoc. 1.15; Lysias 32.14 and 19.15). He was a friend of Socrates (Pl., *Phdr. passim*). If the enthusiasm he shows in that dialogue

---

[79] First published by Sestieri 1960, 156–9 + plates xl–xlii. See also Trendall 1967, 43, no. 58, pl. 3b, Trendall and Webster 1971, 140, and Taplin 1993, 114, for further bibliography.
[80] Storey 1995–6, 137–41.   [81] Storey 2003, 377.

for the subject of Ἔρως ('sexual passion') gently ribs him for a well-known proclivity, then the role of Tereus might be a suitable satirical cover for him. However, Lysias 19.15 says that he married after his return from exile (though for all we know this may be a second marriage).[82] The difficulty of tracking such a profoundly personalised satire with the limited resources at our disposal (despite *PA* and *PAA*) will always mean that we are liable never to be absolutely certain of any given identifcation.

The play's attack, then, is focused upon individuals (possibly three of them, if Tereus does represent a man already in exile after being denounced), some of whom had been implicated in the Mutilation of the Herms. They were all members of the old Athenian aristocracy (always suspect to radical democrats). At this point, we should return to the Sicilian expedition. For it was Nicias, himself widely regarded as representative of this vein of Athenian aristocratic conservatism, who had expressed what may have been a general reluctance among these people to enter upon the venture (Thuc. 6.8–14). Thucydides makes it clear that support for the expedition was so great that people who disliked the notion kept quiet, since anyone voting against it might be thought κακόνους τῇ πόλει 'ill-disposed towards the city' (6.24), which well evokes the atmosphere in which any adverse comment might be satirised and made to seem part of a conspiracy of disloyalty. The incident of the Herms follows seamlessly in Thucydides upon his account of the debate and the enthusiasm of the *demos* for the expedition (6.27), and MacDowell has plausibly written of the Mutilation: 'I do not know what the purpose can have been except to stop the sailing of the fleet to Sicily.'[83] There are, in fact, two other indications that Aristophanes was also connecting the Herms incident not only with oligarchic plots by Laconophiles, but also with resistance to the Sicilian expedition. First, he represents on stage (and not in disguise), as one of the earliest supporters of Nephelococcygia, the astronomer Meton (992f.). There are several anecdotes which suggest that he tried to secure exemption from service in Sicily for himself or his son (Plut. *Nic.* 13.7–8; *Alc.* 17.5–6; Ael. *VH* 13.12). Secondly, in two of these sources (Plut. *Nic.* 13.6 and *Alc.* 17.4),

---

[82] On the other hand, taking the barbarian and Thracian origins of Tereus more seriously, one might suggest he represents Sadocus, son of Sitalces, who had been made an Athenian citizen in 431 (Thuc. 2.29.5; cf. *Ach.* 145). The connection of his family with Tereus through the similarity of the name to Teres, his grandfather, must have been bandied about as part of the public debate. Otherwise it is difficult to understand why Thucydides takes such trouble (*loc. cit.*) to tell his readers that in fact there was no such link. Unfortunately, we have no information about Sadocus after the breakdown of the alliance with Sitalces in 428, and the plot seems to demand that Tereus have a well-known Athenian wife.

[83] MacDowell 1962, 192.

it is also reported that Socrates was against the expedition and made his views known to his friends, whence διῆλθεν εἰς πολλοὺς ὁ λόγος 'the story became widespread'. It does not seem to me, then, to be coincidental that *Birds* has an intellectual theme tied to the Socratic group, a central character (perhaps more than one) who is a leading member of that circle, and a focus on those who have escaped in one way or another from punishment for their involvement in the oligarchically planned Herms incident. Indirectly, the play attacks individuals who were known to have opposed the great democratic adventure.

It is in the circles which fomented resistance, therefore, that we should look for the targets behind the enthusiasts for the new foundation, who arrive in numbers from line 903 onwards and generally treated pretty badly by Peisetairus. It is possible (cf. my account of *Ach.* p. 134) that the comedy is mostly made from the fact that these are friends of his in the real world.[84] Before the procession begins, however, there is a consecration involving a priest (851–94). There are no hints as to his identity, but, given the intellectual focus of the play, it is possible that he represents Socrates. At any rate, the Clouds address him as λεπτοτάτων λήρων ἱερεῦ 'o priest of the subtlest nonsense' (*Clouds* 359), and a scene in which Critias belabours his mentor would have a certain amusement value (for those who disliked Socrates). Aristophanes' vendetta against Socrates, which now seems (from *Clouds II* and *Birds*) to overlap into the 410s, had not necessarily stopped by the time of his trial in 399. At any rate, Aristophanes' known involvement behind the group of prosecutors would account well for the references at Plato *Apology* 18d. and 19c to attacks which were now almost twenty-five years stale, and the charge of 'introducing new gods' is one made against Socrates, if I am right, both in *Clouds* and in *Birds*.

What satirical job does the chorus of birds perform? They may be individualised (note the twenty-four birds listed at 297f.), and so might have been caricaturing real individuals. This certainly seems possible, especially since the prelude to the parodos contains jokes about identifications with real individuals of the second hoopoe (284) and the κατωφαγᾶς 'gobbler' (289). Who would they be? Presumably a group known for their dislike of the status quo, perhaps members of the sort of *hetaireia* which became so influential in the oligarchic revolution (Thucydides 8. 48.3). In their characterisation as birds, there may not only have been satire of the general flightiness and instability of these men (cf. *Birds* 165–70), and their inability

---

[84] I shall deal with the only caricature named on stage apart from Meton, that is, Cinesias, later in this chapter in relation to *Lysistrata*.

to achieve a common purpose (172), but also the implication that their natural inclination will have been to avoid rather than to court combat except with weaker beings (this qualification will explain the presence of two types of vulture, νέρτος 303 and φήνη 304, and two other birds of prey, ἱέραξ 303 and κερχνής 304). In this way we might connect the quest of Peisetairus and Euelpides with an attack on ἀστρατεία 'avoidance of military service' and see these individuals also as men who disapproved of the Sicilian expedition.[85] As I have already said, I suspect that the chorus' dismissive and casual rejection of Prodicus' views on the origins of gods (692) relates to a level of humour about contemporary philosophy, specifically that of the Socratic circle. Aristophanes may have represented in this chorus men associated both with a *hetaireia* opposed to the Sicilian expedition *and* members of the wider Socratic circle, thus, as it were, killing two birds with the same stone.

On this scenario, we still have to explain the relevance of the plot to usurp the power of the gods for the birds and its satiric purpose. There is something to be said still for the notion that Aristophanes continues to cast in Eupolis' face the charge of imitation of Cratinus (note the scholia attributing the hungry Heracles motif to both Eupolis and Cratinus, *Peace* 741b–c) and it will, on my argument, certainly not be mere coincidence that Βασίλεια ('Princess') was mentioned in Cratinus (fr. 423) according to the scholium on *Birds* 1536. In Cratinus' satirical world, the Olympians could represent the Athenian political hierarchy (Pericles as Zeus, Aspasia as Hera: fr. 73, 258, 259). But in Aristophanes too, *Wasps* 1029f. strongly implies that major political figures are not human but, even if monsters, immortals. Hence, the gods who eventually hand over Basileia and the thunderbolt should represent political opponents of the central character, who are nonetheless also opponents of Aristophanes (otherwise they would not be ridiculed on stage). Poseidon's words at 1570f. may be taken, on this interpretation, as revealing the true identity of the ambassadors as elected representatives of a democracy: ὦ δημοκρατία, ποῖ προβιβᾷς ἡμᾶς ποτε, | εἰ τουτονί γ' ἐχειροτόνησαν οἱ θεοί; 'O democracy, where are you taking us, if the gods voted *him* in?' Poseidon, then, will possibly represent a naval commander, Heracles a politician satirised for gluttony and the Triballian an individual often attacked for his barbarian (and specifically Thracian) birth.[86] Prometheus, on the other hand, ought to be someone who could be satirised for betraying the status

---

[85] If Storey is correct (2003, 76) to date Eupolis' *Astrateutoi* 414–412, it might come after *Birds*, and constitute a reply in which the poet cast some of Aristophanes' friends in this unflattering light.
[86] See further MacDowell 1993.

quo. He is a god (therefore in the world of Cratinean allegory, an Athenian), but secretly favourable to the machinations of those who resist them. I will attempt some identifications.

Carcinus, son of Xenotimus of the deme of Thoricus, the tragic poet, was a general in 432/1 (Thucydides 2.32.2; *IG* I³ 365.30–40) and is given Poseidon's epithet ὁ ποντομέδων ἄναξ 'Lord and Master of the Seas' at *Wasps* 1531. Poseidon seems to have appeared in whichever comedy *Knights* 1225 is cited from, since the scholium tells us μιμεῖται δὲ τοὺς εἵλωτας ὅταν στεφανῶσι τὸν Ποσειδῶνα 'He imitates the Helots when they crown Poseidon.' Perhaps he represented Carcinus (whose differentiated appearances in *Wasps* and *Peace* on my arguments suggest that they refer to a common comic intertext in which he appeared as an on-stage caricature)?[87] Since Aristophanes would not have put him on stage in *Wasps* if he were not an enemy, it is possible that he uses Poseidon here to represent Carcinus, perhaps borrowing (from Cratinus?) a common target.

Heracles could well have satirised Cleonymus, whose obesity and gluttony are mentioned at *Birds* 289 and 1476 and also at *Acharnians* 88, *Knights* 958, 1290–9, *Wasps* 16 and 592. I have already suggested (above, pp. 214–15) that the shield-dropping incident associated with him (*Clouds* 353–4; *Wasps* 15–27, 592, 822–3; *Peace* 444–6, 673–8, 1295–1301; *Birds* 1480–1) may belong to a comedy, possibly by Eupolis, but more probably (in the light of the role of Cleonymus' wife in *Thesm.*, on which see pp. 272–3 below) by Cratinus (the greedy Heracles motif is associated with both Eupolis and Cratinus at Σ *Peace* 741b-c).

The Triballian might satirise Execestides, who is mentioned twice in the play as having barbarian ancestry (*Birds* 11, 1527). The second occurrence is in the run-up to the embassy and specifies his Thracian origin.[88] In view of the possible metacomic associations of two of the candidates canvassed above, it is possible that Aristophanes was also expecting his audience to derive amusement from the way in which he recalled characters attacked by Cratinus to make the negotiations which would bring about the collapse of the gods' empire.

And Prometheus? In the circumstances of 414 there is only one figure who could properly focus a betrayal of the Athenians' hierarchy (in allegory,

---

[87] Sommerstein 1980b, 51–3 for the view that the play was Eupolis' *Heilotes*.

[88] Cleophon, son of Cleippides of the deme Acharnae (*PA* 8638) was also satirised for Thracian descent (*Frogs* 678f.). Given that he was already beginning to be a political force in the mid-410s, he could be the individual represented here. But he certainly became after 410 a consistent backer of the war's continuation and is likely enough, therefore, to have been a supporter of the Sicilian expedition. For these very reasons he seems unlikely to me to have been an individual that Aristophanes would have wished to caricature on stage. See further n. 193 at the end of chapter six.

the Olympian gods) to the conservative renegades (Peisetairus, Euelpides and the Birds) – Alcibiades. He had crossed to Sparta on his escape from the custody of the *Salaminia* (Thuc. 6.61.6–7; 88.9–10) and could certainly easily be imagined in spring of 414 to be giving away state secrets to harm his native city, even if no one could have predicted yet the specifics of that advice (cf. Thuc. 6.89–92). It is interesting that in *Birds*, once he uncovers himself – he has been hiding from Zeus's gaze – at 1503, he is greeted at once not just by name, but as a friend by Peisetairus (ὦ φίλε Προμηθεῦ 'My dear Prometheus!'). Immediate recognition alone might be explained by the reuse of the costume from a relatively recent performance of Aeschylus' *Prometheus Bound*.[89] But the familiarity more likely betokens a real-life acquaintance between Peisetairus' original and Prometheus' original (see chapter three, pp. 87–8 on Dicaeopolis and Euripides). If the former represents Critias, the immediacy and warmth of the greeting are both well explained (and the humour enhanced), since the pair were close friends (Pl. *Prt.* 316a, cf. Xen. *Mem.* 1.2.12–39: Critias would later be responsible for Alcibiades' recall Plut. *Alc.* 33.1). It is certainly true that Athens may have been extremely sensitive about Alcibiades' sudden defection, but I suggest that his representation on stage here has two interlinked purposes. The first is, probably, maliciously to connect to Alcibiades' defection the satire on Critias/Peisetairus. This is conspiracy theory on Aristophanes' part which might have gained credence because of Alcibiades' destination, the known proclivities of Critias and the association between both and Eupolis (even if the latter had rejected Alcibiades after his defection to the war party in 422). The second is to underplay by ridicule the potential damage Alcibiades' defection could do. At this point the Athenians had already defeated the Syracusans in battle once (Thuc. 6.67–71) and must still, despite the Herms and Mysteries affairs have retained a good deal of the confidence they had had on the expedition's departure (Thuc. 6.24.3).

If my reading is in essence correct, then *Birds* occupies a very important place in our understanding of internal Athenian political factions and their dramatic accomplices. It cannot have been true at this time that anyone ideologically opposed to the democracy and in the public eye would have dared openly to moot constitutional change. Thucydides has Alcibiades express this view in his speech to the Spartans (Thucydides 6.89.4): ἅμα δὲ καὶ τῆς πόλεως δημοκρατουμένης τὰ πολλὰ ἀνάγκη ἦν τοῖς παροῦσιν ἕπεσθαι ('Besides, in the circumstances of democratic government, it was

---

[89] See Flintoff 1983.

necessary to conform for the most part to existing conditions'). On the other hand, people knew very well that there were many in their midst who would have preferred both peace with Sparta and a quite different system of government, and they had been convinced by the recent issues of the Herms and Mysteries that the danger of action to subvert the democracy was real and present (Thuc. 6.27–8). In *Birds*, Aristophanes took the opportunity once more to implicate Eupolis in this anti-democratic faction by misappropriating and ridiculing his comic techniques and perhaps even by putting him on stage (see above, pp. 245–6) in a plot which in Cratinean allegorical fashion had (some of the worst of) the Athenians defeated by a bunch of cowardly laconisers who had avoided their just punishment through lucky escapes of one kind or another. The ploy was clever and malicious, and it attacked both the oligarchic plotters and the Athenian compromisers who had failed to act effectively against the enemy within. But what it demonstrates is Aristophanes' continued commitment to the radical democracy and its projects even after Hyperbolus' ostracism and his determination to brand his rival as a very present danger to the survival of the constitution. If he represented Critias as Peisetairus, then we can not say that – ultimately – he was mistaken.

LYSISTRATA AND THESMOPHORIAZUSAI

Of these two plays, *Lysistrata* certainly belongs to the festivals of 411 and *Thesmophoriazusai*, despite the lack of direct evidence, almost as certainly. The current consensus is that *Lysistrata* belongs to the Lenaea and *Thesmophoriazusai* to the Dionysia.[90] This is the only occasion on which we have extant two plays from the same year and given that both, in different measure, have plots which involve women, it seems important to ask why Aristophanes chose so suddenly to place his focus here. For it surely can not be put down to coincidence: he had not up to this point, as far as we can tell, produced a play with a female lead character (though *Clouds* had a female chorus); the role of women is rather restricted in the plays of the 420s (possibly limiting itself to metacomic satire, with the bridesmaid in *Acharnians*, Dardanis and Myrtia in *Wasps*, and Opora and Theoria in

---

[90] The evidence for *Lysistrata* is in Hypothesis 1, 33: ἐδιδάχθη ἐπὶ Καλλίου ἄρχοντος τοῦ μετὰ Κλεόκριτον ('It was produced in the archonship of Callias, the one following Cleocritus'). The date of *Thesmophoriazusai* is inferred from a number of correlated pieces of testimony (including *Thesm.* 1060–1, Σ *Frogs* 53, Σ *Thesm.* 190 on the date of Euripides' *Andromeda*). See Sommerstein 1994, 1–3. For the festivals, see Sommerstein 1977, 112–26, Gomme-Andrewes-Dover V 184–93; Henderson 1987, xv–xxv. *Contra* Prato and Del Corno 2001, XII–XVII.

Peace); and Aristophanes had openly criticised satirical attacks on women at *Peace* 751 (perhaps, however, only those with no *public* role).[91] On the other hand, the implication of *Peace* 751 is that his rivals had not scrupled to satirise individual women and it is clear from the scholium to *Clouds* 555 that Eupolis had produced in *Marikas* an on-stage caricature of Hyperbolus' mother. We may reasonably suppose that Euripides' mother had also been subjected to the same treatment, since her comic mentions in Aristophanes as a vegetable-seller (*Ach*. 457, 478, *Thesm*. 387, 456, *Frogs* 840) may be best explained as metacomic allusions to an on-stage caricature by a rival (possibly Cratinus, if it is correct to see his *Idaioi* as an on-stage attack on Euripides: see above, pp. 138–9). It is true that there are two female characters in *Birds*, Iris and Basileia. But the latter is possibly purely metacomic (deriving from Cratinus, cf. fr. 423). Iris, though she almost certainly does represent a real woman (since it would have been perfectly possible for Hermes to be used as Zeus' messenger), possibly an associate of Peisetairus/Critias or Eupolis, or the wife of one of the 'Olympian' Athenian leaders satirised in the embassy scene, has only a bit part (1199–1259). Nonetheless, her relatively important position as a conveyor of political information suggests that we have moved into a period, with an enormous number of male citizens away in Sicily, in which female intervention at the edges of political life might have been possible in a way never dreamed of in earlier times.

In *Lysistrata* the main characters are all women, with men playing only bit parts (the *proboulos*, Cinesias, the Athenian and Spartan ambassadors and the old men of the semi-chorus). *Thesmophoriazusai* once again focuses on male leads – Euripides and the relative (with bit parts for Agathon and Cleisthenes) – but the context is a women's festival, the chorus is female, and individual women have important roles (Critylla and the female speakers at the assembly), while the plot against Euripides (a public political act if carried to its logical conclusion) is the brain-child of the women and its locus a simulacrum of the all-male *ecclesia*. As I have argued, metacomedy – targeted especially upon Eupolis – still plays an important role in both dramas, but the titles and fragments of Eupolis' plays do not encourage the view that he had focused his plots on female themes or characters, despite the attack on Hyperbolus' mother in *Marikas* and the representation of the allied cities as women in *Poleis*. However, the *Deliades* ('Girls from Delos'), *Drapetides* ('Runaway Women'), *Eumenides, Thraittai, Kleoboulinai* and

---

[91] Butrica 2001 dates the first *Thesmophoriazusai* in the 420s, but this is rejected by Austin and Olson 2004, lxxxvi–lxxxvii, mainly on the grounds that Agathon only became well known after 416.

Horai of Cratinus must all predate 411 and probably show that the old rival of Aristophanes and Eupolis had consistently presented female choruses. The nearest other antecedent we get to *Thesmophoriazusai* is Hermippus' *Artopolides* 'Female Bread-Sellers', in which however Hyperbolus seems to have been the main target (*Clouds* 557 with scholium), though his mother may also have had a role (cf. *Clouds* 552).[92]

The conclusion seems inevitable that some specific set of circumstances had impelled Aristophanes towards female targets in 412/11. These will have involved his attitude both to his comic rival Eupolis and to the tragic poet Euripides. The latter's treatment of the Trojan War myth in accordance with the pro-Spartan version of Stesichorus in his *Helen* of 412 had combined a political perspective which must have been distasteful to the radical democrat in Aristophanes with a positive female role-model of a Helen who smacked more of the *sophrosyne* and guile of Penelope than of the traditional adulteress who had appeared on the comic stage in Cratinus' *Dionysalexandros* as central to the causes of both the Trojan War and its modern analogue (the Samian War?). Yet on the hypothesis I have been working through in this book, Lysistrata and her companions should represent *real* women, whose publicly known – presumably because publicly expressed – attitudes have offended the poet and his political backers. To a smaller extent, the same must be true of the women who lead the attack on Euripides in *Thesmophoriazusai*.

Since we are accustomed, from recent studies of the role of women in Athenian culture, to assume that there was no public *political* role for them, only a religious one, it seems that to posit some trespass upon this gendered line of demarcation is to stand against all the available evidence. There are, however, two egregious exceptions to the stereotyping of women as inherently non-political and these may lead us to an understanding of how, in the specific and special circumstances of 411, the rules may have been – to some extent – broken. First is the portrayal, already alluded to, of a positive and actively intelligent female figure in the Helen of Euripides. Although the dramatist was equally capable of demonstrating the potential evil of female power (in *Medea*, *Stheneboia* and *Hecuba*, for example),

---

[92] Unfortunately, we cannot date firmly enough the *Moirai* ('Fates') or *Stratiotides* ('Female Soldiers') of Hermippus (though the latter probably belongs *c.* 400: see below, p. 338), the *Hai aph' Hieron* ('Women Returning from the Sacred Rites') of Plato or the *Mousai* ('Muses') and *Poastriai* ('Grass-cutters') of Phrynichus, though the latter certainly had female characters (fr. 39, 41). Plays with singular female names, Ameipsias' *Sappho*, Cantharus' *Medea*, Crates' *Lamia*, Hermippus' *Europa*, Plato's *Europa*, Strattis' *Atalanta* (if that is the right title) and *Medea*, seem to be centred on mythological or historical characters (the possible exception being Pherecrates' *Corianno*), though that is no guarantee that they did not attack real women in these guises.

one of his other recent plays, *Troiades*, had focused sympathetically upon the females disempowered by war or superior forces (Hecabe, Cassandra, Andromache – and even Helen).[93] Second is the unique focus upon female intelligence and potential for political strategy and action in the thought-world of Plato – and perhaps therefore already in the circle of Socrates. One thinks immediately of Diotima in the *Symposium* as well as the female guardians in the *Republic*. But the figure of Aspasia in the *Menexenus* also demonstrates that the idea of the acquisition of the tools for political action by women was in the air in the last quarter of the fifth century.[94] Indeed, it is generally recognised that there is a family resemblance between the political use of the wool-working metaphor by Lysistrata (574–86) and that of the Eleatic Stranger in Plato's *Politicus* (308c–309b, 310e, 311b–e),[95] which on my argument, however, will not establish influence from Aristophanes to Plato, but rather the Socratic origin of the metaphor and its parody in *Lysistrata*. My conjecture, then, that Eupolis, on one level a target of both plays, was both close to Euripides and a member of the Socratic circle, will be important in understanding the general context in which an attack on women could be associated with him.

However, we come back to the problem: the attack on real women does not seem itself to have a metacomic basis. It must, therefore, arise from some – perhaps minimal – trespass by individual females upon the male preserve of political policy. I suggest that the unique conditions created by the massiveness of the Sicilian expedition's failure may have generated an outcry from a small band of educated females – and this 'assembly' will be the real-world basis also for the *ecclesia* of the *Thesmophoriazusai*. There are certainly signs, at any rate, from jokes made at *Peace* 992 and *Lysistrata* 554 that the incumbent priestess of Athena Polias, Lysimache, had made known publicly her opposition to the war. If *Lysistrata* is a satire of women who wish to interfere in this most male of preserves, then the minimum required to make the plot operate effectively is that, probably after the news of the disaster had reached Athens, a group of upper-class and educated women (for whose existence see Plato, *Laws* 658a-d), including prominent religious figures (priestesses of the major state cults), had found a way to promulgate their desire to end the conflict with Sparta. Possibly, they had

---

[93] It is worth noting that Helen's arguments (1) that Priam ignored divine warnings to kill Paris, and (2) that she is a pawn of the gods (*Tro.* 919f.), are actually well backed up by the mythological tradition, whereas what Hecuba says is not, and that Helen will survive, despite Menelaus' dire words (*Tro.* 1052f.).

[94] On this dialogue, see Coventry 1989.

[95] See Sommerstein 1990, ad loc. Henderson, 1987 on 567–86 makes the same point, but a slip of the pen has *Politicus* referred to as *Republic*.

imparted their views to the board of *Probouloi* and thence to the assembly. Indeed, given the presence on stage of one of the ten *Probouloi*, who is subject to as satirical a treatment as the women themselves, I think it likely that not only was this the way that the news got around, but that the specific *Proboulos* satirised here (and that it is an individual, not the board, is clear from the distinction to be drawn between attacking the *demos'* institutions, e.g. the generalship, and mocking – on stage – individuals serving the *demos* in some official capacity, e.g. Demosthenes and Nicias in *Knights*), had either been instrumental in promoting the publication of the women's statement (in which case the humour is made by turning his actual views inside-out) or had actually opposed them (though still remained an enemy of the poet).

LYSISTRATA

It will be clear by now that in all essentials I agree with the view of Lysistrata articulated first by D. M. Lewis, namely that she represents Lysimache, daughter of Dracontides of Bate (*PA* 4549), the incumbent priestess of Athena Polias.[96] The difference – and it is fundamental – is that I believe the representation was intended to be satirical. First of all, in my view, as an adherent of Hyperbolus Aristophanes had not supported negotiations with Sparta in 425 or in 421, but had mocked unmercifully those he associated with this policy in *Acharnians* and *Peace*. Secondly, in mentioning by name the priestess Lysimache at *Peace* 992 and *Lysistrata* 554, Aristophanes breaks the convention otherwise strictly upheld in comedy that a free man neither addresses nor refers to a respectable living woman by name in public. It is surely not a coincidence that the only other example found by scholars of the breach of this convention is that of Lysistrata at *Lysistrata* 1086, 1103 and 1147.[97] Sommerstein thinks that this breach is to be accounted for by the aura of religious authority and consequential deference from the male characters in the latter part of the play that Aristophanes has, as it were, borrowed from Lysimache. But the evidence is against this view. In court cases, when a living woman is called by name (as with Neaira in [Dem.] 59), it is always in disparagement of her propriety. Thirdly, it is not only the minor female characters who are portrayed as immodest in their attitudes

---

[96] Lewis 1955. This view is slightly modified by Henderson 1987, xxxviii–xl, and Sommerstein 1990, 5–6, of whom the latter prefers to think 'It is not likely... that we should think of Lysistrata as representing Lysimache in the sense in which Paphlagon in *Knights* represents Cleon: it is more a matter of association and reminiscence...' (*loc. cit.* 5).

[97] Schaps 1977, Sommerstein 1980c.

to sexuality and by their language (e.g. Calonice at 134f.). Lysistrata herself complains at 107–10 that there are no μοιχοί 'adulterers' to be found for comfort and she has not seen even a leather dildo since the revolt of Miletus. The word she uses in outlining to her collaborators what the women must abstain from is not euphemistic: it is the primary obscenity τοῦ πέους ('the prick' 124). Given that adultery could be punishable by death (Lysias 1.30; Demosthenes 25.53) and that improper words were not even used in public trials for indecency (witness the euphemistic language of Aeschines 1 *Against Timarchus*),[98] it seems unlikely that there can be any intention to a positive portrayal of figures who promote the first or use the second. Commentators have seemed to think the obvious rightness of the women's *cause* (however fantastic in conception) mitigates or even overrides their portrayal effectively – in Athenian terms – as whores.

Lysimache, then, is the target of a characteristically vicious attack by Aristophanes in this play, as are her confederates. The individual Athenian women behind Calonice and Myrrhine must have been known for much the same reason Lysimache was. I. Papademetriou has shown that a Myrrhine was associated with the temple of Athena Nike in this period[99] and it is possible, though we have no evidence for this proposition, that Calonice too was associated with a civic cult. The satirical edge will only have been the greater if these women were in fact no longer young (cf. the treatment of old women and their lust in *Ecclesiazousai*). The foreign women do not, on the other hand, need to have had a real existence, though Lampito was a royal name at Sparta (Herod. 6.71.2) and Ismenia was at least regarded as typically Theban (cf. *Ach.* 861, 954), so that both might refer to influential actual women. The whole point of the play is that the women have made a totally unrealisable plan for ending the war – both because their sex-plot assumes no access to prostitutes and because they can not affect their husbands if these actually are away from home anyway (cf. 99f.). Moreover, at this juncture making peace with Sparta was the policy of the oligarchs (Thuc. 8.90–1) and, whether it was fair or not, Aristophanes took the opportunity offered by whatever had catapulted Lysimache and her friends into the public eye to tar them with the laconophile brush, just as he had done with Eupolis in *Acharnians*. The representation of Lysistrata as a Euripidean heroine[100] of the Melanippe type (cf. especially 1124, probably quoting Euripides fr. 483 from that play) also suggests, on arguments adumbrated in earlier chapters, a connection

---

[98] See, for example, Aeschines I.38 with Fisher 2001 ad loc.
[99] Papademetriou 1948/9 with Sommerstein 1990, 5 n. 31.   [100] See Finnegan 1995, 164.

with the Euripidaristophaniser, whom I have identifed as Eupolis (above, pp. 88–90). In the context of a satire of Eupolis' inclinations towards peace and a full reconciliation with the Spartans (this is the implication of the final scene), the use of Euripidean material to bolster the plot and its characters adds an extra level of humour. Note as examples: (1) at 706–17 (where Lysistrata's worries about the women's capacity to keep the sex-strike up are heard), the use of tragic diction (and probably of Euripides' *Telephus* fr. 699 at 706 and of fr. 883 at 713); (2) the use of an argument implying the Athenian origin of the Ionians at 582f. which appears at the end of Euripides' *Ion* (1575–88), very probably a recent play.[101]

The *Proboulos*, I have argued above, was an identifiable individual, one whose actions may in reality have led to the dissemination of the women's views, or who had resisted their promulgation through the board of *probouloi* because he was in fact known for his misogynistic and authoritarian character (e.g. 387f., 433f.), but nonetheless was a person disliked by Aristophanes. He is in many ways reminiscent of Sophocles' Creon in *Antigone*, who arrests both sisters for disobeying his edict (cf. the attempt to arrest Lysistrata and the old women who come to her aid, 433f.) and in his conversation with Haemon is insistent that defeat by a *woman* is unthinkable and shameful (e.g. *Ant.* 677–80, 740, 746; *Lys.* 450). In fact, the *proboulos'* line 450 (ἀτὰρ οὐ γυναικῶν οὐδέποτ' ἔσθ' ἡττητέα 'But one must never be beaten by women') is quite remarkably similar to *Antigone* 678 (κοὔτοι γυναικὸς οὐδαμῶς ἡσσητέα 'One must by no means be defeated by a woman'; cf. 680).[102] It surely is not insignificant that one of the ten *probouloi* was an extremely elderly Sophocles (Arist. *Rhet.* 1419a 26–30). That such a satirical treatment would suit him because he could, as I have suggested (above, p. 256), have been *sympathetic* to the women's perspective is shown by two references in *Peace*. At 695 Hermes asks (on behalf of Peace) what has happened to Sophocles. Peace's concern, as with her question about Cratinus (700), must be focused on a known penchant for the cessation of hostilities (and the satirical bent of Trygaeus' reply, which probably also makes fun of Eupolis, shows clearly that Sophocles was not safe from ridicule). Likewise, earlier, at 531, Sophocles' lyrics have been aligned with peace by Trygaeus. And, as we have seen in the satire of Eupolis in *Acharnians* (where the poet is shown, I have argued, attacking his own coterie, Lamachus, Euripides etc.), and shall see again in the case of *Thesmophoriazusai*, Aristophanes did not scruple to make comedy by

---

[101] See Lee 1997, 40, who dates it c. 413.
[102] Noted by Sommerstein 1990 ad loc. but not by Henderson 1987.

reversing realities and creating on-stage conflicts between those who in reality were friends. Later in the year in which *Lysistrata* was produced Sophocles was implicated, as one of the *probouloi*, in the infamous decision to suspend legal safeguards against the proposal of unconstitutional measures (Thuc. 8.67.2; Arist. *Rhet.* 1419a 26–30), which made possible the setting up of the oligarchy. Aristophanes may not have known quite what was going to happen, but his satire here was carefully aimed in early 411 at a figure who might prove dangerous to the rule of the *demos*.

Commentators who are certain that the *Proboulos* does not satirise a recognisable individual are equally sure that the Cinesias who arrives to see his wife Myrrhine at 838 and then goes on to facilitate the settlement with Sparta in the scene with the herald (980f.) is not a real individual and certainly not the only famous Cinesias we know, the dithyrambic poet (*PA* 8438) who was mocked on stage at *Birds* 1372–1409 (and is named in Aristophanes on many other occasions).[103] However, the fundamental basis of the satire in *Birds* and here is the same, namely that the individual is – through weakness of will or inherent flightiness – a fellow-traveller of those who wish to make peace with Sparta. There would have been something bizarre indeed about a love-scene between the gangly poet and the – possibly – ageing Myrrhine, especially if they were not actually married, and this bizarreness would have required no help from textual indicators, rather its humour would have *depended* upon the counterpoint between visual image and text. Lysias (20.21) mentions that Cinesias had a reputation for cowardice and this again suits the undercurrents of both *Birds* and *Lysistrata*, for the former because the bird-colony stands on one level for the alternative to the brave exploit of the Sicilian expedition and for the second because Cinesias *ought* to be away from the city on military service and not available to canoodle with Myrrhine (cf. 99–100). I conclude, then, that there is nothing to prevent the identification of the two figures as one and the same.

There is no solid indication of the targets behind the first Athenian ambassador, who enters at 1086 and negotiates the peace, or the second, who emerges at 1221. However, I doubt that Aristophanes shifted his satirical gaze far from those he had already identified in *Birds* as philo-Laconian. It would certainly have been amusing to see on stage caricatures of such individuals, additionally shamed by the erect phalloi they wore (because it bespoke

---

[103] Henderson 1987 and Sommerstein 1990 on 838. Aristophanes mentions Cinesias at *Frogs* 153, 1437 (and probably he is meant as the target at 366), fr. 156.13 (*Gerytades*), and *Eccl.* 330. Pherecrates has Music complain of his innovations (fr. 155.8–13 *Cheiron*), Plato Comicus has a character speak of his physical debilities (fr. 200) and he was the on-stage target of Strattis' *Cinesias* (see Ath. 12.551d).

their unmanly obsession with sex), by their lubricious behaviour towards Diallage (1168f., 1173, 1178f.), by their glowing praise of the Spartans (1226) and the absurd suggestion that the current Athenian suspiciousness towards the enemy would be alleviated by going on embassies drunk (1229f.). In fact, picking up my identification of Peisetairus in *Birds* as Critias, there is certainly a possibility that he could be behind the first ambassador, given the chorus' joke about the *Hermokopidai* addressed to him at 1094–5 and the fact that Critias had escaped punishment only after Andocides came forward to contradict Diocleides' evidence (Andoc. 1.47 and 60f.).

As I have already noted above (p. 35), there is also a strong metacomic element in *Lysistrata*. It seems very likely that one of its main foci is the chorus. The old men certainly seem to have much generally in common with the earlier groups in *Acharnians*, *Wasps* and *Peace*. (1) Their opening lines are in the same metre as the opening of the parodos of *Wasps* and there is a similarity between the words and structure of the first lines (*Wasps* 230 χώρει, πρόβαιν' ἐρρωμένως. ὦ Κωμία, βραδύνεις. 'March on, step forward strongly. O Comias, you're being slow.' *Lys.* 254 χώρει, Δράκης, ἡγοῦ βάδην, εἰ καὶ τὸν ὦμον ἀλγεῖς 'March on, lead step by step Draces, even if your shoulder's sore') and both songs contain, two lines later, an address to the same chorus-member, Strymodorus (*Wasps* 233, *Lys.* 257), who is also mentioned in Dicaeopolis' phallic song at *Acharnians* 273. (2) Like the earlier choruses, these old men are characterised as jurors, here, and, as in *Wasps* (88), quite specifically attached to the Eliaia court (*Lys.* 380, cf. 270). (3) They specifically associate themselves with the trophy at Marathon (*Lys.* 285), and in this their unbelievable age links them with the chorus of *Wasps* (711) and *Acharnians* (181). (4) They use the cry ἰοὺ ἰού (295, 305), come on stage with at least one torch (308) and try to light more (316), and suggest beating the old women with wood (356–7), motifs criticised by Aristophanes at *Clouds* 541–3 as typical of bad comedy (cf. also the women's wetting of the old men, 381f., and see the promise in the parabasis of *Acharnians* 658 not to 'sprinkle' the audience) (5) Like the chorus of *Wasps* (462f., cf. 488f.), the old men smell a conspiracy to establish a tyranny (*Lys.* 616f., 630–1). (6) Like the *Wasps* chorus (408), the (political) threat makes them remove their cloaks (*Lys.* 614–5), a move associated with that of the women in *Thesmophoriazusai* whose plot against Euripides is threatened by male infiltration (656). Moreover, this undressing carries over to the old women also (636–7) and then degenerates into the removal of all their clothes by both choruses (662, 686). (7) The old men's nostalgia for their glory days (*Lys.* 665f.) is highly reminiscent of that expressed by the choruses of *Acharnians* (209f.) and *Wasps* (1060f.), and the motif of rejuvenation at 669–70 (found in respect of Philocleon at *Wasps* 1333, 1355) is also shared by the chorus of *Peace* (336). (8) When the women's coryphaeus removes a gnat from the male coryphaeus' eye (1025f.), the episode could be construed as a version of 'people fighting with lice', criticised by Aristophanes' chorus on his behalf in the parabasis of *Peace* (740). All this smacks of parodic reuse of choruses, motifs and scenes from earlier rival comedy. The use of an old-man chorus (also jurors) has been traced above ultimately to Cratinus' *Nomoi* and its Eupolidean parody *Chrysoun Genos*. But the device of splitting the chorus into two equal halves (found briefly in the metacomic *Ach.* 557–77) had been used by Eupolis in his *Marikas* of 421 (see frr. 192.98, 117, 118, 120, 186 and 193.5ff.). Quite possibly it was specifically a Eupolidean device, used already before and therefore satirised already by *Acharnians*.[104] The idea of a women's chorus to match the old men – who are ultimately converted, in the same ironical way as was managed in *Acharnians* and *Wasps*, to the 'right' side – need not have direct metacomic roots (despite the use of a metacomic reference at 700f., cf. *Ach.* 883f., *Peace* 1005): the subversion of the Eupolidean hemichorus in the context of a women's plot is enough to explain the humour. However, when Lysistrata summons a women's reserve at 456–7, we may very well suspect that there is here some disparaging cross-reference to market-women such as Euripides' mother (the last element of the sesquipedalian word in 457 is -λαχανοπώλιδες 'female vegetable-sellers'; cf. *Ach.* 457, 478, *Thesm.* 387, *Frogs* 840) and perhaps to the bread-sellers of Hermippus' play *Artopolides* ('Female Bread-sellers') attacking Hyperbolus (the last element of the word in 458 is –αρτοπώλιδες 'female bread-sellers'). The chorus too, then, as in most of the earlier plays (*Clouds* being the exception), far from being a sympathetic intermediary between actors and audience is itself an object of ridicule for its combination of the espousal of philo-Laconian political policies and low-grade comic devices.

Metacomedy is not restricted to the chorus, however. It seems clear that the scene at 1215f. where there is comic business with torches (cf. *Clouds* 543) and a metatheatrical allusion to its low-grade nature (1218f.), though the business is completed anyway, ought to allude to some comic intertext. Perhaps, given that the scene just beginning contains Spartans, it may alert the audience to think about Eupolis' *Heilotes*, one of the few comedies we know to have had (as in Aristophanes) characters speaking in Doric Greek (fr. 147, 149), though we know nothing else about it,[105] or Cratinus' *Lacones*.

---

[104] See Sidwell 2000c for the argument that there had been a (perhaps vestigial) double chorus also in *Knights*.
[105] See Colvin 1999, 271–2 and Storey 2003, 174–9.

Another metacomic reference occurs, on my argument, in the appearance of Diallage in the reconciliation scene (1114–88). Her mention at *Acharnians* (989f.), I have argued, in contrast to Polemos – who appears again in *Peace* – strongly suggests that she belonged in an earlier comedy (possibly Cratinus' *Horai*). If so, then the way she is subverted by Aristophanes here is quite easy to see. Although she is supposed by commentators to stand positively for peace, there is no getting round the fact that she is presented naked (1158–70) and thus as sexually available, a whore just like the two personifications Trygaeus brings back from Olympus (*Peace* 848–9). Moreover, Lysistrata's apparently serious speeches (see further below) arguing for mutual respect between Athenians and Spartans for the past help they have given to each other (1128–35, 1137–46, 1149–56, 1159–61) are spoken in a context where both parties are distracted from their content by their erections and the presence of the alluring Diallage (1136, 1148, 1158, 1168–70, 1173–4). It is in fact difficult to see how this scene could be staged without the intellectual pretensions of Lysistrata (1123–7) being bathetically undercut by the concrete reminders of the success of her plot and the attention of the audience is bound to be drawn away from her pronouncements by the business between the envoys and Diallage.[106]

It is worth reflecting briefly on the question of whether Lysistrata's speeches in this scene and other apparently serious elements are undermined in any other way. (1) Lysistrata's first argument (1128–35) depends on the ideology of Panhellenism, which I have argued (above, p. 210) was also used satirically in *Peace* to undermine Eupolis' political posture. The idea that the rhetoric of the Persian War period might be relevant in the 410s is subverted by the realities known to everyone, in particular that the Spartans had already agreed to recognise Persian claims to territory once ruled by the King's forebears (Thuc. 8.18.37) and that the Athenians themselves knew that their goose would be well and truly cooked if they could not get Persian help and had consequently voted to send envoys to attempt to accomplish this objective (Thuc. 8.53–4). (2) At 1137–44, her argument focuses on the Athenian aid sent to Sparta in 462, but omits the ultimate disgrace of the contingent, sent home 'alone of all the allies' (Thuc. 1.102.3) because they were suspected of sympathy with the revolt, a slight which led to the dissolution of the alliance and, within a few years, war between Athens and the Spartan-led Peloponnesian League (Thuc. 1.102.4–105). Selective use

---

[106] In a production of *Lysistrata* at the University of Lancaster in the early 1980s, the students had decided to use a blow-up sex doll to represent Diallage. The combination of shock and the incredibly funny scene-stealing of the two envoys effectively diverted attention from and eventually drowned out with laughter the words of Lysistrata.

of historical data is apparent in many rhetorical arguments (especially in writers like Isocrates), but such a blatant refusal to acknowledge that the Spartans had actually (according to Athenian opinion) mistreated them badly is intended, in the satirical context I have argued for, to ridicule the whole notion that peace with Sparta is possible or desirable. (3) Her argument to the Athenians at 1149–56 focuses on the aid given by the Spartan king Cleomenes in overturning the tyranny of Hippias in 510. What she omits has already been brought to the attention of the audience by the (democratic) old men of the chorus (271–80), namely that Cleomenes had returned to Athens in 508 at the invitation of Isagoras, to help him establish an oligarchy. He was met, however, with firm resistance and besieged on the acropolis for two days before being permitted to leave unharmed. This was the beginning of the democracy, for Cleisthenes now returned from exile and began the reforms which led to the new constitutional format (Herod. 5.69–73; Arist. *Ath. Pol.* 20.1–4). This was not an obscure episode and once more the point, I think, is to show clearly the bankruptcy of Lysistrata's position by revealing her manipulation of history to establish her argument for peace. It seems entirely possible that Aristophanes was here basing his satire firmly on the ways in which those currently – or during the earlier phase of the war – argued for reconciliation.

To some, the seriousness of Lysistrata's arguments in the scene with the *proboulos* seems if anything rather more impressive. However, we ought to be looking rather for what is *funny* about them, when read as elements which satirise their speakers. I have already suggested that the wool-working metaphor (567–86), which has its analogue in Plato's *Politicus*, is based on current Socratic thought. It is amusing, however, because it appropriates for a *woman's* argument what belongs in the serious discussions of intellectual men, repatriating it, as it were, to its original context (since men did not weave). Its political content, however, with its emphasis upon internal and imperial political cohesion, and especially the idea at 577–8 that the *hetaireiai* (which were working at the time with Peisander to undermine the democracy itself) should be abolished, runs entirely counter to the direction from which the plan to make peace with Sparta would be seen to come. For just as it was the oligarchs who planned to make deals with both Sparta and Persia (Thuc. 8.53–4) by sending out 'embassies here and there' (*Lys.* 570), so the mechanism by which they were trying to achieve the internal conditions which would persuade those parties to agree consisted of the very *hetaireiai* which Lysistrata proposes to abolish. The humour comes, then, from a clear and obvious clash between the known (or presumed) direction of Lysimache's political leanings (i.e. towards oligarchy) and the paradoxical statement by her *altera ego*, Lysistrata, that oligarchic *hetaireiai* are the cause of the city's internal problems. We may indeed presume that this was closer to Aristophanes' own view and that, just as it undercuts Lysistrata's posture and creates laughter because of its contradictory ideology, so it cocks a snook at the people already plotting to remove the democratic constitution.

As to Lysistrata's policy of stopping soldiers from going to market in full armour (556f.), the images evoked (a man on horseback buying porridge and putting it in his helmet 561–2; a Thracian intimidating a fig-stall holder to steal her figs 563–4) are so absurd that they may involve cross-reference to comedy rather than reality. If so, then part of the satire here derives from Lysistrata's use of the world of comedy to sustain her 'serious' arguments. More weighty, however, appear her claim that women bear more than a double burden in war by having sons and then sending them to war (588–90) and her concern for the young women who will remain unmarried because of the shortage of marriageable men (592–7). Henderson comments on 590, where the *proboulos* interrupts Lysistrata with σίγα, μὴ μνησικακήσῃς ('Be quiet! Don't recall past injuries') before she can say 'never to see them again': 'To allow Lys. to complete her statement... would indeed have evoked spectator resentments and in addition would have been ill-omened (cf. 37–8)'.[107] Yet it is, if Henderson is correct, already clear what Lysistrata means. Thucydides' Pericles appears to evoke the normal Athenian view when he speaks of the loss of sons in war almost entirely as a male concern (2.44.3–45.2). Moreover, an expression of the female view of the woman's role in giving birth to children which exactly parallels that of Thucydides' Pericles is found in Euripidean tragedy, in the speech of Praxithea volunteering her daughter for sacrifice to save the city of Athens (*Erechtheus* fr. 360). The very reason for bearing children, she says, is to protect the altars of the gods and the homeland (14–15). If she had had sons rather than daughters and war had come, she would not have refused to send them forth, rather she would have wished for them to be real men, not mere figures brought up for nothing (22–7). She detests women who choose life rather than virtue for their sons (30–1). In any case, as she makes clear at 38, children do not belong to their mothers except through birth: τὴν οὐκ ἐμὴν <δὴ> πλὴν φύσει . . . κόρην ('My daughter, who is not mine except through birth'). It is hard, then, to credit Henderson's conclusion: 'It is difficult to believe that Lys.'s argument here did not reflect the views of many a spectator's wife and was not intended to evoke reflective sympathy'.[108] He may be right where raw emotion is

---

[107] Henderson 1987 on 589–90.   [108] Henderson 1987 on 589–80.

concerned – to lose a child is a dreadful blow. But Lysistrata's bold view appears to cut across accepted *public* postures and seems intended to make her appear crass and foolish, thus inviting from the audience the laughter appropriate to personal ridicule. The same must be true of the following discussion about young girls unable to marry. First, it must be noted that Lysistrata mentions in pride of place married women's sexual gratification (591–2), an issue both improper for public discussion and, for Athenians schooled in the attitudes illustrated from Thucydides and Euripides, absurdly inappropriate as a serious argument against war. Secondly, the very mention by Lysistrata of an issue which was no laughing matter (cf. Lysias 12.21) and which, according to some of our sources (Ath. 13.555d–556a; Diog. Laert. 2.26; Aul. Gell. 15.20.6; Hieron. Rhod. fr. 44–5 Wehrli), was being taken very seriously in the context of the Sicilian defeat by the (male) policy-makers seems designed to arouse exactly the sort of contemptuous laughter as her earlier remarks at 588–90. However, I do not discount that the reference here may be metacomic, given that the same issue is raised by one of the speakers at the assembly in *Thesmophoriazusai* (410f.).

Much as this reading cuts against the grain of our modern sensibilities, the evidence of Athenian perspectives appears to disallow us a sympathetic Lysistrata. Her triumph, like that of other Aristophanic 'heroes' is ironic and illusory, set as it is within a framework which mocks the comic techniques and political attitudes of Eupolis, who is now attacked also, in addition to his laconophilia and Panhellenism, for subscription to the political views of *women*. Moreover, a fundamentally satirical interpretation allows a different answer to the problem of the play's ending, pointed up by Taplin, and so well articulated recently by Revermann: 'Can a comedy performed in Athens in 411 *end* with a celebratory hymn to Athena addressed in her cult function as the protectress of the arch-enemy's city which Athens is at war with at the moment?'[109] Revermann's answer was 'no', and his solution was to propose that our text reflects reperformance in a Laconian city, Taras, in the fourth century.[110] However, if we introduce here an irony which is on my reading absolutely typical of Aristophanes (if not more generally of Old Comedy), the problem of what is missing can now be answered 'a Spartan cult hymn to Athene' (possibly traditional) and the reason clearly seen, namely that such an ending suggests that Lysistrata's 'peace' is simply capitulation.

---

[109] Taplin 1993, 58 n. 7, Revermann 2006, 255.
[110] Revermann 2006, 258. It is difficult to see, however, how such a text would have survived to become part of the *Athenian* set we clearly have in the other plays.

THESMOPHORIAZUSAI

Thesmophoriazusai has always seemed to be the least political of Aristophanes' Peloponnesian War comedies. Indeed, it is this assessment which has tended to be the decisive factor in placing it at the Dionysia rather than at the Lenaea of 411.[111] However, read as satire of Euripides and, more crucially, of Euripides' relative (as well as of Agathon, Cleisthenes, and the individual female targets – the other major players) it may turn out to be less disconnected than has been thought from the ideological conflict raging in Athens during this critical year. As I have already argued above (chapter 2, pp. 36–7), the metacomic material of the play (satire of a tragic poet in a 'borrowing scene', the use of *Telephus* as an intertext) points towards a close connection with the target of *Acharnians*. If the identification of Cratinus' 'Euripidaristophaniser' (fr. 342) as Eupolis is correct and the humour of the Euripides scene in *Acharnians* is based on the overlapping of Cratinus' on-stage satire of the poet with Eupolis' close (family?) relationship to him, then the already established transmutation of the youngish comic into his older rival (managed in *Acharnians* and repeated without fuss in *Peace*) is once again brought to bear in *Thesmophoriazusai*.[112] The relative, then, represents Eupolis[113] and the management of the plot utilises part of Cratinus' critique of his rival: he cannot produce his comic material without help from Euripides – in this case both indirect (the use of the framework from *Telephus*), and direct (the relative's use of *Palamedes* and Euripides' intervention with rescue plans from his own plays, *Helen*, and *Andromeda*). The plot's ultimate irony, however, will be that Euripides' final, successful attempt to rescue his relative has to borrow not from tragedy, but from trygedy. For it seems likely, in a play with other strongly metacomic aspects, that the theme of bamboozling the barbarian in general and of representing the Scythian archer in particular as a booby is taken over – and subverted – from earlier comedy. I note, for example, that a barbarian speaking pidgin Greek features in the *Acharnians* (94f.), as do the wild Thracians (155f.) and Scythian archers (55). The Thracian Triballos, who appears at *Birds* (1565f.), is another example of the barbarian pidgin Greek speaker. If those comedies are as deeply metacomic as I have maintained, then a large part of the humour in these sections must derive from the fact that they have been 'borrowed', with satirical intent, from earlier comedies. In the case

---

[111] See Sommerstein 1994, 1–3. Austin and Olson 2004, xxxiii–xliv.
[112] We need pay no attention to the scholiastic identification of the relative as Mnesilochus, though this shows us both that this information was available and that ancient scholars were looking to identify (some) characters with individuals.
[113] It was Keith Cooke who originally made this identification.

of the Thracians, the use of the circumcised phallus (158, 161) criticised by Aristophanes in the parabasis of *Clouds* (539–40) seems to guarantee the hypothesis. Once more, the general intent to involve a rival in a metacomic critique suggests that the motif derives from earlier comedy. The Scythian archers in *Lysistrata* (433f.) will likewise have the same metacomic point of reference as those in *Acharnians*. It seems very likely, given the way in which, as I have argued, Eupolis is continually represented as using Cratinus' comic material, that all these motifs may go back to his work. Thus part of the satire of the final scene is that Euripides has to borrow a comic scheme from the poet who had ridiculed him (cf. *Idaioi* fr. 90 and *Wasps* 61 with my earlier argument, pp. 139, 181–2). I would not discount the possibility, however, that on-stage caricature is also at work in the Scythian Archer scene of *Thesmophoriazusai*. If so, then the individual so attacked might have been Euathlus, who is not only called a Scythian (*Ach.* 704), but specifically a Scythian archer (*Ach.* 707, cf. 711–12). He had been mentioned by Cratinus (*Thraittai* fr. 82) and is also targeted by Philocleon/Cratinus at *Wasps* 592. So it is possible he is taken over directly from Cratinus, probably because he was a friend of Eupolis, and the humour depends (as so often) upon imagining a conflict between those of the same stripe (cf. e.g. Dicaeopolis/Eupolis versus Lamachus in *Ach.*, above, pp. 143–4). Was he a Knight and the other prosecutor involved (along with Alcibiades, *Ach.* 716) as a *positive* figure in the Cleon trial in *Chrysoun Genos*?

The treatment of the relative, Eupolis, is familiar from *Acharnians*. He is unable to understand the complexities of Euripides' concepts (6f., cf. Dicaeopolis at *Ach.* 397f.); he insults Euripides' penchant for making his characters lame (23–4, cf. Dicaeopolis at *Ach.* 411); he is grossly down to earth in his sexual and scatological comments (50, 57, 59–62, 142–3, 153, 157–8, 200–1, 206–7, 248, 254, 288, 291, 480f., 540, 570, 611, 632; cf. Dicaeopolis at *Ach.* 592, 789, 1060, 1066, 1199,1216–17, 1220–1); yet he knows the theatre and Euripides' plays in particular (134f., 153, 168f.; 275–6, 497, 769f., 847f., 1010f.; cf. Dicaeopolis at *Ach.* 393f.). Two other places also yield more humour if read in conjunction with this identification. At 94, the relative/Eupolis praises Euripides' scheme, but immediately follows it by saying: τοῦ γὰρ τεχνάζειν ἡμέτερος ὁ πυραμοῦς ('when it comes to making plots, we take the biscuit!'). The use of the plural possessive adjective, according to Austin and Olson, 'makes it clear that [the relative] is already wedded to [the plan]', even though it is entirely Euripides'.[114] However, read as the statement of a Eupolis tarred with the Cratinean accusation of 'Euripidism', its humour lies in the claim

---

[114] Austin and Olson 2004 on 94.

that *both* playwrights are good at τεχνάζειν (cf. 198–9, 271; *Frogs* 957 for Euripides), even though Eupolis derives his from his older relative. At 157–8, the relative/Eupolis obscenely offers his writing skills to Agathon in the composition of a satyr-play. The word for collaboration (a rare usage) is συμποιῶ 'I do with'. It can not be a coincidence that this term is used, since Eupolis had (humorously) employed it in defence of his reuse of Aristophanes' *Knights* in the parabasis of *Baptai* (fr. 89): τοὺς Ἱππέας | ξυνεποίησα τῷ φαλακρῷ ('I co-wrote *Knights* with the bald guy'). Now Aristophanes gets his own back by having his rival use his experience in collaborative dramatic writing to express his desire to have anal intercourse with the – very much grown up – Agathon (cf. the defence by Aristophanes of adult male homosexual partnerships in Pl. *Symp.* 189c-193d, which is intended to satirise the poet).[115]

The satire of Euripides has been extensively and well treated by other scholars, most recently Austin and Olson.[116] The most salient points are that he is attacked (as he will be again in *Frogs*) for intellectual pretentiousness (5f.; cf. *Frogs* 98f.), for putting 'bad' women on stage (85, 385f.; cf. *Frogs* 1043f., 1079f.), and for tricksy plots (93–4; cf. *Frogs* 957), will constantly have attributed to him sentiments which his characters utter (e.g. 275–6 = *Hippolytus* 612) and in general represents (as Austin and Olson put it) 'not merely a distillation of his own tragedies, but a highly tendentious reading of them'.[117] What my analysis adds emerges from the observation that with the identification of both Dicaeopolis and the 'relative' as Eupolis, we see here in reverse what was represented in *Acharnians*. There, Euripides was happy, despite his mistreatment (which arose from the superimposition of Cratinus' anti-Euripidean stance onto Eupolis), to help Dicaeopolis with his disguise and becomes implicated as an accessory to his apologia for the Spartans and his self-centred acquisition of peace. Here it is the relative who, despite the ignominies he must undergo, is happy to help out Euripides in his attempt to evade the women's strictures. These are two ways of skinning the same (pair of) cats and despite the lack of an overt political theme, the comparison makes it clear that Aristophanes' purpose in the play was not far different from that of *Acharnians*, namely to vilify both of the individuals in the eyes of the audience. It is for what the public knows – or thinks it knows – about their involvement in the affairs of the city that they have been chosen as targets. What that is, however, is

---

[115] The play with the phrase τὸ δεῖνα 'whatsitsname' at 620f. is rather pronounced and may relate back to Eupolis' use of it at *Prospaltioi* fr. 261, which I suspect may have been in turn part of an attack on Cratinus (as the old man figure).
[116] Austin and Olson 2004, lv–lxiv.   [117] Austin and Olson 2004, lvi.

not addressed by the plot itself, as it is in *Lysistrata*, but is only hinted at by the strong intertextuality with *Acharnians*: Eupolis and Euripides are assumed to be pro-Spartan – and probably, therefore, especially at this time, pro-oligarchic.

The treatment of Agathon, the son of Teisamenos (*PA* 83; *PAA* 105185), the young tragic poet who had won his first victory with his first play at the Lenaea of 416 (Pl. *Symp.* 173a, Ath. 5.216f–217a), probably owes much to metacomic reference. As I have already argued, the scene is highly reminiscent of the Euripides 'borrowing' scene in *Acharnians* and that probably derives its humour from the overlaying of a Cratinean satire onto the persona of Eupolis. Although Agathon was later to leave Athens to serve the artistic agenda of Archelaus, King of Macedon (*Frogs* 83f.; Ael. *VH* 13.4, 2.21), as Euripides also had, writing for him the *Archelaus*, it does not appear on the surface to be for any political motive that he is chosen as a target here.[118] I suspect that, just as Agathon's substitution for Euripides in the 'borrowing' scene of *Acharnians* denotes metacomic play with a Cratinean original, the focus upon Euripides' approach to him rests on rumours about Euripides' homosexual obsession with him which we hear of in the anecdotal tradition (Ael. *VH* 13.4, 2.21). It is against this background that the focus on Agathon's proclivities and his rejection of Euripides' overtures would gain specific bite. However, at another level, his collaboration with Euripides in helping with the dressing-up scheme must reflect the same political charges being made tacitly against Euripides and Eupolis. And the fact that he appears to have been close to Socrates (Pl. *Symp.* 174af.) ties him intellectually into the circle against whose political programme Aristophanes had long been campaigning.

The other major male character is Cleisthenes (574–654), lampooned widely likewise for his lack of a beard, femininity and passive homosexuality (*Ach.* 117–21; *Knights* 1373–4; *Clouds* 355; *Birds* 829–31; *Lys.* 1091–2; *Frogs* 57, 422–4; cf. Cratin. fr. 208.2–3; Pherecrates fr. 143), but also a prominent political – and perhaps military – figure (*Wasps* 1187; *Lys.* 621, *Frogs* 48). He is a friend of the women (574–5) and comes of his own accord to tell them (579f.) the rumours about male infiltration that he has heard in the *agora* (his normal stamping-ground, according to Sausage-Seller at *Knights* 1374). In *Lysistrata* (621), Cleisthenes is regarded as the possible focus of a Spartan plot to get the women to seize the Athenian treasury (620–5). Henderson and Sommerstein both point out that it is the Spartans' inclination towards anal intercourse that makes Cleisthenes' house a good place to locate such a

---

[118] On the question of Euripides' Macedonian connections see most recently Scullion 2003.

conspiracy,[119] but it is also true that the connection between Cleisthenes and women is already assumed there. His representation in *Thesmophoriazusai*, then, as a friend of the women may also be linked to a subtext accusing him (and the women) of pro-Spartan sympathies. His appearance in direct confrontation with Eupolis as Dicaeopolis in *Acharnians* (117–21), whatever is really going on in that strange scene, may suggest that he was actually (like Euripides and Lamachus) an associate of his. If he is identical with the Cleisthenes whom Lysias 25.25 reports as integrally involved with the trials of oligarchs after the collapse of the coup in 411, then this accusation will be factually false, though it is always possible that he acted this way to divert the suspicions of his political sympathies which had been aroused by comedy. He may, however, be a different man.

The *prytanis*, who appears briefly at 929–43, will not represent the *demos* any more than the *proboulos* does in *Lysistrata*, since that would be to demean the *demos* ([Xen.] *Ath. Pol.* 2.18). And although he appears to be presented quite straightforwardly, it is likely that the humour of the scene derives from some relationship known to exist between this specific individual and the relative/Eupolis, since in begging for a favour the latter essentially claims the man is a thief (936–8). There is, in fact, though, a positive ring to the Council's involvement in humiliating the relative (943) – in the sense that the wish for such punishment to fall upon the real individual behind the comic mask is, dramatically speaking, endorsed by the *demos*.

It may also be the case that the theme of male homosexuality (especially anal intercourse) which is present in the Agathon scene (35, 61–2, 133, 157–8, 206) and the archer scene (1118–20, 1123–4) and implied throughout by the theme of male transvestism (Agathon, the relative, Cleisthenes (575–654), and finally Euripides) is meant to stand as a subtext for philo-Laconism, since Spartans were generally reckoned by Athenians to be fond of this practice (Pl. *Laws* 1.636b, 8.836a-c): λακωνίζειν 'to behave like a Spartan' can in some circumstances according to the scholia specifically refer to a predilection for anal penetration of males (Ar. fr. 358).[120] It is here that we may hear more than an echo of Eupolis' *Baptai* (dated by Storey to 415), which had transvestism as a central theme (Σ Juvenal 2.92) and used its parabasis to strike another blow in the war against Aristophanes (fr. 89).

---

[119] Henderson 1987 on 616–24. Sommerstein 1990 on 621.
[120] Henderson 1991, 218 n. 37 collects a rather dubious set of comic references, some of which (e.g. *Lys.* 1148, 1174) clearly relate to anal intercourse with *women* (for which in Sparta see Athenaeus 13.602d). For Spartan pederasty see Cartledge 2001, 91–105 and for further discussion of the comic evidence Hubbard 1998–9, 48–59, 73 n.10.

It would not be in any way surprising to discover that the cross-dressing of *Thesmophoriazusai* has a good deal more to do with Aristophanes' need to respond in kind to the poetic and political attacks of that play than, as Austin and Olson suggest, 'the relationship between men and women'.[121]

The other major hint of an attack upon pro-Spartan elements in the *polis* is the women's involvement in the plot. Their criticism of Euripides is not that what he says about women is untrue, but that his revelations have made it more difficult for them to continue their deceitful behaviour (400–28). The first woman orator's final accusation (545–8) in fact invites the inference that if Euripides wrote about good women (like Penelope) instead of – or as well as – bad ones like Melanippe and Phaedra, there would be no problem. It is no coincidence, then, that an accommodation between the two parties is so easily achieved (1160–71), since Euripides' positive females of the 412 productions (Helen and Andromeda) are already in place, though Aristophanes has reduced them to tales of submissive females rescued by romantically (i.e. sexually) inclined male heroes.[122] Read as satire, the plot reveals at base a conspiracy between Euripides and the women which represents a certain complicity between them. What underlies this will surely be, in the year of *Lysistrata* and the oligarchic revolution, the implication that the women – at least those who are singled out for special satirical attention – are fellow travellers with the anti-democratic forces which currently beset the city. I have already argued (pp. 143–4) that the unexpectedly positive view of Lamachus (via his mother) taken by the chorus in the parabasis (841) allies the women with Eupolidean ideology, just as does their vilification of Hyperbolus' mother (839f.), one of the targets of his *Marikas* (of 421). Even at a desperate point in the fortunes of the radical democratic side, then, Aristophanes could figure the opposition in comedy and ridicule it by relying on a link already more clearly and pungently expressed earlier in the year by his *Lysistrata*.

A few words need to be said finally about the female targets. There is no firm consensus as to their number. The *ecclesia* scene has a woman making the announcements and prayers (295–311, 331–51, 372–9, 380), two orators (A 383–432, B 443–58), and an objector (533–9, 544–8, 551–2, 554, 557, 559, 562, 563, 566–7, 568, 569), plus whoever it is who announces Cleisthenes (571–3) and converses with him (582–3, 586, 589, 592–4, 597–602, 606, 613–14, 626–9, 631, 632, 634–5, 636, 639–40, 642, 645, 649–50, 652). But the general tendency is to reduce these to three voices, by having the announcements and prayers and the conversation with Cleisthenes

---

[121] Austin and Olson 2004, xxxii. [122] On this, see Austin and Olson, 2004, lii–lxviii.

given to the *coryphaeus* or Critylla and by assuming that the objector is identical with the first of the two previous orators; at any rate the exit line given to the Garland-Seller (457) allows one actor to be released to play Cleisthenes, who enters at 574.[123] Since the *ecclesia* scene blends seamlessly into the Cleisthenes scene and thence into the hostage scene, commentators presume that the woman examined by Cleisthenes at 603 and revealed to be Cleonymus' wife (605), the victim of the baby-snatch (688), later given the personal name Mica (764), is identical with the first orator[124] (though if the objector is a separate voice, then this could be her character). The woman who enters at 759 is set to guard the relative (763), and reveals her name at 898 to be Critylla; she remains on stage until 944, when the archer takes over her role. Sommerstein reads her back into the *ecclesia* scene as the announcer,[125] while Austin and Olson and Prato and Del Corno identify her with the Garland-Seller.[126] Rogers and Paduano, however, prefer to see her as a new character.[127] To sum up: the *ecclesia* scene might contain as many as three separate female speakers, assuming the *coryphaeus* takes the announcements and discussion with Cleisthenes; one of these speakers is revealed to be Cleonymus' wife (at 605) and is also later called Mica (764); Critylla (named at 898) may be a new character or reprise the Garland-Seller. However, discussion of the female roles in the play has always hitherto been based on the assumption that all the speakers are generic. The argument of this book and the findings on *Lysistrata* in particular suggest otherwise. Just as a small, but significant, group of real women were the targets of the earlier 411 play, so it is likely that many of the same circle were set up for ridicule in *Thesmophoriazusai*. My hypothesis impels the adoption of a procedure which subordinates consideration of the ascription of parts to that of the poet's satirical agenda.

However, the naming of Cleonymus' wife (605, 760) and Critylla (898) causes certain difficulties from whichever standpoint one approaches the play. Austin and Olson comment on Mica's late naming: 'The poet's decision to name this character (anonymous since her entrance at 294) only now, just before she exits for the final time at 764 is difficult to explain. But something similar occurs with Kritylla, who likewise enters at 294; is named at 898; and exits, never to return, at 944.'[128] Their remarks on

---

[123] For the first role Austin and Olson 2004, Prato and Del Corno 2001 favour the *coryphaeus*, but Sommerstein 1994 reads Critylla back from 898.
[124] Sommerstein 1994, Prato and Del Corno 2001 and Austin and Olson 2004 on line 380.
[125] Sommerstein 1994 on 295.
[126] Austin and Olson 2004 on 758–9, Prato and Del Corno 2001 on 759.
[127] Rogers 1920 on 760. Paduano 1983 n. 93 on line 758.
[128] Austin and Olson 2004 on 760–1.

her identification as Cleonymus' wife (605) make the issue more complex: 'Perhaps Mika's dominance of the women's debate (380–432), her eagerness to get the others to punish a member of their assembly whom she represents as a traitor to their cause (533–9, 544–8, 551–2), and her hot temper (566–8) are all reminiscent of Kleonymus' public behaviour, so that it is funny to identify her as his wife; or perhaps she too is simply immensely fat.'[129] The final remark is referenced across to 570 with its note, which reads: 'The 'Middle Day' of the Thesmophoria involved fasting... and the nasty implication of Inlaw's remark ['the sesame cake you gobbled up'] is that Mika has been snacking surreptitiously.'[130] Both of these notes contain important insights, but they tend to suggest that the audience will have to have recognised the individual behind the character long before her identity is forced from her by Cleisthenes. If that is the case, then the revelation of the name, like that of Dicaeopolis at *Acharnians* 406, will have a humorous impact based on a known relationship between Cleisthenes and Cleonymus' wife. Her reply to his question is indignant: ἔμ' ἥτις <εἴμ'> ἤρου; 'Are you asking *me* who I am?', and this might suggest that in the real world he would be supposed to know the answer. Since Cleisthenes is firmly associated with 'political women' both here (574f.) and at *Lysistrata* 620f., the best inference is that Cleonymus' wife was part of that group. The *formal* response she eventually gives Cleisthenes, then, is funny because he of all people should have known who she was and as a 'fellow-woman' (cf. 574f.) might have expected usually to call her by her first name. The use of that name, Mica, at 760, by Critylla, must also contain humour. It is probably correct to see its basis in the contrast between her size – fat – and the meaning of her name ('Tiny'). But it may also figure some humorous twist in the relationship between herself and Critylla in the real world, since my general argument will imply that Critylla will have been recognised (just as Cleonymus' wife was) as soon as she entered.

Critylla is named among Lysistrata's group of conspirators on the acropolis by the chorus (*Lys.* 323), so that it is possible she had achieved a public profile before *Thesmophoriazusai*. Again, however, we must pay attention to the precise context of the revelation of her name. The relative is playing Helen and Euripides Menelaus, while Critylla continually defuses their game by revealing the true situation. Her naming comes at the culmination of her frustration, when the relative answers Euripides' question about her identity (897) with the revelation that she is Theonoe, Proteus' daughter. What is unusual about the naming is that it occurs in front of

---

[129] Austin and Olson 2004 on 650.   [130] Austin and Olson 2004 on 570.

a man who is, apparently, not related to her. At any rate, Critylla does not recognise him as Euripides and addresses him as ξένε 'stranger' (882, 893, cf. 891), yet she still reveals her personal name, with her patronymic and her father's demotic (or her husband's name and his demotic): εἰ μὴ Κρίτυλλά γ' Ἀντιθέου Γαργηττόθεν 'actually it's Critylla daughter/wife of Antitheus of Gargettus'.[131] It has been suggested that Antitheus is simply a pun on Theonoe and that there may be something inherently amusing about Γαργηττόθεν ('from Gargettus'), if this was not his real deme.[132] However, there was an Antitheus (*PAA* 132995) associated with the Kydathenaion cult of Heracles to which Amphitheus also belonged (*IG* II² 2343) and some commentators have been tempted to identify this Antitheus with him.[133] That would on my earlier argument (see chapter 4, p. 136) draw Antitheus into the circle of Eupolis – and therefore, possibly, of Euripides. It has also been suggested that the Antitheus of the inscription was the brother of Amphitheus.[134] It would make it rather more likely that the genealogy offered by the latter at *Acharnians* 47f. is meant to be pseudo-Euripidean if there had in fact been some family relationship centring on Critylla between Antitheus and Amphitheus and Euripides. It is certainly tempting to see the humour of this scene generally as based upon the audience's recognition of a known relationship between Euripides and Critylla. Prior recognition of her by the audience would be the fuel required to make her frustrated revelation of her name – in *apparent* contravention of propriety – funny. If she was Antitheus' wife, she may have been Euripides' sister. If the daughter of Antitheus, she might even have been Euripides' wife. Either identification materially increases the amusement of the scene, while specifically explaining the humour of the late naming, and draws Euripides into a satirical battle which was quite the opposite of the one he was actually fighting with his recent *Helen* and *Andromeda*. It will be seen from this discussion that I marginally favour seeing Critylla as a new character. Perhaps, however, Sommerstein is right to infer from 759 that she was currently the priestess of the Thesmophoroi and this would account for her public profile (in much the same way as that of Lysimache and

---

[131] For the first, see Sommerstein 1994 on 898, for the second Austin and Olson 2004 on 897–8 (cf. 605).
[132] For the first suggestion, see Prato and Del Corno on 898, for the second Austin and Olson 2004 on 897–8. On (possibly) false demotics, see pp. 87–8 (on *Ach.* 406), pp. 206–7 (on *Peace* 918) and pp. 244, 246 above (on *Birds* 645).
[133] Dow 1969, 234–5, Olson 2002 on *Ach.* 46, Austin and Olson 2004 on *Thesm.* 897–8. Cf. Lind 1990, 132–41.
[134] See Olson 2002 on *Ach.* 46.

Myrrhine, caricatured in *Lysistrata*), in which case his inference that she participates in the *ecclesia* scene as 'herald' could be accepted.[135]

If Critylla does feature in the *ecclesia* scene, it follows that speaker A must be identical with Mica, Cleonymus' wife, since otherwise we have too many actors on stage. This solution, which is certainly plausible, focuses the attack on two women who will have been known to have close associations with male targets (Cleisthenes and Cleonymus on Mica's part and Euripides on Critylla's) who were in Eupolis' circle (cf. *Ach.* 118, 406). The unspoken charge of Laconophilia (cf. *Lys.* 323 and 620f.) lurks malevolently beneath the surface.

The garland-seller may be a metacomic figure, from a play in which Euripides' atheism was central to the plot (450–1; cf. *Frogs* 888f.). Note that she belongs to the market-sellers among whom the mother of Euripides was counted (cf. 456), as possibly also was the mother of Hyperbolus (in Eupolis' *Marikas* and Hermippus' *Artopolides*).[136] This does not necessarily imply, of course, that she does not also represent a real individual, and may in fact argue for it, given the strong possibility that a market occupation was a well-established way of satirising the mothers of important male citizens. However, her identity is impenetrable to us in the current state of the evidence, though it is worth noting that her symposium order (457–8) may have been understood from her identity and, possibly, from the specific number of adherents, to be for a meeting of a well-known – and presumably anti-democratic – *hetaireia*.

Thesmophoriazusai only appears to be non-political. On my reading, it attacks two known circles, that of Eupolis, Euripides, Agathon and Cleisthenes and the women's caucus to which Critylla and Cleonymus' wife belonged (probably the Lysimache group), by showing them together in a plot which simultaneously satirises the men's effeminacy (for which read philo-Laconism) and the women's attempt to make a decision which should belong to the (male) *demos* (for which read imitation of the – from the Athenian viewpoint – Laconian women's control over their menfolk, cf. *Lys.* 168–9, Arist. *Pol.* 1269b 13–1270a15). It is a good deal more circumspect, to be sure, than *Lysistrata*, and that probably does argue for its performance at the Dionysia rather than the Lenaea. By this time, Aristophanes will have known, like his fellow Athenians, that oligarchy was firmly on the march. He was not in this play attacking head on the leaders of that movement. Nonetheless, if my analysis of the reason for Eupolis' burial at Sicyon is correct, his main target was involved enough with the

---

[135] Sommerstein 1994 on 295.   [136] Storey 2003, 204–5.

conspirators – more probably Phrynichus than Peisander, and because of political actions rather than his comedies – to merit disenfranchisement once the democratic government was re-established.

EUPOLIS' *DEMOI*

Storey's early date (417 or 416) is proposed 'principally because it allows the demagogue of fr. 99.23–4 to be Hyperbolus and the reference to Mantineia [fr. 99.30] to be an allusion to something recent and topical, rather than an event over five years in the past.'[137] Telò has recently re-examined the dating indications for this play and concluded, on the basis mainly of arguments linking fr. 99.12–3 to an episode recounted by Thucydides (8.71.1–2), that June 411 is the *terminus post quem* and that the comedy probably belongs to the Lenaea of 410.[138] Telò has in this context also effectively countered the arguments of Storey for earlier demagogues at fr. 99.23–4 (Hyperbolus and Alcibiades in particular), even if his case against Hyperbolus is *a priori* from his new dating, and refocused attention upon the strength of the case for Cleophon.[139] There are, I think, reasons beyond these considerations to agree with this new dating, though naturally given the argument up to this point, I shall be offering a rather different view of the play's purpose from that presented by Telò ('consolidation of the democratic order of the polis').[140] This is both because the so-called 'comic hero', Pyronides, is likely to be a satirical *portavoce* for a real individual under attack, and because Eupolis was in my view never interested in promoting the democratic ideology. But it is also because, as in the case of other fragmentary plays by Eupolis, there are signs of metacomedy within the lacunose material upon which we must perforce base our judgements. Like much of what we have been examining, then, the *Demoi* is not what it looks like on the surface.

The evidence of Platonius (Koster, *Prolegomena* p. 6, II.8–12), who uses *Demoi* to illustrate the seriousness of Eupolis' comedy, is important, but,

---

[137] Storey 2003, 114. See 149–60 on the demagogue of fr. 99.23–4. This is not, given the propensity for metacomedy, a clinching argument. Cf. Labes/Laches' trial in *Wasps* of 422 relating to events no later than 425 (see chapter five).

[138] Telò 2007, 16–24. The central arguments are (a) a linguistic one: ἐν in the phrase τοὺς ἐν μακροῖν τειχοῖν does not have the same value as when the noun phrase is singular and so cannot mean 'those *within* the long walls', but must rather imply 'those *on* the long walls', thus referring not to the populus squeezed into the city (either because they stayed after the end of the war or because they came in again after Decelea was fortified in 413), but to soldiers defending the walls against a specific attack (the one mentioned in Thuc. 8.71.1); (b) political: the scornful treatment of the people within the walls would contradict the 'ideological unity' of the choral voice (Telò 2007, 350).

[139] Telò 2007, 397–401.   [140] Telò 2007, 78: 'consolidamento dell'ordine democratico della πόλις'.

as I argued in chapter three (pp. 58–60) misunderstood. It implies that it was characteristic of Eupolis to *appear on-stage* in his plays. The very way in which the example of *Demoi* is expressed appears to justify this interpretation. For, quite uniquely in this sort of text, it is the poet himself who is said ἀναγαγεῖν ἱκανὸς ὢν ἐξ Ἅιδου νομοθετῶν πρόσωπα καὶ δι' αὐτῶν εἰσηγούμενος ἢ περὶ θέσεως νόμων ἢ καταλύσεως 'to be capable of bringing back from Hades the personages of lawgivers and through them giving advice about the making or repealing of laws'. Platonius appears to be saying, then, that in several of his comedies, including *Demoi*, Eupolis appeared as a character. This is an inference, I have argued above, that certainly seems to have been made about Eupolis by other ancient scholars in respect of other plays, for example, by Apsines (*Rhetoric* 3) and Aelian (*NA* 10.41), probably from Eupolis' *Autolycus*. And it is worth noting that though the type of formulation which definitely identifies the poet as a speaker of lines in the play is not especially common in the scholia, of four clear occurrences that I have noted, two come from *Demoi*, Eupolis fr. 102 and fr. 115 (the others are Eup. fr. 269 from *Taxiarchoi* and Hermippus fr. 36 from *Kerkopes*). There are problems with the way Plutarch introduces fr. 115,[141] but the scholium to Aelius Aristides 3.51 is unequivocal in identifying Eupolis as the *speaker* of fr. 102: Εὔπολις ἐν τοῖς Δήμοις μεμνημένος Περικλέους τούτους φησὶ τοὺς ἰάμβους 'In the *Demoi* Eupolis, referring to Pericles, speaks these iambic lines.'

[141] Plutarch's formulation as he cites fr. 115 at *Per.* 3.4 is curious: ὁ δ' Εὔπολις ἐν τοῖς Δήμοις πυνθανόμενος περὶ ἑκάστου τῶν ἀνεβεβηκότων ἐξ Ἅιδου δημαγωγῶν, ὡς ὁ Περικλέης ἐξωνομάσθη τελευταῖος 'ὅ τι περ κεφάλαιον τῶν κάτωθεν ἤγαγες' 'Eupolis in his *Demoi*, putting questions about each of the demagogues who have come up from Hades, [says] that Pericles was named last – "You have brought from the dead your crowning achievement" (tr. Storey). It sounds as though for some reason here Plutarch saw Eupolis as a *character* in the play, since πυνθανόμενος does not mean, as the Loeb translator (no doubt seeing the problem) has it, 'having enquiries made', but 'making enquiries'. One would not hesitate to blame sloppy writing here were it not for the fact that later, at 24.16, when he cites fr. 110, Plutarch says περὶ οὗ πεποίηκεν Εὔπολις ἐν Δήμοις αὐτὸν μὲν οὕτως ἐρωτῶντα... τὸν δὲ Πυρωνίδην ἀποκρινόμενον '[Pericles' bastard son] about whom Eupolis has represented Pericles as enquiring in his *Demoi*... and Pyronides replying', where his knowledge of the play and his identification of the characters support the inference I have offered from 3.4, that Plutarch thought Eupolis was a character in the play. If, however, Plutarch does imply a comic poet's presence as a character, he does not identify him with Pyronides (see Plut. *Per.* 24.16), since it is Pyronides who must be addressed (cf. ἤγαγες 'you've brought back'). He might, perhaps, be seen in Storey's putative companion for Pyronides, though Telò makes strong arguments against the existence of such a character (Storey 2003, 119–21; Telò 2007, 71). But the speaker is much more likely to be the coryphaeus, given the context of fr. 99.64f. (note especially line 73 πυνθάνῃ 'you ask me', probably spoken by Pyronides: Telò 2007, 462.). Of course, one might argue instead that there is something missing in Plutarch and the text has been adjusted to compensate (for example πυνθανομένο<υ τοῦ Εὐγείτονος> 'when Eugeiton asks' before περὶ etc. and <πεποίηκεν τὸν Πυρωνίδην λέγοντα> '[Eupolis] has shown Pyronides saying' before ὡς). This type of solution is probably best: the theory evidenced by Platonius and utilised by Lucian was thus an alternative tradition, not shared by Plutarch.

Strong support is offered to this reading of Platonius, as I have already noted, by a later imitator of Old Comedy (and of Eupolis in particular), Lucian (see *Bis Acc.* 33, cf. *Piscator* 25), who appears to have made use of *Demoi*, a play he clearly knew (he cites fr. 102 at *Demonax* 10, and uses it at *Nigrinus* 7; cf. [Luc.] *Dem. Enc.* 20). His *Piscator* or *Reviviscentes* has the ancient philosophers arriving back on earth specifically to get their own back on Lucian (presented in disguise: see below) for what he wrote about them in his *Sale of Lives*.[142] Lucian persuades them to allow the judgement to be made by Philosophy herself and her entourage, and a courtroom scene unfolds in which he is able successfully to refute the charges brought against him by Diogenes on the others' behalf, arguing that he was actually attacking false philosophers. Just as Lucian uses Cratinus' *Pytine* in the *Bis Accusatus* as a crucial intertext for an audience he wishes to convince of the validity of his crossing of philosophy with comedy, so he may have been using Eupolis' *Demoi* in *Piscator* to underline once more his unique combination. But as in *Pytine* this could only operate because the ancients saw the comedy as a literary *defence* by the author (since Cratinus was understood to be the comic poet of the play), so the use of *Demoi* also implies that Eupolis was perceived as having had a stage role there and hence was producing a form of *defence* of his serious comic views. Two further relationships between *Piscator* and *Demoi* appear to confirm that this is the intertext Lucian is using to prop up his satirical, but serious, self-presentation. At one point (*Piscator* 30) he calls the philosophers νομοθετὰς ('lawgivers') and since this is an apter description of the central figures in *Demoi* than it is of the angry philosophers, it seems that it is serving as an intertextual signal. Moreover, when Lucian gives his name, it is *Parrhesiades*, which is formed the same way and even sounds rather like *Pyronides*. That this is not pure chance is suggested by the fact that in *Bis Accusatus* he uses the simple ethnic locution 'the Syrian' instead of any sort of name (*Bis Accusatus* 15).

The evidence of Platonius and Lucian – and the seriousness with which the play was received in antiquity – tends to support the inference of a comic poet on stage, naturally identified in antiquity with the author. Note that the implication of Lucian's choice of name for himself in *Piscator* and of Platonius' description of the plot of *Demoi* is that Eupolis played the leading role. It is not implausible to suggest that the perceived message

---

[142] Note that Diogenes is forced (*Piscator* 25) to differentiate the attacks made on Socrates in particular by Aristophanes and Eupolis from those made by Lucian, but in doing so only serves to reinforce the intertextual relationships between the three writers. For Eupolidean *named* attacks on Socrates see frr. 386 and 395 K-A and the scholium on *Clouds* 96.

of the play may have been drawn down most easily had the apparent interventions by the 'author' been in the mouth of Pyronides, since thus the whole notion of the 'Great Idea' of saving the city by recourse to the restoration of the *patrios politeia* could easily be ascribed to the author (in the way that Dicaeopolis' peace plan has been foisted on Aristophanes).

If this is correct, however, on my argument the character could not represent Eupolis, but would have to represent a rival poet. I have already suggested that Aristophanes may well have attacked Eupolis ironically for his original support of Pericles' war policy (in *Acharnians* 530f. and *Peace* 606f.). So Eupolis now brings Pericles face to face with Aristophanes/Pyronides in an ironic confrontation between a 'radical democrat' and a *real* democrat. This identification helps to explain the rude way in which Pyronides treats the great man.

Pyronides is almost certainly the main speaker of fr. 102 and the interlocutor of fr.110.[143] Both of these fragments, however, concern Pericles, whom Storey appears to think comes out of the play well.[144] Telò notes some of the undercurrents which I shall now examine, but plays them down.[145] In fr. 110, in response to Pericles' enquiry about his bastard son, Pyronides replies: καὶ πάλαι γ' ἂν ἦν ἀνήρ, | εἰ μὴ τὸ τῆς πόρνης ὑπορρώδει κακόν ('Yes [he is alive] and he would have been a man long ago, if he weren't so afraid of that evil whore'). If that looks like plain old-fashioned ridicule (for to speak of Aspasia thus is also to demean Pericles, as Cratinus well knew: cf. Cratin. fr. 259), there is ambivalence also in the other passages. The exchange between the characters about Pericles' oratory (fr. 102 as divided by K-A) has the praiser interrupted after his first description by the comment ταχὺν λέγεις γε 'You mean he spoke quickly.' Speed of delivery is a good quality in an orator, but the interruption is surely meant to raise a laugh, and the implication could be 'too quickly' (cf. Aristophanes' description of Cratinus' music at *Ach.* 851), because Pyronides goes on to agree but also amplify his opening statement.[146] What follows – the famous image of persuasion sitting on his lips and the sting he left in his audience – while on the surface again very complimentary contains the seeds of its own refutation, since πειθώ was by no means always a positive force (cf. Xen. *Mem.* 1.7.5, where it is part of a strategy of deceit) and a sting almost by definition is harmful to the person affected (cf. *Ach.*

---

[143] Telò 2007, 171–2, 212–13.
[144] Storey 2003, 133 lists the *aretai* associated with each of the resuscitated leaders. For Pericles, it is 'political leadership'.
[145] Telò 2007, 95–102.   [146] Telò 2007, 187.

376, *Wasps* 225f. etc.).[147] Indeed, as Telò admits, the earliest reception of Eupolis' famous 'eulogy' comes in Plato's *Phd.* 91c, where Socrates says: μὴ ἐγὼ ὑπὸ προθυμίας ἅμα ἐμαυτόν τε καὶ ὑμᾶς ἐξαπατήσας, ὥσπερ μέλιττα τὸ κέντρον ἐγκαταλιπὼν οἰχήσομαι 'in case in my eagerness I end up deceiving both myself and you, leaving my sting behind like a bee'. Telò remarks: 'The strongly negative force of the image in the Platonic text will conceal an implicit polemic against the Eupolidean encomium of the statesman.'[148] On my earlier argument, that Eupolis was a member of the Socratic circle but also an early supporter of Pericles' war policy, the Platonic polemic more likely reveals the underlying satire aimed here by Pyronides against Pericles. When Pericles is addressed along with Miltiades in fr. 104, the context – asking the dead generals not to allow ἄρχειν μειράκια κινούμενα | ἐν τοῖν σφυροῖν ἕλκοντα τὴν στρατηγίαν 'these young bum-boys to hold office, who pull the generalship down around their ankles' – once more undercuts Pericles, if Storey is correct in seeing a specific allusion to Alcibiades here (a proposition with which Telò agrees), since he will be being asked to prevent his own foster-child from holding military office.[149] The use of the word κεφάλαιον in fr. 115 may look innocent, but it contains a joke at the expense of Pericles' well-known strange head shape (cf. again Cratinus' κεφεληγερέταν 'head-gatherer' fr. 258.4).[150]

Identification of Pyronides as the author would help to explain why the underlying negative view was missed in his interactions with Pericles. Aristophanes would have made a good on-stage target at a time when his known frustration with the current state of affairs in Athens might have made risible his fantasy solution of bringing back to 'save the city' the great heroes of the democracy (Solon the ultimate inventor of democracy, Miltiades its mightiest military hero, Aristides the initiator of radical reform and Pericles the radical democrat who was – in Eupolis' eyes at any rate – the most recent great political leader). Aristophanes' radical democratic ideological posture could be ridiculed by the device of having him bring back his great democratic leaders from the past, only to find that they are shocked and disgusted by the type of leaders the audience will know Aristophanes himself supports. If, like Aristophanes, Eupolis was indulging in an ironic game at his rival's expense, Telò's date of Lenaea 410, during the rule of the 5,000, is plausible, and deserves serious consideration.

---

[147] See further Buxton 1982.
[148] Telò 2007, 197 n. 47: 'La valenza fortemente negativa di cui si carica l'immagine nel testo platonico nasconderà... proprio un' implicita polemica contro l'encomio eupolideo dello statista.'
[149] Storey 2003, 114 and 136. Telò 2007, 257.   [150] Telò 2007, 459.

A very great part of what will have been amusing here, then, is provided solely by the political and ideological context of the period during which the democracy was suspended. But, as I have mentioned, I strongly suspect that it was the butts of these apparently friendly resuscitated pro-democratic leaders – the sycophant, the adulterer, possibly the demagogue Demostratus and the generals Laespodias and Damasias – who will have caused the greatest comic sensation.[151] As in Aristophanes antagonists of the 'hero' will most often have been, in reality, his friends (e.g. Lamachus in *Acharnians*), so here, these on-stage targets will surely have been political *friends* of the bald fellow, and to his chagrin the leaders he thought his allies will have savaged them in their new legislation and made the would-be reviver of the radical democracy rue the day he brought them back.

Telò's recent treatment of the iconography of the Pontecagnano vase which illustrates the cover of this book allows us a closer look at another satirical hit at Pyronides/Aristophanes.[152] His view is that the 'hero' encounters Phrynis in the Underworld and that fr. 121 is spoken after he hears him play (cf. *Frogs* 1284–95, where Euripides plays the lyre and 1325f. where Aeschylus criticises his playing). It is part of the scene, whose climax is shown on the vase by Asteas, in which Pyronides attempts to persuade Phrynis to join his expedition to Athens. As the vase-painting shows, however, Phrynis resists forcefully. Telò ascribes Pyronides' desire to resuscitate Phrynis to a conservative agenda, somewhat bizarrely, given that he was the first of the 'new musicians' criticised for their rape of Music in the famous Pherecrates fragment (155 K-A). It seems much more likely that, as in the case of the four leaders, it is personal predilection which leads Pyronides to try to bring him back (as well as, it seems, some apparent linkage of music with his political agenda). The only mention of Phrynis in Aristophanes is at *Clouds* 971, which is critical. But it is put in the mouth of Stronger Argument, who on my argument represents Cratinus. The critique, then, is focalised on Cratinus' character and this says nothing about Aristophanes' own feelings. I conclude that Eupolis chose to have a scene in the Underworld with Phrynis because Aristophanes was known to have liked his cithara-playing or even to have been a friend of his.[153] The satirical amusement of the episode, then, comes from Phrynis' refusal to help out an admirer.

The implication of my argument, of course, is that Asteas' painting contains a representation – at some remove – of Aristophanes. By the

---

[151] See Telò 2007, 72 for this list.
[152] Telò 2007, 28–33, with the commentary on fr. 121 K-A at 285–90.
[153] For Phrynis' dates, see Telò 2007, 29 with n. 70.

time Asteas painted this in Paestum in the mid-fourth century, however, the original costuming and target will have been long forgotten. The iconography will probably represent comic costuming recalled from his – or his teacher's – days in Syracuse. But it seems unlikely that he will have seen an Athenian Old Comedy revived even there. Rather, like other South Italian painters of Old Comic scenes, he is more likely to have been fulfilling a commission from an ex-patriate Athenian who for some reason or other wanted a version of the scene for his dining-room.[154]

That Lenaea 410 would be an altogether more appropriate moment at which the pro-oligarchical Eupolis might make fun of his radical democratic rival will be clear. Turning the ironic tables upon the attack made in *Birds* upon him and his circle, Eupolis will here have shown a desperate Aristophanes heading for Hades to bring back the doyens of radical democracy. Perhaps he will even have individualised the Demes in retaliation for Aristophanes' personalised assault on Eupolis' own circle in that play's chorus. The hare-brained utopian scheme of the 414 comedy will then be the target of the equally mad enterprise of reviving the dead democratic statesmen. If Euelpides had represented Eupolis, then his revenge will have been instantiated in the figure of Pyronides/Aristophanes.

In that case, much of the irony will also be generated by the representation of the chorus, which as Telò has argued, *contra* Storey, embodies the *demos*,[155] and yet expresses strongly anti-demagogic opinions in the epirrhematic sequence which survives as fr. 99.1–34. Exactly this type of ironic chorus, often apparently 'borrowed' from another poet, is now familiar to us from Aristophanic comedies such as *Acharnians* and *Lysistrata*.

That the chorus is intended as an ironic counterweight to the ideology of Pyronides/Aristophanes might gain some support by reconsideration of the text of fr. 99.29, where of the vilified demagogue it is said: ταῖς στρατηγίαις δ' ὑφέρπει καὶ τρυγῳδο [–υ–, which Storey translates as 'He sneaks around the generalships and . . . the comic poets'. He favours interpreting ὑφέρπει as 'attacks', because what follows relates to this theme, and prefers to read a second verb τρυγῳδεῖ with Jensen's τοὺς θεούς or τὴν πόλιν 'and he mocks the gods/the city'. However, Storey does remark that Aristophanes' use of the synonym κωμῳδεῖν usually has the comic poet as subject and the best guess of the editors of the fragment is that the final letter is o.[156] These considerations have led most scholars to look for some form of the word τρυγῳδός plus a verb of which it is the

---

[154] For a good treatment of the Paestan comic scenes see Hughes 2003.
[155] Telò 2007, 61–7. Storey 2003, 124f. with 391f. suggests they are the country towns only.
[156] Storey 2003, 152–3. Cf. Telò 2007, 385–6.

object. Variations on this theme are offered by van Leeuwen (τρυγῳδοῖς μέμφεται 'he blames the comic poets'), Jensen (τρυγῳδοὺς ζημιοῖ 'he fines the comic poets'), and Luppe (τρυγῳδοὺς λοιδορεῖ 'he mocks the comic poets'). However, their underlying assumption, that the demagogue is an *opponent* of the comic poets here, derived as it is from the (I have argued, false) comparison with Cleon and Aristophanes (inferred from *Acharnians* 377f.), may be mistaken. Telò has recently argued convincingly that ὑφέρπει means 'ingratiates himself with'.[157] Why can Eupolis, then, not be accusing this demagogue of *sucking up to* bad comic poets, just as he does to the generals? A supplement such as τρυγῳδοὺς εὐλογεῖ 'he praises low-grade comic poets' (cf. *Knights* 565) would give this sense. Whoever the mystery demagogue is here, then, the added point will be that while he ingratiates himself with the generals (probably because he wants the war to continue), he is also firm friends with Aristophanes, the on-stage target of the play's satire.

Once the *catabasis* had been used for an attack on a comic poet, it could naturally be reappropriated for revenge. Another reason why we perhaps ought to take the new dating seriously is that after the restoration of democracy in summer 410, we have not one, but two Aristophanic comedies with this theme, the *Gerytades*, probably 408, and *Frogs* of 406. We cannot say much that is useful about *Gerytades*, of which we possess only thirty-five fragments, plus nine other 'possibles'.[158] But *Frogs* is a different matter. As I have shown above, it has several specifically Eupolidean aspects. But it also can now be seen to echo quite specifically both the plot-line and the satirical structure of *Demoi* (as well as some details, such as the conversation about the uselessness of contemporary Athenians: cf. *Demoi* fr. 102, 103, 116 on orators with *Frogs* 71f., where Dionysus and Heracles talk about tragic poets). This will have been an act of revenge, in which in like manner to *Demoi*, the poet himself was put on stage attempting – and failing to achieve – a solution to Athens' problems which suited his own political ideology.

FROGS

After *Clouds II*, Aristophanes seems, in the extant plays at any rate, to have moved once more away from the type of parabasis in which he gave – in first or third person – comment upon his own comic agenda and criticism

---

[157] Telò 2007, 380–6.
[158] K-A 156–190. Possibles are: frr. 128, 591, 595, 596, 598, 623, 696, 720, *CGFP* 226.

of that of his rivals. In *Birds*, *Lysistrata* and *Thesmophoriazusai*, the chorus remains in character, but also seems to adopt postures which contradict Aristophanes' own (e.g. the rejection of Prodicus' views at *Birds* 692; the praise of Lamachus and attack on Hyperbolus at *Thesm*. 840–1), and they ridicule themselves (for instance the removal of clothes by men and women at *Lys.* 615,637, 662 and 686). Exactly the same tactic is visible in *Frogs*. The chorus of *mystai* remains in character for its famous call for the re-enfranchisement of those not exiled but disfranchised after the restoration of democracy in the wake of the revolution of 411 (674, 686), and nowhere in the two epirrhemes does it purport to speak for the poet himself, but rather always refers to itself as the originator of the thoughts (687, 690, 692, 695–6, 718). This contrasts firmly with the involvement of the poet himself in *Acharnians*, *Knights*, *Wasps*, *Peace* and *Clouds*. Moreover, the chorus makes clear at 357 its allegiance to the comic style of Cratinus, which cannot but be ironic, given the battle fought between that dramatist and Aristophanes in the 420s (cf. *Ach.* 850–3, 1173; *Knights* 400, 526f.; the ironic reference at *Peace* 700; Cratin. fr. 213 *Pytine*). Like other metacomic aspects of the *Frogs*, then, the quasi-parabatic passage at 354f. (which is in the anapaestic metre often associated with the parabasis), and the epirrhematic parabasis (674–737, formally speaking a *second parabasis*, since it has no anapaests), are part of a ventriloquial attack upon a comic rival, similar to those in *Knights* and *Wasps*.

It is worth considering for a moment how this irony might have been made clear to the original audience, since the parabasis is for the most part taken at face value by scholars as serious political advice.[159] First, it is important to note that the chorus is probably dressed in rags (404f.).[160] Part of the point will presumably be to replicate the actual look of initiates. But it is worth mentioning that in a play which has begun with the search for Euripides (66f.), it is perhaps not insignificant that one of the things thought characteristic of his tragedies in Aristophanic comedy was the clothing of characters (kings, usually) in rags (*Ach.* 412f.; cf. *Frogs* 1063–4). In most scholars' treatments of the problematic doublets at 1422–60, it is Euripides who agrees with the chorus' political agenda (1446–8) – a view which coincides with my reconstruction of the basis for the attack on Euripides in *Thesmophoriazusai* (and even earlier, in *Acharnians*).[161] The audience would not, then, have had to wait until Euripides spoke to see

---

[159] E.g. Heath 1987, 19–20, Arnott 1991, Dover 1993, 73–4, Sommerstein 1996a, 13–14.
[160] Dover 1993 ad loc.
[161] See Dover 1993, 373–5 for arguments supporting the ascription of these lines to Aeschylus. I agree with Sommerstein's counter arguments (1996a on 1442–50). See Goldhill 1991, 218–19 for the

the way the wind was blowing, since the chorus' physical appearance may have trumpeted their complicity with him from the very start. We must also remember here that the scholium on *Peace* 740 (= Eup. fr. 400) takes Aristophanes to be criticising Eupolis ὡς εἰσάγοντα ῥακοφοροῦντας 'for bringing on stage people dressed in rags'. Secondly, it is possible that Aristophanes made at least some members of the chorus – perhaps the *coryphaeus* of each semi-chorus (one man and one woman, if the chorus was split)[162] – recognisable by their masks. This would have given him the opportunity to continue the satire of the women's group which had fuelled his annoyance in 411 and to target specific individuals who either were among the exiles or were – in his view – their advocates in the city. I have argued for something like this individualisation in *Birds*. It would have been a parodic rejoinder to the depiction of individual cities in Eupolis' *Poleis* (fr. 244–7), of semi-choruses of rich and poor men in *Marikas* (fr. 193, cf. fr. 192.186 and 98f., 117, 118, 120) and possibly of individuals in *Demoi*. Such a presentation would have left the audience in absolutely no doubt, right from the parodos, of Aristophanes' intention to *ridicule* the idea that the re-enfranchisement of the oligarchs was the answer to the city's current dilemma.

The rival under attack was, once again, Eupolis. Not only do we find in this play what I have argued (chapter two) are the specific markers of metacomic attack upon him (torches, cries of ἰοὺ ἰού, an old man beating someone with a stick, a hungry Heracles), but there are also quite specifically Eupolidean ideas, scenes and language in it (raising the dead to help the city, cf. Eupolis *Demoi*; the rowing-scene at 197f., cf. Eupolis *Taxiarchoi* frs. 268, 269, 272, 274 ; line 734, cf. Eupolis fr. 392; line 1400, cf. Eupolis fr. 372; perhaps line 1036, cf. Eupolis fr. 318). Soon after the beginning, jokes are made which link Dionysus with the effete Cleisthenes (48, 57), an individual satirised alongside Eupolis (as Euripides' relative) in *Thesmophoriazusai*, and Dionysus is also said to be close to Agathon (83), another on-stage figure of fun in that play. Moreover, the specific mise-en-scène, a descent to Hades to locate a tragic poet, the key to which is Dionysus' desire for Euripides (66–7), suits Eupolis well, if he was related to Euripides, and if he was satirised by Cratinus (fr. 342), as also by Aristophanes (in *Thesm.*), as incapable of writing his comedies without Euripidean help (cf. Dionysus' identification with Euripidean writing at 1228: ἵνα μὴ διακναίσῃ τοὺς προλόγους ἡμῶν 'so that he won't grate up *our* prologues'). It well

---

problem of whether or not the losing contestant's support for the chorus undercuts the seriousness of their advice.
[162] On this question see Dover 1993, 63–9, Sommerstein 1996a, 184 (on 323–49).

ridicules such an individual to have him decide – on political grounds – against Euripides' resuscitation and for that of Aeschylus, a poet who had been used by Eupolis to ridicule Hyperbolus (fr. 207: *Persians*) and possibly Hierocles (fr. 231: *Seven Against Thebes*). It has been argued earlier (pp. 142–3) that Eupolis had put Cratinus on stage (in *Taxiarchoi*) as a Dionysus who was set to learn the military arts from Phormio (an identification which is also made by *Frogs* 357) and that Aristophanes had used this scenario in *Babylonians* (cross-referencing *Ach.* 372 with *Babylonians* fr. 75). Now he revives that early caricature of Cratinus as Dionysus and links it with the Cratinus/Eupolis of *Acharnians* and *Peace* generally to rebut the idea – clearly current in the politics of the city, to judge from the passing of the decree of Patrocleides not long after the play's first performance – that the city needs its former oligarchs and specifically that Eupolis might be re-enfranchised along with the others involved with Phrynichus in that plot. Aristophanes seems to have succeeded – at least ultimately – in the latter but not the former aim: Eupolis, as argued above, died and was buried, in exile, at Sicyon, having thrown his lot in with the Thirty Tyrants and fled there after their fall. The Socratic associations of some of them and the satire of Theramenes at 540f. and especially at 967–70, where he is condemned by Dionysus/Eupolis, may point in this direction, as may Eupolis' association with the Knights (*Clouds* 545), a body which had supported the oligarchic revolution of 411 (Thuc. 8.92.6) and had played an intimate role in sustaining the rule of the Thirty (Xen. *Hell.* 2.4.2, 4, 7, 8, 24, 31, Lysias 16.6).

That the central figure best suits a comic poet seems to emerge also from the opening scene, in which lines 1–20 make play with criticism of the bad comic techniques of rivals (Phrynichus, Lycis and Ameipsias 13–14) while exhibiting precisely those techniques themselves.[163] This is analogous to the dissonance between the parabasis of *Clouds* (537–44) and scenes in the play which use the tropes criticised there. However, in *Clouds* (and one might add *Peace*), the criticism is voiced on behalf of or by the poet himself, and the dissonance is (I have argued) an indication that those scenes are metacomic and intended to satirise a specific poet's specific material. Here, by contrast, it is the characters in the play who are involved in playing out the dissonance and the author – Aristophanes – is nowhere to be seen. The humour of the scene, then, arises from the gap between the pretension and inadequacy of the individual who is being satirised in the role of Dionysus: he claims to know what good comedy is but is incapable

---

[163] As often noted by scholars, for example Sommerstein 1996a, 157 on 1–20.

of avoiding its opposite. This joke of course would require the audience's immediate recognition of Dionysus as Eupolis, but given the longevity of this battle, even the five-year gap since *Thesmophoriazusai* (if there was not some further contribution in between which we have lost: see below Appendix 2, pp. 339–40 on *Wealth*) would not have made the point obscure to an audience who had been witnessing the poets' war for twenty years by this time.

There is a case to be made, in fact, for regarding the whole play as made up from such metacomic scenes, the point of which is the ridicule attracted by Dionysus/Eupolis from participation in what he (or Cratinus) had originally written. Xanthias appears on stage in four earlier plays which, I have argued, involve Cratinean and Eupolidean metacomedy (*Ach.* 243, 259, *Clouds* 1485, *Wasps* 1f., *Birds* 656), though it is not possible to say whether the point is that a particular individual is always being caricatured or something else. The hungry Heracles, criticised at *Wasps* 60 and *Peace* 741 and linked by the scholium on the latter passage to Eupolis and Cratinus, was also an on-stage character in *Birds* (1565f.), no doubt representing an individual whose presence would satirise the target poet.[164] In the Aeacus scene, no doubt the old man who beats Xanthias and Dionysus with a whip (cf. *Clouds* 541–2, and note that Xanthias suggests the ὑστριχίς 'bristle-whip' which features in a criticism of rival comic practice involving slaves getting beaten at *Peace* 746) also represented a recognisable individual whose presence would have given a satiric *frisson* to the ridicule of Dionysus/Eupolis. However, the best example is the rowing-scene, which is now generally accepted to be connected with Eupolis' *Taxiarchoi*, where Dionysus learned naval tactics from Phormio (Σ *Peace* 348, Eupolis frs. 268.53, 269, 272, 274).[165] Sommerstein has suggested that this scene in turn looked back to Cratinus' *Odysses*, where the parodos seems to have been managed in an oared ship (fr. 143, cf. fr. 152).[166] Reinterpretation of these connections on the basis of metacomic satire will involve positing at each point an on-stage caricature figure attacked by the misappropriation of the comic idea. Just as in the case of Eupolis' *Taxiarchoi*, it was argued that Dionysus represented Cratinus (*PCG* IV, Cratinus T15), possibly subverting (among other things) the parodos of his *Odysses*, so in *Frogs* Dionysus represents the poet Eupolis,

---

[164] See my earlier suggestion (p. 250) that Heracles represented Cleonymus. I doubt that this individual could have represented Callias, who is mentioned as a Heracles-imitator at *Frogs* 428–30 (and possibly also at 501; see Sommerstein 1996a ad loc.) and was the main on-stage target of Eup. *Kolakes* of 421, because he may have been a friend of Aristophanes', as the protector of Prodicus and others of the σοφοί who were his patrons (*Clouds* 526, *Wasps* 1049).

[165] Wilson 1974, Dover 1993, Slater 2002, 186–7, 306 n. 22, Storey 2003 256–7.

[166] Sommerstein 1996a, 11 n.49.

acting in a subverted version of his earlier scene with Phormio. The joke will have required, though, an equal and opposite substitution of Phormio with another dead general to have maximum satiric impact. I suggested earlier that Aristophanes in *Acharnians* substituted Lamachus as a Polemos figure for Phormio's Ares (his nickname at Eupolis *Taxiarchoi* fr.268.13–16), possibly following Cratinus' *Horai*. Lamachus would certainly make a good Charon, if I am right in suggesting that he was in fact a close associate of Eupolis. Such a role would suit – satirically speaking – a former naval general (Plut. *Per.* 20, Thuc. 4.75) who was now dead (Thuc. 6.101.6). If this or something like it does represent the metacomic satirical shape of the rowing-scene, then by extension we ought probably to infer that the Frog chorus has its origin also in parody of either Eupolis' *Taxiarchoi* or the parodos of Cratinus' *Odysses*. A mere suggestion will have been enough, perhaps a chance remark by the chorus or by Phormio about the way the rowers can take their time from the song of the swans: this would at any rate explain the very strange formulation of Charon at 207 βατράχων κύκνων 'of frog swans'. As in *Acharnians*, then, the encounters of Dionysus with the Corpse, Persephone's Maid, Plathane and the Innkeeper, and Pluto, and that of Xanthias with Pluto's slave, will all also have operated on a matrix which involved on-stage caricatures interacting with metacomic reference, even if we can not now offer identifications of either reference-point.

The caricature of Euripides has, of course, two major antecedents in Aristophanes, in *Acharnians* and *Thesmophoriazusai*. It has been argued above (pp. 139 and 266), however, that in both cases the caricature owes its origin to Cratinus (probably in his *Idaioi*) and is used as a way of ridiculing Eupolis who, as I have hypothesised, must have been a friend of or closely related to the tragic poet. As I have already said, things will be no different here and the very basis of the plot will have been centred upon the desire to make Eupolis look foolish by having him renege on his promise to Euripides and choose as the city's saviour another poet, whose selection will have inherent comic potential.

The situation with Aeschylus, however, is by no means clear. First of all, he had been dead for about fifty years by the time of *Frogs*, so that few of the audience can have been expected to have had experience of him as a real individual rather than as a name attached to revivals of his tragedies (cf. 868, *Life of Aeschylus* 12, Philostr. *Life of Apollonius* 6.11).[167] Secondly, the only clear evidence we have of a previous on-stage caricature

---

[167] Sommerstein 1996a on 868 suggests that Plato's use of Aeschylus (the only poet named and quoted apart from Homer) in the discussion of poetry and education in the *Republic* may be due to Aeschylus' prominence already in fifth-century education. But *Ach.* 9–11 shows that we are dealing

of the poet belongs to Pherecrates' *Krapataloi*, of unknown date (though his victories at both festivals predate those of Eupolis).[168] Thirdly, though, the contrast between Aeschylus and Euripides was already familiar to the audience of *Frogs* from *Clouds* 1364f. (if this was part of the 423 text as well), where Strepsiades/Alcibiades asks Pheidippides/Phaeax to recite some Aeschylus but is rebuffed and has to put up with Euripides instead; and it may even form part of the metacomic background (in which case *Frogs* is also recalling more generally an earlier comic scenario). Fourthly, the character who expresses delight in the anticipation of seeing an Aeschylus play is the Cratinus-figure played by Eupolis at *Acharnians* 9–11 (and Dionysus/Eupolis tells Pluto at *Frogs* 1411–13 ἄνδρες φίλοι 'the men are my friends'). But it is likely that Cratinus had parodied Aeschylus at least in his *Eumenides*.[169] Fifthly, the *détente* between Aeschylus and Sophocles made clear by 788f., and the positive attitude to Sophocles expressed by Heracles at 76–7 and Dionysus at 82, chime in with *Peace*'s question about him at *Peace* 695 and Trygaeus/Eupolis' mention of his lyrics at 531, which is immediately followed by a positive reference to Euripides. Trygaeus' answer at 696f. may, in the light of all this, be *para prosdokian* and involve a metacomic reference to an on-stage Sophocles satirised for greed. Sixthly, the possibility that the *proboulos* of *Lysistrata* represented Sophocles, argued above, would suggest that the negative attitude of *Peace* 696f. belonged to Aristophanes and that use of Sophocles by Eupolis (e.g. fr. 260.23–6 *Prospaltioi*, cf. *Ant.* 712–15) reflects admiration rather than a desire to ridicule.[170] By the same token, Eupolis' use of Aeschylus to attack Hyperbolus (*Marikas* fr. 207, cf. *Persians* 65) might signal hostility, despite the positive view at *Acharnians* 9–11 and *Frogs* 1411–13. On the whole, a picture seems to emerge in which Eupolis admired Sophocles and Euripides, and also Aeschylus (although his parodies of *Seven against Thebes* at fr. 231 *Poleis* and *Persians* at fr. 207 *Marikas* require further explanation), Cratinus hated Euripides and perhaps disliked Aeschylus, and Aristophanes had problems with all of the above – though there is a *caveat* to which I will return below. The scenario of *Frogs*, though presumably itself original, nonetheless possibly recalls some earlier comedy (in which there was a stand-off between Aeschylean and Euripidean tragedy) and also, very probably, Pherecrates' *Krapataloi*, since that play had presented Aeschylus on stage. Perhaps this had been an attack on Cratinus? The direction of the plot of *Frogs* at any rate, when interpreted as a metacomic

with revivals, and this is confirmed by the inclusion in the discussion of aspects of Aeschylean staging (e.g. 911f., 1028–9). See Dover 1993, 23–4.
[168] *IG* II² 2325.56 and 122.   [169] See Pieters 1946, 157–8.   [170] See Storey 2003, 327–30.

attack on the on-stage target Dionysus/Eupolis, appears to demand that whatever was going on with revivals of Aeschylus could be used to make fun of a comic poet now disenfranchised who was closely associated politically and artistically with Sophocles (*Peace* 531–2, 696) and, as well as in those ways, also by family ties with Euripides.

The key issue, however, is what precisely was going on with Aeschylus? One might be led to suspect, both from the way in which the final choice is focused, and from the foregoing discussion of Aristophanes' underlying association of Euripides first with the laconophile peace party (*Acharnians*) and later with incipient oligarchy (*Thesmophoriazusai*), that it might have something to do with a perceived political stance. The problem will be, of course, that although Euripides could have been 'placed' politically – whether justly or not – and may have adopted political postures, the only people who could have done this for Aeschylus, at the very least by careful choice among his plays and even more careful timing of their production, at the extremes by wholesale rewriting, were the poets who asked for choruses to put on his plays. The Aeschylean political agenda, therefore, will have to have been quite unlike the Euripidean (if either existed apart from its comic manifestation), since it would have depended fundamentally upon other people. If (as the evidence of Quintilian 10.1.66 and the debate over the authenticity of *Prometheus Bound* suggest) producers of Aeschylean revivals adapted the plays – or even wrote new plays with old titles – then Aeschylus might have been appropriated for any number of different ideological postures. On the whole, recent commentators have tended to underplay the evidence for such revisions.[171] But their discussions also tend to ignore the political grounds for the choice of a saviour at *Frogs* 1416f. – the attitude of Aeschylus and Euripides to Alcibiades and concrete suggestions for policy – and the need to explain not only whether the discussion is serious but also in what way it is *funny*. It is time, then, to take a fresh look at what may have been happening to Aeschylus and what Aristophanes may have been trying to do – apart from ridicule Eupolis – in having him brought back to help the city with real issues.

It will be clear enough from my preceding analyses that an audience which recognised Eupolis behind Dionysus would have expected Aristophanes to have him agree with the political views of Euripides (assuming that Sommerstein is correct, against Dover, in assigning 1446–8 and

---

[171] On Aeschylean revivals see Newiger 1961, 427–30, Sommerstein 1996b, 31. See Hutchinson 1985, xliif. for extreme scepticism about fifth-century revivals. See Hamilton 1974 on the external evidence for 'actors' interpolations'.

1449–50 to Euripides).[172] First, the hostile attitude to Alcibiades expressed at 1427–9 is in line with that of Eupolis' *Baptai*, which seems to have satirised Alcibiades, possibly on stage.[173] Secondly, Euripides' support for the reenfranchisement of the oligarchs (probably in the *revised* text of *Frogs*) is in line with the undercurrent of philo-Laconism and conspiracy against the state which I have argued sustains the satire of Euripides and Eupolis (as his relative) in *Thesmophoriazusai*, and this anti-democratic slur is brought to the surface during the contest when Dionysus/Eupolis reminds Euripides (952–3) that his democratic credentials are a bit shaky. It is worth adding that Dionysus/Eupolis' hostile attitude to the law-courts (1466), expressed in response to Aeschylus' policy advice, is closely allied with that of the 411 oligarchs (Thuc. 8.65.3, 8.67.3, 8.97.1) and replicates a point of attack upon Eupolis' own position (opposition to jury-courts) which, on my argument, Aristophanes had been following since at least *Knights* (1316–17, 1332, cf. *Wasps* 410f. and *passim*, *Birds* 109f.). It follows that the advice offered by Aeschylus will be diametrically opposed to this agenda and Dionysus' acceptance of it will be in consequence both paradoxical and amusing.

However, Dionysus/Eupolis is made to choose a poet who has undergone just as much ridicule as Euripides during the tragic contest: he is an innately choleric man, 814, 840, 844, 848 etc.; straight-laced and old-fashioned (1013f., 1043f.) – very reminiscent of the Stronger Argument in *Clouds*, except that Aeschylus uses Socratic questioning against Euripides at 1008f.; Euripides' charges about his stage-techniques, language and lyrics are substantiated with citations; and the 'line-weighing' scene 1365f. is itself probably a parody of the signature scene from Aeschylus' *Psychostasia* ('Weighing of Souls'). It is still not clear, therefore, whether Aristophanes is making a *serious* point about Athenian war policy in the final scene.

Nonetheless, there is, as I mentioned, a *caveat*. At *Peace* 749–50 the poet's claim to greatness (made by the chorus) focuses positively upon his use of language: ἐποίησε τέχνην μεγάλην ἡμῖν κἀπύργωσ᾽ οἰκοδομήσας | ἔπεσιν μεγάλοις 'he has towered up a great art for us, building it with great words'. The scholiast on this line (749a) reports an echo of Pherecrates, fr. 100: ὅστις <γ᾽> αὐτοῖς παρέδωκα τέχνην μεγάλην ἐξοικοδομήσας 'I who built up and handed down to them a great art'. The speaker of this line of Pherecrates was, according to the same scholion, Aeschylus. It is difficult not to see this as a deliberate allusion (especially if it stood out even

---

[172] Dover 1993, 373–6, Sommerstein 1993, 289–90.
[173] See Storey 2003, 103–5 for a measured view. If the elegiac couplet ascribed to Alcibiades (βάπτες μ᾽ ἐν θυμέλῃσιν 'You dipped me in the theatre...' etc.) *are* genuine (West 1989–92: II.29), then his appearance as a character in some later comedy is guaranteed (see above, pp. 222–3).

for a scholiast). Yet the implication, that Aristophanes admired Aeschylean tragedy, especially its language, would run counter to his evident satire of Aeschylus in *Frogs* and the apparent slanting of Aeschylus' arguments towards what I have argued was a Cratinean position (that poetry *teaches*). There was, it seems, scope for an apparently self-contradictory view of Aeschylean tragedy. But before I return to enquire into what the basis for this may have been, I want to examine briefly the policies advocated by Aeschylus in the light of the earlier findings of this study about Aristophanes' political posture.

Aeschylus' reply to Dionysus' enquiry about Alcibiades (1431–2) utilises the lion imagery from *Agamemnon* (717–36) – an amusing and suitable enough riposte purely from the formal viewpoint. The purport of the response, however, is diametrically opposed to Euripides' outright condemnation (1427–9) and, while allowing for discontent about Alcibiades' pattern of behaviour clearly suggests that the city can make use of his skills in the current situation. I have argued earlier that Aristophanes had himself attacked Alcibiades (in *Knights* and the first *Clouds*) as part of the laconophile group supported by Eupolis, but that when his volte-face on the war had brought him into line with Hyperbolus' views, he had probably been constrained to accept the new political reality. This move in turn, I conjectured, allowed Eupolis to mock Aristophanes for a change of allegiance by having Alcibiades contest Hyperbolus' dominance over Demos in *Marikas*. It was only when Alcibiades had treacherously allied with Nicias and/or Phaeax to have Hyperbolus ostracised that Aristophanes once again targeted him on stage in the second version of *Clouds* and again in *Birds* as Prometheus. Since then, however, there had intervened the oligarchic revolution, Hyperbolus' murder, the overthrow of the Four Hundred and, significantly, the reinstatement of Alcibiades as an active general supporting the renewed radical democracy, his recall to Athens (spring 407) and subsequent dismissal from command after his assistant Antiochus' minor defeat at Notium (Xen. *Hell.* 1.5.10f.). Given Alcibiades' military success and his newly rediscovered democratic credentials, it is credible that Aristophanes would have thought his recall an uncomfortable but necessary step: he may have been impossible, but he was also a star. To recap the earlier argument of chapter two (pp. 43–4), the advice given on policy at 1463–5 amounts to (1) concentration of Athenian resources on the fleet, and (2) mounting of attacks on enemy territory while (3) regarding enemy control of Attica as understood and not challenging it.[174] Since this pretty much represented

---

[174] Sommerstein 1996a, 291 on 1463–5.

current *demos* policy, Sommerstein concludes, 'Aeschylus' message is... (i) that the current Athenian strategy is essentially right, (ii) that it must, however, be pursued with more single-mindedness, and above all (iii) that the way to save Athens is by fighting, not by talking.'[175] As the scholiast notes, this is, *mutatis mutandis*, the strategy advocated by Pericles in the early years of the war (Thucydides 1.141–3).[176] On my argument, Aristophanes had always believed that fighting on against the Spartans was the correct course and had used the volte-faces of the pro-Periclean Eupolis and the anti-Periclean Cratinus to satirise both in *Acharnians* and *Peace*. Not only are both pieces of advice given by Aeschylus plausible, then, as strategic policy, but they are also plausible as *Aristophanic* advice, used once more to satirise Eupolis' stubborn adherence to the cause of peace with Sparta *against* the advice of the political hero he had so recently resuscitated in *Demes*.

Uniquely in the case of *Frogs* we have ancient external evidence which tends to support the idea that Aristophanes had sought to give advice in the play. I have reinterpreted this (chapter three, pp. 41–3) to suggest that it reflects a decree passed in 403, after the restoration of the democracy, somewhat as follows:

The *demos* resolved to honour Aristophanes, son of Philippus of Kydathenaion, with a wreath of sacred olive because through his plays he has striven to show that the Athenians' constitution is free and subject to no tyrant's slavery, but that it is a democracy and the *demos* is free and rules itself, and to restage at the next Lenaea the *Frogs* in which he gave sound advice to the *demos*.[177]

This 'sound advice', however, had been offered not in the parabasis, as later commentators assumed, but rather in the final scene – and with irony aimed at Eupolis, his main target – through Aeschylus. It is not, then, absurd to read this final scene as simultaneously ridiculing Euripides and Eupolis (in the guise of Dionysus) for their anti-democratic stance and

---

[175] *Ibid.* 291–2.
[176] So close was the Aeschylus of *Frogs* perceived to be to Pericles that some ancient sources actually *identified* Aeschylus with the general. Valerius Maximus 7.2 says: *remissum ab inferis... Periclem ratiocinantem non oportere in urbe nutriri leonem etc.* ('Pericles returned from the underworld argues that one ought not to bring up a lion-cub in the city'). See Telò 2007, 140 for an example from the ancient argument to Sophocles *OC*. I do not in fact discount that this apparent error may transmit a genuine tradition derived ultimately from the original audience of *Frogs*. For if Pericles had been the author of the famous decree allowing re-performances of Aeschylus, it cannot be doubted that he may have had have had a *political* purpose in mind – the use of Aeschylus' reputation to promote his own policies in the tragic theatre. If so, then to represent Aeschylus as Pericles would have been inherently amusing and also reflect an intertextual satire of Eupolis' Pericles from *Demes*.
[177] Contrast Sommerstein's version 1996a, 21.

suggesting that Aeschylus' true political position when he returns from the dead will be to stand side-by-side with his former *choregos* and Eupolis' hero, Pericles.

The contrast between (a) Aristophanes' appropriation to himself of Pherecrates' description of Aeschylus' language (*Peace* 749–50; Pherecrates fr. 100 *Krapataloi*) and his use of Aeschylus to promote a neo-Periclean war policy in *Frogs* and (b) the thoroughgoing satire of Aeschylus in the contest against Euripides requires a gloss. As argued above, any Aeschylean political posture must have been manipulated by his producers. But the opportunity to do so was provided by a decree (*Life of Aeschylus* 12). It is a guess, but one which emerges naturally from the alignment of Aeschylus with Periclean policy in *Frogs*, that it may have been Pericles who promoted the decree. His relationship with the poet through the *choregia* (for *Persians* in 472) is established from the surviving records of the *didaskaliai* (*IG* II^2 2318.9). Brockmann's recent suggestion that at *Acharnians* 9–11 the call to Theognis to bring on his chorus when the character had been waiting for Aeschylus disappoints because Theognis is the *producer* of the Aeschylus play, and that the joke against Theognis later in the play for frostiness (138–40) hints that the play he produced was *Persians* (cf. 496–7 with *Ach.* 139), may help us to understand the role Aeschylean drama played during the war (and perhaps before it).[178] That Aristophanes at any rate is referring to revival performances and not to the originals is perhaps sufficiently shown by the attention to staging (911f., 1028–9). But the impression is reinforced by the quite specific dating of *Seven against Thebes* (467) before *Persians* (472) at 1021–6 (note εἶτα 'next' in 1026). Commentators are forced to suggest that Aristophanes did not know the real dates and was putting them in the order he needed for Aeschylus' argument.[179] However, it is also possible that he is recalling for humorous – and political – purposes the order in which Athenians had seen these plays during the war. Quite apart from Brockmann's view that Theognis had produced *Persians* before 425,[180] it is clear from Eupolis *Marikas* fr. 207 that the play was in the public mind before 421. The debate on the authenticity of *Prometheus Bound*[181] necessitates that if we accept its spuriousness we must also explain how it came to be in the Aeschylean corpus and more particularly why, as Flintoff has shown, Aristophanes seems to have regarded it as genuine.[182] One

---

[178] Brockmann 2003, 27–41.   [179] Dover 1993 and Sommerstein 1996a on 1026.
[180] Brockmann 2003, 95.
[181] For which see Herington 1970, Griffith 1977, Conacher 1980, Bees 1993, Sommerstein 1996b, 321–7.
[182] Flintoff 1983. See also Herington 1963. Other comic references are: Ar. *Knights* 836 (cf. *Prometheus Bound* 613) and Cratinus *Ploutoi* fr. 171, 20–6 (see further Sommerstein 1996b, 325).

response is, with Flintoff, to suggest that the statistical approach to style does not have enough data to overturn the apparent (statistical!) proof of Aristophanes' view.[183] Another is to consider the idea that the decree had opened the possibility of forgery on a grand scale, that, to put it bluntly, a producer of 'Aeschylus' could have more or less free rein in adapting, adding to or even completely rewriting his plays.[184] Quintilian seems to have had evidence that Aeschylean plays were put on in altered form (*correctas* 10.1.66), though he assumed the changes were merely stylistic. More generally, a gloss on ἐπικαττύειν 'to resole' in Phrynichus specifically refers to the adaptation of existing tragedies for revival.[185] But we do not have to look this far afield for an instance, since we can see for ourselves that we have trouble matching up Dionysus' description of a scene in *Persians* at 1028–9 with what is in our text.[186] This issue obviously requires a much broader discussion than I can offer here. It suffices to say that if it is correct to ascribe to the final scene and to Aeschylus in particular the only serious political advice the play contains and to suggest that it was for this and not for the parabasis that Aristophanes was allowed a second production, then we can not infer that the humour of the dénouement rests on the absurdity of asking tragedians for their political advice. The corollary is, of course, that the poetic skills of tragedians as well as of comic dramatists were involved in the Athenian political arena and in Aeschylus' case it was his various producers, with their manipulations, alterations and (if *Prometheus* is spurious) wholesale reinventions of his work (utilising known titles, of course), who dictated where he stood. If this is the background to *Frogs*, then the audience will have laughed at 868–9, the claim that Aeschylus' poetry has not died with him, for a reason over and above the mere fact of the decree. And they will immediately have understood – and been amused by – the notion that in having the poet finally articulate Periclean ideas, Aristophanes was making the *real* Aeschylus stand up.[187]

In this context, it may turn out to be very significant indeed that it is the two plays specifically mentioned by Aeschylus at 1021–6 as producing warlike responses (*Seven* and *Persians*) that are the only ones specifically

---

[183] Flintoff 1983, 5.
[184] See, for example, Griffith 1977, 254 for the suggestion that Euphorion, Aeschylus' son, or another member of the family may have been involved in 'completing a tragedy or trilogy begun by Aeschylus, for production after his death, perhaps even in his name'.
[185] See Hamilton 1974, 400.
[186] See Dover 1993 and Sommerstein 1996 ad loc. for suggestions. See note 176 above for the possibility that Aeschylus was represented as Pericles.
[187] For Aeschylus as a supporter of Pericles, see Sommerstein 1996b 26 and 391–421.

parodied by Eupolis in our surviving fragments (fr. 231, fr. 207). It is impossible to tell from the surface, though, whether the joke lies in the audience's knowledge that Aeschylus is telling the truth about them or the opposite. Certainly, if he hopes to gain favour with Dionysus/Eupolis, arguing that these dramas were designed to foster a warlike spirit (presumably against the Spartans) when Eupolis had, as has been argued from the attacks upon him in *Acharnians*, *Peace* and *Lysistrata*, been a supporter of the peace party since Pericles' death, these arguments will not produce the result he desires. So it is possible the joke is that these particular plays were not produced with those ideological goals at all, but the *opposite*: *Seven* to demonstrate the futility of internecine conflict (which war among the Greeks always is for subscribers to Panhellenism) and *Persians* to argue that while Panhellenism saved the day for Greece in the Persian Wars, the Persians too are fit objects for sympathy, and it is because Panhellenic solidarity taught them the lesson that invading Greece is futile that they now seek ties of alliance with Greek cities. These interpretations, I suggest, sit a little bit better with the plays we can read now (whether they have been subsequently altered or not) than with Aeschylus' view of them in *Frogs*.[188] In that case, the poet or poets who 'produced' them will have been in the same political camp as Eupolis. Dionysus' responses probably tell in favour of this interpretation: he appears to be objecting to the warlike aspect of *Seven* (τουτὶ μέν σοι κακὸν εἴργασται 'Well this *is* a bad thing you have done' 1023), but then ridiculously asserts that the play made the *Thebans* more warlike; in respect of *Persae*, all he does is express the *enjoyment* he felt during the Darius scene (ἐχάρην 'I enjoyed it' 1028). The humour of *Acharnians* 9–11, which works in a similar way, in fact helps to confirm this interpretation. Dicaeopolis/Eupolis, a fan of Aeschylus, is giving a list of his joys and sorrows (thus providing a link with Dionysus' response here: cf. ἥσθην 'I was delighted' *Ach.* 2, 4, 13 and ἐγανώθην 'I brightened up' *Ach.* 7). His disappointment is caused by the fact that *Theognis* leads the chorus on. As I have already intimated, I find Brockmann's recent suggestion, that Theognis was the poet who had asked for a chorus to produce Aeschylus in accordance with the decree allowing this, by far the best way of understanding the dynamics here.[189] His further insight, that the joke about Theognis at 138–40 (the rivers of Thrace froze when he was contesting at Athens) refers to *Persians* 496–7 and indicates that the Aeschylus play he was producing was *Persians*,

---

[188] That there is a question of fourth-century interference is clear from the problem already mentioned of matching *Frogs* 1028–9 with the surviving text of *Persians* and the widely held view that *Seven* 1005–78 is an interpolation imitating Eur. *Phoen.* (see Hutchinson 1985, xliii and ad loc.).
[189] Brockmann 2003, 28.

helps us to tie the *Frogs* and *Acharnians* passages more tightly together.[190] The audience is invited to laugh because they know (a) that *Persians* as reworked by Theognis promoted an agenda Eupolis would have supported and (b) that Theognis was an *ally* of the young comic poet. A precisely similar joke, which will depend upon a reversal of the known tastes and allegiances of Theognis, occurs at *Thesmophoriazusai* 170, where the relative (alias Eupolis) attacks Theognis for his frigid poetry. Thus, in using *Seven* and *Persians* to attack Hierocles and Hyperbolus, Eupolis is taking *friendly* material to mock his enemies. It should be noted that this interpretation, along with the identification of Peisetairus in *Birds* as Critias (cf. the First Athenian ambassador and the Hermokopidai joke at *Lysistrata* 1093–4), suggests that the scholium on *Acharnians* 11 may not have been wrong to identify Theognis as εἷς τῶν τριάκοντα 'one of the Thirty (Tyrants)' (Xen. *Hell.* 2.3.2; Lysias 12.6 and 13–15). This may help confirm the conjecture I made earlier that Eupolis' hope of return to Athens after 403 was dashed by his intimate involvement with the Thirty.

On this argument, there is a specificity to the references which suggests that fifth-century Athenian tragedy was a good deal less generic in its political agenda than recent scholarship has been prepared to accept.[191] Moreover, there was an ideological battle being fought with Aeschylus which is essential for our understanding of the detail of the jokes in *Frogs*. Our incapacity to see it has disabled our critical understanding not only of the comedy, but also of Aeschylean tragedy.

CONCLUSION

The Aristophanes I have been reconstructing ended the Peloponnesian War as a publicly honoured hero of the democracy – a far cry from the right-wing conservative *laudator temporis acti* that some scholars have made him out to be.[192] The *demos* which voted for the olive wreath had been sophisticated enough to be able to see that what lay behind his sometimes ventriloquial metacomedy had always been a commitment to the radical principles – and the war policy – first of Hyperbolus and then of other unknown popular leaders (possibly among them Cleophon:[193] see

---

[190] Brockmann 2003, 93–5.
[191] For recent debate of the political aspect of Greek tragedy, see Goldhill 1987, Griffin 1998, Goldhill 2000, Rhodes 2003.
[192] E.g. Ste. Croix 1972, Appendix XXIX, 371.
[193] Sommerstein 1993, however, has argued that the decree may have been designed by those who wished to see the fall of the latest radical democratic leader, Cleophon. This popular leader was

above, pp. 276, 283 on *Demoi*), and a deep disdain for laconophiles and oligarchs, and especially for the comic poet Eupolis. The people's desire to see *Frogs* again after the restoration will, on my argument, have had everything to do with its ridicule of Eupolis – in exile now and destined never to return to the city he had more recently betrayed by his close association with Critias and Theognis, two of the Thirty Tyrants. And if on the other side Aristophanes had backed up his dramatic support for the *demos* with a clear choice of Piraeus after the appointment of the Thirty, it would have been all the easier for the newly restored assembly to honour his art in so fulsome a manner.

> put to death in 405 (Lysias 13.12; 30.10–13) at a time when the passing of the decree of Patrocleides shows that there had been a marked shift to the right in Athenian politics. Unfavourable mentions of him are made, it is true, by the chorus at 678f. and 1532, and by Pluto at 1504. But the chorus is, I have argued, the metacomic tool of the oligarchically inclined 'author', Eupolis, and these insults are simply appropriate to his known political position. Thus the re-performance, which in any case ought to be placed in 403, has nothing at all to do with anti-Cleophontic politics. The same argument can be made for other examples of apparently anti-radical democratic invective, for instance those in Pluto's speech at 1500f. Pluto offers an immediate summons to Hades to Cleophon, Myrmex (unknown), Nicomachus (*PA* 10934; Lysias 30), a democrat who worked on the new law code after the restoration in 410, Archenomus (unknown) and Adeimantus (*PA* 202), an associate of Alcibiades who had been attacked by name on stage by Eupolis in *Poleis* (fr.224). The amusement will have depended on the audience's identification of Pluto as an individual associated with Eupolis and regarded as an opponent of democracy. The twist is of course that the Aeschylus who goes back will *support* democratic values and policies.

Conclusions and consequences

The argument of this book proceeded from an analysis of the revised *Clouds* parabasis identifying its audience as an intellectual/political group which had sponsored Aristophanes' plays since his debut in 427. It moved via a re-examination of the consequences of that analysis for the politics and thus comic techniques of Eupolis and Aristophanes, to a reading of the plays of the Peloponnesian War, both extant and fragmentary, on the basis of two major assumptions which appear to underlie Aristophanes' remarks to his sponsors: a play's *characters* are its major theme and attacks on rivals are regularly made by misappropriation of their comic material (of every type and at every level of detail). Both assumptions bring into play serious challenges to the way in which we generally read this material. The second is, however, not especially problematic, unless combined with the first. No sensible reader of Old Comedy is likely to deny *tout court* the possibility that metacomedy was more prominent than we may have thought, since there is so much actual evidence for the criticism of rivals (e.g. Cratin. fr. 213, Ar. fr. 58 etc.). But the idea that the *characters* constitute the focus of the comedians' attacks because they represent real individuals, disguised for the most part because of the danger that open attack posed to the poet (cf. *Ach.* 377f., *Wasps* 1284f.) is much more disturbing, first because it represents a contemporary filter which would fundamentally change the interpretation of almost every play and second because positivistic notions of what constitutes evidence for the interpretation of the comedies will always in some scholars' eyes trump arguments, however strong, which are not based on what is directly reported. I deal with the apparent lack of hard evidence for disguised caricature in Appendix 1, but here it is worth making some general remarks about why there is apparently so little of it and why this should not deter us from following up, as I have in the preceding chapters, the implications of the way Aristophanes treats the genre in the parabasis of *Clouds*.

First, let us follow an insight recently expressed by Jeffrey Rusten, in his treatment of Thucydides and comedy, about the survival and study of the texts with which we are concerned here.[1] After noting that 'the greatest danger to the survival of Cratinus, Aristophanes and Eupolis came in the century after their deaths', and arguing that 'we have no evidence that any Old Comedy was ever re-performed after its authors' death at the Dionysia or Lenaea in Athens', he asks '[w]hy then did Alexandrian scholars... devote such abundant energy to elucidating Old Comedy in particular'? His answer is that 'in this crucial moment it was *historical* interest in Old Comedy that kept its texts alive'. In other words, the survival and the exegesis of these works was fundamentally a phenomenon born of interest in the Peloponnesian War. This seems correct in its fundamentals: but it also misses stating something else of major importance. There is no evidence at all that the texts came to these Alexandrian commentators with any sort of annotation. The student of the scholia is all too painfully aware of how often the ancient scholars have to explain the text by using the text itself as their evidence (a practice we still, perforce, follow today). Occasionally, it is true, there are signs of the deployment of external evidence, sometimes from other plays, sometimes from historical sources (the treatment of the issue of the *Knights* and Eupolis is a case in point). But dramatic satire is a wholly contemporary phenomenon, which depends crucially upon the precise moment of its performance and on the ability of its audience to 'get' the cultural references which fuel its capacity to create laughter. Though everyone will no doubt have talked about the plays and their targets (and indeed there is evidence that they were part even of the political discourse of the city: e.g. Lysias fr. 53 – see Appendix 1, pp. 311–12), no one would have thought for a moment that it was worth preserving such ephemera for posterity. It is true that later writers did occasionally have anecdotes which probably went back to the period (e.g. the one about Alcibiades drowning the poet Eupolis), but they had no interpretative framework in which fragments of information which pointed towards on-stage caricature as the focus of the genre might fit. For the writers of history, such as Thucydides and Xenophon, comedy was either an irrelevance or – more probably – they disapproved of its basis, a fundamentally radical democratic ideology of social control of the aristocratic elite, which, even if it could be appropriated by more politically 'moderate' practitioners, nonetheless had the annoying tic of making fools out of people they considered above that type of public ridicule. The net

---

[1] Rusten 2006, 555–7.

result, then, was that Old Comedy became an object of historical study mostly for the obvious evidence it contained about *named* individuals.

The lack of absolutely direct evidence for disguised caricature ought not in any event to stop us investigating the possibility that this was the basis for Old Comedy (especially given the implication of the *Clouds* parabasis). Not to do so relies on the assumption that the comic texts *must* be what they appear to *us* to be. But such an argument takes no account of the fact that texts can not communicate directly what they have deliberately suppressed. Once we accept the need to investigate along these lines the major difficulty that presents itself is very clearly the one of finding an acceptable method of discovering behind the characters of these plays their contemporary real-life targets, given the apparent care taken to be as enigmatic as possible. I have argued that the direction of the plot is a primary pointer: the satirical scenario will very often help to delimit the range of individuals who might be a play's targets (as it does for example in the case of *Birds*). Knowing the *parti pris* of the author will also help (as I have argued it does, for example, in the cases of Aristophanes' 'peace' plays and in the apparently democratic *Demoi* of Eupolis). Tracking cross-references to incidents involving the same caricature targets can also be of use, as in the allusion to the Telephus scene of *Acharnians* at *Clouds* 920f. (though this method can generally only be a help once certain identifications have been agreed). At the end, however, because of the appropriation of comedy by political and intellectual interest groups, only a set of identifications which makes ideological sense can be deemed acceptable.

This study has only scratched the surface. If others follow its lead, there are a number of potentially important areas where new information and new insights might be gained. (1) Because Aristophanes appears to be intellectually predisposed towards the circle of sophists, further study from this angle should affect our view of the relationship between philosophy and politics. (2) Because many intellectual ideas are satirised which appear only in Plato's dialogues, we may be constrained to re-evaluate the link between Plato's philosophical doctrines and the views of Socrates and of Plato's own use of comedy in the dialogues. (3) Because of the clearly political manner in which both Aeschylus and Euripides are treated in Aristophanes, we will need fundamentally to realign our understanding of the links between fifth-century tragedy and politics. (4) Because on-stage enigmatic caricature has been found to be crucial to Old Comedy, we shall be compelled to rethink the history of the genre, which was misunderstood by Alexandrian scholars, despite their having access to some crucial information (see Appendix 1). (5) Because the comic poets make such detailed use of the personae and plays of their rivals, we must reassess the nature of the audience for whom these comedies were written. (6) Since Cratinus and Eupolis were engaged in a battle with each other and with Aristophanes which was not merely aesthetic, but fundamentally political, we will need to reappraise our understanding of the nature of their comedy and to investigate the possibility that this was not the only meta-show in town.

Comic poets were too powerful not to attract the attentions of political leaders: the consequential laughter induced by on-stage caricature satire was surely hard to ignore in a society where personal honour was central (cf. *Frogs* 367–8, Lysias fr. 53 and Andoc. fr. 5). And comic poets were too engaged in the literary and intellectual currents which surrounded and informed the circles of politicians not to be engaged in politics. Yet it is significant that the only *public* recognitions that we have evidence of for a political role for comedy are the decree of Morychides (and perhaps others, such as the one ascribed to Syracosius) and the crown given to Aristophanes (see Appendix 1).

Further, the attack on Cleon in *Knights* (even if it was slanted in effect as much against Eupolis and Alcibiades) did not prevent his being elected general soon after the contest of 424.[2] The argument of *Frogs* against the re-enfranchisement of the 411 oligarchs was not heeded in the immediate aftermath of its first production. Instead, the decree of Patrocleides was passed, with all that that entailed. It is therefore important not to overrate Old Comedy's effect in terms of *policy*. For the Old Oligarch satirical comedy is a *defensive* measure, not a think tank, and it is never mentioned by the historians of the war (though, as I have said, this might indicate their political colouring as much as the facts). But it is just as significant that the only evidence we have for a real effect is upon an *individual*, Socrates (Pl. *Apol.* 18c–d, 19c; cf. Xen. *Symp.* 6.6–10).

---

[2] MacDowell 1995, 112 suggests that Aristophanes' criticism is more directed towards damaging the political sway in the assembly which his rhetoric gave him and that this may have been (for all we know) effective.

PART III
Appendices

APPENDIX I

The view from the theatron

No ancient writer gives us a dictionary entry on 'Old Comedy'. But the evidence which will be examined in this chapter suggests strongly that if anyone had done so, it might have looked like this:

Old Comedy attacks individuals. Personal attack is politically functional and not confined to the festival context. Two modes of attack exist: (a) by name (Cleon is a bugger) (b) by impersonation (e.g. Paphlagon = Cleon). The second of these is central and fundamental: on-stage caricature is prior to plot, the function of which is to create effective personal attack through the characters. Because these comic characters reflect real individuals, they are made to act in recognisably anti-social ways to provoke laughter *at* (and not *with*) them.

As far as I know, no one has before tried to extract purely from the *external* evidence a contemporary view of Old Comedy. However, it also becomes clear, as one assembles this evidence and interrogates it for its underlying agreements about the nature of the genre, that another factor besides reading of the texts has influenced scholars in their approach. For although material relating to invective comedy can be found from the late fifth to the mid fourth century, a preconceived notion holds sway – a notion found in varying and incompatible forms in later scholiastic material – that Old Comedy developed from an invective form through a middle stage towards New Comedy.[1] This produces a filtering of the evidence for invective comedy in the fourth century that seems to me to be quite arbitrary. As well as our own readings of the texts, we should surely exclude from our considerations the confused and confusing later attempts to make sense of comedy's development.[2] It is the picture and patterns the

---

[1] See, for example, Handley 1985, 398–414, Nesselrath 1990.
[2] Not that this material (conveniently collected in Koster *Prolegomena*) is of no value. Quite the contrary. And I shall be using it later. However, I leave it aside at this point since (a) it is not well understood (b) it can only be understood in the light of the fifth- and fourth-century discussion and (c) I have been criticised for basing my view of Old Comedy too heavily on such dubious material (Storey 2003, 300 n. 26).

contemporary evidence itself suggests that should be our primary guide also to this aspect.

I say this because a review of material related to comedy but outside it from the fifth and fourth centuries makes it clear that invective comedy was still being produced in the 350s and 340s (Isoc. 8.14, from 355; Aesch. 1.157, *c.* 345) and was a live philosophical issue as late as the *Laws* of Plato (816d; 935d–936c, *c.* 347), one with which Aristotle was still wrestling in the *Rhetoric* (1384b 9–11), *Nicomachean Ethics* (1128a, 23–5) and *Politics* (1336a, 39f.), though he had apparently resolved it by the time of the *Poetics* (1449a32–b7; 1451a36–8, b5–15).[3] Thus it seems reasonable to begin from the assumption that whatever later sources say, invective comedy flourished at Athens from 486 (its inception in the competitions) until at least the 340s (and possibly into the 320s). It follows that material related to comedy from this period (including *Poetics*, where Aristotle deals with invective comedy, e.g. at 1448b20 – 1449a5) can be interrogated as a set of responses to a genre which caused deeply diverse evaluations – from acceptance of its truth-telling potential (e.g. Lysias fr. 53) to condemnation of its lies (e.g. Isoc. 8.14) – but whose nature was clearly understood by all. The best index of the latter is, of course, the fact that no one (with the partial exception of the 'Old Oligarch', whose purpose seems to be to describe democracy to a non-Athenian audience) finds it necessary to detail the nature of the genre even when it is under critical examination.

There is, however, a further complication. For if we wish to be guided by contemporary information rather than later guesswork, we may infer that invective comedy was joined, rather earlier than a simplistic developmental model would indicate, by a quite different type of comic drama. Aristotle remarks at *Poetics* 1449b 5–9:

τὸ δὲ μύθους ποιεῖν τὸ μὲν ἐξ ἀρχῆς ἐκ Σικελίας ἦλθεν, τῶν δὲ Ἀθήνησιν Κράτης πρῶτος ἦρξεν ἀφέμενος τῆς ἰαμβικῆς ἰδέας καθόλου ποιεῖν λόγους καὶ μύθους.

Composing plots originated in Sicily, but of the Athenian comic poets Crates was the first to abandon the iambic form and compose arguments, that is plots, of a general nature.

The claim that Crates was the first comic poet to abandon the ἰαμβικὴ ἰδέα and write μῦθοι on the Sicilian model sets the introduction of non-invective

---

[3] Desperate attempts are often made to suggest that Plato and Isocrates are somehow fixed in the past. See e.g. Hornblower 2000, 375 on Isocrates 8.14: 'As a statement *about* the 350s this is simply bizarre; Isokrates is still I suggest in a kind of fifth-century time-warp... I suggest that both *O.O.* and Isokrates derive their knowledge of old comedy from reading it as literature of the past.' Contrast Handley 1985, 405. In my experience, old men do still know what is going on; they simply get grumpier about it and less patient in their criticisms.

comedy in the mid-fifth century (Crates' first victory at the Dionysia was c. 450: *IG* II² 2325, 52). Moreover, Green traces the origins of stock comic characters with standardised mask-types in terracotta to the last quarter of the fifth century.[4] This surely must mean, in conjunction with Aristotle's evidence, that non-invective comedy on the Sicilian model was a fixture alongside the earlier and more contentious form from quite early on (even if its development from Crates through Alexis to Menander may seem at first sight difficult to comprehend).[5] One may suspect that the innovation had something to do with the one decree restricting comic licence to satirise that is accepted by scholars as genuine – the decree of Morychides, evidenced by Σ *Acharnians* 67 ἐπ' Εὐθυμένους ἄρχοντος: οὗτός ἐστιν ὁ ἄρχων ἐφ' οὗ κατελύθη τὸ ψήφισμα τὸ περὶ τοῦ μὴ κωμῳδεῖν γραφὲν ἐπὶ Μορυχίδου ('In the archonship of Euthymenes: this is the archon in whose archonship the decree about not satirising enacted in the archonship of Morychides was repealed'). The decree was enacted in 440 and repealed in 437, and, if the wording of the scholion is accurate, banned attacks on individuals completely. If comedy were to survive, it must necessarily borrow from elsewhere.[6] Of course, this has to remain conjectural. The contemporary evidence, does, however, support the notion of gradual changes in *invective* comedy which has nothing at all to do with the modern orthodoxy whereby the Old Comedy of Aristophanes eventually becomes the New Comedy of Menander. Hence, from the mid-fifth century, we see the coexistence of two utterly different types of comedy, one probably consistent with the injunctions of the decree of Morychides, the other in constant tension with the ideas of elite writers opposed to the democracy ([Xen.] *Ath. Pol.* 2.18; Pl. *Laws* 935d ff.; Arist. *Pol.* 1336a, 39f.). More will be said about the distinction perceived between the two types by Aristotle later on. It should be noted that in the external evidence there is no hint anywhere of a 'mixed' type of play in which satire works hand-in-hand with stock characters. It appears that plays were either 'iambic' or they were not and one can see exactly how the provisions of the decree of Morychides could have been responsible for the production of the non-iambic genre, but not how its repeal could have promoted the creation of yet another type: surely the poets who had not produced during the period of the ban would just have begun once

---

[4] Green 1994, 37 and 63.
[5] Sidwell 2000a (though some aspects of that account have now been revised).
[6] Halliwell 1991b 57–8. His 'unease' at the idea (apparently evidenced in the scholion) of a blanket ban on satire of individuals is tied in with a basic assumption that it was the mention of names rather than on-stage caricature that was central to this function. It is much easier to see what could have motivated a complete ban if on-stage caricature were considered central and this centrality would explain much better the consistent opposition of elite writers to this form of comedy.

more to write the sort of plays they had written before – perhaps with even more critical venom, given that their calling had been put into suspended animation by precisely the sorts of people they had been wont to attack in them.

There are, of course, other basic problems with the material we will need to use for the reconstruction of the way Athenians understood iambic comedy. First, there is its paucity. Nothing can be done about this except to note how consistent nonetheless are the underlying implications about the genre across the period it covers. Secondly, there is its diversity: it ranges from political pamphlets through snippets of law-court speeches to philosophical discussion. Naturally, account must be taken of the diverse motivations and audiences of these sources. Once again, however, it is striking how similar the underlying assumptions turn out to be about the nature of the genre whatever the source. In most cases, it will be clear that the propositions argued below (and already headlined above) can be supported across the range of material. Thirdly, we have access only to written sources, and thus only – effectively – to elite responses. This is a fact of life for the historian of ancient societies. The fact that there is agreement at a deep level about the nature of a phenomenon which causes fundamentally different evaluative responses should, however, suggest that we are not going to be misled as much as if we were trying to use the material to gauge how much enjoyment people got from comedy.

THE ANCIENT EVIDENCE ON INVECTIVE COMEDY

It is time to turn to a detailed analysis of the definition of Old Comedy (or invective comedy – the comedy which Aristotle calls ἰαμβικὴ ἰδέα) given at the beginning of this chapter. I shall take each of the propositions in turn and examine the various pieces of evidence which together support it.

1 Old Comedy attacks individuals

This conclusion is the most straightforward of all and is indicated by the whole range of our sources. First of all it is almost explicitly stated by the Old Oligarch ([Xen.] *Ath. Pol.* 2.18:[7]

κωμῳδεῖν δ᾽ αὖ καὶ κακῶς λέγειν τὸν μὲν δῆμον οὐκ ἐῶσιν, ἵνα μὴ αὐτοὶ ἀκούωσι κακῶς· ἰδίᾳ δὲ κελεύουσιν, εἴ τίς τινα βούλεται, εὖ εἰδότες ὅτι οὐχὶ τοῦ δήμου ἐστὶν οὐδὲ τοῦ πλήθους ὁ κωμῳδούμενος ὡς ἐπὶ τὸ πολύ, ἀλλ᾽

---

[7] For this part of the argument, dating is not a crucial issue. See chapter three n. 21 for suggested dates and bibliography.

ἢ πλούσιος ἢ γενναῖος ἢ δυνάμενος, ὀλίγοι δέ τινες τῶν πενήτων καὶ τῶν δημοτικῶν κωμῳδοῦνται, καὶ οὐδ' οὗτοι ἐὰν μὴ διὰ πολυπραγμοσύνην καὶ διὰ τὸ ζητεῖν πλέον τι ἔχειν τοῦ δήμου, ὥστε οὐδὲ τοὺς τοιούτους ἄχθονται κωμῳδουμένους.

Making fun and insulting of the *demos* they do not allow, so that they do not get a bad reputation. They encourage it in respect of private individuals, however, if anyone wishes to attack anyone else, because they are well aware that for the most part, the person made fun of is not one of the *demos* or the masses, but either a rich man or an aristocrat or someone with power, while few of the poor and ordinary are made fun of (and these only for nosiness and seeking to have a greater part in anything than the *demos*; so they do not get upset even when such men are made fun of).

Focal in this passage is the κωμῳδούμενος, an individual by and large belonging to the rich, aristocratic and power-mongering classes, but also including from time to time less exalted persons who have run foul of a general prejudice against interference (πολυπραγμοσύνη) and vaulting ambition (τό ζητεῖν πλέον τι ἔχειν τοῦ δήμου or πλεονεξία). Even for a writer who seems to be addressing an audience that does not know all the details of Athenian law and culture, this statement is still not as clear cut as it might have been. Its point of departure is not, after all, the desire to give an unambiguous account of comedy, but to demonstrate that even in respect of a public dramatic genre which focuses on satirical attack the *demos* nonetheless knows how to protect itself. It does not specifically even mention comedy, but it is correctly assumed by scholars that this is the context and the evidence to be examined in a moment confirms it. Hence, it focuses on what everyone will presume is the central point – attack on individuals. Working back from this assumption, one might propose that the protection of the *demos* mentioned in this passage must relate to individuals associated with the power of that body.

Later writers agree that satirical attack on individuals was central to the genre. For both Plato and Aristotle, it is what makes comedy problematic. This is clear not only from the specific references back to the attack on Socrates in *Clouds* in the *Apology* (18c–d, 19c) and *Phaedo* (70b–c) (and one might add, in Xenophon's *Symposium* 6.6–8), but also from the legal formulation at *Laws* 935d–936b:

τί δὲ δή; τὴν τῶν κωμῳδιῶν προθυμίαν τοῦ γελοῖα εἰς τοὺς ἀνθρώπους λέγειν ἦ παραδεχόμεθα, ἐὰν ἄνευ θυμοῦ τὸ τοιοῦτον ἡμῖν τοὺς πολίτας ἐπιχειρῶσιν κωμῳδοῦντες λέγειν; ἢ διαλάβωμεν δίχα τῷ παίζειν καὶ μή, καὶ παίζοντι μὲν ἐξέστω τινὶ περί του λέγειν γελοῖον ἄνευ θυμοῦ, συντεταμένῳ δὲ καὶ μετὰ θυμοῦ, καθάπερ εἴπομεν, μὴ ἐξέστω μηδενί; τοῦτο μὲν οὐδαμῶς ἀναθετέον, ᾧ [δʹ] ἐξέστω καὶ μὴ δέ, τοῦτο νομοθετησώμεθα. ποιητῇ δὴ κωμῳδίας ἤ τινος ἰάμβων ἢ μουσῶν μελῳδίας μὴ ἐξέστω μήτε λόγῳ μήτε εἰκόνι, μήτε θυμῷ μήτε ἄνευ θυμοῦ, μηδαμῶς μηδένα τῶν πολιτῶν κωμῳδεῖν· ἐὰν δέ τις ἀπειθῇ, τοὺς ἀθλοθέτας ἐξείργειν ἐκ τῆς χώρας τὸ παράπαν αὐθημερόν, ἢ ζημιοῦσθαι μναῖς τρισὶν ἱεραῖς τοῦ θεοῦ οὗ ἂν ἀγὼν ᾖ. οἷς δ᾽ εἴρηται πρότερον ἐξουσίαν εἶναι περί του ποιεῖν, εἰς ἀλλήλους τούτοις ἄνευ θυμοῦ μὲν μετὰ παιδιᾶς ἐξέστω, σπουδῇ δὲ ἅμα καὶ θυμουμένοισιν μὴ ἐξέστω, τούτου δὴ διάγνωσις ἐπιτετράφθω τῷ τῆς παιδεύσεως ὅλης ἐπιμελητῇ τῶν νέων· καὶ ὃ μὲν ἂν οὗτος ἐγκρίνῃ, προφέρειν εἰς τὸ μέσον ἐξέστω τῷ ποιήσαντι, ὃ δ᾽ ἂν ἀποκρίνῃ, μήτε αὐτὸς ἐπιδεικνύσθω μηδενὶ μήτε ἄλλον δοῦλον μήτε ἐλεύθερόν ποτε φανῇ διδάξας, ἢ κακὸς εἶναι δοξαζέσθω καὶ ἀπειθὴς τοῖς νόμοις.

Are we lending our countenance to the comedians' efforts to raise a laugh against mankind, provided the object of their comedies is to attain their result, to turn the laugh against their fellow-citizens, without such passion? Shall we draw the line between sport and earnest, permitting men to jest upon one another in sport and without anger, but absolutely forbidding all such jesting, as we have already done, where it is in downright earnest and charged with passion? That proviso must certainly not be withdrawn, but the law will proceed to specify the persons to whom permission shall or shall not be granted. No composer of comedy, iambic or lyric verse shall be permitted to hold any citizen up to laughter, by word or by impersonation, with passion or otherwise; in case of disobedience the Presidents of the festival shall give orders for the offender's expulsion from the State's territory within the course of the day, on pain of a fine of three minae to be paid to the deity in whose honour the festival is held. The persons to whom permission has already been granted by an earlier arrangement to compose personal satire shall be free to satirize each other dispassionately and in jest, but not in earnest or with angry feeling. The actual drawing of the distinction shall be left to the Minister in charge of the system of juvenile education. If he approve a piece, its composer shall have licence to produce it in public; if he disapprove, the composer shall neither appear in it himself nor train any other person, slave or free, to perform it, on pain of being declared a bad citizen and a law-breaker. (Tr. A. E. Taylor)

The best one might do with comedy, Plato seems to be saying in his last work, is to control personal satire so that it is turned only against other practitioners of the genre and then only in a spirit of complete jest. The implication is certainly, as with the Old Oligarch, that personal satire was central to the genre, and the same inference must also be drawn from the statement by Aristotle about comic poets at *Rhetoric* 1384b, 9–11 (quoted below in the section 'Aristotle on Comedy'), where comic poets are the same as mockers, interested in their neighbours' faults, and therefore nothing but slanderers and gossips. The specific interest in individual wrongdoing and the publication of the results tally with the focus on attacking the individual already seen above in the Old Oligarch and Plato.

The view from the theatron

To this list, we may add passages from public oratory (Lysias fr. 53, Aeschines 1.157, Andocides fr. 5, for which see under (2) below), in all of which the focus is upon named individuals who are attacked by comic poets. This situation is also reflected in Plato, where Socrates is made to mention at *Phaedo* 70b–c the possibility of his being insulted by a comic poet as a babbler and discusser of irrelevancies. In addition, we have Isocrates' attack upon the freedom of speech of comic poets (8.14):

ἐγὼ δὲ οἶδα μὲν ὅτι πρόσαντές ἐστιν ἐναντιοῦσθαι ταῖς ὑμετέραις διανοίαις, καὶ ὅτι δημοκρατίας οὔσης, οὐκ ἔστι παρρησία, πλὴν ἐνθάδε μὲν τοῖς ἀφρονεστάτοις καὶ μηδὲν ὑμῶν φροντίζουσιν, ἐν δὲ τῷ θεάτρῳ τοῖς κωμῳδοδιδασκάλοις· ὃ καὶ πάντων ἐστὶ δεινότατον, ὅτι τοῖς μὲν ἐκφέρουσιν εἰς τοὺς ἄλλους Ἕλληνας τὰ τῆς πόλεως ἁμαρτήματα τοσαύτην ἔχετε χάριν ὅσην οὐδὲ τοῖς εὖ ποιοῦσι, πρὸς δὲ τοὺς ἐπιπλήττοντας καὶ νουθετοῦντας ὑμᾶς οὕτω διατίθεσθε δυσκόλως ὥσπερ πρὸς τοὺς κακόν τι τὴν πόλιν ἐργαζομένους.

I am well aware that it is an uphill struggle to oppose your ideas, and that although we have democracy, we do not have freedom of speech, except here [the assembly] for the most mindless, who care nothing for you, and in the theatre for the comic poets. The strangest thing of all is that you are as grateful to those who carry the news of the city's misdeeds to the rest of the Greeks as you are to your benefactors, yet your attitude to those who admonish and rebuke you is as bad-tempered as it is towards those who have done the city some real harm.

This shows clearly that even in the 350s comedy was seen by its opponents as a finding-list of 'the city's misdeeds'. This could imply, like the other evidence we have examined, the attack upon individuals for various shortcomings mentioned by the Old Oligarch.

2 Personal attack is politically functional and not confined to the festival context

Two fragments from public orations, one probably from the 410s, the other probably from the 390s, and a remark in an extant speech of the 340s make it clear that the type of personal satire practised by the comic poets at the festivals did not remain bounded by that festival context, but was utilised by political speakers in the discourse of the real world of the city. I will take the fragment from the 390s and the remark from the 340s first, because they are explicit about the source of their prejudicial personal judgements.

(a) In Lysias fr. 53 (Thalheim) the speaker, Phanias, attacked by Cinesias for proposing an illegal decree, says:[8]

---

[8] The trial probably belongs to the 390s: this is the period for which there is evidence of Cinesias' political involvement (*IG* II² 18, 394/3); Lysias' activity as a speechwriter in Athens probably postdates the restoration of democracy in 403. See Carey 1989, 3.

θαυμάζω δὲ εἰ μὴ βαρέως φέρετε ὅτι Κινησίας ἐστὶν ὁ τοῖς νόμοις βοηθός, ὃ ὑμεῖς πάντες ἐπίστασθε ἀσεβέστατον ἁπάντων καὶ παρανομώτατον ἀνθρώπων γεγονέναι. οὐχ οὗτός ἐστιν ὁ τοιαῦτα περὶ θεοὺς ἐξαμαρτάνων, ἃ τοῖς μὲν ἄλλοις αἰσχρόν ἐστι καὶ λέγειν, τῶν κωμῳδοδιδασκάλων <δ'> ἀκούετε καθ' ἕκαστον ἐνίαυτον;

I'm amazed you're not upset that it's Cinesias who is coming to the aid of the laws. You all know that he is the most impious and lawless of men. Is he not the one who commits such crimes against the gods as other people find it shameful even to mention them, though you hear of them every year from the comic poets?

(b) At *Against Timarchus* 1.157, in a law-court speech which was to have serious political fallout for the defendant Timarchus, Aeschines recalls an incident from comedy:[9]

πάλιν ἐκ τῶν μειρακίων καὶ τῶν ἐν παισὶν ἔτι νῦν ὄντων πρῶτον μὲν τὸν ἀδελφιδοῦν τὸν Ἰφικράτους, υἱὸν δὲ Τεισίου τοῦ Ῥαμνουσίου, ὁμώνυμον δὲ τοῦ νυνὶ κρινομένου· ὃς εὐπρεπὴς ὢν ἰδεῖν τοσοῦτον ἀπέχει τῶν αἰσχρῶν, ὥστε πρώην ἐν τοῖς κατ' ἀγροὺς Διονυσίοις κωμῳδῶν ὄντων ἐν Κολλυτῷ, καὶ Παρμένοντος τοῦ κωμικοῦ ὑποκριτοῦ εἰπόντος τι πρὸς τὸν χορὸν ἀνάπαιστον, ἐν ᾧ ἦν εἶναί τινας πόρνους μεγάλους Τιμαρχώδεις, οὐδεὶς ὑπελάμβανεν εἰς τὸ μειράκιον, ἀλλ' εἰς σὲ πάντες· οὕτω κληρονόμος εἶ τοῦ ἐπιτηδεύματος.

Again from the youths and those who are still boys, <I shall mention> first of all the nephew of Iphicrates, the son of Teisias of Rhamnous, who has the same name as the defendant. He is fine-looking, but is so far from shameful behaviour that recently, when there were comedies on at the Rural Dionysia in Kollytos and the comic actor Parmenon in an anapaestic line addressed to the chorus mentioning 'big Timarchian prostitutes', no one thought it was aimed at the youth [the son of Teisias], but everyone took it as referring to you [the defendant], so emblematic are you of the practice.

In both of these extracts, the speaker's assumption is clearly that the prejudices of comedy will help him to establish his case further. There is absolutely no sense in either that there is some disjunction between satire and reality. The comic poets deal thus and thus with Cinesias and Timarchus because the genre tells the truth about individuals. This truth can therefore form part of the evidence used to condemn an individual so attacked.

---

[9] The latest date for this speech is 345. Fisher 2001, 8.

(c) Another fragment (Andoc. fr. 5), from the period of the ostracism of Hyperbolus, fits within the same matrix, although its reference to comedy is only implicit.[10] Here the speaker says:

περὶ Ὑπερβόλου τοίνυν λέγειν αἰσχύνομαι, οὗ ὁ μὲν πατὴρ ἐστιγμένος ἔτι καὶ νῦν ἐν τῷ ἀργυροκοπείῳ δουλεύει τῷ δημοσίῳ, αὐτὸς (MSS ὡς) δὲ ξένος ὢν καὶ βάρβαρος λυχνοποιεῖ.

I am ashamed to speak about Hyperbolus, whose father bears a brand and is still a state slave in the mint, while his son makes lamps, though a barbarian foreigner.

In fact, Hyperbolus was the son of Antiphanes, registered in the deme of Perithoidae (*PA* 13910), so that neither what is said of his father nor his own barbarian status can be true. It was in comedy that Hyperbolus was represented as a barbarian (Eup. *Marikas* of 421; Quint. 1.10.18; cf. Plato Com. *Hyperbolus* fr. 183) and a lamp-maker (e.g. Ar. *Peace* 690–2). Here, then, comic fiction has become fact and is being used as such to berate an individual before the *demos*. This passage is another instance, then, in which, in the public political space of the real world of Athens, the invective fantasies of the comedians are recycled for prejudicial purposes. In this instance also, the speaker is probably implying that the comic poets would not have attacked Hyperbolus without reason, even if he expects his audience to recognise that these images refer to quite specific comic scenes and involve the gross caricature of iambic comedy.

(d) It is in this context, then, that we should seek to understand the two references to comic poetry in Plato's *Apology*: ὃ δὲ πάντων ἀλογώτατον, ὅτι οὐδὲ τὰ ὀνόματα οἷόν τε αὐτῶν εἰδέναι καὶ εἰπεῖν, πλὴν εἴ τις κωμῳδοποιὸς τυγχάνει ὤν. ('The oddest thing of all is that it is impossible to know and speak their names, unless any of them happens to be a comic poet.' 18c–d) and ταῦτα γὰρ ἑωρᾶτε καὶ αὐτοὶ ἐν τῇ τοῦ Ἀριστοφάνους κωμῳδίᾳ, Σωκράτη τινα ἐκεῖ περιφερόμενον, φάσκοντά τε ἀεροβατεῖν καὶ ἄλλην πολλὴν φλυαρίαν φλυαροῦντα, ὧν ἐγὼ οὐδὲν οὔτε μέγα οὔτε μικρὸν πέρι ἐπαΐω. ('You actually saw this yourselves in Aristophanes' comedy, a Socrates being whirled round and claiming to be "walking on air" and talking lots of other nonsense about things of which I have no knowledge, great or small.' 19c). Socrates is imagined, in a replica of public discourse in

---

[10] Wherever this fragment belongs in Andocides' work, it seems to have been written for delivery before the ostracism of Hyperbolus (417–415). For recent discussion of the date of the ostracism, see Rhodes 1994.

the real world of the city, as both accepting the potency of comic invective (18c–d) and rejecting its basis (19c), an understandable inversion of the assumptions of the other passages we have examined which address the actual political world of Athens.[11] A similar analysis can be made of the way the Syracusan's attempt to use Aristophanic invective from *Clouds* against the real Socrates is rebutted in Xenophon's *Symposium* (6.6f.).[12]

Invective comedy, then, is conceived of as a mode of attack, one which was meant to sting. Writers working within the context of the democratic system assume with their public that such attacks reflect the truth (a), (b), and so can even use the comic fantasy itself to engage their audience's distaste for an individual (c), while critics of the system, though recognising the power the genre has to create prejudice, nonetheless refuse to accept the proposition that such attacks are necessarily based on reality (d). This amounts to an acceptance on both sides that the genre aims at laughter which is 'consequential' rather than 'playful', to use the terms of Halliwell's acute analysis of Greek constructions of laughter.[13] Consequential laughter is distinguished, according to Halliwell, by being directed 'towards some definite result other than autonomous pleasure (e.g. causing embarrassment or shame, signalling hostility, damaging a reputation, contributing to the defeat of an opponent, delivering public chastisement)', by 'its deployment of an appropriate range of ridiculing tones, from mild derision to the vitriolic or outrageously offensive' and by 'its arousal of feelings which may not be shared or enjoyed by all concerned, and which typically involve some degree of antagonism'.[14] The connection between comedy, laughter, abuse and spite (θυμός) seen in Plato's legislative proposal for comedy at *Laws* 935d discussed above puts the whole

---

[11] Contrast Heath 1987, 9–12.
[12] τοιούτων δὲ λόγων ὄντων ὡς ἑώρα ὁ Συρακόσιος τῶν μὲν αὑτοῦ ἐπιδειγμάτων ἀμελοῦντας, ἀλλήλοις δὲ ἡδομένους, φθονῶν τῷ Σωκράτει εἶπεν· Ἆρα σύ, ὦ Σώκρατες, ὁ φροντιστὴς ἐπικαλούμενος; Οὐκοῦν κάλλιον, ἔφη, ἢ εἰ ἀφρόντιστος ἐκαλούμην. Εἰ μή γε ἐδόκεῖς τῶν μετεώρων φροντιστὴς εἶναι. Οἶσθα οὖν, ἔφη ὁ Σωκράτης, μετεωρότερόν τι τῶν θεῶν; ... Ταῦτα μὲν, ἔφη, ἔα· ἀλλ' εἰπέ μοι πόσους ψύλλα πόδας ἐμοῦ ἀπέχει. ταῦτα γάρ σέ φασι γεωμετρεῖν. 'With the discussion going on like this, the Syracusan saw that they were neglecting his spectacles and just enjoying one another's company. So he said to Socrates, in a spirit of nastiness, 'Are you, Socrates, the man nicknamed 'the thinker'?' 'Well,' replied Socrates, 'That's a good deal better than being called 'unthinking'.' 'It would be if people didn't consider you to be a thinker about things in the air.' 'Well,' said Socrates, 'Do you know anything more 'in the air' than the gods?' ... 'Well, let's leave that subject,' he said. 'Tell me instead how many feet a flea is way from me. That's the sort of measurements people say you make.' Cf. *Clouds* 360 (τῶν νῦν μετεωροσοφιστῶν 'of the current air-thinkers') and 144f. (measuring how many of its own feet a flea has jumped).
[13] Halliwell 1991a.   [14] Halliwell 1991a, 283.

picture together neatly. Comedy invites laughter *at* individuals which is *consequential* and therefore politically functional – and this is the foundation of both Plato's and Aristotle's problem with it.

3 Two modes of attack exist: (a) by name; (b) by impersonation
If attack on individuals is, according to our sources, central to the genre, we can also discern from these same sources indications of the two ways in which such attacks were conducted: by naming of names and by impersonation.

The first mode, in which an individual is named in conjunction with some incident, vice or foible to engender in the audience the laughter of derision, is evidenced in several passages written from differing perspectives. It is clearly the mode used in the comedy mentioned at Aeschines 1.157, quoted above, where we are told the speaker (a comic actor, identified as Parmenon), the dramatic addressee (the chorus), and the type of verse used (anapaestic), and also given the precise phrase containing the insult (πόρνους μεγάλους Τιμαρχώδεις 'big Timarchian prostitutes'). The phrasing of Lysias fr. 53 (also quoted above) makes it likely that the comic poets mentioned there also attacked Cinesias in this way, since he is named and we are told that while other people are ashamed to mention them, you *hear* of them every year (though as we shall see below, this formulation need not exclude the other mode). It is likely that Plato means naming of this sort when he mentions, in the new law he is creating to govern comedy, attacks against citizens λόγῳ᾽ ('by word') that comic poets (among others) are not allowed to utilise (*Laws* 935e).

In the case of Plato, *Phaedo* 70b–c, where Socrates is made to say οὔκουν γ᾽ ἂν οἶμαι ... εἰπεῖν τινα νῦν ἀκούσαντα, οὐδ᾽ εἰ κωμῳδοποιός εἴη, ὡς ἀδολεσχῶ καὶ οὐ περὶ προσηκόντων τοὺς λόγους ποιοῦμαι ('I don't think anyone who heard this present discussion ... even if he were a writer of comedies, would say that I am babbling and discussing irrelevancies'), it is not entirely clear what εἰπεῖν implies, given that there survives a fragment of Eupolis (fr. 386.1–2) which both names Socrates and uses the word ἀδολέσχης ('babbler') to describe him and at *Apology* 19c Socrates is made to describe an attack on him by impersonation (in *Clouds*) which includes the idea of his φλυαρίαν φλυαροῦντα ('talking nonsense'). The indeterminacy of some of this evidence together with the lack of any indication of mode in [Xen.] *Ath. Pol.* 2.18, is in fact rather important and will be analysed below.

The second mode, impersonation, is firmly evidenced by Plato *Apology* 19c (quoted above). Here, it is Socrates who is represented on stage, though once more there is a subtle twist which reflects the antagonistic perspective from which Plato characteristically views this genre. For Socrates' comment makes it clear that the Socrates on stage had nothing to do with *him*, the real Socrates. That gap allows us to infer that such representations were not portraits, but caricatures (as one might expect they would be, given the satirical intention already established for the genre). If my reading of Andocides fr. 5 above is correct, then the passage recalls a play in which Hyperbolus' father was represented on stage as a state-slave, working in the mint, and in which (or perhaps it was a different play) Hyperbolus was represented as a lamp-maker (though since there are many instances in extant plays and fragments of comedy in which Hyperbolus is *named* and associated with lamp-making, the latter inference is not quite cut and dried). Finally, Plato's legal formulation against the comedy of personal attack (*Laws* 935e) mentions the prohibition of attacks εἰκόνι ('by impersonation' Saunders) in conjunction with λόγῳ ('by word'). It is not quite clear how 'impersonation' could apply to attack in an iambic or lyric verse and, given the evidence already cited, it seems reasonable to infer that this is inserted here specifically to cover a mode typical of invective comedy – the representation on stage of a real individual as a character in the drama.

As has already been noted, however, although these modes are quite distinct from each other, the ancient writers we are examining do not seem normally to make any thoroughgoing distinction between them (the opposite of the way Aristophanes treats the issue, p. 26 above), even as they display a clear agreement that individual attack is the central focus of the genre. Thus when Lysias mentions the comic poets' treatment of Cinesias' vices, he may be evoking not merely named attacks ('Cinesias is impious and lawless') but also caricature attacks (Cinesias as a character in comedies, displaying such features by his words and actions). The Old Oligarch, too, who is notably silent about mode, may simply be assuming that the κωμῳδούμενος – the focus of invective comedy – is commonly attacked in both ways: like the others, he does not have to say it in so many words, because nobody who has ever attended an invective comedy will need to be told and in any case the modal distinction is not central to his point.

One of these two modes, however, impersonation, is inherently *dramatic* and must, therefore, have originated with the emergence of the dramatic genre. It would therefore be distinctly odd, since attack on individuals appears to be assumed by our ancient sources to be what invective comedy is all about, if impersonation were not of crucial importance to the nature of the dramatic form as opposed to its non-dramatic forebear, iambic. A

The view from the theatron 317

late source of indeterminate date and provenance, Platonius, *On Differences* (Koster *Prolegomena*, p. 5, 1.57–9) does in fact focus in an interesting way upon the centrality of impersonation:

ἐν μὲν γὰρ τῇ παλαιᾷ κωμῳδίᾳ εἴκαζον τὰ προσωπεῖα τοῖς κωμῳδουμένοις ἵνα, πρίν τι καὶ τοὺς ὑποκριτὰς εἰπεῖν, ὁ κωμῳδούμενος ἐκ τῆς ὁμοιότητος τῆς ὄψεως κατάδηλος ᾖ.

In Old Comedy, they made the masks like the targets of the satire, so that before the actors actually said anything the target was clear from the likeness of his face.

We do not know his source (but I will return to that later), and his words have been much maligned because of general scepticism about the idea of 'portrait-masks'.[15] Nonetheless, we ought to pay more attention, not because of what he says about masks, but because, very unusually, he uses the term κωμῳδούμενος in the sense of an individual attacked by impersonation rather than as a person attacked by named invective attack. Plutarch also used the word in exactly the same way of Hyperbolus in Eupolis' *Marikas*: ὁ δ' ὑπ' Εὐπόλιδος κωμῳδούμενος ἐν τῷ Μαρικᾷ (*Nicias* 4.5). Thus while the whole discussion about masks just might be a theoretical excursus based very largely upon *Knights* 230f.,[16] it is hard to believe that this use of the word κωμῳδούμενος does not have ancient authority, since impersonation of this kind must have originated with the dramatic genre.

The only contemporary evidence we can bring to bear on this topic that comes from a source who might have known at first hand the reality of invective comedy in Athens is contained in Aristotle's *Poetics*, a text of the 320s. An examination of his *obiter dicta* on the history and nature of comedy will confirm the logic of the inference made above, that impersonation was regarded as the central satirical ploy of invective comedy.

ARISTOTLE ON COMEDY

Aristotle's discussion of comedy, as of the role of poetry *tout court*, is dependent upon that of Plato. He shares the basic notion that poetry is *mimesis* (e.g. *Republic* 394e f., 595a; *Poetics* 1447a etc.). He also takes from Plato the basic division of all poetry into two antithetical categories, serious and comic (*Poetics* 1448b). In Plato, these are given the generalised

---

[15] See particularly Dover 1967.
[16] It will be clear from my discussion (above, pp. 66–8) that I do not think this is the explanation, even though scholiastic variance on the issue of the development of comedy shows that such theorising did occur.

names τραγῳδία ('tragedy') and κωμῳδία ('comedy') (see *Republic* 595b–c, 598d, 607a for Homer as the inventor of tragedy, and *Theaetetus* 152e for the division between the two types of poetry). More importantly, Aristotle's discussion of both tragedy and comedy is constructed in antithesis with Plato's views. While Plato rejects tragedy and comedy from his ideal state (*Republic* 10) and severely limits its scope in his legislative model for an actual state (*Laws* 816–17, 935–6), Aristotle prefers to prescribe generic objectives and regulations which will allow them to be retained and serve specific social and educational goals. Hence, to answer the critique of Plato against the harmful indulgence of emotions induced by tragedy, Aristotle develops his theory of *katharsis* and recommends models for plots which will allow the correct education of the emotions thus evoked.[17] We may presume that the rather positive reading which Aristotle gives to comedy in *Poetics* 1449a, linked as it is back to a Homeric model (1448b–1449a), represents his answer to Plato's strictures. Possibly, though this is uncertain, the type of comedy he commends would evoke laughter linked to an appropriate model of comic *katharsis*.[18]

However, that part of Plato's critique of comedy concerned with the harmfulness to society of *satirical attack on individuals* (*Laws* 935c–d) is shared by Aristotle, as can be seen from the following three passages:

EN 1128a, 23–5: ἴδοι δ' ἄν τις καὶ ἐκ τῶν κωμῳδιῶν τῶν παλαιῶν καὶ τῶν καινῶν· τοῖς μὲν γὰρ ἦν γελοῖον ἡ αἰσχρολογία, τοῖς δὲ μᾶλλον ἡ ὑπόνοια· διαφέρει δ' οὐ μικρὸν ταῦτα πρὸς εὐσχημοσύνην.

One can see this from the 'old' and the 'new' comedies. The humour in the first was open treatment of shameful things (*aiskhrologia*) but in the second rather merely hinting at them (*hyponoia*). This makes a big difference as far as decorum is concerned.

Rhetoric 1384b.9–11: καὶ οἷς ἡ διατριβὴ ἐπὶ ταῖς τῶν πέλας ἁμαρτίαις, οἷον χλευασταῖς καὶ κωμῳδοποιοῖς· κακολόγοι γάρ πως οὗτοι καὶ ἐξαγγελτικοί.

(And men are ashamed) also before those who spend their time in looking for their neighbours' faults, for instance mockers and comic poets; for they are also in a manner slanderers and gossips.

Aristotle, *Politics* 1336a39f.: ἐπισκεπτέον δὲ τοῖς παιδονόμοις τὴν τούτων διαγωγὴν τήν τ' ἄλλην καὶ ὅπως ὅτι ἥκιστα μετὰ δούλων ἔσται. ταύτην γὰρ τὴν ἡλικίαν, καὶ μέχρι τῶν ἑπτὰ ἐτῶν, ἀναγκαῖον οἴκοι τὴν τροφὴν ἔχειν· εὔλογον οὖν ἀπολαύειν ἀπὸ τῶν ἀκουσμάτων καὶ τῶν ὁραμάτων ἀνελευθερίαν

---

[17] Halliwell 1986, 184f.
[18] On comic *katharsis*, see Janko 1984, Halliwell 1986, 274f. and Sutton 1994.

καὶ τηλικούτους ὄντας. ὅλως μὲν οὖν αἰσχρολογίαν ἐκ τῆς πόλεως, ὥσπερ ἄλλο τι, δεῖ τὸν νομοθέτην ἐξορίζειν (ἐκ τοῦ γὰρ εὐχερῶς λέγειν ὁτιοῦν τῶν αἰσχρῶν γίνεται καὶ τὸ ποιεῖν σύνεγγυς), μάλιστα μὲν οὖν ἐκ τῶν νέων, ὅπως μήτε λέγωσι μήτε ἀκούωσι μηδὲν τοιούτων... τοὺς δὲ νεωτέρους οὔτ᾽ ἰάμβων οὔτε κωμῳδίας θεατὰς ἐατέον, πρὶν ἢ τὴν ἡλικίαν λάβωσιν ἐν ᾗ καὶ κατακλίσεως ὑπάρξει κοινωνεῖν ἤδη καὶ μέθης καὶ τῆς ἀπὸ τῶν τοιούτων γιγνομένης βλάβης ἀπαθεῖς ἡ παιδεία ποιήσει πάντας.

The tutors must supervise the children's pastimes, and in particular must see that they associate as little as possible with slaves. For children of this age, and up to seven years old, must necessarily be reared at home; so it is reasonable to suppose that even at this age they may acquire a taint of illiberality from what they hear and see. The lawgiver ought therefore to banish *aiskhrologia*, as much as anything else, out of the state altogether (for light talk about anything disgraceful soon passes into action) - so most of all from among the young, so that they may not say or hear anything of the sort... But the younger ones must not be allowed in the audience at lampoons and at comedy, before they reach the age at which they have the right to recline at table in company and to drink deeply, and at which their education will render all of them immune to the harmful effects of such things. (Tr. H. Rackham)

For Aristotle here, comic poets are satirists, whose use of αἰσχρολογία is harmful, especially to the ethical formation of the young. It is important to note that we have in fr. 53 of Lysias, quoted above, contemporary evidence which links αἰσχρολογία directly with individual satirical attack: what is shameful for others even to mention (αἰσχρόν ἐστι καὶ λέγειν) in Cinesias' case is precisely what comic poets do mention. Though some change has occurred in the course of time to ameliorate the problem, according to Aristotle's formulation in the *EN* passage, namely, the introduction of ὑπόνοια for αἰσχρολογία, this does not mean the substitution of the coy euphemism in sexual matters which is characteristic of what we call New Comedy (cf., e.g. Men. *Sam.* 49–50) for the primary obscenities of Old Comedy. Rather it implies the substitution of covert for open attack (e.g. Xen. *Symp.* 3.6, Pl. *Rep.* 378d). The antithesis is understood by Aspasios (*CAG* 19.1, p. 125, 31–5 (Heylbut]) as φανερῶς αἰσχρολογεῖν ('saying disgraceful things openly') versus μόνον ἐμφαίνειν ('merely hinting'): specifically, τὸ μεθ᾽ ὑπονοίας σκώπτειν, τουτέστιν μετὰ τοῦ αἰνίττεσθαῖ 'joking with *hyponoia* means joking enigmatically'. Whatever had happened to the genre which we call Old Comedy by the time of the *Nicomachean Ethics*, it had not changed its basic nature. It still involved an attack on the vices of individuals, even if that attack was now covert rather than completely open, and it was still, therefore, a source of irritation for its deleterious moral effects. I shall return to this passage later.

In *Poetics*, however, Aristotle's focus is not on the invective form of comedy, but on a type which concentrates on generic human foibles, though he seems always to have the invective form at the back of his mind. Evidence for this latter contention can be found at *Poetics* 1451a36–8 and b 5–15:

φανερὸν δὲ ἐκ τῶν εἰρημένων καὶ ὅτι οὐ τὰ γενόμενα λέγειν, τοῦτο ποιητοῦ ἔργον ἐστίν, ἀλλ' οἷα ἂν γένοιτο καὶ τὰ δυνατὰ κατὰ τὸ εἰκὸς ἢ τὸ ἀναγκαῖον... διὸ καὶ φιλοσοφώτερον καὶ σπουδαιότερον ποίησις ἱστορίας ἐστίν· ἡ μὲν γὰρ ποίησις μᾶλλον τὸ καθόλου, ἡ δ' ἱστορία τὰ καθ' ἕκαστον λέγει. ἔστιν δὲ καθολοῦ μέν, τῷ ποίῳ τὰ ποῖα ἄττα συμβαίνει λέγειν ἢ πράττειν κατὰ τὸ εἰκὸς ἢ τὸ ἀναγκαῖον, οὗ στοχάζεται ἡ ποίησις ὀνόματα ἐπιτιθεμένη· τὸ δὲ καθ' ἕκαστον, τί Ἀλκιβιάδης ἔπραξεν ἢ τί ἔπαθεν. ἐπὶ μὲν οὖν τῆς κωμῳδίας ἤδη τοῦτο δῆλον γέγονεν· συστήσαντες γὰρ τὸν μῦθον διὰ τῶν εἰκότων οὕτω τὰ τύχοντα ὀνόματα ὑποτιθέασιν, καὶ οὐχ ὥσπερ οἱ ἰαμβοποιοὶ περὶ τὸ καθ' ἕκαστον ποιοῦσιν.[19]

> From what has been said it is also clear that the poet's job is not to report what has happened, but what is likely to happen: that is, what is capable of happening according to the rule of probability or necessity. Hence poetry is a more philosophical and serious business than history; for poetry speaks more of universals, history of particulars. 'Universal' in this case is what kind of person is likely to do or say certain kinds of things, according to probability or necessity; that is what poetry aims at, though it gives its persons particular names afterward; while the 'particular' is what Alcibiades did or what happened to him. In the field of comedy this has now become clear. Comic poets construct the plot on the basis of general probabilities and then assign names to the persons quite arbitrarily; they do not compose (sc. plots) dealing with the particular like the *iambopoioi*.

After asserting that poetry's task is to deal with the general and history's the particular, Aristotle defines what he means, ending with an example of the particular (what Alcibiades did or had done to him). He then provides an illustration in terms of comedy: ἤδη τοῦτο δῆλον γέγονεν 'this has now become clear' (sc. from my earlier discussion).[20] The way comic poets compose is by starting from a realistic plot, which is peopled with

---

[19] Malcolm Heath pointed out to me during discussion at the 'Rivals of Aristophanes' conference in September 1996 that the text περὶ τὸν καθ' ἕκαστον obscured the antithesis between 'general' and 'particular' which is the theoretical substructure of the sentence. I accept that the reading τὸ is more likely, though it makes no difference to my interpretation.

[20] It is possible (as I argued in Sidwell 2000a) that Aristotle here alludes to some sort of historical development in comedy. The commentators (e.g. Lucas 1968) certainly make heavy weather of ἤδη, which they do not interpret as temporal because they cannot associate Aristotle with a chronologically developmental model of comedy: but the passage of *EN* cited earlier also suggests an historical change in comedy. Oliver Ranner suggests to me, however, that this is merely a way Aristotle has of referring to things he regards as established by the current discussion and I now accept this as a more likely interpretation.

individuals whose names are not those of specific individuals, but only whatever chance dictates. The implication is that only this form is actually *comedy*. Comedies based on plot had been in the picture since Crates, as Aristotle himself says elsewhere in the work (1449b7f., quoted above). The definition is formulated in terms of a contrast to the work of the poets he calls ἰαμβοποιοί ('composers of iamboi'). But who are the ἰαμβοποιοί? In contrast to comic poets, who construct their plots according to normal rules of causality and then give their characters chance names, the ἰαμβοποιοί composed (but what?) beginning from the particular. The contrast makes no sense if the implicit object of the first part of the sentence, namely the comic plot, is not also the implicit object of the second. If we insert that object, then ἰαμβοποιοί are writers of another – fundamentally different – form of comic drama, to which, however, Aristotle denies the name 'comedy'. Since Aristotle ascribed to Crates what for him was a truly significant development and contrasted it fundamentally with a form of comedy he called ἰαμβική, and this development specifically involved the focus on *plot*, then it seems reasonable to suspect that ἰαμβοποιοί does not mean iambic poets, but poets of the iambic form of comedy.[21]

We are thus left with important fourth-century support for Platonius' contention that the κωμῳδούμενος was not just a person attacked by name, but was a dramatic character. For once we see that Aristotle is speaking of invective comedy as the contrast to plot-based comedy, it follows that he is telling us that the fundamental particularity of such dramas was that of their characters, who must have been representing real individuals, as opposed to the generic characters of the type of comedy that had its foundation in a realistic plot, who were only given names in response to the requirement for them and not because they reflected the fact that these were specific real individuals.

Once this explicit contrast between the two genres of comedy is perceived, it will be immediately obvious from Aristotle's cross-reference that it must underlie his earlier discussions too. The passage where Aristotle defines comedy can help us further with his implicit assumptions about what comedy should and should not be. At *Poetics* 1449a 32f., Aristotle writes:

---

[21] It is difficult to sustain the argument that the focus here is upon *names*, and that is why iambic poets are mentioned. This would be a peculiar way to say that iambic poets used real names, while it is not an odd way to speak about two different ways of composing plots. Moreover, the emphasis on names is subordinate to the argument about the general versus the particular. Aristotle cannot defend the type of comedy assumed in our other sources from the period precisely because it is based on the principle of attacking particular individuals. He can defend a type of comedy which is based not on *psogos*, but upon *to geloion*.

ἡ δὲ κωμῳδία ἐστὶν ὥσπερ εἴπομεν μίμησις φαυλοτέρων μέν, οὐ μέντοι κατὰ πᾶσαν κακίαν, ἀλλὰ τοῦ αἰσχροῦ ἐστι τὸ γελοῖον μόριον. τὸ γὰρ γελοῖον ἐστιν ἁμάρτημά τι καὶ αἶσχος ἀνώδυνον καὶ οὐ φθαρτικόν, οἷον εὐθὺς τὸ γελοῖον πρόσωπον αἰσχρόν τι καὶ διεστραμμένον ἄνευ ὀδύνης.

Comedy is, as we said, an imitation of persons who are inferior; not, however, going all the way to full villainy, but imitating the shameful (*aiskhron*), of which the laughable (*to geloion*) is one part. For the laughable (*to geloion*) is a failing or a piece of ugliness which causes no pain or destruction; thus, to go no farther, the laughable mask is something ugly (*aiskhron*) and distorted, but painless.

It now becomes clearer that here, as elsewhere, Aristotle is struggling against another type of comedy which is not based on τὸ γελοῖον, but on some other principle. That other genre, unlike the one he now defines as 'comedy', did have characters who were entirely villainous (κατὰ πᾶσαν κακίαν), and whose failings (ἁμάρτημά τι καὶ αἶσχος) did cause harm. His specific example of what this comedy does not do, the mask, confirms Platonius' observation about masks. For the πρόσωπον αἰσχρόν τι καὶ διεστραμμένον ἄνευ ὀδύνης ('an ugly and distorted, but painless, mask') surely implies the existence of an opposite, one intended to cause pain by its distortion of the features of a specific individual, the κωμῳδούμενος, the real individual caricatured as a dramatic character in the invective comedy.

Underlying Aristotle's account of comedy, then, is a contrast he expects his readers to have picked up from his earlier discussion between the invective and the plot-based comedy. His clear dislike for the invective form can be seen for the first time, in fact, in the more general discussion of the development of poetry, where we can find further support for the centrality of critical impersonation to the invective genre, and which is probably, therefore, the place cross-referenced from 1451b. At *Poetics* 1448b20–1449a5 Aristotle writes:

κατα φύσιν δὲ ὄντος ἡμῖν τοῦ μιμεῖσθαι καὶ τῆς ἁρμονίας καὶ τοῦ ῥυθμοῦ... ἐξ ἀρχῆς οἱ πεφυκότες πρὸς αὐτὰ μάλιστα κατὰ μικρὸν προάγοντες ἐγέννησαν τὴν ποίησιν ἐκ τῶν αὐτοσχεδιασμάτων. διεσπάσθη δὲ κατὰ τὰ οἰκεῖα ἤθη ἡ ποίησις· οἱ μὲν σεμνότεροι τὰς καλὰς ἐμιμοῦντο πράξεις καὶ τὰς τῶν τοιούτων, οἱ δὲ εὐτελέστεροι τὰς τῶν φαύλων, πρῶτον ψόγους ποιοῦντες, ὥσπερ ἕτεροι ὕμνους καὶ ἐγκώμια. τῶν μὲν οὖν πρὸ Ὁμήρου οὐδενὸς ἔχομεν εἰπεῖν τοιοῦτον ποίημα, εἰκὸς δὲ εἶναι πολλούς, ἀπὸ δὲ Ὁμήρου ἀρξαμένους ἔστιν, οἷον ἐκείνου ὁ Μαργίτης καὶ τὰ τοιαῦτα. ἐν οἷς κατὰ τὸ ἁρμόττον καὶ τὸ ἰαμβεῖον ἦλθε μέτρον - διὸ καὶ ἰαμβεῖον καλεῖται νῦν, ὅτι ἐν μέτρῳ τούτῳ ἰάμβιζον ἀλλήλους. καὶ ἐγένοντο τῶν παλαιῶν οἱ μὲν ἡρωικῶν οἱ δὲ ἰάμβων ποιηταί. ὥσπερ δὲ καὶ τὰ σπουδαῖα μάλιστα ποιητὴς Ὅμηρος ἦν (μόνος γὰρ οὐχ ὅτι εὖ ἀλλὰ καὶ μιμήσεις δραματικὰς ἐποίησεν), οὕτω καὶ τὸ τῆς κωμῳδίας σχῆμα πρῶτος ὑπέδειξεν, οὐ ψόγον ἀλλὰ τὸ γελοῖον δραματοποιήσας· ὁ γὰρ Μαργίτης ἀνάλογον ἔχει, ὥσπερ Ἰλιὰς καὶ ἡ Ὀδυσσεία πρὸς τὰς τραγῳδίας, οὕτω καὶ οὗτς πρὸς τὰς κωμῳδίας. παραφανείσης δὲ τῆς τραγῳδίας καὶ κωμῳδίας οἱ ἐφ᾽ ἑκατέραν τὴν ποίησιν ὁρμῶντες κατὰ τὴν οἰκείαν φύσιν οἱ μὲν ἀντὶ τῶν ἰάμβων κωμῳδοποιοὶ ἐγένοντο, οἱ δὲ ἀντὶ τῶν ἐπῶν τραγῳδοδιδάσκαλοι...

Since, then, imitation comes naturally to us, and melody and rhythm too... it was those who were most gifted in these respects who, developing them little by little, brought the making of poetry into being out of improvisations. And the poetic enterprise split into two branches, in accordance with the two kinds of character. Namely, the more serious were imitating noble actions and the actions of noble persons, while the less serious ones were imitating the actions of the worthless, producing invectives (*psogoi*) at first, just as the others were producing hymns and encomia. Now it happens that we cannot name anyone before Homer as the author of the former kind of poem (i.e. an invective), though it stands to reason that there were many who were; but from Homer on we can do so; thus his *Margites* and other poems of that sort. In them (i.e. invectives), in accordance with what was suitable and fitting, iambic verse also put in an appearance; indeed that is why it is called 'iambic' now, because it is the verse in which they used to 'iambize', that is lampoon, each other. And so of the early poets some became composers of epic, the others of iambic, verses. However, just as on the serious side Homer was most truly a poet, since he was the only one who not only composed well but constructed dramatic imitations, so too he was the first to mark out the (sc. proper) form of comedy by dramatising not invective (*psogos*) but the ludicrous (*to geloion*). For as the *Iliad* and the *Odyssey* stand in relation to (our?) tragedies, so the *Margites* stands in relation to (our?) comedies. Once tragedy and comedy had been brought to light, those who were in pursuit of the two kinds of poetic activity, in accordance with their own respective natures, became in the one case comic poets instead of iambic poets, and in the other tragic poets instead of epic poets.

According to Aristotle, the earliest period of poetry is the pre-Homeric, during which it emerged from the human instinct to imitate, and split into two streams (1448b). The more serious individuals imitated fine actions and those of the same sort of people, the meaner the deeds of the low. Hymns and encomia are the result on the serious side, invectives on the other. There seems then to be a development towards epic on the serious side and iambic on the other. Homer gives examples of both, though his *Margites* did not dramatise invective (*psogos*), but the ridiculous (*to geloion*). When drama was invented, epic poets became tragedians and iambic poets became writers of comedy (1449a). This taxonomy, however, produces a straight line on the serious side (hymns and encomia → epic → tragedy), but a forking path on the non-serious (invective → iambic → comedy of invective [*psogos*] or comedy of the ridiculous [*to geloion*]). The fork favours the comedy of the ridiculous, in seeming to elide the very existence of the comedy of invective, exactly what we have seen happens in the later passages of the treatise which refer to comedy.

There is, then, an important lacuna of thought here which can be filled by asking what distinction Aristotle made between the comedy of Crates (the first Athenian to leave behind the iambic form, 1449b7f., quoted above) and that of other fifth-century poets, such as Cratinus, contemporary with Crates. In this passage, Aristotle seems to be focusing on Homer's responsibility for producing a model for comedy by suggesting there was no development of an iambic form into which the energies of the iambic poets were now funnelled. He is certainly looking forward in the formulation 'dramatising not invective but the ridiculous' to his definition of comedy at 1449a. But he cannot have meant that invective was not dramatised, since this was, in his formulation, the basis of the type of poetry which in the non-serious tradition preceded the emergence of the iambic and presumably informed it, and he specifically tells us at 1449b7f. that there was an ἰαμβικὴ ἰδέα an 'iambic form' of comedy. Besides, a few lines earlier (at the start of 1449a), he tells us that comedy developed from improvisational beginnings from those who led off the phallic processions still held in many cities. It is generally and reasonably assumed that the characteristics of these improvisations in Dionysiac processions were obscenity and personal attack.[22] This form of comedy must be meant by Aristotle as the precursor of the Athenian mode we have found assumed in our other sources (as well as by Aristotle himself). It is the comedy of Crates at Athens which first deviates from this invective mode and adopts the Sicilian form. This occurred in the middle of the fifth century (Crates' first of three victories at the Dionysia was around 450).[23]

In looking at Aristotle's theory of the history of literature, we can see that the moment when drama was invented was absolutely crucial. For him, it led to direct *mimesis*, which suited his philosophical goals better than that of narration or even the epic mix of the two. His formulation about Homer's *Margites*, 'dramatising the ridiculous and not invective', can now be seen to be highly significant. Other Athenian sources mention comedy in its invective form. Aristotle is implicitly accepting that invective was dramatised to form comedy. But he wishes to underpin his argument that it was not what he would call comedy. Comedy is poetry and poetry deals with the general. But invective comedy centres upon the particular and so

---

[22] As found, for example, in the phallic song of the old farmer at *Acharnians* 263f., where the metre is iambic.
[23] *IG* II² 2325, 52 (= II 977 i 9). See Bonanno 1972, 19f.

is not poetry. The missing part of his antithesis with τὸ γελοῖον, then, is ψόγος. When ψόγος was dramatised, the effect was as crucial as was the transition from the semi-dramatic form of epic to the fully dramatic form of tragedy. Since he states at 1449a38–b5 that the stages of comedy's development are unknown, Aristotle here can only be thinking back to an imagined moment – which he infers from the standard form of invective comedy – where the static insults of iambic poetry leap into life on the stage as the individuals attacked are mercilessly caricatured in imitation of their real-life counterparts. Moreover, this fundamental division of the non-serious branch of poetry between *psogos* and *to geloion* accords with the basic polarities 'consequential' and 'festive', which, as we have seen, underlie the Greek construction of laughter, on Halliwell's model.[24]

It is important to notice that Aristotle treats comedy in *Poetics* in exactly the same way as he does tragedy. The work is not *descriptive*, it is *prescriptive*. We should not, therefore, be surprised to see the type of comedy of which Aristotle disapproved elided in favour of the form of which he approved, just as his illustrations of tragedy are made to support his theory of how tragedy ought to be composed, and not as a reader's guide to the genre as it exists.

Nonetheless, despite his elision, we can now see, in the antithesis with what Aristotle defined as plot-based comedy,[25] the nature of the sort of comedy we have been hearing about from our other fifth- and fourth-century sources.[26]

1 Its characters are real individuals, not fictional persons with chance names (thus when invective was dramatised, greater effect was gained because now the objects of satire were actually represented on the stage instead of merely being named).

2 Its masks are meant to hurt (the people they represent?), rather than merely being generically ugly.

---

[24] Halliwell 1991a.

[25] It is overwhelmingly probable, then, that the example from comedy given at 1453a is from a comedy which Aristotle would have called plot-based. Its mythological plot may suggest that at 1449b the use of μῦθος as opposed to λόγος refers specifically to the Sicilian mythological burlesque associated especially with Epicharmus. Later commentators thought instinctively of this poet when commenting on *Poetics* 1449b (the names of Epicharmus and Phormis have actually entered the text). It is worth noting that Plato ascribed to Epicharmus the invention of comedy (*Theaetetus* 152e). Aristotle's argument that *Sicilian* comedy was the correct form was an excellent riposte to Plato's strictures on the invective form. For Epicharmus, see Rodriguez-Noriega Guillén 1996.

[26] Heath 1989, 352, followed by Freudenburg 1992, 69 argues: 'it is important to grasp that Aristotle's characterisation of the laughable at 1449a34–5 is meant to place comedy in opposition to tragedy, not one kind of comedy in opposition to another'. This formulation does not take account of the problems internal to Aristotle's discussion of comedy or the external evidence for a different type of comedy (see above).

3 The individuals represented are meant to be thoroughgoing rogues, as opposed to the merely low fictional characters of the plot-based type of comic drama.

It is possible to add to this general picture an inference about an aspect of invective comedy which clearly does derive from the iambic tradition. The use of obscenity was an invective technique in iambic verse.[27] It is unlikely that its function was altered significantly in comedy, except that it is now subordinated to the dramatic. In other words, where it occurs in invective comedy, its function will be not to break taboos, but to invite the ridicule of shame upon the character who employs it. As I have argued, one part of the costume also, the mask, seems to have been designed with the intention of causing harm, i.e. of ridiculing the individual whose features are grotesquely distorted in it. The same ought to be true, *mutatis mutandis*, about the other parts of the costume also (the phallus, the padded buttocks etc.). These too, then, are the dramatic manifestations of a desire to ridicule and shame individuals in a society where the sexual was entirely private and the public discussion of such matters was rigorously – even occasionally absurdly – restricted.[28]

NAMING AND NOT NAMING CHARACTERS

The information we have from our external sources says nothing about the use of names for characters in invective comedy. It might, however, be possible to infer what the normal practice was from the way Aristotle formulates the contrast between the plot-based comedy and the comedy of the ἰαμβοποιοί. He specifically mentions the addition of names to generic characters in plot-based comedy, but only says that the ἰαμβοποιοί compose (their plays) with the specific in mind (1451b10f.). In invective comedy, then, naming of characters may not be as important as ensuring that the point of attack is recognised. It is an obvious fact about our extant texts that only a very small proportion of the characters carry the names of real individuals. However, the external evidence shows that characters who bear fictitious names (or none) would still somehow have been recognised as real individuals by the audience. I suggested above (pp. 65–6) that fear of prosecution may have been the fundamental reason for enigma. But we need also to take account of the evidence for legal restrictions on naming, contentious though it is.

[27] Rosen 1988, 3f.
[28] For example, take the reluctance of Aeschines in his prosecution of Timarchus for prostitution (Aeschines 1) in using the term *pornos* (37–8, 40–1, 45, 51–2, 74–6). Fisher 2001, 42.

It is generally agreed that the decree of Morychides, operative from 440–437, restricted in some way – perhaps completely – the freedom of comic poets to engage in personal attacks. However, there is no agreement, and much scepticism, about the other decrees for which we have evidence as restricting what is variously described as κωμῳδεῖν ἐξ ὀνόματος (Σ *Acharnians* 1150) or κωμῳδεῖν ὀνομαστί (Σ *Birds* 1297a; Σ Aelius Aristides *Orationes* 3.8 L-B), 'satirising by name'.[29] But scholars have failed to notice an obvious anomaly which virtually guarantees that this phrase was not generated by conjecture. Ancient scholars spent much energy on compiling information about the individuals named in Old Comedy: Ammonius' and Herodicus' κωμῳδούμενοι ('Individuals attacked in comedy') are examples, of which the latter contained at least six books (Σ *Wasps* 947c, 1238a; Ath. 13.586a), and Galen *On his own Books* 17, mentions three books of his on Eupolis' 'political names', five on Aristophanes' and two on Cratinus'. They clearly regarded this as central to the genre. Had there been no mention somewhere in their sources of such legal restrictions using the phrase κωμῳδεῖν ὀνομαστί, it is difficult to understand why they would have invented them, when the evidence before them so overwhelmingly made satirical naming a fundamental aspect of the genre. Given the contrast between the inference I have made from the external evidence that on-stage caricature was central and the state of our texts apropos of the ascription of real names to characters, there is, therefore, something to be said for renewing the proposal of Cobet that 'satire by name' meant calling an on-stage caricature by his or her real name.[30] Halliwell doubted, in respect of the decree of Morychides, the one restrictive measure that seems to be difficult to write off as scholiastic misinterpretation, 'that the Athenians engaged in the casuistry of banning names but not personalities'.[31] However, there are, as I mentioned earlier, signs of a tradition in which the form κωμῳδούμενος means 'on-stage caricature' (Plut. *Nic.* 4.5, Platonius *On Differences in Comedy* = Koster, *Prolegomena* I, 57–9). So, although scholiasts – against the evidence before their eyes – took this as meaning 'to satirise by (mentioning a person's) name', it can just as readily be interpreted as 'to satirise by on-stage caricature with the individual's real name attached'. There can be little doubt that when political leaders found themselves the butt of on-stage caricature they did not enjoy it (cf. *Frogs* 367–8): as I have shown, the exposure was meant to be demeaning. They might, it

---

[29] Halliwell 1991b, 54–66.
[30] Halliwell 1991b, 54–66, 58, Cobet 1840, 12–3, 39. However, the phrase is not used in respect of the Morychides *psephisma*, where it is κωμῳδεῖν *tout court* which is banned.
[31] Halliwell 1991b, 58.

seems reasonable to suggest, at times of national emergency have tried with the *ecclesia* the argument that conditions of war required a much tighter definition of the relationship between the individual who served the *demos* and the *demos* itself. It does, therefore, seem to me reasonable to suggest that the situation we encounter in the Aristophanic corpus is the result of a reaction against what had happened in the period in which the Morychides decree (μὴ κωμῳδεῖν 'not to satirise') was in force. For it seems not unlikely that Crates' introduction of a non-satiric comedy (Arist. *Poetics* 1449b 5–9) was the result of a blanket ban on the iambic type during the Samian War. On its repeal, on-stage attacks, even upon the *demos'* acknowledged leader Pericles, seem to have returned with vigour (Cratinus fr. 73 *Thraittai*, 118 *Nemesis* with Plut. *Per.* 3.3–4). At the beginning of the Archidamian War, an attempt to argue for a complete ban on invective comedy (such as I have suggested the Morychides decree had introduced) might well have run up against firm opposition from the emerging breed of radical democrats who took the *demos'* side rather than showed it what it should do. In such circumstances, the proponents of a ban (especially if they were the same people behind the Morychides decree) may have been able to arrive only at the 'casuistry' of allowing on-stage caricature attacks, but banning the addition of names for certain categories of servants of the *demos*, while placing no restriction at all upon the mention of individuals by name. Hence while Cleon as a serving general had to be presented on stage under a pseudonym, he could still be attacked by name by the chorus at *Knights* 976. This compromise might seem bizarre to us, but it will have been an effective protection, if I am correct in seeing such on-stage caricature as central to the genre, since in the case of foreigners visiting the Dionysia the targets might be somewhat obscured. The Athenians in the audience could see and hear for themselves that an individual was being targeted: the signals would be visual and vocal and could escape the confines of the text completely.

SCHOLIASTIC MISREADING

All this demonstrates that what we see in the plays of Aristophanes (and more dimly in those of Cratinus and others) is perfectly consistent with a situation in which poets were (sometimes) constrained to avoid naming on stage caricatures of certain groups of people (probably those with official positions representing the *demos*) and chose to avoid naming others. And it explains how, despite those restrictions, the poets could expect their audience to 'get' what was going on. What it does not explain is why, apparently, the scholars of the Alexandrian period who had access to complete plays of many of the comic poets did not read them as I am claiming their original audience was expected to do.

In fact, the picture is not quite as black and white as that. The scholia do have a scattering of attempts to identify unnamed characters. The scholia on *Acharnians* 395 identify the slave who answers the door at Euripides' house as Cephisophon. In *Thesmophoriazusai*, the scholia give the relative the name of Euripides' father-in-law, Mnesilochus. The identification of Marikas as Hyperbolus in Eupolis' play is also made clear by the scholiasts (Eup. fr. 192.150). But we ought to consider the probability that, since our texts are substantially what they had, they came without a set of keys. Thus even if ancient commentators had understood the evidence they possessed of their true nature, they would not have been able, any more than we are, to do more than hazard intelligent guesses. Brockmann has recently expressed the view that we cannot accept the notion of enigmatic comedy, since texts of plays were already available in the fifth century and had to be self-explanatory, yet no traces are found in the Alexandrian tradition of the type of notes needed to unlock the enigmas of Old Comedies. This analysis is based on a number of fundamental misconceptions.[32] First, we have no evidence at all that copies of Old Comedy texts were generally available in the fifth century. Secondly, the way the scholiasts attempt to deal with explaining jokes about individuals does not encourage the notion that, even if such texts were produced, they ever contained annotations, since patently the ancient scholars were often simply constructing their gloss by inference from the text itself.[33] Thirdly, Old Comedy was a topical genre and the contemporary audience would not have required glosses. In the age of the internet, perhaps it has become normal for 'nerds' to write up at once lists of the filmic cross-references in *The Simpsons*, but in what was still effectively an oral culture, it does not seem bizarre to think that no one recorded for posterity what individual was meant by which character in which comedy, though occasionally (as in Andocides fr. 5) snippets will have passed down.

A LOST HISTORY OF COMEDY?

In fact, I think there is substantive evidence that someone in a position to know what Old Comedy had been like wrote a *general* account of its development. It is reflected in different ways in many of the texts

---

[32] Brockmann 2003, 160 n.40. [33] Halliwell 1984, 83–4.

collected by Koster in his *Prolegomena*. Though these accounts differ in minor details, they are consistent in the following: (a) applying a set of periodic titles, 'old', 'middle', 'new' or 'first', 'second' and 'third' to the development of invective comedy ('Old Comedy': note that nowhere do they attempt a history of the non-invective form introduced by Crates); (b) distinguishing each period by whether its attitude to the mode of attack allowed open attack, disguised attack, or no attack upon citizens.[34] In particular, these scholars wrote of an 'enigmatic' or 'symbolic' stage of Old Comedy's development, variously called ψόγος κεκρυμμένος ('hidden invective'), κωμῳδεῖν ἐσχηματισμένως ('satirising figuratively'), συμβολικὰ σκώμματα ('allegorical jokes'), ἐλέγχουσα αἰνιγματωδῶς ('attacking enigmatically').[35] This stage is sometimes said to have begun with the start of Eupolis' career (*PCG* Aristophanes T83b 3–4 = Koster XIa 1, 87–8), and Aristophanes, among others, is claimed to have operated this manner of satirical attack (*PCG* Aristophanes T83b 6). In some accounts, this 'enigmatic turn' is associated with the abandonment of ὀνομαστὶ κωμῳδεῖν ('satirising by name'), e.g. the *Anonymus Cranmeri* (Koster XIb 29) and the scholia to Dionysius Thrax (Koster XVIIIa 31–2). I have already said that such an account could hardly have been constructed by scholars who manifestly thought that satirising by name meant what I have termed 'invective attack'. It is equally difficult to believe that scholars in a tradition which nowhere seriously manifests any interest in reading Eupolis, Aristophanes or Plato as 'enigmatic' or 'symbolic' could have invented such a schema.

Hence I am certain that there had existed at some point a history of Old Comedy which made the following basic points: (1) around the beginning of Eupolis' career (429), the comedy of open named attack (i.e. named on-stage caricatures) was hamstrung by legislation which impelled poets to disguise their targets (at least some of them), by not giving them their real names, that is by partially banning ὀνομαστὶ κωμῳδεῖν; (2) that further legislation removed completely the possibility of ὀνομαστὶ κωμῳδεῖν, naming on-stage caricatures, and produced the necessity of disguised attack, but still against anyone; (3) that a final piece of legislation disallowed comic poets from making caricature attacks on citizens, leaving invective comedy only as a vehicle for attacks upon slaves and foreigners. But clearly, this account cannot have gone into details or even been

---

[34] This final stage is mentioned e.g. by the scholia to Dionysius Thrax: ἡ δὲ νέα ἡ μηδὲ ὅλως τοῦτο ποιοῦσα πλὴν ἐπὶ δούλων ἢ ξένων 'New comedy is the one which does not to this (sc. satirise individuals) except only in the case of slaves or foreigners.'

[35] The first three are Tzetzes' formulations (*PCG* Aristophanes T83a and b), the last of the scholium on Dionysius Thrax (*PCG* Aristophanes T84).

generally available. Otherwise, later ancient readers would have been able to match it to their texts. This they did not do.

I infer, then, that this 'brief history of comedy' (which underlies, with a bit of individual theorising at various points, most of the 'histories of Old Comedy' we possess) was constructed by someone who did not approve of the genre or wish to make too much of it, yet needed to explain the developments for some purpose to do with the understanding of comedy. This person, I suggest, may very well have been Aristotle, and, if so, probably in the lost second book of the *Poetics*. We know from *Poetics* 1449b 21–2 that he planned to discuss comedy further. *Rhetoric* 1371b 33 and 1419b 2 assure us that that he actually wrote such an account. The first of these notices is curt: διώρισται δὲ περὶ γελοίων χωρὶς ἐν τοῖς περὶ ποιητικῆς ('a definition of things which are laughable has been provided separately in the *Poetics*'). The second is more specific: εἴρηται πόσα εἴδη γελοίων ἐστὶν ἐν τοῖς περὶ ποιητικῆς, ὧν τὸ μὲν ἁρμόττει ἐλευθέρῳ τὸ δ' οὔ· ὅπως οὖν τὸ ἁρμόττον αὐτῷ λήψεται. ἔστι δ' ἡ εἰρωνεία τῆς βωμολοχίας ἐλευθεριώτερον· ὁ μὲν γὰρ αὐτοῦ ἕνεκα ποιεῖ τὸ γελοῖον, ὁ δὲ βωμολόχος ἑτέρου. ('I have listed all the types of the laughable in the *Poetics*. One sort is fitting for a free man and the other not. He should make sure he chooses the one which is suitable. Irony is more the province of a free man than buffoonery. The ironic man produces laughter on his own account, the buffoon at someone else's expense'). This taxonomy of humour may in fact relate only to the principle which Aristotle allows for comedy, namely τὸ γελοῖον 'the laughable', which does not involve the sort of harm which he ascribes to the iambic comedy (as I argued earlier). However, if Landi is correct to see evidence for *Poetics II* at *Poetics* 1462b 19f. in the phrase περὶ δὲ ἰάμβων καὶ κωμῳδίας 'about iambus and comedy', then the fundamental distinction which underlies his remarks on comedy in the first book will have been subject to further clarification in the second.

That it was Aristotle whose account was behind later scholars' confused attempts to track Old Comedy's history can, I think, be further supported. It is he, as we have seen, who makes a distinction between 'old' and 'new' comedies at *EN* 1128a 23–5 (quoted earlier). As I have already argued, he is clearly referring to the iambic genre, invective comedy ('Old Comedy') since 'speaking of *aischra*' is fundamental only to that genre of comedy (cf. Lysias fr. 53 Thalheim). Moreover, the periodic distinction he makes here operates on another matrix also, the change from *aischrologia* to *hyponoia*, from open attack on vice to covert attack. This is, though expressed in different language, precisely the basis of the changes located by the later scholars, from 'open' to 'covert' attack. What Aristotle is expecting his readers to understand in the *Nicomachean Ethics*, then, as he slips into his discussion of propriety in laughter an historical example to illustrate the difference between wit and buffoonery, is that iambic comedy developed away from open on-stage caricature attack on citizens to covert on-stage caricature attack. The formulation 'old' and 'new' also tells us that he composed his *Nicomachean Ethics* after the complete ban on satirising citizens (the third stage).

Since Aristotle himself uses the terms 'old' and 'new', it seems best to assume that the periods he reported were in fact 'old' 'middle' and 'new' (rather than 'first' 'second' and 'third') and that these were appropriated later (probably by Aristophanes of Byzantium)[36] to produce the entirely spurious developmental model which is most widely used today, according to which Old Comedy went through a series of structural changes (loss of chorus, loss of parabasis etc.) via Middle Comedy (mainly mythological) into the New Comedy of situation written by Alexis, Diphilus, Philemon and Menander.[37] This confuses the development of iambic comedy with that of plot-based comedy of the type Aristotle tells us (*Poetics* 1449b) was introduced to Athens from Sicily by Crates, a contemporary of Cratinus, which is shown by a continuous series of terracotta statuettes to continue uninterruptedly from the last quarter of the fifth century right down to the period of Menander, and which itself must have undergone fundamental shifts in the types of plot favoured.[38]

We must now try to locate the comedies we have on Aristotle's map. First of all, it is important to note that some real individuals are named caricatures in Aristophanic comedies of 411 (e.g. Cleisthenes at *Thesm.* 574f., Cinesias at *Lys.* 831f.) and that Plato's *Cleophon* of Lenaea 405 (Hypothesis I(c) of *Frogs*) showed the demagogue as an on-stage caricature along with his mother (fr. 61).[39] These facts strongly suggest that the only restriction placed on iambic comedy during the war was the ban on ὀνομαστὶ κωμῳδεῖν, which can therefore only have meant 'naming on-stage caricatures' and must have had a restricted remit, designed to protect the *demos* from

---

[36] Nesselrath 1990, 186–7, suggests that Aristophanes of Byzantium developed the Old-Middle-New model with which we are now familiar.

[37] See Sidwell 2000a. However, I now withdraw my view (255) that Aristotle did not use the term 'middle'. Indeed, it was very probably his use of the word to describe a stage in the development of iambic comedy which led to its appropriation for what we now call 'Middle Comedy'. See previous note.

[38] Green 1994, 63.

[39] καὶ Πλάτων ἐν Κλεοφῶντι δράματι βαρβαρίζουσαν πρὸς αὐτὸν πεποίηκε τὴν μητέρα 'And Plato in his play *Cleophon* had his mother speaking in barbarian language to him.'

the implication that its elected officials at least were not fit to serve and perhaps to obfuscate these targets for foreign visitors. Moreover, the fact that Plato Comicus is sometimes singled out as the major exponent of the 'middle comedy' (i.e. 'middle *iambic* comedy'), sometimes included along with Cratinus, Aristophanes, Eupolis, Pherecrates and Hermippus as part of the second phase, when ἦν ὁ ψόγος κεκρυμμένος ('when invective was hidden'); that Eupolis is sometimes an exponent of the first phase, sometimes belongs to the second and is once the person with whom the second begins; and that it was possible to make the elementary mistake of designating any play by Cratinus 'middle comedy'(as was done with the *Odysses*) suggests that Aristotle either did not give examples to back up his tripartite analysis or mentioned the names of Eupolis and Plato in such a way as to suggest that the first marked the start of the restriction of *onomasti komoidein* and the second illustrated the practice of 'enigmatic comedy'.[40] Since it was obviously not clear to Alexandrian scholars what *onomasti komoidein* could possibly mean, they were naturally at a disadvantage when they turned to the attempt to classify their extant corpus according to the Aristotelian scheme. This explains, I think, why the confusion in the accounts rests more upon the details of playwrights and plays than (generally speaking) upon the scheme itself. If there were three phases, then policy on naming and masking, but not on the principle that anyone could be attacked by on-stage caricature, must have changed completely with the second, since (a) the evidence of the plays shows that as late as 405, on-stage named caricature occurred, (b) the notion of the caricature-mask was still current in the 420s (*Knights* 230f.), (c) Platonius' description of changes in masking convention is strictly tied to the tripartite historical model and, since it seems accurately to depict the situation in the plays of the 420s, and since there appears to be no fundamental change in the general situation before 405, it seems likely that what he reports about masking in stages two and three should be taken to belong to Aristotle's own account, even if the writer introduces a confusion (the Macedonians) because of his own inability to understand the real purport of what he is relaying. Thus the 'middle comedy' will have been characterised by (a) enigma (b) the absence of caricature-masks (c) a continued licence nonetheless to use on-stage caricature to attack any individual at all, without restriction. It

---

[40] Plato as exponent of 'middle comedy', Koster, *Prolegomena*, p. 40 XIb.37, p. 71 XVIIIa.42, p. 115, XXIII.11; included alongside Aristophanes etc. in the second ('enigmatic') phase p. 44 XIc.40, p. 88 XXIa.84. Eupolis in the first phase, Koster *Prolegomena*, p. 3, 1.11f. (cf. Vell. Pat. 1.16.3); in the second p. 88 XXIa.83; the first poet of the second p. 27, XIa 1.87–8. Cratinus' *Odysses* as 'middle comedy' Koster *Prolegomena*, p. 4, 1.30.

is worth noting that there is nowhere in *Ecclesiazusai* or *Wealth* any sign of a named on-stage caricature, although my analysis (Appendix 2) makes it clear that these are still iambic comedies. Plato's career also overlapped into the fourth century (his *Phaon* was produced in 391), and, if it was not Aristotle's doing, this fact, plus the normal bracketing of Aristophanes with Cratinus and Eupolis and the relatively large number of mythological titles for Plato's plays, may have dictated the choice of Plato Comicus as the chief exponent of the 'middle comedy'.[41]

Nuggets of the original account may surface anywhere in the confused babble of the later commentators. In fact Platonius (who preserves more than most) does give an indication that Aristotle may have dated the beginning of the second phase to the period of the Thirty Tyrants (Koster, *Prolegomena* p. 3, Platonius *On Differences* 1.13–18):

λοιπὸν δὲ τῆς δημοκρατίας ὑποχωρούσης ὑπὸ τῶν κατὰ τὰς Ἀθήνας τυραννιώντων καὶ καθισταμένης ὀλιγαρχίας καὶ μεταπιπτούσης τῆς ἐξουσίας τοῦ δήμου εἰς ὀλίγους καὶ κρατυνομένης τῆς ὀλιγαρχίας ἐνέπιπτε τοῖς ποιηταῖς φόβος· οὐ γὰρ ἦν τινα προφανῶς σκώπτειν δίκας ἀπαιτούντων τῶν ὑβριζομένων παρὰ τῶν ποιητῶν

In the end, when the democracy fell at the hands of the tyrants at Athens and an oligarchy was established and the power of the *demos* was transferred to a few and the oligarchy became strong, the poets became afraid: for they could not ridicule anyone openly, because those who were mistreated demanded recompense from the poets.

It is certainly imaginable that the Thirty would have been eager to restrict such a fundamentally democratic genre (cf. [Xen.] *Ath. Pol.* 2.18). It is also possible to see how the re-established democracy might have resisted its suppression, but, as a compromise in the new spirit of reconciliation that settled on the city in 403, have offered a ban on named on-stage satire and on caricature-masks. This certainly did nothing to assuage the doubts of the 'right', as we have seen in Plato's legislation in *Laws* and in Aristotle's treatment of comedy.

It may also be possible to detect the moment by which the third stage had begun, in which only slaves and foreigners could be attacked, because Aristotle's remark at *Nicomachean Ethics* 1128a 23–5 refers to 'new comedies'. If, as seems likely, Aristotle was working to the surviving schema, the change must have occurred before that work was written. Unfortunately, we can not date the *Nicomachean Ethics* securely. However, it does seem unlikely that any legislation against attacks by comedy on citizens had been introduced

---

[41] Σ Ar. *Wealth* 179.

before the completion of Plato's *Laws*. We are, therefore, in the mid-340s. Timocles for example wrote plays in this period with the names of real individuals in the title, and of those *Neaira* can certainly be construed as an attack on a slave (cf. [Dem.] 59), while *Orestautokleides* may not have been attacking a *citizen*, since even if we do not know precisely what Autocleides' status was, Aeschines' contemptuous listing of him among other low-lifes (1.52) may suggest that he was not a *polites*.

One could certainly suggest that the arguments of opponents of iambic comedy (people like Plato, Isocrates and Aristotle) might well have had an impact eventually and that the threat from Macedon was enough to induce a feeling of the need for citizen solidarity. As to what eventually happened to the genre, Horace's famous dictum (*Ars Poetica* 281–4) suggests a final curtain. Once more Platonius (*On Differences* Koster, *Prolegomena* pp. 5–6, 1.59–63; cf. Pollux 4.133f.), albeit in a garbled manner, because he had no real idea what he was talking about, gives us a clue to the socio-political circumstances which led to the ban on all satire, not merely that of citizens. In his section on caricature-masks, he says:

ἐν δὲ τῇ μέσῃ καὶ νέᾳ κωμῳδίᾳ ἐπίτηδες τὰ προσωπεῖα πρὸς τὸ γελοιότερον ἐδηιούργησαν δεδοικότες τοὺς Μακεδόνας καὶ τοὺς ἐπηρτημένους ἐξ ἐκείνων φόβους, ἵνα δὲ μὴ ἐκ τύχης τινὸς ὁμοιότης προσώπου συμπέσῃ τινὶ Μακεδόνων ἄρχοντι καὶ δόξας ὁ ποιητὴς ἐκ προαιρέσεως κωμῳδεῖν δίκας ὑπόσχῃ.

But in the middle and new comedy they deliberately made the masks tending towards the merely risible in fear of the Macedonians and the terrors which they threatened, and so that it might not happen by some chance that a mask might bear a resemblance to one of the Macedonian governors and the poet might be subject to judicial process because he had been thought to have deliberately satirised the man.[42]

This situation could only occur (a) if the iambic comedy had entered its third stage (so 340s at the earliest) and (b) if Macedonians were in control in Athens (so after 322). I conclude, then, that Aristotle still regarded as 'open' attack the period I have been dealing with in this book, even if some of the names of the on-stage targets were suppressed. His 'middle iambic comedy' ran from 403 to around 345 and his 'new iambic comedy' from *c.* 345 until 322.

---

[42] The phrase ἐπὶ τὸ γελοιότερον ('with the emphasis rather on the laughable') echoes Aristotle's description of non-iambic comedy at *Poetics* 1449a 32- b7, but is probably not, as I thought in Sidwell 2000a 249, confusing the two traditions of comedy, since Aristotle, I surmise, made no attempt to give a history of the plot-based variety.

CONCLUSION

It is an observable fact that 'allegorical' interpretation was much more usual in the early nineteenth century than it became later.[43] The gradual reduction of interest in such interpretation probably has something to do with a general movement in literary aesthetics (which after all has its roots in Aristotle's *Poetics*) against the cotidian and specific and towards the eternal and generic. Silk's recent analysis of Aristophanes' 'literary greatness', for example, involves the search for a deeper and more satisfying meaning than 'the creator of pure ridicule or pure satire'.[44] For '[e]ven if Aristophanes in some moods may be taken for a pure ridiculer or satirist, his pathos by itself reveals a larger perspective and a deeper vision'.[45] Silk's conclusions reflect a deep-seated aversion to the essential negativity of satire that had already taken root among German writers on Aristophanes' imitator Lucian in the early twentieth century. To suggest that the basis of Old Comedy is the ridicule of individuals on stage is seen as reducing Aristophanes to a 'pure satirist', which is, apparently, inherently contradictory to any argument about his merits as a writer.[46] I can see no special justification for this view.

---

[43] Süvern 1826, Cobet 1840. But see Katz 1976 and Vickers 1997.
[44] Silk 2000, 1 and 421.   [45] Silk 2000, 421.
[46] Silk 2000, 367. Helm 1906, 1. Vickers 1997 is an exception to the general rule, since he assumes that characters are satirically calqued on individuals. For critiques of his methodology see Sidwell 1997 and Dover 2004, 243f.

APPENDIX 2

Metacomedy and caricature in the surviving fourth-century plays of Aristophanes

Aristophanes continued writing for some twenty years after the success of *Frogs*. His last two extant plays are *Ecclesiazusai* (late 390s) and *Wealth* (388), the second of that name, the first having been produced in 409/8 (Σ *Wealth* 179). Despite the lack of many of their choral lyrics (the position of which is marked in the MSS by the legend XOPOY), the plays conform in the essential aspects of their plots to the format of his earlier plays.[1] They also have in common with each other the political theme of wealth and poverty, though the approach of their plots is very different, the first based on a philosophical idea – communism – the second on a quirk of the divinely ordained lot of man – the blindness of Wealth and his consequent inability to go to the righteous. Their closeness in time and their shared concerns make it likely that in different ways both plays are responding satirically to the same stimuli (though a similar one was presumably also present when the first *Wealth* was produced during the war in 408, if it was anything like the later play). However, they have always been read – like Aristophanes' earlier plays – as though the fantasy were wish-fulfilment rather than a construction built around the desire to ridicule the individuals shown bringing it to pass.[2] In the light of the analysis of the history of the genre offered above in Appendix 1, it now seems reasonable to suggest that these plays belong to the second or 'middle' period of iambic comedy (according to the ancient schema) and are still based upon the on-stage attack on individuals, but with even fewer clues offered by the text (and by the visual aspects of production) than was the case in the Peloponnesian War plays.

In the case of *Ecclesiazusai*, there is, of course, the fundamental problem of just who could be the object of a satire of communistic ideas, when Plato was – according to Aristotle (*Pol.* 1266a 31–6, 1274b 9–10) – the only

---

[1] Sommerstein 1998, 22, 2001 23.
[2] Rothwell 1990, 5–10, Sommerstein 1998, 11–22 and 2001 13–22, MacDowell 1995, 320–3 and 349.

thinker to have included common ownership of property and wives and children in his model of the ideal state, yet the *Republic* was probably still twenty years in the future, and the central figure in the play, Praxagora, is female.[3] Yet, given the closeness of the ideas in the comedy and the philosophical work,[4] the only logical alternatives to Aristophanes' satirical use of Platonic material – a common source, or use of Aristophanes by Plato – can be ruled out: the first because of Aristotle's statement (presuming he did not miss anything obvious), the second because of Plato's hostile attitude to comedy (for which see Appendix 1). In fact the passages from *Republic* 452a–d cited by Sommerstein in defence of the second explanation both reinforce Plato's hostility to satirical comedy and may in fact suggest rather that these ideas have *already* been subject to comic appropriation.[5] Theopompus had, a few years earlier (around 400) produced a play called *Stratiotides* ('Female Soldiers') which might be taken as satire on what would later become another of Plato's radical signatures in the *Republic* – the military training of women (457a). I argued above (p. 263), in respect of a passage from *Lysistrata* (574f., the wool-working metaphor) which has a later manifestation in Plato's *Politicus* (308c f.), that what lies behind it is a formulation of Socrates which is being made fun of. Despite Athens' relatively large size (though its citizen body was actually no larger than the staff/student body of a modern university), stories, gossip and even philosophical ideas circulated very quickly. I do not find it hard to believe that Plato's (or Socrates'?) communistic ideas were already being discussed by his circle when Plato was in his late twenties, nor that – novel and outrageous as they were – they very quickly gained a wide circulation, wide enough, like many sophistic ideas before them (e.g. the 'sky as a baking-dish'), to be intelligibly used as the basis for satirical attack. And since, as argued above, the sudden public profile of certain intellectual women was very likely attributable to the influence of the Socratic circle, and could lead in 411 to their appearance on stage (though they were not the first individual women to be so caricatured), it does not seem strange to read Praxagora as a later manifestation of the same 'movement'. Once she is seen as an individual in the circle of Plato, the plot becomes what Socrates fears at *Republic* 452a–d, a satire of the ideas which centre on the equality of the male and female intellect and their equal capacity for political action and oversight. As in the other plays, the other figures will represent individuals whom Aristophanes wishes to attack and who can be included in such a

---

[3] See Sommerstein 1998, 13f.   [4] Tabulated by Sommerstein 1998, 14.
[5] Sommerstein 1998, 16–17.

plot because of their views, their individual foibles, or their relationships in the real world with the original of Praxagora.

With *Wealth*, the problem is slightly different, since the premiss of the plot is the banishment of poverty (from the just), rather than the redistribution of existing wealth. As with *Ecclesiazusai*, however, there does need to have been some debate against which the satire could operate. In the 420s, as I argued in chapter five (pp. 194–5), there seems to have been some discussion of redistribution, albeit within the parameters of the vast income in tribute which the city then enjoyed, since the arguments of Bdelycleon at *Wasps* 703f. would otherwise have no satirical referent either. However, it could have taken as little as a politician saying 'if only wealth were not blind, we could all have enough to live on', within a debate about poverty and redistribution, for him to have become instantly a candidate for caricature as Wealth. In this case, though, I doubt if it is as simple as that. For there is a problem in respect of the relationship between the text of this play and that of the first version, produced in 409/8 (Σ *Wealth* 179). MacDowell argued that the evidence shows the second version to have been altered only in minor ways (as with *Clouds II*, though in this case we have no direct blow-by-blow account of the major changes).[6] Sommerstein has recently re-examined this evidence and concluded that (a) there were two versions of the 388 play (so probably a second performance, as with *Frogs*) (b) that the 408 version did not exist in the library at Alexandria and that the few fragments we have of the first version – which was a completely different play – came through a copy held at Pergamum.[7] However, even if Sommerstein is right, and the 408 play was very different (witness the fragments), the fact is that, unlike in *Ecclesiazusai*,[8] there are several indications of metacomic hits at Eupolis in the play: (1) cries of ἰοὺ ἰού (276, 478, 852); (2) (the threat of) an old man beating someone with a stick (271–2); (3) torches on stage (1194f.); (4) use of the catch-phrase μεταβαλόντα τοὺς τρόπους ('changing his ways'; Eup. fr. 392.7, cf. *Wasps* 1461, *Frogs* 734); (5) quotation from Eur. *Telephus* fr. 713

---

[6] MacDowell 1995, 324–7.   [7] Sommerstein 1998, 28–33.

[8] There is *one* torch brought on stage (978), but it appears simply because torch and garland indicate a night visit to a lover and in any case here Aristophanes is, according to Davidson 2000, 50–1, parodying the *paignia* genre (and possibly Gnesippus in particular). However, the scene where Blepyrus is brought on stage to defecate (311f.) does seem to have a metacomic aspect. The scholium to *Clouds* 296c, glossing οἱ τρυγοδαίμονες οὗτοι 'these wretched low-grade comic poets', remarks: οἱ ἄλλοι κωμικοί· οὗτοι γὰρ ἐν τοῖς ποιήμασιν αὐτῶν ἀνθρώπους εἰσῆγον χέζοντάς τε καὶ ἕτερα αἰσχρὰ ποιοῦντας. λέγει δὲ δι' Εὔπολιν καὶ Κρατῖνον καὶ τοὺς ἄλλους. 'The other comic poets: for in their poems they brought on stage men shitting and doing other vile things. He says this because of Eupolis and Cratinus and the rest.'

(*Wealth* 601, *Knights* 813; cf. *Ach. passim*). There are also several overlaps with the language and themes of earlier plays which suggest a metacomic intent: (1) the theme of defeat of the gods (28f., 1112f.) is shared with *Birds*; (2) Hermes (1097f.) appears in a door-knocking scene at *Peace* 179f., where (in contrast to *Wealth*) he is the answerer and he appears equally susceptible to the allure of food (1135f.; cf. *Peace* 192f.) and where the anger of the gods at Athens is expressed by the same image (salad-making; 1107–9; cf. *Peace* 226f.); (3) the chorus (like those of *Acharnians* and *Peace*) are farmers (223) and very old men (258); (4) line 763 ὡς ἄλφιτ' οὐκ ἔνεστιν ἐν τῷ θυλάκῳ ('that there are no groats in the bag') has the same structure as *Clouds* 56 and *Birds* 1589. Moreover, the scene where the Just Man appears (823f.) along with a sycophant (850f.) bears a family resemblance to that between Aristeides and a sycophant in Eupolis' *Demes* (fr. 99.79f.) and the idea of gaining wealth unjustly is found in Cratinus' *Ploutoi* ('Wealth Gods', fr. 171. 46 and 69). All this makes more sense at a period when Aristophanes seems still to have needed to attack his rival Eupolis (on my argument, when he was disenfranchised, but still in Athens) than in the early 380s. I am inclined, then, despite Sommerstein's arguments, to think that the first *Wealth* was aimed at Eupolis and his circle and then, in 388, that Aristophanes saw (as he had with *Clouds II*), an opportunity to adapt the original to suit a new set of individual on-stage targets and that he made quite substantial changes (as our fragments of the first play show) which did not involve abandoning the metacomic structure, but did involve inclusion of new metacomic material like the parody of Philoxenus of Cythera's *Cyclops* at 290f. The characters, then, will represent individuals caught up in a debate about wealth and poverty. Perhaps Poverty was based upon a rich woman nonetheless inclined to a philosophical doctrine which emphasised the virtues of hard work. Possibly the old woman and her young lover represented a well-known pair whose mutual – but unequal – dependence is ridiculed by their inclusion in the comedy. At any rate, even if we cannot suggest precise identifications, it is not difficult to see how the principle of satirical attack on on-stage caricatures would operate in *Wealth* nor to glimpse the impact that reference to earlier comedies might have upon the audience's level of amusement.

APPENDIX 3

Timeline and proposed relationships between comedies

This list is an attempt to pull together for ease of reference various suggestions made in the course of the argument. The evidence for the relationships and relative dates is discussed in the text and is not repeated here. Everything (apart from a few solid dates and one or two names of characters) is conjectural. However, it is worth mentioning again that the basis for the conjectures made is: (1) the centrality of on-stage caricature in Old Comedy; (2) the hypothesis that antagonism between poets was based on the real political agenda of each participant; (3) that poets were themselves on-stage targets; (4) that therefore their plays formed part and parcel of the attempt to satirise each other's political postures and circles; (5) that we can spot the points where such antagonistic misappropriations are being made by a number of methods which include: (a) looking for scenes which contradict Aristophanes' parabatic strictures (they are parodic); (b) finding close linguistic or thematic relationships between extant plays and the fragments of rival comedies; (c) tracking passages of 'self-imitation' (they are parodying specific material from a rival poet or poets).

AUTHOR	TITLE	DATE	RELATIONSHIP
Cratinus	*Dionysalexandros* ('Dionysus plays Paris')	437/6 (?)	The play criticised Pericles for bringing the Samian war on Athens. Portrayed Aspasia as Helen and the real Paris as Pericles.
Cratinus	*Horai* ('Seasons')	430 (?)	The play criticised Pericles for bringing another war on Athens for personal reasons, including revenge for problems actually caused by Alcibiades and Aspasia. Caricatured Lamachus as War? Had a chorus of grape-farmers?

(cont.)

Appendix 3

AUTHOR	TITLE	DATE	RELATIONSHIP
Eupolis	*Prospaltioi* ('Demesmen of Prospalta')	429	A response to *Horai*, portraying Cratinus as a stubborn old man(?), while exonerating Pericles from responsibility for the war and attacking Cleon.
Cratinus	*Ploutoi* ('Wealth Gods')	428 (?)	Celebrated Pericles' suspension from the generalship and the return of democracy. Possibly introduced Cleon as Typhoeus, combating the tyrannical Zeus/Pericles.
Eupolis	*Taxiarchoi* ('Taxiarchs')	427 (?)	Satirised Phormio as Ares and Cratinus as Dionysus.
Aristophanes	*Daitales* ('Banqueters')	427	Represented Cratinus as the father of Eupolis?
Cratinus	*Nomoi* ('Laws')	427 (?)	A pro-Cleonian chorus of Laws, represented as bees, judged cases against individuals opposed to Cleon. Marks Cratinus' shift of allegiance to Cleon.
Eupolis	*Chrysoun Genos* ('The Golden Race')	426	A response to Cratinus' *Nomoi* and Aristophanes' *Banqueters*? Contained a scene in which young knight prosecutors (Alcibiades and Euathlus?) indicted Cleon (represented as a dog, possibly Cerberus) for theft and a jury including Cratinus and Aristophanes condemned him. Possibly also attacked Hyperbolus.
Aristophanes	*Babylonians*	426	A satire of Cratinus, representing him as Dionysus. Contained a scene in which Cleon attacked Cratinus in the *boule* and Cratinus agreed not to attack him again.
Aristophanes	*Acharnians*	L425	Attacked Cratinus and his 'imitator' Eupolis and his coterie for their anti-democratic attitude to the war.
Eupolis	*Noumeniai* ('New Moon Days')	L425	Represented Cleon as Paphlagon the leather-seller and Cratinus as Demos in a plot in which Hyperbolus the lamp-seller took over the *prostasia* of the *demos* from Cleon. Possibly satirised Aristophanes as a rejuvenated Demos.
Aristophanes	*Knights*	L424	A response to Eupolis' *Noumeniai* in Eupolis' voice in which Aristophanes borrowed Paphlagon/Cleon and Demos/Cratinus and the basic idea of a 'seller' taking the *prostasia* from Cleon and possibly the rejuvenation motif, but subverted Eupolis' comedy by subsituting Alcibiades for Hyperbolus and possibly the rejuvenated Demos/Eupolis for Eupolis' Demos/Aristophanes.

Timeline and relationships between comedies

AUTHOR	TITLE	DATE	RELATIONSHIP
Eupolis	*Poleis* ('Cities')	D424 (?)	An attack on a radical democratic proposal (Cleon's?) to use the tribute to relieve Athenian poverty.
Eupolis	*Autolycus I*	L423 (?)	An attack on Lycon's son (but probably targeting his lover Callias). May have attacked Aristophanes on stage as Ephialtes for stealing the comedies of the 'Aeginetan' poet of *Acharnians*.
Aristophanes	*Clouds I*	D423	An attack on Eupolis and his intellectual and political circle, especially Socrates and Alcibiades, repudiating Eupolis' or Cratinus' attack on Prodicus by making Socrates an atheistic, money-grubbing sophist, concerned with meteorology and grammar.
Cratinus	*Pytine* ('The Wine-Flask')	D423	An attack upon Aristophanes (the drunken comic poet character) for plagiarising Eupolis' work in *Knights* and attacking Cratinus as Demos.
Aristophanes	*Wasps*	L422	A response to Cratinus' *Pytine* in Cratinus' voice in which Cratinus was portrayed as Philocleon and Eupolis as the hedonist Bdelycleon, his son (as perhaps already in *Banqueters*), attempting to wean his father from his jury-obsessed ways (based on *Nomoi*) into a more sophisticated way of life. The attack on Eupolis was probably motivated by *Autolycus I*.
Eupolis	*Marikas*	L421	A response to recent attacks by Aristophanes which remodelled Eupolis' *Noumeniai* of L425 and thereby also subverted *Knights*, which had been a parody of *Noumeniai*. Here, Marikas/Hyperbolus took the place of Paphlagon/Cleon, probably Demos/Aristophanes took the place of Demos/Cratinus, and the *prostasia* was claimed (as in *Knights*) by an Alcibiades with whom Aristophanes has now had to make an unwilling and uncomfortable pact.
Aristophanes	*Peace*	D421	A further attack on Eupolis and the peace-party on the eve of the treaty. Once again, Eupolis is portayed as a vulgar Cratinean figure, Trygaeus the vine-farmer, in a parody of motifs from his enemy Cratinus' *Horai*. Eupolis' attitude to the war's origins (in *Prospaltioi*?) is also satirised.

(*cont.*)

AUTHOR	TITLE	DATE	RELATIONSHIP
Eupolis	*Kolakes* ('Flatterers')	D421	An attack on Callias and his sophistic circle (including Protagoras). Possibly a reply to *Clouds I*.
Eupolis	*Autolycus II*	420	Eupolis' reply to the most recent Aristophanic attack on him (in *Peace*) represented Aristophanes as the play-stealing slave Ephialtes, and Cratinus now as the fellow-slave from whom he stole comedies.
Eupolis	*Baptai* ('Dippers')	L415 (?)	Attacked Alcibiades, but also replied to Aristophanes' accusation (in *Anagyros*?) of having plagiarised *Knights* and possibly used the theme of cross-dressing to satirise Aristophanes and his circle.
Aristophanes	*Clouds II*	415	Recast with Alcibiades as the central character and Phaeax as his son, with Eupolis as Unjust Argument and Cratinus as the Just, the play was designed as a response to the ostracism of Hyperbolus via a renewed attack on the Socratic circle. It was never performed at a state festival because of Alcibiades' defection to Sparta that summer.
Aristophanes	*Anagyros*	after 415 (?)	Attacked Eupolis for plagiarising one of his comedies three times.
Aristophanes	*Birds*	D414	A reply to Eupolis' *Baptai*, the play attacked figures from the Socratic circle, including Critias, opposed to the Sicilian expedition.
Aristophanes	*Lysistrata*	L411	An attack on the pro-oligarchic circle of intellectual women led by Lysimache.
Aristophanes	*Thesmophoriazusai*	D411	An attack on Eupolis (the relative), Euripides and other closet Laconophiles, for their oligarchic leanings, along with prominent members of Lysimache's circle. The play possibly borrows and subverts the cross-dressing theme from Eupolis' *Baptai*.
Eupolis	*Demoi* ('Demes')	L410 (?)	Presented the return from Hades of four dead politicians (Solon, Aristides, Miltiades and Pericles), to satirise contemporary Athens and perhaps to suggest a return to an earlier model of democracy. Aristophanes was the main character, attacked for his political credo.

AUTHOR	TITLE	DATE	RELATIONSHIP
Aristophanes	*Frogs*	L405	An attack on Eupolis (represented as Dionysus) and the conservative tragedians (including the appropriators of Aeschylus), aimed at persuading the Athenians of the lack of wisdom of re-enfranchising the 411 oligarchs and the importance of continuing to pursue the *demos'* current war policy with vigour.

Various other currently undatable plays must have formed contributions of one or another kind to this battle. Cratinus' *Idaioi* ('Men of Mt Ida') was probably one of the sources for Aristophanes' *Acharnians* and the subsequent satires of Euripides in *Thesmophoriazusai* and *Frogs*. Cratinus' *Boukoloi* ('Herdsmen') may be reflected in *Wasps* and *Peace*. His *Cheimazomenoi* ('Storm-tossed Men') of L425 was already lost in antiquity, while of his *Satyroi* ('Satyrs') of L424 (the year after *Acharnians*) all we have is the title. Since *Dionysalexandros* had also had a chorus of satyrs, this play may have returned to the attack against Pericles' policies. No doubt Eupolis' *Aiges* ('Nanny-goats'), *Heilotes* ('Helots'), *Philoi* ('Friends') and *Astrateutoi* ('Evaders of Military Service') all featured in some way now all but invisible in the 'poets' war', but the most we can hazard is that Aristophanes may have used the Spartan language from *Heilotes* to satirise Eupolis and that *Astrateutoi* might have been a reply to *Birds*.

APPENDIX 4

The date of Eupolis' Taxiarchoi

It seems worthwhile to examine briefly once more the arguments for the dating of this play. The 427 date was set on the basis that (a) Phormio was a character in the play (Σ *Peace* 348; fr. 268.15 and 34) and (b) he vanishes from Thucydides after 428. Handley 1982, however, dated the play to 415 on the basis of a series of *oinochoai* which probably have reference to comedy (photographs in *DFA*² plates 86 and 87). One has two characters whose names]ΟΝΥΣΟΣ [onysos] and ΦΟΡ[[Phor]) can be reasonably restored as ΔΙ]ΟΝΥΣΟΣ (Dionysus) and ΦΟΡ[ΜΙΩΝ (Phormio). The other has a man rowing astride a fish. With the vases was discovered an *ostrakon* 'inscribed for the ostracism held in 415 BC or a neighbouring year, at which Hyperbolos was exiled' (Handley 1982, 24–5. See Crosby 1955, 81f.). We know from Σ *Peace* 348 that Dionysus was a character in *Taxiarchoi*, and went to Phormio to learn the 'laws of generals and wars'. Wilson 1974 has demonstrated that the play contained a rowing scene, possibly the antecedent of that in *Frogs*. But the proximity of the *ostrakon* does not prove that the play which the painting represents was recent, because the pots may have been around some years before they were buried. Our dating system for these artefacts could certainly not be said to be accurate within ten years, so that the play may still be *Taxiarchoi* and the date of production back in the early 420s. Storey (1990, 22–4 and 2003, 246–8) also prefers the later date, but for different reasons, as follows. (1) Opountios is mentioned in fr. 282, and elsewhere only at 'Callias' fr. 4 (*Atalantai*) and *Birds* 1294 (414 BC). The ascription to Callias and the date of his *Atalantai* are uncertain. *Birds* gives a certain date. (2) Fr. 268.7–12 shows that Eupolis parodied Sophocles' *Tereus*, also made fun of by *Birds* 100–1. (3) Fr. 268.43 mentions a λωποδύτης ('mugger'). The only target of this kind we know of is Orestes in *Acharnians* 1165f. and *Birds* 712, 1491. (4) Phormio vanishes from Thucydides after 428, but is found in comedy (*Babylonioi* fr. 88, *Knights* 562, *Clouds I* fr. 397, *Peace* 347–8, *Lys.* 804). If he was dead, there may have been either a necromancy (as, on Storey's reconstruction, in *Demoi*) or a visit to Hades (as in *Frogs*). Of Storey's arguments, (2) and (3) are weak. *Thesmophoriazusai* of 411 satirises Euripides' *Telephus* of 438, as did *Acharnians* of 425. Parody of tragedy does not necessarily occur topically, though it may (e.g. of *Helen* and *Andromeda* in *Thesmophoriazusai*). For what it is worth, Tereus' name was apparently important during the debate over the enfranchisement of Sitalces' son Sadocus, in the early 420s (Thuc. 2.29). The story as it is told by Thucydides follows the lines of what is probably the surviving hypothesis (*P. Oxy.* 3013). Given the interest in Thracian pre-history at that time, Sophocles' play may well have belonged c. 430–428. Parody in *Taxiarchs* would, then, have been topical had the play been produced in 428/7. We do not have the name of the λωποδύτης ('mugger') at fr. 268.43 and Storey cites a play of 425 (*Acharnians*) as the first mention of the only mugger in comedy, Orestes. But (a) K-A report Handley's conjecture on line 41: λέγων Ἰάσονι with the comment that Iason may be the name of the mugger; (b) no rule I know of makes it imperative to see a mention in Aristophanes as the first in a series; (c) the scholiast may have inferred that Orestes was a mugger from the text, but a link between this mention of Orestes and Cratinus' *Eumenides* is more likely in the context; (d) Storey omits from his account the commentator's remark that this same person was also attacked by Telecleides (fr. 73). Telecleides is a comic poet of the same generation as Cratinus and Crates (*IG* II² 2325). His *Sterroi* was possibly produced for a second time in 431/0 (*PCG* T5 with commentary). We have at the most seven titles of plays by him (*PCG* T1). It seems likeliest that his λωποδύτης ('mugger') was attacked at the latest in the early 420s. On Storey's criteria, this makes it more likely that *Taxiarchs* belongs to that period too. Argument (4), the series of mentions in Aristophanic comedy over a long period is not unusual. Lamachus appears first in *Acharnians*, but then after his death in *Thesmophoriazusai*. Cratinus is first named at *Acharnians* 849, but is mentioned as late as *Frogs* 357 (again, after his death?). It is important to note also that the proposed existence of metacomedy would make it impossible to know simply from the mention of a name whether the attack was direct or evoked, through its context, some earlier attack in another comedy. Eupolis' *Taxiarchs* could well have generated all the mentions of Phormio and provided an intertext which would be central to the humour at these points. This consideration would affect Storey's strongest argument (1), if we could show that *Birds* has metacomic elements (see further chapter five). If parody of tragedy has such broad temporal boundaries, there does not seem any reason to suppose that parody of comedy was notably different. In any case, one might note that Storey's argument challenging the ascription of the mention of Opountios to Callias' *Atalantai* is not especially strong. He might be right, but he has to convict the scholiasts of an error or move Callias' *Atalantai* down to the 410s with no substantive evidence.

APPENDIX 5

Clouds *868–73* and τραυλίζω

It is clear from the *Wasps* joke (45) that at least one thing which could be understood as τραυλίζειν is substituting λ for ρ. Dover and Sommerstein on 872 agree that the pronunciation of κρέμαιο is criticised by Socrates for the slurring of the final vowel to [aew] or [ae]. But this seems most unlikely, since the final vowel is elided in Socrates' response and in any case there will have been a tendency for such final short vowels to be very unobtrusive even when the word is fully pronounced as at 870. In that case it is more likely that it is the consonant ρ which is the focus of the jibe. Is there in fact any positive evidence to connect τραυλίζειν with a fault of vowel as opposed to consonant pronunciation? Dover's interpretation of χείλεσιν διερρυηκόσιν is as follows: 'In κρέμαιο the lips meet on μ, part on α, stretch a little on ι and are rounded on ο. μ is an easy sound for infants; difficulty in pronouncing rolled ρ (unlike difficulty in pronouncing the very rare sound written 'r' in English) is not apparent in the movement of the lips; thus the only pronunciation which makes sense of Socrates' words is something like [k(r)emaew].' But his argument on [ρ] misses the point. If Socrates is criticising a slight mispronunciation, then we might speak of 'difficulty in pronouncing rolled ρ'. But if, as our evidence on the usage of τραυλίζειν suggests, the criticism is aimed at the substitution of [λ] for [ρ], then the significant move will be to examine what happens when the phoneme [λ] is inserted into the word κρέμαι' in place of [ρ]. Of course, we do not know what type of [l] Greek had, nor whether, like for example Russian, there were two distinct phonemes which are expressed by the same grapheme. If we began from the evidence for τραυλίζειν and worked outwards, we might in fact suggest that Greek medial [λ] was like the Polish **l** in Vaclav, which is in fact a phoneme much closer to [w], where the lips spread out as in Socrates' description of Pheidippides' speech habit. It follows from this argument that it is not only the generic notion of τραυλίζειν which Pheidippides has in common with Alcibiades. The pronunciation of κρέμαι' is of a piece with that of κόρακος in *Wasps* 45.

APPENDIX 6

Michael Vickers on Strepsiades and Pericles

In chapter six (pp. 227–8) I suggested that Alcibiades might have been Pericles' stepson. If my reconstruction of Alcibiades' and Pericles' family history is correct, then it helps to explain some of the coincidences found by Vickers between Strepsiades and Pericles (1997 chapters two and three *passim*). We do not need Pericles' stinginess to account for the humour of Alcibiades' debt problems and there need be no relationship between *Clouds* 1160 and Timon of Phlius' verses on Pericles' use of Zeno's logic (Plut. *Per.* 4.3). However, the fact that Pericles was also interested in the μετεωρολογία of Anaxagoras (Plut. *Per.* 4.4, 5.1) is not easily dismissed, since it is his theory of thunder which underlies the scene in which Strepsiades first meets the Clouds (374f.; Diog. Laert. 2.9). An anecdote reported in Frontinus (*Strat.* 1.11.10) tells us that Pericles allayed 'the panic of his men by knocking two stones together in order to explain the underlying mechanism of thunderbolts' (Vickers 1997, 37). If this anecdote was generally known at the time of *Clouds I* and is relevant, it does not, as Vickers supposes, suggest that Strepsiades represents Pericles, but in the first version makes fun of old man/Eupolis' (or old man/Hipponicus': see chapter five n. 58) inability to grasp intellectual concepts and in the second ridicules Alcibiades for not even having listened to theories beloved of his guardian. References in the play to Zeus will operate in a similar way, if the audience is meant to pick them up as relating to Pericles' sobriquet (most associated with Cratinus' comedy – see e.g. frr. 73, 258). It will have raised a laugh to hear Alcibiades invoking his guardian in the opening line of the play. And the discussion about Zeus' loss of the kingship ends with lines which may have a double point in reference to the political situation at Athens (380–1): Δῖνος; τουτὶ μ' ἐλελήθει, | ὁ Ζεὺς οὐκ ὢν, ἀλλ' ἀντ' αὐτοῦ Δῖνος νυνὶ βασιλεύων. 'Whirlwind? I hadn't noticed this, that Zeus was dead and Whirlwind is now king in his place.' If Zeus was a name given to Pericles, now dead, it was Cleon who was associated with Typhoeus (*Knights* 511), the monster usually identified with the whirlwind. Here this known identity of Cleon would be cleverly assimilated to the Democritean theory to make Alcibiades say he did not know (a) that Pericles was dead (b) that Cleon had taken his place at the top of the political hierarchy. But this would have been a better joke in 423 than in 415. Other aspects mentioned by Vickers as showing Strepsiades as Periclean include accusations against Pericles of cowardice (Plut. *Per.* 33.7–8 with *Clouds* 267–8, 293–5, 481, 497, 506–9), Pericles' use of siege-engines at Samos (*ibid.* 27.3 with *Clouds* 479–81), his hatred of Sparta (*ibid.* 10.3–4 etc. with *Clouds* 215–16), and his involvement with the grain-supply (Σ *Ach.* 548 with *Clouds* 260, 262 etc.). But these, if they are intended, do not show that Strepsiades represents Pericles, but rather implicate Alcibiades in Periclean characteristics (as I argue at pp. 174 and 229 is done with Socrates and Prodicus and Pheidippides and Alcibiades). If the mention of 'enoplian' and 'dactylic' metres at *Clouds* 636–54 do contain a reference to Damon's book on metre, the comic point will be: (a) Damon was Pericles' music-teacher (Pl. *Rep.* 400b); (b) thus Alcibiades is ignorant of material which his guardian knew well. Vickers' contention that the scene in which Strepsiades is bothered by bed bugs and is finally caught masturbating (694–745) is a re-enactment of Pericles' plague-symptons is not backed by any solid evidence. An equally unpleasant joke made about Megarian hunger at *Ach.* 751 can now be seen as part of a satire of Aristophanes' rival Eupolis. Vickers has certainly seen something which does exist in Aristophanes, namely the association with another individual of characteristics which belong to someone else. It is a technique of ridicule and is used in the cases of both Socrates and Pheidippides in this play.

Bibliography

Arnott, W. G. (1991) 'A lesson from the *Frogs*' *G&R* 38: 18–23.
Atkinson, J. E. (1992) 'Curbing the comedians: Cleon versus Aristophanes and Syracosius' decree', *CQ* 42: 56–64.
Austin, C. (1973) *Comicorum Graecorum Fragmenta in Papyris Reperta*, Berlin.
Austin, C. and Olson, S. D. (2004) *Aristophanes' Thesmophoriazusai*, Oxford.
Bees, R. (1993) *Zur Datierung des Prometheus Desmotes*, Stuttgart.
Bergk, Th. (1838) *Commentationum de reliquiis comoediae Atticae antiquae libri duo*, Leipzig.
Bianchetti, S. (19779) 'L'ostracismo di Iperbolo e la seconda relazione delle *Nuvole* di Aristofane', *SIFC* 51: 221–48.
Baker, W. W. (1904) 'De comicis Graecis litterarum iudicibus', *HSCP* 15: 121–240.
Biles, Z. P (2002) 'Intertextual biography in the rivalry of Cratinus and Aristophanes', *AJP* 123: 169–204.
Bonanno, M. G. (1972) *Studi su Cratete Comico*, Padua.
Borthwick, E. K. (1970) 'P. Oxy. 2738: Athena and the Pyrrhic dance', *Hermes* 98: 318–31.
Bowie, A. M. (1982) 'The parabasis in Aristophanes: prolegomena, *Acharnians*', *CQ* 32: 27–40.
  (1993) *Aristophanes: Myth, Ritual and Comedy*, Cambridge.
Bowie, E. L. (1988) 'Who is Dicaeopolis?' *JHS* 108: 183–5.
Braun, T. (2000) 'The choice of dead politicians in Eupolis's *Demoi*: Themistocles' exile, hero-cult and delayed rehabilitation; Pericles and the origins of the Peloponnesian War', in Harvey and Wilkins 2000, 191–231.
Braund, D. (2005) 'Pericles, Cleon and the Pontus: the Black Sea in Athens c. 440–421', in D. Braund, ed., *Scythians and Greeks*, Exeter, 80–99.
Braund, D. and Wilkins, J., eds. (2000) *Athenaeus and His World*, Exeter.
Brock, R. W. (1986) 'The double plot in Aristophanes' *Knights*', *GRBS* 27: 15–27.
  (1990) 'Plato on Comedy' in E. M. Craik, ed., *Owls to Athens: Essays on Classical Subjects Presented to Sir Kenneth Dover*, Oxford, 39–49.
Brockmann, C. (2003) *Aristophanes und die Freiheit der Komödie: Untersuchungen zu den frühen Stücken unter besonderer Berücksichtigung der Acharner*, Munich and Leipzig.

Burkert, W. (1993) 'Bacchic *Teletai* in the Hellenistic Age' in T. H. Carpenter and C. A. Faraone, eds., *Masks of Dionysus*, Ithaca and London, 259–75.
Butrica, J. (2001) 'The lost *Thesmophoriazusai* of Aristophanes', *Phoenix* 55: 44–76.
Buxton, R. G. A. (1982) *Persuasion in Greek Tragedy: A Study of Peitho*, Cambridge.
Byl, S. (1994) 'Les Mystères d'Éleusis dans les *Nuées*', in S. Byl and L. Couloubaritsis, eds., *Mythe et Philosophie dans les Nuées d'Aristophane*, Brussels, 11–68.
Carawan, E. M. (1990) 'The five talents Cleon coughed up (Schol. Ar. *Ach.* 6)', *CQ* n.s. 50: 137–47.
Carey, C. (1989) *Lysias: Selected Speeches*, Cambridge.
  (1994) 'Comic ridicule and democracy', in R. Osborne and S. Hornblower, eds., *Ritual, Finance, Politics: Athenian Democratic Accounts Presented to David Lewis*, Oxford, 69–83.
Cartledge, P. (2001) *Spartan Reflections*, London.
Cassio, A. C. (1985) 'Old Persian *Marika-*, Eupolis *Marikas* and Aristophanes *Knights*' *CQ* 35: 38–42.
Cobet, C. G. (1840) *Observationes Criticae in Platonis Comici Reliquias*, Amsterdam.
Colvin, S. (1999) *Dialect in Aristophanes: The Politics of Language in Ancient Greek Literature*, Oxford.
Conacher, D. J. (1980) *Aeschylus' Prometheus Bound: A Literary Commentary*, Toronto, Buffalo, and London.
Cornford, F. M. (1961) *The Origins of Attic Comedy*, New York.
Coventry, L. (1989) 'Philosophy and rhetoric in the *Menexenus*', *JHS* 109: 1–15.
Crosby, M. (1955) 'Five comic scenes from Athens', *Hesperia* 24: 76–84.
Csapo, E. (1993) 'Deep ambivalence: notes on a Greek cockfight', *Phoenix* 47: 1–28, 115–24.
Davidson, J. (1997) *Courtesans and Fishcakes: The Consuming Passions of Classical Athens*, London.
  (2000) '*Paignia* as sympotic mimes: Gnesippus, *Ecclesiazusae*, adultery and the hetaera', in Harvey and Wilkins 2000, 41–64.
Davies, J. K. (1971), *Athenian Propertied Families 600–300 B.C.*, Oxford.
  (2000) 'Athenaeus' use of public documents', in Braund and Wilkins 2000, 203–17.
Dearden, C. W. (1976) *The Stage of Aristophanes*, London.
Degani, E. (1993) 'Aristofane e la tradizione dell'invettiva personale in Grecia', in *Entretiens Fondation Hardt* 38: 1–36.
Develin, R. (1989) *Athenian Officials, 684–321 B.C.*, Cambridge.
Dindorf, G. (1829) *Aristophanis Fragmenta*, Leipzig.
  (1835) *Aristophanis Fragmenta*, Oxford (= *Aristophanis Comoediae* II, 495–723).
Dover, K. J. (1963) 'Notes on Aristophanes' *Acharnians*', *Maia* 15: 6–25.
  (1967) 'Portrait-masks in Aristophanes' in *Komoidotragemata: Studia Aristophanea viri Aristophanei W. J. W. Koster in Honorem Amsterdam*, 16–28 (reprinted in K. J. Dover, *Greek and the Greeks*, Oxford 1987, 267–78).
  (1968) *Aristophanes: Clouds*, Oxford.
  (1972) *Aristophanic Comedy*, Berkeley and Los Angeles.

(1974) *Greek Popular Morality in the Time of Plato and Aristotle*, Oxford.
(1980) *Plato, Symposium*, Cambridge.
(1987) 'The style of Aristophanes', in Dover, *Greek and the Greeks*, Oxford, 224–36 (originally published as '*Lo stile di Aristofane*', *QUCC* 9:7–23).
(1993) *Aristophanes: Frogs*, Oxford.
(2004) 'The limits of allegory and allusion in Aristophanes', in D. L. Cairns and R. A. Knox, eds., *Law, Rhetoric and Comedy in Classical Athens: Essays in Honour of Douglas M. MacDowell*, Swansea, 239–49.
Dow, S. (1969) 'Some Athenians in Aristophanes', *AJA* 73: 234–5.
Dunbar, N. V. (1970) 'Three notes on Aristophanes (*Acharnians* 593 and 1073–4, *Peace* 991–2, *Birds* 1229), *CR* n.s. 20: 269–73.
(1995) *Aristophanes' Birds*, Oxford.
Eco, U. (2003) *Mouse or Rat? Translation as Negotiation*, London.
Edmunds, L. M. (1980) 'Aristophanes' *Acharnians*', *YCS* 26: 1–41.
(1987) *Cleon, Knights and Aristophanes' Politics*, Lanham, New York, and London.
Edwards, A. T. (1993) 'Historicizing the popular grotesque: Bakhtin's *Rabelais* and Attic Old Comedy' in R. S. Scodel, ed., *Theater and Society in the Classical World*, Ann Arbor, 89–117.
Finnegan, R. (1995) *Women in Aristophanes*, Amsterdam.
Fisher, N. R. E. (1992) *Hybris: A Study in the Values of Honour and Shame in Ancient Greece*, Warminster.
(1993) 'Multiple personalities and Dionysiac festivals: Dicaeopolis in Aristophanes' *Acharnians*', *G&R* 40: 31–47.
(1994) 'Sparta re(de)valued' in Anton Powell and Stephen Hodkinson, eds., *The Shadow of Sparta*, London and New York, 347–400.
(2001) *Aeschines: Against Timarchos*, Oxford.
Fisher, R. K. (1984) *Aristophanes' Clouds: Purpose and Technique*, Amsterdam.
Flintoff, E. (1983) 'Aristophanes and the *Prometheus Bound*', *CQ* 33: 1–5.
Foley, H. (1988) 'Tragedy and politics in Aristophanes' *Acharnians*', *JHS* 108: 33–47 (reprinted in E. Segal, *Oxford Readings in Aristophanes*, Oxford 1996, 117–42).
Freudenburg, K. (1992) *The Walking Muse: Horace on the Theory of Satire*, New Jersey.
Geissler, P. (1925) *Chronologie der altattischen Komödie*, Berlin.
Gilula, D. (1989) 'A career in the navy (Arist. *Kn.* 541–4)', *CQ* n.s. 39: 259–61.
(1995) 'The *choregoi* vase – comic yes, but angels?', *ZPE* 109: 5–10.
Goldhill, S. (1987) 'The Great Dionysia and civic ideology', *JHS* 107: 58–76.
(1991) *The Poet's Voice*, Cambridge.
(2000) 'Civic ideology and the problem of difference: the politics of Aeschylean tragedy, once again', *JHS* 120: 34–56.
Gomme, A. W. (1938) 'Aristophanes and politics', *CR* 52: 97–109.
Goosens, R. (1935) 'Un nouveau fragment des Προσπάλτιοι d'Eupolis', *RPh* 61: 333–49.
Green, J. R. (1985) 'A representation of the *Birds* of Aristophanes', in *Greek Vases in the J. Paul Getty Museum*, vol. II, 95–118.

(1994) *Theatre in Ancient Greek Society*, London.
Green, P. (1979) 'Strepsiades, Socrates and the abuses of intellectualism', *GRBS* 20: 15–25.
Griffin, J. (1998) 'The social function of Attic tragedy', *CQ* 48: 39–61.
Griffith, J. G. (1974) 'Amphitheos and Anthropos in Aristophanes', *Hermes* 102: 367–9.
Griffith, M. (1977) *The Authenticity of the Prometheus Bound*, Cambridge.
Habicht, C. (1985) *Pausanias' Guide to Ancient Greece*, Berkeley (new edn 1998).
Halliwell, F. S. (1980) 'Aristophanes' apprenticeship', *CQ* 30: 33–45.
  (1984) 'Ancient interpretations of ὀνομαστὶ κωμῳδεῖν in Aristophanes', *CQ* 34: 83–8.
  (1989) 'Authorial collaboration in the Athenian comic theatre', *GRBS* 30: 515–28.
  (1991a) 'The uses of laughter in Greek culture', *CQ* 41: 279–96.
  (1991b) 'Comic satire and freedom of speech in classical Athens' *JHS* 111: 48–70.
  (1986) *Aristotle's Poetics*, London (2nd edn 1998).
Hamilton, R. (1974) 'Objective evidence for actors' interpolations in Greek tragedy', *GRBS* 15: 387–42.
Handley, E. W. (1982) 'Aristophanes' rivals', *PCA* 79: 24–5.
  (1985) 'Comedy' in P. E. Easterling and B. M. W. Knox, eds., *The Cambridge History of Classical Literature*, vol. 1 *Greek Literature*, Cambridge, 355–425.
  (1993) 'Aristophanes and his theatre' in *Fondation Hardt Entretiens XXXVIII*, Geneva, 97–117.
Harriott, Rosemary (1962) 'Aristophanes' audience and the plays of Euripides', *BICS* 9: 1–8.
Harvey, D. (1994) 'Lacomica: Aristophanes and the Spartans' in Anton Powell and Stephen Hodkinson, eds., *The Shadow of Sparta*, London and New York 1994, 35–58.
Harvey, D. and Wilkins, J., eds. (2000) *The Rivals of Aristophanes: Studies in Athenian Old Comedy*, London and Swansea.
Heath, M. (1987) *Political Comedy in Aristophanes*, Göttingen.
  (1989) 'Aristotelian comedy', *CQ* 39: 344–54.
  (1990) 'Aristophanes and his rivals' *G&R* 37: 43–158.
Helm, R. (1906) *Lukian und Menipp*, Leipzig.
Henderson, J. (1975) *The Maculate Muse: Obscene Language in Attic Comedy*, Yale (2nd edn, Oxford 1991).
  (1987) *Aristophanes: Lysistrata*, Oxford.
  (1993) 'Problems in Greek literary history: the case of Aristophanes' *Clouds*', in R. M. Rosen and Joseph Farrell, eds., *Nomodeiktes. Greek Studies in Honor of Martin Ostwald*, Ann Arbor, 591–602.
Herington, C. J. (1963) 'A study in the *Prometheia* part II: *Birds* and *Prometheus*', *Phoenix* 17: 236–43.
  (1970) *The Author of the Prometheus Bound*, Austin.
Heylbut, G. (1889) *Aspasii in Ethica Nicomachea quae supersunt commentaria*, Berlin (= *Commentaria in Aristotelem Graeca*, vol. XIX, part 1).

Hofmann, H. (1976) *Mythos und Komödie*, Hildesheim.
Hornblower, S. (1991) *A Commentary on Thucydides*, vol. I, Books I–III, Oxford.
 (1996) *A Commentary on Thucydides*, vol. II, Books IV – V. 24, Oxford.
 (2000) 'The *Old Oligarch* (Pseudo-Xenophon's *Athenaion Politeia*) and Thucydides. A fourth-century date for the *Old Oligarch?*' in P. Flensted-Jensen, T. H. Nielsen and L. Rubinstein, eds., *Polis and Politics: Studies in Ancient Greek History*, Copenhagen, 363–84.
Hubbard, T. K. (1986) 'Parabatic self-criticism and the two versions of Aristophanes' *Clouds*', *CA* 5: 182–97.
 (1991) *The Mask of Comedy: Aristophanes and the Intertextual Parabasis*, Cornell.
 (1998–9) 'Popular perceptions of elite homosexuality in classical Athens', *Arion* 6: 48–78.
Hughes, Alan (2003) 'Comedy in Paestan vase painting', *Oxford Journal of Archaeology* 22 (3): 281–301.
Hutchinson, G. O. (1985) *Aeschylus: Seven against Thebes*, Oxford.
Janko, R. (1984) *Aristotle on Comedy: Towards a Reconstruction of Poetics II*, London.
Kaibel, G. (1907) 'Eupolis', *RE* VI.1, 1230–5.
Katz, B. R. (1976) 'The *Birds* of Aristophanes and politics', *Athenaeum* n.s. 54: 353–81.
Kloss, G. (2001) *Erscheinungsformen komischen Sprechens bei Aristophanes*, Berlin and New York.
Kopff, E. C. (1990) 'The date of Aristophanes *Nubes II*', *AJP* III: 318–29.
Koster, W. J. W., ed. (1975) *Scholia in Aristophanem*, Pars I, Fasc. IA: *Prolegomena de Comoedia*, Groningen.
Koster, W. J. W. and Holwerda, D., eds. (1960–2007) *Scholia in Aristophanem*, Groningen.
Krentz, P. (1982) *The Thirty at Athens*, Ithaka, NY and London.
Kyriakidi, Natalia (2007) *Aristophanes und Eupolis: zur Geschichte einer dichterischen Rivalität*, Berlin and New York.
Lambert, C. (1993) *The Phratries of Attica*, Ann Arbor.
Lapini, W. (1997) *Commento all'Athenaion Politeia dello Pseudo-Senofonte*, Florence.
 (1998) 'L'*Athenaion Politeia* dello Pseudo-Senofonte e i "ricordi di distanza"', *Sileno* 24 (1–2): 109–34.
Lee, K. H. (1997) *Euripides: Ion*, Warminster.
Leeuwen, J. van (1898) *Aristophanis Nubes*, Leiden.
Lewis, D. M. (1955) 'Notes on Attic inscriptions (II)', *ABSA* 50: 1–36.
 (1961) 'Double representation in the strategia', *JHS* 81: 118–123.
 (1977) *Sparta and Persia*, Leiden.
Lind, H. (1990) *Der Gerber Kleon in den 'Rittern' des Aristophanes*, Frankfurt am Main.
Lübke, H. (1883) *Observationes Criticae in Historiam Veteris Graecorum Comoediae*, Berlin.
Lucas, D. W. (1968) *Aristotle: Poetics*, Oxford.
Luppe, W. (1966) 'Die Hypothesis zu Kratinos' Dionysalexandros', *Philologus* 110: 169–93.

(1972) 'Die Zahl der Konkurrenten an den komischen Agonen zur Zeit des peloponnesischen Kriegs', *Philologus* 116: 53–75.
MacDowell, D. M. (1962) *Andokides On the Mysteries*, Oxford.
  (1971) *Aristophanes*: Wasps, Oxford.
  (1978) *The Law in Classical Athens*, London.
  (1982) 'Aristophanes and Kallistratos', *CQ* 32: 21–6.
  (1983) 'The nature of Aristophanes' *Acharnians*', *G&R* 30: 143–62.
  (1993) 'Foreign birth and Athenian citizenship in Aristophanes' in Sommerstein, Halliwell, Henderson and Zimmermann, 1993, 359–71.
  (1995) *Aristophanes and Athens*, Oxford.
Mansfield, J. (1979) 'The chronology of Anaxagoras' Athenian period and the date of his trial. Part I', *Mnemosyne*, 32: 39–69.
  (1980) 'The chronology of Anaxagoras' Athenian period and the date of his trial. Part II', *Mnemosyne*, 33: 17–95.
Mariotta, G. (2001) 'Il decreto di Antimaco, Aristofane e la "Costituzione degli Ateniesi"', *Prometheus* 27 (2): 113–18.
Mastromarco, G. (1979) 'L'esordio "segreto" di Aristofane', *QS* 10: 153–96.
  (1993) 'Il commediografo e il demagogo', in Sommerstein, Halliwell, Henderson and Zimmermann, 341–57.
Mattingly, H. B. (1997) 'The date and purpose of the Pseudo-Xenophontic *Constitution of Athens*', *CQ* n.s. 47: 352–7.
Molitor, M. V. (1969) 'Aristophanes, *Acharnians* 593 and 1073–4' *CR* n.s. 19: 141.
Möllendorff, P. von (1995) *Grundlagen einer Ästhetik der Alten Komödie: Untersuchungen zu Aristophanes und Michail Bachtin*, Tübingen.
  (2000) *Auf der Suche mach der verlogenen Wahrheit: Lukians Wahre Geschichten*, Tübingen.
Moorton, R. F. (1988) 'Aristophanes on Alcibiades', *GRBS* 29: 345–59.
Morgan, J. D. (1986) 'ΜΑΡΙΚΑΣ', *CQ* 36: 529–31.
Murray, G. (1933) *Aristophanes: A Study*, Oxford.
Murray, R. J. (1987) 'Aristophanic protest', *Hermes* 115: 146–54.
Nails, D. (2002) *The People of Plato: A Prosopography of Plato and Other Socratics*, Indianapolis and Cambridge.
Nesselrath, H.-G. (1990) *Die attische Mittlere Komödie: ihre Stellung in der antiken Literaturkritik und Literaturgeschichte*, Berlin.
  (2000) 'Eupolis and the periodization of Athenian comedy', in Harvey and Wilkins 2000, 233–46.
Newiger, H. J. (1961) 'Elektra in Aristophanes' Wolken', *Hermes* 89: 422–30.
Norwood (1931) *Greek Comedy*, London.
Ober, J. (1989) *Mass and Elite in Democratic Athens: Rhetoric, Ideology, and the Power of the People*, Princeton.
  (1998) *Political Dissent in Democratic Athens: Intellectual Critics of Popular Rule*, Princeton.
Olson, S. D. (1991) 'Dicaeopolis' motivations in Aristophanes' *Acharnians*', *JHS* 111: 200–3.
  (1992) 'Names and naming in Aristophanic comedy', *CQ* 42: 304–19.

(1998) *Aristophanes: Peace*, Oxford.
(1999) 'Kleon's eyebrows (Cratin. fr. 228 K–A) and late fifth-century portrait-masks', *CQ* n.s. 49: 320–1.
(2002) *Aristophanes: Acharnians*, Oxford.
(2007) *Broken Laughter: Select Fragments of Greek Comedy*, Oxford.
Ostwald, M. (1986) *From Popular Sovereignty to the Sovereignty of Law*, Berkeley.
Paduano, G. (1983) *Aristofane: La Festa delle Donne*, Milano.
Panofka, T. (1849) 'Komödienscenen auf Thongefässen', *Archäologische Zeitung* 7: 33–8.
Papademetriou, I. (1948/9) 'ἡ πρώτη ἱερεία τοῦ ναοῦ τῆς Ἀθηνᾶς Νίκης καὶ ἡ Μυρρίνη τῆς Λυσιστράτης τοῦ Ἀριστοφάνους', *AE*: 146–53.
Papageorgiou, N. (2004) 'Prodicus and the agon of the Logoi in Aristophanes' *Clouds*', *QUCC* 78: 61–9.
Parker, L. P. E. (1983) Review of Sommerstein *Acharnians* (1981), *CR*, n.s. 33: 10–12.
(1991) 'Eupolis or Dicaeopolis?', *JHS* 111: 203–8.
(1997) *The Songs of Aristophanes*, Oxford.
Perusino, F. (1982) 'Aristofane poeta e didascalo', *Corolla Londiniensis* 2: 137–45.
Pickard-Cambridge, A. W. (1946) *The Theatre of Dionysus*, Oxford (reprinted 1956).
(1988) *The Dramatic Festivals of Athens*, 2nd edn, revised by J. Gould and D. M. Lewis, reissued with a new supplement, Oxford.
Pieters, J. Th. M. F. (1946) *Cratinus: Bijdrage tot de geschiedenis der vroeg-attische comedie*, Leiden.
Platnauer, M. (1949) 'Three notes on Aristophanes, *Wasps*', *CR* 63: 6–7.
(1964) *Aristophanes: Peace*, Oxford (reprint Bristol 1981, 1990).
Platter, C. (2007) *Aristophanes and the Carnival of Genres*, Baltimore.
Podlecki, A. J. (1987) *Plutarch's Life of Pericles*, Bristol.
Poole, W. (1994) 'Euripides and Sparta' in Anton Powell and Stephen Hodkinson, eds., *The Shadow of Sparta*, London and New York 1994, 1–33.
Prato, C., trans. D. Del Corno (2001) *Aristofane: Le Donne alle Tesmoforie*, Milan.
Rau, P. (1967) *Paratragodia: Untersuchungen einer komischen Form des Aristophanes*, Munich (= *Zetemata* 45).
Reckford, K. J. (1987) *Aristophanes' Old-And-New Comedy*, Chapel Hill and London.
Revermann, M. (1997) 'Cratinus' Διονυσαλέξανδρος and the head of Pericles', *JHS* 117: 197–200.
(2006) *Comic Business: Theatricality, Dramatic Technique, and Performance Contexts of Aristophanic Comedy*, Oxford.
Rhodes, P. J. (1994) 'The ostracism of Hyperbolus', in R. Osborne and S. Hornblower, eds., *Ritual, Finance, Politics: Athenian Democratic Accounts Presented to David Lewis*, Oxford, 85–98.
2003 'Nothing to do with democracy: Athenian drama and the *polis*', *JHS* 123: 104–19.
Riu, X. (1992) 'El procés de Cleó contra Aristòfanes', in *Actes del Xè Simposi de la secció Catalana de la SEEC*, Tarragona 1992, 427–9.

(1995) 'Gli insulti alla polis nella parabasi degli *Acarnesi*', *QUCC* n.s. 50: 59–66.
(1999) *Dionysism and Comedy*, Lanham, Boulder, New York, Oxford.
Robson, J. (2006) *Humour, Obscenity and Aristophanes*, Tübingen.
Rodriguez-Noriega Guillén (1996) *Epicarmo de Siracusa: Testimonios y fragmentos*, Oviedo.
Rogers, B. B. (1920) *The Thesmophoriazusae of Aristophanes*, London.
Roscalla, F. (1995) 'Περὶ δὲ τῆς Ἀθηναίων πολιτείας...', *QUCC* n.s. 50: 105–30.
Rosen, R. M. (1988) *Old Comedy and the Iambographic Tradition*, Georgia.
(2000) 'Cratinus' *Pytine* and the construction of the comic self' in Harvey and Wilkins 2000, 23–39.
Rothwell, K. S. (1990) *Politics and Persuasion in Aristophanes' Ecclesiazusae*, Leiden (= *Mnemosyne* Supplement 111).
Ruffell, I. (2002) 'A total write-off: Aristophanes, Cratinus and the rhetoric of comic competition', *CQ* n.s. 52: 138–63.
Russo, C. F. (1962) *Aristofane autore di teatro*, Florence (trans. Kevin Wren as *Aristophanes: An Author for the Stage*, London, 1994).
Rusten, J. (2006) 'Thucydides and comedy' in A. Rengakos and A. Tsakmakis, eds., *Brill's Companion to Thucydides*, Leiden and Boston, 547–58.
Saunders, T. J. (1970) *Plato, The Laws*, Harmondsworth.
Schaps, D. (1977) 'The woman least mentioned: etiquette and women's names', *CQ* 27: 323–30.
Scullion, S. (2003) 'Euripides and Macedon, or the silence of the *Frogs*', *CQ* 53: 389–400.
Sestieri, P. C. (1960) 'Vasi pestani di Pontecagnano', *ArchClass* 12: 155–69.
Sidwell, K. (1989) 'The sacrifice at *Wasps* 860–90', *Hermes* 117: 271–7.
(1990) 'Was Philocleon cured? The *nosos* theme in Aristophanes' *Wasps*', *C&M* 41: 9–31.
(1993) 'Authorial collaboration? Aristophanes' *Knights* and Eupolis', *GRBS* 34: 365–89.
(1994) 'Aristophanes' *Acharnians* and Eupolis', *C&M* 45: 71–115.
(1995) 'Poetic rivalry and the caricature of comic poets', in A. Griffiths, ed., *Stage Directions: Essays in Honour of E. W. Handley* (*BICS* Supplement 66), London, 56–80.
(1996) 'The politics of Aeschylus' *Eumenides*', *Classics Ireland* 3: 182–203.
(1997) Review of Vickers 1997, *CR* 47: 254–5.
(2000a) 'From Old to Middle to New? Aristotle's *Poetics* and the history of Athenian comedy', in Harvey and Wilkins 2000, 247–58.
(2000b) 'Athenaeus, Lucian and fifth century comedy', in Braund and Wilkins 2000, 136–52.
(2000c) 'The Parodos of Aristophanes' *Knights*', in *Theatre: Ancient and Modern*, Open University, 45–52.
(2005a) Review discussion of Storey 2003, *Classics Ireland* 12: 62–71.
(2005b) 'Some thoughts on the sophist in bed', *Hermathena* 179: 67–76.
Silk, M. (1980) 'Aristophanes as a lyric poet', *YCS* 26: 99–151.

(1990) 'The people of Aristophanes', in C. B. R. Pelling, ed., *Characterisation and Individuality in Greek Literature*, Oxford, 150–173.
(2000) *Aristophanes and the Definition of Comedy*, Oxford.
Slater, N. W. (2002) *Spectator Politics: Metatheatre and Performance in Aristophanes*, Philadelphia.
Smith, C. F. (1930) *Thucydides. History of the Peloponnesian War*, Cambridge Mass. (Loeb Classical Library).
Solomos, A. (1974) *The Living Aristophanes*, Ann Arbor.
Sommerstein, A. H. (1974) 'Aristophanes, *Frogs* 1463–5', *CQ* 24: 24–7.
(1977) 'Aristophanes and the events of 411', *JHS* 97: 112–26.
(1978) 'Notes on Aristophanes' *Acharnians*' *CQ* 28: 377–82.
(1980a) *Acharnians*, Warminster.
(1980b) 'Notes on Aristophanes' *Knights*', *CQ* 30: 46–56.
(1980c) 'The naming of women in Greek and Roman comedy', *QS* 11: 393–418.
(1981) *Knights*, Warminster.
(1982) *Clouds*, Warminster.
(1983) *Wasps*, Warminster.
(1985) *Peace*, Warminster.
(1986) 'The decree of Syrakosios', *CQ* 36: 101–8.
(1987) *Birds*, Warminster.
(1990) *Lysistrata*, Warminster.
(1992) 'Old Comedians on Old Comedy', *Drama* 1: 14–33.
(1993) 'Kleophon and the restaging of *Frogs*', in Sommerstein, Halliwell, Henderson and Zimmermann, 1993, 461–76.
(1994) *Thesmophoriazusae*, Warminster.
(1996a) *Frogs*, Warminster.
(1996b) *Aeschylean Tragedy*, Bari.
(1997a) 'The silence of Strepsiades and the *agon* of the first *Clouds*' in Pascal Thierry and Michael Menu, eds, *Aristophane: La Langue, La Scène, La Cité* (Actes du colloque de Toulouse, 17–19 mars 1994), Bari, 269–82.
(1997b) 'The theatre audience, the *Demos*, and the *Suppliants* of Aeschylus', in C. Pelling, ed., *Greek Tragedy and the Historian*, Oxford, 63–79.
(1998) *Ecclesiazusae*, Warminster.
(2000) 'Platon, Eupolis and the "demagogue-comedy"', in Harvey and Wilkins 2000, 437–51.
(2001) *Wealth*, Warminster.
(2004) 'Comedy and the unspeakable', in D. L. Cairns and R. A. Knox, eds., *Law, Rhetoric and Comedy in Classical Athens*, Swansea, 205–22.
Sommerstein, A. H., Halliwell, S., Henderson, J. and Zimmerman, B., eds (1993) *Tragedy, Comedy and the Polis*, Bari.
Sordi, M. (2002) 'L'*Athenaion Politeia* e Senofonte', *Aevum* 76 (1): 17–24.
Sourvinou-Inwood, C. (1989) 'Assumptions and the creation of meaning: reading Sophocles' *Antigone*', *JHS* 109: 134–48.
(1991) '*Reading' Greek Culture: Texts and Images, Rituals and Myths*, Oxford.
Ste Croix, G. E. M. de (1972) *The origins of the Peloponnesian War*, London.

Stevens, P. T. (1971) *Euripides: Andromache*, Oxford.
Stone, L. M. (1981) *Costume in Aristophanic Comedy*, New York.
Storey, I. C. (1985) 'The symposium at *Wasps* 1299ff.', *Phoenix* 39: 317–33.
　(1989) 'The 'blameless shield' of Kleonymos', *RhM* 132: 247–61.
　(1990) 'Dating and redating Eupolis', *Phoenix* 44: 1–30.
　(1993a) 'Notus est omnibus Eupolis?' in Sommerstein, Halliwell, Henderson and Zimmermann, 373–96.
　(1993b) 'The dates of Aristophanes' *Clouds II* and Eupolis' *Baptai*: a reply to E. C. Kopff', *AJP* 114: 71–84.
　(1995–6) 'Notes on unassigned fragments of Eupolis', *MCr* 30–1: 137–57.
　(2003) *Eupolis: Poet of Old Comedy*, Oxford.
　(2006) 'On first looking into Kratinus' *Dionysalexandros*', in L. Kozak and J. Rich, eds., *Playing Around Aristophanes: Essays in Celebration of the Completion of the Edition of the Comedies of Aristophanes by Alan Sommerstein*, Oxford, 105–25.
Sutton, D. F. (1990) 'Aristophanes and the transition to Middle Comedy', *LCM* 15.6 (June): 81–95.
　(1994) *The Catharsis of Comedy*, Lanham.
Süvern, J. W. (1826) *Über die Wolken des Aristophanes*, Berlin.
　(1827) *Über Aristophanes Vögel*, Berlin (trans. W. R. Hamilton as *Essay on the Birds of Aristophanes*, London, 1835).
Talbot, J. F. (1963) 'Aristophanes and Alcibiades', *CB* 39: 65–8.
Taplin, O. (1986) 'Fifth century tragedy and comedy: a *synkrisis*', *JHS* 106: 163–74.
　(1987) 'Phallology, phlyakes, iconography and Aristophanes', *PCPhS* 33: 92–104 and *Dioniso* 57: 95–109.
　(1993) *Comic Angels*, Oxford.
Tarrant, H. (1989) 'Alcibiades in Aristophanes' *Clouds I* and *II*', *AH* 19: 13–20.
Taylor, A. E. (1926) *Plato, the Man and his Work*, London.
Telò, Mario (2007) *Eupolidis: Demi*, Florence.
Thompson, W. E. (1967) 'The marriage of first cousins in Athenian society', *Phoenix* 21: 273–82.
　(1970) 'The kinship of Perikles and Alkibiades', *GRBS* 11: 27–33.
Todd, S. (1990) '*Lady Chatterley's Lover* and the Attic Orators', *JHS* 110: 146–73.
Totaro, P. (1999) *Le seconde parabasi di Aristofane*, Stuttgart and Weimar (= *Drama: Beiträge zum antiken Drama und seiner Rezeption*, Beiheft 7).
Trendall, A. D. (1967) *Phlyax Vases*, 2nd edn (*BICS* Supplement 19), London.
　(1991) 'Farce and tragedy in South Italian vase-painting', in T. Rasmussen and N. Spivey, eds., *Looking at Greek Vases* (for R. M. Cook), Cambridge, 151–82.
Trendall, A. D. and Webster, T. B. L. (1971) *Illustrations of Greek Drama*, London.
Vaio, J. (1971) 'Aristophanes' *Wasps*. The relevance of the final scenes', *GRBS* 12: 335–51.
　(1901) *Aristophanis Acharnenses cum prolegomenis et commentariis*, Leiden.
　(1904) *Aristophanis Thesmophoriazusae*, Leiden.
Vickers, M. (1987a) 'Alcibiades on stage: *Philoctetes* and *Cyclops*', *Historia* 36: 171–97.

(1987b) 'Lambdacism at Aristophanes *Clouds* 1381–2', *LCM* 12: 143.
(1989) 'Alcibiades on stage: *Thesmophoriazusae* and *Helen*', *Historia* 38: 41–65.
(1997) *Pericles on Stage: Political Comedy in Aristophanes' Early Plays*, Texas.
Wees, H. van (2004) *Greek Warfare: Myths and Realities*, London.
Welsh, D. (1979) '*Knights* 230–3 and Kleon's eyebrows', *CQ* 29: 214–15.
(1983a) 'The chorus of Aristophanes' *Babylonians*', *GRBS* 24: 137–50.
(1983b) '*IG* ii^2 2343, Philonides and Aristophanes' *Banqueters*', *CQ* 33: 51–5.
West, M. L. (1989–92) *Iambi et Elegi Graeci*, 2nd edn (2 vols.), Oxford.
Whitley, James (2001) *The Archaeology of Ancient Greece*, Cambridge.
Wilamowitz-Moellendorff, U. von (1935) *Kleine Schriften*, Berlin (reprinted Amsterdam 1971).
Willink, C. W. (1983) 'Prodikos, "Meteorosophists" and the "Tantalos" paradigm', *CQ* 33: 25–33.
Wilson, A. M. (1974) 'A Eupolidean precedent for the rowing scene in Aristophanes' *Frogs*?', *CQ* n.s. 24: 250–2.
(1976) 'Addendum to "A Eupolidean precedent for the rowing scene in Aristophanes' *Frogs*?"', *CQ* n.s. 26: 318.
Wilson, P. (2000) *The Athenian Institution of the Khoregia: The Chorus, the City and the Stage*, Cambridge.

Index

Acharnae (*see* demes/demotics)
Acharnians x, 31–2, 52, 68, 80, 94, 107–54, 202,
    209, 210, 215, 216, 245, 246, 262, 266,
    283, 288, 294, 342, 343
  and Cratinus 32, 33, 79–80, 345 (*see also*
    Acharnians, caricature targets,
    disguised, Dicaeopolis)
  (apparent) self-representation by poet 60,
    75–6, 86
  as a 'peace' play 4, 28, 29, 76, 81, 207
  Boeotians 134, 144–7
  caricature targets 154, 342
    disguised
      Bridesmaid 205, 252
      Dicaeopolis x, 32, 36, 37, 57, 75–6, 77–8,
        80–1, 83, 85–6, 87, 89, 94, 96, 97, 107,
        117–18, 120, 122, 123–4, 127, 128–9,
        130, 133–5, 139–41, 143, 145, 147, 148,
        160–3, 177, 181, 182, 186, 197, 198, 203,
        206, 207, 208–9, 210, 213, 225, 234–5,
        246, 251, 258, 260, 266, 267, 268, 270,
        273, 279, 286, 289, 296, 301
      Herald of Assembly 134
      Informer 134
      Slave of Euripides 36, 87, 329
      Slave of Lamachus 139, 140, 141, 211
      Xanthias 287
    named
      Amphitheus 126, 134, 135–8, 144, 211, 274
      Cleisthenes 270
      Dercetes 134–5, 144
      Euripides 36, 80, 86–91, 134, 138–9,
        143–4, 182, 207, 251, 258, 267, 268,
        269, 270, 284, 288, 290, 345
      Lamachus 37, 66, 132, 134, 139–44, 208,
        210, 213, 258, 267, 270, 281, 288, 347
      Nicarchus 134, 144
      Theorus 134–5, 144
  causes of war/defence speech 144, 145, 146,
    147–53, 195
  voice 80

chorus 32, 81, 92, 96, 124–53, 161, 163, 184, 186,
    213, 260–1, 282, 284, 340
Cleon and the comic poet 65–6, 75, 77–8,
    117–22, 123, 283
comic motifs criticised by Aristophanes 144
  circumcised phallus 5, 17, 23, 31, 144, 266–7
  old man beating someone with stick 32, 144
conventional view 4, 28
cross-referenced in *Clouds* 93–4, 175, 234–5,
    301
cross-referenced in *Thesmophoriazusai* 36–7,
    266, 268–9
dialects 147
market scene 145–7
Megarians 134, 144–7, 181, 351
metacomedy 17, 23, 31–2, 124–5, 128, 132, 134,
    137, 141, 142, 144, 145–7, 153–4, 161,
    164, 186, 187, 209
  ventriloquial 164, 180
parabasis 5, 6–7, 16, 23, 32, 33, 47, 107–11,
    117–22, 211, 260, 284
  authorial voice 6, 107–11, 112, 117–22, 164,
    180, 284
  epirrhemes 130–2, 164
  'Persian King' anecdote 118, 120–1
  pnigos 120, 122
  second 132–3, 209
parody of Euripidean tragedy 36, 45, 86–91,
    94, 209, 347
Persian embassy scene 192, 200, 266, 270
phallic song 141, 260, 324
'piggy' scene 32, 146, 181
political stance 4, 28, 29, 147–54, 195, 202,
    207, 256, 257, 268–9, 279, 293
relationships between Dicaeopolis and other
    caricature targets 134–5, 288
Scythian archers 266–7
sycophant scene 144, 146
'Thracians' scene 23, 31, 137, 144, 266–7
vomiting scene 144
actors 46, 81, 236, 261, 275, 290, 312, 315

363

Adeimantus 298
Adrestos 135
Aegeis 244
Aegina 39, 111–12, 114, 115–16, 118
Aeginetan poet 116, 117, 118, 121, 122, 123, 219, 343
Aegospotamoi, battle of 43
Aelian (Claudius Aelianus) 58
Aeschines *Against Timarchus* 257, 312, 326
Aeschylus 214, 218, 288–9, 301
  caricatured by Aristophanes 43–4, 141–2, 285–6, 288–97 (*see also* parodied by Aristophanes)
  as Pericles (?) 293, 295
  caricatured by Pherecrates 288–9
  decree allowing revivals 290, 293, 294–5
  parodied by Aristophanes 141–2 (*see also* caricatured by Aristophanes)
  revivals 288–90
    politically motivated 294–7, 301
  rewriting of plays 290, 295–6
  Choephoroi 13
  Eumenides 126
  Persians 120, 210, 286, 289, 294–7
  Prometheus Bound 141, 251, 290, 294–5
  Psychostasia 291
  Seven Against Thebes 286, 289, 294–7
Aeson 162
Agamemnon 94, 125, 135
Agariste 227
Agathon (son of Teisamenos) 175, 253, 268, 269, 270, 275, 285 (*see also Thesmophoriazusai*, caricature targets, named)
Agoracritus 158 (*see also Knights*, caricature targets, disguised, Sausage-Seller)
aiskhrologia 318–19, 331–2
Akamantis 228
Alcaeus 64
Alcibiades (son of Cleinias) 27, 38, 40, 43, 55, 131, 151, 154, 160, 175, 192, 217, 222–3, 234, 237, 241, 243, 276, 280, 290–1, 292–3, 298, 320, 341, 342–4, 349
  and Eupolis 38–9, 55, 115, 151, 154, 158, 192, 200, 209, 251, 267
  anecdotal tradition 222–3, 230–2, 300
  attitudes to Peloponnesian War 153–4, 158, 201, 209
  caricatured by Aristophanes (?)
    in *Birds* 250–1, 292
    in *Clouds* 164, 174, 177–8, 224–32, 292, 350–1
    in *Knights* 158–60, 163–5, 192, 200, 292
  'dipping' anecdote 55, 115, 222–3, 300
  family history 226–9, 280, 350
  membership of Knights 160, 177, 229, 232, 267

  political career 159, 164, 178, 222, 231–2, 235–6, 240–1, 251–2, 292
  'whirlwind' sobriquet 158–9
Alcibiades the Younger 229
Alexander the Great 210, 229
Alexis 307, 332
Alkmeonidai 226
Ameipsias 16, 48, 203, 204, 286
  Komastai 236
  Konnos 165, 178
  Sappho 254
Ammonius *Komoidoumenoi* 327
Amphitheus 135–6, 211, 274 (*see also Acharnians*, caricature targets, named)
Amynias 192
Anaxagoras 131, 174, 350
Andocides 240–2, 244, 260, 311, 313
Andromache 255
Andromeda 271 (*see also* Euripides, *Andromeda*)
Antimachus 79, 124–5
Antiochis 244
Antiochus 292
Antiphanes 313
Antiphon 196
Antisthenes 228
Antitheus 136, 274–5
Anthropos 135
Apsines 58
Aphthonius 59
Aphrodite 64, 132
Apostolius 82
apragmosyne (*see polypragmosyne*)
Araros (son of Aristophanes) 86, 111
Archelaus of Macedon 269
Archenomus 298
Archestratos 19
Archidamian War 146, 151, 194, 215, 217, 328 (*see also* Peloponnesian War)
Archilochus 63
Archippus 229
archon
  role in festival productions 10, 13, 47, 105, 217–18
  use of in naming years 108, 126, 165, 218, 236, 252, 307
Ares 142, 208, 288, 342 (*see also* Phormio)
Arete 173–4, 235 (*see also* Prodicus of Ceos)
Argives 210
Aristides 148, 160, 163, 280, 344
Aristion 218
Aristomenes 76, 203, 204
Aristonymus 147
Aristophanes (son of Philippos) ix–xi, 342–5
  accused of *xenia* (foreignness) 60, 111–12
  (alleged) drunkenness 4, 64, 175, 183, 198

baldness 14, 16, 19–20, 25, 49, 64, 84, 85, 89, 92, 111, 116, 218, 221, 268
biographical background 86, 111–12
career 14–5, 108–11, 216, 217
caricatured (?)
  in Cratinus 60–4, 75, 85, 102, 178–9, 183, 191, 343
  in Eupolis 89, 130, 219–20, 245, 279–83
civic crown 4, 41–4, 237, 293–4, 297–8, 302
comic practice, contrasted with rivals' 15–23, 28, 202–6, 219
conflicts with rivals 28 (*see also* Cratinus; Eupolis; poets' war; rivalry, poetic)
and enigmatic attack 330, 333, 334
fragmentary or lost plays
  Amphiaraus 236
  Anagyros 21, 120–3, 220–2, 344
    dating 221
  Babylonians 77, 79, 84, 108, 112, 115, 179, 200, 286, 342
    caricature targets 79, 83, 114, 123, 124, 179, 213–14, 286, 342
    chorus 200
    dating 79
    metacomedy 194
  Banqueters (*Daitales*) 10–15, 86, 108–9, 136, 342
    caricature targets 86, 136, 342
    chorus 136
    dating 342
    patrons/sponsors 10–11, 12–13, 17, 20, 111
    personified as 'Electra' 13–15
    private pre-festival performance 10–11, 14–15
    production history 10, 13–15
  Georgoi 167
  Gerytades 259, 283
  Holkades 167
  Odomantopresbeis 127, 221
  Proagon 216
  Skenas Katalambanousai ('Women Pitching Tents') 86, 90, 186
  Tagenistai 172
intellectual/philosophical outlook 4, 12, 27–9, 48, 173–5, 202, 284, 301
other writers' attacks on 4–5, 16, 64, 72, 75, 89, 164–5, 175, 179, 191, 268 (*see also* Cratinus, caricature attack on Aristophanes; Eupolis, caricatures of Aristophanes; plagiarism, accusations of; Plato (philosopher))
parody of Eupolis' plays
  in *Acharnians* 127–33, 142–3, 145–52
  in *Clouds* 18–20, 93–4, 175–7, 234–5
  in *Frogs* 37–8, 285–8
  in *Lysistrata* 260–2, 265
  in *Wasps* 188–91, 193–5
  in *Wealth* 339–40
political outlook ix-x 20, 24–6, 27–8, 38, 41–4, 48, 49–50, 51, 54–5, 91–103, 105–6, 165, 200, 217, 237–8, 252, 254, 256, 279–81, 282, 284, 292–4, 297–8, 301 (*see also* radical democracy)
'self-imitation' 144–5, 147, 208
sexual proclivities 175, 183
see also titles of individual extant works
Aristophanes of Byzantium 332
Aristotle
  conjectured 'lost history' of Old Comedy (in *Poetics II*?) 329–35
  Nicomachean Ethics 319, 332, 334
  on comedy 306–7, 309, 310, 315, 317–26
  Poetics 317–26
Aspasia 127, 131, 148, 149, 211, 249, 255, 279, 341
Aspasios 319
Asteas 281–2
Athena 140, 226, 265
  Nike 257
  Polias 212, 256
Athenaeus 64, 73, 176, 210–11, 218–19, 220, 231
Athenian Constitution (*see* 'Old Oligarch')
Athens /Athenian(s) 135, 137, 149–53, 164, 210, 230–1, 237, 240, 244–5, 247, 249, 251, 253, 258, 262, 264
  allegations of mistreatment of by comic poet 119–20
  as a 'village' 67–8, 338
  citizenship laws (*see xenia*)
  civic awards 41–4, 293
  constitution 42–4, 293
  culture 309
  finances 194–5
  fleet 41–2, 43, 72–3, 91, 222–3, 249–50, 288, 292
    personified triremes 96
  law 309
  military conflicts (*see* Peloponnesian War; Persia; Sparta/Spartans)
  political factions 251–2
  relations
    with allies 149–50, 164, 194–5, 210–11, 253
    with Persia 262
    with Sparta 262–3, 265
Athmonum (*see* demes/demotics)
Atlantis 243
audiences xi, 7, 11–13, 23, 27, 29, 47, 66, 68, 78, 81, 86, 87, 88–9, 93, 94, 111, 125, 128, 130, 154, 164, 176, 201, 210, 261, 264, 274, 278, 284–5, 290, 296, 301–2, 306, 308, 309, 314, 328, 340

audiences (*cont.*)
  specific targeting of in *Clouds II* 7–15, 111, 217, 299 (*see also Clouds II*, parabasis, audience (intended))
  tragic/comic 45–6 (*see also Clouds II*, parabasis; Old Comedy)
Augeas 113–14, 115
Autocleides 335
Autolycus 197, 219–20, 343–4 (*see also* Eupolis, *Autolycus*)

Bakhtin, Mikhail x
barbarians, bad Greek spoken by 266
Bate (*see* demes/demotics)
bees, (hypothetical) comedic referencing 185–6, 187–8
Birds 34–5, 41, 68, 69, 70, 108, 217, 236–52, 301, 340, 344, 345, 346
  apragmosyne/polypragmosyne 69, 237–8, 243
  caricature targets 237, 247, 301, 344
    disguised
      Basileia 249, 253
      Euelpides 35, 237, 238, 239, 241, 242, 243, 244–6, 249, 251, 252, 282
      Heracles 181, 238, 245, 249, 250, 253, 287
      Iris 253
      Messenger 35
      Peisetairus 35, 237, 238, 239, 240–4, 246, 248, 249, 251, 252, 253, 260, 297
      Poseidon 238, 249, 250, 253
      Priest 248
      Procne 244, 245
      Prometheus 249–50, 250–1, 292
      Tereus 35, 239, 240, 241, 244, 245, 246–7
      Tereus' servant 239
      Triballian 238, 249, 250, 253, 266
      Xanthias 287
    named
      Cinesias 246, 248, 259
      Meton 243, 247, 248
  chorus 35, 248–9, 282, 284, 285
  dating 34, 236
  dithyrambic poets 239
  intellectual themes 238, 239, 240, 248
  links with *Demoi* 246, 282
  metacomedy 34–5, 238, 243–4, 245, 250, 251, 253
  Nephelococcygia 238, 247
  parabasis 6, 69, 249, 284
  Sicilian Expedition, relevance 69, 237–8, 240, 247–9, 250, 259
  tyranny 238, 239, 243
  wedding-scene 215
Black Sea 140, 155

Boeotians, comic depictions of (*see* Megarians)
Brasidas 141

calendar 210
Callias (wealthy Athenian) 176, 179, 188, 202, 218–19, 227, 252, 287, 344
Callias (comic poet)
  Atalantai 346, 348
  Pedetai (Men in Fetters) 139, 182
Callimachus 8, 168
Callimedes 207
Callistratus 35, 76, 107, 108, 236
  production/supposed authorship of *Acharnians* 6, 76, 107–10
  production/supposed authorship of *Banqueters* 14
Camirus 112
Cantharus 108
  Medea 254
Carcinus (son of Xenotimus) 144, 250
  sons 144, 208
caricature
  centrality to Old Comedy 22, 28–9, 54, 61, 64–9, 117, 219, 245, 299, 301, 305, 315–17, 321–2, 324–9, 329–36
  masks 53, 67–8, 81, 85, 191, 212, 285, 317, 322, 325, 326, 333, 334, 335
  means of identification 68–9
  named 26
  of comic poets x, 56–64, 69–86, 92–6, 97, 98–100, 102–3, 107–54, 155, 159, 161–4, 177, 178–80, 181, 188–99, 200–1, 206–15, 219–20, 234–5, 246, 266–8, 276–83, 285–8
  of real individuals x, 21–2, 26, 53, 61, 64–9, 91, 102, 105, 113, 133–44, 324–8, 332–6, 337–9, 339–40
  disguised 26, 27–30, 91–103, 301
  recognisability 26, 67–8
  same individual in different disguises 71–2, 74–5, 77, 90, 92, 93–4, 95, 211, 248, 250–1, 260, 266, 285–7
  scholiastic attempts at identification 329
  two modes of (named *and* disguised) 21–3, 28–9, 91–103, 315–17
  (enforced) switch to latter 326–8, 330–1
  (*see also* Old Comedy; naming; Pauson; *personal names, e.g.* Alcibiades, Cleon, Hyperbolus, Socrates; *see also under individual play titles and chapters 3, 4, 5 and 6 passim*)
Carthage 96
Cassandra 255
Cephisodemus 131
Cephisophon 329

Index

Cerberus 84, 110, 190–1, 342
Chaerephon 232–3, 239
Charias 236
chariot-racing, metaphor of 108–9, 172
Cholleidae (*see* demes/demotics)
choregos/choregia 10, 43, 124–5, 218, 294
chorus 46, 96–8, 105, 124–33, 163, 183–8, 248–9, 260–1, 282–3, 284–5
 double 161, 261
 (*see also* parabases; *under individual plays by Aristophanes, Cratinus and Eupolis*)
Cinesias 248, 259, 311, 312, 316, 319, 332 (*see also* Birds; *Thesmophoriazusai*, caricature targets, named)
Cleinias (father/son) 178, 227–8
Cleisthenes (founder of Athenian democracy) 263
Cleisthenes (politician) 68, 102, 163, 269, 273, 275, 285, 332 (*see also* Acharnians; *Thesmophoriazusai*, caricature targets, named)
Cleocritus 252
Cleomenes of Sparta 263
Cleon 24, 56, 66, 70, 73, 97, 111–12, 119–22, 155–7, 159, 188, 193, 214, 217, 221, 328, 342–3, 350–1
 accusations of cowardice 122, 215
 accusations of theft 84, 95, 128–9, 144, 188, 190, 236
 and the Knights 128, 129, 144, 146, 190
 attacked by name 6, 11, 20, 23, 79
  in *Acharnians* 117–18, 126, 127–9, 184
  in *Babylonians* (?) 77–8, 112, 115
  in *Clouds* 8, 15, 16, 22–3, 25, 97, 236
  in *Knights* 23, 128, 178–9, 221, 302, 328
  in *Peace* 20, 23, 149–51
  in *Wasps* 71, 123–4, 167, 171, 180, 183, 196, 221
 attacked as 'jag-toothed' 169, 191
 as a leather-seller/shoemaker 98, 155, 158
 caricatured by
  Aristophanes
   in *Knights* (*see* Knights, caricature targets, disguised, Paphlagon)
   in *Wasps* (*see* Wasps, caricature targets, disguised, Kuon)
  Cratinus
   in *Ploutoi* (?) 84–5, 191
  Eupolis
   in *Chrysoun Genos* (?) 190–1, 267
 death 22–3, 199, 216, 221, 223
 (implied) relationship with Cratinus 84–5, 103, 148, 196, 199, 216, 235
 political support base 122, 165

public life/political career 85, 156, 159, 164, 165, 195, 302
 (representations of) conflict with poets 65–6, 70, 75, 77–8, 80, 111–12, 120, 123–4, 179–80, 182, 213–14, 283
 satirised
  as Typhon (*see* Typhoeus/Typhon)
  by Cratinus 84 (*see also* Cratinus, *Ploutoi*, caricature targets)
  by Eupolis 151, 182, 188–91
 support for attacks on 12, 15, 20, 22–3, 24–6
Cleonymus 96, 145, 214, 215, 250, 272–3, 275, 287
 shield-dropping incident 214–15, 250
Cleonymus' son (*see Peace*, caricature targets, named)
Cleonymus' wife 215, 250, 272–3
Cleophon (son of Cleippides) 250, 276, 297–8, 332
Cleophon's mother (caricatured) 332
Clouds I 8–10, 12, 17, 20–1, 27, 165–78, 229, 343
 caricature targets 12, 15, 17, 22, 25, 27, 66, 99, 166, 167–9, 171–2, 174–8, 188, 224, 229, 230, 232, 234, 289, 292, 313–14, 315–16, 343, 350
 dating 8, 165
 defeat at Dionysia 16, 72, 165, 172, 177–8, 191, 216
Clouds II 34
 caricature targets x, 22, 166, 167, 224–5, 344
 disguised
  debtors 177
  Logoi 5, 27, 92, 93–4, 96, 99–100, 173–7, 224, 233, 234–5, 281, 291, 301
  Pheidippides 22, 64, 99, 169, 170, 171, 173, 177–8, 225, 229, 232–4, 289, 292, 349, 351
  Strepsiades 22, 34, 64, 87, 169, 170, 171, 172, 173, 177–8, 203, 213, 225–32, 240, 289, 350–1
  Student 87, 177, 230–1
  Xanthias 287
 named
  Socrates x, 4, 22, 26, 66, 87, 92, 99–100, 160, 172, 174–5, 188, 224, 233, 239, 240, 248, 309, 349, 351
 Chaerephon 232–3, 239
 chorus 12, 92, 96–7, 170, 172, 173, 174–5, 252, 261, 350
 dating 10, 23, 219, 220–2, 223–4, 235, 236
 lack of public performance 8–9, 229
 metacomedy 17–20, 34, 174–6, 223–4, 231, 233, 236, 239
 parabasis ix-x 5–7, 34, 91, 120, 166, 219, 221, 283–4, 299

Clouds II (cont.)
  attacks on rival playwrights 15–23, 24–6, 31–8, 46–7, 53, 96–7, 180–1, 199–202, 245, 260, 284, 286
  audience (intended) 7–15, 16, 24–5, 98, 105, 172, 217, 236, 299
  authorial voice 6–7
  epirrhemes 96–7
  political stance 11–12, 15, 20, 24–6, 28–30, 224
  pre-festival performance 10–11, 12, 14, 236
  venue 10
  revisions 8–9, 17, 21–2, 165–6, 172, 175, 178, 223, 236, 339
    change of caricature targets 22, 178, 219, 340
  title 8, 27
Coisyra 226–7
collaboration 18, 48–9, 121, 268 (*see also* *Knights*; Eupolis, and *Knights*)
comedy
  Aristotle on 306–7, 309, 310, 317–26, 329–35
  personified 13, 61, 69, 101, 178
  Plato on 103, 306, 309–10, 315–16, 317–18
  two distinct forms 306–8, 320–6 (*see also* Old Comedy; Sicilian type of comedy)
Comias 260
comic poets
  attacks
    general/unnamed 6, 16
    named 6
    on-stage representations (*see* caricature (of) comic poets)
  (supposed) self-depiction 57–60, 86
Connus 63
Corybants 186
Crates 6, 306–7, 321, 324, 328, 330, 332, 347
  Lamia 254
Cratinus 48, 100, 302, 332, 333, 334, 339, 341–5, 347
  accused of *xenia* (?) 112–13
  (alleged) cowardice 82
  allegory 66, 185–8, 249–50, 252
  Aristophanes' comments on 6, 16, 32, 33, 37, 38, 46, 79–81, 115–16, 124–6, 142, 145, 199, 235, 284, 347
  as Dionysus 79, 82–3, 86, 112, 179, 213–14, 286, 342 (*see also* Aristophanes, fragmentary or lost plays, *Babylonians*, caricature targets; Eupolis, *Taxiarchoi*, caricature targets)
  association with wine production/consumption 62–3, 82–3, 115, 143, 197–9
  attacks on Hyperbolus 101–2, 152

  attacks on Pericles 85, 137, 146, 147–8, 149, 151, 152–3, 171, 204, 209, 211, 249, 279, 280, 293, 328
  biography/writing career 76, 199
  caricature attack on Aristophanes (?) 60–4, 75, 85, 178–9, 191, 218, 343
  caricature attack on Lamachus (?) 140–2
  caricatured by(?)
    Aristophanes
      in *Acharnians* (*see* *Acharnians*, caricature targets, disguised, Dicaeopolis)
      in *Babylonians* 77, 79, 84, 112, 123, 342
      in *Clouds II* (*see* *Clouds II*, caricature targets, disguised, Logoi)
      in *Knights* (*see* *Knights*, caricature targets, disguised, Demos)
      in *Peace* (*see* *Peace*, caricature targets, disguised, Trygaeus)
      in *Wasps* (*see* *Wasps*, caricature targets, disguised, Philocleon)
    Eupolis (?) 81, 85–6, 132–3, 145, 146, 220
      in *Chrysoun Genos* (*see* Eupolis, *Chrysoun Genos*, caricature targets)
      in *Noumeniai* (*see* Eupolis, *Noumeniai*, caricature targets)
      in *Prospaltioi* (*see* Eupolis, *Prospaltioi*, caricature targets)
      in *Taxiarchoi* (*see* Eupolis, *Taxiarchoi*, caricature targets)
  comments on rivals' work 5
  complaints of Aristophanes' plagiarism 18, 49, 50, 60–1, 81, 164–5
  dancing-teacher 73
  death 63, 115, 199
  Euripidaristophaniser fragment 86, 88–90, 138, 182, 209, 266, 285
  female choruses 253–4
  (hypothetical) 426 BC festival entry (referenced in *Acharnians*) 78
  imitated by Eupolis 38, 82, 144, 200, 204, 206, 209, 249, 267
  parody of Aeschylus 126, 289
  physical characteristics 64, 81, 162–3
  poetic persona 180–3
  political allegiance 76–7, 84–6, 103, 124, 148, 153–4, 179–80, 183, 188, 191–7, 216, 235
  reception in antiquity 60–4
  retirement 83, 199, 206, 215–16, 235
  satire of Euripides 138–9, 182, 209, 266, 268, 269, 288 (*see also* Idaioi)
  satire/parody of works 73, 101, 132–3, 138–9, 142, 144–54, 178–88, 249
  Boukoloi 345
  Bousiris 181

Cheimazomenoi 52, 345
Deliades 253
Dionysalexandros 66, 68, 76–7, 89, 137–8, 146, 211, 254, 341, 345
  caricature targets 137–8, 211, 341
  dating 66, 76–7, 133, 137, 146, 254, 341
  political stance 76–7, 146
Drapetides 253
Eumenides 46, 125, 141–2, 220, 253, 289
Euneidae 142, 220, 347
  dating 126
Horai 32, 33, 100, 101, 132–3, 146–7, 150, 151, 175, 181, 206, 208–9, 210, 213, 254, 262, 341, 342
  caricature targets 140, 143, 151, 158, 162, 181, 206, 208, 213, 288, 341, 343
  dating 101, 132–3, 151–2, 209
  political stance 146–7, 148, 151
Idaioi 138–9, 288, 345
  caricature targets 138–9, 253, 345
Kleoboulinai 253
Lacones 33, 261
Malthakoi ('*Softies*') 187
Nomoi 72, 85, 130, 133, 161, 184, 188, 220, 235, 261, 342
  chorus 126–7, 186–8
  political stance 188
Odysses 73, 287–8, 333
Ploutoi 103, 124, 340, 342
  caricature targets 85, 103, 124, 183, 191, 342
  political stance 124, 342
Pytine x, 13, 16, 56–8, 60–4, 69–73, 83, 85–6, 92, 94, 123, 125, 165, 178–80, 183, 191, 199, 215–16, 278, 343
  and *Knights* 60–1, 64, 73
  and *Wasps* 69–70, 75, 178–91, 198
  caricature targets 60–4, 75, 101–2, 178–9, 191, 218, 343
  dating 165
  metacomedy 60–4
  parabasis 72, 179, 191
Satyroi 345
Seriphioi 183
'*Softies*' (*see Malthakoi*)
Thraittai 253
  caricature targets 148
Creon 258
Cretans 139
Crioa (*see* demes/demotics)
Critias 242–4, 248, 251, 252, 253, 260, 297, 344
  (*see also* Birds, caricature targets, disguised, Peisetairus; *Lysistrata*, caricature targets, disguised, Athenian Ambassadors)
Ctesias 96

Cybele 138
Cynossema, battle of 39

Daitales (*see* Aristophanes, fragmentary or lost plays, *Banqueters*)
Damasias 281
Damon 351
Danaans 135
dancing 15, 17, 20, 33, 34, 73, 191, 202, 208
Darius 126, 296
Deinomache 227–8
Delium, battle of 178
Delphic Amphictyony 97
demes/demotics
  Acharnae 127, 130, 143, 250 (*see also* Acharnians, chorus)
  Athmonum 95, 206–7
  Bate 212, 256
  Cholleidae 80, 87–8, 206–7, 246
  Crioa 244, 245, 246
  Gargettus 274
  Kikynna 228
  Kollytos 312
  Konthyleus 122
  Kydathenaion 44, 80, 136, 274
  Myrrhinous 246
  Oe 139
  Perithoidae 313
  Phlya 122
  Phyle 44, 135
  Prospalta 127 (*see also* Eupolis, *Prospaltioi*)
  Rhamnous 312
  Skambonidae 228
  Thoricus 250
  Thumoitadai 127
  comic
    Pyknites 77
Democritus 351
demos
  insult to/avoidance of insult to 4, 51, 80, 120–1, 142, 194, 256, 270, 308–9, 332–3
  political decisions/positions of 4, 41–2, 43, 44, 119, 122, 137–8, 165, 210, 237, 247, 290, 292–3, 294–5, 297–8, 302, 307, 309
  punishment for offences against 40
Demos (as character) 223
  in Cratinus (?) 85
  in Eupolis 50–1
  in *Knights* (*see Knights*, caricature targets, disguised, Demos)
Demosthenes (general) 66, 155–6, 158, 256 (*see also* Knights, caricature targets, disguised, Slave 1)
Demostratus 281

Derketes of Phyle 135 (*see also* Acharnians, caricature targets, named, Dercetes)
diaballein 119–20
dialect, use of 147, 261
Diallage (*see* Reconciliation; *see also Lysistrata*, caricature targets, disguised, Diallage)
Dicaearchus 37, 41–3
Dicaeopolis (*see Acharnians*, caricature targets, disguised)
didaskalos 5, 14, 107–10, 111, 171, 235
Dike 175
Diocleides 244, 260
Diodorus 228
Diodotus 119
Diogenes 176, 278
Dionysia (City and Rural) (*see* festivals (of drama))
Dionysius Thrax 330
Dionysus 7, 37, 64, 79, 89, 151, 204
  Dionysiac processions 324
  (*see also* Aristophanes, fragmentary or lost plays, *Babylonians*; *Frogs*, caricature targets, disguised, Dionysus; Eupolis, *Taxiarchoi*, caricature targets)
Diopeithes 76
Diotima 255
Diotimos 108
Diphilus 332
Draces 260
Dracontides of Bate 212, 256
drama, invention/evolution (in Aristotelian theory) 324–5
dress, significance of 192–3 (*see also* Persia, clothing)
Dunphy, Eamon 67

Ecclesiazousai 257, 333–4, 337–9
  caricature targets 337–9
  chorus 337
  metacomedy 339
  political themes 337–9
Ecphantides 76
Eirene (*see* Peace (goddess))
Elaphebolion 224
Electra (tragic character), Aristophanes' referencing of 8, 13
Eleusinian mysteries
  chorus of *mystai* 6, 38, 284–5
  profanation of 236, 240, 251–2
Eleusis 113
Eliaia court 260
Epeios 82
Ephialtes (comic character in Eupolis?) x, 39, 113–15, 219–20, 343–4
  identified as Aristophanes 115, 219–20

Epicharmus 325
Epicurus 231
Epilycus 192
Ephorus 80, 149
Eratosthenes 8, 38, 115, 168
Erechtheis 244–5
Erechtheus 190, 244
Eresistratos 233
Erichthonios 233
eriole 158–9
Euathlus 130–1, 194, 267, 342
Euboea 112–13
Eucrates 244
Eudaimonia 173–4, 175 (*see also* Prodicus)
Eunomie 175
Euphemus 244, 245
Euphorion (son of Aeschylus) 295
Eupolis ix–x 6, 37, 48, 66, 153, 173, 174, 302, 330, 333, 334, 339, 342–5, 351
  accused of *xenia* 113–14, 115
  allegory 55, 189–91
  and *Acharnians* 80
  and Cleon 21, 119, 121–2, 182
  and *Clouds* 92–4, 96–7, 99–100, 175–8 (*see also Clouds I*, caricature targets; *Clouds II*, caricature targets, disguised, Logoi)
  and *Frogs* 37–8, 40–1, 72, 285–8 (*see also* Frogs, caricature targets, disguised, Dionysus)
  and *Knights* 11, 32–3, 47, 48–56, 60–1, 97, 121, 152, 155, 159, 161–5, 199–202, 220–1, 223, 268, 271, 300
  and *Peace* 202–15 (*see also* Peace, caricature targets, disguised, Trygaeus)
  as *epibates* 41, 91, 223
  as Euripidaristophaniser 88–90, 138, 182, 257–8, 266, 285
  attacks on Cratinus (*see* Cratinus, caricatured by Eupolis(?))
  attacks on Hyperbolus (*see* Hyperbolus, caricatured by Eupolis)
  attacks (named) on Socrates in Eupolis 176–7
  as focus of Aristophanes' satire 25, 38, 254
  career x, 39, 41, 217
  caricatures of Aristophanes (?) 89, 246, 279–83
  caricatured by Aristophanes (?) 136
    in *Acharnians* (*see Acharnians*, caricature targets, disguised, Dicaeopolis)
    in *Birds* (*see Birds*, caricature targets, disguised, Euelpides)
    in *Clouds* (*see Clouds I*, caricature targets; *Clouds II*, caricature targets, disguised, Logoi)

in *Frogs* (see *Frogs*, caricature targets, disguised, Dionysus)
in *Knights* (see *Knights*, caricature targets, disguised, Demos)
in *Peace* (see *Peace*, caricature targets, disguised, Trygaeus)
in *Thesmophoriazousai* (see *Thesmophoriazusai*, caricature targets, disguised, Relative of Euripides)
in *Wasps* (see *Wasps*, caricature targets, disguised, Bdelycleon)
comments on rivals' work 5, 218, 220–1
complaints of Aristophanes' plagiarism 18
criticisms in *Clouds* parabasis 15–26, 34
death/burial 38–9, 40, 115–16, 275–6, 286
double chorus 161, 261, 285
exile/disenfranchisement 40–1, 42, 212–13, 222–3, 275–6, 286, 290, 297, 298, 340
festival successes 215–16, 217
feud with Aristophanes, scope/duration 30, 38, 45, 48–55, 103, 121–2, 215–16, 287, 302
imitator of Cratinus 38, 82, 144, 161, 183, 191, 193, 200, 204, 206, 209, 249, 267
links with Alcibiades 38–9, 115, 151, 154, 158, 159, 160, 192, 200, 209, 251, 300
links with Euripides 86–91, 138–9, 176–7, 207, 209, 255, 266, 267–8, 274, 285–6, 288, 290
links with Pericles 148, 151, 154, 279–80
links with Socrates 99–100, 176–7, 189, 235, 240, 255, 280
parody of his plays by Aristophanes
in *Acharnians* 127–33, 142–3, 145–52
in *Clouds* 18–20, 93–4, 175–7, 234–5
in *Frogs* 37–8, 285–8
in *Lysistrata* 260–2, 265
in *Wasps* 188–91, 193–5
in *Wealth* 339–40
parodying of Aeschylus 200, 214, 286, 289, 295–7
physical characteristics 25, 81, 92, 162–3, 192–3
political stance ix–x 25, 38–41, 42, 97, 103, 119, 120, 153–4, 156–7, 158, 163, 182–3, 191–7, 200, 209, 210, 257, 265, 276, 279, 280, 282, 286, 290, 295–8, 301
reception in antiquity 58–60, 276–9, 280, 330
satirised by Cratinus 61–2, 64, 75, 89, 179, 183
satirised via chorus 96–8
(supposed) self-representations 56–7, 60, 113–14, 276–9
Aiges 174, 345
caricature targets 174
dating 174
Astrateutoi ('*Evaders of Military Service*') 187, 249, 345

Autolycus 39, 47, 56–7, 113–16, 179, 197, 217, 218–20, 277, (*I*) 343, (*II*) 344
caricature targets x, 39, 114–16, 219–20, (*I*) 343, (*II*) 344
dating 116, 217, 220
production history 218–20
(supposed)self-representation by Eupolis 39, 114
two versions 197, 218–19
Baptai 22, 54, 115, 158, 160, 217, 220–1, 222–3, 268, 270–1, 291, 344
caricature targets 158, 222–3, 291, 344
dating 221, 222
links with *Thesmophoriazusai* 223, 270–1
Chrysoun Genos 20, 38, 49, 83–4, 85, 89, 111, 114, 129–30, 131–2, 133, 162, 182, 184, 188–91, 193–4, 199–200, 261, 342
caricature targets 84, 85, 130, 163, 184, 189–91, 267, 342
chorus 83, 182
dating 49, 84, 121, 182
positive on-stage representations 131, 160, 267, 342
relation to *Knights* 49, 189, 199–200
relation to *Wasps* 189–90, 193–4
Demoi 37, 59–60, 69, 154, 220, 223, 233, 245–6, 276–83, 285, 293, 301, 340, 344, 347
caricature targets 281, 344
disguised; adulterer 281; Pyronides 246, 276, 277, 278–83; sycophant 281, 340
named; Damasias (?) 281; Demostratus (?) 281; Laespodias (?) 281; Phrynis 246, 281
chorus 282, 285
dating 223, 246, 276, 280, 282, 283
links with *Birds* 246, 282
metacomedy 276
political stance 223, 276–83, 301
positive on-stage representations 148, 154, 160, 163
Aristides 148, 160, 163, 280, 340
Miltiades 148, 160, 163, 280
Pericles 148, 154, 160, 163, 279–80, 293
Solon 148, 160, 163, 280
referenced by Lucian 278
'*Evaders of Military Service*' (see Eupolis *Astrateutoi*)
Heilotes 33, 245, 261, 345
Hybristodikai 114–15, 220
Kolakes 160, 202, 216, 217, 344
caricature targets 160, 176, 219, 238, 287, 344
dating 202, 217, 219

Eupolis (*cont.*)
  Marikas 8, 20, 22, 25, 49–53, 54–5, 56, 89, 91, 92, 94, 95, 98, 101, 103, 105, 152, 156–7, 161, 179, 199–202, 206, 209, 216, 217, 220, 253, 261, 271, 285, 317, 329, 343
    caricature targets 20, 26, 49, 50, 200, 201, 253, 271, 275, 292, 317, 343
    chorus 161, 183
    relation to *Knights* 48–56, 201, 343
  Noumeniai 52–6, 75, 80, 84, 94, 96, 99, 102, 105, 128, 150, 155, 156, 157, 158, 160, 162, 165, 174, 179, 182, 183, 189, 199, 200–1, 223, 205, 220, 223, 342, 343
    caricature targets 84, 99, 103, 150, 155, 156, 157, 160, 162, 174, 199, 201, 208, 342
    dating 52, 99
    reconstruction 53–5, 205
    relation to *Knights* 53–6, 182, 189, 200
  Philoi 345
  Poleis 187, 194–5, 211, 214, 215, 220, 285, 298, 343
    caricature targets 214, 285
    chorus 211, 253
  Prospaltioi 19, 83, 85, 127, 146, 151–2, 180–1, 194, 209, 342, 343
    caricature targets 85, 148, 151, 181, 206, 268, 342
    dating 151–2
    political stance 151–2, 153, 342
  Taxiarchoi 37, 82–3, 85, 90, 142–3, 204, 208, 285, 286, 287–8, 342
    caricature targets 82–3, 142–3, 286, 287–8, 342, 346
    dating 83, 346–8
    parabasis (?) 152
Euripides 80, 86, 180, 181, 228, 254, 275, 301
  caricatured by
    Aristophanes 45, 66, 86–91, 182, 301
      in *Acharnians* (see *Acharnians*, caricature targets, named)
      in *Frogs* (see *Frogs*, caricature targets, named)
      in *Thesmophoriazusai* (see *Thesmophoriazusai*, caricature targets, named)
    Cratinus (?)138–9 182, 209, 253
    other comic poets 139, 181–2
  caricatures of mother (?) 253, 261, 275
  parodied by Aristophanes 45, 209, 257–8 (see also parody of Euripidean tragedy under *Acharnians*, *Frogs*, *Peace*, *Thesmophoriazusai*)
  political stance 291
  portrayal of women 254–5, 257–8, 271
  relationship with Eupolis 86–91, 138–9, 143, 176, 207, 209, 255, 266, 267–8, 274, 285–6, 288, 290
  Aeolus 228
  Andromeda 45, 252, 266, 271, 274, 347
  Archelaus 269
  Erechtheus 264–5
  Hecuba 254
  Helen 45, 254, 266, 271, 273, 274, 347
  Ion 258
  Medea 254
  Melanippe Sophe 257
  Palamedes 266
  Stheneboia 254
  Telephus 36–7, 45, 75, 81, 93–4, 203, 234–5, 258, 266, 347
  Trojan Women (Troiades) 255
Eurycles 109–11
Euthymenes 307
Evenus of Paros 172
Execestides 250

festivals (of drama) 6, 8–9, 10, 11, 12, 14, 16, 34, 35, 37, 42, 46–7, 48, 75, 76, 78, 101, 105, 111, 124–5, 142, 152, 165, 168, 178, 187, 195, 199, 202, 206, 209, 216, 217–18, 219, 220, 221, 223, 235, 236, 252, 266, 269, 275, 276, 289, 293, 300, 306, 307, 310, 311, 312, 324, 332
  decline in Aristophanes' success rate 117
  judging 29, 105
  Proagon 126
  selection of material 10, 105, 217–18
  timing of Dionysia 224
financing (of productions) 10–11, 29, 217–18
Frogs 37–8, 40–4, 69, 223, 283–98, 337, 345, 347
  and *Acharnians* 37–8
  caricature targets 345
  disguised
    Aeacus 287
    Charon 37, 288
    Corpse 288
    Dionysus 37, 81, 87, 91, 283, 285–8, 291, 292, 293, 295, 296, 345
    Heracles 81, 87, 89, 283, 287
    Innkeeper 288
    Persephone's Maid 288
    Pluto 288, 298
    Pluto's Slave 288
    Xanthias 81, 89, 283, 287, 288
  named
    Aechylus 43–4, 141, 143, 148, 281, 284, 286, 288–90, 291–5, 298

Index

Euripides 43–4, 87, 89, 90, 91, 148, 281, 284–6, 288, 289, 290–1, 345
  Plathane 92, 100–1, 288
  chorus of *mystai* 6, 38, 284–5, 298
  chorus of Frogs 288
  Cratinus and 79, 284
  dating 37, 283
  didactic content 41–4, 292–4
  Eupolis and 37–8, 40–1, 285–8, 346
  metacomedy 37–8, 43, 101, 284, 286–8, 289, 290, 298
    ventriloquial 284, 297–8
  parabasis 4, 6, 41–3, 72, 283–4
  parody of Euripidean tragedy 45, 209, 284–5, 288–91
  political position 4, 30, 41–4, 290–8, 302
  second production 4, 37, 41, 42–3, 293, 295, 298, 339

Gaia 85
Gargettus (*see* demes/demotics)
geloion, to 321, 322–5, 331
general (*strategos*)/generalship 142–3, 155–6, 249–50, 256, 282–3, 288, 302, 328, 346
Giants 233
Glaucetes 145
Gnesippus 218, 339
Gorgias 178, 238
Graces 132

Haemon 258
Hecuba 255
Hegemon 231
Helen 137, 211, 254, 255, 271, 273, 341 (*see also* Euripides, *Helen*; Euripides, *Trojan Women*)
Hellespont 200
Helots 250
Hera 135, 249 (*see also* Aspasia)
Heracles 29, 31, 34, 101, 125, 136, 172, 173, 175, 180, 181, 203, 204, 238, 245, 249, 274, 285, 287 (*see also* Birds, caricature targets, disguised; Frogs, caricature targets, disguised)
Hermae, Mutilation of 236, 240–8, 251–2, 260
Hermes 132, 137, 253 (*see also* Peace, caricature targets, disguised, Hermes)
Hermippus 333
  Aristophanes' comments on 6, 21–2, 34, 120
  Artopolides ('*Female Bread-Sellers*') 21–2, 101, 254, 261, 275
  Europa 254
  Kerkopes 277
  Moirai 254
  Stratiotides 254, 338

Hermogenes 59
Herodicus *Komoidoumenoi* 327
Hesiod 175
Hesychius 82
hetaireiai, oligarchic 136, 210, 243, 248, 249, 252, 263–4, 275
hieromnemon 97
Hipparete 178, 227–8, 229
Hippias 263
Hippocrates 178, 227
Hipponicus 178, 227–8, 230, 232
Hippyllos 196–7
Hitchcock, Alfred xi
Homer
  Iliad, Odyssey 322–3
  inventor of *tragoidia* 318, 322–3
  Margites 322–3, 324
Horae (Seasons – goddesses) 132, 175, 209
homosexuality 160, 173–4, 179, 198, 235, 268, 269–71
humour, understanding of 3–4, 9, 16–18, 27–8, 46, 53, 54, 76, 78, 80, 81, 125, 126, 129, 131, 132, 133, 138, 139, 144, 150, 151, 153, 156, 162, 164, 173, 178, 182, 185, 187, 191, 192, 195, 196, 202, 204, 209–10, 225, 226, 228–34, 243, 249, 250, 256, 259, 261, 263–4, 267, 270, 273, 274, 281, 290, 291, 294, 296–7, 329, 331, 347
hybris 198, 213
Hyperbolus (son of Antiphanes) 152, 173, 175, 188, 217, 223, 276, 286, 342–4
  as barbarian 157, 313
  as lamp-maker/merchant 55, 94, 95, 96, 98, 101–2, 155, 157, 160, 174, 313, 316
  Aristophanes' support of x, 6, 24–5, 27–8, 43, 51, 54–5, 91, 95, 162, 165, 173, 200, 210, 223–4, 237, 256, 284, 297
  career 152
  caricatured 23
    by Eupolis 20, 21, 22, 26, 91, 144, 157, 206, 209, 317, 329 (*see also* Eupolis, *Marikas*, caricature targets)
    by Hermippus 22, 254
    by Plato 22
  caricature of his father (?) 316
  caricature of his mother 20, 91, 98, 101, 179, 201–2, 205–6, 253, 254, 271, 275
  death 221, 223, 292
  named attacks on in Aristophanes 25–6, 28, 91–102, 105, 143–4, 145–6, 201, 284
  named attack on his mother in Aristophanes 97, 143
  ostracism 23, 221, 223–4, 225, 234, 235, 252, 292, 313, 346
  political stance 28, 50, 162, 200–1

hypodidaskalos 108
hyponoia 318–19, 331–2

'iambic' comedy (*see* Old Comedy; caricature)
iambic poetry 309–10, 316, 319, 321, 322–3, 325, 326
Iason 347
Ida 139
I Keano (musical) 67
individuals, attacks on (*see* caricature; Old Comedy, defining features)
intertextuality x–xi, 23, 72, 128, 130, 141, 144, 147, 149, 154, 162, 187, 202, 206, 208, 209, 229, 250, 261, 278, 293, 347 (*see also* metacomedy)
invective comedy (*see* Old Comedy; caricature)
Ionians 258
Iphicrates 312
Iris 137 (*see also Birds*, caricature targets, disguised)
irony ix 16–17, 26, 28, 40, 43, 51, 53, 60, 84, 91, 98, 157, 158, 162, 164, 173, 182, 186, 195, 201, 206, 213, 223, 228, 230, 231, 234, 261, 265, 266, 279, 280, 282, 284, 293
= *eironeia* 331
Isagoras 263
Isarchus 165
Isocrates 210, 263, 306, 311, 335
Isthmian games 227

Jason 162
jurors/jury system 72, 73, 93, 126, 128–32, 152, 161, 183–4, 188, 191, 193–4, 207, 220, 241, 260 (*see also* lawcourts)

Kakia 173–4, 175 (*see also* Prodicus of Ceos)
katharsis 318
kaunakes (*see* Persia, clothing)
Keane, Roy 67
Kekropis 207
Kikynna (*see* demes/demotics)
Knights (cavalrymen) 25, 27, 54, 127, 128, 129, 130, 131, 146, 159, 160, 161, 163, 177, 192, 200, 229, 232, 267, 286, 342, 343
Knights 4, 11, 20–1, 32–3, 48–56, 70, 81, 84–5, 105, 110, 126–7, 128–9, 150, 155–65, 178, 183–4, 189, 190–1, 193, 203, 233, 302
and Cratinus 60–4, 70, 73, 75, 80, 235, 246
and Eupolis 11, 18–21, 24, 32, 47, 48–56, 60–1, 64, 66, 73, 75, 91, 92, 95–6, 102–3, 121, 152, 155, 159, 161–5, 179, 183, 189–91, 199–202, 219, 220–1, 223, 246, 268, 271, 300, 302

caricature targets 342
disguised
Demos 50–6, 64, 70, 71, 73–5, 77–8, 80, 84, 92–3, 98–9, 103, 128–9, 148, 155, 161–5, 179, 192–4, 199, 200, 201, 207, 225, 342
Paphlagon x, 11, 15, 16, 21, 22, 23, 24, 25, 26, 49, 50, 52, 54, 55, 66, 74, 96, 99, 128, 151, 155, 161, 162, 163–4, 171, 179, 183, 191, 207, 221, 256, 302, 305, 328, 342
Sausage-Seller 50, 53, 54–5, 56, 64, 92–3, 96, 98, 99, 129, 150, 151, 155, 157–60, 161–2, 163–4, 165, 171, 174, 179, 189, 190, 192, 193, 207, 269, 292, 302
Slave 1, 53, 66, 155–6, 158, 256
Slave 2, 53, 155–7, 158, 256
chorus 92, 96, 161, 164, 183, 261
metacomedy 32–3, 48–56, 156, 162, 164, 182
ventriloquial 33, 123, 164–5, 284
opening scene 205
parabasis 5–6, 32–3, 46–7,107 109, 110, 159, 164, 284
second 96, 164–5, 205
political stance 4, 12, 20–1, 22–3, 29, 160, 165, 194
Spondai ('Peace-Terms') 162, 199
Kollytos (*see* demes/demotics)
Konthyleus (*see* demes/demotics)
komoidoumenos/oi 65, 133, 309, 316–17, 321, 322, 327
kordax 14, 17, 20, 31, 33, 34, 202
Kronos 85
Kydathenaion (*see* demes/demotics)

Lacedaimon 242
Laches 66, 207
caricatured
in *Wasps* x, 66, 152, 188–91
political career 188–9
Laconophilia (*see* Sparta/Spartans)
Lacrateides 85, 126
Lady and the Tramp (1955) 46
Laespodias 281
Lamachus 4, 37, 132, 134, 139–44, 207, 210, 211, 213, 271, 284, 288, 347
biography/military career 139–40, 141, 142
caricatured 4, 341
by Aristophanes
in *Acharnians* (*see Acharnians*, caricature targets, named, Lamachus)
in *Frogs* (*see Frogs*, caricature targets, disguised, Charon)
in *Peace* (*see Peace*, caricature targets, disguised, Polemos (War))

by Cratinus
  in *Horai* (*see* Cratinus, *Horai*, caricature targets)
  mother 97, 142–3
  named attacks 4
Lampsacus 131
laughter 26, 27, 67, 129, 147, 164, 229, 234, 262, 265, 279, 297, 300, 305, 318, 331–2, 350
  consequential 302, 305, 314–15, 325
  festive/playful 314, 325
lawcourts 69, 71, 73, 75, 77, 92, 126, 160, 171, 177, 193, 230, 231, 237, 240–2, 246, 278, 291 (*see also* jurors)
Laws (personified) 186–8, 342
Lenaea (*see* festivals (of drama))
Leontis 228, 246
Leucon 203, 204
Lindos 112
Lucian 57–8, 60, 62, 63, 100, 176, 190, 204, 231, 278–9, 336
  Sale of Lives 278
Lycis 286
Lycon 113, 196–7, 220, 343
Lysanias 136
Lysias 63, 311–12, 315, 316, 319
Lysimache 212, 255–6, 257, 263–4, 274, 275, 344
  (*see also* Lysistrata, caricature targets, disguised, Lysistrata)
Lysistrata 35, 108, 158, 252–65, 296, 344
  caricature targets 338, 344
    disguised
      Athenian Ambassadors 35, 253, 259, 297
      Diallage 260, 262
      Lysistrata 35, 212, 254, 255, 256–8, 262–5, 274–5, 338, 344
      Proboulos 253, 256, 258–9, 263–4, 270, 289
      Spartan Ambassadors 253
    named
      Calonice (?) 35, 257
      Cinesias 35, 248, 253, 259, 332
      Ismenia (?) 257
      Lampito (?) 257
      Myrrhine 257, 259, 274–5
  chorus 35, 253, 260–1, 273, 282, 284
  dating 35, 252
  metacomedy 35, 253, 260–2, 264, 265, 267
  modern productions 262
  parabasis 284
  parody of Euripidean tragedy 257–8
  undercutting of anti-war arguments 260–5, 296
Lysistratus 96, 145–6, 196–7

Macedon 269
  threat to Athens 335
Magnes 6
Major, John and Norma 98
Mantineia, battle of 276
Marathon, battle of 74, 126, 163, 260
masks,
  portrait (*see* caricature, masks)
  stock characters 307, 322
McCarthy, Mick 67
Medon 135, 162
Megacles (father/son) 225–6, 227–8
Megarian comedy 179–80
Megarian decree 148, 149, 150, 151
Megarians/Boeotians, comic depictions of 134, 145–7, 149, 151, 180–1, 207, 209, 210, 351
Melanippe 271 (*see also* Euripides, *Melanippe Sophe*)
Melanthius 145
Menander (comic poet) 76, 307, 332
Menelaus 135, 255, 273
Menippus 231
metacomedy x, 18–19, 28–30, 31–8, 43, 45–8, 78, 85–6, 91–103, 105, 111, 113, 144–7, 152, 162, 182, 184, 202–6, 252, 253, 255, 276, 286, 299, 347–8 (*see also* chapters 3, 4, 5 and 6 passim; metacomedy under individual plays)
  metre and 130
  techniques 110–11, 144–6
  ventriloquial 19, 33, 111, 297 (*see also* metacomedy, ventriloquial *under* Acharnians; Frogs; Knights; Wasps)
metics 150, 170–1
Meton 247
Metroon 44, 231
Middle Comedy 332 (*see also* Old Comedy, history of)
Miletus 257
Miltiades 148,160 163, 280, 344
Mnesilochus 266, 329
moneylending 97–8
Moon (personified) 210
Morychides
  archon year of 307
  decree of 302, 307–8, 327–8
Morychus 145–6
Muses 108, 130
Music (personified) 259, 281
Myrmex 298
Myrrhine 257, 259, 274–5 (*see also* Lysistrata, caricature targets, named)
Myrrhinous (*see* demes/demotics)

naming 16, 26, 28, 29, 91–102, 105, 176, 219, 301, 307, 311, 315–16, 321, 326–8, 331, 332–4
Naucratis 112
Neaira 256
Nepos 228
New Comedy, development of 305, 307, 319, 332
Nicias 67, 89, 95, 122, 155–6, 157, 158, 201, 207, 224, 237, 247, 256, 292
  caricatured in *Knights* (*see Knights*, caricature targets, disguised, Slave 2),
  Peace of 55, 140, 156, 160, 189, 211, 216, 217
Nicomachus 298
Nicostratus/Philetairus (son of Aristophanes) 86, 111
Nikochares 125
Nile 112
Notium, battle of 292

Odeon 68
Odysseus 135
Oe (*see* demes/demotics)
Oeneis 82, 143
Old Comedy (= iambic comedy *or* invective comedy) ix–xi, 305, 307–8, 308–17, 321, 324, 325–6
  allegorical interpretation 66–7, 237, 336
  (apparent) impartiality of attacks 29, 105
  (apparent) self-satire by poets 56–8, 61–2
  bans/legal restrictions 125, 307, 308, 326–8, 330–1, 332–3, 334–5
  criticisms of 309–11, 318–25, 331
  defining features 21, 25, 26, 28, 61, 91, 133, 299, 301, 305–6, 308–17, 321, 325–6
  distinguished from plot-based (by Aristotle) 321, 324, 325–6, 332
  'enigmatic' stage of development 330, 333
  history of 58, 301, 305–6, 329–35
  irony in 265
  'middle iambic comedy' 333–4, 337
  modern interpretation 66–7
  naming 16, 26, 28, 29, 91–102, 105, 176, 219, 311, 315–16, 321
    of characters 301, 305, 321, 326–8, 332–4
    restrictions on 326–8, 331, 332–4
  'new (iambic) comedy' 330–2, 334–5
  obscenity 27, 34, 180–1, 257, 319, 324, 326
  oratory, public, references to Old Comedy in 310–13
  originality in Old Comedy 24, 172
  overlaying of one character on another 12, 81, 142, 157, 160, 174, 351
  plagiarism, attacks on 47
  plot, function of 69, 133
  political function 3–7, 11, 27–8, 30, 154, 300, 302, 311–15

reception in antiquity 58–60, 83, 278–9, 300–1
revival performances in antiquity 48, 64, 281–2, 300
scholiastic misreading 328–9
texts, availability of 46–7, 329
  without notes 46, 329
topicality 329
(*see also* caricature; metacomedy)
'Old Oligarch,' *Athenian Constitution* 4, 51, 302, 306, 308–9, 310, 311, 316
  dating 4, 51, 308
oligarchic revolution (411) 40–1, 163, 197, 210, 217, 243, 248, 259, 264, 266, 270, 271, 275–6, 281, 282, 284, 286, 291, 292, 302
  feared coup (415) 240–1, 252
  rule of 5,000 280
Olympia 108
onomasti komoidein 327, 330, 332–3, 334–5
on-stage caricature (*see* caricature; *individual plays under* caricature targets, disguised and named)
Opountios 346, 348
Orestes 13, 124–6, 346–7
ostracism 131, 224–5 (*see also* Hyperbolus, ostracism)

Paestum 282
Panathenaia 219
Pandeletus 94
Pandionis 111, 244–5, 246
Panhellenism 210, 262, 265, 296
pankration 219
parabases 4–7, 16, 29, 41–3, 46–8, 88, 116, 125, 144, 206, 283–4 (*see also under specific plays, especially Acharnians, Clouds, Frogs, Knights, Peace, Wasps*)
Paralos 227–8
paratragedy 45–6, 48, 125, 347 (*see also* parody of Euripidean tragedy *under Acharnians, Frogs, Peace, Thesmophoriazusai*)
Parmenon 312
parrhesia 311
Parrhesiades 278
Paris 89, 137, 211, 255, 341 (*see also* Cratinus, *Dionysalexandros*)
Parmenon 312, 315
parody 46
  of comedy (*see* metacomedy)
  of tragedy (*see* paratragedy)
patrios politeia 279
Patrocleides, decree of 41, 286, 298, 302
Pausanias 39–40
Pauson 68, 96, 145 (*see also* caricature)

Peace (goddess) 132, 149, 150, 175 (*see also Peace*, caricature targets, disguised, Peace)
Peace 4, 16, 19, 20, 23, 28, 29, 34, 45, 52, 55, 115–16, 129, 132, 137, 140–1, 142, 149, 158, 194, 195–6, 199, 202–16, 245, 258, 291–2, 343
  as a 'peace' play 28
  caricature targets 220, 343
    disguised
      Arms Dealer 208, 210, 212, 213
      Hermes 95, 149, 194, 208–10, 211, 212, 258, 340
      Kudoimos 140, 211
      Opora 208, 215, 252, 262
      Peace 95, 99, 199, 206, 208–9, 210, 211, 212, 218, 258, 289
      Polemos 140, 207, 208–9, 211, 262
      Sickle-Merchant 208, 212, 213
      Theoria 208, 252, 262
      Slave of Trygaeus 210
      Trygaeus 34, 90, 92, 95–6, 99, 140, 145, 149–50, 158, 162, 181, 191, 199, 206–15, 225, 258, 262, 266, 286, 289, 296, 343
    named
      Hierocles 39, 212–14
      Lamachus (?) 208–9, 211
      son of Cleonymus 208, 212, 214–15
      son of Lamachus 208, 212, 213
  causes of war speech (Hermes) 149–51, 207, 209
  chorus 34, 207, 208, 260–1, 284, 340
  critique of portrayal of women 205–6, 252–3
  dating 34, 202
  defeat at Dionysia 34, 216
  exodus 207, 208, 215
  metacomedy 34, 144–7, 149–51, 181, 199, 202–15, 250
  opening scene 205
  parabasis 5–6, 34, 208, 284
    authorial voice 6
    critiques of rivals' comic motifs 27, 31, 32, 34–5, 46–7, 137, 145, 181, 202–6, 213, 245, 253, 261, 285, 286, 287
    second 209
  parody of Euripidean tragedy 45, 207, 209
  political stance 208, 256, 279, 293
  satirised by Eupolis 218
  wedding scene (*see Peace,* exodus)
Pegasus 209
Peisander 263, 276
Peisistratus 243
Peloponnesian War 4, 30, 39–40, 43–4, 102, 118–19, 122, 153–4, 194, 215, 217, 218, 276, 292, 297, 299, 300, 328, 337
  advice on conduct of, in *Frogs* 292–7

Aegospotamoi, battle of 43
  causes 147–53, 262
Cynossema, battle of 39
Decelea 276
Delium, battle of 178
Mantineia, battle of 276
Megarian decree 148, 149, 150, 151
Notium, battle of 292
Peace of Nicias 55, 140, 156, 160, 189, 211, 216, 217
Pylos and Spacteria 122, 156, 165
revolt of Miletus 257
(*see also* oligarchic revolution; Sicilian Expedition)
Penelope 254, 271
Pericles 32, 43, 68–9, 77, 118, 131, 133, 148, 160, 163, 209–10, 211, 216, 218, 264, 277, 279, 280, 293, 294, 295, 328, 341, 342, 344, 350–1
  family history/relationships 226–8, 280, 350
  prosecutors of 85, 152
  relations with Alcibiades 151, 178, 226–7, 230, 231–2
  role in Peloponnesian War 148–54, 207
  satirised by Cratinus 85, 137, 146, 147–8, 149, 151, 152–3, 171, 204, 209, 211, 249, 279, 280, 293, 328 (*see also* caricature targets *under* Cratinus, *Dionysalexandros*; Cratinus, *Thraittai*)
  supported by Eupolis 148–54, 163, 209–10, 279–80, 293–4
Perithoidae (*see* demes/demotics)
Persia,
  and Eupolis 163, 192, 200, 210
  Athenian relations with 50, 157, 163, 200, 210, 262, 263
  clothing 74, 159, 163, 192, 200, 207, 246
  in Aristophanes 118, 120–1, 200, 210, 262–4
  Spartan relations with 262
Phaeax (son of Eresistratos) 224–5, 292
  caricatured in *Clouds II* (?) 224–5, 228, 232–4
Phaedra 271
Phaedrus (son of Pythocles) 246–7
Phales 141
Phanias 311
Phayllus of Croton 126
phantasia 58–60
Pheidias 149
Pheidippides (*see Clouds II,* caricature targets, disguised)
Pheidon 228, 234
Pherecrates 76, 269, 281, 291–2, 294, 333
  Cheiron 259, 281
  Corianno 254
  Krapataloi 288–9, 291, 294

Philemon 332
Philetairus (son of Aristophanes) (*see* Nicostratus)
Philippos/Philippides (father of Aristophanes) 111
Philippus (son of Aristophanes) 86, 111
Philippus (son of Gorgias) 185
Philocleon (*see Wasps*, caricature targets, disguised)
Philonides 14, 37, 108, 109, 136, 236
  Proagon 216
Philosophy (personified) 278
Philoxenus of Cythera, *Cyclops* 340
Phlya (*see* demes/demotics)
Phormio 82–3, 142–3, 208, 286, 287–8, 342, 346–7
Phormis 325
Photius 82
Phrynichus (comic poet) 6, 24, 48, 98, 206, 286
  Monotropos 236
  Mousai 254
  Poastriai 254
Phrynichus (grammarian) 295
Phrynichus (politician) 40, 196–7, 276, 286
Phrynichus (tragic poet) 73, 186
Phrynis 281
Phyle (*see* demes/demotics)
plagiarism, accusations of 18, 47, 80, 115, 116, 219–20 (*see also Knights*, and Eupolis; Eupolis, *Autolycus*)
Piraeus 298
Plato (comic poet) 48, 212, 259, 330, 333, 334
  Cleophon 332
  Europa 254
  Hai aph' Hieron 254
  Hyperbolus 22, 120
  Phaon 334
  Rhabdouchoi 206
Plato (philosopher) 172, 174, 186, 202, 228, 255, 301, 306, 317–18, 337–8
  commentary on comedy 103, 306, 309–10, 315–16, 317–18, 334, 335, 338
  dating of works 239
  depiction of Aristophanes 4–5, 175, 178, 268
  Apology 47, 309, 313–14, 315–16
  Critias 243
  Euthyphro 169
  Gorgias 178
  Laches 189
  Laws 103, 306, 309–10, 314–15, 316, 334
  Menexenus 255
  Phaedo 280, 309, 311, 315
  Politicus 255, 263, 338
  Protagoras 188, 202

Republic 238–9, 253, 337–9
Symposium 173, 175, 178, 255, 268
Platonius 58–60, 276–9, 316–17, 321, 322, 333, 334, 335
pleonexia 309
plot-based comedy 320–1
Plutarch 57–8, 85, 277, 317
Plutus 85
poetry, Aristotelian theory of 322–4
'poets' war', rival support bases x–xi, 24–6, 89, 103, 117, 199, 222, 287; *see* 105–302 *passim*
poietes 25, 108–10
polemarch 166, 170–1
Polemos (*see* War, personification of; *Peace*, caricature targets, disguised)
Polish 349
politicians, distinguished from private individuals 171
polypragmosyne/apragmosyne 69, 170, 171, 309 (*see also Birds, apragmosyne/polypragmonsyne*)
Pontecagnano vase 281
'portrait-masks' (*see* caricature, masks)
Pnyx 95
Poseidon 238, 250 (*see also Birds*, caricature targets, disguised)
Pratinas 73
Praxagora 337–9
Praxithea 264
Prepis 96, 145
Priam 255
Proagon 126
Probouloi 256, 258–9 (*see also Lysistrata*, caricature targets, disguised, Proboulos)
Procne 245 (*see also Birds*, caricature targets, disguised)
Prodicus of Ceos 5, 12, 27, 100, 170, 172–5, 181, 188, 202, 235, 238, 239, 249, 284, 287, 343, 351
Prometheus 85 (*see also Birds*, caricature targets, disguised)
Prospalta (*see* demes/demotics)
prostasia/prostates 53–5, 95–6, 102, 155, 157, 162, 199, 210, 223, 342
Protagoras 170, 172, 174, 176, 235, 238, 344
Proteus 273
prytaneis 135
prytanies 224, 236
psogos 321, 323–5
Psycho (1960) xi
Pylos 122, 156, 165
Pyronides (*see* Eupolis, *Demoi*, caricature targets, disguised)
Pythian games 227

radical democracy 163, 165, 194, 197, 200, 211, 223, 247, 279, 292, 300, 328
  as Aristophanes' standpoint ix 25, 41–3, 200, 217, 223, 237–8, 252, 254, 279–81, 297–8
  expansionism 223
Reconciliation (Diallage) 132,150 209, 260, 262
redistribution of wealth, as contemporary political issue 194–5, 337, 339
rejuvenation, in comedy 74 92, 155, 162–4, 225, 261
Rhamnous (*see* demes/demotics)
Rhodes 112
rivalry, poetic x–xi, 6, 16, 17, 23, 24, 26, 27, 28, 29, 30, 34, 38, 47, 55, 69, 83, 106, 120, 125, 179, 203–5, 208, 223–4, 245, 268, 299 (*see also generally under* Aristophanes, Cratinus, Eupolis)
Roman Satire 60
Russian 349

Sacas 241
Sadocus 247, 347
Salaminia 251
Salamis, battle of 126
Samian War /Samos 66, 77, 137, 146, 211, 254, 328, 341, 351 (*see also* Cratinus, *Dionysalexandros*)
Sardis 192
Satyrus 131
Sausage-Seller (*see Knights*, caricature targets, disguised)
scatology 213, 267
Scythia 131
Scythian archers 266–7
scholia
  fallibility 328–9
  sources 46
self-contradiction (apparent) 17–21, 23
Semele 204
Sicilian type of comedy 306–8, 324, 325, 332
Sicilian Expedition 115, 140, 217, 222–3, 235, 237–8, 251, 253, 255, 259 (*see also Birds*, Sicilian Expedition, relevance)
Sicyon,
  as place of Eupolis' death 39–41, 115, 244, 275, 286
  as Spartan ally 39–41
Simaitha 151
Simmias 85
Simon 136
The Simpsons (TV) xi, 46, 329
Sinope 140
Sitalces 247, 347

Skambonidae (*see* demes/demotics)
Socrates 12, 24, 25, 27, 29, 34, 87, 89, 169, 171, 172–3, 178, 186, 228, 229, 232–3, 234, 238–40, 242, 255, 263, 278, 280, 291, 301, 302, 309, 311, 313–14, 315–16, 338
  attitude to Sicilian Expedition 247–8
  caricatured
    in *Birds* (?) 248
    in *Clouds I* 12, 15, 17, 22, 24, 25, 27, 29, 166, 168, 173–5, 177, 224, 309, 313, 315–16, 343
    in *Clouds II* 22, 99–100, 160, 224, 239, 240, 248, 344, 351
  in other comedy 230–1
    Ameipsias *Konnos* 178
    Eupolis (?) 176–7
  political/philosophical associates 167–72, 176–7, 178, 189, 192, 225, 229, 230–1, 232–3, 242, 246, 255, 269, 286
  satirical attacks (on his philosophical material)
    in *Ecclesiazusai* 338–9
    in *Lysistrata* 255, 263
  responses to 309, 311, 313–14, 315–16
Solon 148, 160, 163, 280, 344
sophists 12–13, 27, 100, 172, 174, 176, 225, 233, 238, 301, 338
sophos/sophoi 7, 8, 12, 18, 27, 172, 240, 287 (*see also* sophists)
Sophocles 186, 218, 258–9, 289–90
  Antigone 258
  Tereus 346–7
Sopolis 190
South Italian vase-painting 282
Sparta/Spartans 43, 76, 89, 118, 121, 137, 157, 159, 162, 178, 189, 192–3, 207, 210, 212, 218, 235, 236, 242, 243, 244, 251–2, 255, 257, 260, 261, 269–71, 344, 351
  allies 39–41
  and Cratinus 192–3
  and Eupolis 25, 39, 193, 210
  army 68
  Athenian relations with 149–51, 262–4, 265, 270–1
  homosexuality among 269–70
  in comedy 35, 118, 120–1
  invasions of Attica 153, 199
  Laconophilia/Laconophiles 25, 153, 192, 216, 242, 244, 247, 252, 257, 259–60, 261, 265, 275, 290, 291, 292, 298, 344
  peace offers/negotiations 4, 81, 118, 121, 150, 153, 189, 256, 257, 263, 268
  (*see also* Peloponnesian War)
Sphacteria 156
Spitting Image (TV) xi, 98

Stesichorus 254
strategos (*see* general)
Strattis
    Atalanta 254
    Cinesias 259
    Medea 254
    Phoinissae 147
Strepsiades (*see Clouds II*, caricature targets, disguised)
Strymodorus 184, 260
Suda 82
sycophants 170–1
Sun (personified) 210
Syracosius, decree of 236, 302
Syracuse/Syracusans 251, 282, 314

taktes 164
Taras 265
taxiarch 142–3 (*see* also Eupolis, *Taxiarchoi*)
Teisias 229
    of Rhamnous 312
Teleas 145
Telecleides 182, 347
Telemachus 135
Telephus 93–4 (*see* also Euripides, *Telephus*; *Acharnians*, parody of Euripidean tragedy; *Thesmophoriazusai*, parody of Euripidean tragedy)
Teres 247
Tereus 247, 347 (*see* also *Birds*, caricature targets, disguised)
terracottas (of stock comic characters/masks) 307, 332
Teucrus 245–6
Theatre of Dionysus 32, 120
    architecture/capacity 68
theatrical performances, private 9–11, 12, 13, 14
theatrical production 10, 46–7, 212, 288–9, 294
Thebes/Thebans 257
Themis 175
Theonoe 273–4
Theogenes 112
Theognis 294, 296–7
Theopompus, *Stratiotides* 338
Theramenes 286
Thesmophoria 273
Thesmophoriazusai 4, 35–7, 68, 98, 142–3, 203, 252–5, 258, 265, 266–76, 287, 291, 329, 344, 347
    and *Acharnians* 36–7, 38, 266
    and Cratinus 36, 138–9
    caricature targets 266, 271–2, 338, 344
        disguised
            Agathon's slave 35
            Garland-Seller 253, 272, 275

Prytanis 270
Relative of Euripides 90, 92, 143, 253, 266, 267–9, 270, 272, 273, 285, 291, 297, 329
Scythian Archer 267, 270
named
    Agathon 36, 253, 266, 268, 269, 270, 275, 285
    Cleisthenes 68, 163, 253, 266, 269–70, 271–2, 273, 275, 285, 332
    Critylla 253, 272, 273–5
    Euripides 35, 36–7, 86–7, 90–1, 143, 226, 253, 254, 260, 266–9, 271, 273–4, 275, 284, 288, 290, 291, 344, 345
    Wife of Cleonymus/Mica 215, 253, 272–3, 275
chorus 92, 97–8, 143, 260, 284
    coryphaeus 271–2
dating 35, 252, 266, 275
    first version 253
metacomedy 35–7, 38, 223, 253, 266, 270–1, 266, 269, 275
parabasis 6, 97–8, 271, 284
parody of Euripidean tragedy 36, 45, 94, 266, 268, 347
political stance 268–9, 275–6
Thesmophoroi 274
Thespis 73
thiasos 136, 274
Thirty Tyrants 40–1, 43, 163, 234, 244, 286, 297, 298, 334
Thoricus (*see* demes/demotics)
Thouphrastos 196–7
Thrace/Thracians 23, 137, 247, 249, 250, 264, 266–7, 296, 347
Thucydides (historian) 40, 147, 152, 156, 197, 247, 251–2, 264, 300, 346, 347
Thucydides son of Melesias (politician) 130–2, 189, 193–4
Thumoitadai 127 (*see* also demes/demotics)
Thurii 241
Timarchus 198, 257, 312
Timesias 185
Timesilaos 140
Timocles
    Neaira 335
    Orestautokleides 335
Timon of Phlius 350
Titans 85
tragedy
    Aristotle on 317–18, 322–4
    parodied by Aristophanes 45–6
    Plato on 317–18
    (*see also* Aeschylus, Euripides)
traulizo 349

Triballian 238 (*see also Birds*, caricature targets, disguised)
tribes 82, 111, 143, 207, 228, 244–5, 246
Trojan War 66, 77, 254
Trygaeus (*see Peace*, caricature targets, disguised)
Tydeus 141
Typhoeus/Typhon 84–5, 103, 110, 124, 158, 159, 191, 342, 350 (*see also* Cleon, satirised, as Typhon)
tyrant/tyranny 216, 238–9, 243, 260, 263, 293 (*see also* Thirty Tyrants)
Tzetzes, Johannes 222, 330

utopianism 238–9, 240

vases, depictions of comic scenes on 47–8, 64–5, 125, 204, 245, 281–2, 346
ventriloquial metacomedy (*see* metacomedy; *Acharnians*; *Frogs*; *Knights*; *Wasps*)
vomiting, metaphor of 77, 84, 129, 188, 190

War, personification of 132, 140–3, 149, 150, 207, 209, 262, 288 (*see also Peace*, caricature targets, disguised, Polemos)
war dead, Athenian burial traditions 39–41
Wasps 16, 23, 29, 33, 64, 69–75, 80, 85, 101, 105, 108, 122, 131, 178–99, 201, 202, 210, 216, 343
  and Cratinus 69–73, 84, 123, 178–88, 193, 195–8, 202, 220 (*see also Wasps*, caricature targets, disguised, Philocleon)
  caricature targets 123–4, 220, 249, 343
    disguised
      Bdelycleon 33, 57, 70–2, 74, 80, 84, 92, 97, 98, 112–13, 119, 121, 131–2, 146, 159, 163, 164, 179–80, 182, 183, 184–5, 187, 191–9, 200, 202, 211, 220, 246, 339, 343
      Chrysus 197
      Kuon 23, 188–91, 221
      Labes x, 66, 131, 132, 146, 152, 183, 188–9, 191, 276
      Philocleon 70, 71, 72–5, 83–4, 92, 95, 96, 98, 103, 112–13, 123, 124, 127, 129, 132, 145–6, 148, 153, 159, 162, 163, 179, 185, 186, 188–9, 192–4, 196–9, 202, 208, 213, 244, 246, 261, 267, 343
      Xanthias 180, 182, 189, 287
    named
      Carcinus 70, 208, 250
      Chaerephon 33
      Dardanis (?) 198, 252
      Myrtia (?) 33, 205, 252

chorus 122, 166–73, 175, 177, 183–8, 207, 208, 213, 260–1
metacomedy 33, 66, 126–7, 131, 144, 182, 184–8, 188–91, 193, 203, 205, 208, 213, 250
ventriloquial 123, 164, 180–3, 203, 284, 297
opening scene 205
parabasis 5, 6, 12, 23, 33, 47, 84, 108–11, 121, 123, 177, 183, 187, 218, 249, 284
epirrhemes 187
pnigos 172
references to *Clouds I* 12, 22, 166–73, 177
second 203
symposium scenes 196–7
wasps *versus* bees 185–8
Wealth 287, 337, 339–40
caricature targets
  Old Woman and Young Lover 340
  Poverty 340
  Wealth 339–40
metacomedy 339–40
two versions 337, 339
wedding scenes 35, 215
'the wise,' (*see sophos/sophoi*)
women
  Aristophanes' portrayals of 33, 143, 205, 212, 252–6, 271–6, 337–9
  as immodest 256–7
  as trespassing on male preserve 255–6, 275
  as characters in others' plays 205–6, 254 (*see also* Euripides, portrayal of women)
  mention by name, social taboo on 256, 272–4
Women Pitching Tents (*see* Aristophanes, fragmentary or lost plays, *Skenas Katalambanousai*)

Xanthias 287
Xanthippos (father/son of Pericles) 226–8
xenia (foreignness), accusations of 111–16, 170–1
  see also accused of *xenia* under Aristophanes, Cratinus *and* Eupolis)
xenoi 170–1
Xenophanes 139
Xenophon 40, 43, 174, 300
Xerxes 200

Zeno 350
Zenobius 82
Zeus 32, 77, 85, 137, 146, 148, 171, 175, 204, 209, 249, 251, 253, 342, 350 (*see also* Pericles, satirised by Cratinus)

Index Locorum

Aelian
  Varia Historia (VH)
    2.13 29
    2.21 269
    3.28 230
    10.21 185
    12.45 185
    13.4 269
    13.12 247
  De Natura Animalium (NA)
    1.9 186
    1.9–11 185
    1.58 186
    1.58–60 185
    5.11 186
    5.13 185
    10.41 39, 47, 57, 113, 219, 277
Aelius Aristides
    28.91 84
Aeschines
    1.37–8 198, 326
    1.38 257
    1.40 198
    1.40–1 326
    1.42 198
    1.45 326
    1.51–2 326
    1.52 335
    1.74–6 326
    1.157 306, 311, 312, 315
    3.67 224
Aeschylus
  Agamemnon
    717–36 292
  Award of the Arms
    fr. 174N 146
  Persians
    65 50, 200, 289
    496–7 294, 296
  Prometheus Bound
    613 294

  Seven against Thebes
    39 214
    384 141
    1005–78, 296
Andocides
    1.15 246
    1.34 245
    1.40 245
    1.47 242, 245, 260
    1.60f. 260
    1.78 40
    1.96–8 239
    fr. 5 157, 302, 311, 313, 316, 329
  [Andocides]
    4.10 229
    4.10f. 177
    4.11 164
    4.13 227
    4.32 228, 234
Anonymous *De comoedia*; see Koster *Prolegomena*
Anonymous *Cranmeri*; see Koster *Prolegomena*
Aphthonius
  Progymnasmata (Prog.)
    11 59
Apollodorus
  Library
    1.6.3 85
Apsines
  Ars Rhetorica (Rhet.)
    3 57, 113, 277
Archippus
    fr. 48 229
Aristophanes
  Acharnians
    2 296
    3 81
    4 296
    5–8 77, 84, 127, 128, 129, 130, 160, 182, 184, 188, 190, 236
    7 296
    8 235

382

Index Locorum 383

9–11 142, 288, 289, 294, 296
13 296
30 77
32–3 80, 87
32f. 77
34 174
35 174
37f. 119
46 135, 136, 274
47f. 274
55 266
57 134
61f. 200
71–2 77
88 214, 250
94f. 266
117–21 269, 270
118 275
128f. 127
129–32 137
131–2 118
135 134
138–40 294, 296
145 247
155f. 144, 266
158 267
158f. 5, 17, 23, 31
161 267
162 127
175 137
177f. 126
179 186
179–81 126
181 163, 260
188 174
191 174
209f. 260
214 126
238–9 126
243 287
254 133
255 133
259 287
266–7 80, 87
270 141
273 133, 184, 260
299–302 126, 127, 129, 207
299f. 130, 133, 160, 182, 184
325f. 36
350 133
372 286
375–6 126, 127, 185, 207
375–7 184
376 279–80
377–8 78

377–82 57, 117
377f. 60, 65, 75, 77, 79, 80, 85, 86, 112, 123, 179, 180, 283, 299
378 32, 86
378f. 70, 120
387 77
393f. 36, 90, 267
397f. 267
405 87
405f. 81
406 80, 87, 90, 206, 207, 245, 273, 274, 275
408–9 36
411 267
412f. 203, 284
426–9 127, 207
430f. 235
440–4 81
441 81, 87
443 81
457 253, 261
478 253, 261
479 36
496 75
496–556 57
496f. 75, 94, 123, 164
497–8 235
499 32, 75, 123
499–500 34
499f. 60, 69, 80, 85, 86, 146, 180, 216
500 90
501 118
501–3 117
502–8 36
502f. 65
504 125
509–12 36
509f. 118
512 63, 82, 132, 206, 207
514 36
515 149
515f. 144, 207
517 149
519 145, 147
519f. 146
520 145
521 146
524 151
524f. 127
525 149
526f. 149
530 32, 146
530f. 77, 148, 279
535–9 150
541 235

384 Index Locorum

Aristophanes (cont.)
543   235
546f. 246
555–6 36
557f. 161
557–77 261
566f. 4, 140
569–71 142
572   134, 140
572–4 139
573   140
575   37, 141
578   37
579   141
580f. 32
581f. 139
582f. 133
585f. 144
592   267
593   142
595f. 194
614   226
628f. 107, 109, 123
629   5
630   119
630–1 117
630–2 32, 47, 120
630f. 222
633f. 23, 29, 118
634f. 211
636f. 47
645   117, 118, 120
649   120
649–51 118
652–3 153
652–5 121, 154
652f. 219
653   107
653–5 4
655   118, 122
656f. 29, 56
657–8 16
657–64 6
658   213, 260
659–62 117
659f. 118, 119, 122, 123, 215
665–7 130
665f. 133
668   184
672–3 130
676f. 126
676–702 131
696f. 163
703   194
703f. 130, 189

704   267
705   131, 194
707   267
710   130, 194
711–12 267
716   131, 160, 230, 267
719f. 144, 207
748   134
748–9 80
751   351
761   145
769f. 32
789   267
818f. 146
823   80
824   134
824f. 32, 127, 144
834f. 133
836–9 81
836f. 99, 213
836–59 132, 145
839f. 96
842f. 146
846–7 25, 92, 96, 98, 101, 152
848   32, 96
848–9 64
848f. 206
849   163, 347
849f. 63
850   79
850–3 284
851   279
852–3 235
854   68, 197
857–9 203
861   257
862f. 146
864f. 32, 127, 144
875   145
878   145
880   145
883   146
883f. 261
886   32
887   146
908   134
920f. 175, 177
924–5 144
924f. 127
933f. 144
935   133
954   257
959   80
959f. 139
963   140

Index Locorum 385

964 140, 141
965 141
971–99 132
971f. 213
974–99 209
978f. 140, 150
979–87 63
979f. 207
989f. 262
993f. 32
1008f. 213
1015f. 213
1019 134
1027 134
1028 135
1037f. 213
1044–6 125
1048 80
1056f. 205
1058 143
1060 267
1066 267
1071 141
1071f. 139
1073 142
1080 140
1085 80
1130 77
1132 140
1143 125
1149 127
1150–73 79, 124
1165f. 346
1173 284
1151 125
1153 184
1154f. 32
1173 32, 79
1197f. 198
1199 213, 267
1202f. 198
1216 213
1216–17 267
1220 213
1220–1 267
1228 77
Anagyros
  fr. 58 21, 54, 55, 199, 220, 299
Babylonians
  fr. 75 79, 112, 179, 286
  fr. 88 346
Banqueters (Daitales)
  Tiii 136
  fr. 205 86, 160, 230
  fr. 244 160

Birds
11 250
12 243
30–8 241
33f. 237
36f. 240
39–42 241
40–1 246
43–5 237
44 69, 243
48 237
54–5 243
71–3 239
87–8 243
96f. 239
100–1 346
108–10 241
109–10 240
109f. 246, 291
110 237
121f. 237
123–4 238
145–7 236, 237, 240
145–8 241
165–70 248
172 249
194 35
284 248
289 248, 250
290 214
295 35
297f. 248
302f. 246
303–4 249
305 35
318 240
320 35
363–4 237
368 244, 246
428 240
429–30 240
462–3 240
465–6 240
465f. 238
492f. 246
494–6 245
554f. 237
585 245
637 240
639 237
640 89
643–5 87
645 80, 244, 245
654–5 239
656 287

386 *Index Locorum*

Aristophanes (*cont.*)
688 6
688f. 172
692 238, 239, 249, 284
712 346
748 186
801f. 239
809–14 242
814–16 243
819 35
820f. 238
829–31 269
845–6 244
848 238
851–8 246
851–94 248
862 238
889 35
903 248
904f. 239
959f. 214
992f. 243, 247
999f. 35
1000–1 239
1017–18 35
1029f. 35
1130f. 243
1170 35
1199–1259 253
1207 35
1256 35
1281–3 242
1281f. 192
1282 239
1294 346
1304f. 239
1321 237
1372–1409 246, 259
1377f. 239
1397f. 35
1401 35
1410–69 246
1464f. 35
1473–81 214
1476 250
1480–1 250
1491 346
1503 251
1510 35
1527 250
1536 249
1555 239
1564 239
1565f. 266, 287
1570f. 249

1583f. 34, 203
1589 340
1596f. 238
1632f. 238
1708 239
1720f. 35
Clouds I
fr. 397 346
fr. 399 167
Clouds II
1 5, 17, 19, 34
6 140
10 170
25 177, 229
28 177, 229
32 177, 229
35–6 229
38 229
41–2 226
45–6 225
46 226, 245
46–7 227
48 226
56 340
60f. 225
63–4 227
64 226
65 228
70 226
80 87
96f. 239
99 171
102–4 232
104 239
112f. 171
116 99
120 177, 229
124 226
124–5 177, 229
134 87, 228
144f. 239, 314
146–7 17
153 240
156f. 239
171–3 17
206–17 230
215–16 351
222 87
225 47
230f. 240
239f. 171
247–8 238
252–3 238
260 240, 351
262 351

264f.	238
267–8	351
269f.	238
272	112
293–5	351
296	34
320	240
353–4	214, 250
355	269
358f.	172
359	240, 248
360	314
360–2	239
361	240
365	238
367	238
374f.	350
380–1	350
398	232
361	12, 175
412–13	230
420	170
429–34	230
431–2	171
433–4	171
439–40	267
439–56	17
443–51	230
445–51	240
446	171
449–50	121, 179
468–75	230
479–81	351
481	351
483	225
497	351
501f.	239
506–9	351
510	125
518	76
518–36	7–15
518–62	224
520	172
520–36	236
521	88
523–4	22
524	16
525–6	22, 25
526	29, 105, 172, 287
527	88
528	29
528–33	109
529	47, 86
529–31	111
530–1	107

535	88
537–43	25, 31, 34, 49, 50, 92, 286
537–50	15–23
537f.	175
538	46
538–9	5
539	35, 181
540	14, 33, 34
540–3	46
541	33
541–2	34, 36, 37, 181, 213, 287
541–3	260
542–3	46
543	5, 32, 33, 34. 35, 37, 213, 215, 261
544	46, 147
545	14, 25, 29, 38, 49, 51, 55, 64, 92, 160, 286
545f.	91
546	47, 54, 220
546–7	166
546–8	25
546f.	225
547	24
549	11, 15
549–50	47, 97, 182
549–58	6
549f.	69
550	223
550–1	221
551	29, 54, 91, 152, 200
551–2	95, 100
551–9	24–6, 46
551f.	21, 51, 69, 92, 103, 144, 175
552	98, 200, 254
553	9, 20, 21, 46, 50, 54, 91, 101, 120
553–5	19, 20, 49
553–6	91, 199
553–9	16, 47, 55, 61
553f.	89
554	11, 18, 47, 48, 105, 162, 201
555	15, 20, 91, 179
555–6	46, 98, 202, 205
557	9, 120, 254
559–61	11
560–2	26–7
560–3	175
561–2	206
563–74	174
575–94	8, 20, 96, 236
595–606	174
581f.	97
607–26	96
607f.	210
623f.	25, 92, 97
634	34

Aristophanes (*cont.*)
  636–54 351
  669f. 174
  694–745 351
  694f. 170
  698f. 203
  707f. 34
  710 185
  728 225
  739 171
  747 225
  757–74 231
  758f. 171
  789–90 232
  791–3 230
  800 226
  810–11 174
  844–6 169, 232
  853 232
  862 177
  865 232
  868–73 177, 229, 349
  876 25, 55, 92, 99, 100, 165, 174, 175, 188
  886–1111 173–4
  888 8, 236
  889–948 27
  891–2 235
  920f. 93, 224, 234, 301
  922 93
  971 281
  978 235
  988–9 174
  1031 169
  1065 25, 92, 94, 95, 96, 98
  1077 233
  1084–104 5, 175
  1112 233
  1113 125
  1113–14 173, 174
  1160 351
  1163 136
  1167 233
  1171f. 231
  1178–200 233
  1206f. 213
  1209–11 171
  1214–302 232
  1248f. 174
  1297–300 17, 19, 34
  1303–20 174
  1321 17, 19, 34
  1321–475 233
  1321f. 169, 229, 234
  1336f. 100
  1364f. 289
  1371–2 228
  1381 177
  1385–90 169
  1401–2 232, 233
  1432 233
  1458–61 174
  1465 239
  1467 233
  1485 287
  1490f. 17, 19, 34
  1493 17, 19, 34
Ecclesiazousai
  311f. 339
  330 259
  850 192
  978 339
Frogs
  13–14 286
  35f. 87
  48 269, 285
  48f. 91
  57 269, 285
  66f. 284, 285
  71f. 283
  76–7 289
  82 289
  83f. 269, 285
  98f. 268
  153 259
  207 288
  313 37
  340 37
  354f. 284
  357 37, 38, 79, 82, 86, 91, 142, 284, 286, 347
  366 259
  367–8 302, 327
  404f. 284
  422–4 269
  428–30 287
  499 89, 140
  500 81
  501 287
  540f. 286
  550–1 100
  570 25, 92, 100
  575 143
  579 143
  605f. 37
  674–737 284
  653 37
  674 6
  678f. 250, 298
  686 6
  687–737 42

689   40
697f.   91
699–702   40
734   37, 72, 285, 339
788f.   289
814   291
840   253, 261, 291
844   291
848   291
868–9   295
888f.   275
911f.   289, 294
952–3   291
957   268
967–70   286
1008f.   291
1009–10   90
1013f.   291
1016f.   141
1021–6   294, 295
1023   296
1025–7   200
1028–9   289, 294, 295, 296
1036   37, 285
1039   4, 37, 134, 141
1043f.   268   291
1063–4   284
1079f.   268
1228   285
1284–95   281
1325f.   281
1365f.   291
1400   37, 285
1411–13   289
1416f.   290
1422–60   284
1427–9   291, 292
1431–2   292
1437   259
1437–41   43
1442–50   43
1445–7   43
1446–8   290–1
1449–50   290–1
1451–3   43
1463–5   43, 292
1466   291
1491f.   177
1500f.   298
1504   298
1525   37
1532   298
Geras (perhaps *Gerytades*?)
   fr. 128   283
Gerytades

fr. 156   259
fr. 156–90, 283
Knights
1–10   32
2   52, 155
2f.   73
40   77
42   52, 77
43–4   52
50–2   52
55   158
75   47, 121
162f.   47
167   160
191–3   12, 122
228   88
230f.   66, 67, 85, 191, 317, 333
233   88
242   136
255–7   183
255f.   161, 193
258f.   161
266   161
299   18
315–21   98, 155, 156, 192
326   171
328f.   53
346–50   160, 171
400   63, 235, 284
423–6   160
451   32
498   125
507–9   161
507–50   33, 164
510–11   29
511   85, 158, 159, 192, 350
513   5, 47
513f.   107, 109, 110
520   6
520f.   29, 46, 47
526   6, 16
526f.   284
529–30   46, 126
531f.   63
534   235
535   63
537   6, 16
541–4   14
544f.   206
550   20
562   346
565   283
580   25, 192
721   160
728   52

Aristophanes (cont.)
    729 74
    730f. 73
    738–40 92, 98, 102, 155, 157
    739 25
    754–5 73
    755 77
    760 159
    792–6 77
    792–804 150
    794–6 156
    797f. 74
    805–8 129
    805f. 77
    808 73
    813 340
    836 294
    868–70 192
    881f. 74, 163
    893 74
    899 74
    908 74
    958 214, 250
    976 23, 79, 328
    977f. 127, 183, 184, 188
    986 12, 122, 165
    997f. 74
    1006 74
    1017 84, 169, 191
    1030–4 189, 190
    1065 73
    1065–6 164
    1078–9 164
    1089 74
    1096 32
    1100f. 74
    1111–50 51, 70
    1121 25
    1121f. 84
    1125–30 236
    1141f. 84
    1145–50 77, 236
    1145f. 124, 128
    1148 129, 190
    1225 33, 205, 250
    1257 87
    1261 74
    1268–73 203
    1288 32
    1290–9 214, 250
    1300–4 28
    1300–15 92, 96
    1302f. 25
    1304 157
    1309 164
    1314–15 102
    1315–16 98
    1316–17 246, 291
    1317 71, 73, 193
    1319 164
    1321 162
    1321f. 74
    1325 161, 163
    1325f. 216
    1331 192
    1331–32 92, 163
    1332 73, 193, 246, 291
    1334 74, 163
    1336f. 73
    1340–4 163
    1349 162
    1350–4 163
    1350–5 194
    1356–61 163
    1357–61 93
    1359–82 163
    1362–3 25, 92
    1366–7 73, 164
    1373–4 269
    1375–80 233
    1377 224
    1381 233
    1384 163
    1384–6 179
    1384–7 246
    1386–7 199
    1388–9 156, 162, 163
    1388f. 148
    1391 199
    1392–3 122
    1395–403 163
    1404–5 164
    1408 171
Lysistrata
    37–8 264
    67 35
    99–100 259
    99f. 257
    107–10 257
    124 257
    134f. 257
    168–9 275
    254 260
    257 260
    270 260
    271–80 263
    278 192
    285 260
    295 35, 260
    305 35, 260

Index Locorum 391

308   260
316   260
323   273, 275
356–7   260
380   260
381f.   260
384f.   213
387f.   258
433f.   258, 267
450   258
456–8   261
554   212, 255, 256
556f.   264
561–2   264
563–4   264
567–86   263
574–86   255, 338
582f.   258
588–90   264, 265
591–2   265
592–7   264
614–15   260
615   284
616f.   260
619   239
620–5   269
620f.   273
630–1   260
636–7   260
637   284
662   260, 284
665f.   260
669–70   261
686   260, 284
700f.   261
706–17   258
804   346
829   35
831f.   332
838   259
980f.   259
990   132
994   132
979   35
1086   256, 259
1090–1   269
1093–4   236, 241–2, 297
1094–5   260
1103   256
1114–88   262
1124   257
1025f.   261
1133   210
1147   256
1148   270
1149–56   263
1168f.   260
1173   260
1174   270
1178f.   260
1215f.   261
1218f.   261
1217   16
1217f.   35
1221   259
1226   260
1229f.   260

Peace
1–288   208
43–9   88
43f.   52
47–8   20
56f.   209
76f.   207, 209
102–8   209
108   210
114–23   209
154f.   209
179f.   340
190   34, 95, 206, 207, 228
192f.   211, 340
205   140
226f.   340
234–5   140
236–88   208
236f.   140, 207
241   140
255f.   140, 211
269–72   20
289–600   208
292   210
293   141
302   210
304   4, 211
313   191
313–20   20
317   145
321f.   34
336   261
345   34, 145
347–8   346
348–9   142
348–53   207
349–57   210
352–3   141
356   132
378f.   211
406f.   210
444–6   250
446   214

Aristophanes (*cont.*)
   455   209
   466   210
   473   207, 210, 211
   473–4   4, 141
   478–80   210
   481–2   210
   493   210
   500f.   210
   503f.   210
   508   210
   511   210
   520f.   207
   531   258, 289
   531–2   290
   601–728   208
   603–4   150
   603f.   137, 149
   605f.   207, 209, 211
   606f.   279
   610–11   150
   615–16   150
   617   150
   619–24   150
   635–48   171
   635f.   194
   637–8   150
   647–8   150
   647–56   20
   661f.   212
   664–7   210
   673–8   214, 250
   680–92   95
   680f.   201
   681f.   55
   682–4   28
   683–4   210
   689f.   99
   690–2   96, 102, 313
   692   55
   695   258, 289
   696   290
   696f.   289
   700   258, 284
   700–3   63, 115
   700f.   115, 199, 206, 207
   703   83
   709f.   199
   729   125
   729–31   133
   729–74   34, 145
   734–5   206
   734–51   29
   736–53   206
   738   5
   739–53   202
   739f.   6, 16, 46
   740   34, 261, 285
   740–5   203
   740–7   31, 46
   741   35, 101, 181, 287
   742   211
   743f.   32, 33
   746   287
   746–7   46
   747   205
   748   16
   748–50   24
   748f.   47
   749–50   18, 147, 291, 294
   750   27, 32, 46
   751   31, 33, 171, 205, 253
   752f.   29, 121, 175, 182
   752–60   20
   753   179
   754   191
   754f.   179
   754–74   6, 206
   755f.   85
   762–3   218, 220
   767f.   19–20
   771–4   64
   775–818   208
   781f.   144
   819–921   208
   848–9   262
   856f.   213
   860–1   162
   860f.   213
   862   199, 213
   865f.   213
   885f.   213
   894f.   213
   909f.   213
   912   213
   913f.   213
   916   213
   918   245, 274
   918–19   95, 207
   918f.   213
   921   25, 92, 95, 206, 209
   922–1126   208
   931–6   210, 211
   938f.   213
   962–7   181
   962f.   213
   969   213
   971–2   213
   986–7   209
   992   143, 205, 212, 255, 256

Index Locorum

995–9   209
999f.   144, 145, 147
1000f.   207, 246
1005   261
1022   125
1026   213
1027f.   213
1033f.   213
1049–50   214
1051f.   213
1058f.   213
1111   214
1117–18   214
1119f.   213
1120   214
1121f.   34
1122f.   214
1127–90   209
1128–9   141
1150   196
1155   208
1191   34, 213
1191–359   208
1228f.   213
1264   213
1266   213
1290–4   4
1291   207
1295–301   250
1296–304   214
1317   213
1319   206
1321   25, 92, 95

Skenas Katalambanousai (Women Pitching Tents)
fr. 488   57, 86, 89, 90, 182

Tagenistai
fr. 506   172

Thesmophoriazusai
5f.   268
6f.   267
23–4   267
35   270
39   36
50   267
57   267
59–62   267
61–2   270
85   268
93–4   268
94   267
96   36
101   35
133   270
134f.   267

142–3   267
153   267
157–8   267, 268, 270
168f.   267
170   297
198–9   268
200–1   267
206   270
206–7   267
215   36
230   35
248   267
254   267
265   36
271   268
275–6   267, 268
280   35
288   267
291   267
294   272
295   272
295–311   271
331–51   271
338   239
372–9   271
380   271, 272
383–432   271, 273
385f.   268
387   253, 261
400–28   271
410f.   265
443–58   271
450–1   275
456   253, 275
457   272
457–8   275
468–519   36
480f.   267
497   267
533–9   273
540   267
545–8   271, 273
553–9   271
544–8   271
551–2   271, 273
554   271
557   271
559   271
562   271
563   271
566–7   271
566–8   273
568   271
569   271
570   267, 273

Aristophanes (*cont.*)
571–3   271
574   68, 272
574f.   273, 332
574–654   269, 270
582–3   271
586   271
589   271
592–4   271
597–602   271
603   272
605   272, 273, 274
606   271
611   267
613–14   271
620f.   275
626–9   271
631   271
632   267, 271
634–5   271
635   68
636   271
639–40   271
642   271
645   271
649–50   271
650   273
652   271
688   272
688f.   36
758–9   272
759   272, 274
760   272, 273
763   272
764   272
769f.   267
786   6
832–3   142
839f.   25, 92, 97, 144, 271
840–1   284
841   4, 143, 271
847f.   267
882   274
893   274
891   274
897   273, 274
898   136, 272, 274
917   35
929–43   270
944   272
948–52   203
1010f.   267
1060–1   252
1118–20   270
1123–4   270
1160–71   271
Wasps
1f.   287
11–12   205
15–27   214, 250
34   192
44–6   177, 229
45   349
55–66   180
58–9   213
60   181, 287
61   267
63   182
66   16
68   81
88   260
88–1008   73
88f.   73
105   81
107   81, 186
126–7   81
129   81
133   73
140–1   81
142–3   81
197   183
199   185
205   81
206   81
207–9   81
211–13   184
214–29   185
225f.   279–80
230   260
230f.   122
232   208
233   184, 260
333   73
343–4   72, 73
349   73, 163
363   81
366   81, 186
398–9   74
408   184, 260
410f.   71, 216, 291
411   92
411f.   246
412–14   73, 193
414   92
417   239
420–1   185
463   239
462f.   260
466   192
466f.   216

481 184	946–8 131
488f. 260	947 194
490f. 239	950 119
505 193	953 188
515f. 73	958 188
517 193	963–6 189
521 193	972 185
548–630 193	984 74
592 194, 214, 250, 267	1003f. 70, 74
616–18 198	1007 25, 92, 96, 98, 146
631–3 193	1015–59 33
636–41 193	1016 5
643 194	1017–22 110
644–9 193	1018f. 47, 109, 206
650–1 33, 57, 69, 70, 92, 184	1022 108, 172
650–724 193	1023f. 218, 220
653–63 195	1024–9 29
655–724 194	1025f. 70
655f. 187	1026–9 179
698f. 211	1029 171
703f. 339	1029f. 29, 110, 167, 179, 182, 249
706f. 164	1030f. 175
706–11 195	1031 191
711 74, 163, 260	1031–5 171
715f. 74, 112	1033 85, 159
720f. 73	1036 84, 179
724–7 193	1037–42 22, 167, 168, 171, 230
757–9 95, 184, 188, 193, 214, 236	1037–45 166
758–9 129	1037f. 121
787–93 99	1038 23
787f. 96, 145, 197	1039 169
788 146	1040–1 169
798–804 74	1042–59 172
798f. 74	1043f. 22, 167
811 74	1044 23
814 74	1044f. 179
822 146	1045 177, 229
822–3 214, 250	1049 12, 287
836–8 189	1050 179
838 188	1060–121 187
875f. 191	1060f. 260
878f. 197	1078f. 163
891f. 69	1107 186
894f. 23	1122f. 70, 74, 83, 130, 163, 192
896 188	1131 83
900 188	1131–2 192
902f. 221	1134 74
911 188	1136f. 192
924–5 188, 189	1137f. 200, 246
925 190	1139f. 192
927–8 188	1144 159
931 33	1146–8 159
933 188	1148 74, 192
937–9 189	1157 192
940–1 213	1158f. 192

Aristophanes (cont.)
   1159–65 244
   1161–5 153
   1206 126
   1219–48 196
   1251–5 197
   1252f. 69
   1267–74 203
   1283 236
   1284 124
   1284–91 203
   1284f. 70, 123, 180, 182, 299
   1290 124
   1299f. 69, 192, 196
   1301 220
   1306 198
   1307 33
   1310 198
   1326f. 33
   1333 74, 162, 261
   1345–6 70
   1346 198
   1352–5 74
   1355 162, 261
   1388f. 33, 205
   1408 33
   1417f. 213
   1444f. 70
   1448 208
   1450f. 213
   1459–61 69, 71
   1461 37, 339
   1474f. 208
   1482 70
   1498f. 144
   1516–37 208
   1531 250
  Wealth
   28f. 340
   223 340
   258 340
   271–2 339
   276 339
   478 339
   601 340
   714 192
   763 340
   794–801 213
   823f. 340
   842–6 192
   850f. 340
   852 339
   882 192
   1097f. 340
   1107–9 340
   1112f. 340
   1135f. 340
   1194f. 339
  Testimonia
   T1 (=*Life of Aristophanes*; see below)
   T12 112
   T83a–b58 330
   T83b 330
   T84 58, 330
  Fragments
   fr. 591 283
   fr. 595 283
   fr. 596 283
   fr. 598 283
   fr. 604 57, 86
   fr. 623 283
   fr. 696 283
   fr. 720 283
   CGFP 226
Aristotle
  Athenaion Politeia (*Ath. Pol.*)
   16.20 239
   20.1–4 263
   39 40
   43.5 224
   61.3 142
  Historia Animalium (*HA*)
   8.627b–628b 187
   8.629a 186, 187
  Nicomachean Ethics (*EN*)
   1128a 23–5, 306, 318–19, 331, 334
  Poetics
   1447a 317
   1448a6 68
   1448b 317
   1448b20–1449a5 306, 318, 322–4
   1449a 318
   1449a32-b7 306, 321–2, 335
   1449a 34–5, 325
   1449a38-b5 325
   1449b 325, 332
   1449b 5–9, 306, 328
   1449b7f. 321, 324
   1449b 21–2, 331
   1451a 36–8, 306, 320–1
   1451b 69, 322
   1451b 5–15, 320–1
   1451b 10f.326
   1462b19 331
  Politics
   1266a31–6 337
   1269b13–1270a15 275

Index Locorum

1274b9–10 337
1336a39f. 306, 307, 318–19
Rhetoric
  1371b33 331
  1384b 9–11 306, 310, 318–19
  1419a26–30 258, 259
  1419b2 331
Aspasios
  In Ethica Nicomachea Commentaria
  CAG 19.1
  p.125, 31–5 (Heylbut) 319
Athenaeus
  1.22a 73
  5.187c 175
  5.216c–d 218
  5.216f–217a 269
  5.218b–c 176
  5.219e 229
  5.220c 228
  6.229 112
  9.407b–c 231
  10.429a 64
  12.551d 259
  13.555d–556a 265
  13.586a 327
  13.602d 270
Aulus Gellius
  15.20.6 265

Callias
  Atalantai
    fr. 4 346
  Pedetai
    fr. 15 139, 182
Cicero
  Ad Atticum
    6.1.18 39, 115
    12.6.3 80
  Orator
    29 80
Clement of Alexandria
  Stromateis
    VI.26.4 138
Comica Adespota (*PCG* VIII)
  fr. 498 127
  fr. 952 82
  fr. 1151.5 215
  Tituli 8 127
Cratinus
  Archilochoi
    fr. 2 186
    fr. 6 130
  Boukoloi
    fr. 17 218
    fr. 19 209

Cheirones
  fr. 255 84
  fr. 258 32, 77, 85, 146, 280, 350
  frr. 258–9 84, 204, 249
  fr. 259 85, 279
  fr. 260 235
Dionysalexandros
  Ti 44f. 32
Dionysoi
  fr. 52 56, 118, 188
Eumenides
  fr. 70 126
Horai
  fr. 271 32, 133
  fr. 273 32, 133
  fr. 277 133
  fr. 278 133, 151
  fr. 283 101, 152
  fr. 291 133
  fr. 297 133
Idaioi
  fr. 90 36, 138, 182, 267
  fr. 91 138
Nemesis
  fr. 117 243
  fr. 118 32, 77, 85, 146, 328
Nomoi
  fr. 133 72, 126, 184
Odysses
  fr. 143 287
  fr. 149 196
  fr. 152 287
Ploutoi
  fr. 170 85
  fr. 171 85, 151, 294, 340
Pytine
  Ti 16
  Tii 56, 69
  fr. 193 61, 62
  fr. 195 63
  fr. 198 63
  fr. 199 69
  fr. 208 57, 102, 179, 269
  fr. 209 57, 101, 102, 179
  fr. 210 72
  fr. 211 150
  fr. 213 5, 16, 18, 23, 24, 32, 47, 49, 50, 55, 60, 64, 69, 70, 72, 80, 81, 90, 121, 164, 179, 191, 284, 299
Pylaia
  fr. 184 125
Seriphioi
  fr. 228 84, 153

Cratinus (*cont.*)
  Thraittai
    fr. 73   32, 77, 85, 146, 148, 171, 209, 249, 328, 350
    fr. 82   130, 267
  Trophonius
    fr. 237   130
  Testimonia
    T2a   76
    T15   82, 287
    T19   188
  Fragments
    fr. 321   81
    fr. 342   57, 86, 88, 90, 182, 190, 209, 266, 285
    fr. 346   101, 181
    fr. 355   125
    fr. 363   82
    fr. 423   249, 253
    fr. 512   164
Critias
  D-K fr. 6–9 and 32–7   242
Ctesias
  Persica
    52   197

Demosthenes
  18.227   18
  21.204   103
  25.50   142
  25.53   257
  32.29   171
  54.33–4   192
[Demosthenes]
  59 (*Neaira*)   256, 335
Dio Chrysostom
  16.9   42
Diodorus Siculus
  12.38   230
  12.39–40   149
Diogenes Laertius
  2.9   350
  2.18   139
  2.26   265

Eupolis
  Aiges
    fr. 1   174
    fr. 10   174
    fr. 13   82, 246
    fr. 17   174
    fr. 18   174
    fr. 21   174
  Autolycus
    Tiii   113

    fr. 50   218
    fr. 61   197
    fr. 62   16, 212, 218
    fr. 65   218
  Baptai
    Tiii–vi   55
    fr. 89   5, 11, 16, 18, 20, 23, 24, 32, 33, 47, 48, 49, 50, 54, 55, 61, 69, 121, 160, 199, 220, 221, 222, 223, 268, 270
  Chrysoun Genos
    fr. 298   19, 49, 83, 84, 89, 121, 130, 163, 184, 188, 191
    fr. 299   189, 190
    fr. 302   47
    fr. 304   194
    fr. 308   81
    fr. 316   47, 121, 130, 182, 189
    fr. 318   38, 285
  Demoi (*Demes*)
    Ti   148, 154
    fr. 99   32, 68, 89, 246, 276, 277, 282, 340
    fr. 102   82, 89, 277, 278, 279, 283
    fr. 103   283
    fr. 104   280
    fr. 106   89
    fr. 110   277, 279
    fr. 115   83, 277, 280
    fr. 116   233, 283
    fr.121   281
  Heilotes
    fr. 147   261
    fr. 149   261
  Hybristodikai
    T   114, 220
  Kolakes
    fr. 157   176, 238
    fr. 158   176, 238
    fr. 171   160
  Marikas
    fr. 192   161, 261, 285, 329
    fr. 193   157, 161, 261, 285
    fr. 207   50, 200, 214, 286, 289, 294, 296
    fr. 209   55, 101
  Poleis
    fr. 224   298
    fr. 231   214, 286, 289, 296
    fr. 243   195
    frr. 244–7   195, 285
    fr. 252   101
    fr. 254   187, 195
  Prospaltioi
    fr. 259   152
    fr. 260   83, 127, 152, 289
    fr. 261   127, 180, 268

Index Locorum

fr. 262 127
fr. 267 127
Taxiarchoi (*Taxiarchs*)
fr. 268 142, 208, 285, 287, 288, 346, 347
fr. 269 82, 277, 285, 287
fr. 272 285, 287
fr. 274 82, 204, 285, 287
fr. 280 90
Testimonia
T1 190
T2a.7 38, 82
Fragments
fr. 326 246
fr. 329 125
fr. 346 50, 201
fr. 351 157
fr. 352 215
fr. 372 37, 285
fr. 386 100, 176, 278, 315
fr. 392 37, 71, 72, 100, 116, 150, 285, 339
fr. 395 176, 278
fr. 400 285
Euripides
Aeolus
frr. 17–18, 209
Bacchae
200 18
Bellerophon
frr. 306–7, 209
Cretes
fr. 472N 139
Electra
184–5 90
Erechtheus
Fr. 300 264
Hippolytus
612 268
Iphigenia in Aulis (*IA*)
744 18
Ion
1575–88, 258
Medea
529 240
Melanippe Sophe
fr. 483 257
Telephus
fr. 699 258
fr. 713 339
fr. 722 235
fr. 883 258
Trojan Women (*Troiades*)
919f. 137, 255
1052f. 255

FrGrH (Jacoby)
70 F 196 (Ephorus) 80
300 F 2 (Theogenes) 112
328 F 30 (Philochorus) 224
328 F 202
 (Philochorus) 126
Frontinus
Strategemata
1.11.10 350

Galen
Commentary on Hippocrates' On Regimen in Acute Diseases
1.4 219
On his own Books
17 327

Hermippus
Kerkopes
fr. 36 82, 277
Hermogenes
Peri methodou deinotetos (*Meth.*)
34 233
Progymnasmata
9 R. 59
Herodotus
1.82.8 25, 192
1.60.3 240
5.69–73 263
6.71.2 257
8.47 126
9.45 135
Hesiod
Theogony
624f. 85
711f. 85
824–30 84, 85
901 132
901f. 27, 175, 209
Hieronymus Rhodius
fr. 44–5 (Wehrli) 265
Homer
Iliad
1.56 135
1.196 135
6.55–6 135
7.204 135
17.572 185
Odyssey
22.358 135
Homeric Hymn to Aphrodite
6.5f. 132
Horace
Ars Poetica
281–4 335

400 Index Locorum

Hypotheses
  Aristophanes
    Acharnians
      32   107
    Birds
      I   108, 236
      II   108, 236
    Clouds
      I (Dover)   20, 165–6
      II (Dover)   16, 165
    Frogs
      Ic   4, 37, 41, 332
    Knights
      A3   156
    Lysistrata
      I   108, 252
    Wasps
      I   108, 216
  Cratinus
    Dionysalexandros   77, 133, 137, 138, 146

IG
  XIV 1140   111
  I^1 63   164
  I^3 365.30–40   250
  I^3 1190.52   39
  II^2 18   311
  II^2 75   135
  II^2 1698   135
  II^2 2318.9   294
  II^2 2321   127, 221
  II^2 2325   76, 108, 111, 307, 324, 347
  II^2 2343   135, 136, 274
  II^2 3018   245
Isaeus
  9.30   136
Isocrates
  8.14   306, 311
  16.31   227
  16.45   229
  16.46   229
  17.12   171
Koster *Prolegomena*
  3 (= Platonius 1.11f.)   333
  3 (= Platonius 1.13–18)   334
  3 (= Platonius 1.18–19)   115
  4 (= Platonius 1.30)   333
  4 (= Platonius 1.35–7)   42, 59
  5 (= Platonius 1.57–9)   317, 327
  5–6 (= Platonius 1.59–63)   335
  6 (= Platonius II.1–5)   63
  6 (= Platonius II.8–12)   58, 276
  8 (= Anon. *De comoedia* III.23)   199
  9 (= Anon. *De comoedia* III.34)   38, 82
  9 (= Anon. *De comoedia* III.38)   108

  14 (= Anon. *De comoedia* V.17)   188
  27. (= Tzetzes XIaI, 87–8)   330, 333
  27 (= Tzetzes XIa I.88–95)   222
  40 (= Anon. Cranmeri XIb.29)   330
  40 (= Anon. Cranmeri XIb.37)   333
  40 (= Anon. Cranmeri XIb.49)   58
  44 (= Anon. Cranmeri II.XIc.40)   333
  71 (= Scholia to Dionysius Thrax
      XVIIIa.31–2)   58, 330
  71 (= Scholia to Dionysius Thrax XVIIIa.42)
      333
  88 (=*Carmina* Tzetzae XXIa.83–4), 333
  115 (= Ps. Andronicus XXIII.11)   333
  141 (= Aristophanes *Life* XXXa.2)   112
Life of Aeschylus
  12   288, 294
Life of Aristophanes (=*PCG* T1)
  1–2   111
  19   112
  21–2   112
  27   112
  32–5   42
  33–5   168
  35   169
  35–9   4, 41
  55   57
  55–6   111
  56–7   86
[Longinus]
  De Sublimitate (*Peri Hypsous*)
    15.1   59
Lucian
  Bis Accusatus
    14   57, 62
    15   278
    27   60
    33   57, 137, 185, 190, 204, 231, 278
  Demonax
    10   278
  Dialogues of the Gods
    8(5).2   204
  Dearum Iudicium   137
  Icaromenippus
    18   231
  Lexiphanes
    20–1   190
  Muscae Encomium
    2   186
    6   185
  Nigrinus
    7   278
  Piscator (Fisherman)
    19   62
    25   100, 176, 278
    30   278

Index Locorum

Verae Historiae
  1.2 58
  1.29 60
[Lucian]
  Demosthenis Encomium
    20 278
  Longaevi
    25 199
Lysias
  1.30 257
  12.6 297
  12.13–15 297
  12.21 265
  12.54f. 234
  13.12 298
  16.6 163, 286
  16.18 25, 192
  16.19 192
  19.15 246, 247
  20.21 259
  25.24 40
  25.25 270
  30.10–3 298
  32.14 246
  32.16 192
  fr. 53
    (Thalheim) 29, 300, 302, 306, 311–12, 315, 319, 331

Menander
  Samia
    49–50 319

Nepos
  Alcibiades
    2.1 227
Nostoi
  fr. 6 Allen 162

Olympiodorus
  Vita Platonis
    3 175

P. Oxy. (Oxyrhynchus Papyri)
  2737 206
  3013 347
  4301.5 215
Pausanias
  2.7.3 39, 115
  9.35.2 132
Pherecrates
  Cheiron
    fr. 155 259, 281
  Krapataloi
    fr. 100 291, 294

Petale
  fr. 143 269
Philochorus (see *FrGrH*)
Philostratus
  Life of Apollonius
    6.11 288
Phrynichus
  Poastriai
    fr. 39 254
    fr. 41 254
Pindar
  Nemeans
    11.1 142
Plato (comic poet)
  Cleophon
    fr. 61 332
  Hyperbolus
    fr. 182–7, 22
    fr. 183 313
  Nikai
    fr. 81 212
    fr. 86 16, 23, 206
  Testimonia
    T7 206
  Fragments
    fr. 200 259
Plato (philosopher)
  Apology
    18a 100
    18c–d 47, 302, 309, 313–14
    18d 175, 248
    19c 12, 22, 100, 175, 248, 302, 309, 313–14, 315–16
    20a 12, 172
    20b 100
    23c 172
    24b 238
  Charmides
    161b 243
    162cf. 243
    173a 135
  Cratylus
    384b 100
  Critias
    115f. 243
  Crito
    50af. 186
  Ion
    536a 108
  Laws
    54d 186
    658a–d 255
    636b 270
    816–17 318
    836a–c 270

Plato (philosopher) (cont.)
    935–6 318
    935c–d 318
    935d 307, 314
    935d–936b 309–10
    935e 315, 316
    936a 103
  Phaedo
    70b–c 309, 311, 315
    91c 280
  Phaedrus
    236c 16
  Politicus
    308c–309b 255, 338
    310e 255
    311b–e 255
  Protagoras
    309a–c 229
    309b 12, 172
    314c–e 170
    315b 170
    315cf. 202
    315d 170
    316a 242, 251
    316b 188
    336d 242
  Republic
    2.369c–f 238
    2.378d 319
    3.394ef. 317
    3.400b 351
    4.433a 243
    5.452a–d 338
    5.457a 338
    8.545cf. 239
    8.550c–f 239
    8.551c 239
    8.555d–e 185
    8.557b–e 239
    8.564a–f 185
    8.564d 186
    8–9.565a–576 239
    10.595a 317
    10.595b–c 318
    10.598d 318
    10.607a 318
  Sophist
    252c 110
  Symposium
    173a 269
    174a 269
    176b 64
    177d–e 4, 64, 175
    185c–e 175
    189c–193d 268
    192a 175
    212df. 159, 229
    218a7–b4 27
    221a 131, 160, 177, 229
    221b 175
    223a 175
  Theaetetus
    152e 318, 325
  Timaeus
    20a 242
    23d 142
    25f. 243
    90d 239
    107b 243
Platonius; see Koster *Prolegomena*
Pliny
  NH
    11.16.46–9 187
    11.19.60 187
    11.24.74 187
Plutarch
  Alcibiades
    1.7 229
    3.1 232
    7 131, 160, 177, 229
    7.2–3 230
    8 177, 229
    8.1 232
    8.1–3 227
    12.2f. 232
    13 224
    13.1 233
    16 243
    16.1 160
    17.4–6 247
    18.2 140
    21.2–4 241
    21.9 140
    33.1 251
  Aristides
    7.3–4 224
  Moralia
    96b 185
    414e 110
    634d 57
    853a–854d 57
  Nicias
    2 156
    4.5 317, 327
    9 156
    11 224
    13.6–8 247
    15.1 140

Index Locorum 403

Pericles
 3.3–4 328
 3.4 277
 4.3 350
 4.4 350
 5.1 350
 10.3–4 351
 20 140, 288
 24.5 227
 24.16 277
 27.3 351
 31 149
 33.7–8 351
 35.3–4 85
Pollux
 4.133f. 335
 9.102 82
Prodicus
 D-K fr. 7
  (= Xen. *Mem.* 2.1.24) 5, 175

Quintilian
 1.10.18 20, 21, 313
 10.1.66 290, 295

Scholia
 Aelius Aristides
  3.8 327
  3.51 277
 Aristophanes
  Ach.
   8a 139
   11 297
   67 307
   378 42, 79, 108, 112, 194
   395 329
   525 151
   548 351
   614 226
   654b 112
   993a 139
   1150a 125, 327
   1167c 125
  Birds
   1297a 327
  Clouds
   88 201
   96 176, 277
   109 218
   179e 176
   296c 339
   541a 19, 83, 127, 181
   555 20, 91, 98, 179, 253
   557 254

 Frogs
  53 252
  1356a 139
 Knights
  1c, 1d 156
  55b 156
  400a 56, 61, 62, 69
  531a 60
  1225 139
  1288 96
  1321 162
 Peace
  348e 204, 287, 346
  702d 63
  740 203
  741b,c 101, 148, 181, 204, 249, 250
  763 204
 Thesm.
  190 252
  215 138, 182
 Wasps
  366 186
  462b 186
  749a 291
  947a 327
  1025b,c 218, 219
  1038a, c 22, 167
  1039a 169
  1238a 327
 Wealth
  179 334, 337, 339
 Dionysius Thrax; see Koster *Prolegomena*
 Juvenal
  2.92 270
 Plato
  Apol. 19c 57, 88, 89, 112, 212
 SEG
  XIII 12–22 246
  XVI 13 246
 Sophron
  fr. 68 (Kaibel) 171
 Sophocles
  Antigone
   677–80 258
   712–15 289
   740 258
   746 258
 Stobaeus
  3.4.32 71
 Suda
  α 3737 111
  ε 3657 39, 115, 190
  ψ 308 111

Telecleides
Sterroi 347
Fragments
  fr. 41 182
  fr. 42 182
  fr. 73 347
Testimonia
  T1 347
  T5 347
Theogenes see *FrGrH*
Thucydides
  1.70.3 244
  1.102.3 262
  1.102.4–105 262
  1.108.5 40
  1.111.2 40
  1.114.1 40
  1.141–3 43, 293
  2.7.1 200
  2.9.3 39
  2.27 116
  2.29 347
  2.29.5 247
  2.32.2 250
  2.34.5 39
  2.44.3–45.2 264
  2.59.2 121
  2.65.2 121
  2.65.4 152
  2.80.3 39
  3.37.3 165
  3.37.3–5 12, 122, 188
  3.42 119
  3.90.2 188
  3.115.2 188
  4.27f. 156
  4.28 122
  4.28.5 156
  4.29 156
  4.29.2 156
  4.30.4 156
  4.41.3–4 121
  4.50.3 200
  4.70.1 39
  4.75 140, 288
  4.101.3–4 39
  5.11.1 141
  5.16 156
  5.16.1 95
  5.19 156
  5.19.2 140, 189, 211
  5.24.1 189
  5.43.2 189
  5.52.3 39
  5.58–60 39

  5.81.2 39
  6.8.14 247
  6.14 135
  6.15 237
  6.15.3 159, 177, 230
  6.15.4 239
  6.18.3–7 237
  6.18.6 69
  6.24 247
  6.24.3 251
  6.27 247
  6.27–8 252
  6.27–9 240
  6.60–1 241
  6.61 240
  6.61.6–7 251
  6.67–71 251
  6.88.9–10 251
  6.89–92 251
  6.89.4 251
  6.101.6 140, 288
  7.19.4 39
  7.58.3 39
  8.3.2 39
  8.6 210
  8.18.37 262
  8.27.5 197
  8.48.3 243, 248
  8.48.4–7 197
  8.53–4 262, 263
  8.65.3 291
  8.67.2 259
  8.67.3 291
  8.68.3 40, 197
  8.70.2 210
  8.71.1–2 276
  8.73.3 40, 157, 221
  8.90.1 257
  8.92.6 163, 286
  8.97.1 291
Tzetzes (see Koster *Prolegomena*)

Valerius Maximus
  7.2 293

Xenophon
  Anabasis
    5.8.3 198
  Hellenica
    1.5.10f. 292
    2.1.25–6 43
    2.3.2 234, 297
    2.4 163, 286
    2.4.43 40
    3.1.4 163

Index Locorum

Lacedaemonion Politeia
  7.3   25, 192
  11.6   68
Memorabilia
  1.2.12–39   251
  1.2.40–6   231
  1.2.49   232
  1.2.49f.   169
  1.7.5   279
  2.1.21   12, 172, 240
  2.1.21f.   173–4, 175
  2.1.24   5
  2.1.28   173
  2.1.30–3   173–4

  2.12–39   242
  2.14   243
Symposium
  1.2   218
  3.6   319
  6.6f.   314
  6.6–8   175, 309
  6.6–10   302

[Xenophon] [= *Old Oligarch*]
Athenian Constitution (Ath. Pol.)
  1.10   68
  2.18   4, 25, 51, 121, 194, 270, 307, 308–9, 315, 334

Index of Modern Scholars

Note: This index for the most part includes only modern scholars who are mentioned in the *text*. However, where an important argument is conducted in a footnote, such references are also included. The same is true when I owe an idea to another scholar which is articulated in the text, but recognised only in the footnote.

Austin, Colin, 112, 267–8, 271, 272–3

Bergk, Theodor, 174, 176
Biles, Zachary P. 69, 179
Bowie, E.L. 80, 107, 117–18, 120, 143
Brockmann, Christian 14, 46, 110, 294, 296–7, 329
Byl, S. 236

Cobet, Carel Gabriel 66, 327
Colvin, Stephen 147
Cooke, Keith 85, 266
Cornford, Francis M. 215

Davies, J.K. 228
Del Corno, Dario 272
Develin, R. 164
Dover, Kenneth 6, 8–9, 21, 66–7, 93–4, 141, 165–6, 172–3, 226, 290, 349
Dow, Sterling 136
Dunbar, Nan 237, 240, 242, 243–4, 245

Edwards, Anthony ix

Flintoff, Everard 294–5

Geissler, P. 187
Gomme, A.W. 161–2
Goossens, Roger 152
Green, J.R. 307

Halliwell, Stephen 10, 11, 14, 109–10, 124, 236, 314, 325, 327

Handley, Eric W. 143, 346–8
Heath, Malcolm 3, 4, 320
Henderson, Jeffrey ix 235, 264, 269, 270
Hubbard, Thomas K. 17, 33, 164, 167, 168

Jensen, Christian 282–3

Kaibel, Georg 47, 72, 82
Kassel, R. 112
Katz, B.R. 68, 237
Kinzl, Konrad 39
Kloss, Gerrit x
Kock, Theodor 82
Kopff, E.C. 235
Körte, Werner 39, 137
Koster, W.J.W. 330
Kyriakidi, Natalia 18, 38, 48, 80, 83, 113

Landi, C. 331
Leeuwen, Johannes van 125, 138, 283
Lewis, D.M. 256
Lübke, Heinrich 88, 128
Luppe, Wolfgang 283

MacDowell, Douglas M. 6, 36, 108–10, 111, 136–7, 147, 148, 169–70, 196, 197, 204, 205, 214, 247, 302, 339
Mastromarco, Giuseppe 14, 109–10
Meineke, August 72
Moellendorf, Peter von x

Ní Mheallaigh, Karen 58
Norwood, Gilbert 215

Index of Modern Scholars

Olson, Douglas 122, 127, 138, 152–3, 203, 205–6, 212, 267–8, 271, 272–3

Paduano, Guido 272
Papademetriou, I. 257
Parker, L.P.E. 117–18, 119, 122
Pickard-Cambridge, A.W. 68
Pieters, J.Th.M.F. 57, 102, 179
Platnauer, M. 213
Platter, Charles x
Prato, Carlo 272

Ranner, Oliver 320
Revermann, Martin x 265
Rhodes, P. 235
Riu, Xavier 78–9
Robson, James x
Rogers, B.B. 272
Rosen, Ralph M. 63, 65
Russo, Carlo Fernando 124
Rusten, Jeffrey 300

Silk, Michael S. 5–6, 29, 336
Solomos, Alexis 158

Sommerstein, Alan H. ix 8–9, 13, 17, 32–3, 41–4, 51, 65, 75–6, 77–8, 87, 93–4, 97, 99, 100, 107, 127–8, 141, 142, 156, 168–9, 170, 174–5, 181–2, 199, 200, 203, 226, 236–7, 242, 243, 244, 245, 256, 269–70, 272, 274–5, 287, 290, 292–3, 297–8, 338–40, 349
Storey, Ian C. 39, 47, 48–51, 56–7, 83, 84, 87, 90, 103, 113, 116, 121, 143, 152, 195, 197, 201, 213, 214, 218, 219, 220–1, 222, 223, 235, 245–6, 270, 276, 279, 280, 282, 346–8
Ste Croix, G.E.M. de ix 3, 161–2
Süvern, J.W. 66, 237

Taplin, Oliver 48, 265
Telò, Mario 59, 223, 246, 276, 279–81, 282, 283
Thompson, W.E. 228

Vickers, Michael 68–9, 158–9, 233, 237, 336, 350–1

Welsh, David 136
West, Martin L. 222
Wilamowitz-Moellendorf, Ulrich von 142
Willink, Charles W. 12, 100, 174
Wilson, A.M. 346

Printed in Great Britain
by Amazon